GREEN LANTERN

SECTOR 2814

VOLUME 2

STEVE ENGLEHART
LEN WEIN
PAUL KUPPERBERG
WRITERS

JOE STATON
BRUCE PATTERSON
DAVE GIBBONS
MARK FARMER
BILL WILLINGHAM
RICH RANKIN
ARTISTS

GREEN SECT

JOHN COSTANZA
HELEN VESIK
L. LOIS BUHALIS
LETTERERS

ANTHONY TOLLIN
COLORIST

DAVE GIBBONS
COLLECTION COVER ARTIST

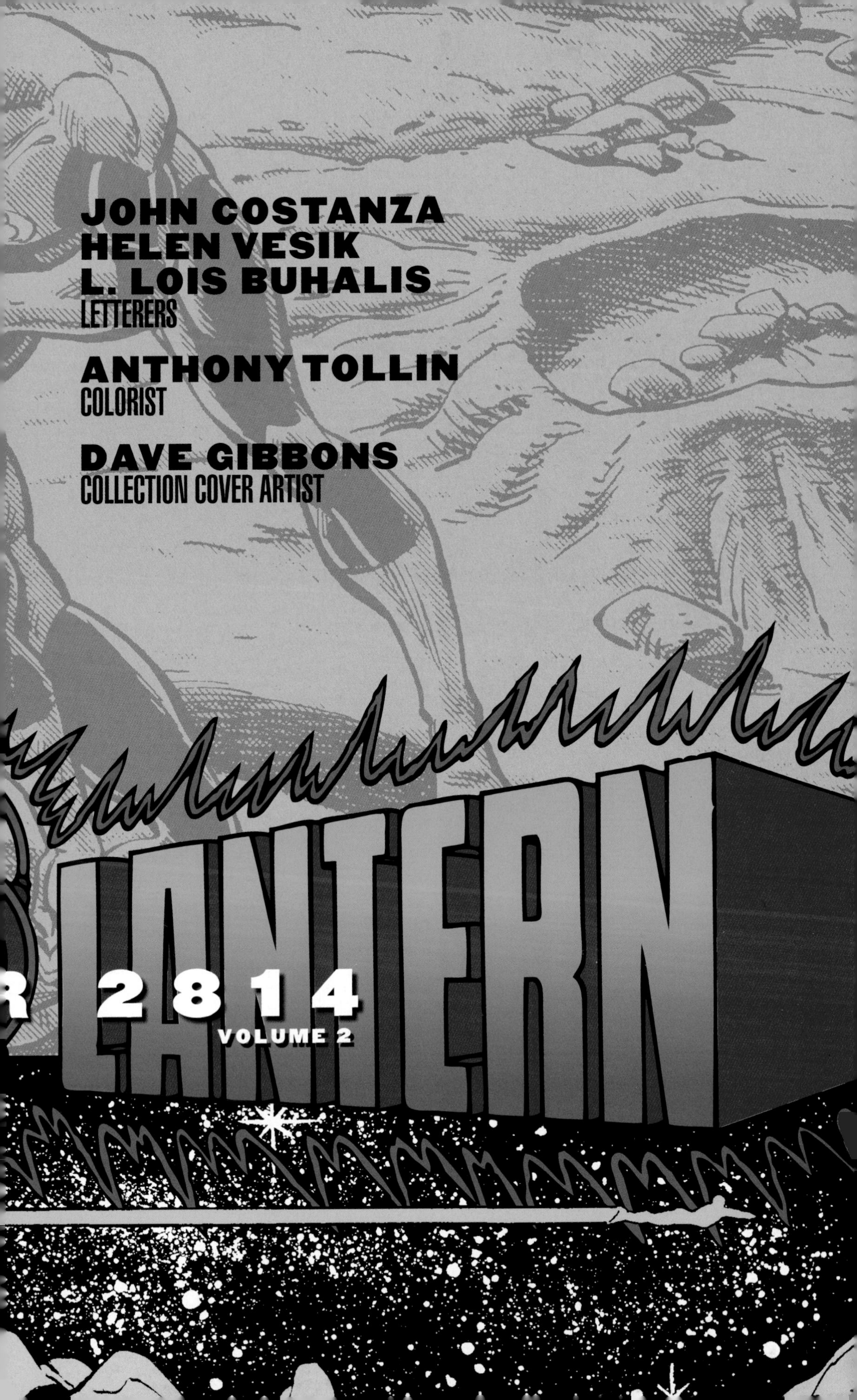
LANTERN
R 2814
VOLUME 2

LEN WEIN
ANDY HELFER
Editors – Original Series
ROWENA YOW
Editor
ROBBIN BROSTERMAN
Design Director – Books
DAMIAN RYLAND
Publication Design

BOB HARRAS
Senior VP – Editor-in-Chief, DC Comics

DIANE NELSON
President
DAN DIDIO and **JIM LEE**
Co-Publishers
GEOFF JOHNS
Chief Creative Officer
JOHN ROOD
Executive VP – Sales, Marketing and Business Development
AMY GENKINS
Senior VP – Business and Legal Affairs
NAIRI GARDINER
Senior VP – Finance
JEFF BOISON
VP – Publishing Planning
MARK CHIARELLO
VP – Art Direction and Design
JOHN CUNNINGHAM
VP – Marketing
TERRI CUNNINGHAM
VP – Editorial Administration
ALISON GILL
Senior VP – Manufacturing and Operations
HANK KANALZ
Senior VP – Vertigo and Integrated Publishing
JAY KOGAN
VP – Business and Legal Affairs, Publishing
JACK MAHAN
VP – Business Affairs, Talent
NICK NAPOLITANO
VP – Manufacturing Administration
SUE POHJA
VP – Book Sales
COURTNEY SIMMONS
Senior VP – Publicity
BOB WAYNE
Senior VP – Sales

GREEN LANTERN: SECTOR 2814, VOLUME 2

DC Comics, 1700 Broadway, New York, NY 10019
A Warner Bros. Entertainment Company.
Printed by RR Donnelley, Salem, VA, USA. 7/19/13. First Printing.
ISBN: 978-1-4012-4078-3

Library of Congress Cataloging-in-Publication Data

Wein, Len.
  Green Lantern, Sector 2814. Volume 2 / Len Wein, Dave Gibbons.
    pages cm
  "Originally published in single magazine form in Green Lantern 182-183, 185-193."
  ISBN 978-1-4012-4078-3
  1. Graphic novels. I. Gibbons, Dave. II. Title. III. Title: Sector 2814.
  PN6728.G74W46 2013
  741.5·973—dc23
                                        2013012655

SUSTAINABLE
FORESTRY
INITIATIVE
Certified Chain of Custody
At Least 20% Certified Forest Content
www.sfiprogram.org
SFI-01042
APPLIES TO TEXT STOCK ONLY

Cover art by Dave Gibbons

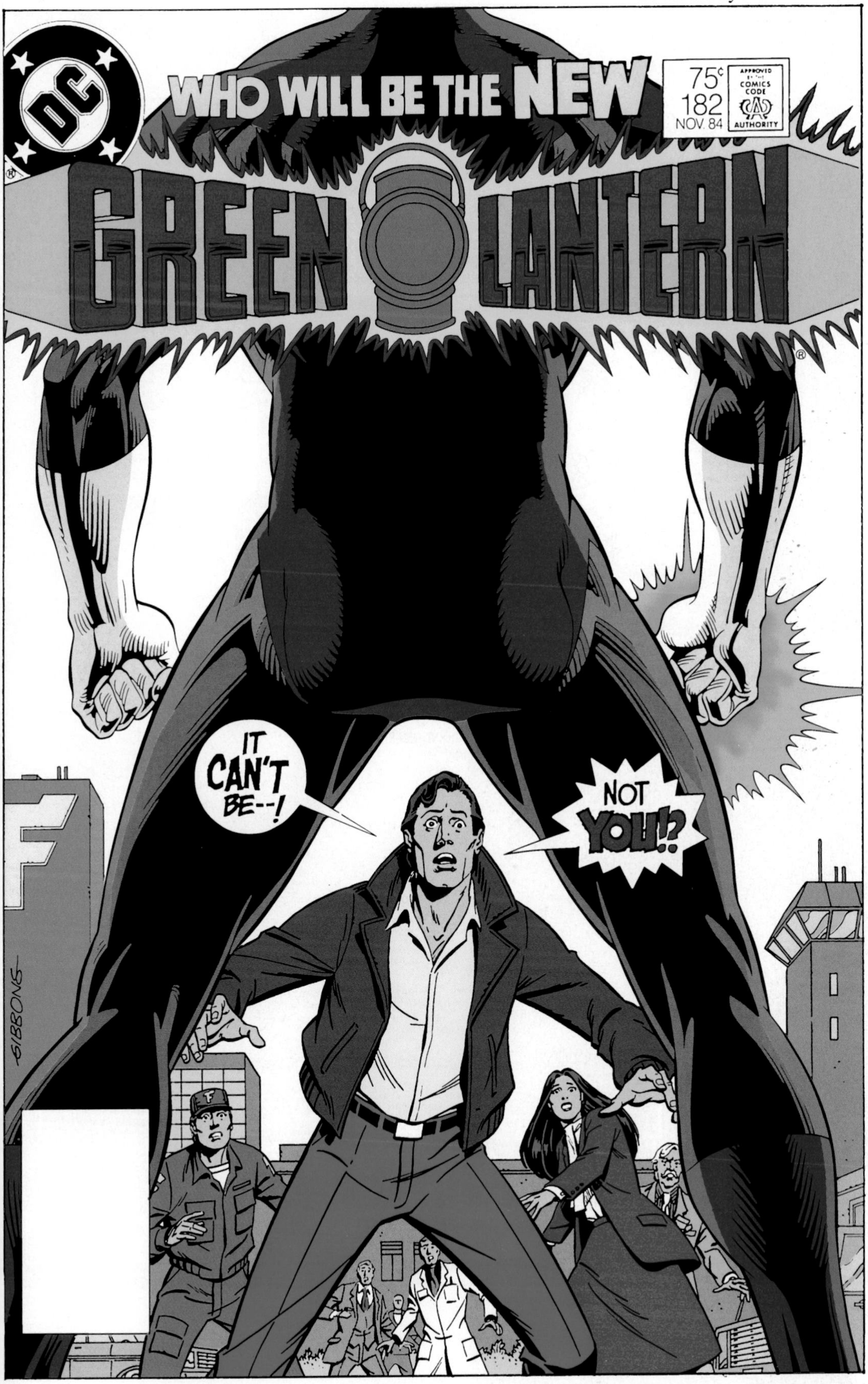
WHO WILL BE THE NEW
75¢
182
NOV. 84
APPROVED BY THE COMICS CODE AUTHORITY
GREEN LANTERN
IT CAN'T BE--!
NOT YOU!?
GIBBONS

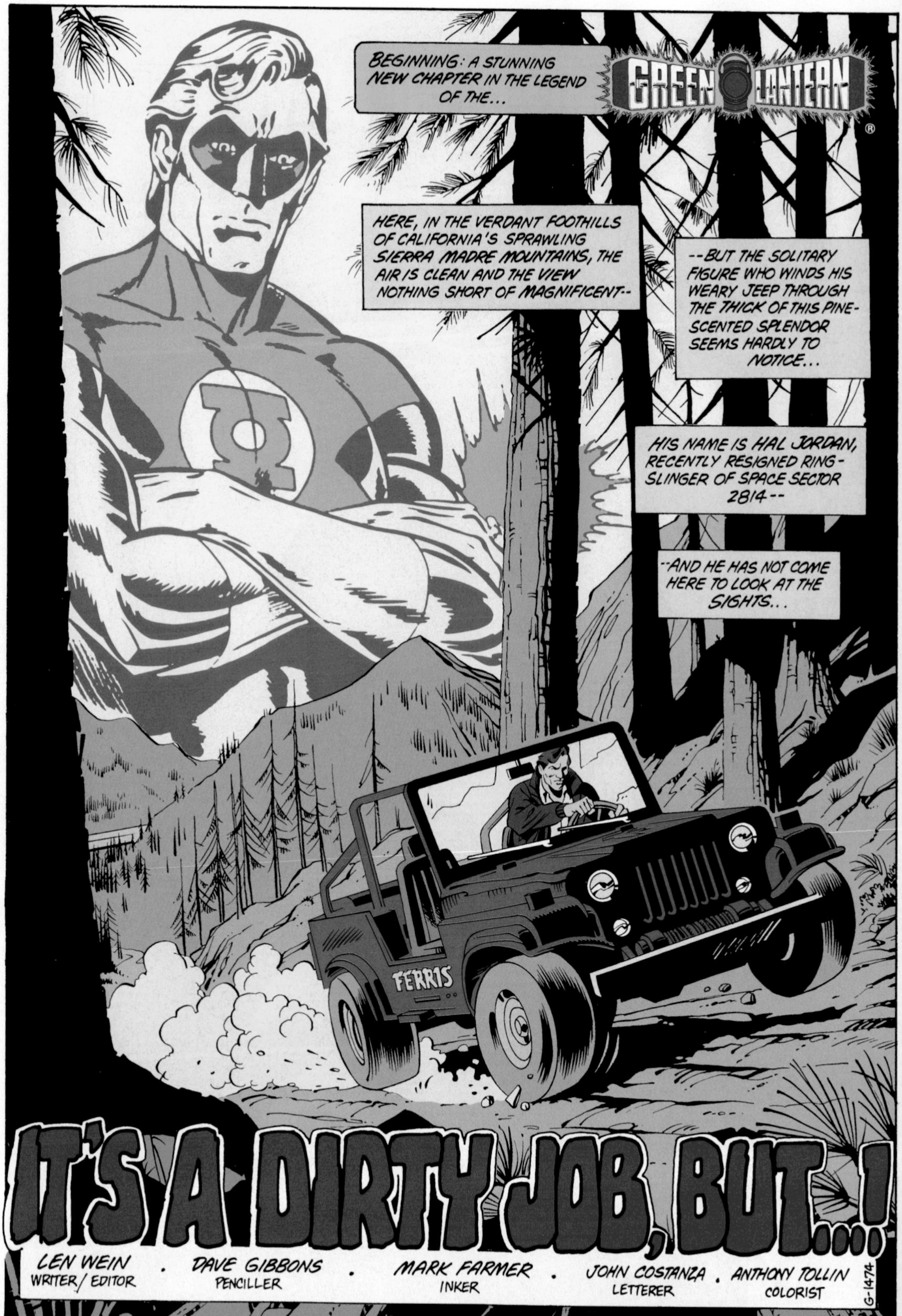
BEGINNING: A STUNNING NEW CHAPTER IN THE LEGEND OF THE...
GREEN LANTERN®
HERE, IN THE VERDANT FOOTHILLS OF CALIFORNIA'S SPRAWLING SIERRA MADRE MOUNTAINS, THE AIR IS CLEAN AND THE VIEW NOTHING SHORT OF MAGNIFICENT--
--BUT THE SOLITARY FIGURE WHO WINDS HIS WEARY JEEP THROUGH THE THICK OF THIS PINE-SCENTED SPLENDOR SEEMS HARDLY TO NOTICE...
HIS NAME IS HAL JORDAN, RECENTLY RESIGNED RING-SLINGER OF SPACE SECTOR 2814--
--AND HE HAS NOT COME HERE TO LOOK AT THE SIGHTS...
FERRIS
IT'S A DIRTY JOB, BUT...!
LEN WEIN WRITER/EDITOR · DAVE GIBBONS PENCILLER · MARK FARMER INKER · JOHN COSTANZA LETTERER · ANTHONY TOLLIN COLORIST
G-1474

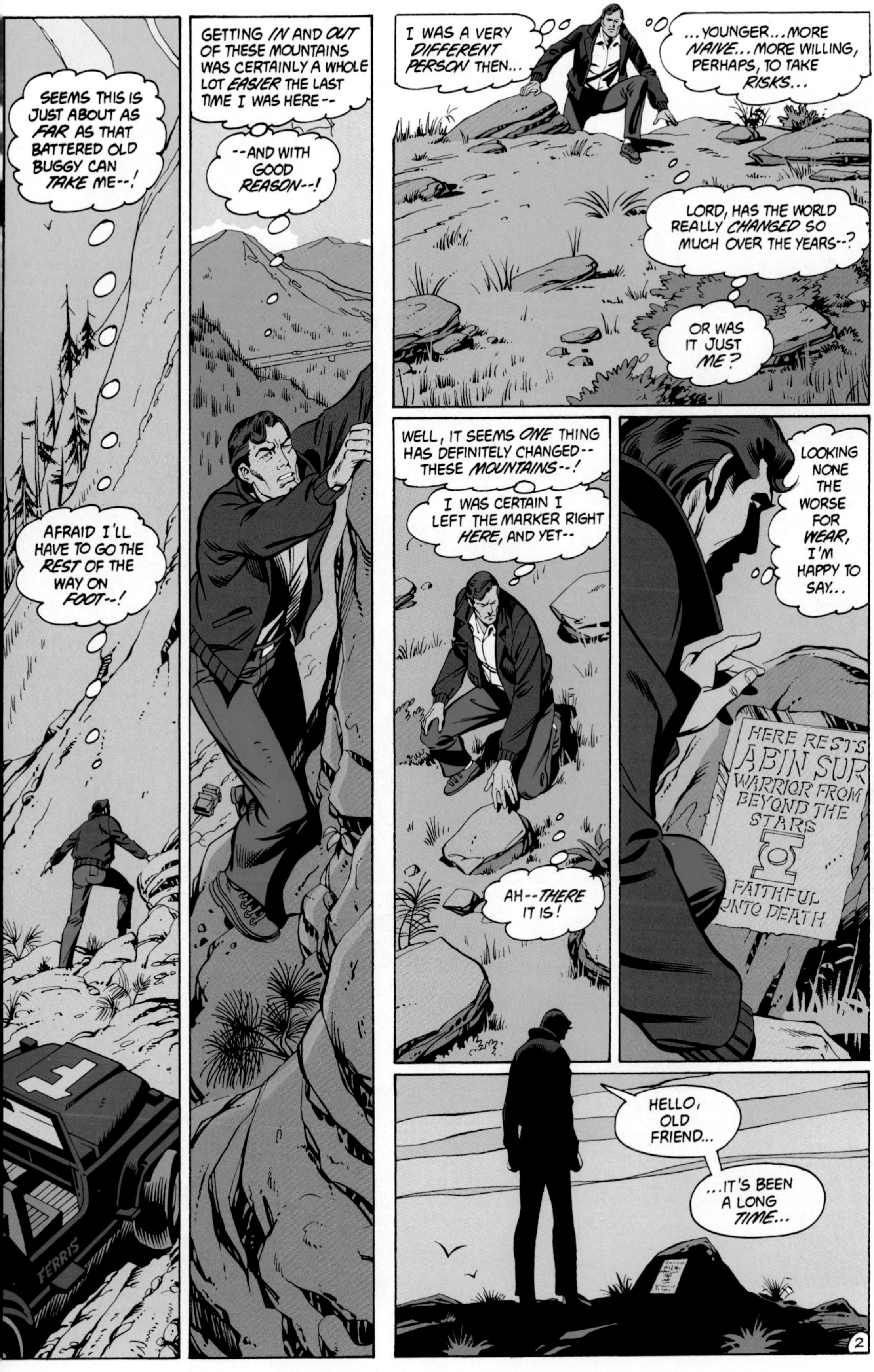
SEEMS THIS IS JUST ABOUT AS FAR AS THAT BATTERED OLD BUGGY CAN TAKE ME--!
AFRAID I'LL HAVE TO GO THE REST OF THE WAY ON FOOT--!
FERRIS
GETTING IN AND OUT OF THESE MOUNTAINS WAS CERTAINLY A WHOLE LOT EASIER THE LAST TIME I WAS HERE--
--AND WITH GOOD REASON--!
I WAS A VERY DIFFERENT PERSON THEN...
...YOUNGER...MORE NAIVE...MORE WILLING, PERHAPS, TO TAKE RISKS...
LORD, HAS THE WORLD REALLY CHANGED SO MUCH OVER THE YEARS--?
OR WAS IT JUST ME?
WELL, IT SEEMS ONE THING HAS DEFINITELY CHANGED-- THESE MOUNTAINS--!
I WAS CERTAIN I LEFT THE MARKER RIGHT HERE, AND YET--
AH--THERE IT IS!
LOOKING NONE THE WORSE FOR WEAR, I'M HAPPY TO SAY...
HERE RESTS
ABIN SUR
WARRIOR FROM BEYOND THE STARS
FAITHFUL UNTO DEATH
HELLO, OLD FRIEND...
...IT'S BEEN A LONG TIME...
2

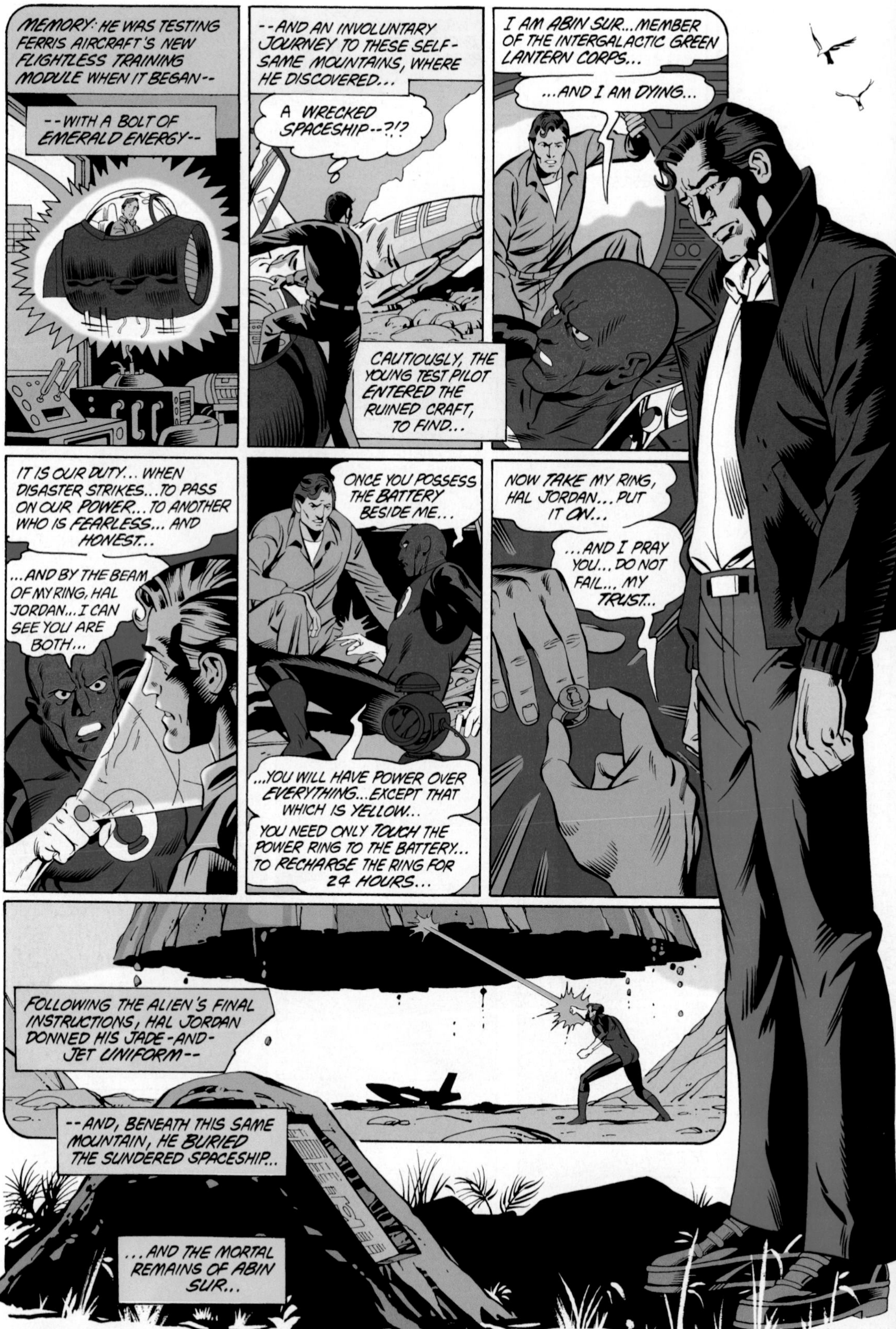
MEMORY: HE WAS TESTING FERRIS AIRCRAFT'S NEW FLIGHTLESS TRAINING MODULE WHEN IT BEGAN--
--WITH A BOLT OF EMERALD ENERGY--
--AND AN INVOLUNTARY JOURNEY TO THESE SELF-SAME MOUNTAINS, WHERE HE DISCOVERED...
A WRECKED SPACESHIP--?!?
CAUTIOUSLY, THE YOUNG TEST PILOT ENTERED THE RUINED CRAFT, TO FIND...
I AM ABIN SUR... MEMBER OF THE INTERGALACTIC GREEN LANTERN CORPS...
...AND I AM DYING...
IT IS OUR DUTY... WHEN DISASTER STRIKES... TO PASS ON OUR POWER... TO ANOTHER WHO IS FEARLESS... AND HONEST...
...AND BY THE BEAM OF MY RING, HAL JORDAN... I CAN SEE YOU ARE BOTH...
ONCE YOU POSSESS THE BATTERY BESIDE ME...
...YOU WILL HAVE POWER OVER EVERYTHING... EXCEPT THAT WHICH IS YELLOW...
YOU NEED ONLY TOUCH THE POWER RING TO THE BATTERY... TO RECHARGE THE RING FOR 24 HOURS...
NOW TAKE MY RING, HAL JORDAN... PUT IT ON...
...AND I PRAY YOU... DO NOT FAIL... MY TRUST...
FOLLOWING THE ALIEN'S FINAL INSTRUCTIONS, HAL JORDAN DONNED HIS JADE-AND-JET UNIFORM--
--AND, BENEATH THIS SAME MOUNTAIN, HE BURIED THE SUNDERED SPACESHIP...
...AND THE MORTAL REMAINS OF ABIN SUR...
3

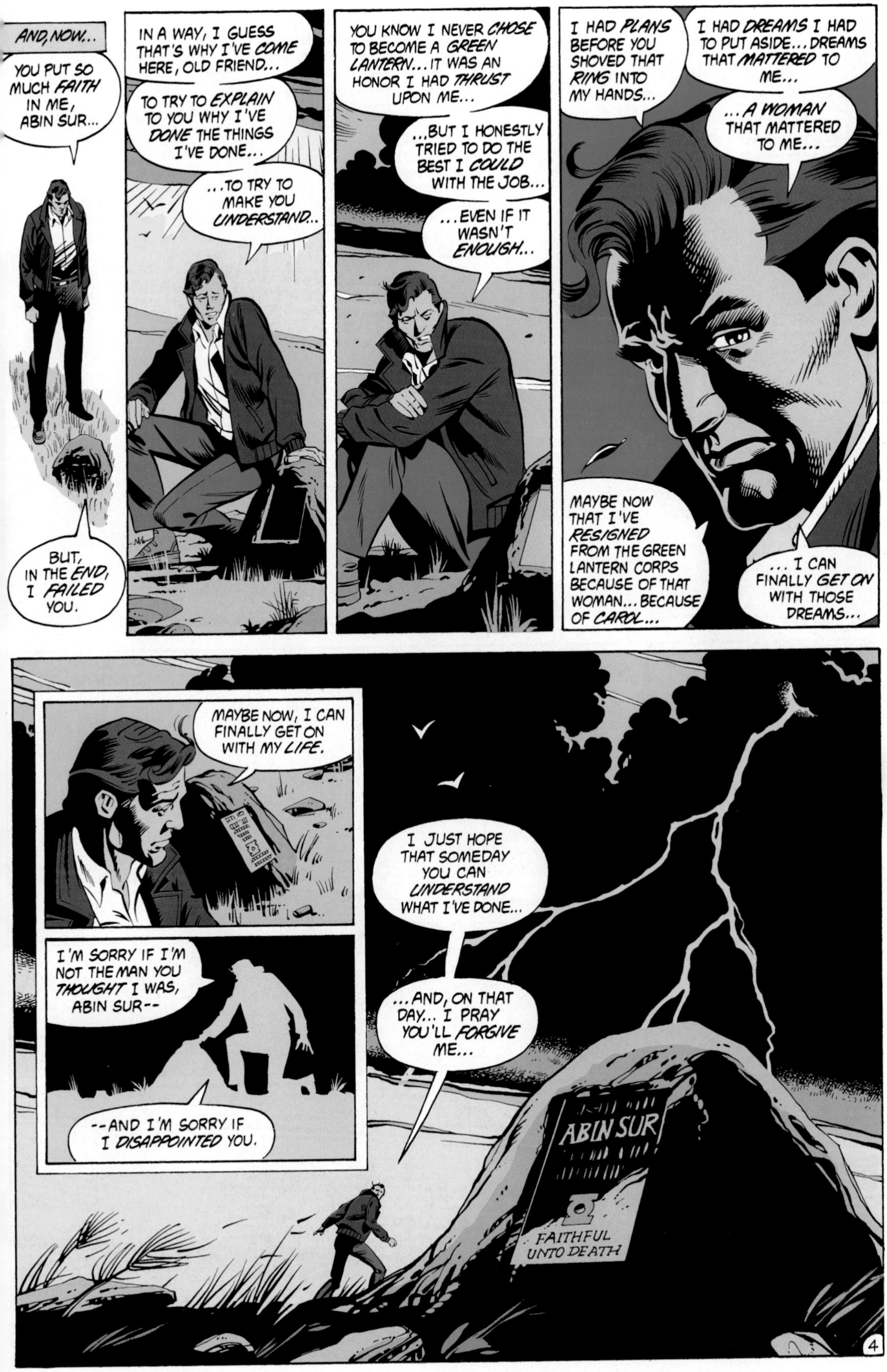
AND, NOW...
YOU PUT SO MUCH FAITH IN ME, ABIN SUR...
BUT, IN THE END, I FAILED YOU.
IN A WAY, I GUESS THAT'S WHY I'VE COME HERE, OLD FRIEND...
TO TRY TO EXPLAIN TO YOU WHY I'VE DONE THE THINGS I'VE DONE...
...TO TRY TO MAKE YOU UNDERSTAND...
YOU KNOW I NEVER CHOSE TO BECOME A GREEN LANTERN... IT WAS AN HONOR I HAD THRUST UPON ME...
...BUT I HONESTLY TRIED TO DO THE BEST I COULD WITH THE JOB...
...EVEN IF IT WASN'T ENOUGH...
I HAD PLANS BEFORE YOU SHOVED THAT RING INTO MY HANDS...
I HAD DREAMS I HAD TO PUT ASIDE... DREAMS THAT MATTERED TO ME...
...A WOMAN THAT MATTERED TO ME...
MAYBE NOW THAT I'VE RESIGNED FROM THE GREEN LANTERN CORPS BECAUSE OF THAT WOMAN... BECAUSE OF CAROL...
... I CAN FINALLY GET ON WITH THOSE DREAMS...
MAYBE NOW, I CAN FINALLY GET ON WITH MY LIFE.
I'M SORRY IF I'M NOT THE MAN YOU THOUGHT I WAS, ABIN SUR--
--AND I'M SORRY IF I DISAPPOINTED YOU.
I JUST HOPE THAT SOMEDAY YOU CAN UNDERSTAND WHAT I'VE DONE...
...AND, ON THAT DAY... I PRAY YOU'LL FORGIVE ME...
ABIN SUR
FAITHFUL UNTO DEATH
4

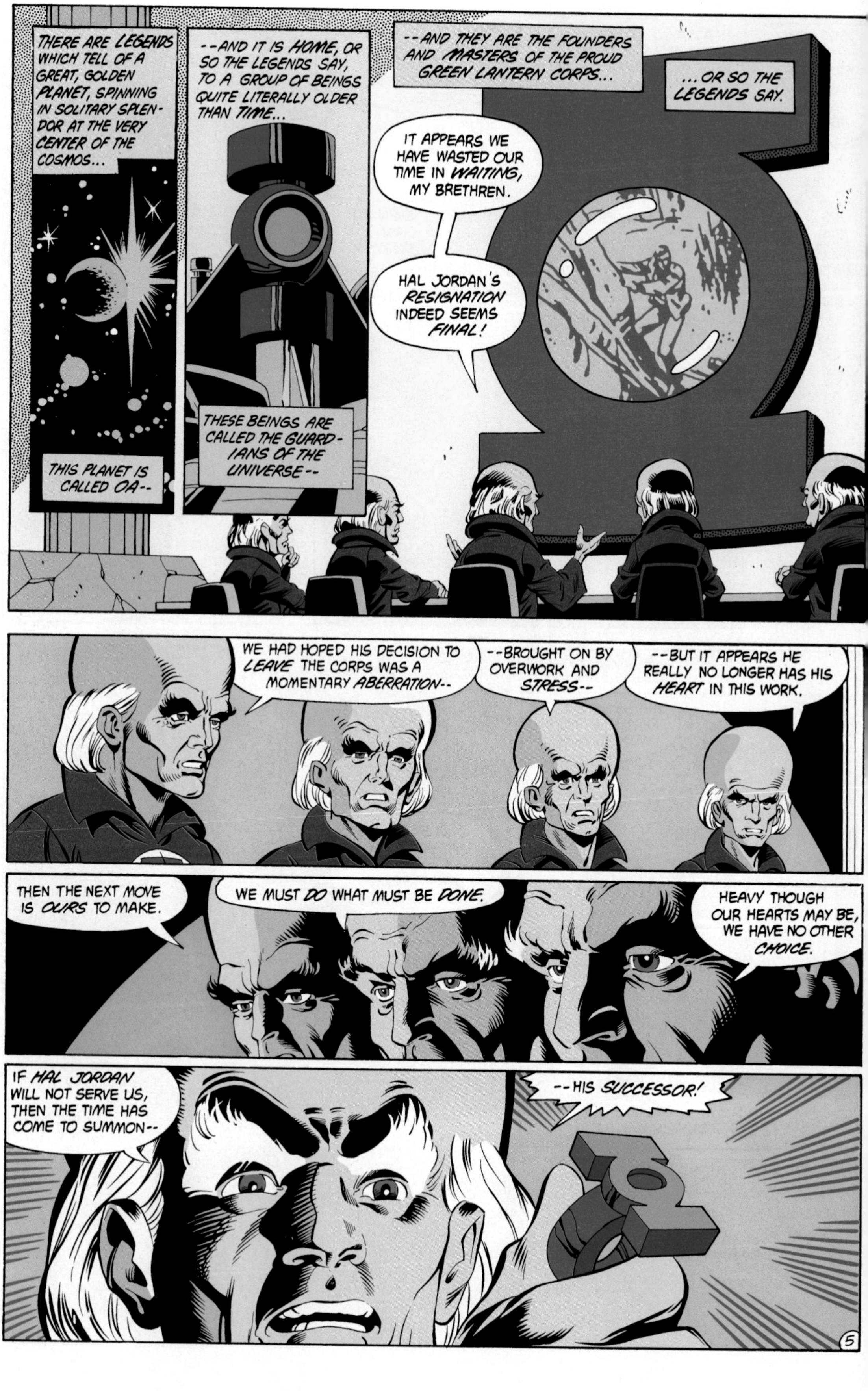
THERE ARE LEGENDS WHICH TELL OF A GREAT, GOLDEN PLANET, SPINNING IN SOLITARY SPLENDOR AT THE VERY CENTER OF THE COSMOS...
THIS PLANET IS CALLED OA--
--AND IT IS HOME, OR SO THE LEGENDS SAY, TO A GROUP OF BEINGS QUITE LITERALLY OLDER THAN TIME...
THESE BEINGS ARE CALLED THE GUARDIANS OF THE UNIVERSE--
--AND THEY ARE THE FOUNDERS AND MASTERS OF THE PROUD GREEN LANTERN CORPS...
...OR SO THE LEGENDS SAY.
IT APPEARS WE HAVE WASTED OUR TIME IN WAITING, MY BRETHREN.
HAL JORDAN'S RESIGNATION INDEED SEEMS FINAL!
WE HAD HOPED HIS DECISION TO LEAVE THE CORPS WAS A MOMENTARY ABERRATION--
--BROUGHT ON BY OVERWORK AND STRESS--
--BUT IT APPEARS HE REALLY NO LONGER HAS HIS HEART IN THIS WORK.
THEN THE NEXT MOVE IS OURS TO MAKE.
WE MUST DO WHAT MUST BE DONE.
HEAVY THOUGH OUR HEARTS MAY BE, WE HAVE NO OTHER CHOICE.
IF HAL JORDAN WILL NOT SERVE US, THEN THE TIME HAS COME TO SUMMON--
--HIS SUCCESSOR!
5

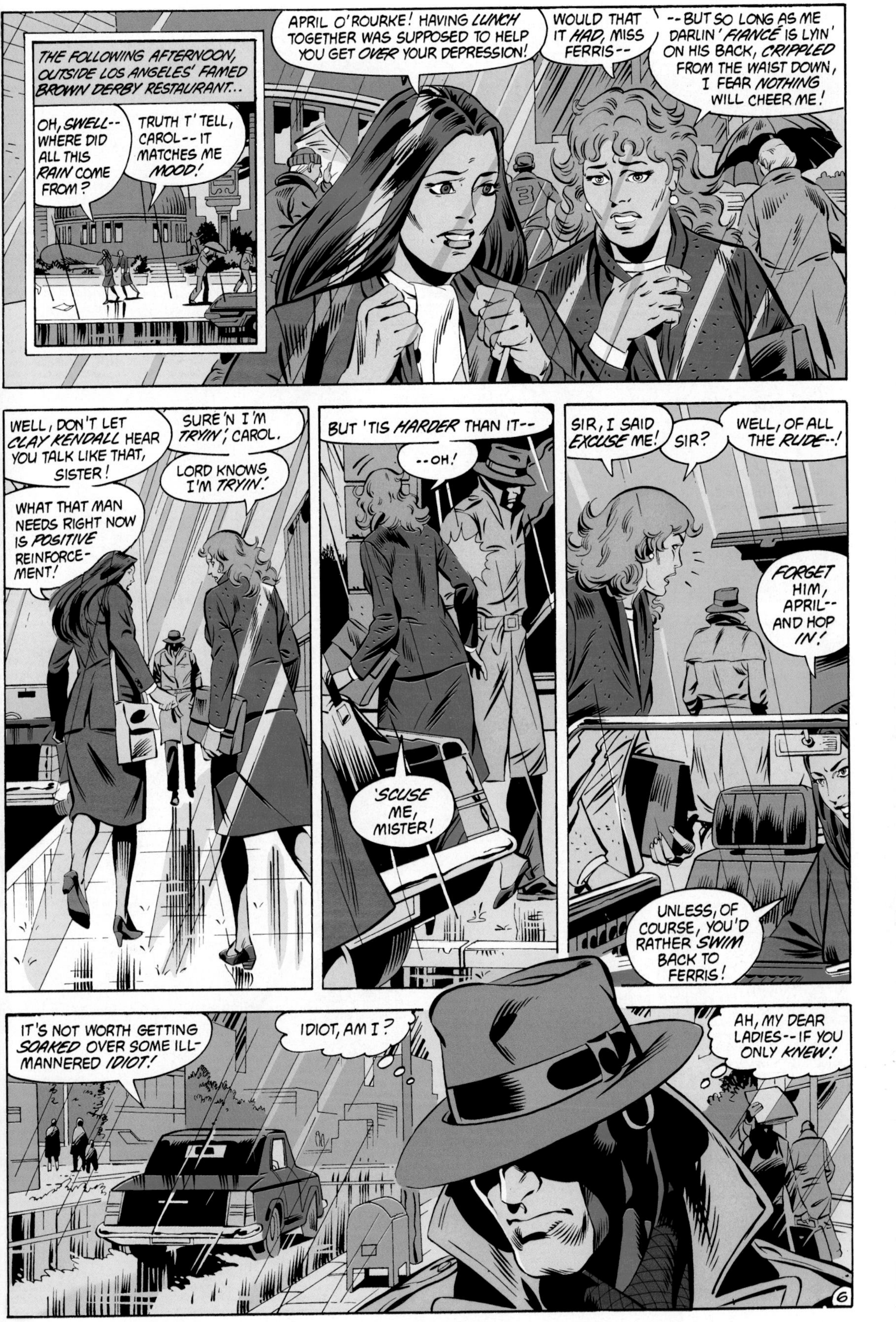
THE FOLLOWING AFTERNOON, OUTSIDE LOS ANGELES' FAMED BROWN DERBY RESTAURANT...
OH, SWELL-- WHERE DID ALL THIS RAIN COME FROM?
TRUTH T' TELL, CAROL-- IT MATCHES ME MOOD!
APRIL O'ROURKE! HAVING LUNCH TOGETHER WAS SUPPOSED TO HELP YOU GET OVER YOUR DEPRESSION!
WOULD THAT IT HAD, MISS FERRIS--
--BUT SO LONG AS ME DARLIN' FIANCÉ IS LYIN' ON HIS BACK, CRIPPLED FROM THE WAIST DOWN, I FEAR NOTHING WILL CHEER ME!
WELL, DON'T LET CLAY KENDALL HEAR YOU TALK LIKE THAT, SISTER!
SURE'N I'M TRYIN', CAROL.
LORD KNOWS I'M TRYIN'.
WHAT THAT MAN NEEDS RIGHT NOW IS POSITIVE REINFORCEMENT!
BUT 'TIS HARDER THAN IT--
--OH!
'SCUSE ME, MISTER!
SIR, I SAID EXCUSE ME!
SIR?
WELL, OF ALL THE RUDE--!
FORGET HIM, APRIL-- AND HOP IN!
UNLESS, OF COURSE, YOU'D RATHER SWIM BACK TO FERRIS!
IT'S NOT WORTH GETTING SOAKED OVER SOME ILL-MANNERED IDIOT!
IDIOT, AM I?
AH, MY DEAR LADIES--IF YOU ONLY KNEW!
6

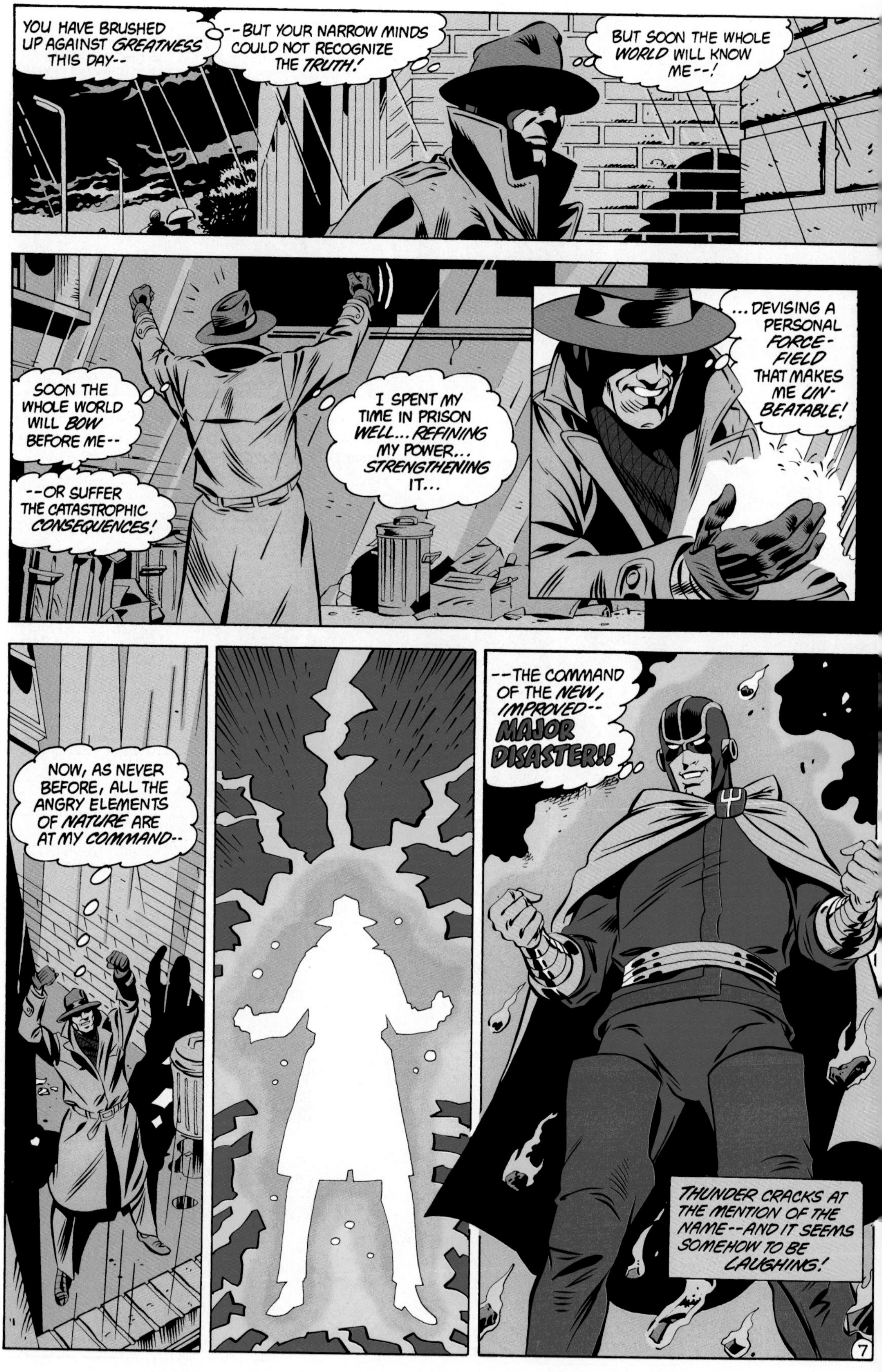
YOU HAVE BRUSHED UP AGAINST GREATNESS THIS DAY--
--BUT YOUR NARROW MINDS COULD NOT RECOGNIZE THE TRUTH!
BUT SOON THE WHOLE WORLD WILL KNOW ME--!
SOON THE WHOLE WORLD WILL BOW BEFORE ME--
--OR SUFFER THE CATASTROPHIC CONSEQUENCES!
I SPENT MY TIME IN PRISON WELL... REFINING MY POWER... STRENGTHENING IT...
...DEVISING A PERSONAL FORCE-FIELD THAT MAKES ME UN-BEATABLE!
NOW, AS NEVER BEFORE, ALL THE ANGRY ELEMENTS OF NATURE ARE AT MY COMMAND--
--THE COMMAND OF THE NEW, IMPROVED--MAJOR DISASTER!!
THUNDER CRACKS AT THE MENTION OF THE NAME--AND IT SEEMS SOMEHOW TO BE LAUGHING!
7

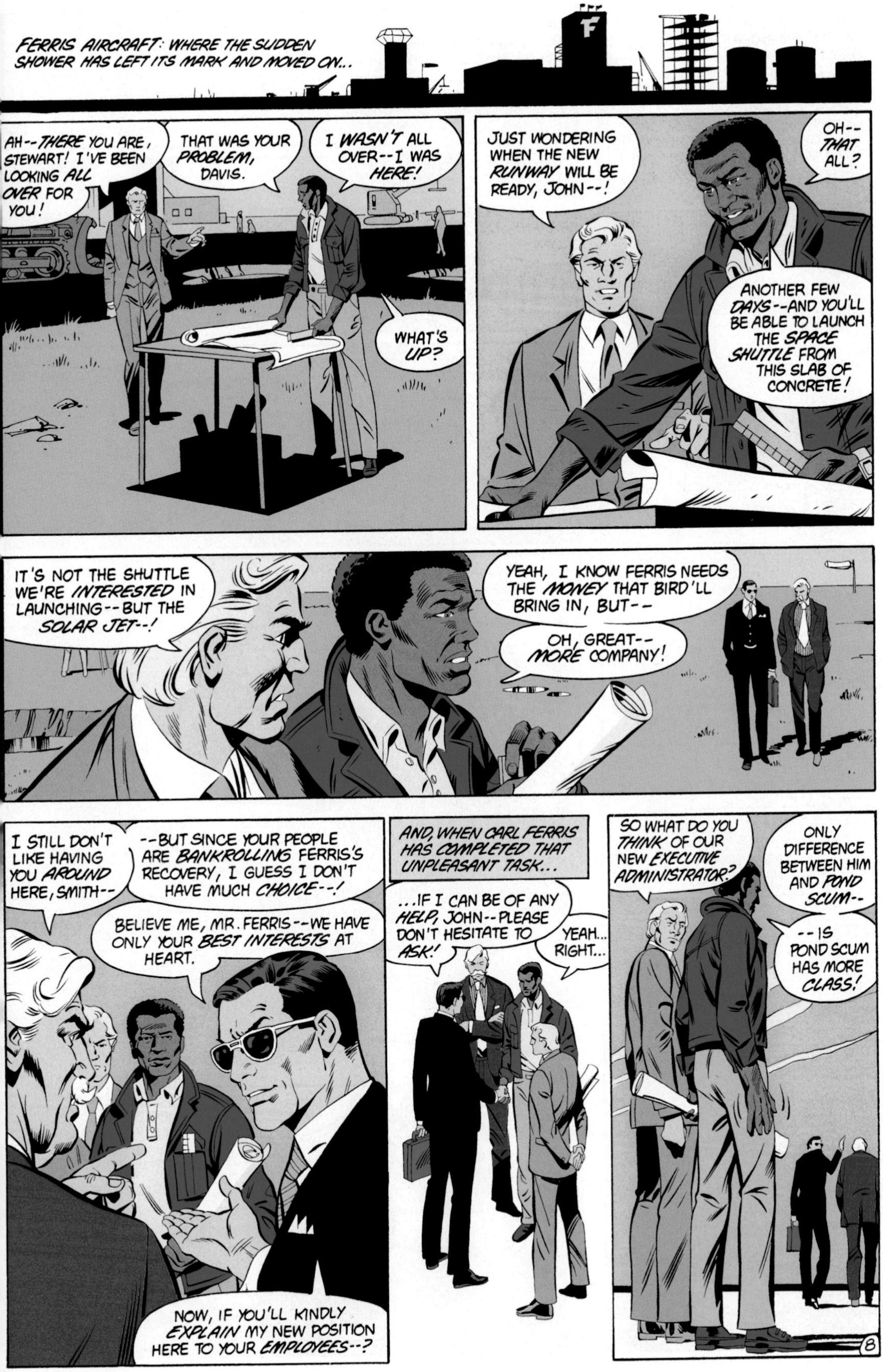
FERRIS AIRCRAFT: WHERE THE SUDDEN SHOWER HAS LEFT ITS MARK AND MOVED ON...
AH--THERE YOU ARE, STEWART! I'VE BEEN LOOKING ALL OVER FOR YOU!
THAT WAS YOUR PROBLEM, DAVIS.
I WASN'T ALL OVER--I WAS HERE!
WHAT'S UP?
JUST WONDERING WHEN THE NEW RUNWAY WILL BE READY, JOHN--!
OH--THAT ALL?
ANOTHER FEW DAYS--AND YOU'LL BE ABLE TO LAUNCH THE SPACE SHUTTLE FROM THIS SLAB OF CONCRETE!
IT'S NOT THE SHUTTLE WE'RE INTERESTED IN LAUNCHING--BUT THE SOLAR JET--!
YEAH, I KNOW FERRIS NEEDS THE MONEY THAT BIRD'LL BRING IN, BUT--
OH, GREAT--MORE COMPANY!
I STILL DON'T LIKE HAVING YOU AROUND HERE, SMITH--
--BUT SINCE YOUR PEOPLE ARE BANKROLLING FERRIS'S RECOVERY, I GUESS I DON'T HAVE MUCH CHOICE--!
BELIEVE ME, MR. FERRIS--WE HAVE ONLY YOUR BEST INTERESTS AT HEART.
NOW, IF YOU'LL KINDLY EXPLAIN MY NEW POSITION HERE TO YOUR EMPLOYEES--?
AND, WHEN CARL FERRIS HAS COMPLETED THAT UNPLEASANT TASK...
...IF I CAN BE OF ANY HELP, JOHN--PLEASE DON'T HESITATE TO ASK!
YEAH... RIGHT...
SO WHAT DO YOU THINK OF OUR NEW EXECUTIVE ADMINISTRATOR?
ONLY DIFFERENCE BETWEEN HIM AND POND SCUM--
--IS POND SCUM HAS MORE CLASS!
8

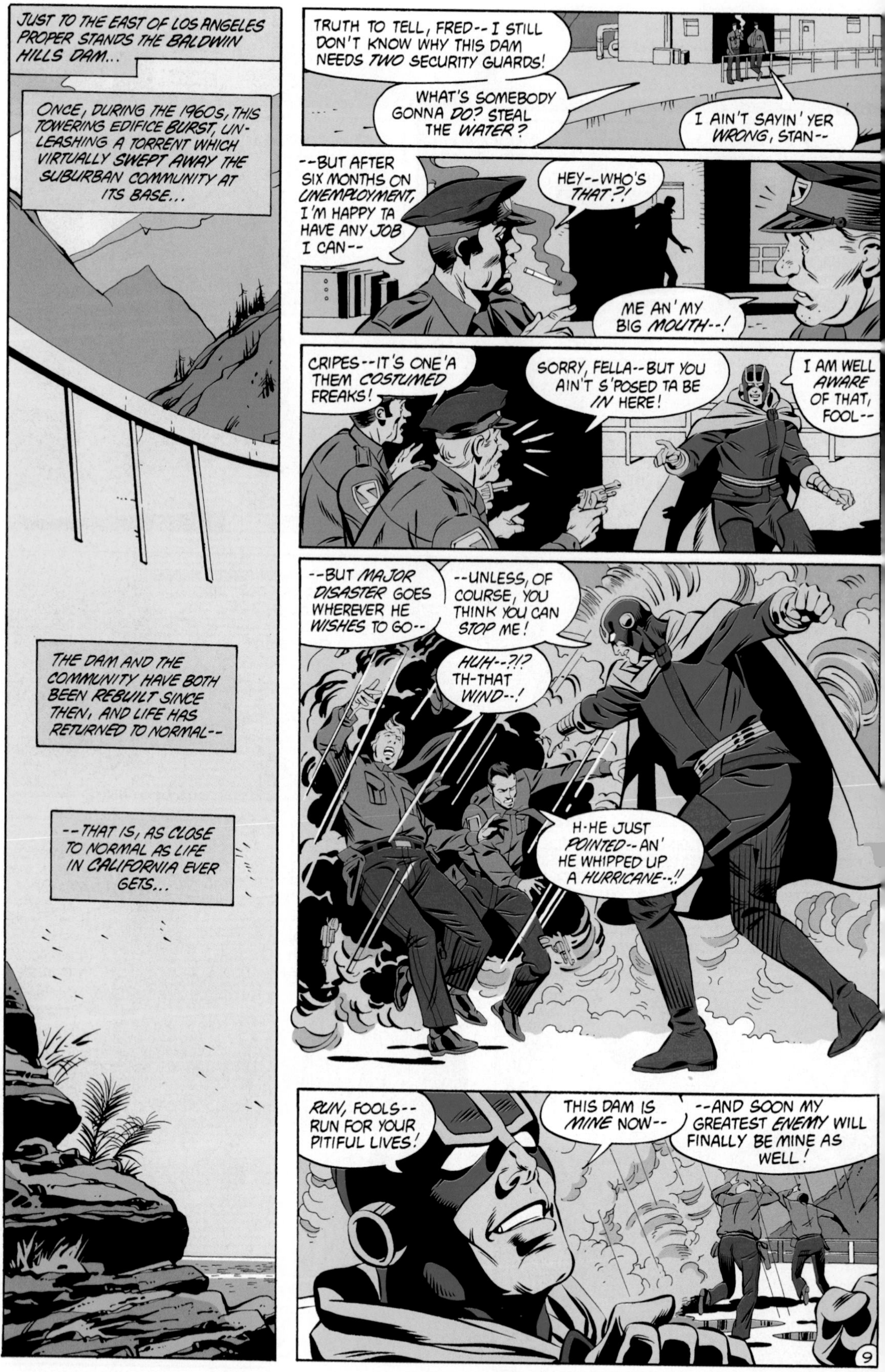

JUST TO THE EAST OF LOS ANGELES PROPER STANDS THE BALDWIN HILLS DAM...
ONCE, DURING THE 1960s, THIS TOWERING EDIFICE BURST, UNLEASHING A TORRENT WHICH VIRTUALLY SWEPT AWAY THE SUBURBAN COMMUNITY AT ITS BASE...
THE DAM AND THE COMMUNITY HAVE BOTH BEEN REBUILT SINCE THEN, AND LIFE HAS RETURNED TO NORMAL--
--THAT IS, AS CLOSE TO NORMAL AS LIFE IN CALIFORNIA EVER GETS...
TRUTH TO TELL, FRED--I STILL DON'T KNOW WHY THIS DAM NEEDS TWO SECURITY GUARDS!
WHAT'S SOMEBODY GONNA DO? STEAL THE WATER?
I AIN'T SAYIN' YER WRONG, STAN--
--BUT AFTER SIX MONTHS ON UNEMPLOYMENT, I'M HAPPY TA HAVE ANY JOB I CAN--
HEY--WHO'S THAT?!
ME AN' MY BIG MOUTH--!
CRIPES--IT'S ONE'A THEM COSTUMED FREAKS!
SORRY, FELLA--BUT YOU AIN'T S'POSED TA BE IN HERE!
I AM WELL AWARE OF THAT, FOOL--
--BUT MAJOR DISASTER GOES WHEREVER HE WISHES TO GO--
--UNLESS, OF COURSE, YOU THINK YOU CAN STOP ME!
HUH--?!? TH-THAT WIND--!
H-HE JUST POINTED--AN' HE WHIPPED UP A HURRICANE--!!
RUN, FOOLS--RUN FOR YOUR PITIFUL LIVES!
THIS DAM IS MINE NOW--
--AND SOON MY GREATEST ENEMY WILL FINALLY BE MINE AS WELL!
9

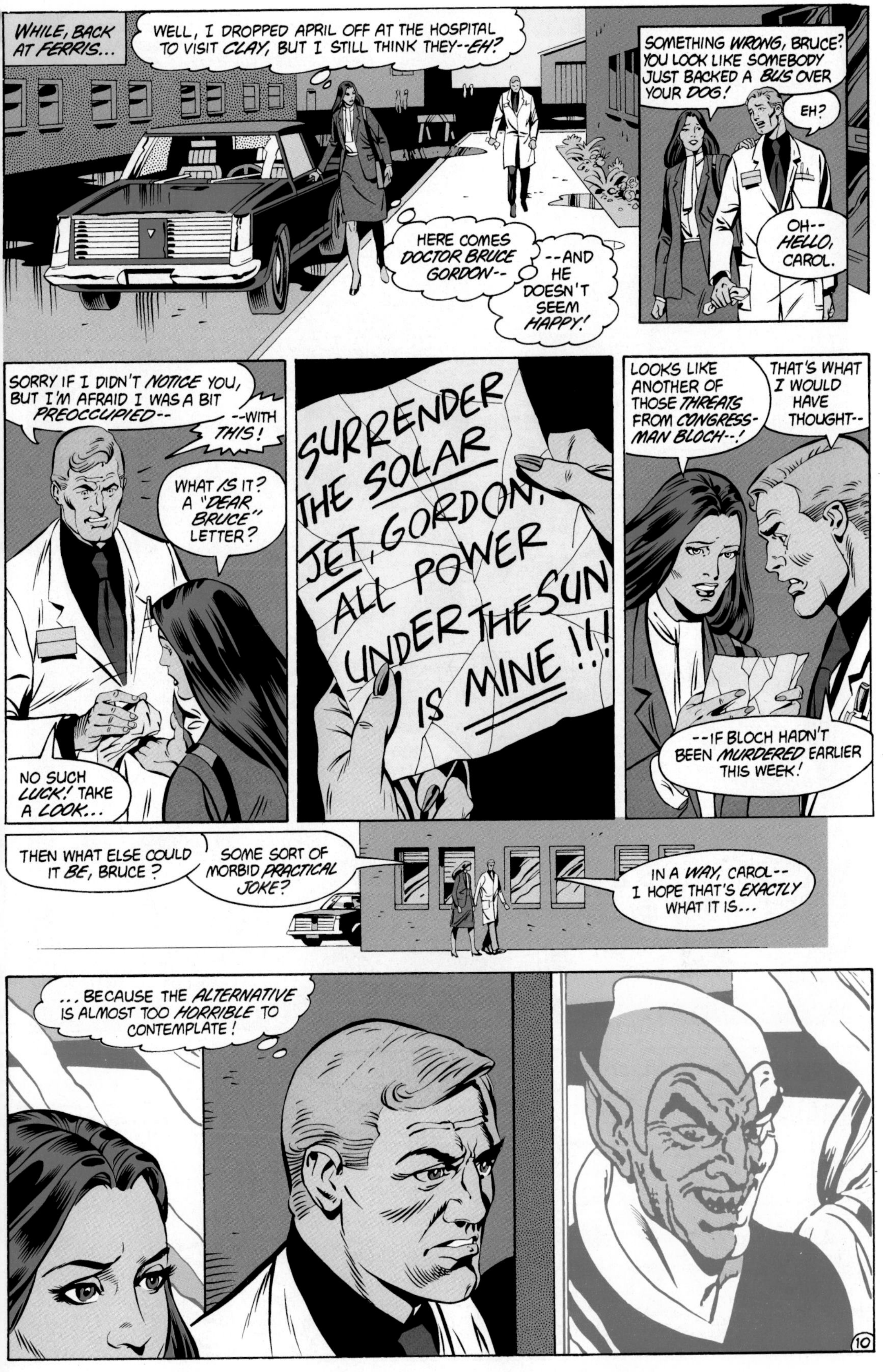

WHILE, BACK AT FERRIS...
WELL, I DROPPED APRIL OFF AT THE HOSPITAL TO VISIT CLAY, BUT I STILL THINK THEY--EH?
HERE COMES DOCTOR BRUCE GORDON--
--AND HE DOESN'T SEEM HAPPY!
SOMETHING WRONG, BRUCE? YOU LOOK LIKE SOMEBODY JUST BACKED A BUS OVER YOUR DOG!
EH?
OH-- HELLO, CAROL.
SORRY IF I DIDN'T NOTICE YOU, BUT I'M AFRAID I WAS A BIT PREOCCUPIED--
--WITH THIS!
WHAT IS IT? A "DEAR BRUCE" LETTER?
NO SUCH LUCK! TAKE A LOOK...
SURRENDER THE SOLAR JET, GORDON, ALL POWER UNDER THE SUN IS MINE !!!
LOOKS LIKE ANOTHER OF THOSE THREATS FROM CONGRESSMAN BLOCH--!
THAT'S WHAT I WOULD HAVE THOUGHT--
--IF BLOCH HADN'T BEEN MURDERED EARLIER THIS WEEK!
THEN WHAT ELSE COULD IT BE, BRUCE?
SOME SORT OF MORBID PRACTICAL JOKE?
IN A WAY, CAROL-- I HOPE THAT'S EXACTLY WHAT IT IS...
...BECAUSE THE ALTERNATIVE IS ALMOST TOO HORRIBLE TO CONTEMPLATE!
10

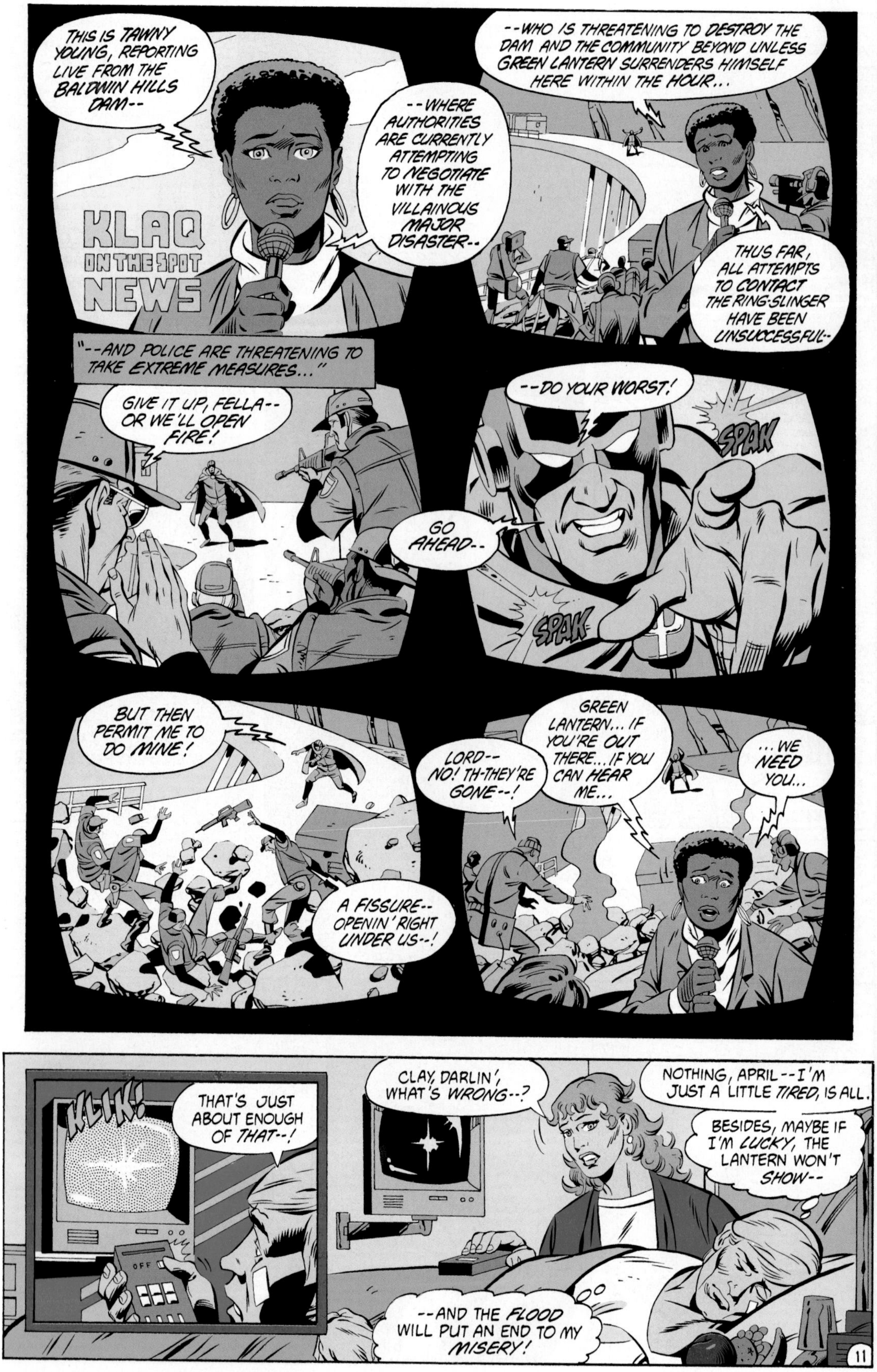
THIS IS TAWNY YOUNG, REPORTING LIVE FROM THE BALDWIN HILLS DAM--
KLAQ ON THE SPOT NEWS
--WHERE AUTHORITIES ARE CURRENTLY ATTEMPTING TO NEGOTIATE WITH THE VILLAINOUS MAJOR DISASTER--
--WHO IS THREATENING TO DESTROY THE DAM AND THE COMMUNITY BEYOND UNLESS GREEN LANTERN SURRENDERS HIMSELF HERE WITHIN THE HOUR...
THUS FAR, ALL ATTEMPTS TO CONTACT THE RING-SLINGER HAVE BEEN UNSUCCESSFUL--
"--AND POLICE ARE THREATENING TO TAKE EXTREME MEASURES..."
GIVE IT UP, FELLA-- OR WE'LL OPEN FIRE!
--DO YOUR WORST!
SPAK
GO AHEAD--
SPAK
BUT THEN PERMIT ME TO DO MINE!
A FISSURE-- OPENIN' RIGHT UNDER US--!
LORD-- NO! TH-THEY'RE GONE--!
GREEN LANTERN... IF YOU'RE OUT THERE... IF YOU CAN HEAR ME...
...WE NEED YOU...
KLIK!
THAT'S JUST ABOUT ENOUGH OF THAT--!
CLAY, DARLIN', WHAT'S WRONG--?
NOTHING, APRIL--I'M JUST A LITTLE TIRED, IS ALL.
BESIDES, MAYBE IF I'M LUCKY, THE LANTERN WON'T SHOW--
--AND THE FLOOD WILL PUT AN END TO MY MISERY!
OFF
11

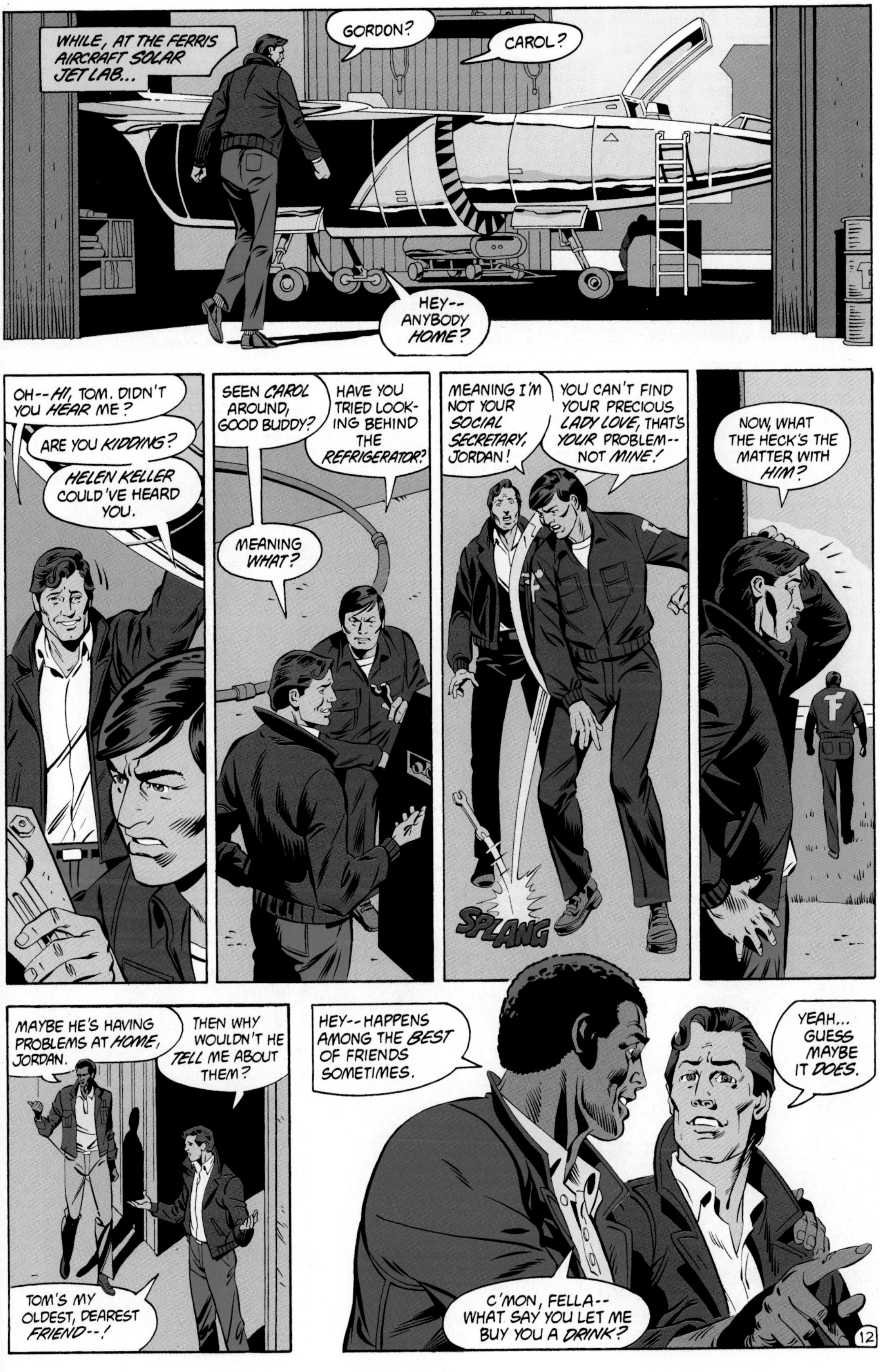
WHILE, AT THE FERRIS AIRCRAFT SOLAR JET LAB...
GORDON?
CAROL?
HEY-- ANYBODY HOME?
OH--HI, TOM. DIDN'T YOU HEAR ME?
ARE YOU KIDDING?
HELEN KELLER COULD'VE HEARD YOU.
SEEN CAROL AROUND, GOOD BUDDY?
HAVE YOU TRIED LOOKING BEHIND THE REFRIGERATOR?
MEANING WHAT?
MEANING I'M NOT YOUR SOCIAL SECRETARY, JORDAN!
YOU CAN'T FIND YOUR PRECIOUS LADY LOVE, THAT'S YOUR PROBLEM-- NOT MINE!
SPLANG
NOW, WHAT THE HECK'S THE MATTER WITH HIM?
MAYBE HE'S HAVING PROBLEMS AT HOME, JORDAN.
THEN WHY WOULDN'T HE TELL ME ABOUT THEM?
TOM'S MY OLDEST, DEAREST FRIEND--!
HEY--HAPPENS AMONG THE BEST OF FRIENDS SOMETIMES.
YEAH... GUESS MAYBE IT DOES.
C'MON, FELLA-- WHAT SAY YOU LET ME BUY YOU A DRINK?
12

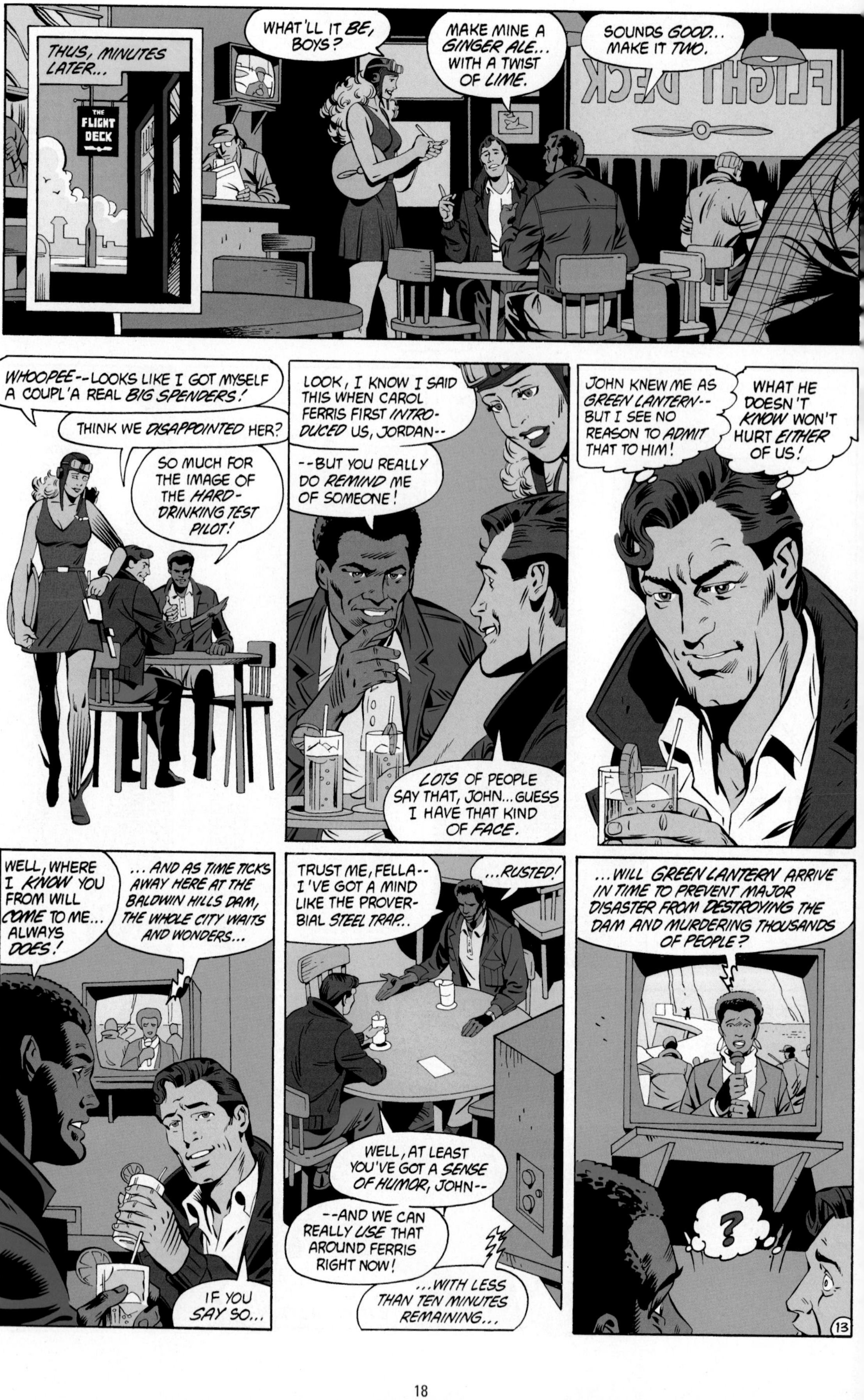
THUS, MINUTES LATER...
THE FLIGHT DECK
WHAT'LL IT BE, BOYS?
MAKE MINE A GINGER ALE... WITH A TWIST OF LIME.
SOUNDS GOOD.. MAKE IT TWO.
FLIGHT DECK
WHOOPEE--LOOKS LIKE I GOT MYSELF A COUPL'A REAL BIG SPENDERS!
THINK WE DISAPPOINTED HER?
SO MUCH FOR THE IMAGE OF THE HARD-DRINKING TEST PILOT!
LOOK, I KNOW I SAID THIS WHEN CAROL FERRIS FIRST INTRODUCED US, JORDAN--
--BUT YOU REALLY DO REMIND ME OF SOMEONE!
LOTS OF PEOPLE SAY THAT, JOHN... GUESS I HAVE THAT KIND OF FACE.
JOHN KNEW ME AS GREEN LANTERN--BUT I SEE NO REASON TO ADMIT THAT TO HIM!
WHAT HE DOESN'T KNOW WON'T HURT EITHER OF US!
WELL, WHERE I KNOW YOU FROM WILL COME TO ME... ALWAYS DOES!
... AND AS TIME TICKS AWAY HERE AT THE BALDWIN HILLS DAM, THE WHOLE CITY WAITS AND WONDERS...
IF YOU SAY SO...
TRUST ME, FELLA--I'VE GOT A MIND LIKE THE PROVERBIAL STEEL TRAP...
...RUSTED!
WELL, AT LEAST YOU'VE GOT A SENSE OF HUMOR, JOHN--
--AND WE CAN REALLY USE THAT AROUND FERRIS RIGHT NOW!
...WITH LESS THAN TEN MINUTES REMAINING...
...WILL GREEN LANTERN ARRIVE IN TIME TO PREVENT MAJOR DISASTER FROM DESTROYING THE DAM AND MURDERING THOUSANDS OF PEOPLE?
?
13

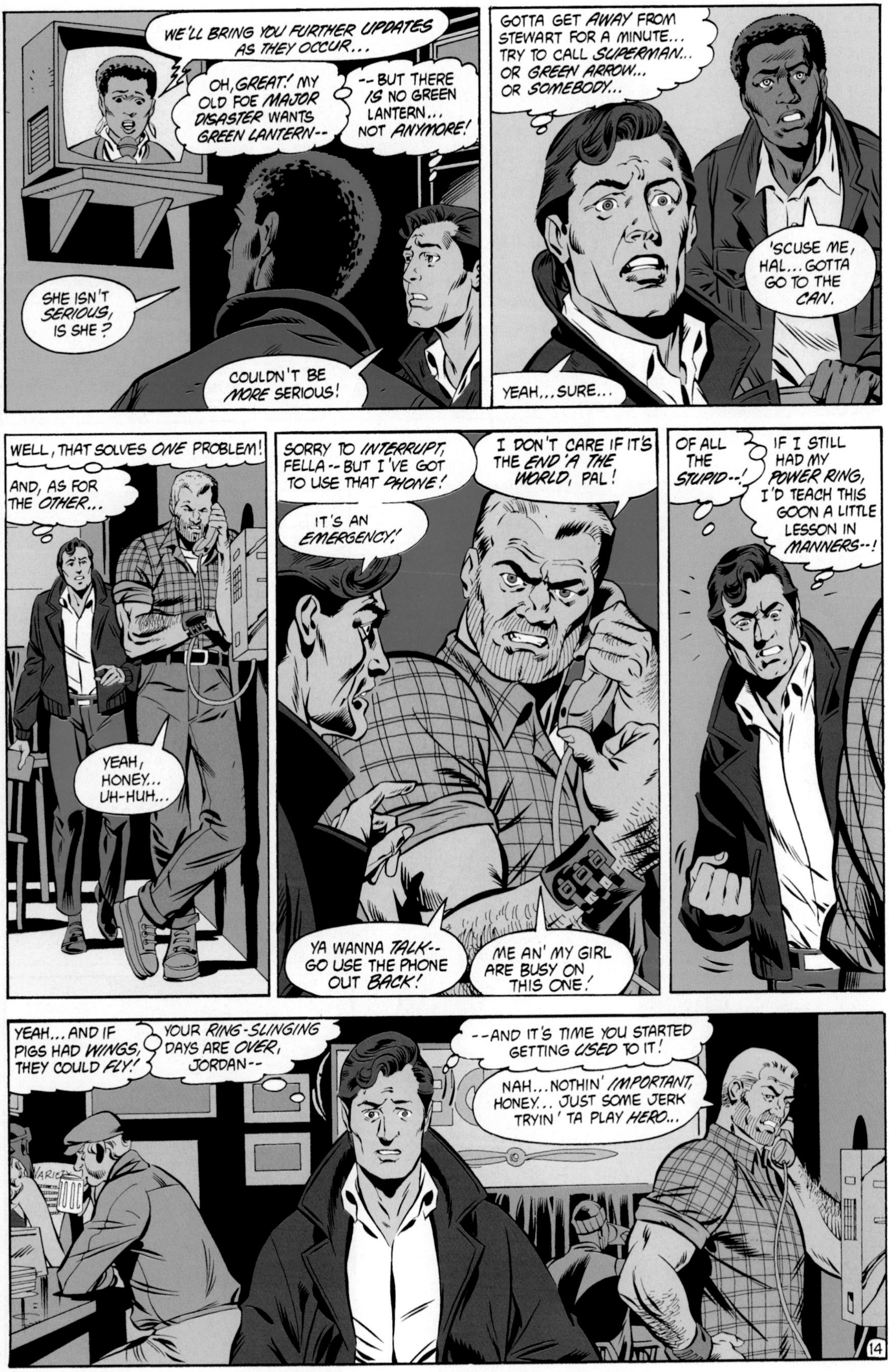
WE'LL BRING YOU FURTHER UPDATES AS THEY OCCUR...
OH, GREAT! MY OLD FOE MAJOR DISASTER WANTS GREEN LANTERN--
--BUT THERE IS NO GREEN LANTERN... NOT ANYMORE!
SHE ISN'T SERIOUS, IS SHE?
COULDN'T BE MORE SERIOUS!
GOTTA GET AWAY FROM STEWART FOR A MINUTE... TRY TO CALL SUPERMAN... OR GREEN ARROW... OR SOMEBODY...
'SCUSE ME, HAL... GOTTA GO TO THE CAN.
YEAH... SURE...
WELL, THAT SOLVES ONE PROBLEM!
AND, AS FOR THE OTHER...
YEAH, HONEY... UH-HUH...
SORRY TO INTERRUPT, FELLA--BUT I'VE GOT TO USE THAT PHONE!
I DON'T CARE IF IT'S THE END 'A THE WORLD, PAL!
IT'S AN EMERGENCY!
YA WANNA TALK--GO USE THE PHONE OUT BACK!
ME AN' MY GIRL ARE BUSY ON THIS ONE!
OF ALL THE STUPID--!
IF I STILL HAD MY POWER RING, I'D TEACH THIS GOON A LITTLE LESSON IN MANNERS--!
YEAH... AND IF PIGS HAD WINGS, THEY COULD FLY!
YOUR RING-SLINGING DAYS ARE OVER, JORDAN--
--AND IT'S TIME YOU STARTED GETTING USED TO IT!
NAH... NOTHIN' IMPORTANT, HONEY... JUST SOME JERK TRYIN' TA PLAY HERO...
14

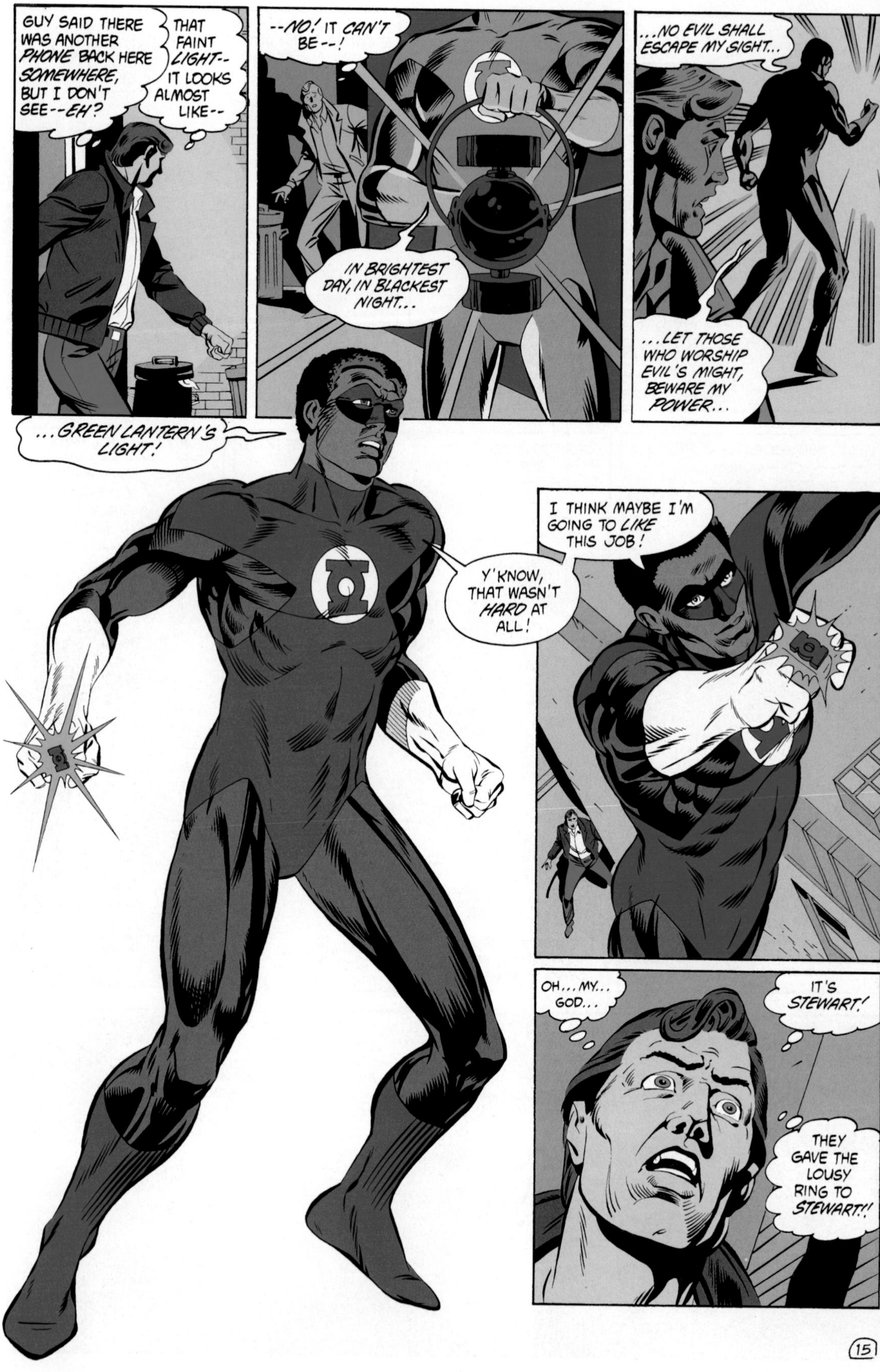
GUY SAID THERE WAS ANOTHER PHONE BACK HERE SOMEWHERE, BUT I DON'T SEE--EH?
THAT FAINT LIGHT-- IT LOOKS ALMOST LIKE--
--NO! IT CAN'T BE--!
IN BRIGHTEST DAY, IN BLACKEST NIGHT...
...NO EVIL SHALL ESCAPE MY SIGHT...
...LET THOSE WHO WORSHIP EVIL'S MIGHT, BEWARE MY POWER...
...GREEN LANTERN'S LIGHT!
Y'KNOW, THAT WASN'T HARD AT ALL!
I THINK MAYBE I'M GOING TO LIKE THIS JOB!
OH...MY... GOD...
IT'S STEWART!
THEY GAVE THE LOUSY RING TO STEWART!!
15

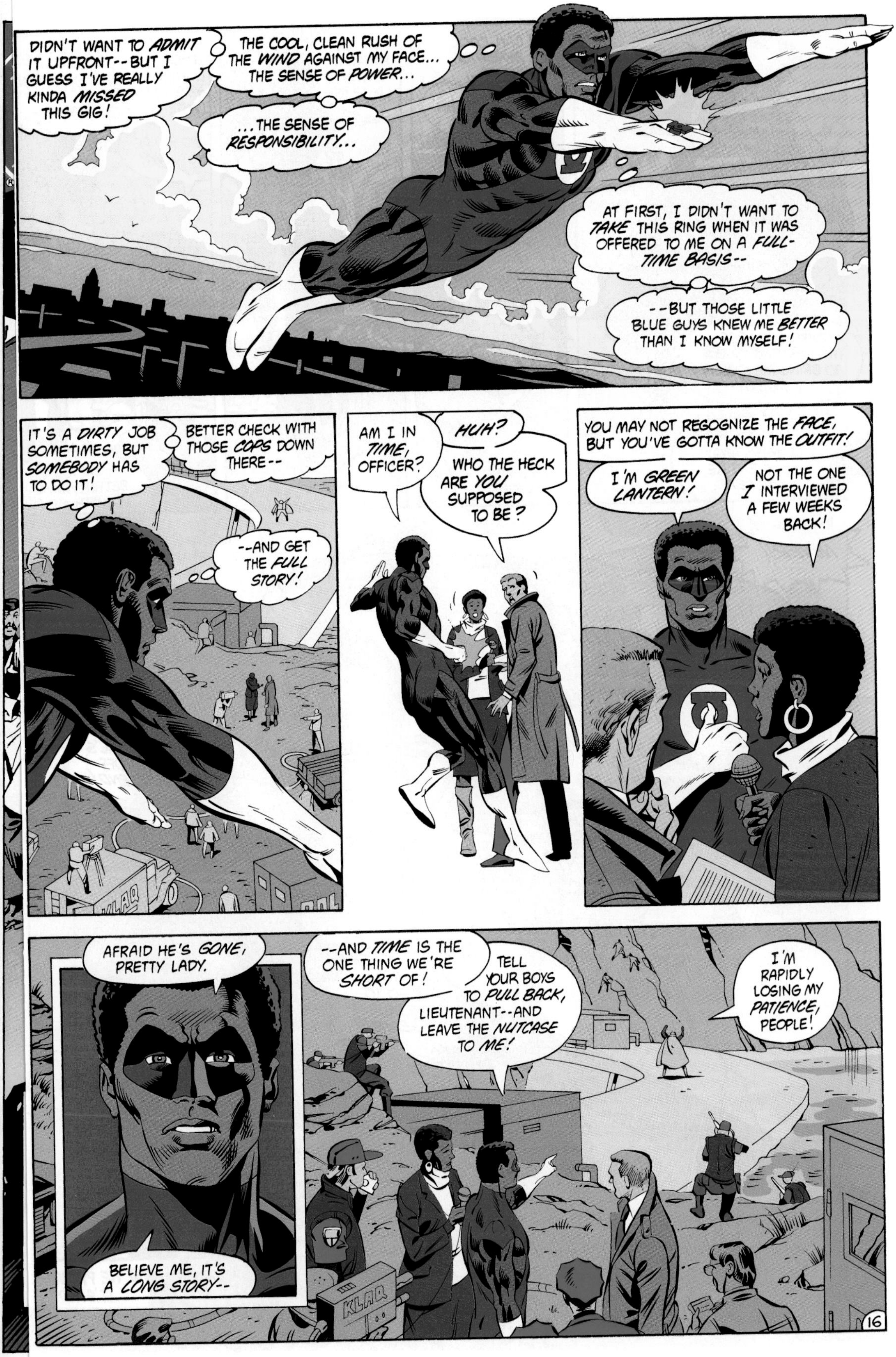
DIDN'T WANT TO ADMIT IT UPFRONT--BUT I GUESS I'VE REALLY KINDA MISSED THIS GIG!
THE COOL, CLEAN RUSH OF THE WIND AGAINST MY FACE... THE SENSE OF POWER...
...THE SENSE OF RESPONSIBILITY...
AT FIRST, I DIDN'T WANT TO TAKE THIS RING WHEN IT WAS OFFERED TO ME ON A FULL-TIME BASIS--
--BUT THOSE LITTLE BLUE GUYS KNEW ME BETTER THAN I KNOW MYSELF!
IT'S A DIRTY JOB SOMETIMES, BUT SOMEBODY HAS TO DO IT!
BETTER CHECK WITH THOSE COPS DOWN THERE--
--AND GET THE FULL STORY!
AM I IN TIME, OFFICER?
HUH?
WHO THE HECK ARE YOU SUPPOSED TO BE?
YOU MAY NOT RECOGNIZE THE FACE, BUT YOU'VE GOTTA KNOW THE OUTFIT!
I'M GREEN LANTERN!
NOT THE ONE I INTERVIEWED A FEW WEEKS BACK!
AFRAID HE'S GONE, PRETTY LADY.
BELIEVE ME, IT'S A LONG STORY--
--AND TIME IS THE ONE THING WE'RE SHORT OF!
TELL YOUR BOYS TO PULL BACK, LIEUTENANT--AND LEAVE THE NUTCASE TO ME!
I'M RAPIDLY LOSING MY PATIENCE, PEOPLE!
KLAQ
16

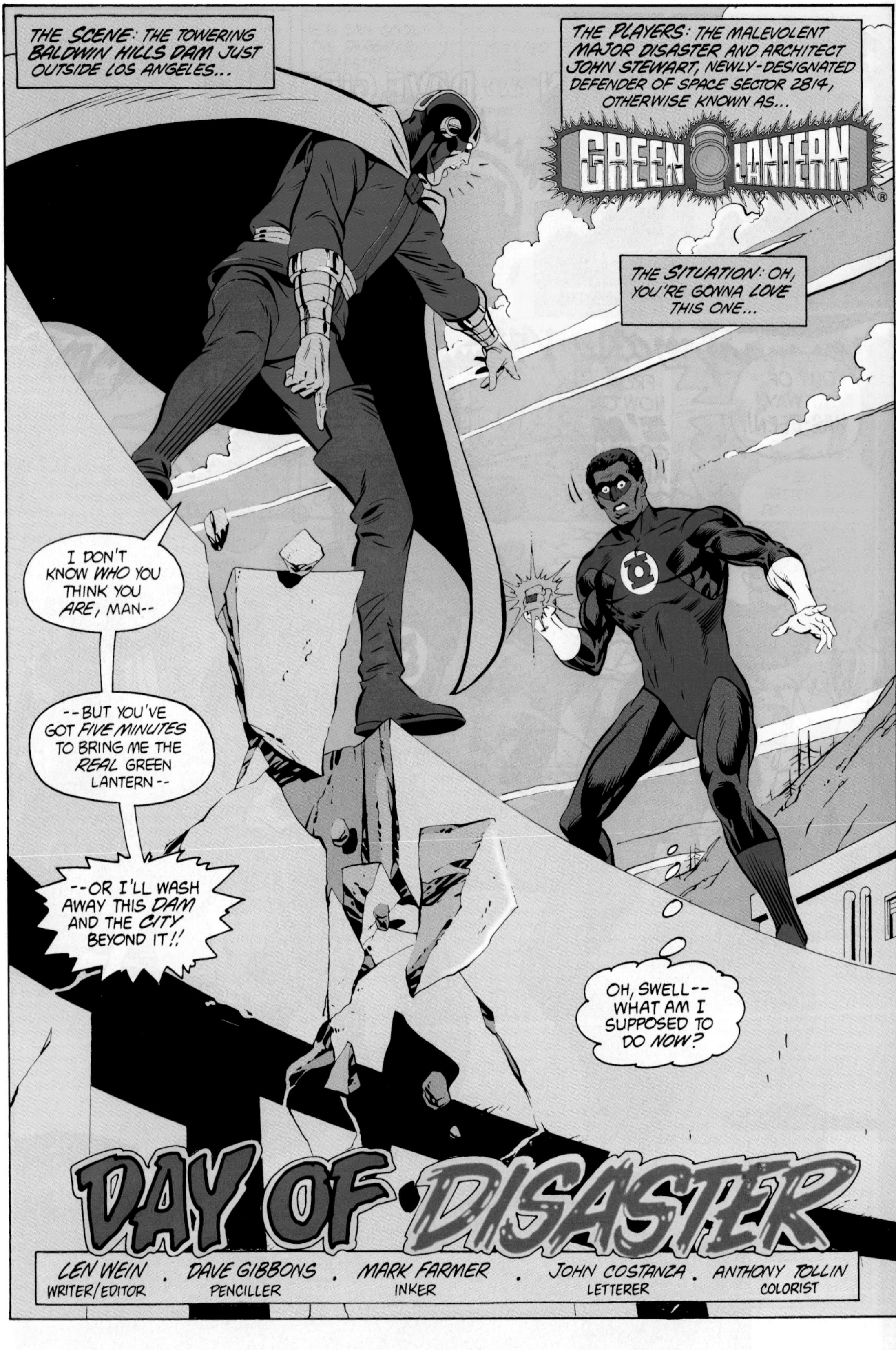
THE SCENE: THE TOWERING BALDWIN HILLS DAM JUST OUTSIDE LOS ANGELES...
THE PLAYERS: THE MALEVOLENT MAJOR DISASTER AND ARCHITECT JOHN STEWART, NEWLY-DESIGNATED DEFENDER OF SPACE SECTOR 2814, OTHERWISE KNOWN AS...
GREEN LANTERN
THE SITUATION: OH, YOU'RE GONNA LOVE THIS ONE...
I DON'T KNOW WHO YOU THINK YOU ARE, MAN--
--BUT YOU'VE GOT FIVE MINUTES TO BRING ME THE REAL GREEN LANTERN--
--OR I'LL WASH AWAY THIS DAM AND THE CITY BEYOND IT!!
OH, SWELL--WHAT AM I SUPPOSED TO DO NOW?
DAY OF DISASTER
LEN WEIN WRITER/EDITOR . DAVE GIBBONS PENCILLER . MARK FARMER INKER . JOHN COSTANZA LETTERER . ANTHONY TOLLIN COLORIST

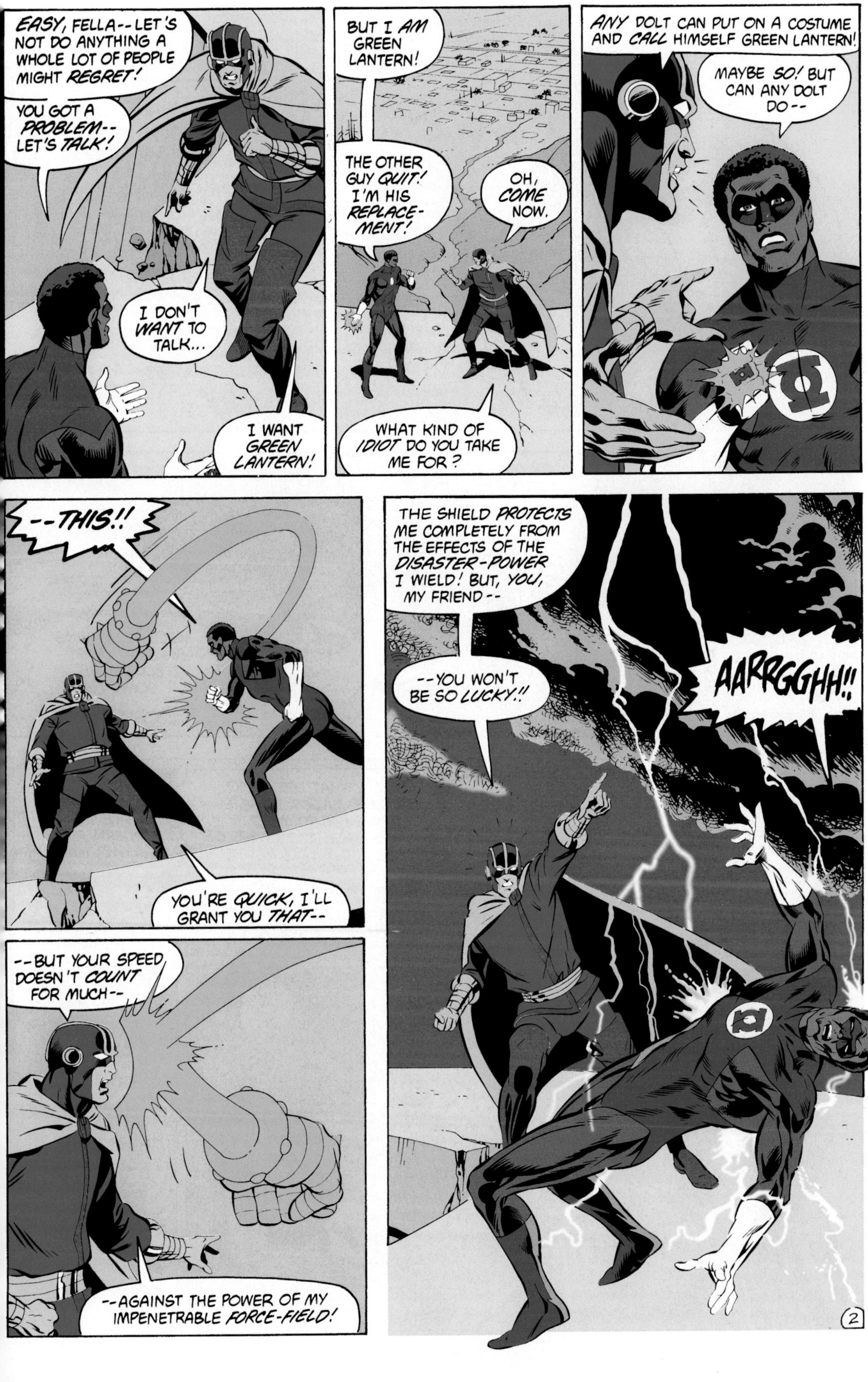
EASY, FELLA--LET'S NOT DO ANYTHING A WHOLE LOT OF PEOPLE MIGHT REGRET!
YOU GOT A PROBLEM--LET'S TALK!
I DON'T WANT TO TALK...
I WANT GREEN LANTERN!
BUT I AM GREEN LANTERN!
THE OTHER GUY QUIT! I'M HIS REPLACEMENT!
OH, COME NOW.
WHAT KIND OF IDIOT DO YOU TAKE ME FOR?
ANY DOLT CAN PUT ON A COSTUME AND CALL HIMSELF GREEN LANTERN!
MAYBE SO! BUT CAN ANY DOLT DO--
--THIS!!
YOU'RE QUICK, I'LL GRANT YOU THAT--
--BUT YOUR SPEED DOESN'T COUNT FOR MUCH--
--AGAINST THE POWER OF MY IMPENETRABLE FORCE-FIELD!
THE SHIELD PROTECTS ME COMPLETELY FROM THE EFFECTS OF THE DISASTER-POWER I WIELD! BUT, YOU, MY FRIEND--
--YOU WON'T BE SO LUCKY!!
AARRGGHH!!
2

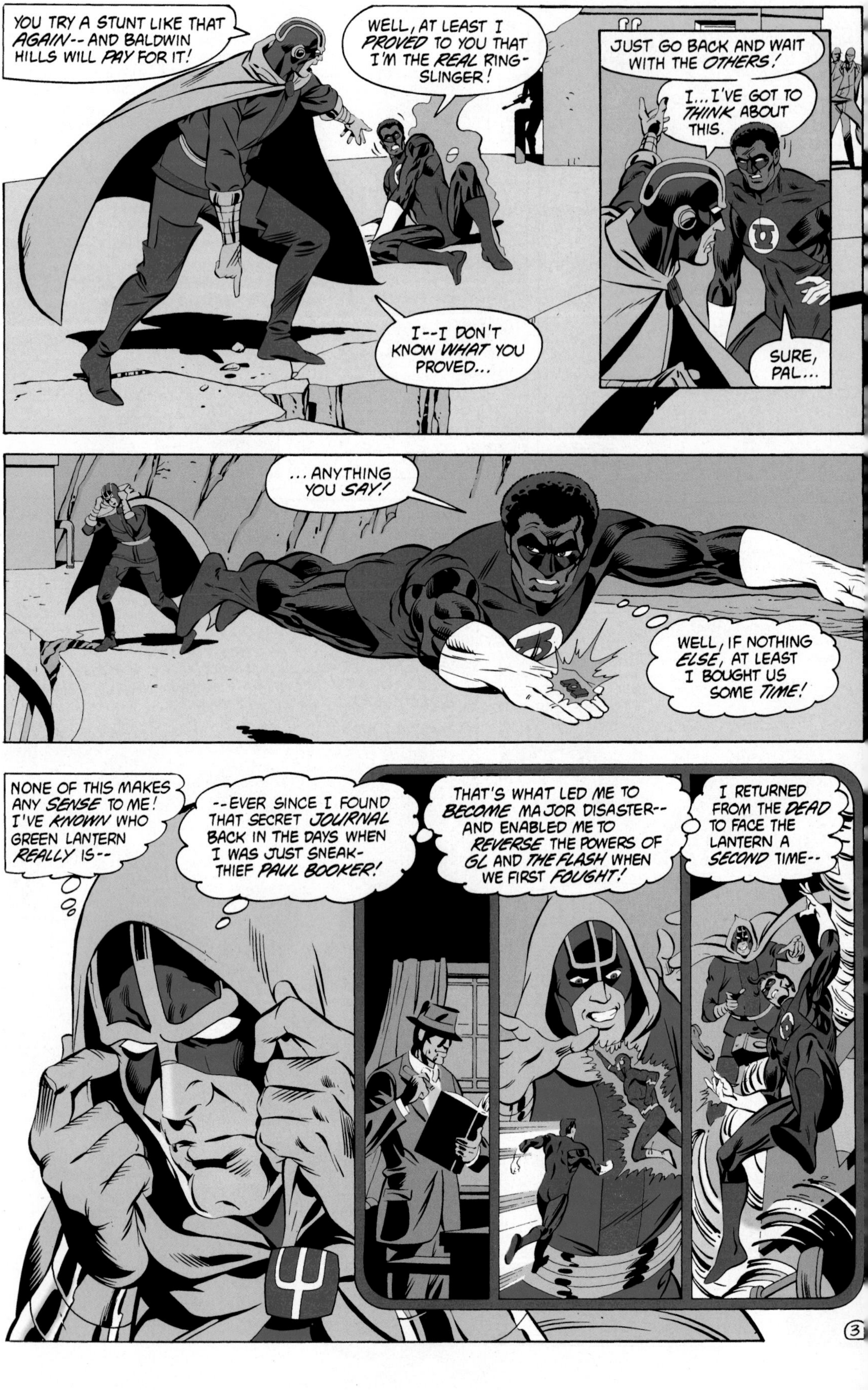

YOU TRY A STUNT LIKE THAT AGAIN-- AND BALDWIN HILLS WILL PAY FOR IT!
WELL, AT LEAST I PROVED TO YOU THAT I'M THE REAL RING-SLINGER!
I--I DON'T KNOW WHAT YOU PROVED...
JUST GO BACK AND WAIT WITH THE OTHERS!
I...I'VE GOT TO THINK ABOUT THIS.
SURE, PAL...
...ANYTHING YOU SAY!
WELL, IF NOTHING ELSE, AT LEAST I BOUGHT US SOME TIME!
NONE OF THIS MAKES ANY SENSE TO ME! I'VE KNOWN WHO GREEN LANTERN REALLY IS--
--EVER SINCE I FOUND THAT SECRET JOURNAL BACK IN THE DAYS WHEN I WAS JUST SNEAK-THIEF PAUL BOOKER!
THAT'S WHAT LED ME TO BECOME MAJOR DISASTER-- AND ENABLED ME TO REVERSE THE POWERS OF GL AND THE FLASH WHEN WE FIRST FOUGHT!
I RETURNED FROM THE DEAD TO FACE THE LANTERN A SECOND TIME--
3

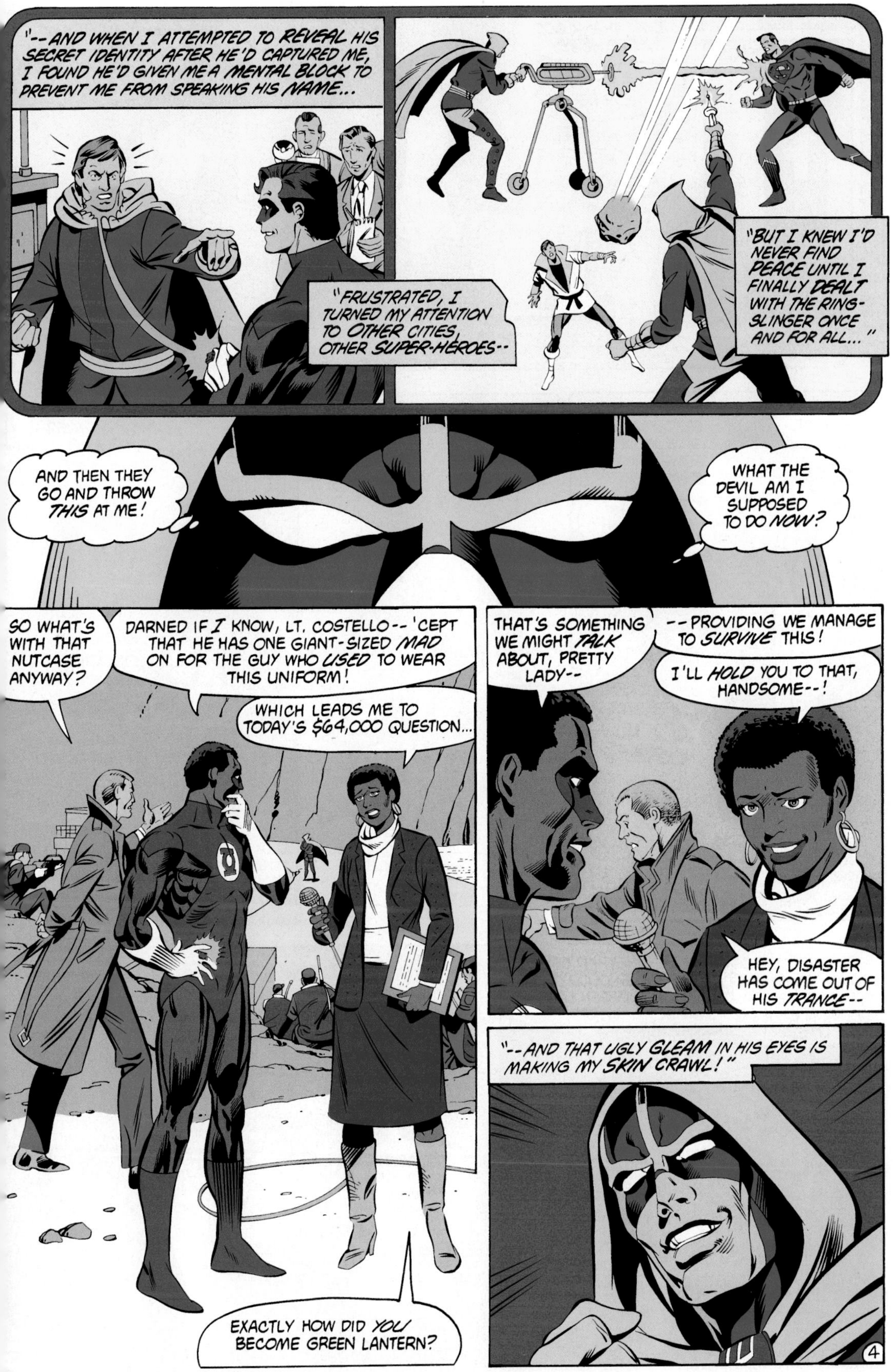
"--AND WHEN I ATTEMPTED TO REVEAL HIS SECRET IDENTITY AFTER HE'D CAPTURED ME, I FOUND HE'D GIVEN ME A MENTAL BLOCK TO PREVENT ME FROM SPEAKING HIS NAME...
"FRUSTRATED, I TURNED MY ATTENTION TO OTHER CITIES, OTHER SUPER-HEROES--
"BUT I KNEW I'D NEVER FIND PEACE UNTIL I FINALLY DEALT WITH THE RING-SLINGER ONCE AND FOR ALL..."
AND THEN THEY GO AND THROW THIS AT ME!
WHAT THE DEVIL AM I SUPPOSED TO DO NOW?
SO WHAT'S WITH THAT NUTCASE ANYWAY?
DARNED IF I KNOW, LT. COSTELLO--'CEPT THAT HE HAS ONE GIANT-SIZED MAD ON FOR THE GUY WHO USED TO WEAR THIS UNIFORM!
WHICH LEADS ME TO TODAY'S $64,000 QUESTION...
EXACTLY HOW DID YOU BECOME GREEN LANTERN?
THAT'S SOMETHING WE MIGHT TALK ABOUT, PRETTY LADY--
--PROVIDING WE MANAGE TO SURVIVE THIS!
I'LL HOLD YOU TO THAT, HANDSOME--!
HEY, DISASTER HAS COME OUT OF HIS TRANCE--
"--AND THAT UGLY GLEAM IN HIS EYES IS MAKING MY SKIN CRAWL!"
4

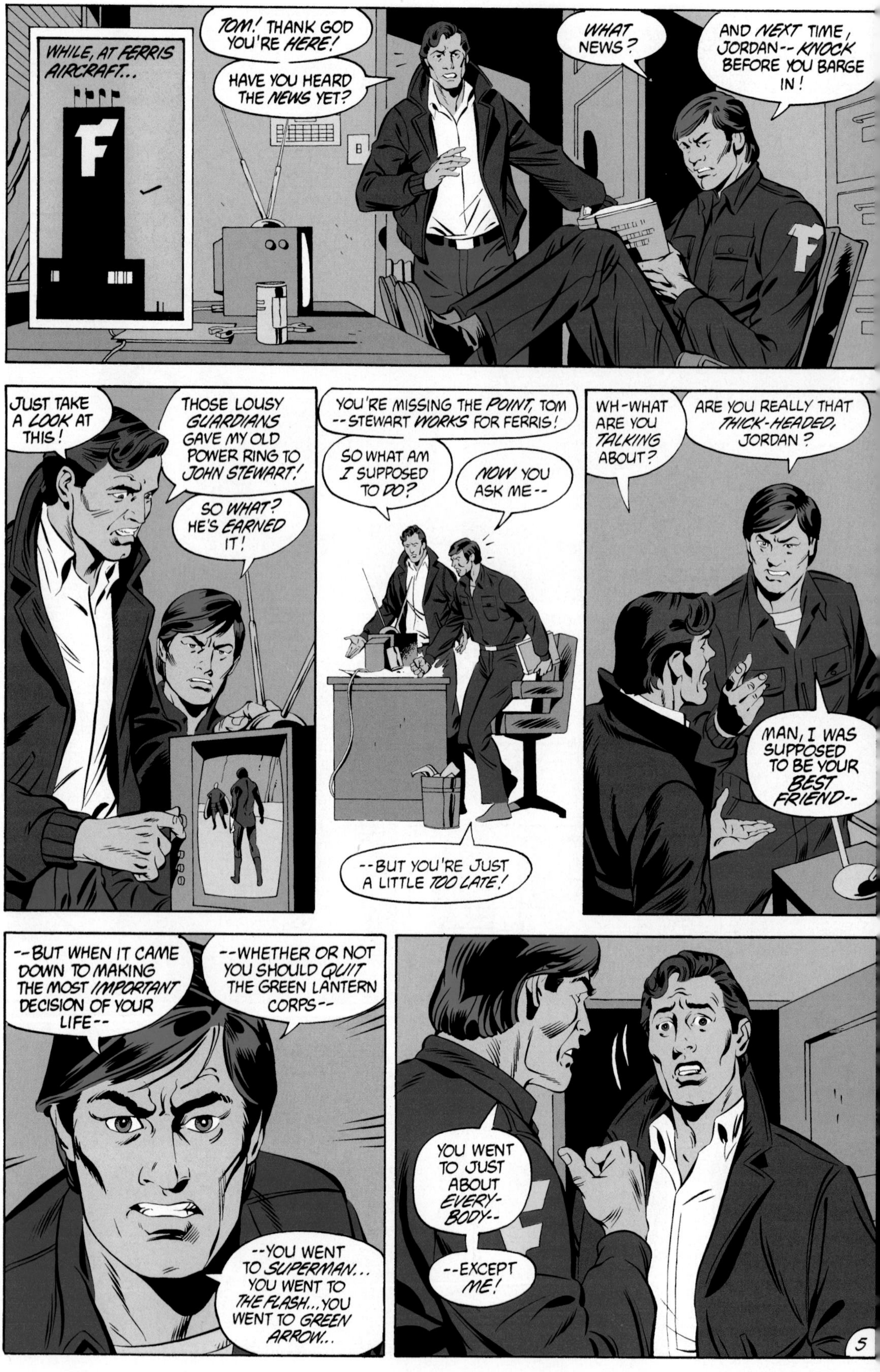
WHILE, AT FERRIS AIRCRAFT...
TOM! THANK GOD YOU'RE HERE!
HAVE YOU HEARD THE NEWS YET?
WHAT NEWS?
AND NEXT TIME, JORDAN--KNOCK BEFORE YOU BARGE IN!
JUST TAKE A LOOK AT THIS!
THOSE LOUSY GUARDIANS GAVE MY OLD POWER RING TO JOHN STEWART!
SO WHAT? HE'S EARNED IT!
YOU'RE MISSING THE POINT, TOM --STEWART WORKS FOR FERRIS!
SO WHAT AM I SUPPOSED TO DO?
NOW YOU ASK ME--
--BUT YOU'RE JUST A LITTLE TOO LATE!
WH-WHAT ARE YOU TALKING ABOUT?
ARE YOU REALLY THAT THICK-HEADED, JORDAN?
MAN, I WAS SUPPOSED TO BE YOUR BEST FRIEND--
--BUT WHEN IT CAME DOWN TO MAKING THE MOST IMPORTANT DECISION OF YOUR LIFE--
--WHETHER OR NOT YOU SHOULD QUIT THE GREEN LANTERN CORPS--
--YOU WENT TO SUPERMAN... YOU WENT TO THE FLASH...YOU WENT TO GREEN ARROW...
YOU WENT TO JUST ABOUT EVERY-BODY--
--EXCEPT ME!
5

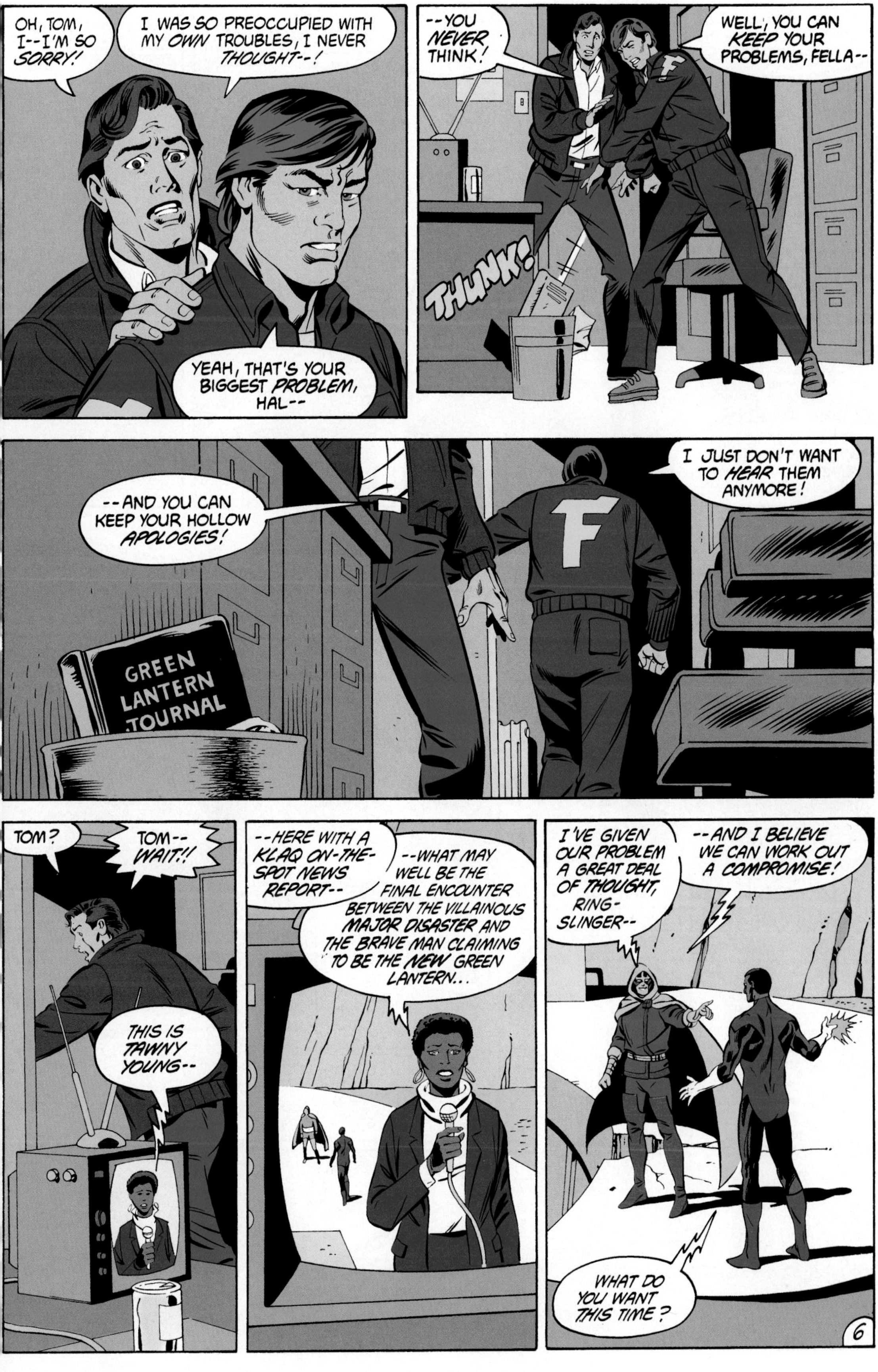
OH, TOM, I--I'M SO SORRY!
I WAS SO PREOCCUPIED WITH MY OWN TROUBLES, I NEVER THOUGHT--!
YEAH, THAT'S YOUR BIGGEST PROBLEM, HAL--
--YOU NEVER THINK!
WELL, YOU CAN KEEP YOUR PROBLEMS, FELLA--
THUNK!
--AND YOU CAN KEEP YOUR HOLLOW APOLOGIES!
I JUST DON'T WANT TO HEAR THEM ANYMORE!
GREEN LANTERN JOURNAL
TOM?
TOM-- WAIT!!
THIS IS TAWNY YOUNG--
--HERE WITH A KLAQ ON-THE-SPOT NEWS REPORT--
--WHAT MAY WELL BE THE FINAL ENCOUNTER BETWEEN THE VILLAINOUS MAJOR DISASTER AND THE BRAVE MAN CLAIMING TO BE THE NEW GREEN LANTERN...
I'VE GIVEN OUR PROBLEM A GREAT DEAL OF THOUGHT, RING-SLINGER--
--AND I BELIEVE WE CAN WORK OUT A COMPROMISE!
WHAT DO YOU WANT THIS TIME?
6

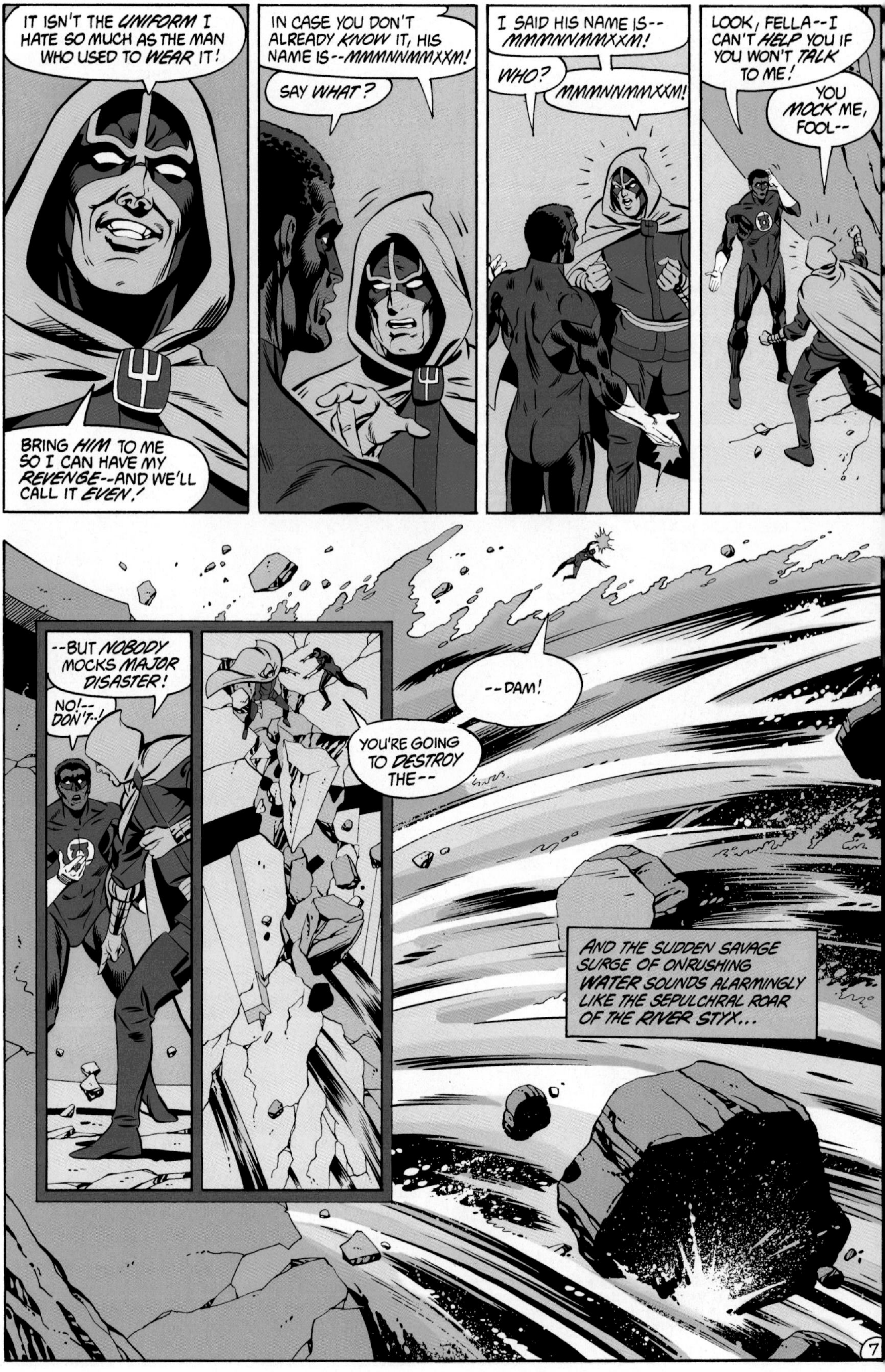
IT ISN'T THE UNIFORM I HATE SO MUCH AS THE MAN WHO USED TO WEAR IT!
BRING HIM TO ME SO I CAN HAVE MY REVENGE--AND WE'LL CALL IT EVEN!
IN CASE YOU DON'T ALREADY KNOW IT, HIS NAME IS--MMMNNMMXXM!
SAY WHAT?
I SAID HIS NAME IS--MMMNNMMXXM!
WHO?
MMMNNMMXXM!
LOOK, FELLA--I CAN'T HELP YOU IF YOU WON'T TALK TO ME!
YOU MOCK ME, FOOL--
--BUT NOBODY MOCKS MAJOR DISASTER!
NO!--DON'T--!
YOU'RE GOING TO DESTROY THE--
--DAM!
AND THE SUDDEN SAVAGE SURGE OF ONRUSHING WATER SOUNDS ALARMINGLY LIKE THE SEPULCHRAL ROAR OF THE RIVER STYX...
7

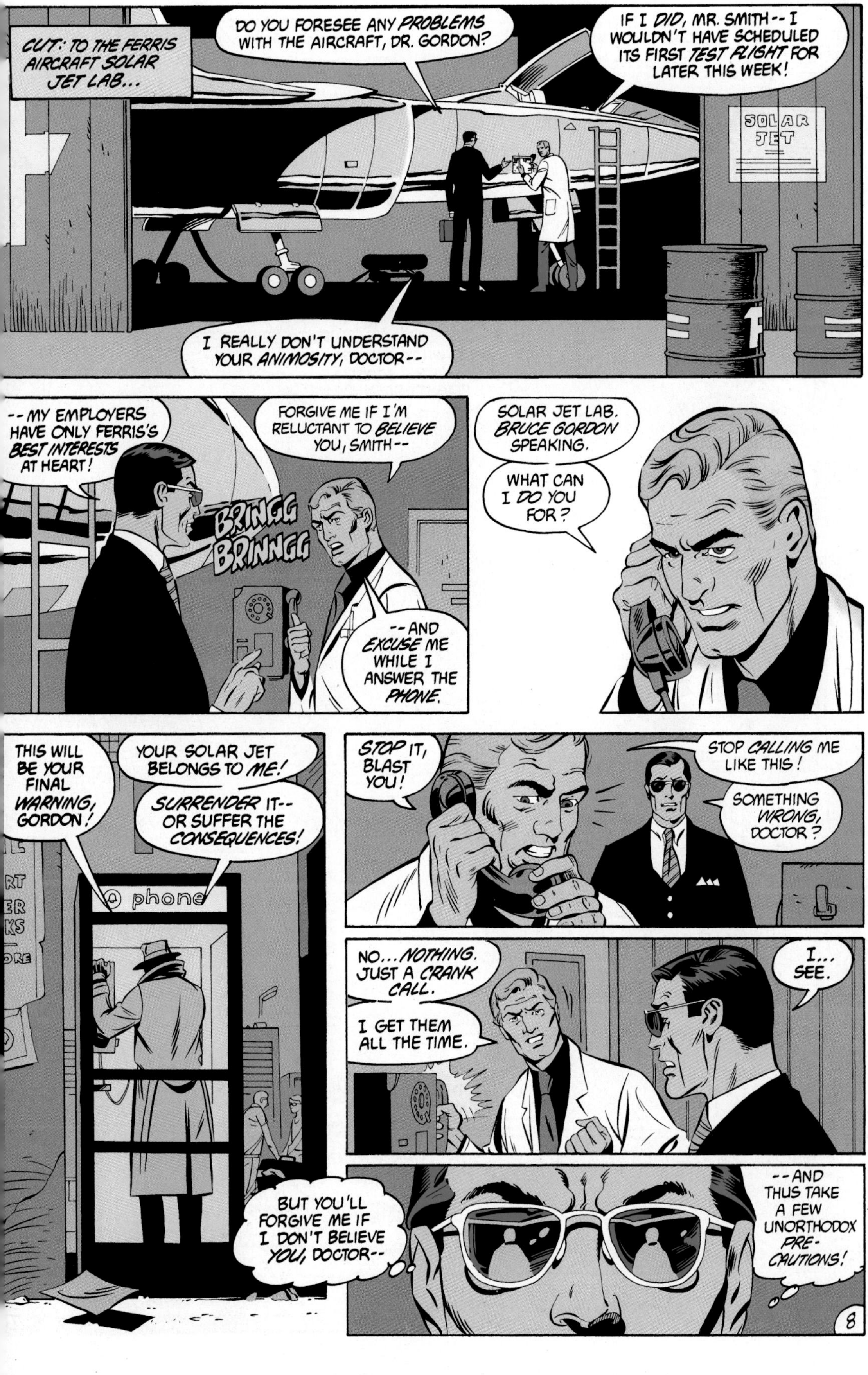
CUT: TO THE FERRIS AIRCRAFT SOLAR JET LAB...
DO YOU FORESEE ANY PROBLEMS WITH THE AIRCRAFT, DR. GORDON?
IF I DID, MR. SMITH-- I WOULDN'T HAVE SCHEDULED ITS FIRST TEST FLIGHT FOR LATER THIS WEEK!
SOLAR JET
I REALLY DON'T UNDERSTAND YOUR ANIMOSITY, DOCTOR--
--MY EMPLOYERS HAVE ONLY FERRIS'S BEST INTERESTS AT HEART!
FORGIVE ME IF I'M RELUCTANT TO BELIEVE YOU, SMITH--
BRINGG BRINNGG
--AND EXCUSE ME WHILE I ANSWER THE PHONE.
SOLAR JET LAB. BRUCE GORDON SPEAKING.
WHAT CAN I DO YOU FOR?
THIS WILL BE YOUR FINAL WARNING, GORDON!
YOUR SOLAR JET BELONGS TO ME!
SURRENDER IT-- OR SUFFER THE CONSEQUENCES!
phone
STOP IT, BLAST YOU!
STOP CALLING ME LIKE THIS!
SOMETHING WRONG, DOCTOR?
NO... NOTHING. JUST A CRANK CALL.
I GET THEM ALL THE TIME.
I... SEE.
BUT YOU'LL FORGIVE ME IF I DON'T BELIEVE YOU, DOCTOR--
--AND THUS TAKE A FEW UNORTHODOX PRE-CAUTIONS!
8

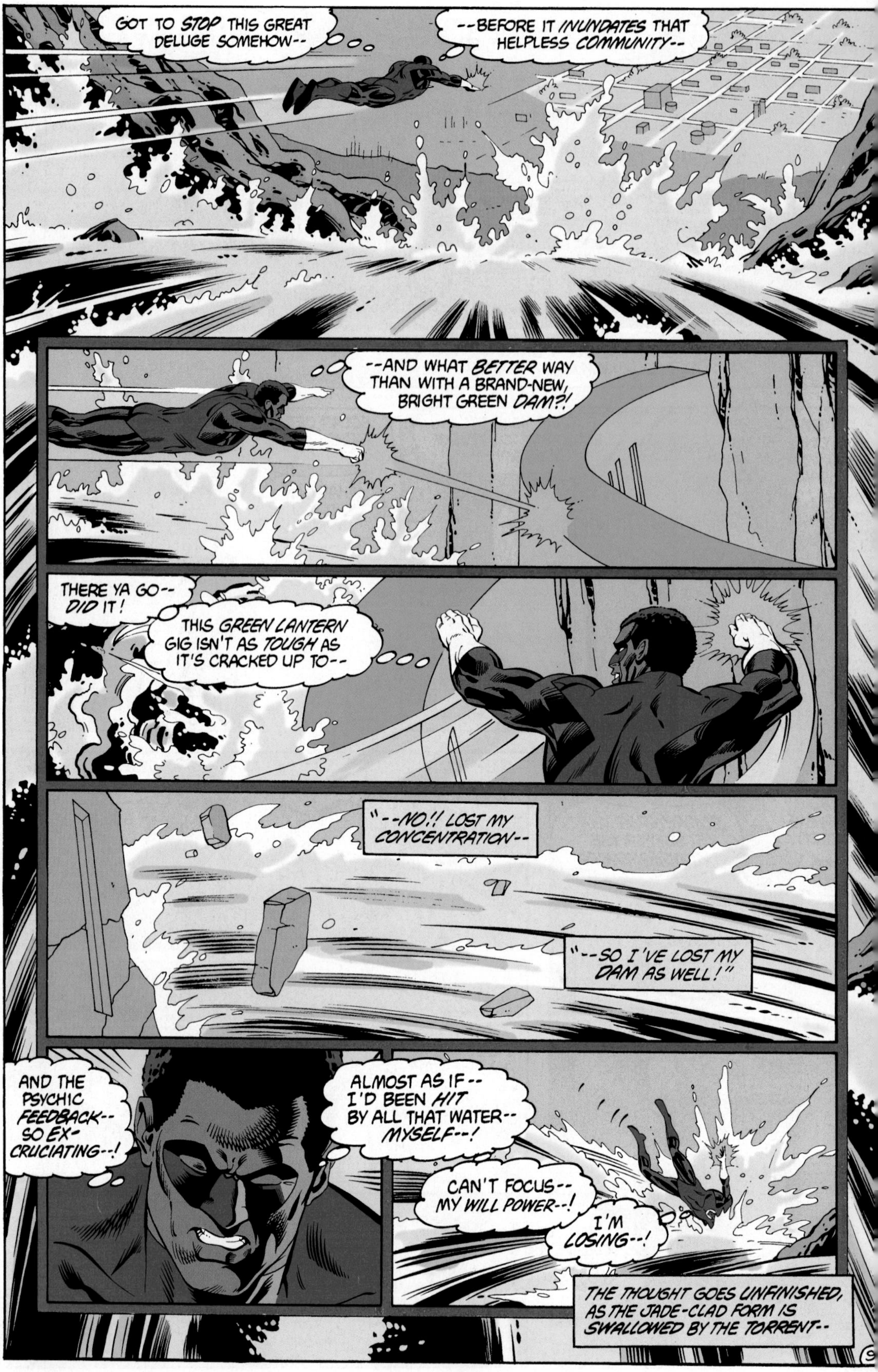
GOT TO STOP THIS GREAT DELUGE SOMEHOW--
--BEFORE IT INUNDATES THAT HELPLESS COMMUNITY--
--AND WHAT BETTER WAY THAN WITH A BRAND-NEW, BRIGHT GREEN DAM?!
THERE YA GO-- DID IT!
THIS GREEN LANTERN GIG ISN'T AS TOUGH AS IT'S CRACKED UP TO--
"--NO!! LOST MY CONCENTRATION--
"--SO I'VE LOST MY DAM AS WELL!"
AND THE PSYCHIC FEEDBACK-- SO EXCRUCIATING--!
ALMOST AS IF-- I'D BEEN HIT BY ALL THAT WATER-- MYSELF--!
CAN'T FOCUS-- MY WILL POWER--!
I'M LOSING--!
THE THOUGHT GOES UNFINISHED, AS THE JADE-CLAD FORM IS SWALLOWED BY THE TORRENT--
9

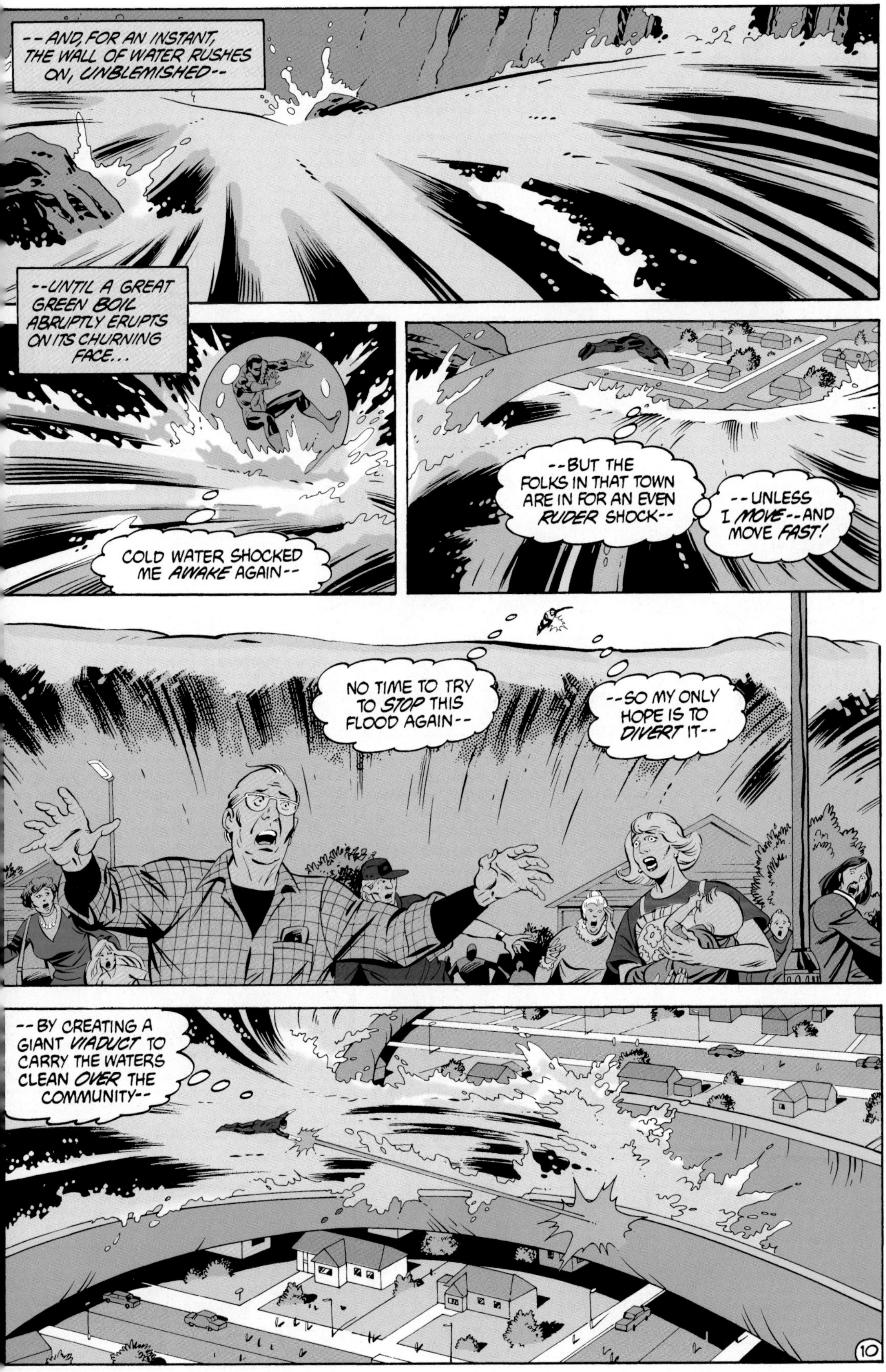
--AND, FOR AN INSTANT, THE WALL OF WATER RUSHES ON, UNBLEMISHED--
--UNTIL A GREAT GREEN BOIL ABRUPTLY ERUPTS ON ITS CHURNING FACE...
COLD WATER SHOCKED ME AWAKE AGAIN--
--BUT THE FOLKS IN THAT TOWN ARE IN FOR AN EVEN RUDER SHOCK--
--UNLESS I MOVE--AND MOVE FAST!
NO TIME TO TRY TO STOP THIS FLOOD AGAIN--
--SO MY ONLY HOPE IS TO DIVERT IT--
--BY CREATING A GIANT VIADUCT TO CARRY THE WATERS CLEAN OVER THE COMMUNITY--
10

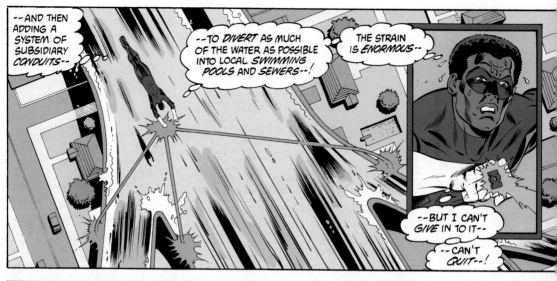

--AND THEN ADDING A SYSTEM OF SUBSIDIARY CONDUITS--

--TO *DIVERT* AS MUCH OF THE WATER AS POSSIBLE INTO LOCAL *SWIMMING POOLS* AND *SEWERS*--!

THE STRAIN IS *ENORMOUS*--

--BUT I CAN'T *GIVE* IN TO IT--

--CAN'T *QUIT*--!

NEXT TIME I BRAG ABOUT HOW *EASY* THIS JOB IS--

--REMIND ME TO BITE MY *TONGUE!*

AND, WHEN THE REMAINING FLOOD WATERS HAVE SUBSIDED...

HEY, YOU ALL RIGHT?

JUST A LITTLE... *BREATHLESS...*

JOB TOOK A LOT *OUT* OF ME...

BUT IT WAS A JOB WELL DONE...*GREEN LANTERN!*

APPRECIATE THE *COMPLIMENT,* PRETTY LADY--

--BUT IT'S ALL JUST PART OF THE *SERVICE!*

NOW, ABOUT THAT *DINNER* YOU PROMISED ME...

HATE TO COME *BETWEEN* YOU TWO LOVEBIRDS, LANTERN-- BUT THERE'S SOMETHING YOU SHOULD *KNOW!*

WHICH IS...?

WE'VE SCOURED THE ENTIRE AREA FOR THE *BODY*-- BUT CAME UP *EMPTY!*

APPARENTLY, *MAJOR DISASTER* IS STILL *ALIVE!*

11

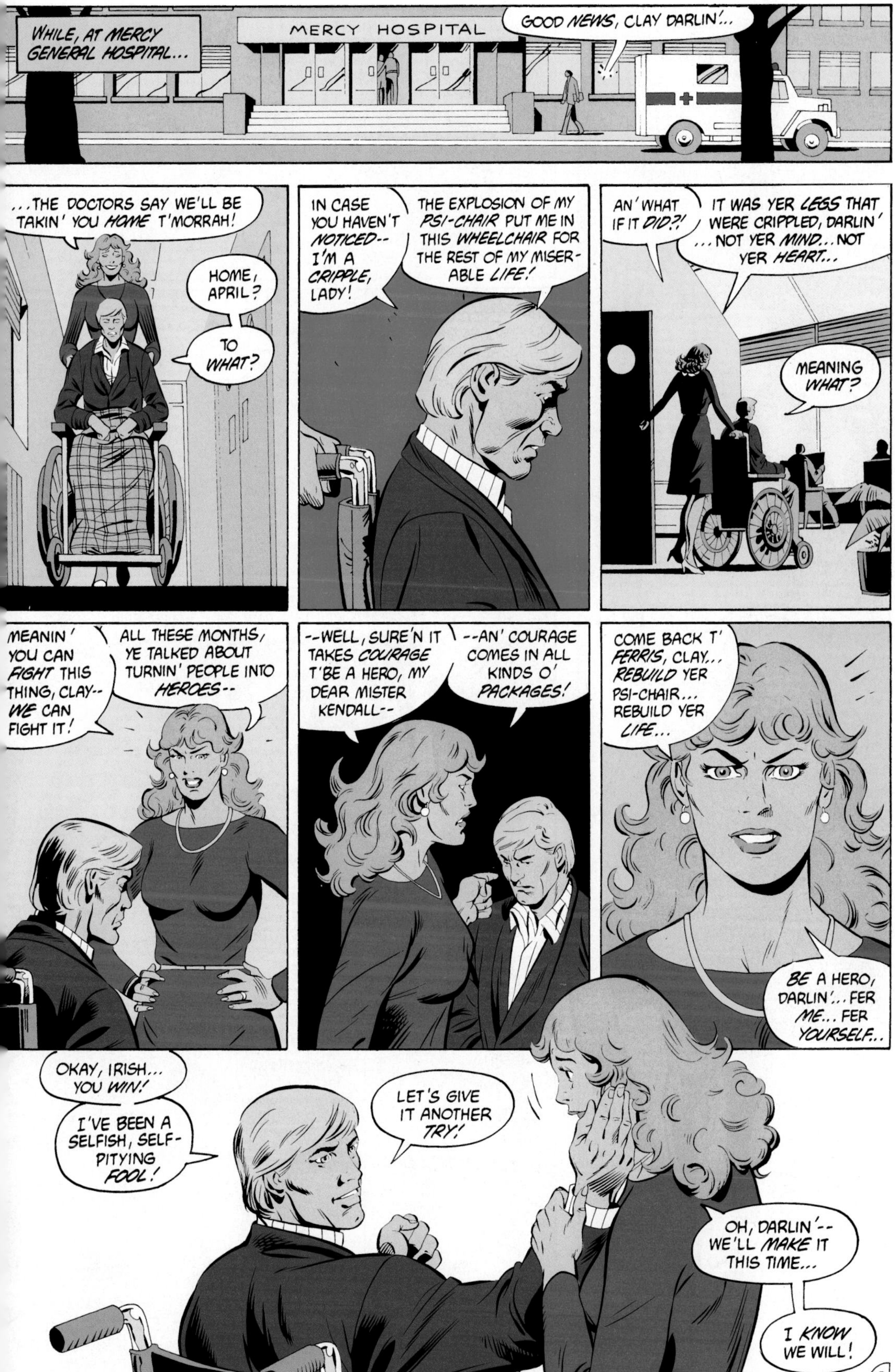
WHILE, AT MERCY GENERAL HOSPITAL...
MERCY HOSPITAL
GOOD NEWS, CLAY DARLIN'...
...THE DOCTORS SAY WE'LL BE TAKIN' YOU HOME T'MORRAH!
HOME, APRIL?
TO WHAT?
IN CASE YOU HAVEN'T NOTICED-- I'M A CRIPPLE, LADY!
THE EXPLOSION OF MY PSI-CHAIR PUT ME IN THIS WHEELCHAIR FOR THE REST OF MY MISERABLE LIFE!
AN' WHAT IF IT DID?!
IT WAS YER LEGS THAT WERE CRIPPLED, DARLIN' ...NOT YER MIND... NOT YER HEART...
MEANING WHAT?
MEANIN' YOU CAN FIGHT THIS THING, CLAY-- WE CAN FIGHT IT!
ALL THESE MONTHS, YE TALKED ABOUT TURNIN' PEOPLE INTO HEROES--
--WELL, SURE'N IT TAKES COURAGE T'BE A HERO, MY DEAR MISTER KENDALL--
--AN' COURAGE COMES IN ALL KINDS O' PACKAGES!
COME BACK T' FERRIS, CLAY... REBUILD YER PSI-CHAIR... REBUILD YER LIFE...
BE A HERO, DARLIN'... FER ME... FER YOURSELF...
OKAY, IRISH... YOU WIN!
I'VE BEEN A SELFISH, SELF-PITYING FOOL!
LET'S GIVE IT ANOTHER TRY!
OH, DARLIN'-- WE'LL MAKE IT THIS TIME...
I KNOW WE WILL!
12

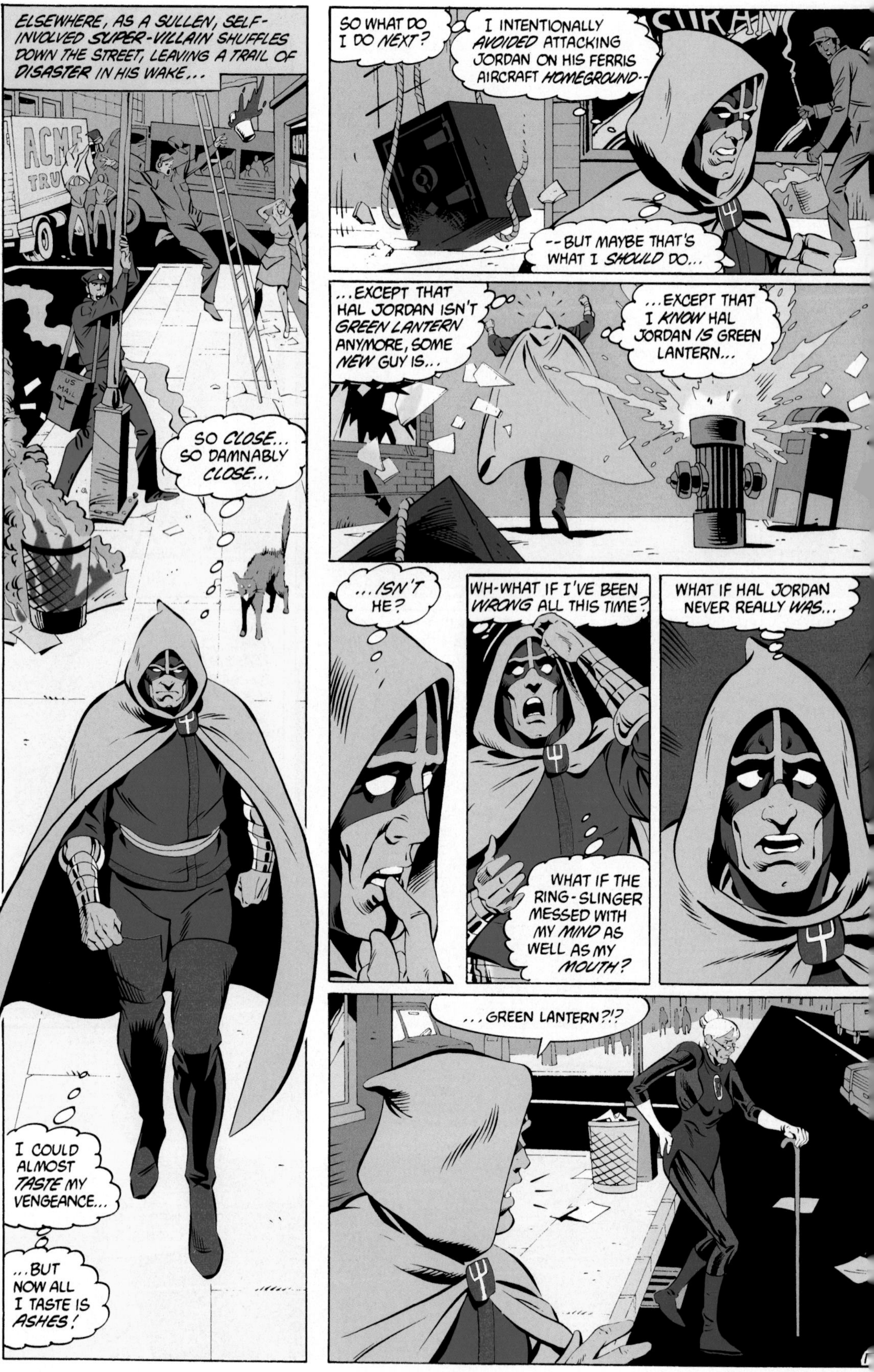
ELSEWHERE, AS A SULLEN, SELF-INVOLVED SUPER-VILLAIN SHUFFLES DOWN THE STREET, LEAVING A TRAIL OF DISASTER IN HIS WAKE...
SO CLOSE... SO DAMNABLY CLOSE...
I COULD ALMOST TASTE MY VENGEANCE...
...BUT NOW ALL I TASTE IS ASHES!
SO WHAT DO I DO NEXT?
I INTENTIONALLY AVOIDED ATTACKING JORDAN ON HIS FERRIS AIRCRAFT HOMEGROUND--
--BUT MAYBE THAT'S WHAT I SHOULD DO...
...EXCEPT THAT HAL JORDAN ISN'T GREEN LANTERN ANYMORE, SOME NEW GUY IS...
...EXCEPT THAT I KNOW HAL JORDAN IS GREEN LANTERN...
...ISN'T HE?
WH-WHAT IF I'VE BEEN WRONG ALL THIS TIME?
WHAT IF THE RING-SLINGER MESSED WITH MY MIND AS WELL AS MY MOUTH?
WHAT IF HAL JORDAN NEVER REALLY WAS...
...GREEN LANTERN?!?

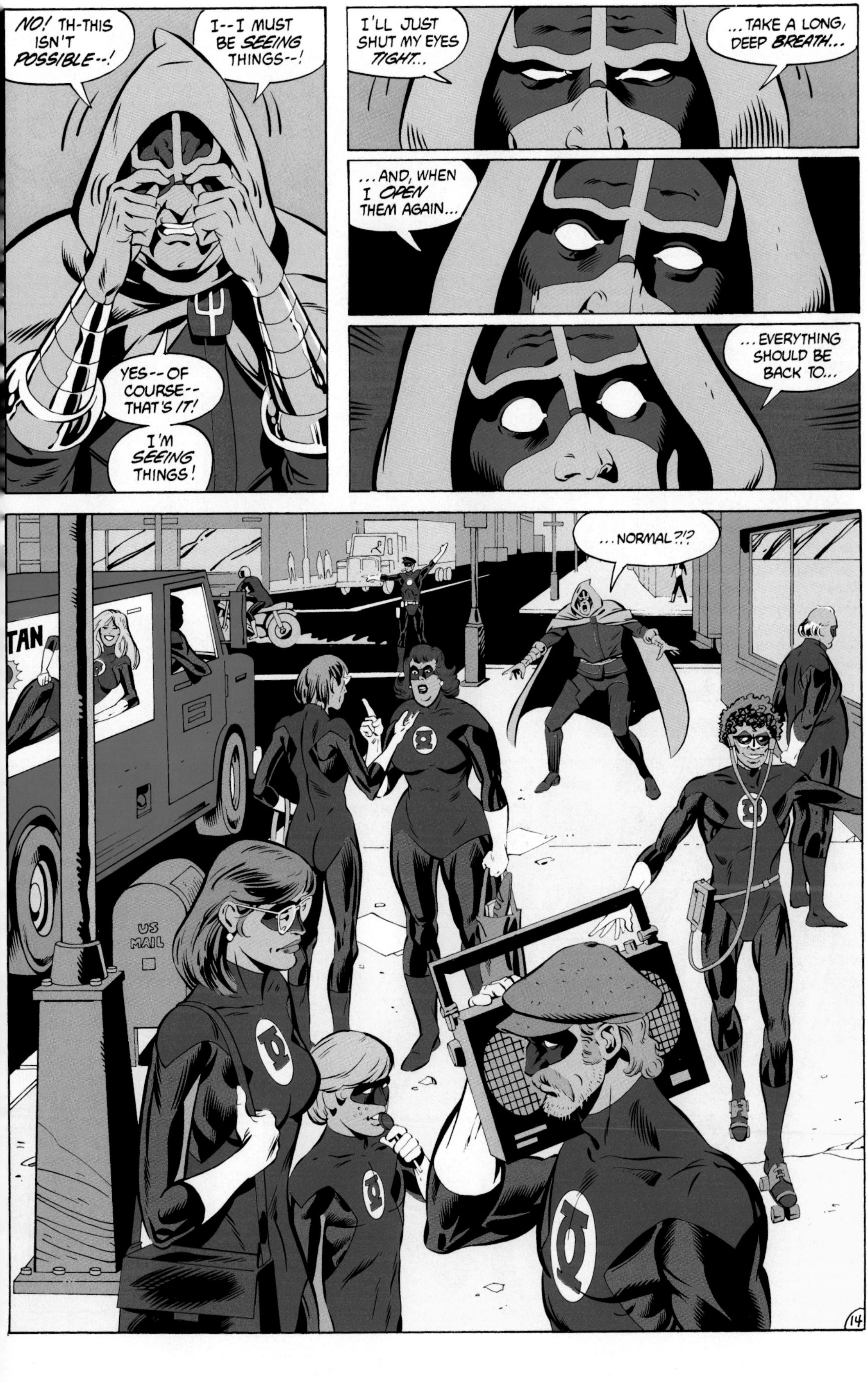
NO! TH-THIS ISN'T POSSIBLE--!
I--I MUST BE SEEING THINGS--!
YES--OF COURSE--THAT'S IT!
I'M SEEING THINGS!
I'LL JUST SHUT MY EYES TIGHT...
...TAKE A LONG, DEEP BREATH...
...AND, WHEN I OPEN THEM AGAIN...
...EVERYTHING SHOULD BE BACK TO...
...NORMAL?!?
TAN
US MAIL
14

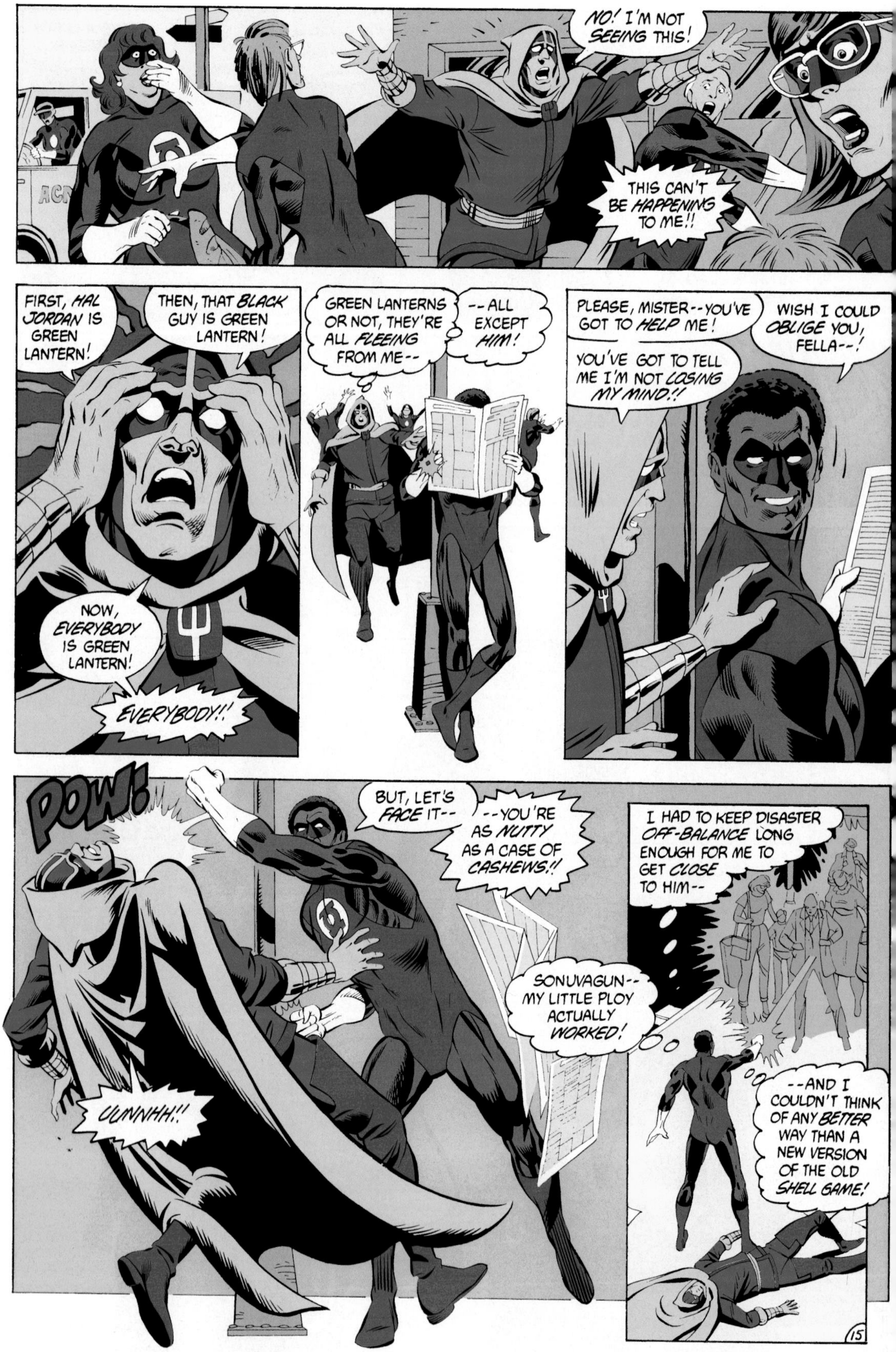
NO! I'M NOT SEEING THIS!
THIS CAN'T BE HAPPENING TO ME!!
FIRST, HAL JORDAN IS GREEN LANTERN!
THEN, THAT BLACK GUY IS GREEN LANTERN!
NOW, EVERYBODY IS GREEN LANTERN!
EVERYBODY!!
GREEN LANTERNS OR NOT, THEY'RE ALL FLEEING FROM ME--
--ALL EXCEPT HIM!
PLEASE, MISTER--YOU'VE GOT TO HELP ME!
YOU'VE GOT TO TELL ME I'M NOT LOSING MY MIND!!
WISH I COULD OBLIGE YOU, FELLA--!
POW!
BUT, LET'S FACE IT--
--YOU'RE AS NUTTY AS A CASE OF CASHEWS!!
UUNNHH!!
SONUVAGUN--MY LITTLE PLOY ACTUALLY WORKED!
I HAD TO KEEP DISASTER OFF-BALANCE LONG ENOUGH FOR ME TO GET CLOSE TO HIM--
--AND I COULDN'T THINK OF ANY BETTER WAY THAN A NEW VERSION OF THE OLD SHELL GAME!
15

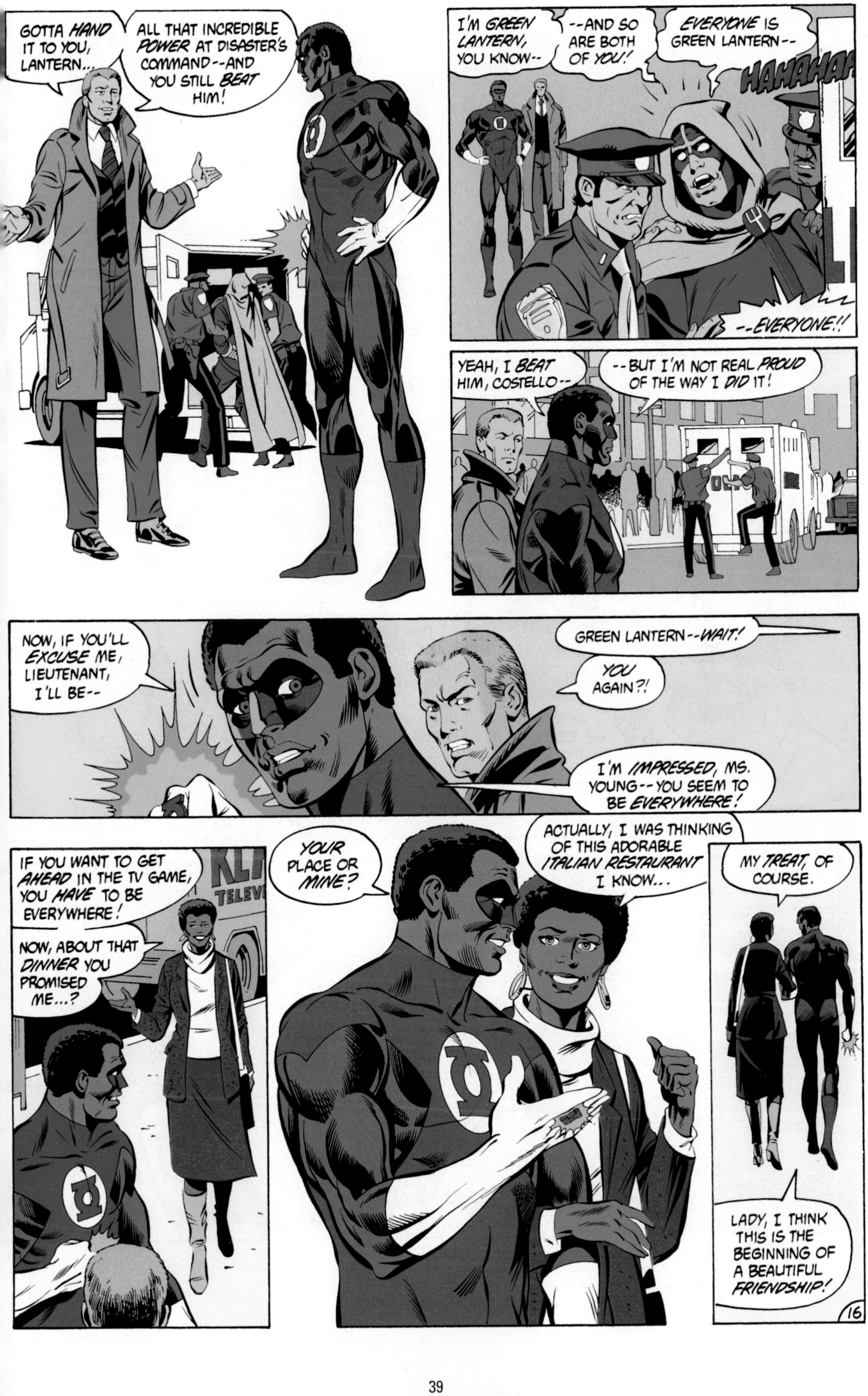
GOTTA HAND IT TO YOU, LANTERN...
ALL THAT INCREDIBLE POWER AT DISASTER'S COMMAND--AND YOU STILL BEAT HIM!
I'M GREEN LANTERN, YOU KNOW--
--AND SO ARE BOTH OF YOU!
EVERYONE IS GREEN LANTERN--
HAHAHAH
--EVERYONE!!
YEAH, I BEAT HIM, COSTELLO--
--BUT I'M NOT REAL PROUD OF THE WAY I DID IT!
NOW, IF YOU'LL EXCUSE ME, LIEUTENANT, I'LL BE--
GREEN LANTERN--WAIT!
YOU AGAIN?!
I'M IMPRESSED, MS. YOUNG--YOU SEEM TO BE EVERYWHERE!
IF YOU WANT TO GET AHEAD IN THE TV GAME, YOU HAVE TO BE EVERYWHERE!
NOW, ABOUT THAT DINNER YOU PROMISED ME...?
YOUR PLACE OR MINE?
ACTUALLY, I WAS THINKING OF THIS ADORABLE ITALIAN RESTAURANT I KNOW...
MY TREAT, OF COURSE.
LADY, I THINK THIS IS THE BEGINNING OF A BEAUTIFUL FRIENDSHIP!
16

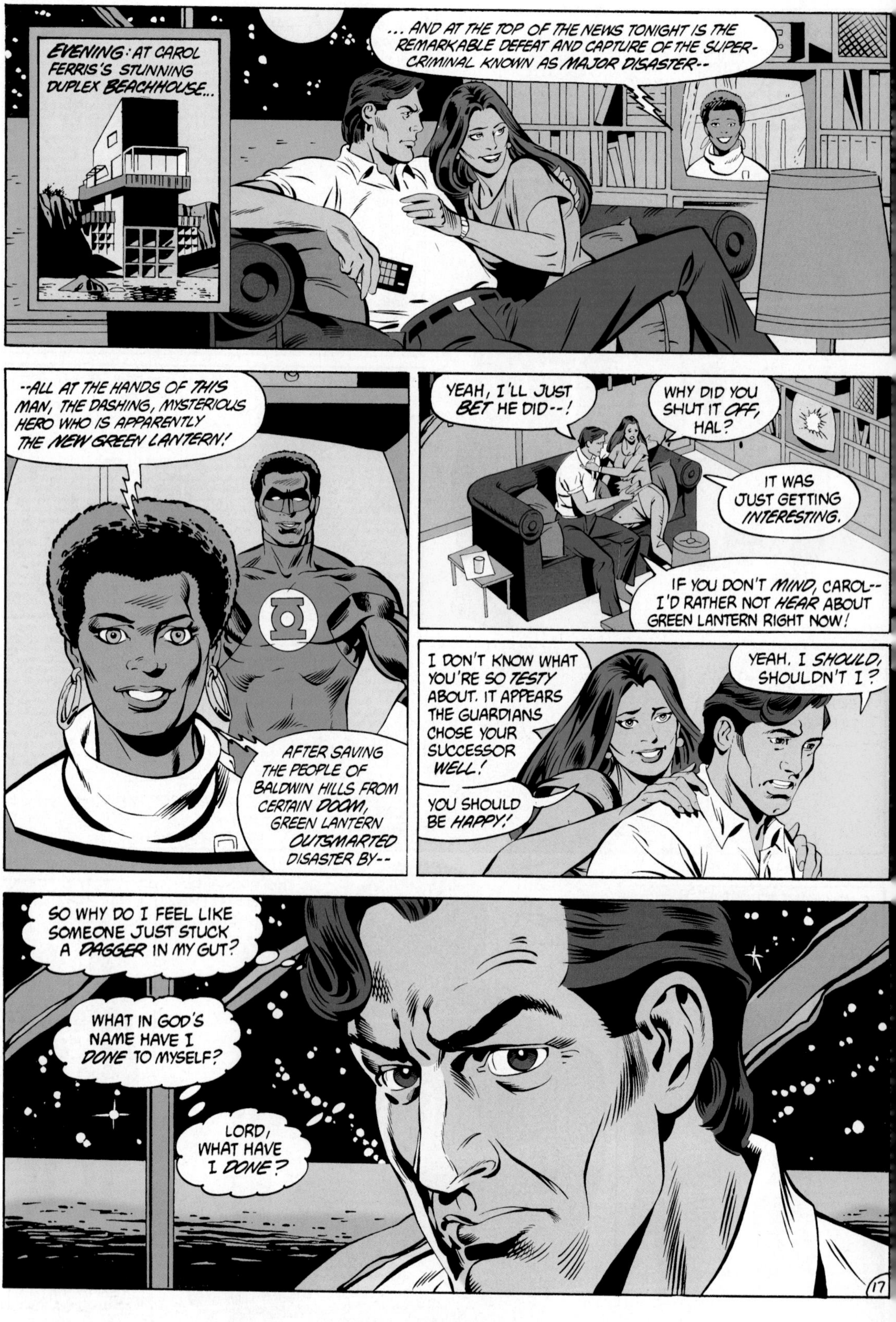
EVENING: AT CAROL FERRIS'S STUNNING DUPLEX BEACHHOUSE...
...AND AT THE TOP OF THE NEWS TONIGHT IS THE REMARKABLE DEFEAT AND CAPTURE OF THE SUPER-CRIMINAL KNOWN AS MAJOR DISASTER--
--ALL AT THE HANDS OF THIS MAN, THE DASHING, MYSTERIOUS HERO WHO IS APPARENTLY THE NEW GREEN LANTERN!
AFTER SAVING THE PEOPLE OF BALDWIN HILLS FROM CERTAIN DOOM, GREEN LANTERN OUTSMARTED DISASTER BY--
YEAH, I'LL JUST BET HE DID--!
WHY DID YOU SHUT IT OFF, HAL?
IT WAS JUST GETTING INTERESTING.
IF YOU DON'T MIND, CAROL-- I'D RATHER NOT HEAR ABOUT GREEN LANTERN RIGHT NOW!
I DON'T KNOW WHAT YOU'RE SO TESTY ABOUT. IT APPEARS THE GUARDIANS CHOSE YOUR SUCCESSOR WELL!
YOU SHOULD BE HAPPY!
YEAH. I SHOULD, SHOULDN'T I?
SO WHY DO I FEEL LIKE SOMEONE JUST STUCK A DAGGER IN MY GUT?
WHAT IN GOD'S NAME HAVE I DONE TO MYSELF?
LORD, WHAT HAVE I DONE?
17

Cover art by Dave Gibbons

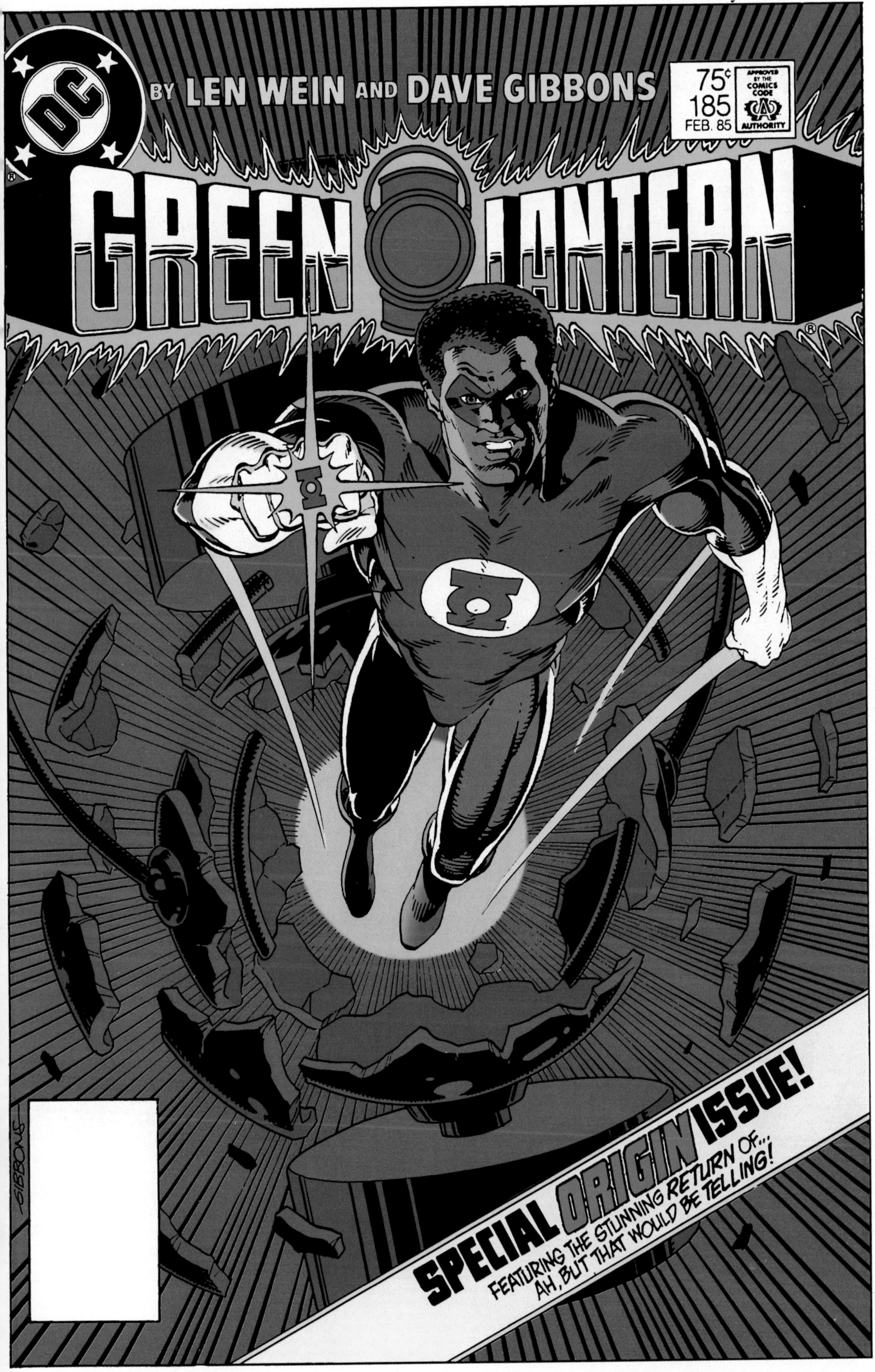
DC
BY LEN WEIN AND DAVE GIBBONS
75¢
185
FEB. 85
APPROVED BY THE COMICS CODE AUTHORITY
GREEN LANTERN
SPECIAL ORIGIN ISSUE!
FEATURING THE STUNNING RETURN OF... AH, BUT THAT WOULD BE TELLING!
GIBBONS

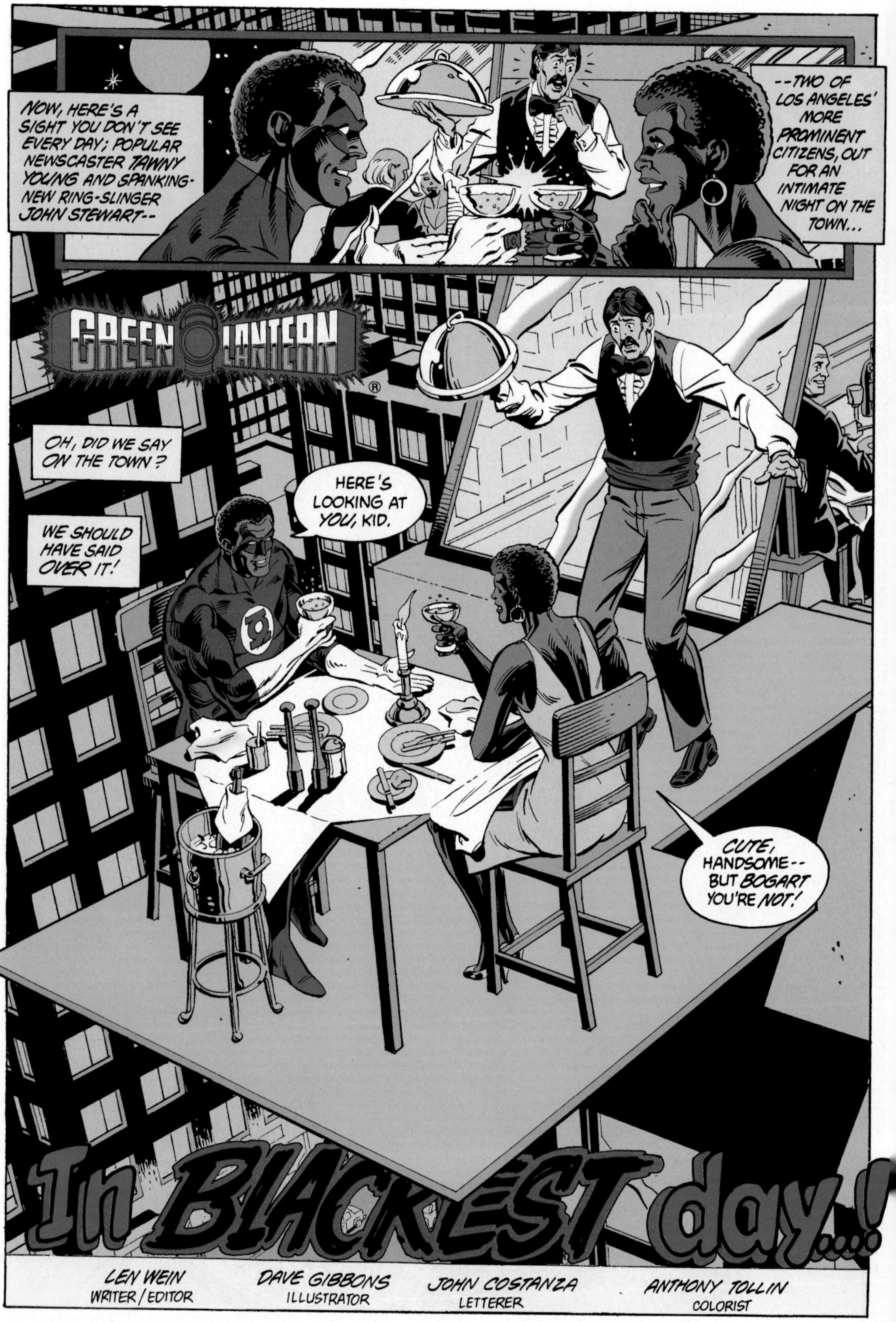
NOW, HERE'S A SIGHT YOU DON'T SEE EVERY DAY; POPULAR NEWSCASTER TAWNY YOUNG AND SPANKING-NEW RING-SLINGER JOHN STEWART--
--TWO OF LOS ANGELES' MORE PROMINENT CITIZENS, OUT FOR AN INTIMATE NIGHT ON THE TOWN...
GREEN LANTERN
OH, DID WE SAY ON THE TOWN?
WE SHOULD HAVE SAID OVER IT!
HERE'S LOOKING AT YOU, KID.
CUTE, HANDSOME-- BUT BOGART YOU'RE NOT!
In BLACKEST day...!
LEN WEIN WRITER/EDITOR
DAVE GIBBONS ILLUSTRATOR
JOHN COSTANZA LETTERER
ANTHONY TOLLIN COLORIST

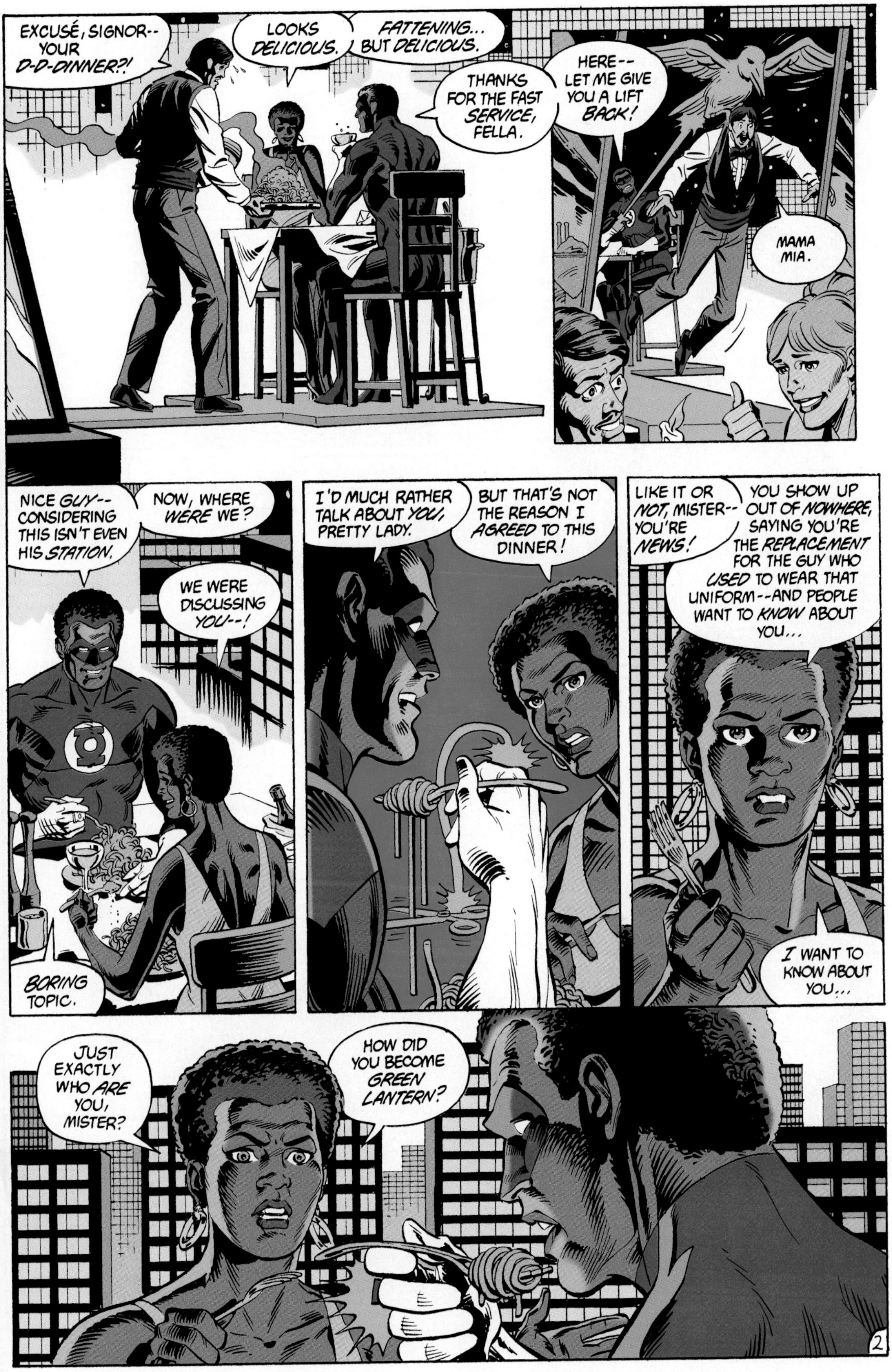
EXCUSÉ, SIGNOR-- YOUR D-D-DINNER?!
LOOKS DELICIOUS.
FATTENING... BUT DELICIOUS.
THANKS FOR THE FAST SERVICE, FELLA.
HERE-- LET ME GIVE YOU A LIFT BACK!
MAMA MIA.
NICE GUY-- CONSIDERING THIS ISN'T EVEN HIS STATION.
NOW, WHERE WERE WE?
WE WERE DISCUSSING YOU--!
BORING TOPIC.
I'D MUCH RATHER TALK ABOUT YOU, PRETTY LADY.
BUT THAT'S NOT THE REASON I AGREED TO THIS DINNER!
LIKE IT OR NOT, MISTER-- YOU'RE NEWS!
YOU SHOW UP OUT OF NOWHERE, SAYING YOU'RE THE REPLACEMENT FOR THE GUY WHO USED TO WEAR THAT UNIFORM--AND PEOPLE WANT TO KNOW ABOUT YOU...
I WANT TO KNOW ABOUT YOU...
JUST EXACTLY WHO ARE YOU, MISTER?
HOW DID YOU BECOME GREEN LANTERN?
2

HOW DID I **BECOME** GREEN LANTERN?

I REMEMBER IT LIKE IT WAS *YESTERDAY*... BECAUSE IT *WAS* YESTERDAY...

"I WAS IN MY NEW APARTMENT, FIXING MYSELF SOME *BREAKFAST--*"

GOD, I JUST LOVE TO HEAR THESE LITTLE SUCKERS *SNAP*, *CRACKLE*, AND *POP*--!

"--WHEN I SUDDENLY GOT A FAMILIAR, UNCOMFORTABLE FEELING..."

UH-OH.

"THERE WAS A MOMENTARY *RUSH* OF *IMPLODING* AIR, AND THEN I WAS--"

"--*SOMEWHERE ELSE!*"

YEAH-- I KIND 'A FIGURED IT WAS *YOU!*

WHAT DO YOU WANT FROM ME *THIS* TIME?

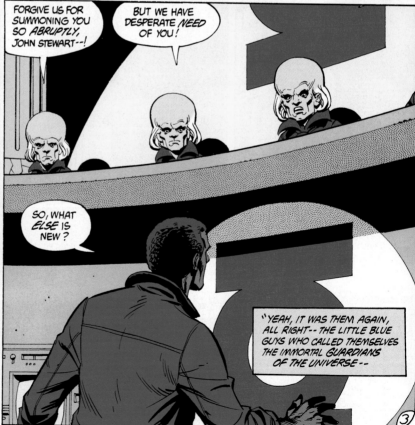

FORGIVE US FOR SUMMONING YOU SO *ABRUPTLY*, JOHN STEWART--!

BUT WE HAVE DESPERATE *NEED* OF YOU!

SO, WHAT *ELSE* IS NEW?

"YEAH, IT WAS THEM AGAIN, ALL RIGHT-- THE LITTLE BLUE GUYS WHO CALLED THEMSELVES THE IMMORTAL *GUARDIANS* OF THE UNIVERSE--"

3

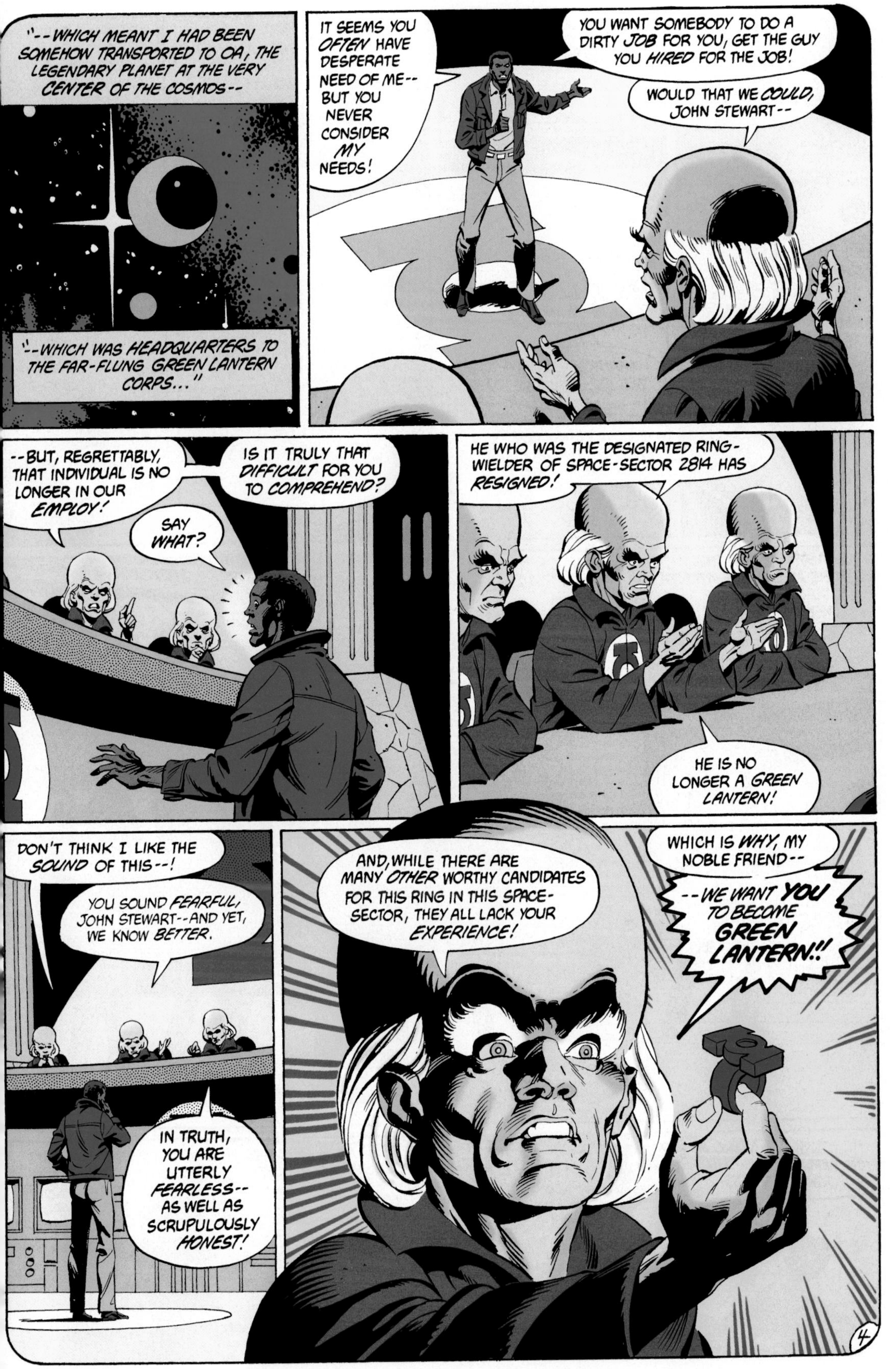
"--WHICH MEANT I HAD BEEN SOMEHOW TRANSPORTED TO OA, THE LEGENDARY PLANET AT THE VERY CENTER OF THE COSMOS--
"--WHICH WAS HEADQUARTERS TO THE FAR-FLUNG GREEN LANTERN CORPS..."
IT SEEMS YOU OFTEN HAVE DESPERATE NEED OF ME--BUT YOU NEVER CONSIDER MY NEEDS!
YOU WANT SOMEBODY TO DO A DIRTY JOB FOR YOU, GET THE GUY YOU HIRED FOR THE JOB!
WOULD THAT WE COULD, JOHN STEWART--
--BUT, REGRETTABLY, THAT INDIVIDUAL IS NO LONGER IN OUR EMPLOY!
SAY WHAT?
IS IT TRULY THAT DIFFICULT FOR YOU TO COMPREHEND?
HE WHO WAS THE DESIGNATED RING-WIELDER OF SPACE-SECTOR 2814 HAS RESIGNED!
HE IS NO LONGER A GREEN LANTERN!
DON'T THINK I LIKE THE SOUND OF THIS--!
YOU SOUND FEARFUL, JOHN STEWART--AND YET, WE KNOW BETTER.
IN TRUTH, YOU ARE UTTERLY FEARLESS--AS WELL AS SCRUPULOUSLY HONEST!
AND, WHILE THERE ARE MANY OTHER WORTHY CANDIDATES FOR THIS RING IN THIS SPACE-SECTOR, THEY ALL LACK YOUR EXPERIENCE!
WHICH IS WHY, MY NOBLE FRIEND--
--WE WANT YOU TO BECOME GREEN LANTERN!!
4

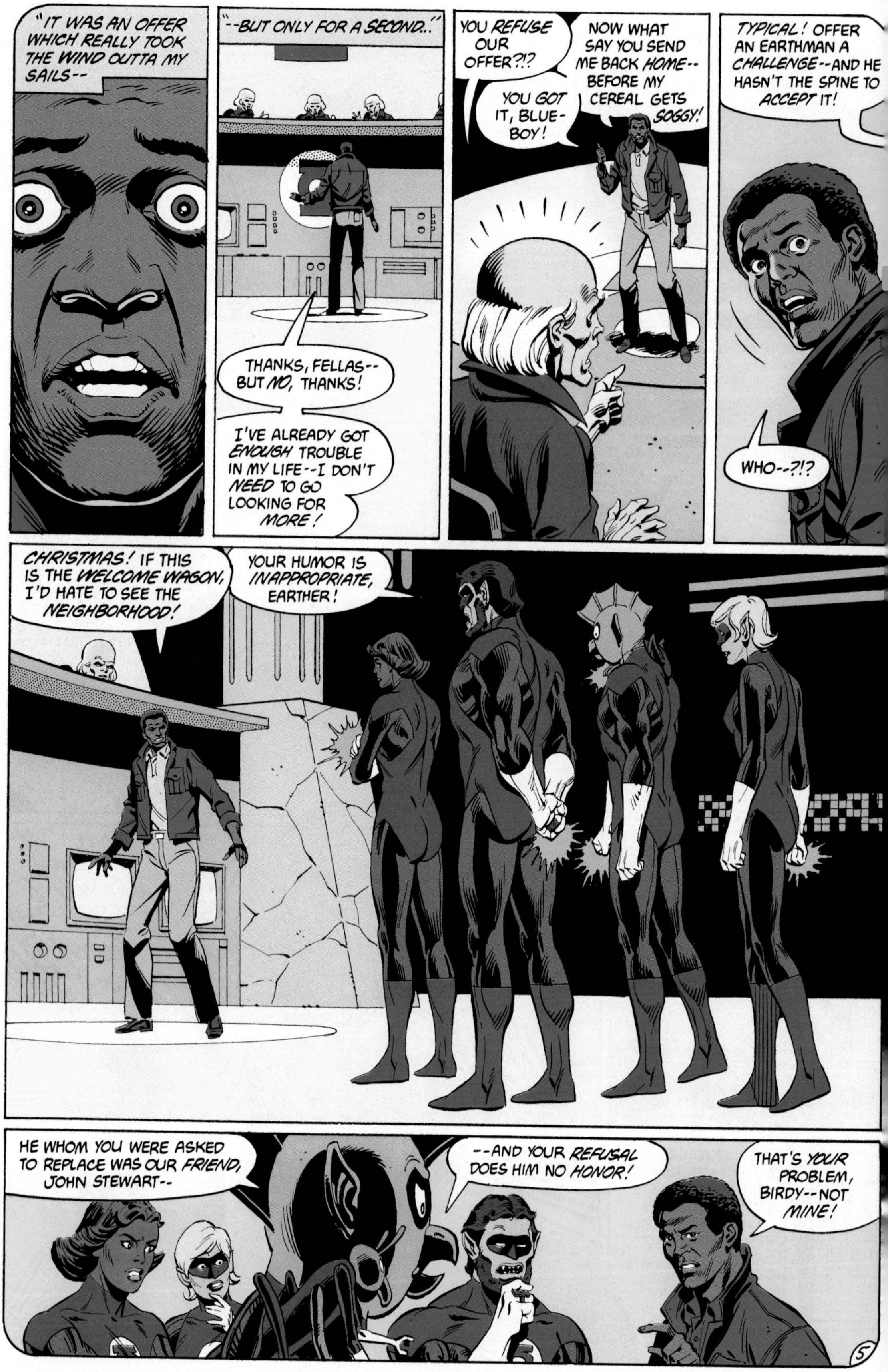
"IT WAS AN OFFER WHICH REALLY TOOK THE WIND OUTTA MY SAILS--
"--BUT ONLY FOR A SECOND.."
THANKS, FELLAS-- BUT NO, THANKS!
I'VE ALREADY GOT ENOUGH TROUBLE IN MY LIFE--I DON'T NEED TO GO LOOKING FOR MORE!
YOU REFUSE OUR OFFER?!?
YOU GOT IT, BLUE-BOY!
NOW WHAT SAY YOU SEND ME BACK HOME-- BEFORE MY CEREAL GETS SOGGY!
TYPICAL! OFFER AN EARTHMAN A CHALLENGE--AND HE HASN'T THE SPINE TO ACCEPT IT!
WHO--?!?
CHRISTMAS! IF THIS IS THE WELCOME WAGON, I'D HATE TO SEE THE NEIGHBORHOOD!
YOUR HUMOR IS INAPPROPRIATE, EARTHER!
HE WHOM YOU WERE ASKED TO REPLACE WAS OUR FRIEND, JOHN STEWART--
--AND YOUR REFUSAL DOES HIM NO HONOR!
THAT'S YOUR PROBLEM, BIRDY--NOT MINE!
5

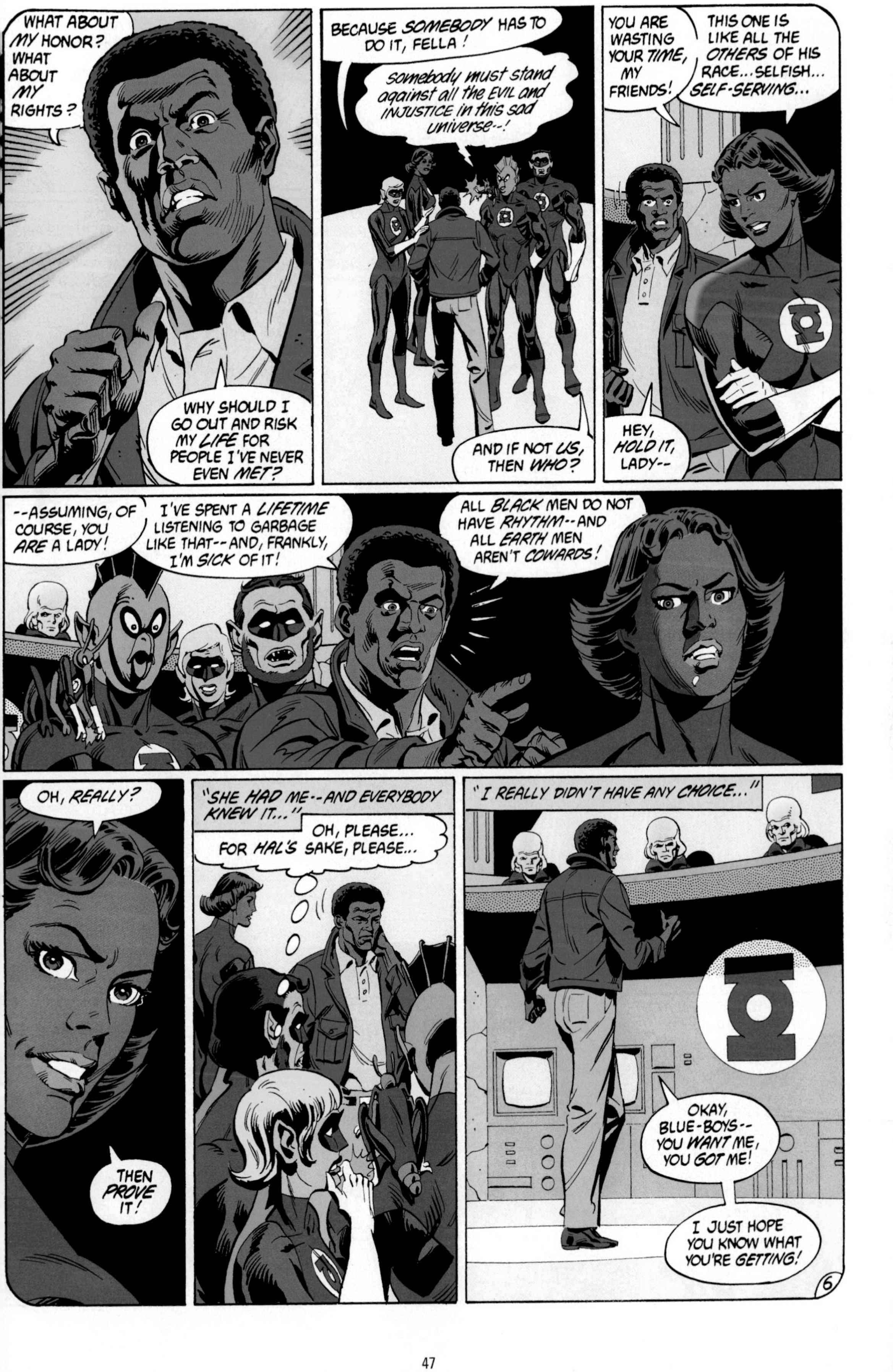
WHAT ABOUT MY HONOR? WHAT ABOUT MY RIGHTS?
WHY SHOULD I GO OUT AND RISK MY LIFE FOR PEOPLE I'VE NEVER EVEN MET?
BECAUSE SOMEBODY HAS TO DO IT, FELLA!
somebody must stand against all the EVIL and INJUSTICE in this sad universe--!
AND IF NOT US, THEN WHO?
YOU ARE WASTING YOUR TIME, MY FRIENDS!
THIS ONE IS LIKE ALL THE OTHERS OF HIS RACE... SELFISH... SELF-SERVING...
HEY, HOLD IT, LADY--
--ASSUMING, OF COURSE, YOU ARE A LADY!
I'VE SPENT A LIFETIME LISTENING TO GARBAGE LIKE THAT--AND, FRANKLY, I'M SICK OF IT!
ALL BLACK MEN DO NOT HAVE RHYTHM--AND ALL EARTH MEN AREN'T COWARDS!
OH, REALLY?
THEN PROVE IT!
"SHE HAD ME--AND EVERYBODY KNEW IT..."
OH, PLEASE... FOR HAL'S SAKE, PLEASE...
"I REALLY DIDN'T HAVE ANY CHOICE..."
OKAY, BLUE-BOYS--YOU WANT ME, YOU GOT ME!
I JUST HOPE YOU KNOW WHAT YOU'RE GETTING!
6

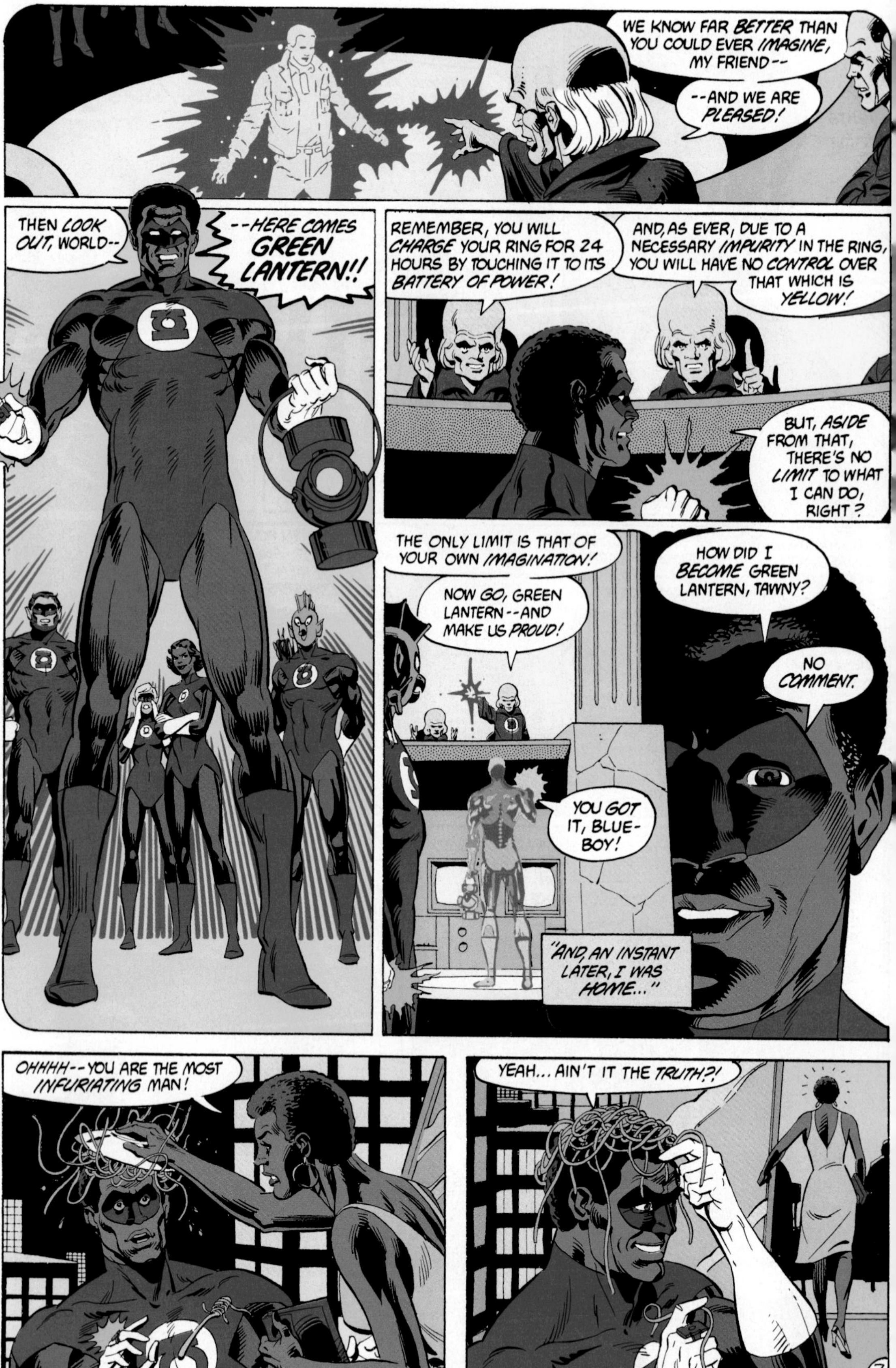
WE KNOW FAR BETTER THAN YOU COULD EVER IMAGINE, MY FRIEND--
--AND WE ARE PLEASED!
THEN LOOK OUT, WORLD--
--HERE COMES GREEN LANTERN!!
REMEMBER, YOU WILL CHARGE YOUR RING FOR 24 HOURS BY TOUCHING IT TO ITS BATTERY OF POWER!
AND, AS EVER, DUE TO A NECESSARY IMPURITY IN THE RING, YOU WILL HAVE NO CONTROL OVER THAT WHICH IS YELLOW!
BUT, ASIDE FROM THAT, THERE'S NO LIMIT TO WHAT I CAN DO, RIGHT?
THE ONLY LIMIT IS THAT OF YOUR OWN IMAGINATION!
NOW GO, GREEN LANTERN--AND MAKE US PROUD!
YOU GOT IT, BLUE-BOY!
"AND, AN INSTANT LATER, I WAS HOME..."
HOW DID I BECOME GREEN LANTERN, TAWNY?
NO COMMENT.
OHHHH--YOU ARE THE MOST INFURIATING MAN!
YEAH... AIN'T IT THE TRUTH?!
7

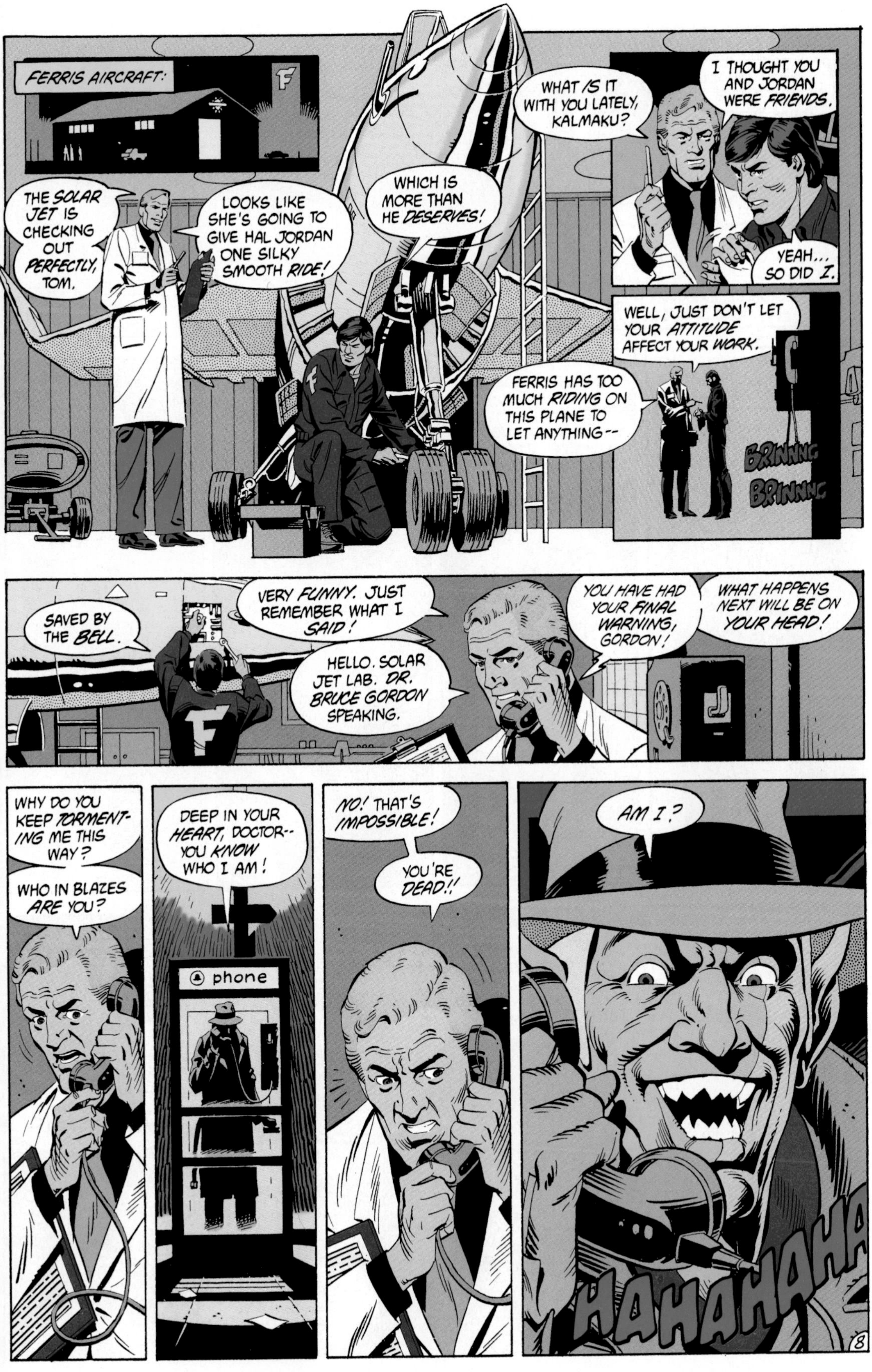
FERRIS AIRCRAFT:
THE SOLAR JET IS CHECKING OUT PERFECTLY, TOM.
LOOKS LIKE SHE'S GOING TO GIVE HAL JORDAN ONE SILKY SMOOTH RIDE!
WHICH IS MORE THAN HE DESERVES!
WHAT IS IT WITH YOU LATELY, KALMAKU?
I THOUGHT YOU AND JORDAN WERE FRIENDS.
YEAH... SO DID I.
WELL, JUST DON'T LET YOUR ATTITUDE AFFECT YOUR WORK.
FERRIS HAS TOO MUCH RIDING ON THIS PLANE TO LET ANYTHING--
BRINNNG
BRINNNG
SAVED BY THE BELL.
VERY FUNNY. JUST REMEMBER WHAT I SAID!
HELLO. SOLAR JET LAB. DR. BRUCE GORDON SPEAKING.
YOU HAVE HAD YOUR FINAL WARNING, GORDON!
WHAT HAPPENS NEXT WILL BE ON YOUR HEAD!
WHY DO YOU KEEP TORMENTING ME THIS WAY?
WHO IN BLAZES ARE YOU?
DEEP IN YOUR HEART, DOCTOR-- YOU KNOW WHO I AM!
phone
NO! THAT'S IMPOSSIBLE!
YOU'RE DEAD!!
AM I?
HAHAHAHA
8

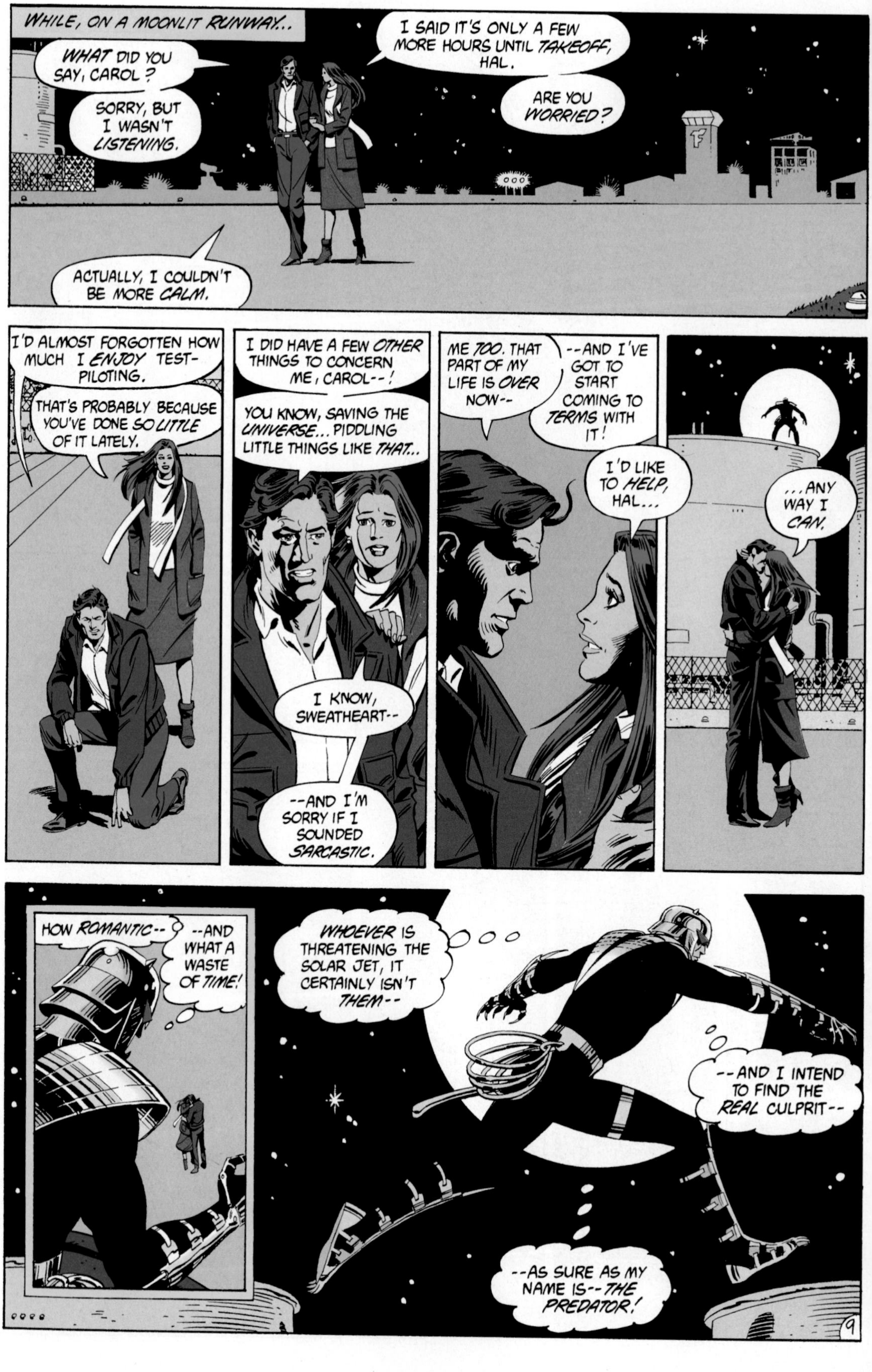
WHILE, ON A MOONLIT RUNWAY...
WHAT DID YOU SAY, CAROL?
SORRY, BUT I WASN'T LISTENING.
I SAID IT'S ONLY A FEW MORE HOURS UNTIL TAKEOFF, HAL.
ARE YOU WORRIED?
ACTUALLY, I COULDN'T BE MORE CALM.
I'D ALMOST FORGOTTEN HOW MUCH I ENJOY TEST-PILOTING.
THAT'S PROBABLY BECAUSE YOU'VE DONE SO LITTLE OF IT LATELY.
I DID HAVE A FEW OTHER THINGS TO CONCERN ME, CAROL--!
YOU KNOW, SAVING THE UNIVERSE... PIDDLING LITTLE THINGS LIKE THAT...
I KNOW, SWEATHEART--
--AND I'M SORRY IF I SOUNDED SARCASTIC.
ME TOO. THAT PART OF MY LIFE IS OVER NOW--
--AND I'VE GOT TO START COMING TO TERMS WITH IT!
I'D LIKE TO HELP, HAL...
...ANY WAY I CAN.
HOW ROMANTIC--
--AND WHAT A WASTE OF TIME!
WHOEVER IS THREATENING THE SOLAR JET, IT CERTAINLY ISN'T THEM--
--AND I INTEND TO FIND THE REAL CULPRIT--
--AS SURE AS MY NAME IS--THE PREDATOR!
9

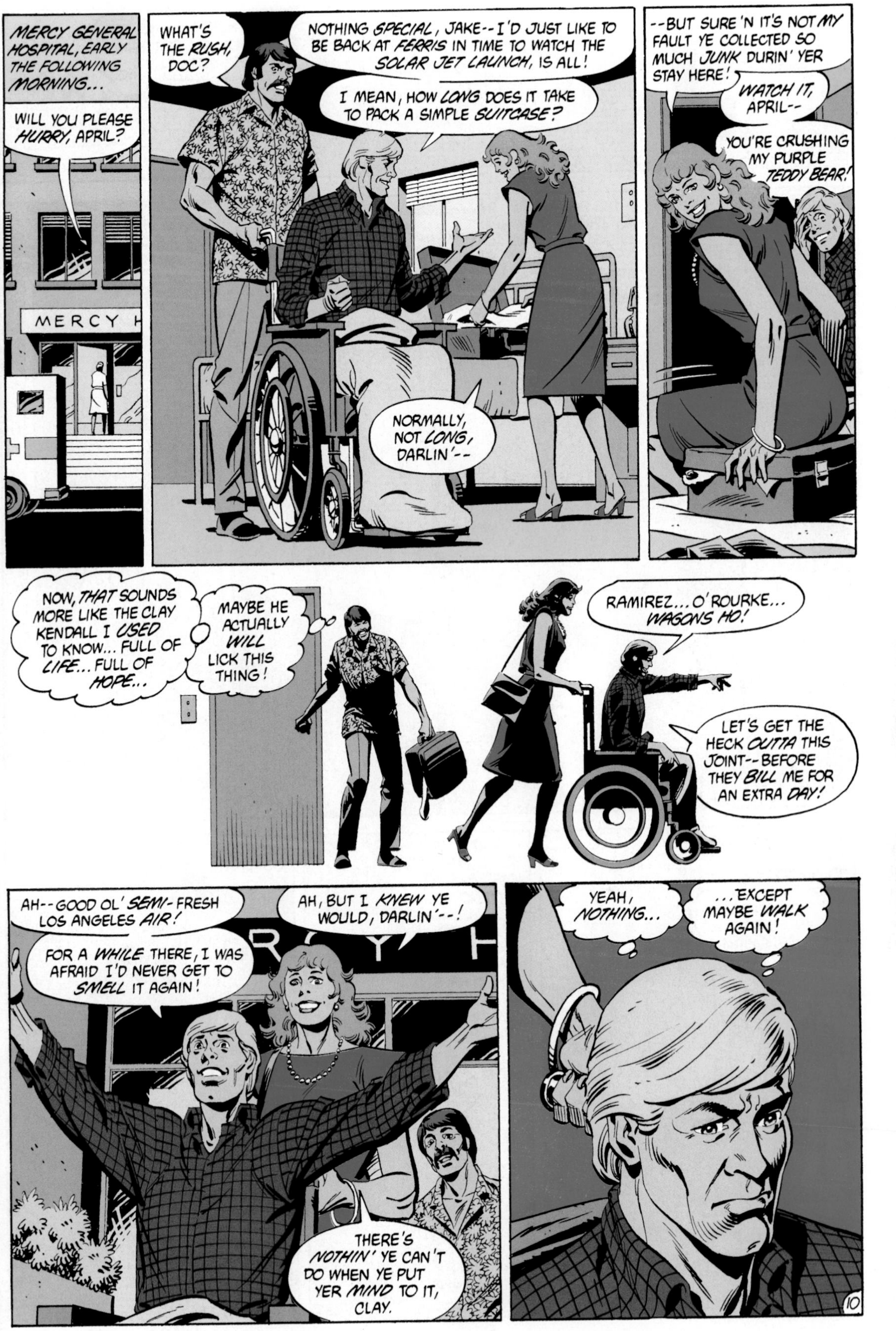
MERCY GENERAL HOSPITAL, EARLY THE FOLLOWING MORNING...
WILL YOU PLEASE HURRY, APRIL?
MERCY H
WHAT'S THE RUSH, DOC?
NOTHING SPECIAL, JAKE--I'D JUST LIKE TO BE BACK AT FERRIS IN TIME TO WATCH THE SOLAR JET LAUNCH, IS ALL!
I MEAN, HOW LONG DOES IT TAKE TO PACK A SIMPLE SUITCASE?
NORMALLY, NOT LONG, DARLIN'--
--BUT SURE 'N IT'S NOT MY FAULT YE COLLECTED SO MUCH JUNK DURIN' YER STAY HERE!
WATCH IT, APRIL--
YOU'RE CRUSHING MY PURPLE TEDDY BEAR!
NOW, THAT SOUNDS MORE LIKE THE CLAY KENDALL I USED TO KNOW... FULL OF LIFE... FULL OF HOPE...
MAYBE HE ACTUALLY WILL LICK THIS THING!
RAMIREZ... O'ROURKE... WAGONS HO!
LET'S GET THE HECK OUTTA THIS JOINT--BEFORE THEY BILL ME FOR AN EXTRA DAY!
AH--GOOD OL' SEMI-FRESH LOS ANGELES AIR!
FOR A WHILE THERE, I WAS AFRAID I'D NEVER GET TO SMELL IT AGAIN!
AH, BUT I KNEW YE WOULD, DARLIN'--!
THERE'S NOTHIN' YE CAN'T DO WHEN YE PUT YER MIND TO IT, CLAY.
YEAH, NOTHING...
...EXCEPT MAYBE WALK AGAIN!
10

AND, AT LAST...

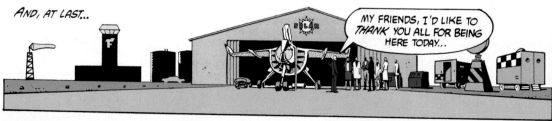

MY FRIENDS, I'D LIKE TO *THANK* YOU ALL FOR BEING HERE TODAY...

...TO WITNESS THE BEGINNING OF A *BOLD* NEW *ERA* HERE AT FERRIS...

...THE COMING-OF-AGE OF THE *SOLAR JET!*

WITH THE MONEY WE STAND TO MAKE FROM THE *PATENTS* IF TODAY'S TEST GOES AS *EXPECTED,* FERRIS WILL BE ABLE TO *REBUILD...EXPAND...*

FERRIS AIRCRAFT WILL BE ON TOP AGAIN!!

AS YOU *KNOW,* CARL--MY EMPLOYERS ARE PREPARED TO *GUARANTEE* THAT!

SO YOU PERSIST IN *REMINDING* ME, SMITH!

THEY COULD *ARGUE* LIKE THAT FOR HOURS--

--AND I HAVE MORE *IMPORTANT* MATTERS TO ATTEND TO!

IF NOT FOR A CRUEL *FATE,* TODAY COULD HAVE BELONGED TO *ME,* INSTEAD OF--

--HAL JORDAN!

HEY, RICH--*THOUGHT* YOU MIGHT STOP BY TO WISH ME *LUCK.*

14

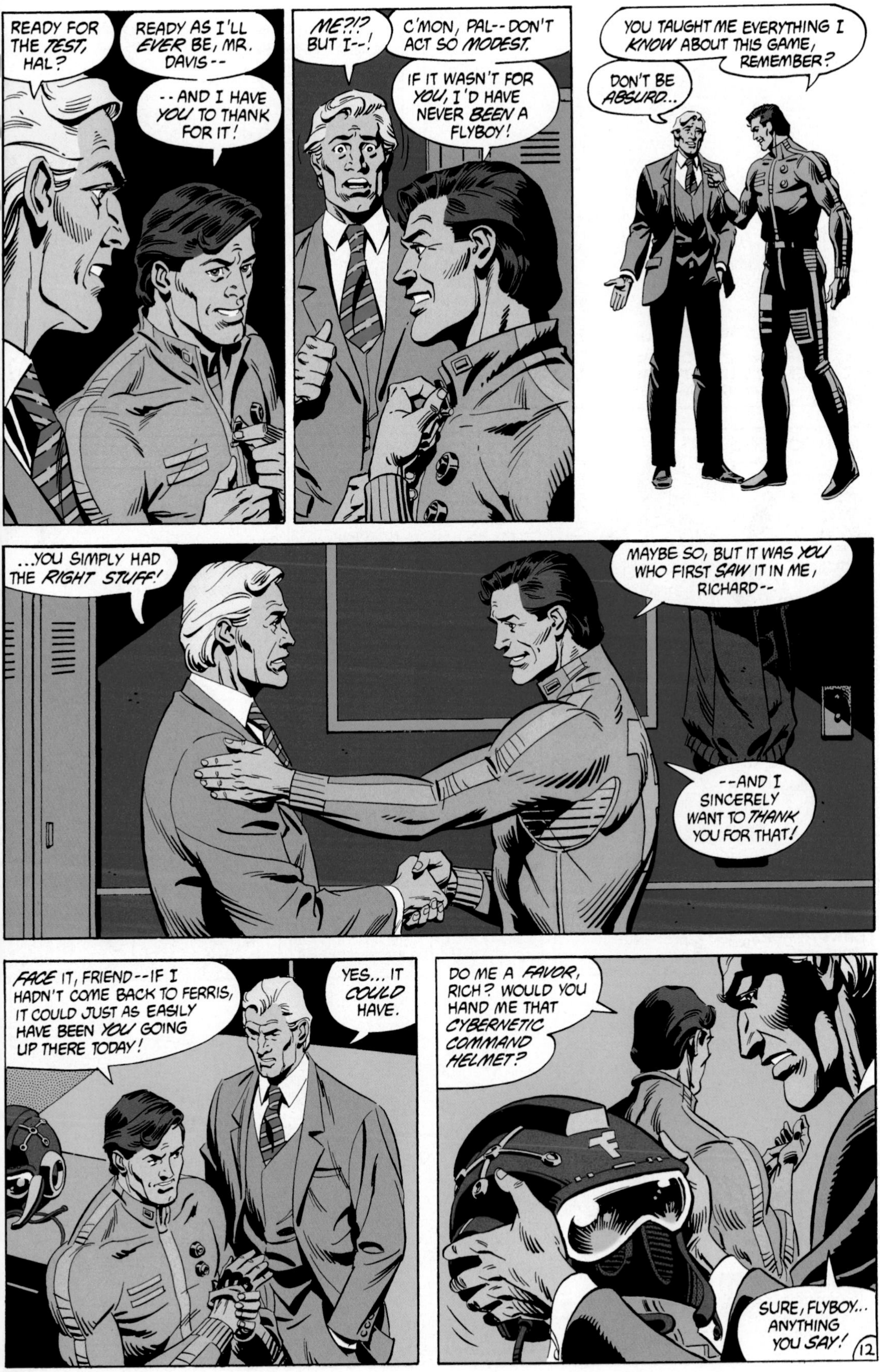
READY FOR THE TEST, HAL?
READY AS I'LL EVER BE, MR. DAVIS--
--AND I HAVE YOU TO THANK FOR IT!
ME?!? BUT I--!
C'MON, PAL--DON'T ACT SO MODEST.
IF IT WASN'T FOR YOU, I'D HAVE NEVER BEEN A FLYBOY!
YOU TAUGHT ME EVERYTHING I KNOW ABOUT THIS GAME, REMEMBER?
DON'T BE ABSURD...
...YOU SIMPLY HAD THE RIGHT STUFF!
MAYBE SO, BUT IT WAS YOU WHO FIRST SAW IT IN ME, RICHARD--
--AND I SINCERELY WANT TO THANK YOU FOR THAT!
FACE IT, FRIEND--IF I HADN'T COME BACK TO FERRIS, IT COULD JUST AS EASILY HAVE BEEN YOU GOING UP THERE TODAY!
YES... IT COULD HAVE.
DO ME A FAVOR, RICH? WOULD YOU HAND ME THAT CYBERNETIC COMMAND HELMET?
SURE, FLYBOY... ANYTHING YOU SAY!
12

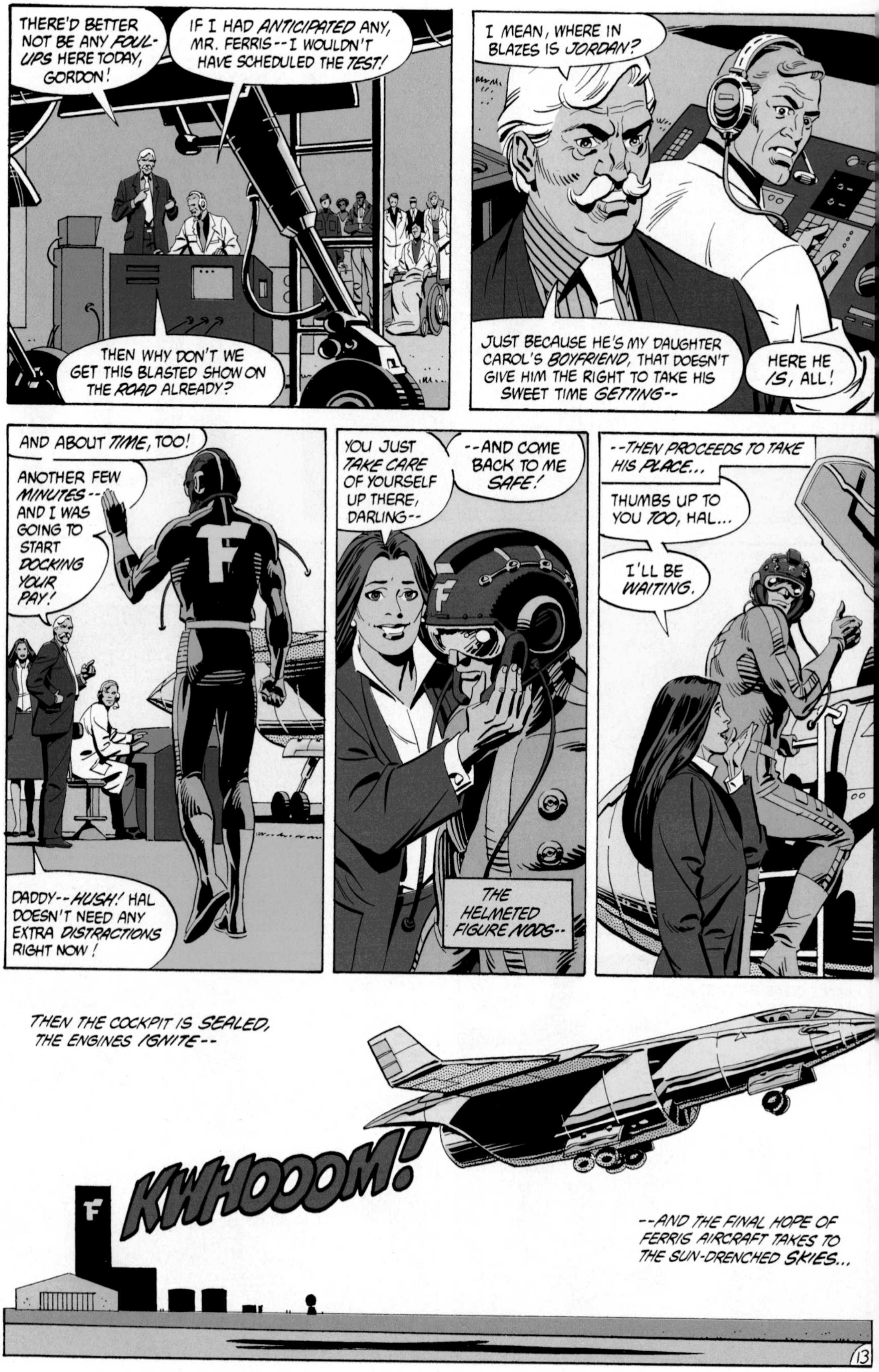
THERE'D BETTER NOT BE ANY FOUL-UPS HERE TODAY, GORDON!
IF I HAD ANTICIPATED ANY, MR. FERRIS--I WOULDN'T HAVE SCHEDULED THE TEST!
THEN WHY DON'T WE GET THIS BLASTED SHOW ON THE ROAD ALREADY?
I MEAN, WHERE IN BLAZES IS JORDAN?
JUST BECAUSE HE'S MY DAUGHTER CAROL'S BOYFRIEND, THAT DOESN'T GIVE HIM THE RIGHT TO TAKE HIS SWEET TIME GETTING--
HERE HE IS, ALL!
AND ABOUT TIME, TOO!
ANOTHER FEW MINUTES--AND I WAS GOING TO START DOCKING YOUR PAY!
DADDY--HUSH! HAL DOESN'T NEED ANY EXTRA DISTRACTIONS RIGHT NOW!
YOU JUST TAKE CARE OF YOURSELF UP THERE, DARLING--
--AND COME BACK TO ME SAFE!
THE HELMETED FIGURE NODS--
--THEN PROCEEDS TO TAKE HIS PLACE...
THUMBS UP TO YOU TOO, HAL...
I'LL BE WAITING.
THEN THE COCKPIT IS SEALED, THE ENGINES IGNITE--
KWHOOOOM!
--AND THE FINAL HOPE OF FERRIS AIRCRAFT TAKES TO THE SUN-DRENCHED SKIES...
13

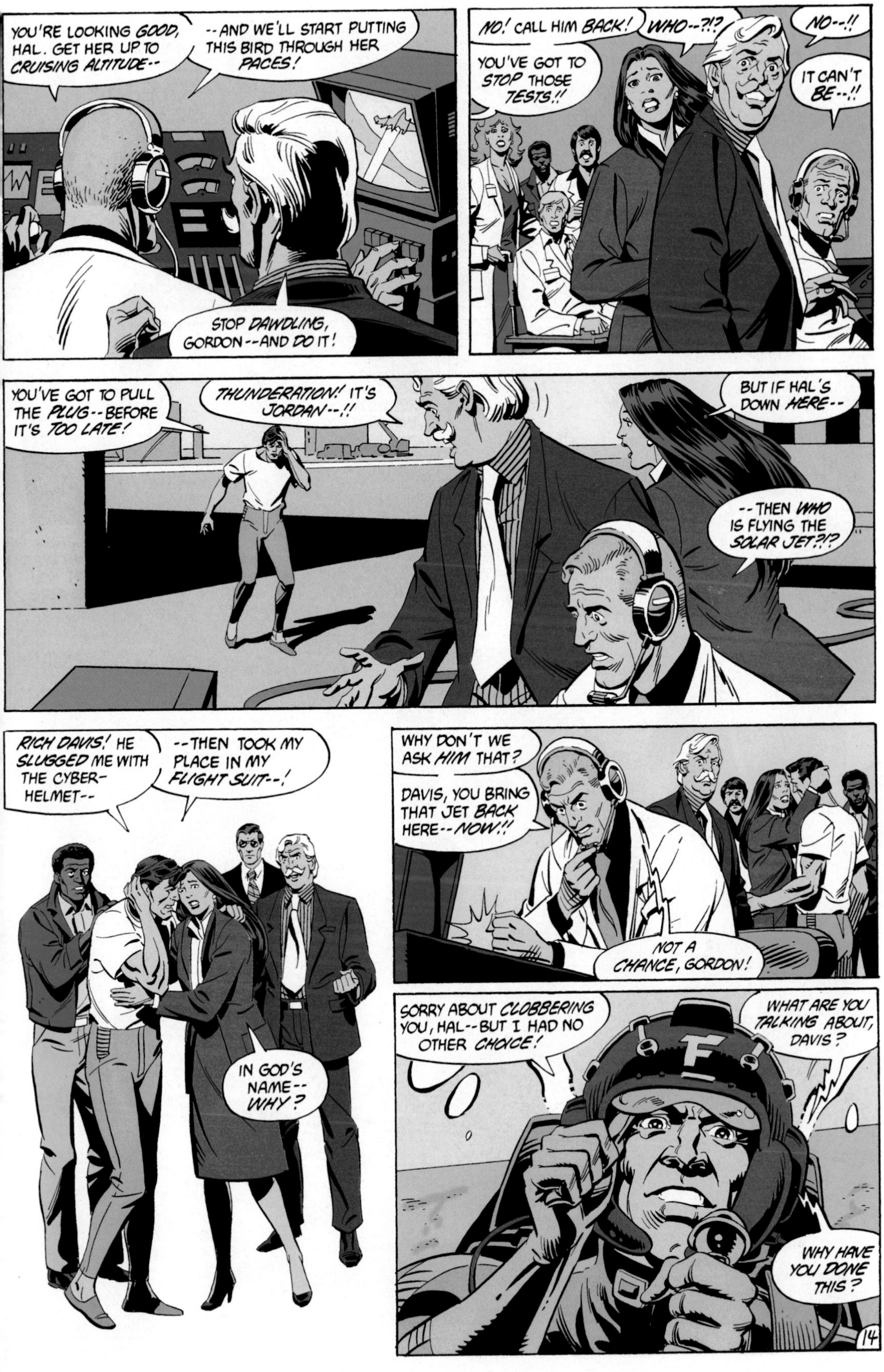

YOU'RE LOOKING GOOD, HAL. GET HER UP TO CRUISING ALTITUDE--
--AND WE'LL START PUTTING THIS BIRD THROUGH HER PACES!
STOP DAWDLING, GORDON--AND DO IT!
NO! CALL HIM BACK!
YOU'VE GOT TO STOP THOSE TESTS!!
WHO--?!?
NO--!!
IT CAN'T BE--!!
YOU'VE GOT TO PULL THE PLUG--BEFORE IT'S TOO LATE!
THUNDERATION! IT'S JORDAN--!!
BUT IF HAL'S DOWN HERE--
--THEN WHO IS FLYING THE SOLAR JET?!?
RICH DAVIS! HE SLUGGED ME WITH THE CYBER-HELMET--
--THEN TOOK MY PLACE IN MY FLIGHT SUIT--!
IN GOD'S NAME--WHY?
WHY DON'T WE ASK HIM THAT?
DAVIS, YOU BRING THAT JET BACK HERE--NOW!!
NOT A CHANCE, GORDON!
SORRY ABOUT CLOBBERING YOU, HAL--BUT I HAD NO OTHER CHOICE!
WHAT ARE YOU TALKING ABOUT, DAVIS?
WHY HAVE YOU DONE THIS?
14

I'VE GOT A *BUM HEART,* REMEMBER?

THIS WAS MY *LAST* CHANCE TO GET UP INTO THE *BIG BLUE* AGAIN-- AND I HAD TO *TAKE* IT, NO MATTER *WHAT!*

BUT WHAT ABOUT OUR *TESTING?*

HEY, I USED TO BE THE *BEST* TEST PILOT IN THE BUSINESS-- JUST ASK *HAL!*

YOU JUST TELL ME WHAT YOU NEED *DONE*--AND I'LL *DO* IT!

WELL...?

WHAT OTHER *CHOICE* HAVE WE GOT?

OKAY, DAVIS, YOU'LL PROBABLY BE OUT OF A *JOB* WHEN YOU *LAND*--BUT FOR NOW, YOU'RE ALL WE'VE *GOT!*

HERE'S WHAT WE WANT YOU TO DO...

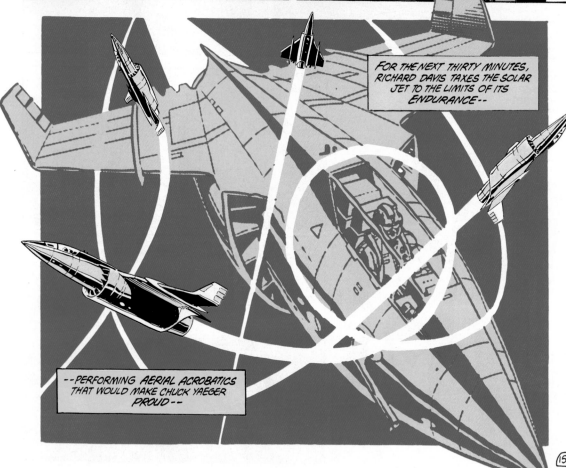

FOR THE NEXT THIRTY MINUTES, RICHARD DAVIS TAXES THE SOLAR JET TO THE LIMITS OF ITS *ENDURANCE*--

--PERFORMING *AERIAL ACROBATICS* THAT WOULD MAKE CHUCK YAEGER *PROUD*--

15

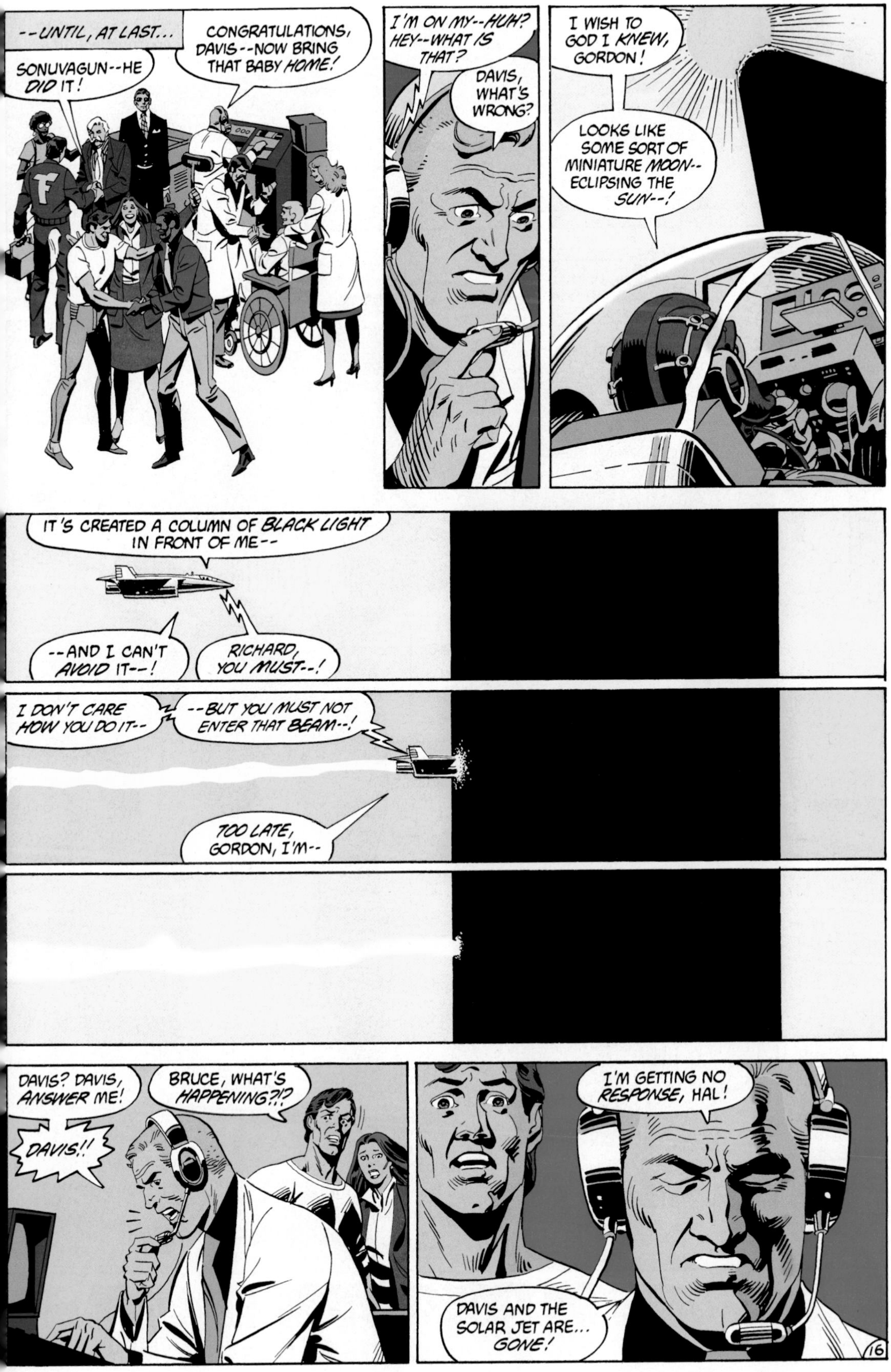
--UNTIL, AT LAST...
SONUVAGUN--HE DID IT!
CONGRATULATIONS, DAVIS--NOW BRING THAT BABY HOME!
I'M ON MY--HUH? HEY--WHAT IS THAT?
DAVIS, WHAT'S WRONG?
I WISH TO GOD I KNEW, GORDON!
LOOKS LIKE SOME SORT OF MINIATURE MOON--ECLIPSING THE SUN--!
IT'S CREATED A COLUMN OF BLACK LIGHT IN FRONT OF ME--
--AND I CAN'T AVOID IT--!
RICHARD, YOU MUST--!
I DON'T CARE HOW YOU DO IT--
--BUT YOU MUST NOT ENTER THAT BEAM--!
TOO LATE, GORDON, I'M--
DAVIS? DAVIS, ANSWER ME!
DAVIS!!
BRUCE, WHAT'S HAPPENING?!?
I'M GETTING NO RESPONSE, HAL!
DAVIS AND THE SOLAR JET ARE... GONE!
16

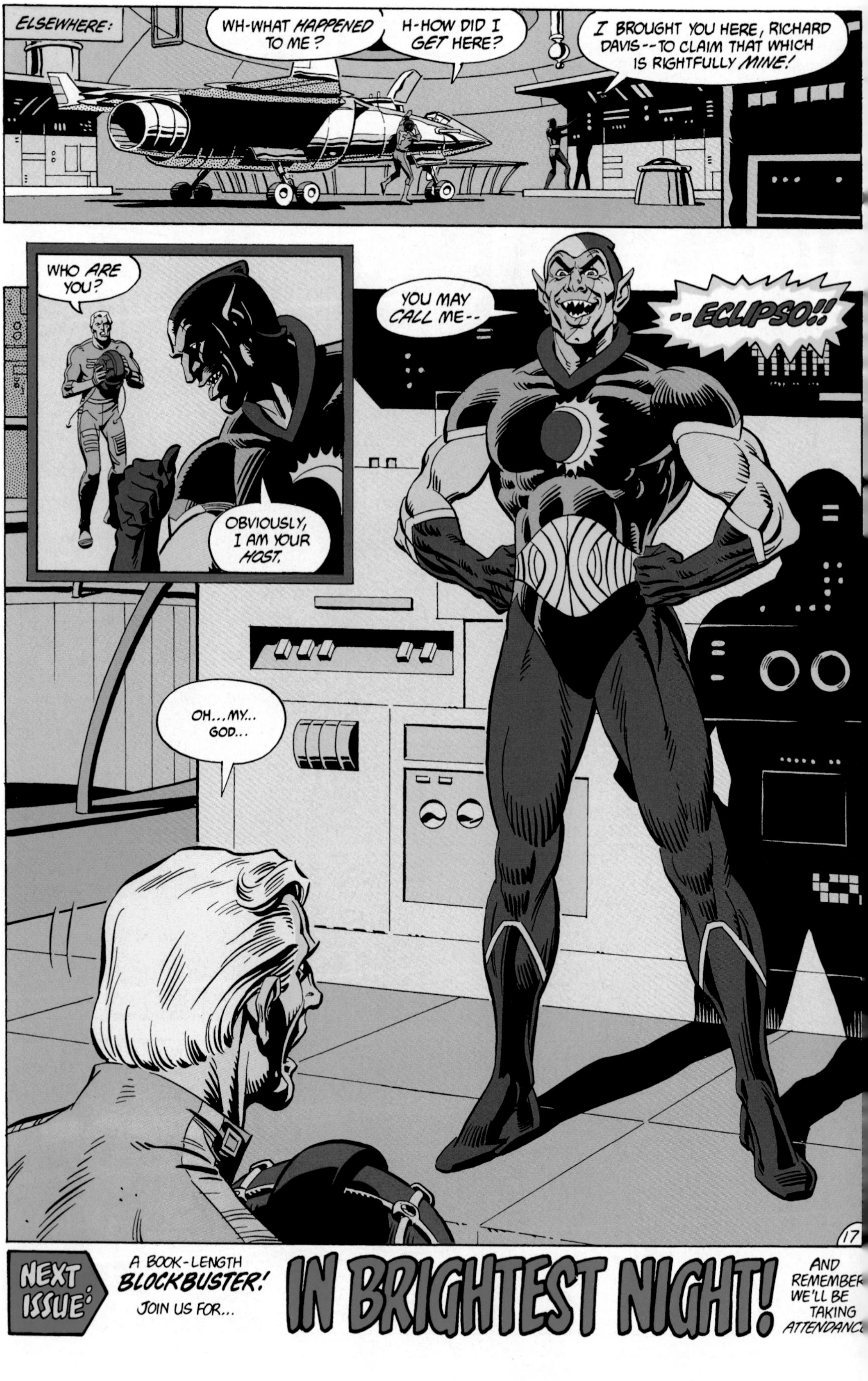
ELSEWHERE:
WH-WHAT HAPPENED TO ME?
H-HOW DID I GET HERE?
I BROUGHT YOU HERE, RICHARD DAVIS--TO CLAIM THAT WHICH IS RIGHTFULLY MINE!
WHO ARE YOU?
OBVIOUSLY, I AM YOUR HOST.
YOU MAY CALL ME--
--ECLIPSO!!
OH...MY... GOD...
17
NEXT ISSUE:
A BOOK-LENGTH BLOCKBUSTER!
JOIN US FOR...
IN BRIGHTEST NIGHT!
AND REMEMBER WE'LL BE TAKING ATTENDANC

Cover art by Dave Gibbons

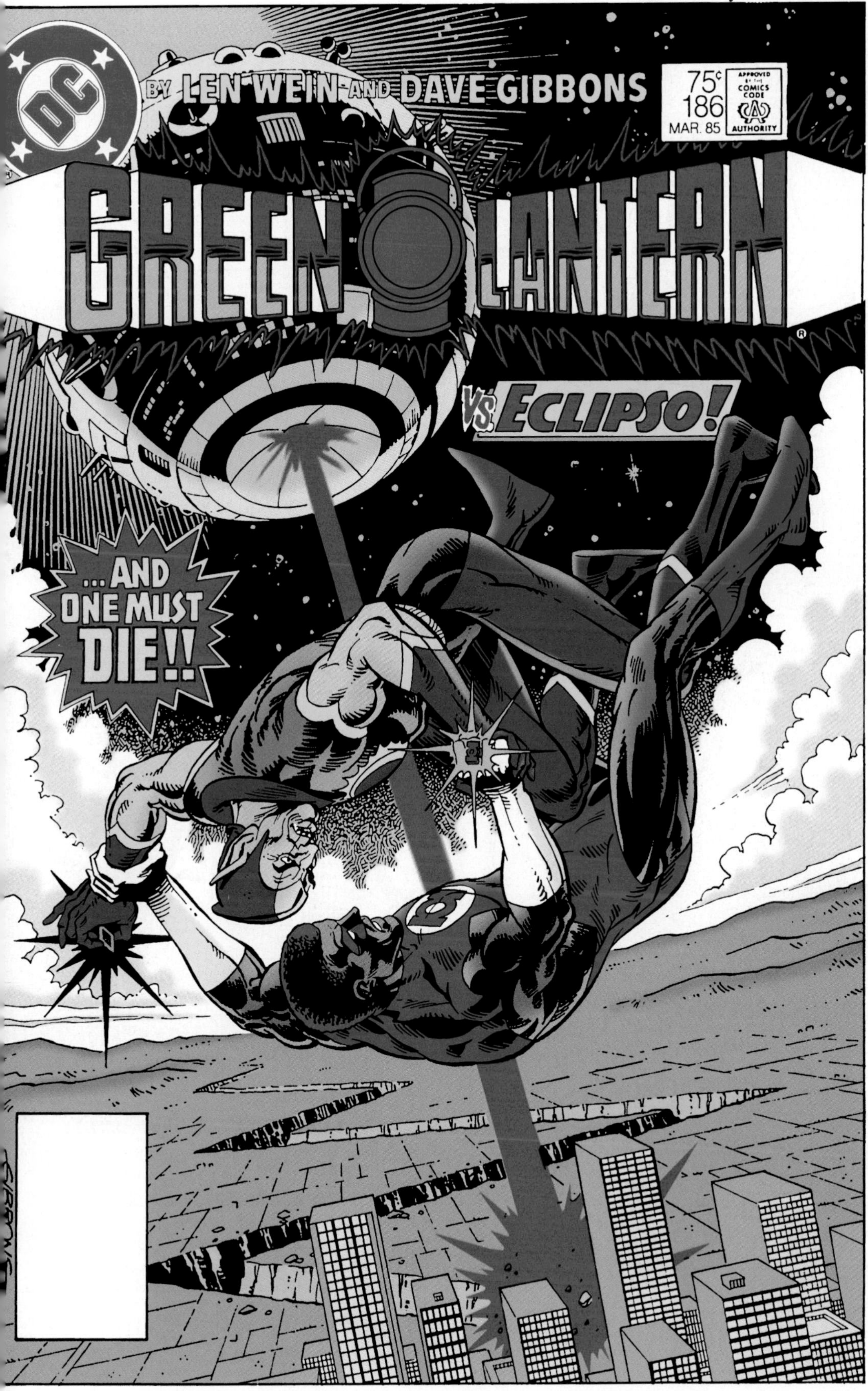

BY LEN WEIN AND DAVE GIBBONS
75¢
186
MAR. 85
APPROVED BY THE COMICS CODE AUTHORITY
GREEN LANTERN
VS. ECLIPSO!
...AND ONE MUST DIE!!

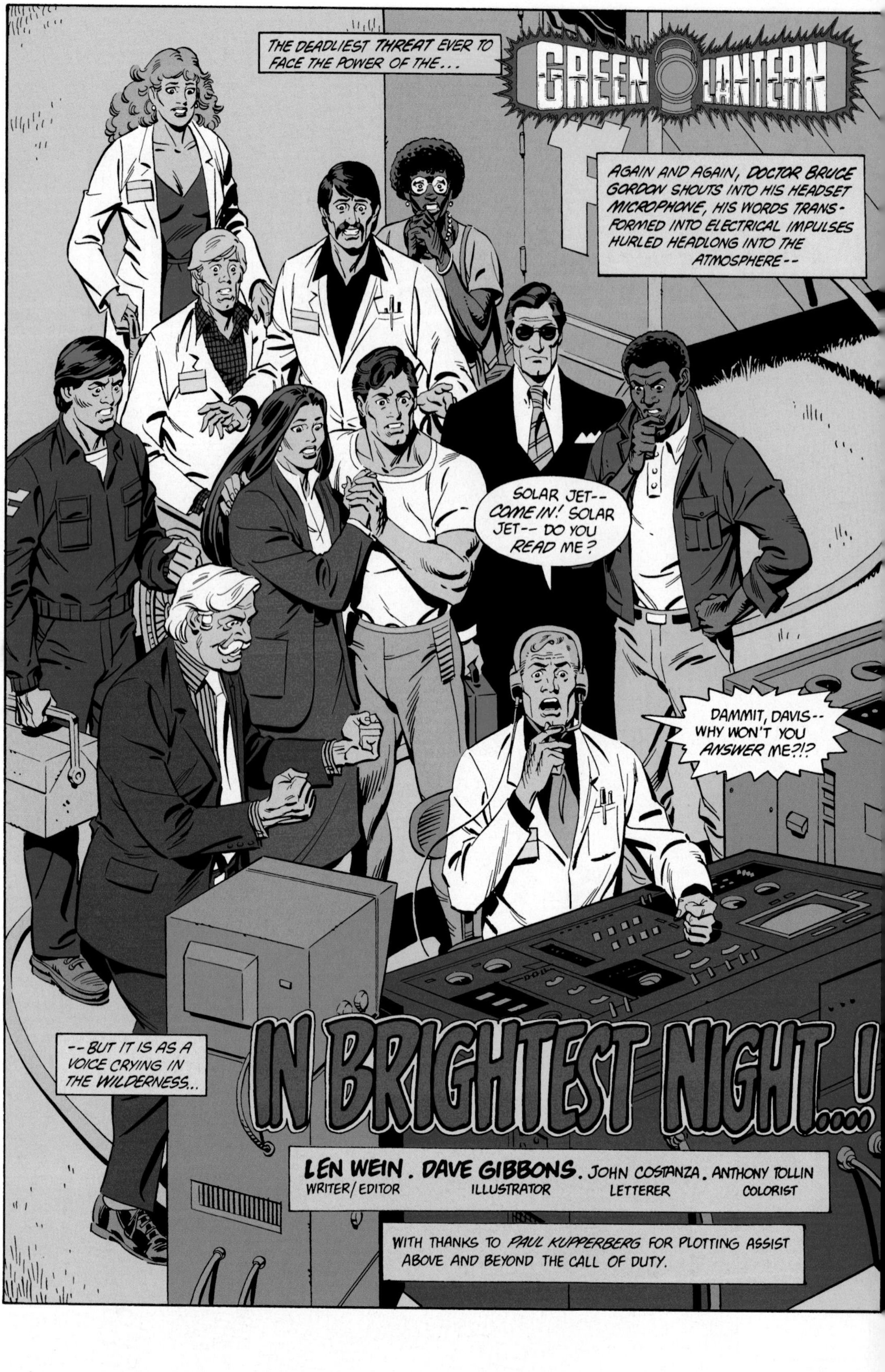
THE DEADLIEST THREAT EVER TO FACE THE POWER OF THE...
GREEN LANTERN
AGAIN AND AGAIN, DOCTOR BRUCE GORDON SHOUTS INTO HIS HEADSET MICROPHONE, HIS WORDS TRANSFORMED INTO ELECTRICAL IMPULSES HURLED HEADLONG INTO THE ATMOSPHERE--
SOLAR JET-- COME IN! SOLAR JET-- DO YOU READ ME?
DAMMIT, DAVIS-- WHY WON'T YOU ANSWER ME?!?
--BUT IT IS AS A VOICE CRYING IN THE WILDERNESS...
IN BRIGHTEST NIGHT...!
LEN WEIN . DAVE GIBBONS . JOHN COSTANZA . ANTHONY TOLLIN
WRITER/EDITOR ILLUSTRATOR LETTERER COLORIST
WITH THANKS TO PAUL KUPPERBERG FOR PLOTTING ASSIST ABOVE AND BEYOND THE CALL OF DUTY.

IT'S NO *USE*-- THE RADIO'S GONE *DEAD!*

RICH DAVIS AND THE SOLAR JET ARE -- *GONE!*

THIS IS ALL *MY* FAULT!

DON'T BE *ABSURD*, HAL! YOU DIDN'T KNOCK *YOURSELF* UNCONSCIOUS SO DAVIS COULD *REPLACE* YOU IN THE SOLAR JET!

IT WAS ALL *HIS* IDEA... AND NOW HE'S PAID THE *PRICE!*

SO WHAT DO WE DO *NOW?*

REPLAY THE *AUDIO-TAPE.* MAYBE IT'LL GIVE US A *CLUE*--!

"DAVIS, WHAT'S *WRONG?*"

"I WISH TO GOD I *KNEW*, GORDON!"

"LOOKS LIKE SOME SORT OF MINIATURE *MOON*-- ECLIPSING THE SUN--!"

"IT'S CREATED A COLUMN OF *BLACK LIGHT* IN FRONT OF ME-- AND I CAN'T *AVOID* IT!"

"RICHARD, YOU *MUST*--! I DON'T CARE *HOW* YOU DO IT--

--BUT YOU MUST NOT ENTER THAT *BEAM*--!"

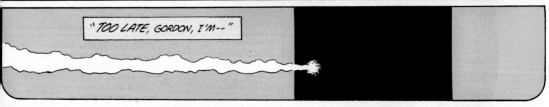

"*TOO LATE*, GORDON, I'M--"

EITHER DAVIS AND THE JET HAVE BEEN *DESTROYED*, OR THEY'VE BEEN *SNATCHED* SOMEHOW--

--AND IT'S UP TO *ME* TO FIND OUT *WHICH!*

THERE GOES JOHN STEWART--

--AND IT ISN'T DIFFICULT FOR ME TO GUESS *WHY!*

2

61

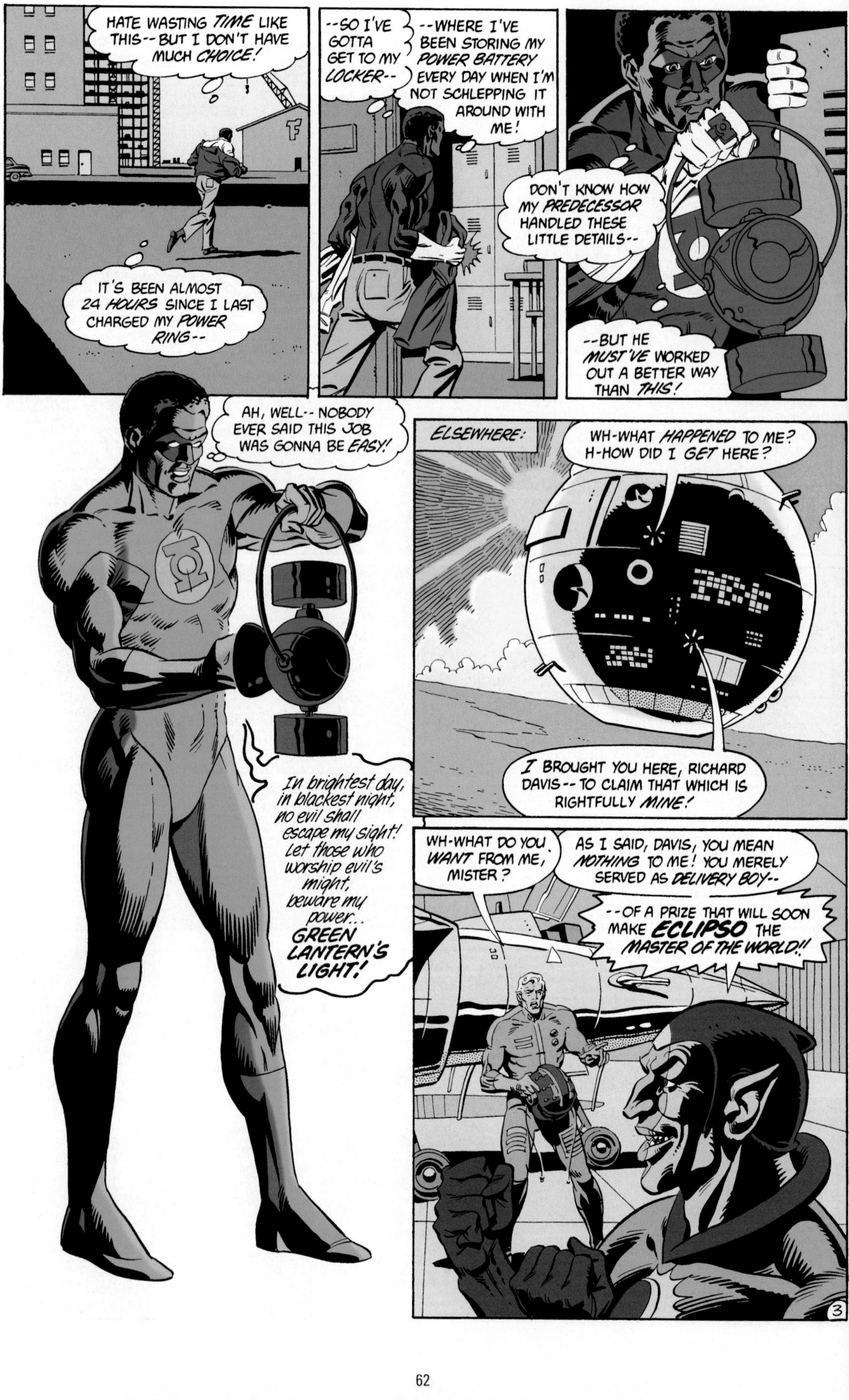
HATE WASTING TIME LIKE THIS--BUT I DON'T HAVE MUCH CHOICE!
IT'S BEEN ALMOST 24 HOURS SINCE I LAST CHARGED MY POWER RING--
--SO I'VE GOTTA GET TO MY LOCKER--
--WHERE I'VE BEEN STORING MY POWER BATTERY EVERY DAY WHEN I'M NOT SCHLEPPING IT AROUND WITH ME!
DON'T KNOW HOW MY PREDECESSOR HANDLED THESE LITTLE DETAILS--
--BUT HE MUST'VE WORKED OUT A BETTER WAY THAN THIS!
AH, WELL--NOBODY EVER SAID THIS JOB WAS GONNA BE EASY!
In brightest day, in blackest night, no evil shall escape my sight! Let those who worship evil's might, beware my power... GREEN LANTERN'S LIGHT!
ELSEWHERE:
WH-WHAT HAPPENED TO ME? H-HOW DID I GET HERE?
I BROUGHT YOU HERE, RICHARD DAVIS--TO CLAIM THAT WHICH IS RIGHTFULLY MINE!
WH-WHAT DO YOU WANT FROM ME, MISTER?
AS I SAID, DAVIS, YOU MEAN NOTHING TO ME! YOU MERELY SERVED AS DELIVERY BOY--
--OF A PRIZE THAT WILL SOON MAKE ECLIPSO THE MASTER OF THE WORLD!!
3

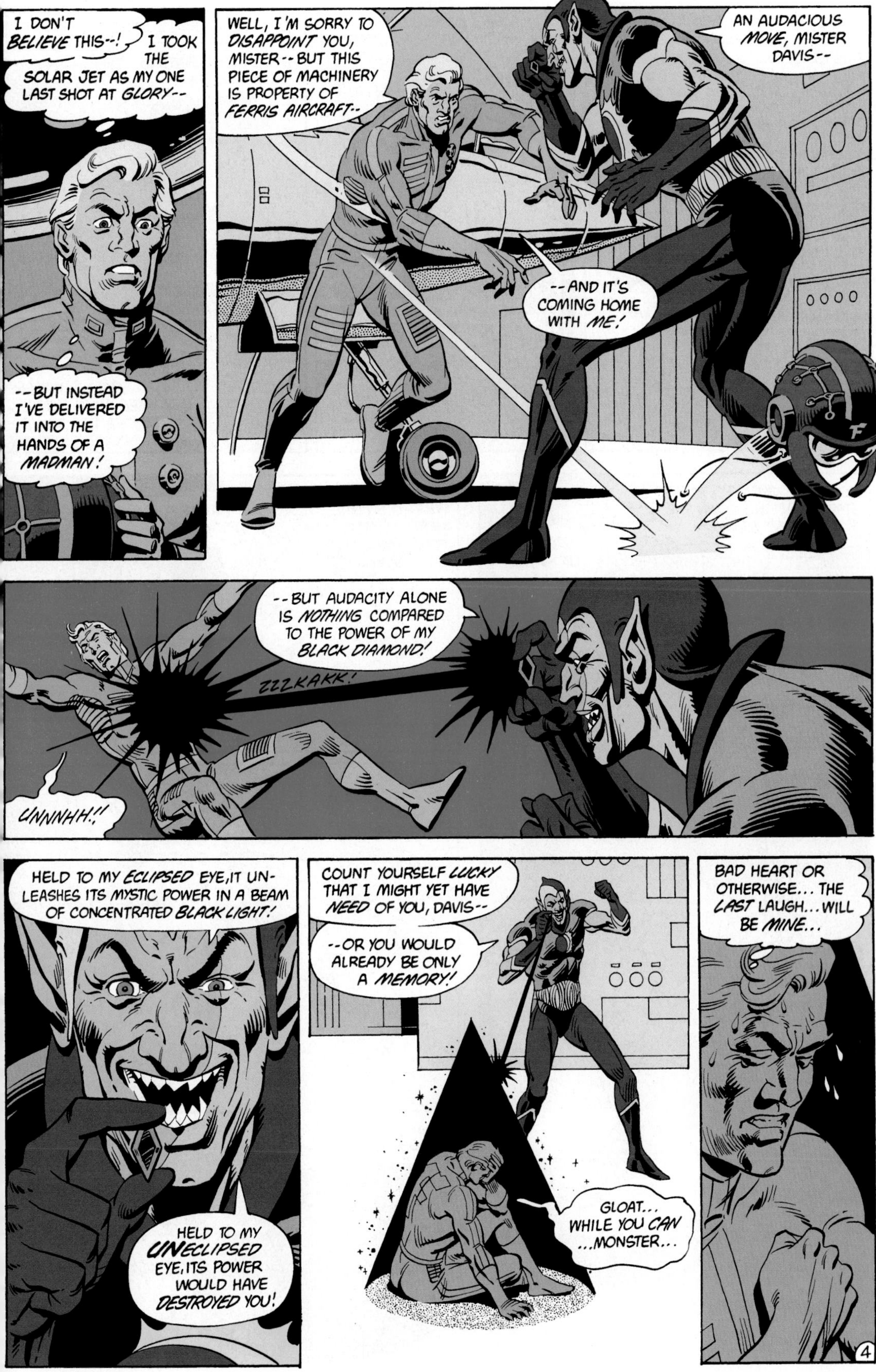
I DON'T BELIEVE THIS--! I TOOK THE SOLAR JET AS MY ONE LAST SHOT AT GLORY--
--BUT INSTEAD I'VE DELIVERED IT INTO THE HANDS OF A MADMAN!
WELL, I'M SORRY TO DISAPPOINT YOU, MISTER--BUT THIS PIECE OF MACHINERY IS PROPERTY OF FERRIS AIRCRAFT--
AN AUDACIOUS MOVE, MISTER DAVIS--
--AND IT'S COMING HOME WITH ME!
--BUT AUDACITY ALONE IS NOTHING COMPARED TO THE POWER OF MY BLACK DIAMOND!
ZZZKAKK!
UNNNHH!!
HELD TO MY ECLIPSED EYE, IT UNLEASHES ITS MYSTIC POWER IN A BEAM OF CONCENTRATED BLACK LIGHT!
HELD TO MY UNECLIPSED EYE, ITS POWER WOULD HAVE DESTROYED YOU!
COUNT YOURSELF LUCKY THAT I MIGHT YET HAVE NEED OF YOU, DAVIS--
--OR YOU WOULD ALREADY BE ONLY A MEMORY!
GLOAT... WHILE YOU CAN ...MONSTER...
BAD HEART OR OTHERWISE... THE LAST LAUGH... WILL BE MINE...
4

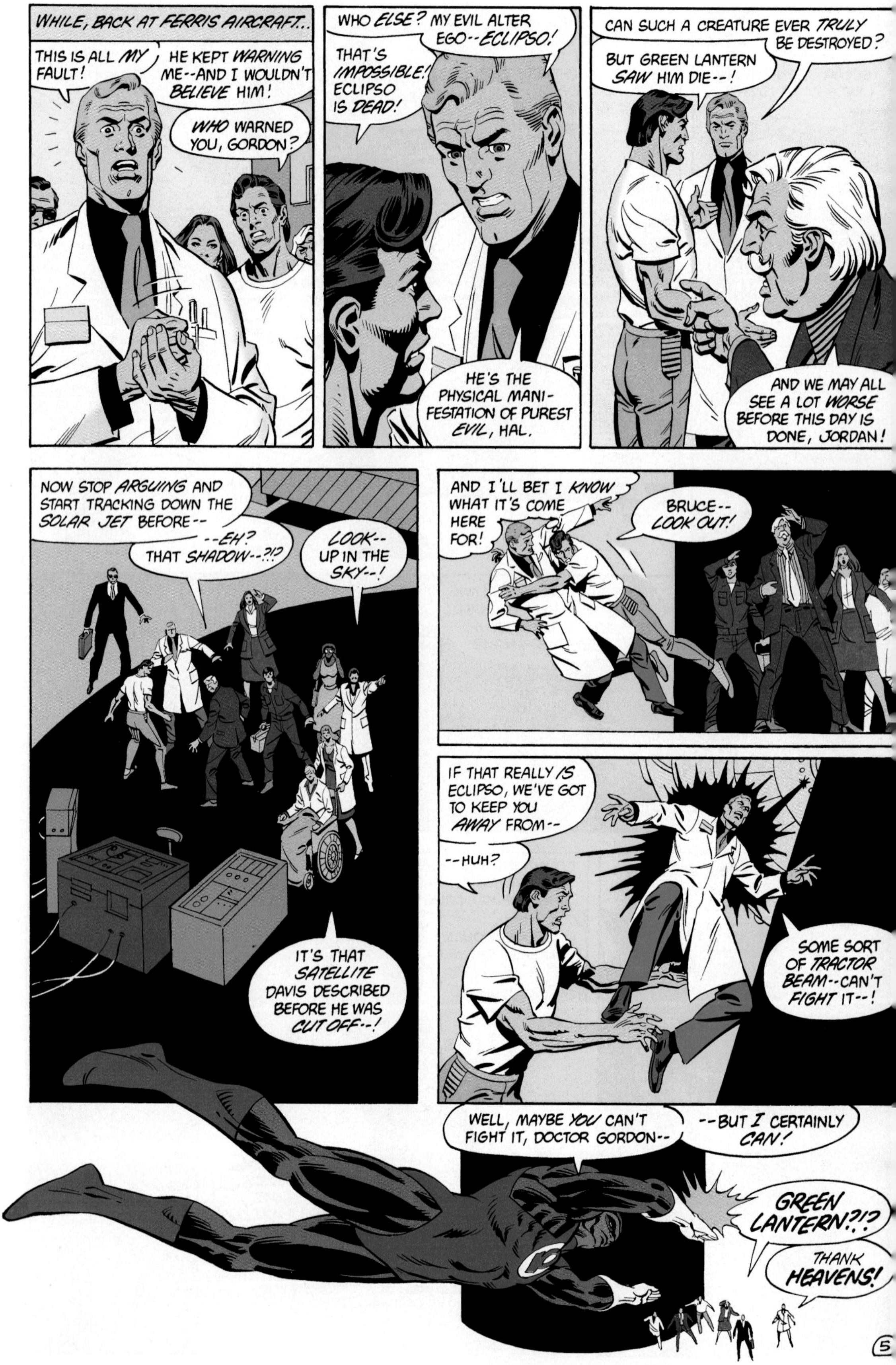

WHILE, BACK AT FERRIS AIRCRAFT...
THIS IS ALL MY FAULT!
HE KEPT WARNING ME--AND I WOULDN'T BELIEVE HIM!
WHO WARNED YOU, GORDON?
WHO ELSE? MY EVIL ALTER EGO--ECLIPSO!
THAT'S IMPOSSIBLE! ECLIPSO IS DEAD!
HE'S THE PHYSICAL MANIFESTATION OF PUREST EVIL, HAL.
CAN SUCH A CREATURE EVER TRULY BE DESTROYED?
BUT GREEN LANTERN SAW HIM DIE--!
AND WE MAY ALL SEE A LOT WORSE BEFORE THIS DAY IS DONE, JORDAN!
NOW STOP ARGUING AND START TRACKING DOWN THE SOLAR JET BEFORE--
--EH? THAT SHADOW--?!?
LOOK-- UP IN THE SKY--!
IT'S THAT SATELLITE DAVIS DESCRIBED BEFORE HE WAS CUT OFF--!
AND I'LL BET I KNOW WHAT IT'S COME HERE FOR!
BRUCE-- LOOK OUT!
IF THAT REALLY IS ECLIPSO, WE'VE GOT TO KEEP YOU AWAY FROM--
--HUH?
SOME SORT OF TRACTOR BEAM--CAN'T FIGHT IT--!
WELL, MAYBE YOU CAN'T FIGHT IT, DOCTOR GORDON--
--BUT I CERTAINLY CAN!
GREEN LANTERN?!?
THANK HEAVENS!
5

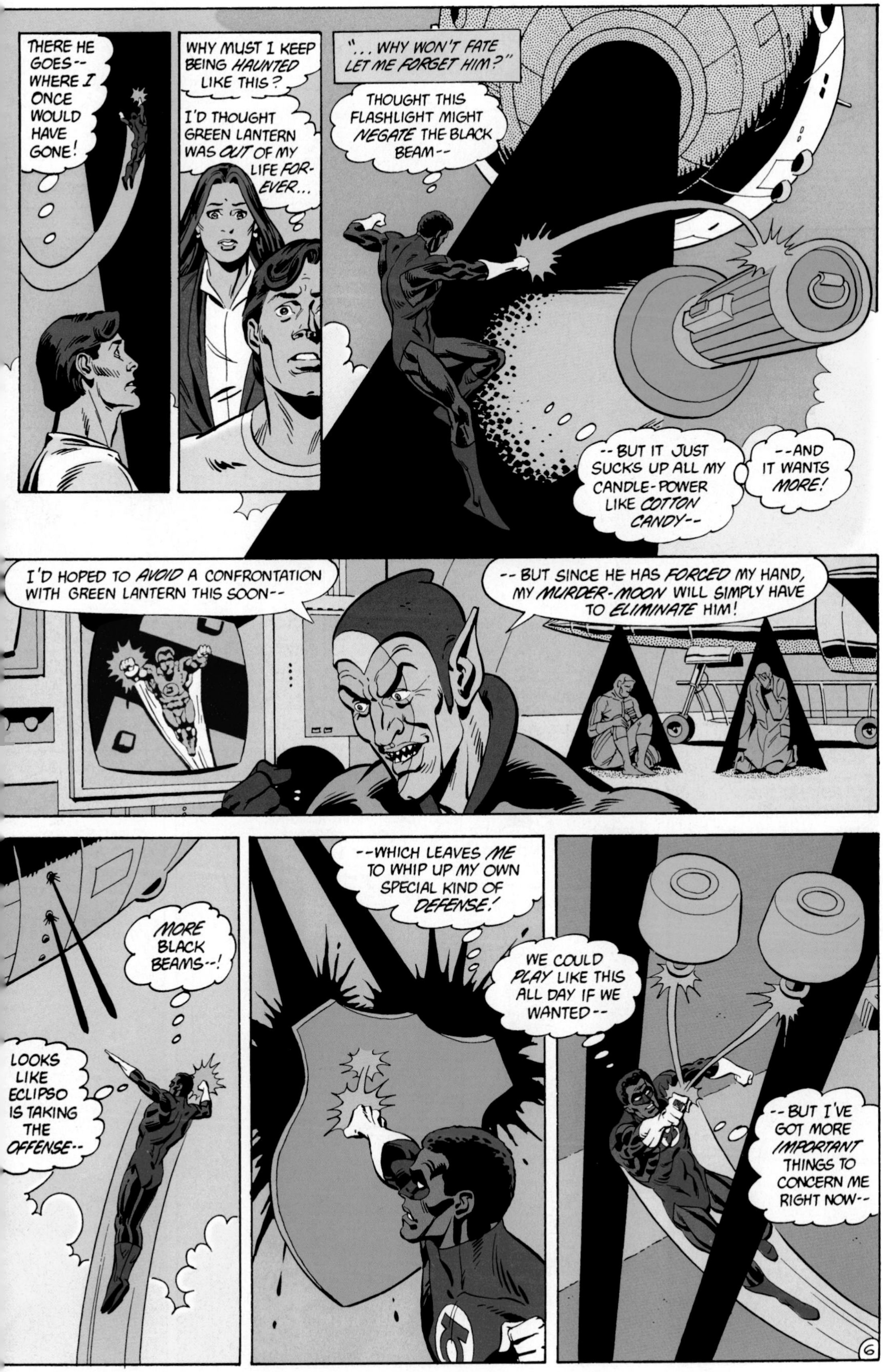
THERE HE GOES-- WHERE I ONCE WOULD HAVE GONE!
WHY MUST I KEEP BEING HAUNTED LIKE THIS? I'D THOUGHT GREEN LANTERN WAS OUT OF MY LIFE FOR-EVER...
"...WHY WON'T FATE LET ME FORGET HIM?"
THOUGHT THIS FLASHLIGHT MIGHT NEGATE THE BLACK BEAM--
--BUT IT JUST SUCKS UP ALL MY CANDLE-POWER LIKE COTTON CANDY--
--AND IT WANTS MORE!
I'D HOPED TO AVOID A CONFRONTATION WITH GREEN LANTERN THIS SOON--
--BUT SINCE HE HAS FORCED MY HAND, MY MURDER-MOON WILL SIMPLY HAVE TO ELIMINATE HIM!
MORE BLACK BEAMS--!
LOOKS LIKE ECLIPSO IS TAKING THE OFFENSE--
--WHICH LEAVES ME TO WHIP UP MY OWN SPECIAL KIND OF DEFENSE!
WE COULD PLAY LIKE THIS ALL DAY IF WE WANTED--
--BUT I'VE GOT MORE IMPORTANT THINGS TO CONCERN ME RIGHT NOW--
6

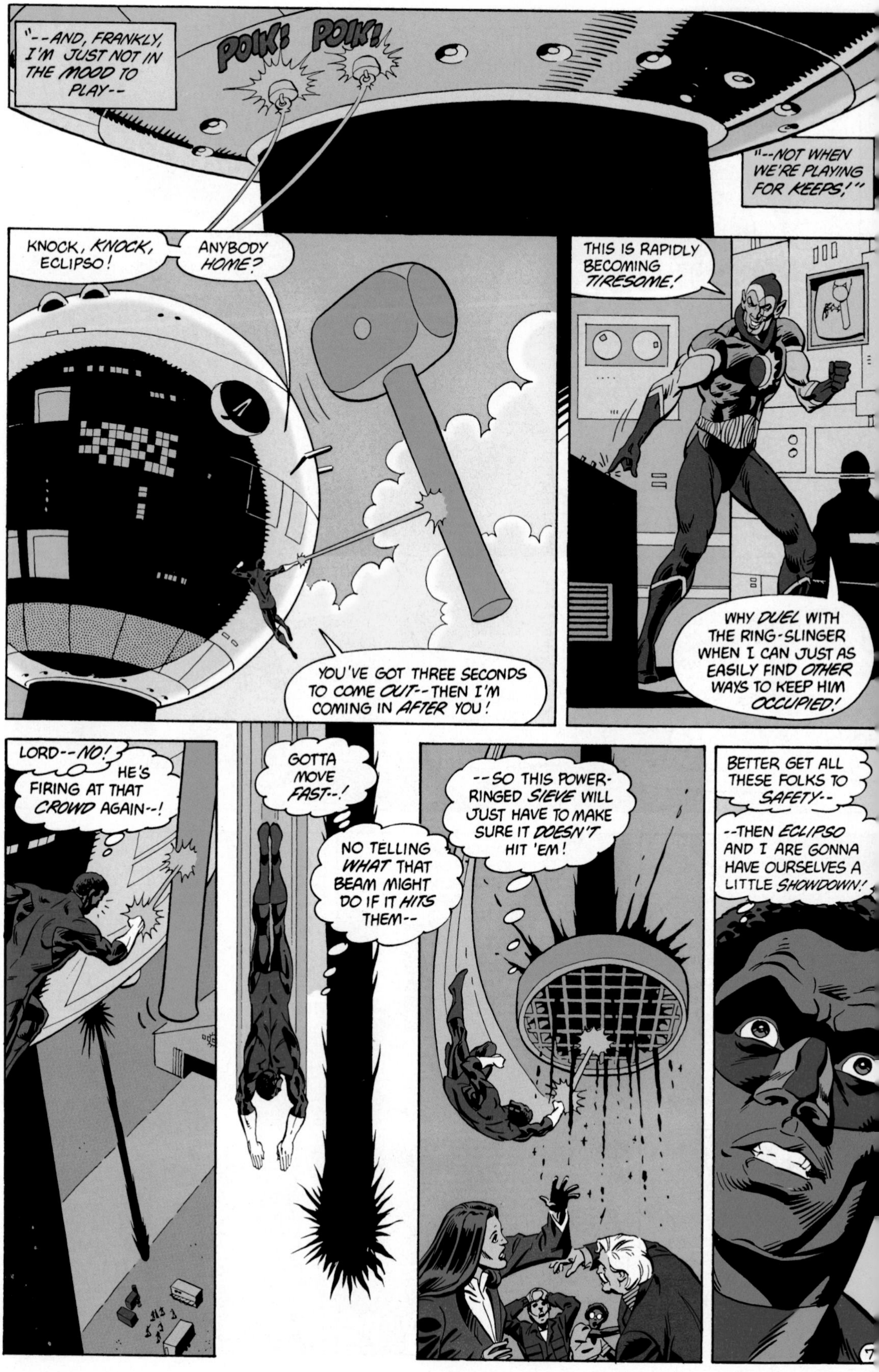
"--AND, FRANKLY, I'M JUST NOT IN THE MOOD TO PLAY--
POIK! POIK!
"--NOT WHEN WE'RE PLAYING FOR KEEPS!"
KNOCK, KNOCK, ECLIPSO!
ANYBODY HOME?
YOU'VE GOT THREE SECONDS TO COME OUT--THEN I'M COMING IN AFTER YOU!
THIS IS RAPIDLY BECOMING TIRESOME!
WHY DUEL WITH THE RING-SLINGER WHEN I CAN JUST AS EASILY FIND OTHER WAYS TO KEEP HIM OCCUPIED!
LORD--NO! HE'S FIRING AT THAT CROWD AGAIN--!
GOTTA MOVE FAST--!
NO TELLING WHAT THAT BEAM MIGHT DO IF IT HITS THEM--
--SO THIS POWER-RINGED SIEVE WILL JUST HAVE TO MAKE SURE IT DOESN'T HIT 'EM!
BETTER GET ALL THESE FOLKS TO SAFETY--
--THEN ECLIPSO AND I ARE GONNA HAVE OURSELVES A LITTLE SHOWDOWN!
7

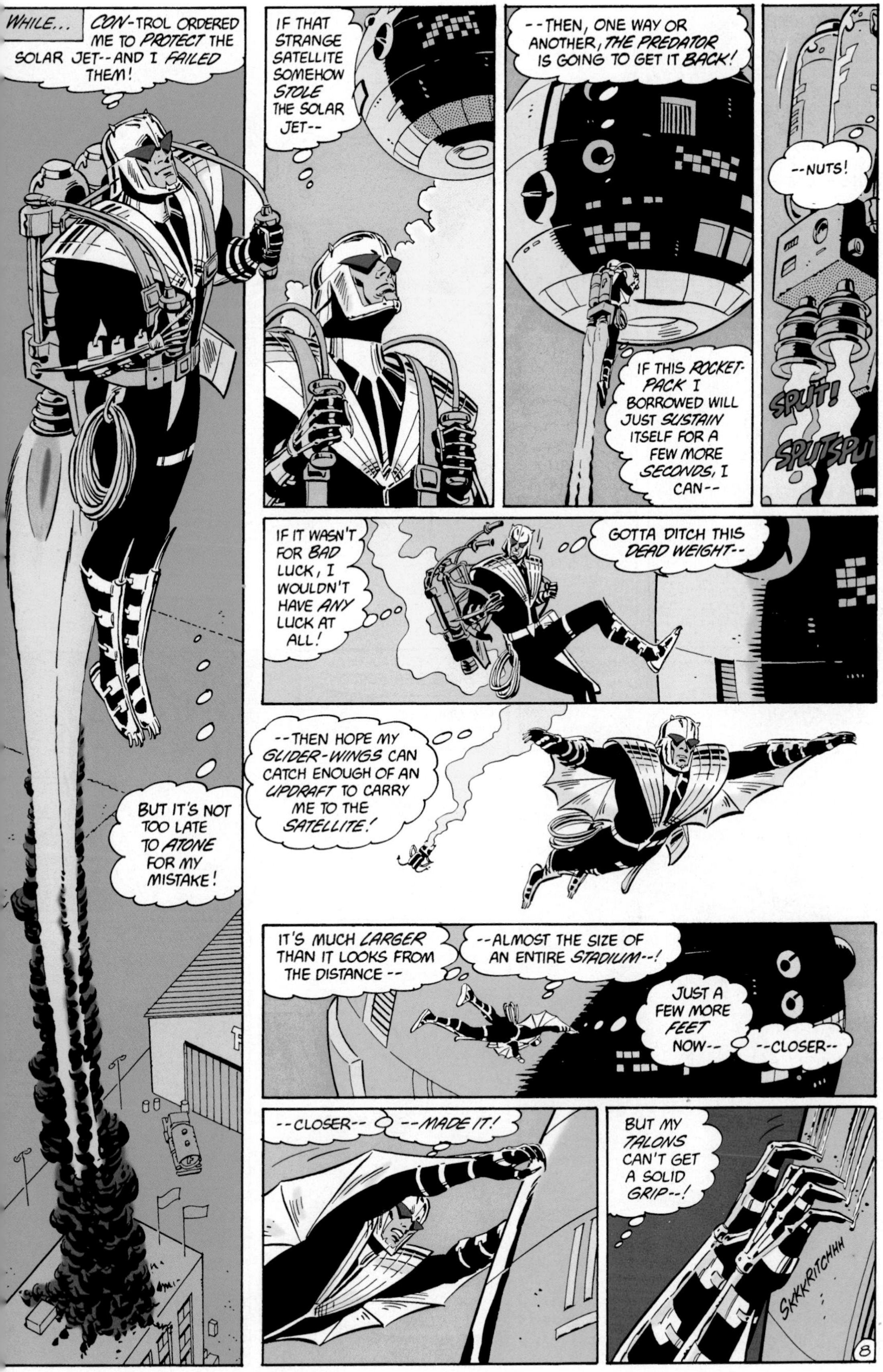

WHILE...
CON-TROL ORDERED ME TO PROTECT THE SOLAR JET--AND I FAILED THEM!
BUT IT'S NOT TOO LATE TO ATONE FOR MY MISTAKE!
IF THAT STRANGE SATELLITE SOMEHOW STOLE THE SOLAR JET--
--THEN, ONE WAY OR ANOTHER, THE PREDATOR IS GOING TO GET IT BACK!
IF THIS ROCKET-PACK I BORROWED WILL JUST SUSTAIN ITSELF FOR A FEW MORE SECONDS, I CAN--
--NUTS!
SPUT!
SPUTSPUT
IF IT WASN'T FOR BAD LUCK, I WOULDN'T HAVE ANY LUCK AT ALL!
GOTTA DITCH THIS DEAD WEIGHT--
--THEN HOPE MY GLIDER-WINGS CAN CATCH ENOUGH OF AN UPDRAFT TO CARRY ME TO THE SATELLITE!
IT'S MUCH LARGER THAN IT LOOKS FROM THE DISTANCE--
--ALMOST THE SIZE OF AN ENTIRE STADIUM--!
JUST A FEW MORE FEET NOW--
--CLOSER--
--CLOSER--
--MADE IT!
BUT MY TALONS CAN'T GET A SOLID GRIP--!
SKKRITCHHH
8

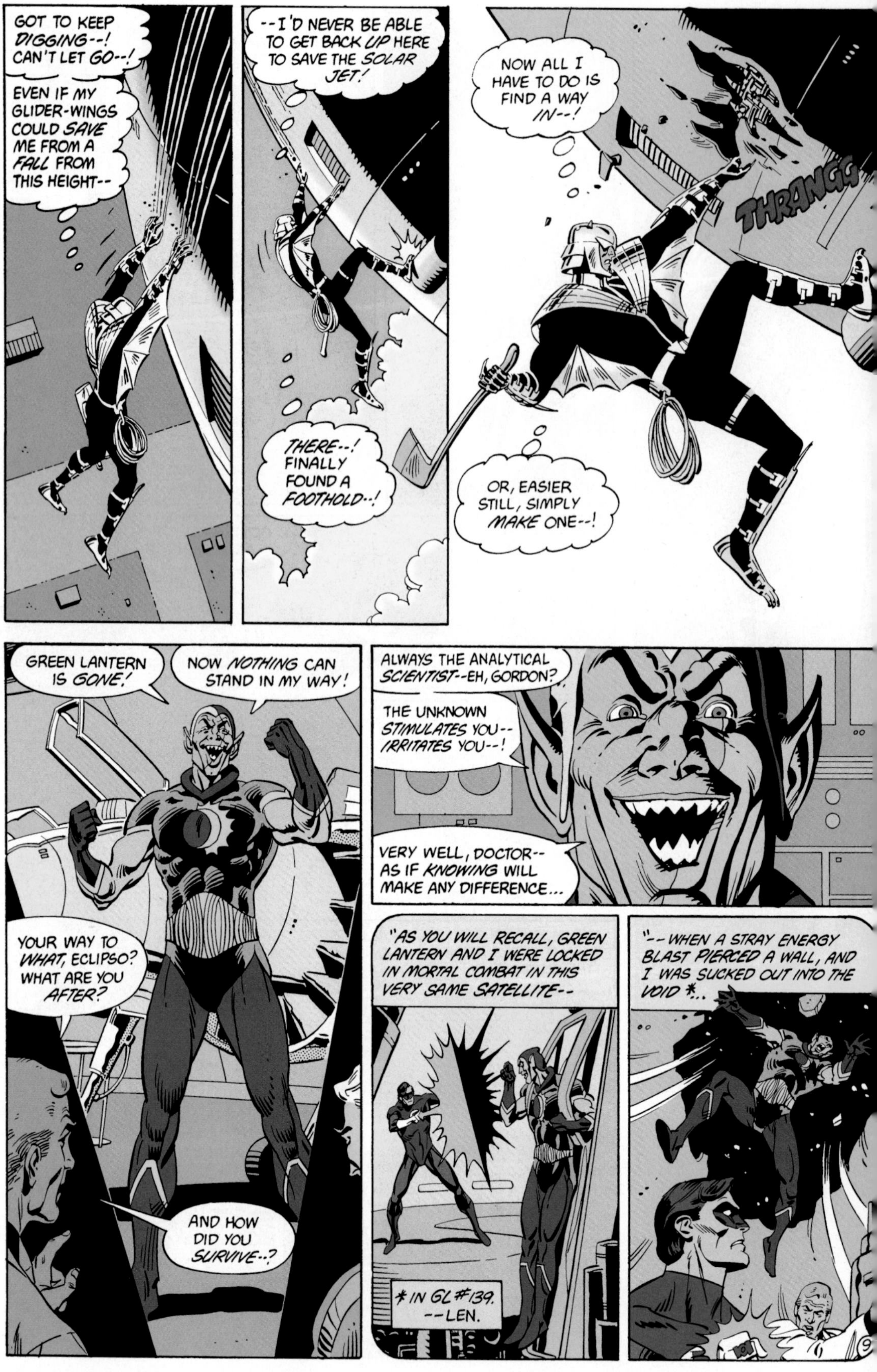
GOT TO KEEP DIGGING--! CAN'T LET GO--!
EVEN IF MY GLIDER-WINGS COULD SAVE ME FROM A FALL FROM THIS HEIGHT--
--I'D NEVER BE ABLE TO GET BACK UP HERE TO SAVE THE SOLAR JET!
THERE--! FINALLY FOUND A FOOTHOLD--!
NOW ALL I HAVE TO DO IS FIND A WAY IN--!
THRANGG
OR, EASIER STILL, SIMPLY MAKE ONE--!
GREEN LANTERN IS GONE!
NOW NOTHING CAN STAND IN MY WAY!
YOUR WAY TO WHAT, ECLIPSO? WHAT ARE YOU AFTER?
AND HOW DID YOU SURVIVE--?
ALWAYS THE ANALYTICAL SCIENTIST--EH, GORDON?
THE UNKNOWN STIMULATES YOU--IRRITATES YOU--!
VERY WELL, DOCTOR--AS IF KNOWING WILL MAKE ANY DIFFERENCE...
"AS YOU WILL RECALL, GREEN LANTERN AND I WERE LOCKED IN MORTAL COMBAT IN THIS VERY SAME SATELLITE--
*IN GL #139. --LEN.
"--WHEN A STRAY ENERGY BLAST PIERCED A WALL, AND I WAS SUCKED OUT INTO THE VOID*...
9

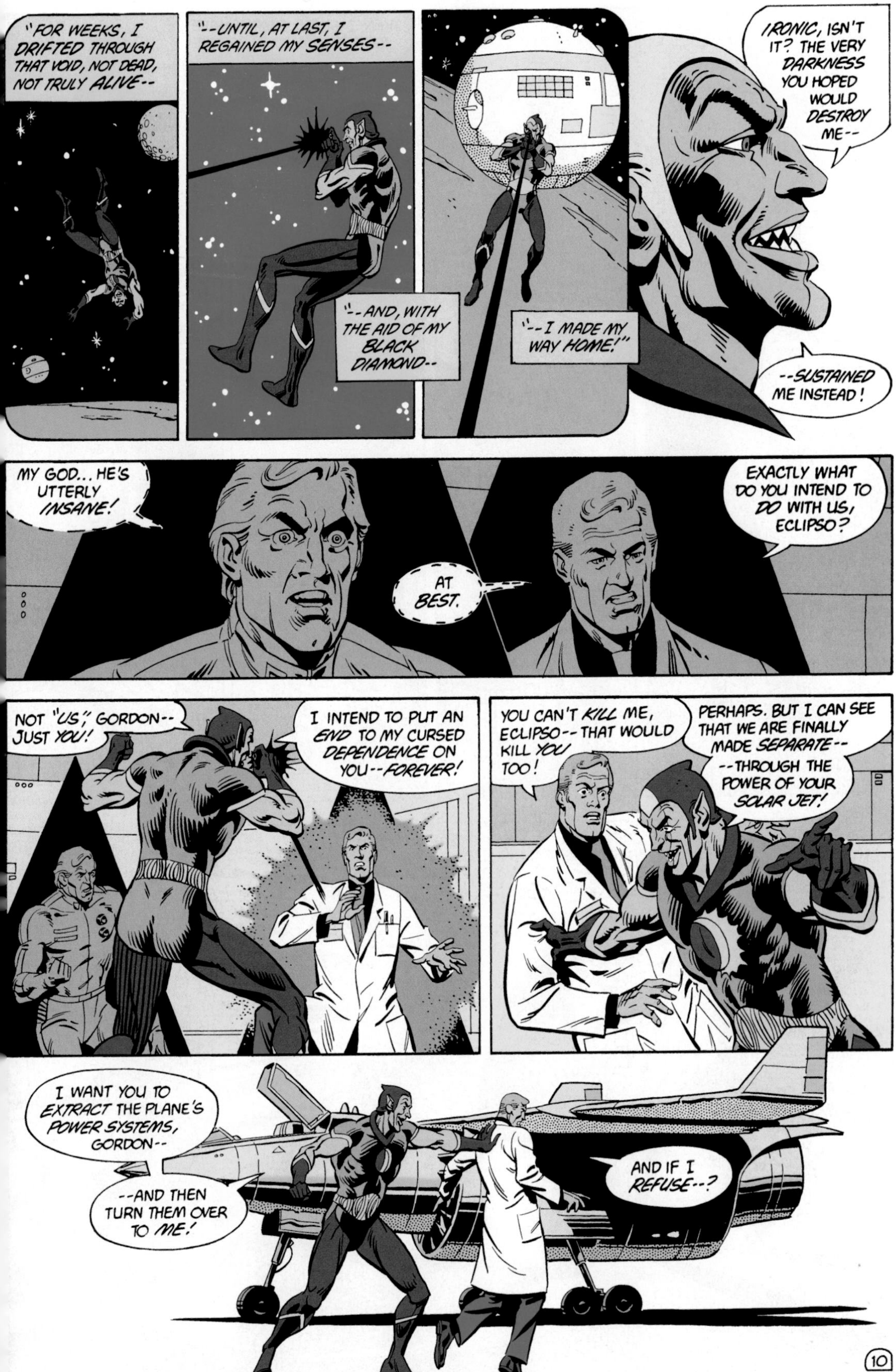
"FOR WEEKS, I DRIFTED THROUGH THAT VOID, NOT DEAD, NOT TRULY ALIVE--
"--UNTIL, AT LAST, I REGAINED MY SENSES--
"--AND, WITH THE AID OF MY BLACK DIAMOND--
"--I MADE MY WAY HOME!"
IRONIC, ISN'T IT? THE VERY DARKNESS YOU HOPED WOULD DESTROY ME--
--SUSTAINED ME INSTEAD!
MY GOD... HE'S UTTERLY INSANE!
AT BEST.
EXACTLY WHAT DO YOU INTEND TO DO WITH US, ECLIPSO?
NOT "US," GORDON-- JUST YOU!
I INTEND TO PUT AN END TO MY CURSED DEPENDENCE ON YOU--FOREVER!
YOU CAN'T KILL ME, ECLIPSO--THAT WOULD KILL YOU TOO!
PERHAPS. BUT I CAN SEE THAT WE ARE FINALLY MADE SEPARATE--
--THROUGH THE POWER OF YOUR SOLAR JET!
I WANT YOU TO EXTRACT THE PLANE'S POWER SYSTEMS, GORDON--
--AND THEN TURN THEM OVER TO ME!
AND IF I REFUSE--?
10

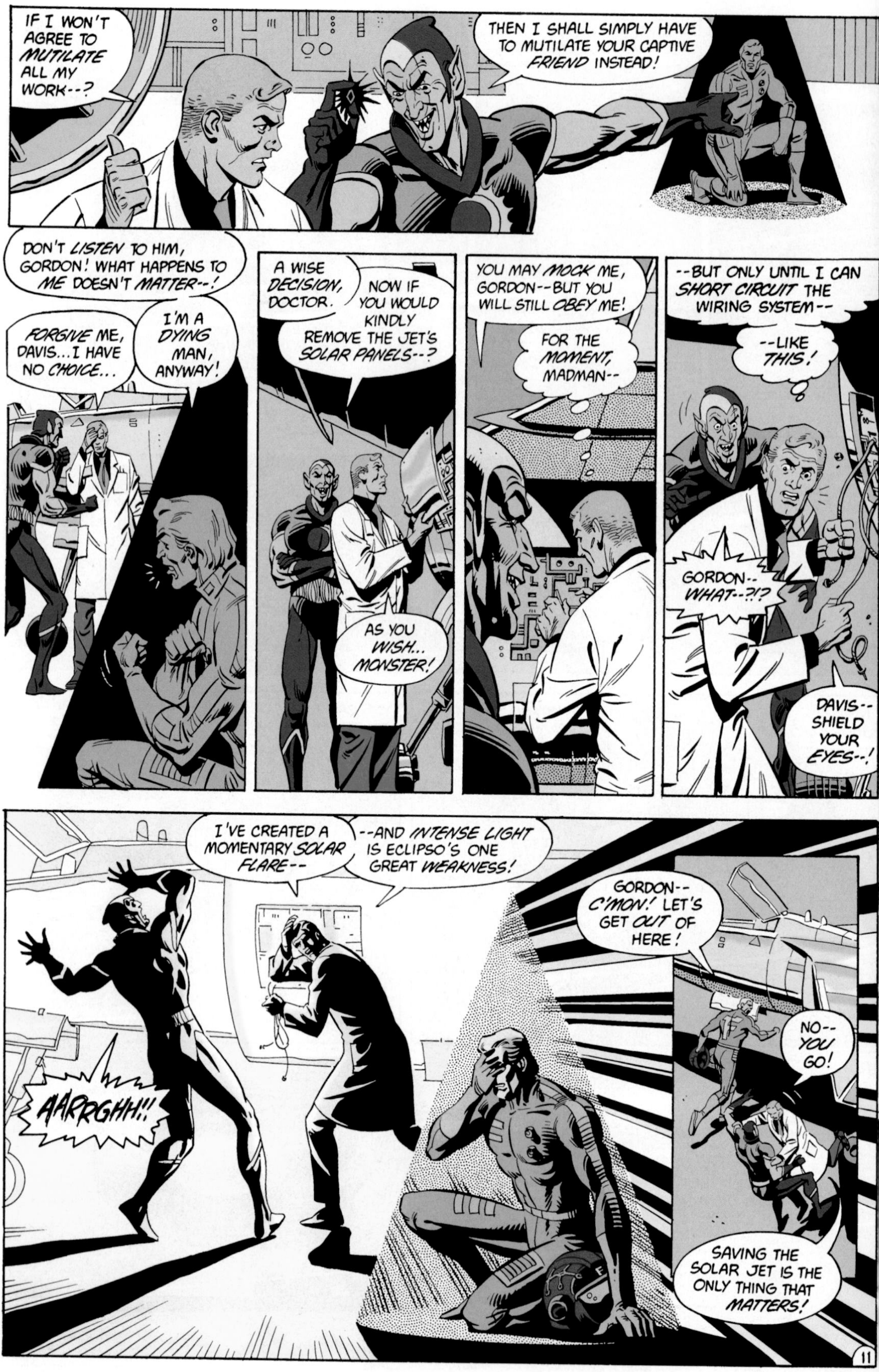
IF I WON'T AGREE TO MUTILATE ALL MY WORK--?
THEN I SHALL SIMPLY HAVE TO MUTILATE YOUR CAPTIVE FRIEND INSTEAD!
DON'T LISTEN TO HIM, GORDON! WHAT HAPPENS TO ME DOESN'T MATTER--!
I'M A DYING MAN, ANYWAY!
FORGIVE ME, DAVIS...I HAVE NO CHOICE...
A WISE DECISION, DOCTOR.
NOW IF YOU WOULD KINDLY REMOVE THE JET'S SOLAR PANELS--?
AS YOU WISH... MONSTER!
YOU MAY MOCK ME, GORDON--BUT YOU WILL STILL OBEY ME!
FOR THE MOMENT, MADMAN--
--BUT ONLY UNTIL I CAN SHORT CIRCUIT THE WIRING SYSTEM--
--LIKE THIS!
GORDON-- WHAT--?!?
DAVIS-- SHIELD YOUR EYES--!
I'VE CREATED A MOMENTARY SOLAR FLARE--
--AND INTENSE LIGHT IS ECLIPSO'S ONE GREAT WEAKNESS!
AARRGHH!!
GORDON-- C'MON! LET'S GET OUT OF HERE!
NO-- YOU GO!
SAVING THE SOLAR JET IS THE ONLY THING THAT MATTERS!
11

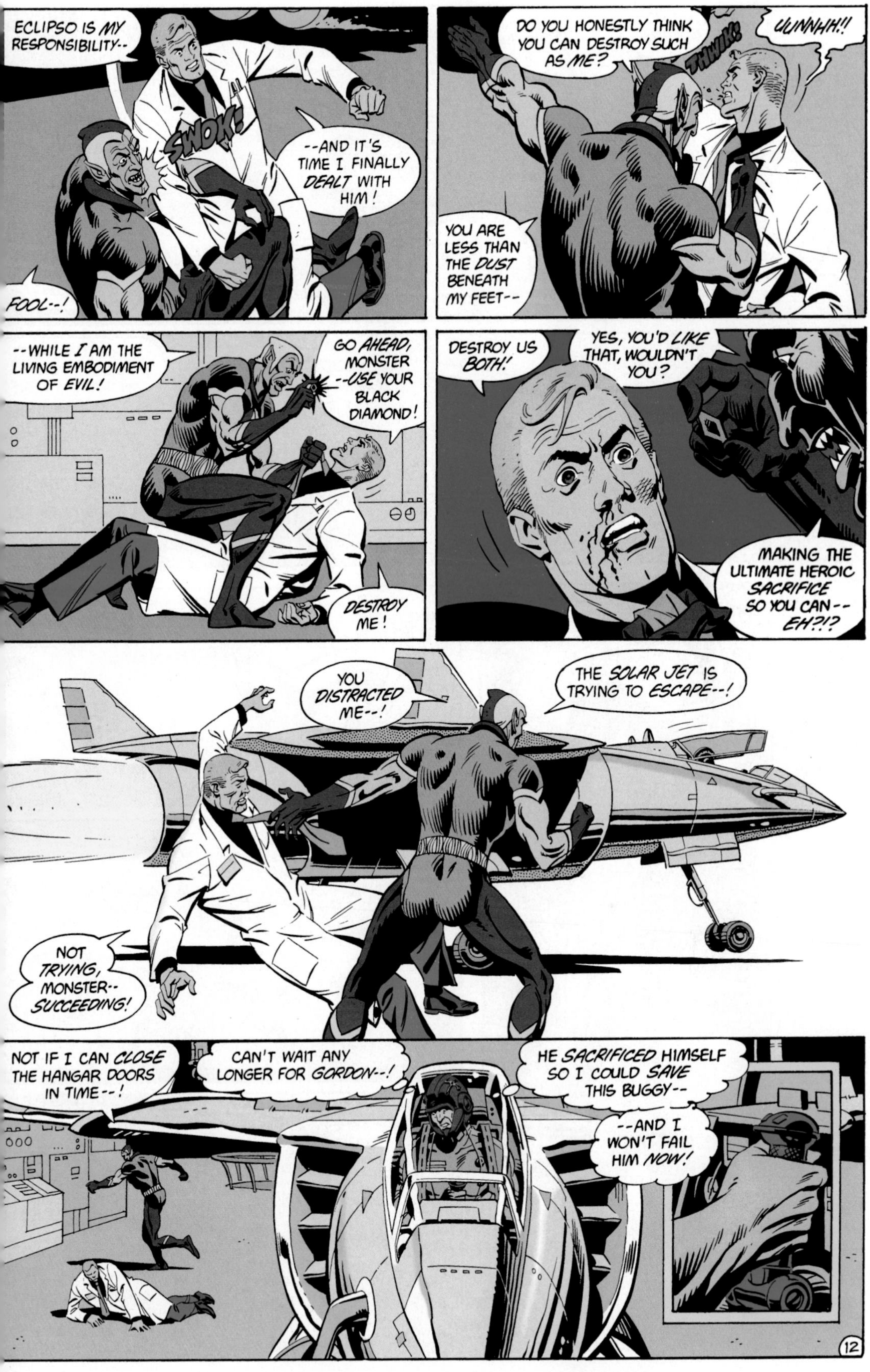
ECLIPSO IS MY RESPONSIBILITY--
SWOK!
--AND IT'S TIME I FINALLY DEALT WITH HIM!
FOOL--!
DO YOU HONESTLY THINK YOU CAN DESTROY SUCH AS ME?
THWAK!
UUNNHH!!
YOU ARE LESS THAN THE DUST BENEATH MY FEET--
--WHILE I AM THE LIVING EMBODIMENT OF EVIL!
GO AHEAD, MONSTER --USE YOUR BLACK DIAMOND!
DESTROY ME!
DESTROY US BOTH!
YES, YOU'D LIKE THAT, WOULDN'T YOU?
MAKING THE ULTIMATE HEROIC SACRIFICE SO YOU CAN-- EH?!?
YOU DISTRACTED ME--!
THE SOLAR JET IS TRYING TO ESCAPE--!
NOT TRYING, MONSTER-- SUCCEEDING!
NOT IF I CAN CLOSE THE HANGAR DOORS IN TIME--!
CAN'T WAIT ANY LONGER FOR GORDON--!
HE SACRIFICED HIMSELF SO I COULD SAVE THIS BUGGY--
--AND I WON'T FAIL HIM NOW!
12

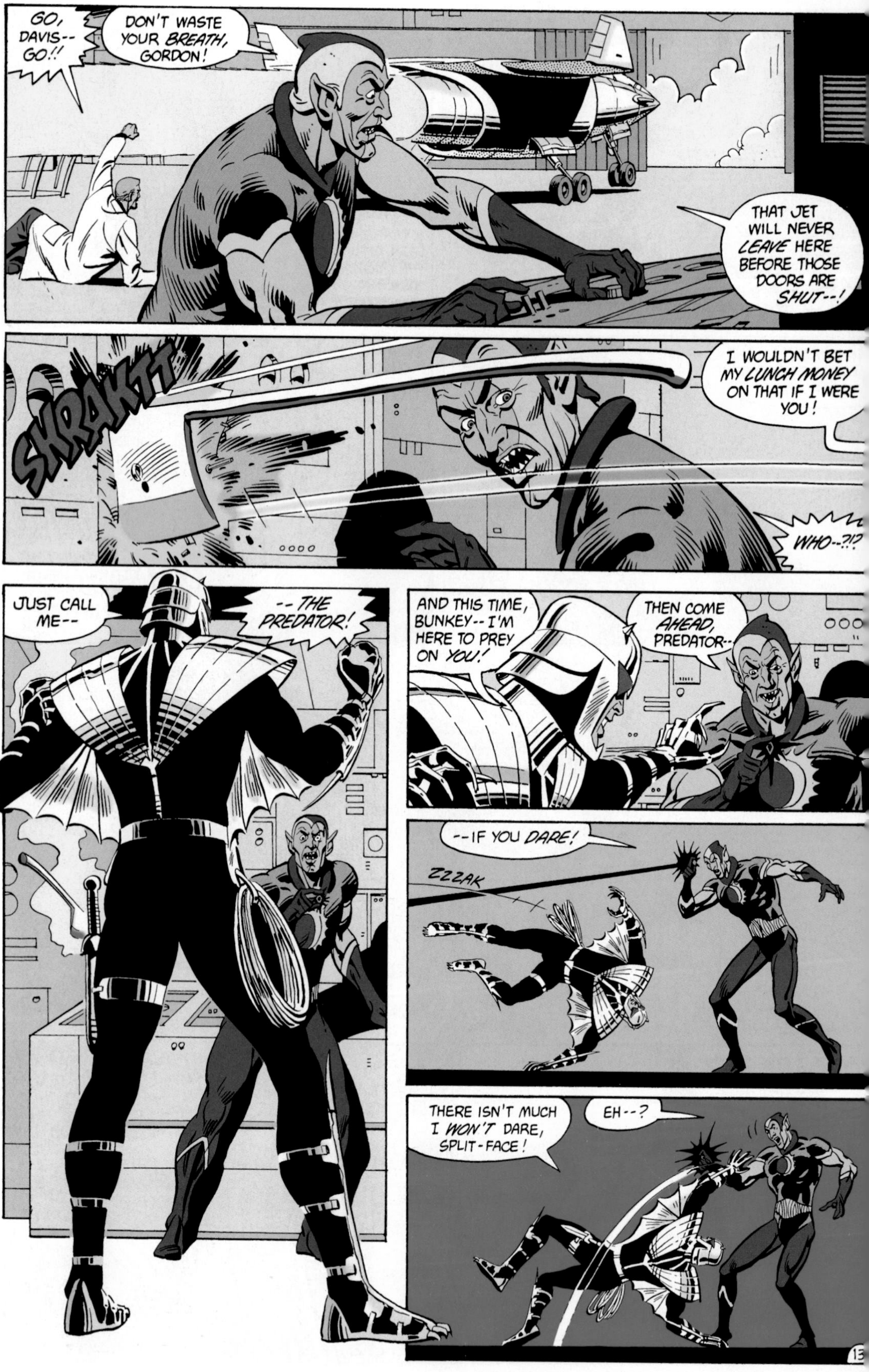
GO, DAVIS-- GO!!
DON'T WASTE YOUR BREATH, GORDON!
THAT JET WILL NEVER LEAVE HERE BEFORE THOSE DOORS ARE SHUT--!
SHRAKTT
I WOULDN'T BET MY LUNCH MONEY ON THAT IF I WERE YOU!
WHO--?!?
JUST CALL ME--
--THE PREDATOR!
AND THIS TIME, BUNKEY--I'M HERE TO PREY ON YOU!
THEN COME AHEAD, PREDATOR--
--IF YOU DARE!
ZZZAK
THERE ISN'T MUCH I WON'T DARE, SPLIT-FACE!
EH--?
13

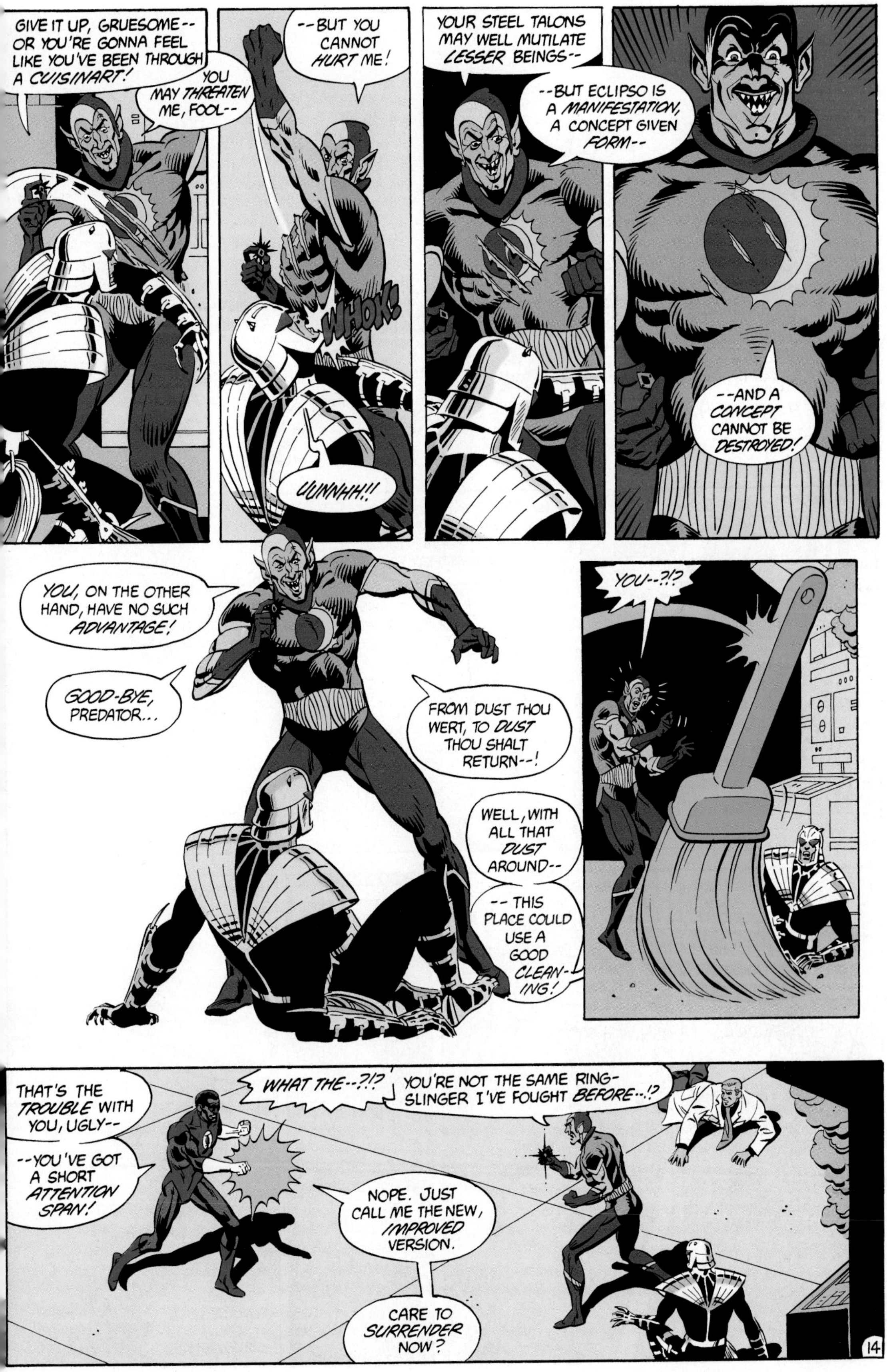
GIVE IT UP, GRUESOME-- OR YOU'RE GONNA FEEL LIKE YOU'VE BEEN THROUGH A CUISINART!
YOU MAY THREATEN ME, FOOL--
--BUT YOU CANNOT HURT ME!
WHOK!
UUNNHH!!
YOUR STEEL TALONS MAY WELL MUTILATE LESSER BEINGS--
--BUT ECLIPSO IS A MANIFESTATION, A CONCEPT GIVEN FORM--
--AND A CONCEPT CANNOT BE DESTROYED!
YOU, ON THE OTHER HAND, HAVE NO SUCH ADVANTAGE!
GOOD-BYE, PREDATOR...
FROM DUST THOU WERT, TO DUST THOU SHALT RETURN--!
YOU--?!?
WELL, WITH ALL THAT DUST AROUND--
-- THIS PLACE COULD USE A GOOD CLEAN-ING!
THAT'S THE TROUBLE WITH YOU, UGLY--
--YOU'VE GOT A SHORT ATTENTION SPAN!
WHAT THE--?!?
YOU'RE NOT THE SAME RING-SLINGER I'VE FOUGHT BEFORE--!?
NOPE. JUST CALL ME THE NEW, IMPROVED VERSION.
CARE TO SURRENDER NOW?
14

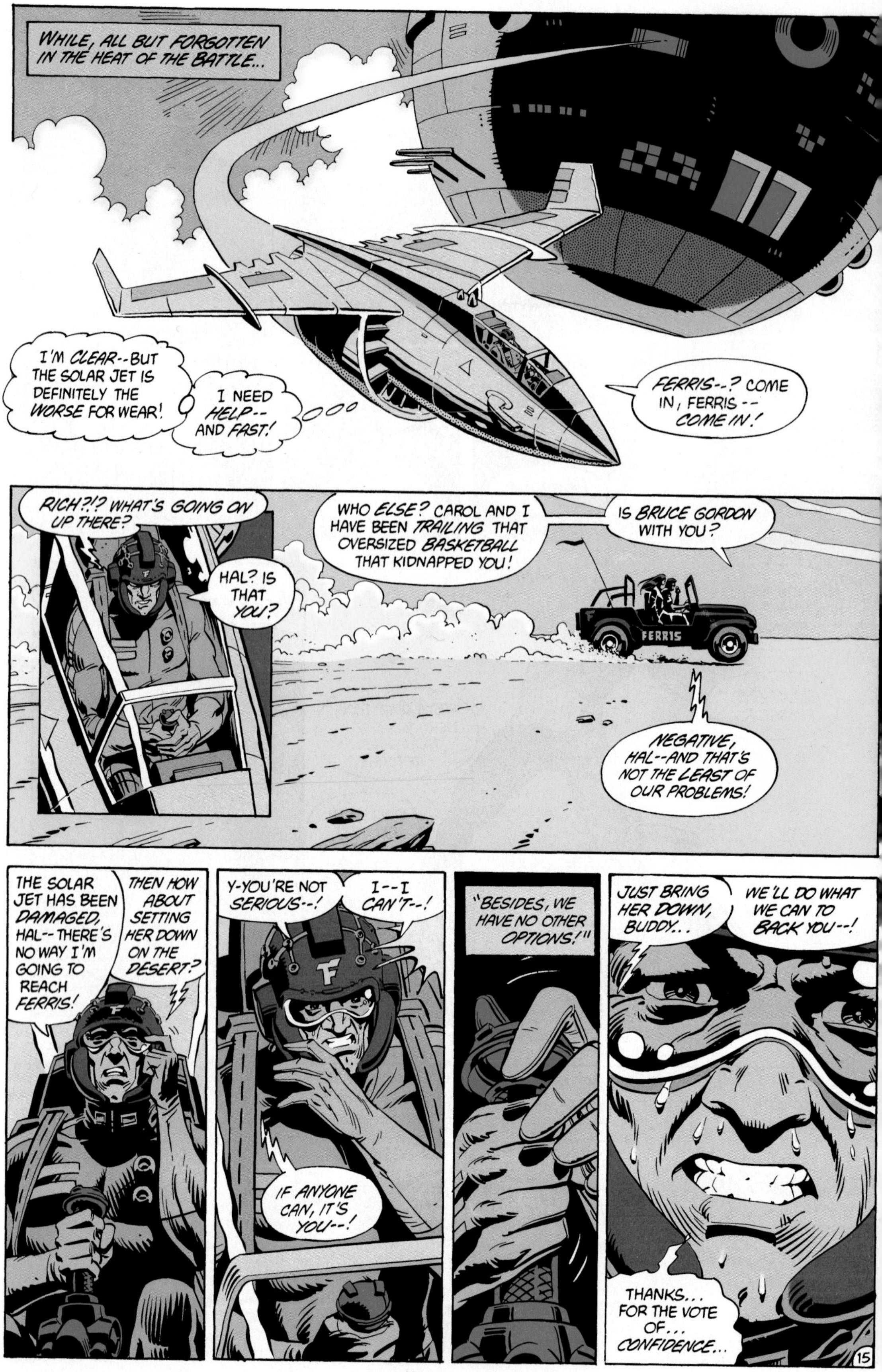
WHILE, ALL BUT FORGOTTEN IN THE HEAT OF THE BATTLE...
I'M CLEAR--BUT THE SOLAR JET IS DEFINITELY THE WORSE FOR WEAR!
I NEED HELP--AND FAST!
FERRIS--? COME IN, FERRIS--COME IN!
RICH?!? WHAT'S GOING ON UP THERE?
HAL? IS THAT YOU?
WHO ELSE? CAROL AND I HAVE BEEN TRAILING THAT OVERSIZED BASKETBALL THAT KIDNAPPED YOU!
IS BRUCE GORDON WITH YOU?
FERRIS
NEGATIVE, HAL--AND THAT'S NOT THE LEAST OF OUR PROBLEMS!
THE SOLAR JET HAS BEEN DAMAGED, HAL--THERE'S NO WAY I'M GOING TO REACH FERRIS!
THEN HOW ABOUT SETTING HER DOWN ON THE DESERT?
Y-YOU'RE NOT SERIOUS--!
I--I CAN'T--!
IF ANYONE CAN, IT'S YOU--!
"BESIDES, WE HAVE NO OTHER OPTIONS!"
JUST BRING HER DOWN, BUDDY...
WE'LL DO WHAT WE CAN TO BACK YOU--!
THANKS... FOR THE VOTE OF... CONFIDENCE...
15

CAN HE REALLY *DO* IT, HAL?

I MEAN, WITH HIS *BAD HEART*, THE *STRESS* ALONE COULD--!

DON'T *SAY* IT, CAROL-- DON'T EVEN *THINK* IT!

RICHARD DAVIS *TAUGHT* ME EVERY-THING I *KNOW* ABOUT THIS GAME--!

IF *ANYONE* CAN BRING THAT BUGGY DOWN *INTACT*--

--I'D BET ON *HIM*!

PLEASE, LORD...

...THIS ONE LAST TIME...

...LET ME HAVE...WHAT IT TAKES...

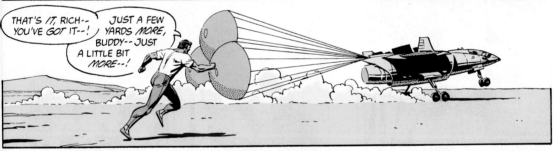

THAT'S *IT*, RICH-- YOU'VE *GOT* IT--!

JUST A FEW YARDS *MORE*, BUDDY-- JUST A LITTLE BIT *MORE*--!

ALL RIGHT-- A PERFECT *DEADSTICK* LANDING--!

I *TOLD* YOU HE COULD DO IT, CAROL--!

BAD HEART OR *OTHERWISE*, RICH DAVIS IS JUST ABOUT THE *BEST* DAMN PILOT THERE IS--!

WELCOME BACK TO THE LAND OF THE *LIVING*, GOOD BUDDY!

LET ME GIVE YOU A HAND *OUT* OF THERE AND WE CAN--

16

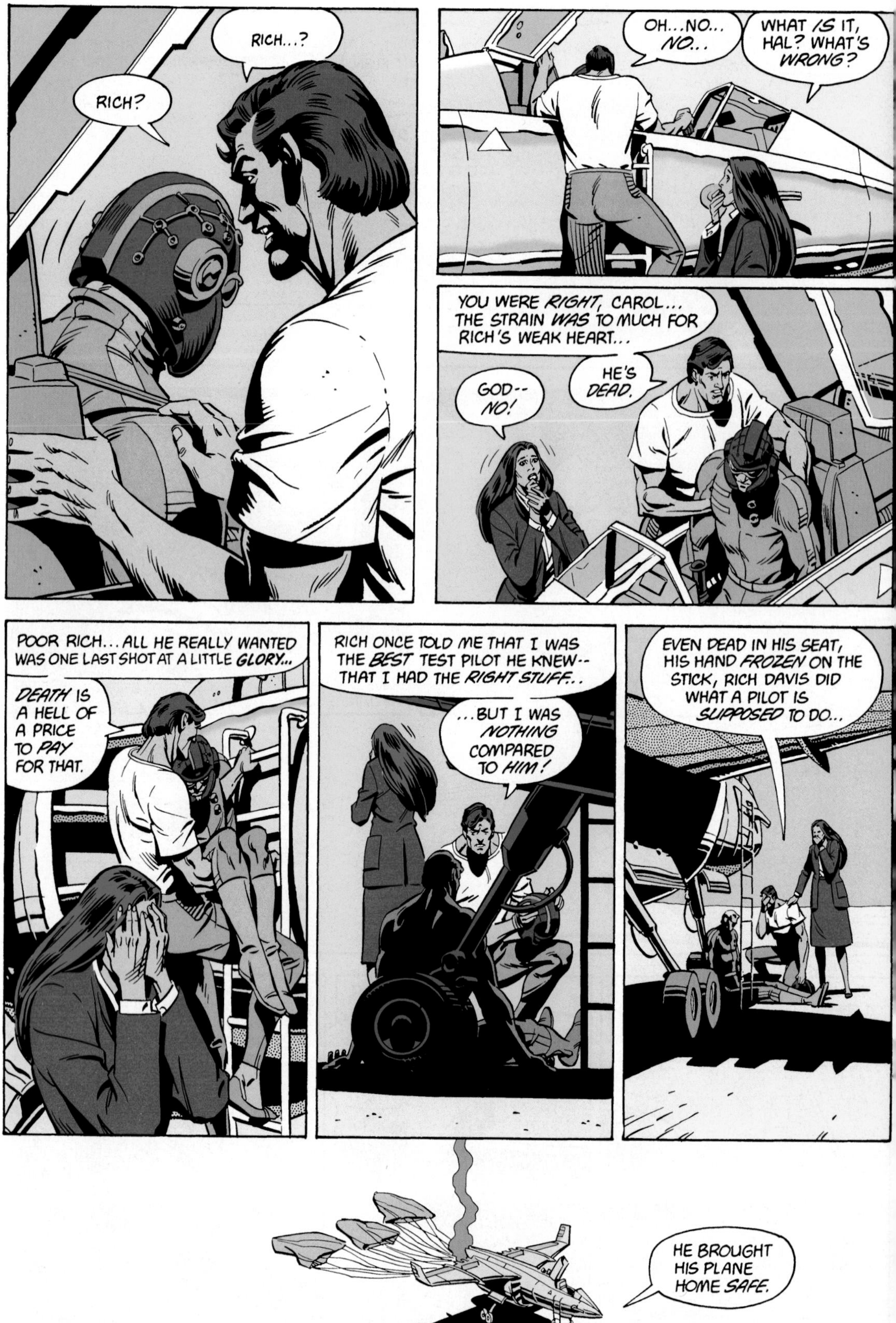
RICH...?
RICH?
OH...NO... NO...
WHAT IS IT, HAL? WHAT'S WRONG?
YOU WERE RIGHT, CAROL... THE STRAIN WAS TO MUCH FOR RICH'S WEAK HEART...
HE'S DEAD.
GOD-- NO!
POOR RICH... ALL HE REALLY WANTED WAS ONE LAST SHOT AT A LITTLE GLORY...
DEATH IS A HELL OF A PRICE TO PAY FOR THAT.
RICH ONCE TOLD ME THAT I WAS THE BEST TEST PILOT HE KNEW-- THAT I HAD THE RIGHT STUFF...
...BUT I WAS NOTHING COMPARED TO HIM!
EVEN DEAD IN HIS SEAT, HIS HAND FROZEN ON THE STICK, RICH DAVIS DID WHAT A PILOT IS SUPPOSED TO DO...
HE BROUGHT HIS PLANE HOME SAFE.
17

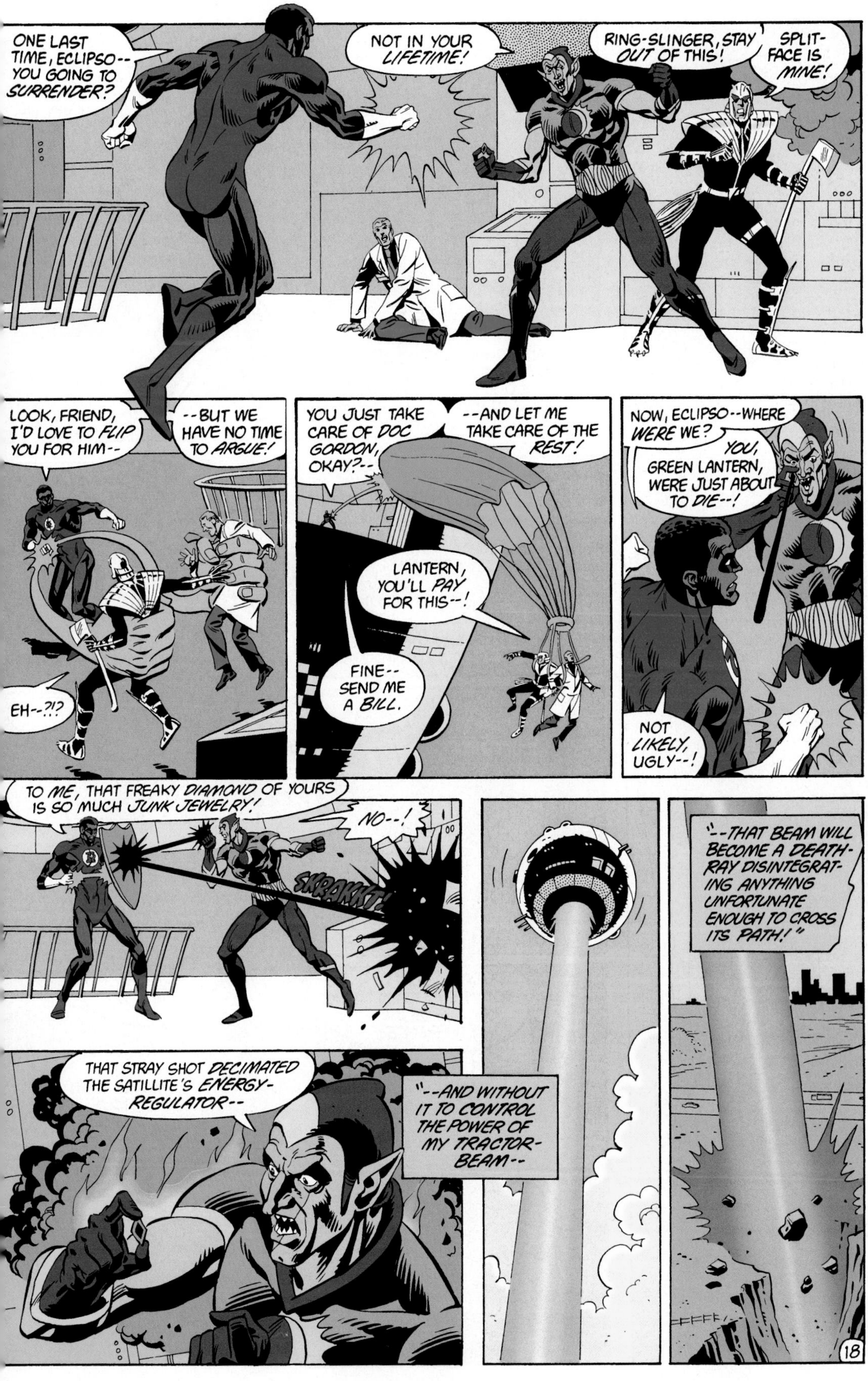
ONE LAST TIME, ECLIPSO-- YOU GOING TO SURRENDER?
NOT IN YOUR LIFETIME!
RING-SLINGER, STAY OUT OF THIS!
SPLIT-FACE IS MINE!
LOOK, FRIEND, I'D LOVE TO FLIP YOU FOR HIM--
--BUT WE HAVE NO TIME TO ARGUE!
EH--?!?
YOU JUST TAKE CARE OF DOC GORDON, OKAY?--
--AND LET ME TAKE CARE OF THE REST!
LANTERN, YOU'LL PAY FOR THIS--!
FINE-- SEND ME A BILL.
NOW, ECLIPSO--WHERE WERE WE?
YOU, GREEN LANTERN, WERE JUST ABOUT TO DIE--!
NOT LIKELY, UGLY--!
TO ME, THAT FREAKY DIAMOND OF YOURS IS SO MUCH JUNK JEWELRY!
NO--!
SKRAKKT!
THAT STRAY SHOT DECIMATED THE SATILLITE'S ENERGY-REGULATOR--
"--AND WITHOUT IT TO CONTROL THE POWER OF MY TRACTOR-BEAM--
"--THAT BEAM WILL BECOME A DEATH-RAY DISINTEGRATING ANYTHING UNFORTUNATE ENOUGH TO CROSS ITS PATH!"
18

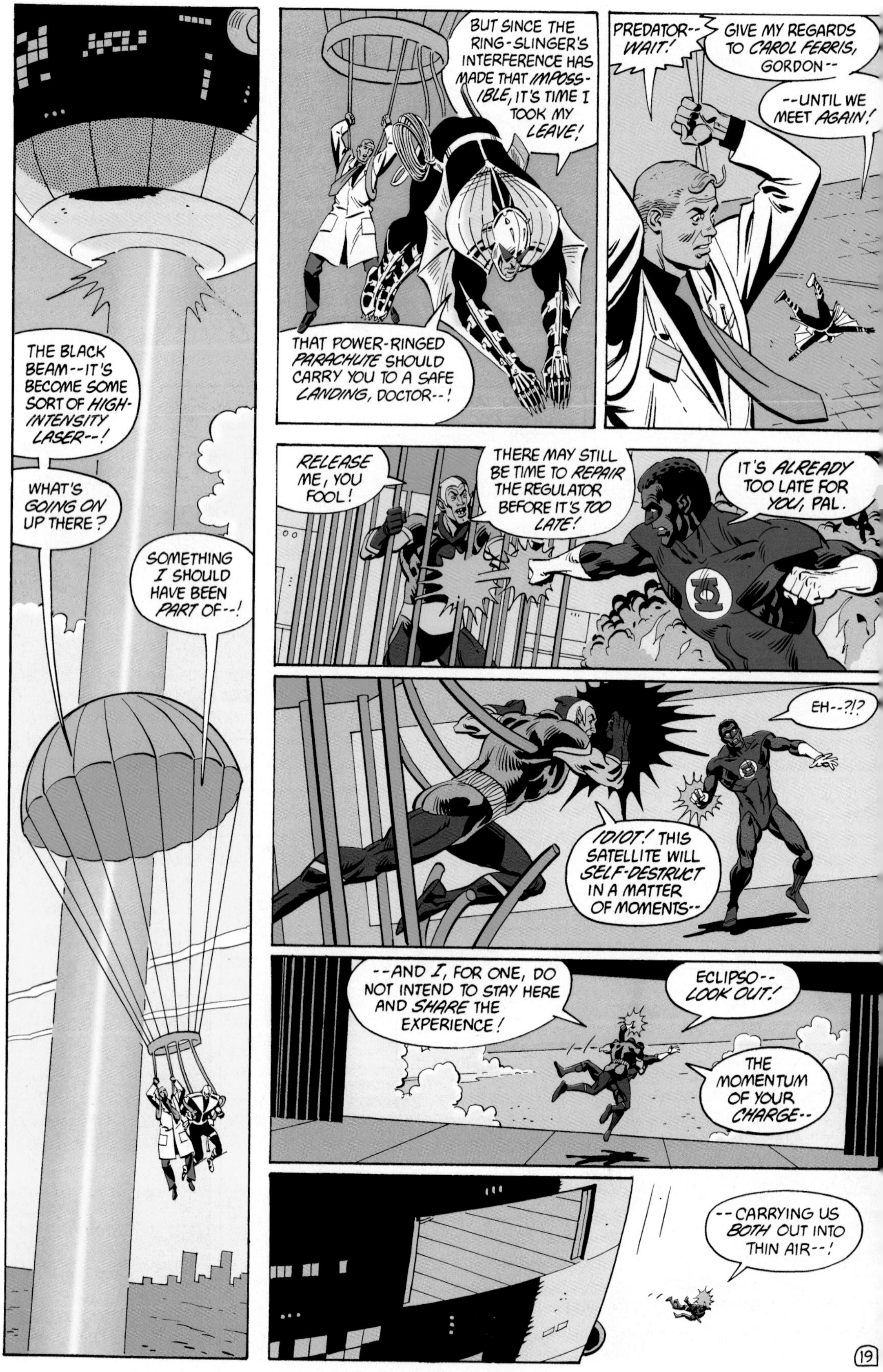
THE BLACK BEAM--IT'S BECOME SOME SORT OF HIGH-INTENSITY LASER--!
WHAT'S GOING ON UP THERE?
SOMETHING I SHOULD HAVE BEEN PART OF--!
BUT SINCE THE RING-SLINGER'S INTERFERENCE HAS MADE THAT IMPOSSIBLE, IT'S TIME I TOOK MY LEAVE!
THAT POWER-RINGED PARACHUTE SHOULD CARRY YOU TO A SAFE LANDING, DOCTOR--!
PREDATOR--WAIT!
GIVE MY REGARDS TO CAROL FERRIS, GORDON--
--UNTIL WE MEET AGAIN!
RELEASE ME, YOU FOOL!
THERE MAY STILL BE TIME TO REPAIR THE REGULATOR BEFORE IT'S TOO LATE!
IT'S ALREADY TOO LATE FOR YOU, PAL.
EH--?!?
IDIOT! THIS SATELLITE WILL SELF-DESTRUCT IN A MATTER OF MOMENTS--
--AND I, FOR ONE, DO NOT INTEND TO STAY HERE AND SHARE THE EXPERIENCE!
ECLIPSO--LOOK OUT!
THE MOMENTUM OF YOUR CHARGE--
--CARRYING US BOTH OUT INTO THIN AIR--!
19

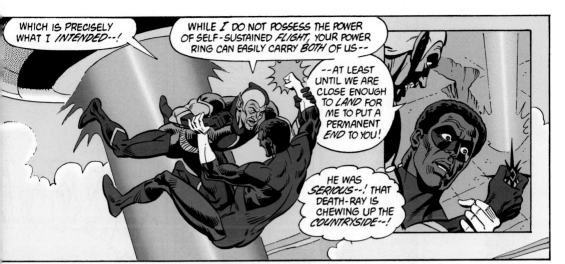

WHICH IS PRECISELY WHAT I *INTENDED*--!

WHILE *I* DO NOT POSSESS THE POWER OF SELF-SUSTAINED *FLIGHT*, YOUR POWER RING CAN EASILY CARRY *BOTH* OF US--

--AT LEAST UNTIL WE ARE CLOSE ENOUGH TO *LAND* FOR ME TO PUT A PERMANENT *END* TO YOU!

HE WAS *SERIOUS*--! THAT DEATH-RAY IS CHEWING UP THE *COUNTRYSIDE*--!

GOTTA *STOP* HIM-- THEN STOP HIS SCREWY *SATELLITE*...

...BEFORE IT CARVES *LOS ANGELES* LIKE A THANKSGIVING *TURKEY*!

ONLY *QUESTION* IS... *HOW?*

THE WAY WE'RE ANGLED NOW, ECLIPSO WILL BREAK HIS FALL WITH *MY BODY*--

--WHILE *I* BREAK MY *NECK*--

--BUT MAMA STEWART DIDN'T RAISE ANY STUPID *CHILDREN*--

AND THE GUARDIANS GAVE ME THIS *POWER RING* FOR A REASON!

CUSHION BROKE OUR FALL--

--AND THIS *FAN* SHOULD KEEP GRUE-SOME *OFF-BALANCE* LONG ENOUGH FOR ME TO--

--UNNNHH!!

THANK YOU FOR THE *RIDE*, RING-SLINGER--

-- AND GOOD-BYE!

RING'S *ABSORBING* MOST OF HIS BLACK LIGHT...

...BUT IT CAN'T...KEEP IT UP... FOREVER...

20

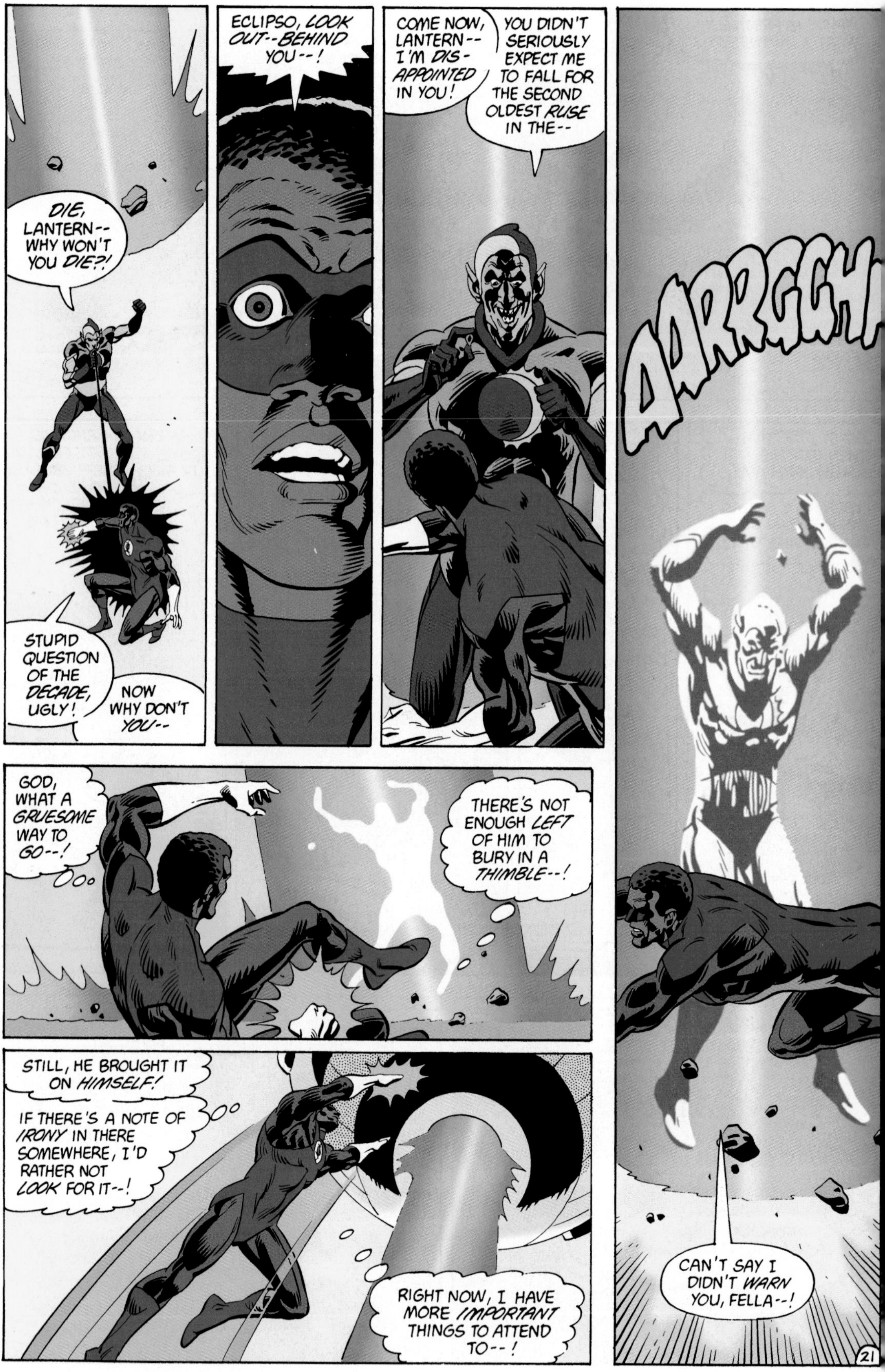
DIE, LANTERN-- WHY WON'T YOU DIE?!
STUPID QUESTION OF THE DECADE, UGLY!
NOW WHY DON'T YOU--
ECLIPSO, LOOK OUT--BEHIND YOU--!
COME NOW, LANTERN-- I'M DIS-APPOINTED IN YOU!
YOU DIDN'T SERIOUSLY EXPECT ME TO FALL FOR THE SECOND OLDEST RUSE IN THE--
AARGGH
CAN'T SAY I DIDN'T WARN YOU, FELLA--!
GOD, WHAT A GRUESOME WAY TO GO--!
THERE'S NOT ENOUGH LEFT OF HIM TO BURY IN A THIMBLE--!
STILL, HE BROUGHT IT ON HIMSELF!
IF THERE'S A NOTE OF IRONY IN THERE SOMEWHERE, I'D RATHER NOT LOOK FOR IT--!
RIGHT NOW, I HAVE MORE IMPORTANT THINGS TO ATTEND TO--!
21

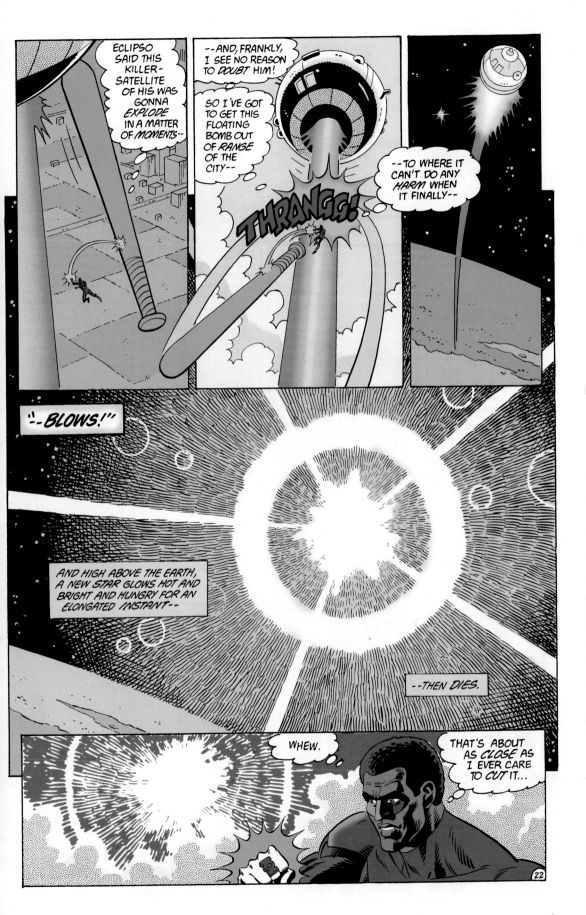

ECLIPSO SAID THIS KILLER-SATELLITE OF HIS WAS GONNA EXPLODE IN A MATTER OF *MOMENTS*--

--AND, FRANKLY, I SEE NO REASON TO *DOUBT* HIM!

SO I'VE GOT TO GET THIS FLOATING BOMB OUT OF *RANGE* OF THE CITY--

--TO WHERE IT CAN'T DO ANY *HARM* WHEN IT FINALLY--

THRANGG!

"--BLOWS!"

AND HIGH ABOVE THE EARTH, A NEW *STAR* GLOWS HOT AND BRIGHT AND HUNGRY FOR AN ELONGATED *INSTANT*--

--THEN DIES.

WHEW.

THAT'S ABOUT AS *CLOSE* AS I EVER CARE TO *CUT* IT...

22

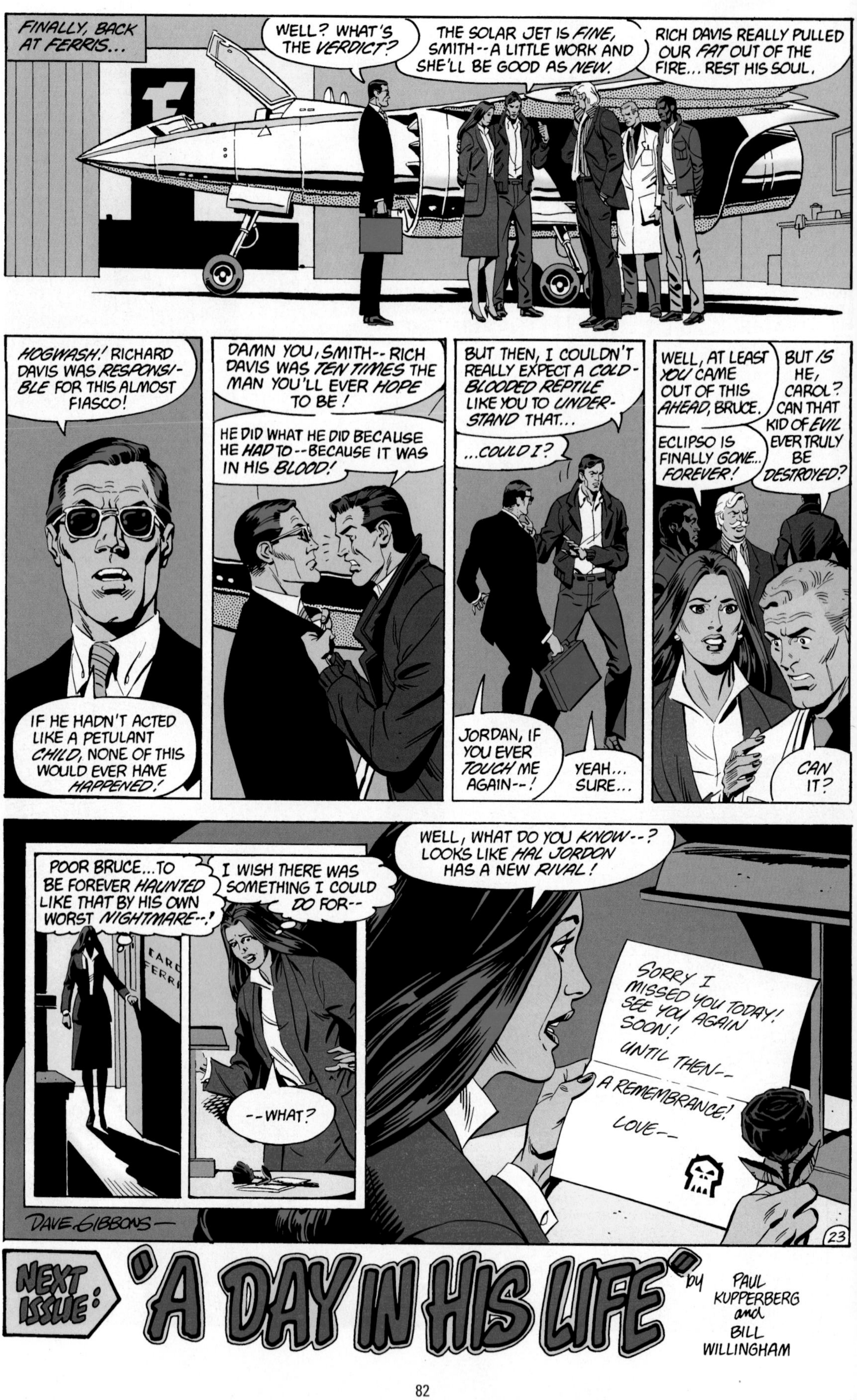
FINALLY, BACK AT FERRIS...
WELL? WHAT'S THE VERDICT?
THE SOLAR JET IS FINE, SMITH--A LITTLE WORK AND SHE'LL BE GOOD AS NEW.
RICH DAVIS REALLY PULLED OUR FAT OUT OF THE FIRE... REST HIS SOUL.
HOGWASH! RICHARD DAVIS WAS RESPONSI-BLE FOR THIS ALMOST FIASCO!
IF HE HADN'T ACTED LIKE A PETULANT CHILD, NONE OF THIS WOULD EVER HAVE HAPPENED!
DAMN YOU, SMITH--RICH DAVIS WAS TEN TIMES THE MAN YOU'LL EVER HOPE TO BE!
HE DID WHAT HE DID BECAUSE HE HAD TO--BECAUSE IT WAS IN HIS BLOOD!
BUT THEN, I COULDN'T REALLY EXPECT A COLD-BLOODED REPTILE LIKE YOU TO UNDER-STAND THAT...
...COULD I?
JORDAN, IF YOU EVER TOUCH ME AGAIN--!
YEAH... SURE...
WELL, AT LEAST YOU CAME OUT OF THIS AHEAD, BRUCE.
ECLIPSO IS FINALLY GONE... FOREVER!
BUT IS HE, CAROL? CAN THAT KID OF EVIL EVER TRULY BE DESTROYED?
CAN IT?
POOR BRUCE...TO BE FOREVER HAUNTED LIKE THAT BY HIS OWN WORST NIGHTMARE--!
I WISH THERE WAS SOMETHING I COULD DO FOR--
--WHAT?
WELL, WHAT DO YOU KNOW--? LOOKS LIKE HAL JORDON HAS A NEW RIVAL!
SORRY I MISSED YOU TODAY! SEE YOU AGAIN SOON!
UNTIL THEN--
A REMEMBRANCE!
LOVE--
DAVE GIBBONS
23
NEXT ISSUE: "A DAY IN HIS LIFE" by PAUL KUPPERBERG and BILL WILLINGHAM

Cover art by Paris Cullins & Romeo Tanghal

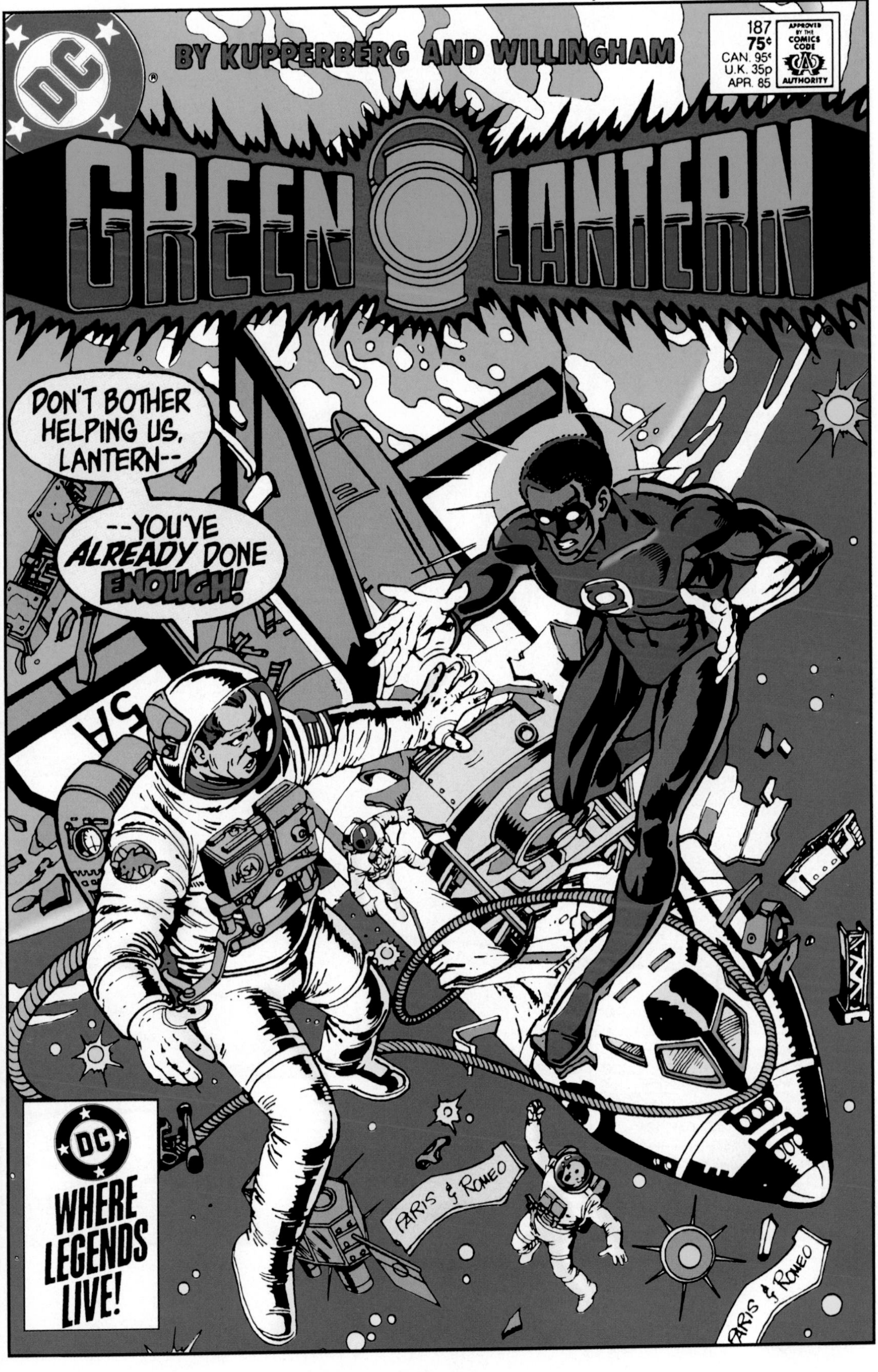

BY KUPPERBERG AND WILLINGHAM
187
75¢
CAN. 95¢
U.K. 35p
APR. 85
APPROVED BY THE COMICS CODE AUTHORITY
GREEN LANTERN
DON'T BOTHER HELPING US, LANTERN--
--YOU'VE ALREADY DONE ENOUGH!
DC
WHERE LEGENDS LIVE!
PARIS & ROMEO
PARIS & ROMEO

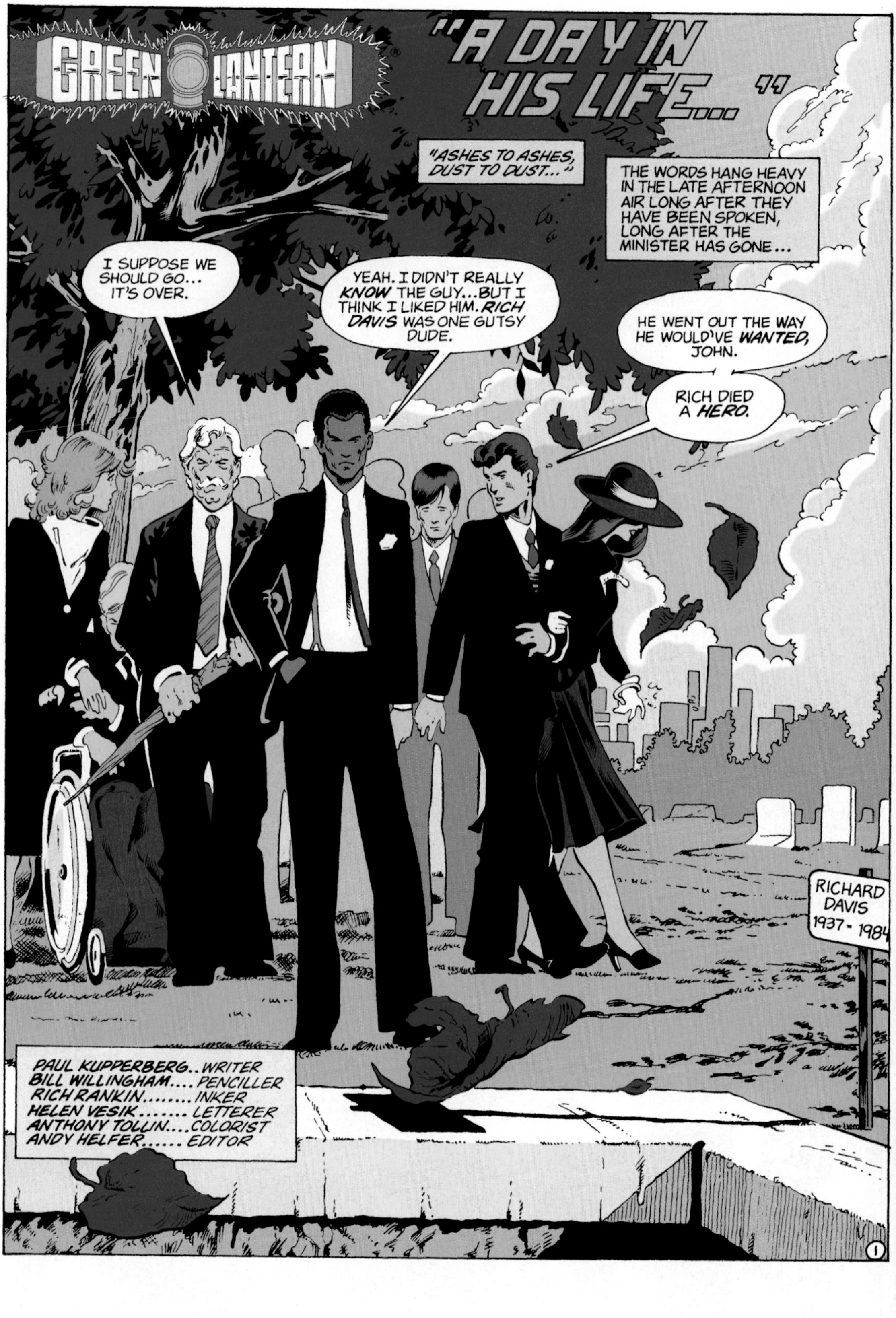
GREEN LANTERN®
"A DAY IN HIS LIFE..."
"ASHES TO ASHES, DUST TO DUST..."
THE WORDS HANG HEAVY IN THE LATE AFTERNOON AIR LONG AFTER THEY HAVE BEEN SPOKEN, LONG AFTER THE MINISTER HAS GONE...
I SUPPOSE WE SHOULD GO... IT'S OVER.
YEAH. I DIDN'T REALLY KNOW THE GUY...BUT I THINK I LIKED HIM. RICH DAVIS WAS ONE GUTSY DUDE.
HE WENT OUT THE WAY HE WOULD'VE WANTED, JOHN.
RICH DIED A HERO.
RICHARD DAVIS 1937 - 1984
PAUL KUPPERBERG..WRITER
BILL WILLINGHAM....PENCILLER
RICH RANKIN........INKER
HELEN VESIK.......LETTERER
ANTHONY TOLLIN....COLORIST
ANDY HELFER.....EDITOR
1

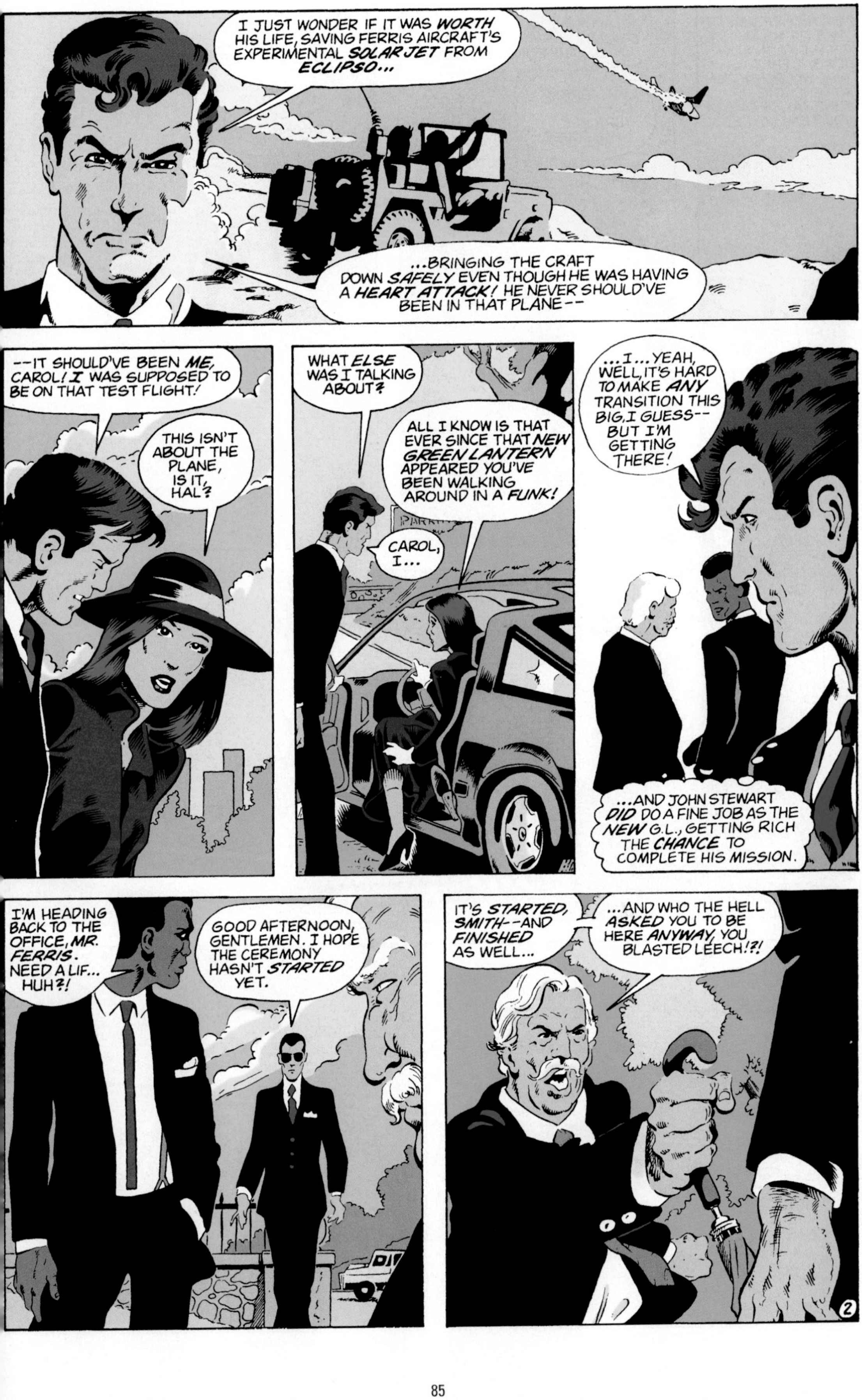
I JUST WONDER IF IT WAS WORTH HIS LIFE, SAVING FERRIS AIRCRAFT'S EXPERIMENTAL SOLAR JET FROM ECLIPSO...
...BRINGING THE CRAFT DOWN SAFELY EVEN THOUGH HE WAS HAVING A HEART ATTACK! HE NEVER SHOULD'VE BEEN IN THAT PLANE--
--IT SHOULD'VE BEEN ME, CAROL! I WAS SUPPOSED TO BE ON THAT TEST FLIGHT!
THIS ISN'T ABOUT THE PLANE, IS IT, HAL?
WHAT ELSE WAS I TALKING ABOUT?
ALL I KNOW IS THAT EVER SINCE THAT NEW GREEN LANTERN APPEARED YOU'VE BEEN WALKING AROUND IN A FUNK!
CAROL, I...
...I...YEAH, WELL, IT'S HARD TO MAKE ANY TRANSITION THIS BIG, I GUESS-- BUT I'M GETTING THERE!
...AND JOHN STEWART DID DO A FINE JOB AS THE NEW G.L., GETTING RICH THE CHANCE TO COMPLETE HIS MISSION.
I'M HEADING BACK TO THE OFFICE, MR. FERRIS. NEED A LIF... HUH?!
GOOD AFTERNOON, GENTLEMEN. I HOPE THE CEREMONY HASN'T STARTED YET.
IT'S STARTED, SMITH--AND FINISHED AS WELL...
...AND WHO THE HELL ASKED YOU TO BE HERE ANYWAY, YOU BLASTED LEECH!?!
2

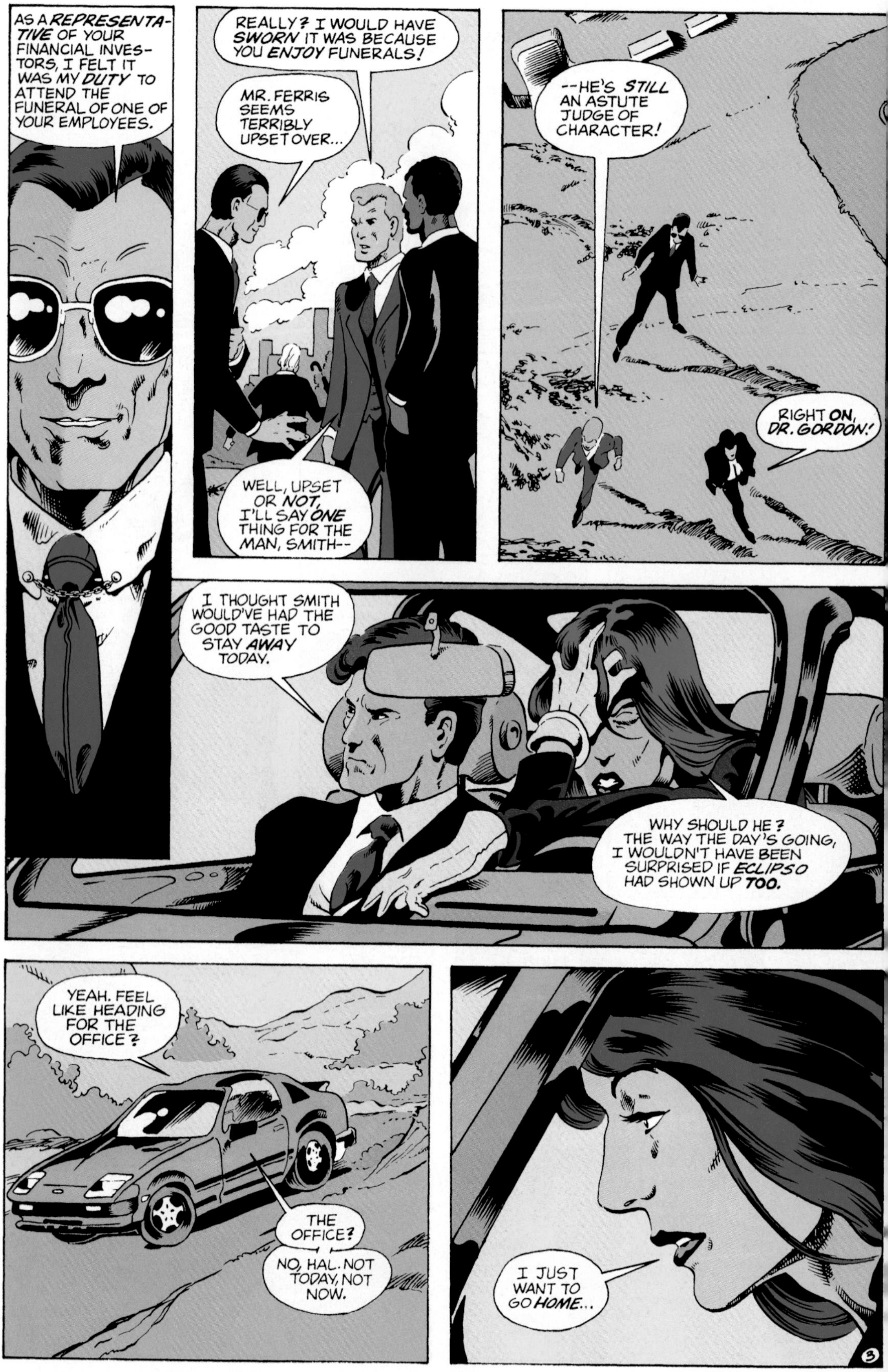
AS A REPRESENTATIVE OF YOUR FINANCIAL INVESTORS, I FELT IT WAS MY DUTY TO ATTEND THE FUNERAL OF ONE OF YOUR EMPLOYEES.
REALLY? I WOULD HAVE SWORN IT WAS BECAUSE YOU ENJOY FUNERALS!
MR. FERRIS SEEMS TERRIBLY UPSET OVER...
WELL, UPSET OR NOT, I'LL SAY ONE THING FOR THE MAN, SMITH--
--HE'S STILL AN ASTUTE JUDGE OF CHARACTER!
RIGHT ON, DR. GORDON!
I THOUGHT SMITH WOULD'VE HAD THE GOOD TASTE TO STAY AWAY TODAY.
WHY SHOULD HE? THE WAY THE DAY'S GOING, I WOULDN'T HAVE BEEN SURPRISED IF ECLIPSO HAD SHOWN UP TOO.
YEAH. FEEL LIKE HEADING FOR THE OFFICE?
THE OFFICE?
NO, HAL. NOT TODAY, NOT NOW.
I JUST WANT TO GO HOME...
3

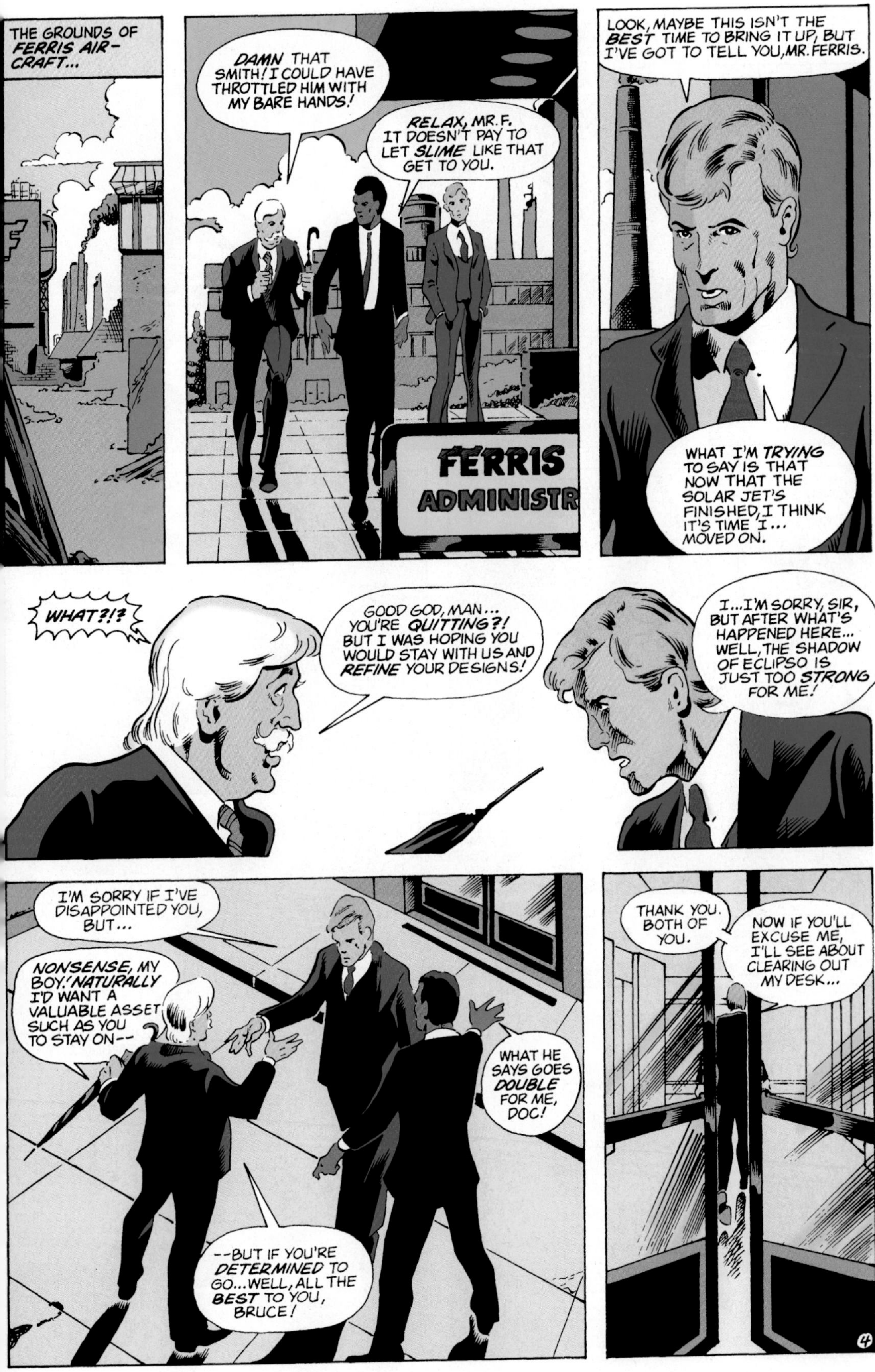
THE GROUNDS OF FERRIS AIR-CRAFT...
DAMN THAT SMITH! I COULD HAVE THROTTLED HIM WITH MY BARE HANDS!
RELAX, MR. F. IT DOESN'T PAY TO LET SLIME LIKE THAT GET TO YOU.
FERRIS ADMINISTR
LOOK, MAYBE THIS ISN'T THE BEST TIME TO BRING IT UP, BUT I'VE GOT TO TELL YOU, MR. FERRIS.
WHAT I'M TRYING TO SAY IS THAT NOW THAT THE SOLAR JET'S FINISHED, I THINK IT'S TIME I... MOVED ON.
WHAT?!?
GOOD GOD, MAN... YOU'RE QUITTING?! BUT I WAS HOPING YOU WOULD STAY WITH US AND REFINE YOUR DESIGNS!
I...I'M SORRY, SIR, BUT AFTER WHAT'S HAPPENED HERE... WELL, THE SHADOW OF ECLIPSO IS JUST TOO STRONG FOR ME!
I'M SORRY IF I'VE DISAPPOINTED YOU, BUT...
NONSENSE, MY BOY! NATURALLY I'D WANT A VALUABLE ASSET SUCH AS YOU TO STAY ON--
WHAT HE SAYS GOES DOUBLE FOR ME, DOC!
--BUT IF YOU'RE DETERMINED TO GO... WELL, ALL THE BEST TO YOU, BRUCE!
THANK YOU. BOTH OF YOU.
NOW IF YOU'LL EXCUSE ME, I'LL SEE ABOUT CLEARING OUT MY DESK...
4

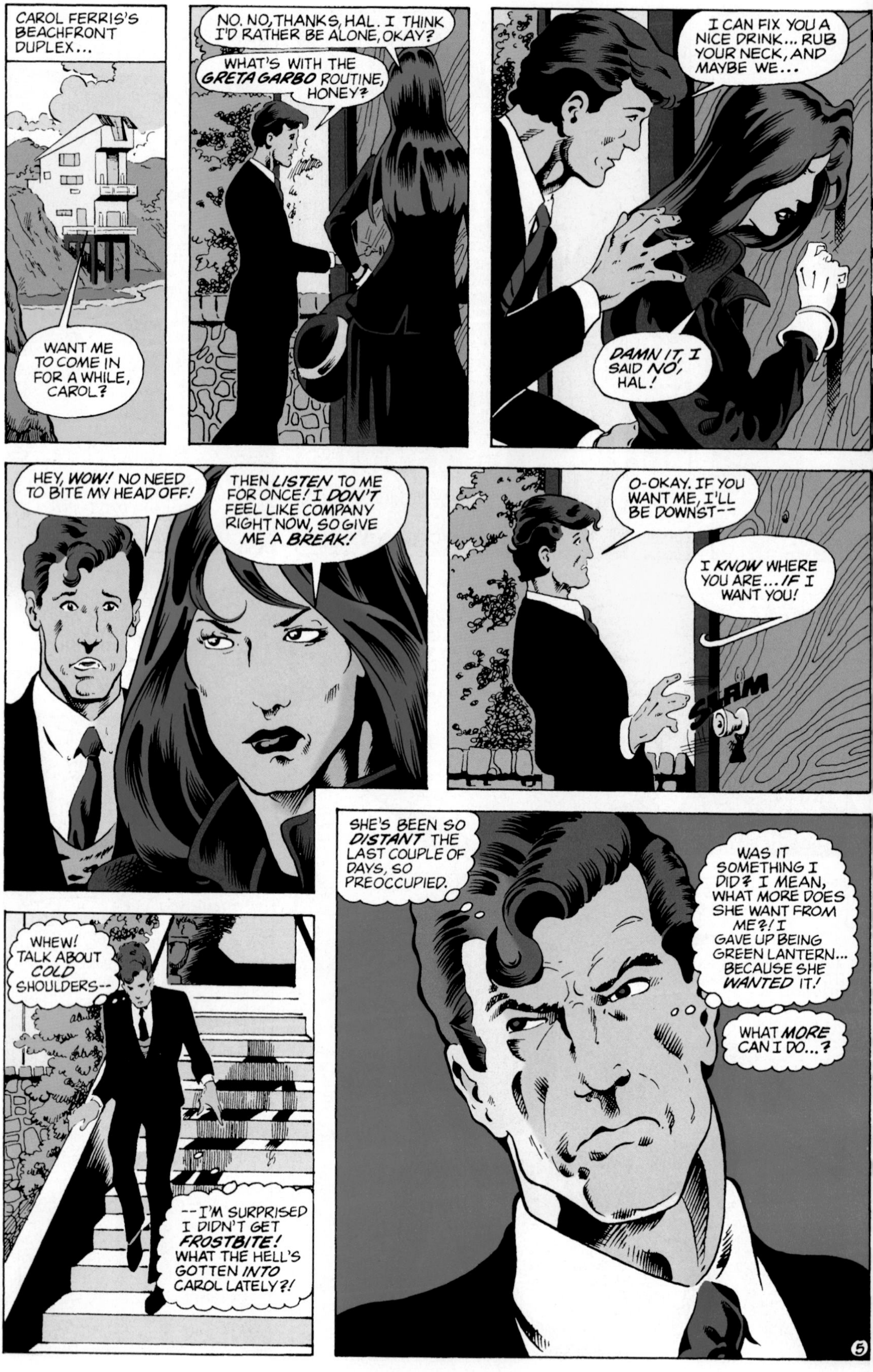

CAROL FERRIS'S BEACHFRONT DUPLEX...
WANT ME TO COME IN FOR A WHILE, CAROL?
NO. NO, THANKS, HAL. I THINK I'D RATHER BE ALONE, OKAY?
WHAT'S WITH THE GRETA GARBO ROUTINE, HONEY?
I CAN FIX YOU A NICE DRINK... RUB YOUR NECK, AND MAYBE WE...
DAMN IT, I SAID NO, HAL!
HEY, WOW! NO NEED TO BITE MY HEAD OFF!
THEN LISTEN TO ME FOR ONCE! I DON'T FEEL LIKE COMPANY RIGHT NOW, SO GIVE ME A BREAK!
O-OKAY. IF YOU WANT ME, I'LL BE DOWNST--
I KNOW WHERE YOU ARE... IF I WANT YOU!
SLAM
WHEW! TALK ABOUT COLD SHOULDERS--
--I'M SURPRISED I DIDN'T GET FROSTBITE! WHAT THE HELL'S GOTTEN INTO CAROL LATELY?!
SHE'S BEEN SO DISTANT THE LAST COUPLE OF DAYS, SO PREOCCUPIED.
WAS IT SOMETHING I DID? I MEAN, WHAT MORE DOES SHE WANT FROM ME?! I GAVE UP BEING GREEN LANTERN... BECAUSE SHE WANTED IT!
WHAT MORE CAN I DO...?
5

FERRIS AIRCRAFT:

YUCH! I KEEP COMING UP WITH DESIGNS LIKE *THIS* AND MY *NEXT* COMMISSION'S GONNA BE FOR *RESTROOMS!*

MAN, I JUST *CAN'T* GET MY MIND INTO IT! MAYBE I *AM* THE NEW KID ON THE BLOCK HERE AT FERRIS--

--BUT DAVIS' FUNERAL WAS *STILL* ONE MAJOR DOWNER!

'COURSE, NOWADAYS I GOT *OPTIONS* WHEN IT COMES TO LETTIN' OFF STEAM--

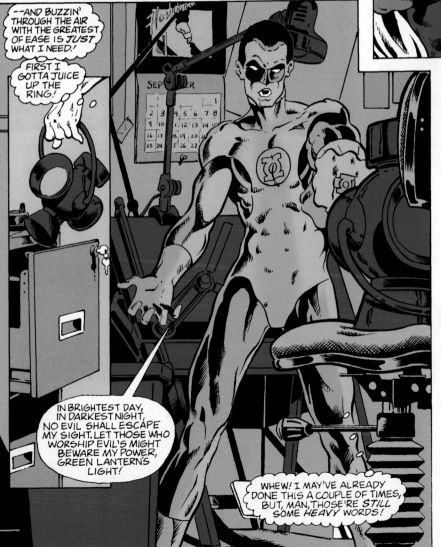

--AND BUZZIN' THROUGH THE AIR WITH THE GREATEST OF EASE IS *JUST* WHAT I NEED!

FIRST I GOTTA JUICE UP THE RING!

IN BRIGHTEST DAY, IN DARKEST NIGHT, NO EVIL SHALL ESCAPE MY SIGHT. LET THOSE WHO WORSHIP EVIL'S MIGHT BEWARE MY POWER, GREEN LANTERN'S LIGHT!

WHEW! I MAY'VE ALREADY DONE THIS A COUPLE OF TIMES, BUT, MAN, THOSE'RE *STILL* SOME *HEAVY* WORDS!

SHORTLY...

OKAY. I'M OUT... NOW WHERE DO I WANNA *PLAY?* GUESS I'LL JUST *CRUISE* THE NEIGHBORHOOD.

6

89

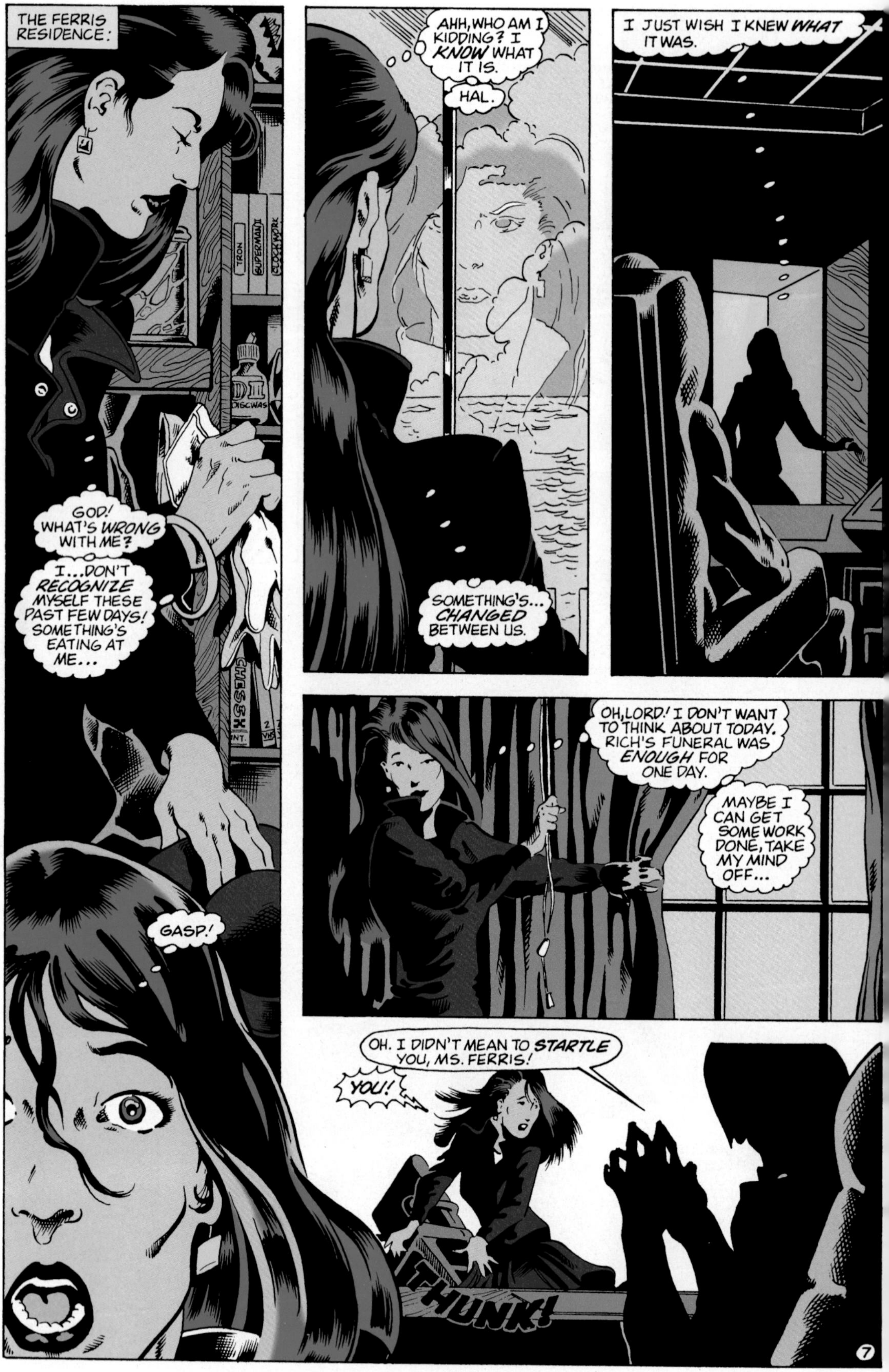
THE FERRIS RESIDENCE:
GOD! WHAT'S WRONG WITH ME?
I...DON'T RECOGNIZE MYSELF THESE PAST FEW DAYS! SOMETHING'S EATING AT ME...
AHH, WHO AM I KIDDING? I KNOW WHAT IT IS.
HAL.
SOMETHING'S... CHANGED BETWEEN US.
I JUST WISH I KNEW WHAT IT WAS.
OH, LORD! I DON'T WANT TO THINK ABOUT TODAY. RICH'S FUNERAL WAS ENOUGH FOR ONE DAY.
MAYBE I CAN GET SOME WORK DONE, TAKE MY MIND OFF...
GASP!
OH. I DIDN'T MEAN TO STARTLE YOU, MS. FERRIS!
YOU!
THUNK!
7

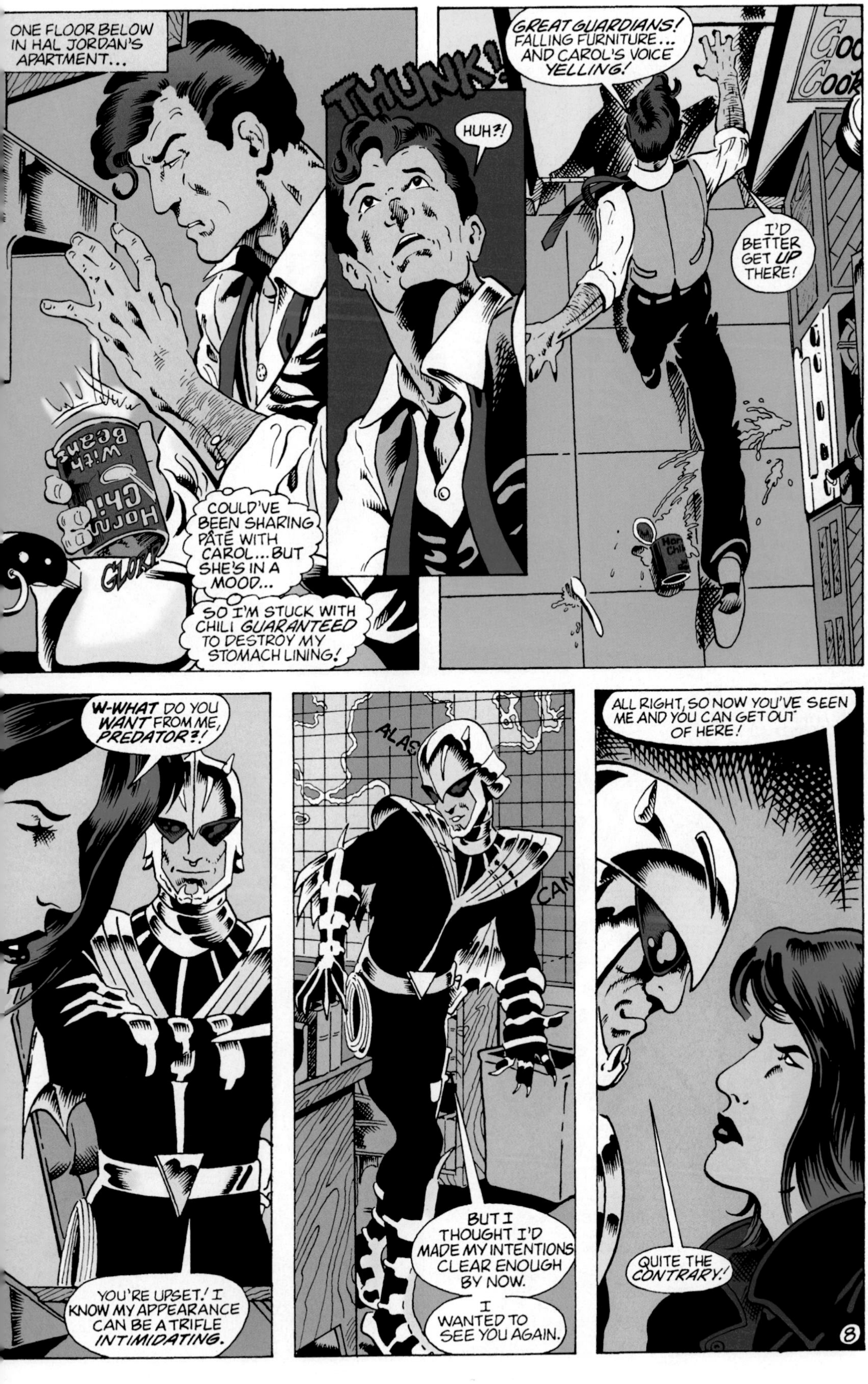
ONE FLOOR BELOW IN HAL JORDAN'S APARTMENT...
Hormel Chili with Beans
GLORK
COULD'VE BEEN SHARING PÂTÉ WITH CAROL... BUT SHE'S IN A MOOD...
SO I'M STUCK WITH CHILI GUARANTEED TO DESTROY MY STOMACH LINING!
THUNK!
HUH?!
GREAT GUARDIANS! FALLING FURNITURE... AND CAROL'S VOICE YELLING!
I'D BETTER GET UP THERE!
W-WHAT DO YOU WANT FROM ME, PREDATOR?!
YOU'RE UPSET! I KNOW MY APPEARANCE CAN BE A TRIFLE INTIMIDATING.
BUT I THOUGHT I'D MADE MY INTENTIONS CLEAR ENOUGH BY NOW.
I WANTED TO SEE YOU AGAIN.
ALL RIGHT, SO NOW YOU'VE SEEN ME AND YOU CAN GET OUT OF HERE!
QUITE THE CONTRARY!
8

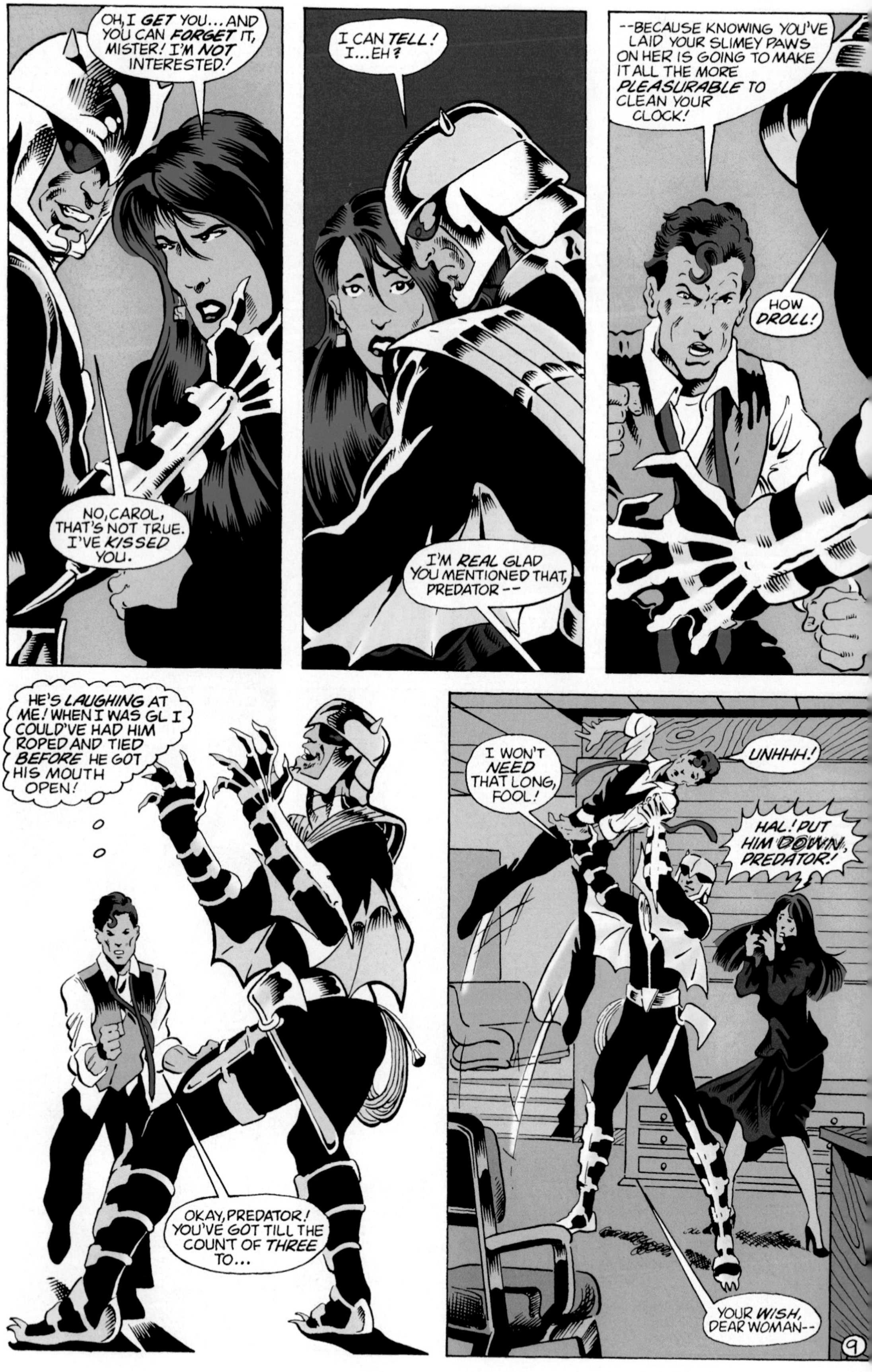
OH, I GET YOU... AND YOU CAN FORGET IT, MISTER! I'M NOT INTERESTED!
NO, CAROL, THAT'S NOT TRUE. I'VE KISSED YOU.
I CAN TELL! I...EH?
I'M REAL GLAD YOU MENTIONED THAT, PREDATOR --
--BECAUSE KNOWING YOU'VE LAID YOUR SLIMEY PAWS ON HER IS GOING TO MAKE IT ALL THE MORE PLEASURABLE TO CLEAN YOUR CLOCK!
HOW DROLL!
HE'S LAUGHING AT ME! WHEN I WAS GL I COULD'VE HAD HIM ROPED AND TIED BEFORE HE GOT HIS MOUTH OPEN!
OKAY, PREDATOR! YOU'VE GOT TILL THE COUNT OF THREE TO...
I WON'T NEED THAT LONG, FOOL!
UNHHH!
HAL! PUT HIM DOWN, PREDATOR!
YOUR WISH, DEAR WOMAN--
9

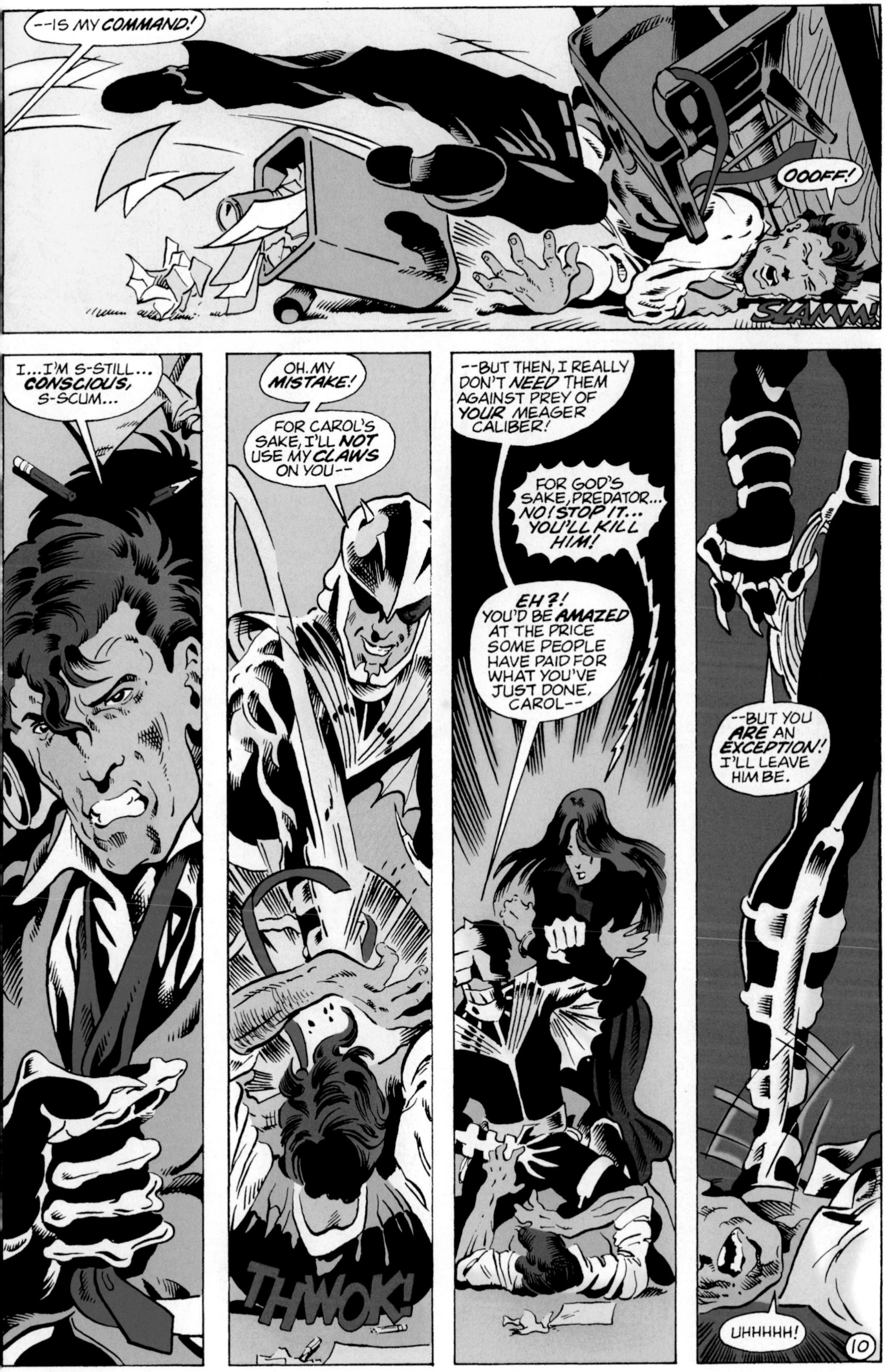
--IS MY COMMAND!
OOOFF!
SLAMM!
I...I'M S-STILL... CONSCIOUS, S-SCUM...
OH. MY MISTAKE!
FOR CAROL'S SAKE, I'LL NOT USE MY CLAWS ON YOU--
THWOK!
--BUT THEN, I REALLY DON'T NEED THEM AGAINST PREY OF YOUR MEAGER CALIBER!
FOR GOD'S SAKE, PREDATOR... NO! STOP IT... YOU'LL KILL HIM!
EH?! YOU'D BE AMAZED AT THE PRICE SOME PEOPLE HAVE PAID FOR WHAT YOU'VE JUST DONE, CAROL--
--BUT YOU ARE AN EXCEPTION! I'LL LEAVE HIM BE.
UHHHHH!
10

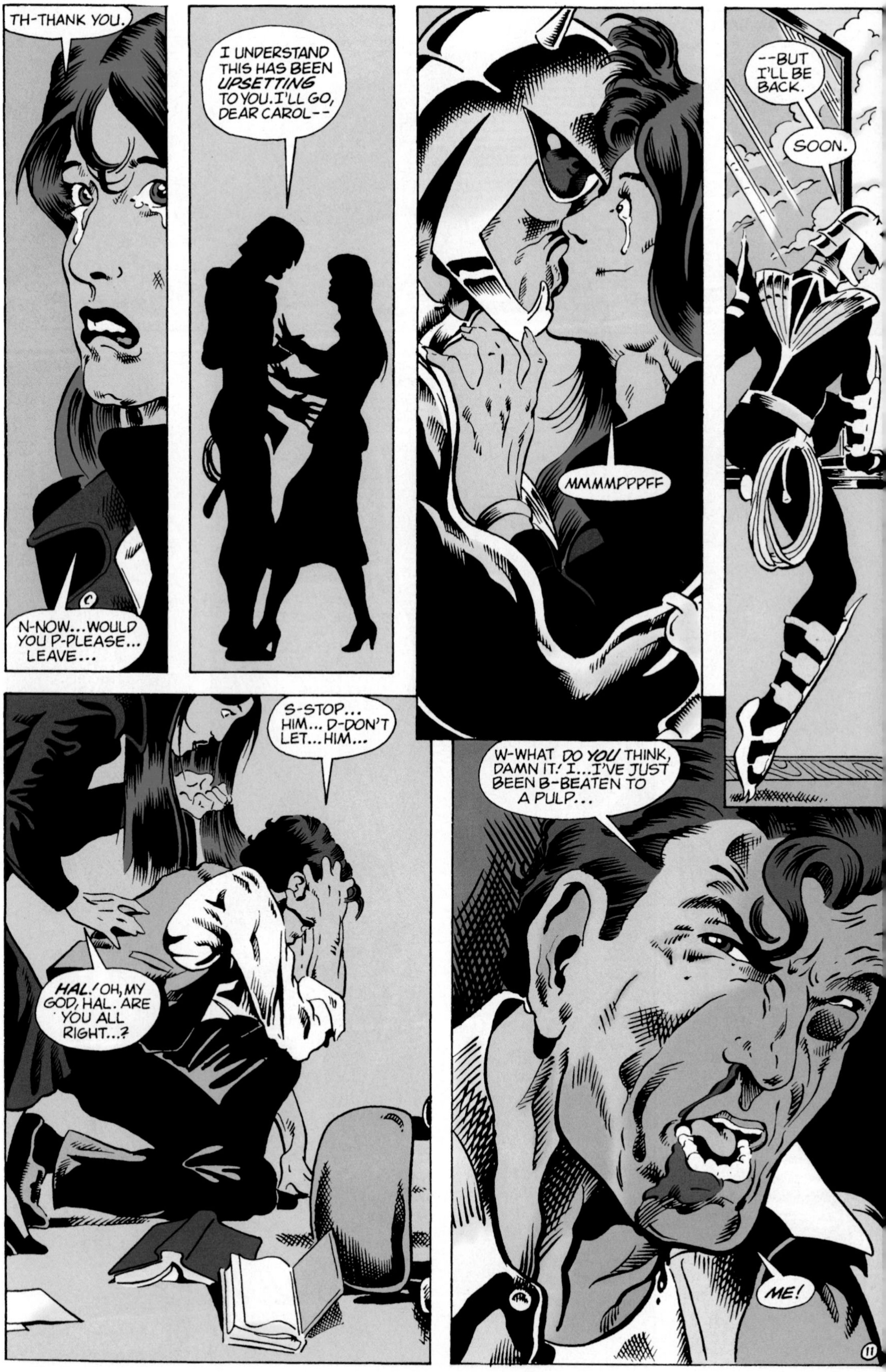
TH-THANK YOU.
N-NOW...WOULD YOU P-PLEASE... LEAVE...
I UNDERSTAND THIS HAS BEEN *UPSETTING* TO YOU. I'LL GO, DEAR CAROL--
MMMMPPPFF
--BUT I'LL BE BACK.
SOON.
HAL! OH, MY GOD, HAL. ARE YOU ALL RIGHT...?
S-STOP... HIM... D-DON'T LET... HIM...
W-WHAT *DO YOU* THINK, DAMN IT! I...I'VE JUST BEEN B-BEATEN TO A PULP...
ME!
11

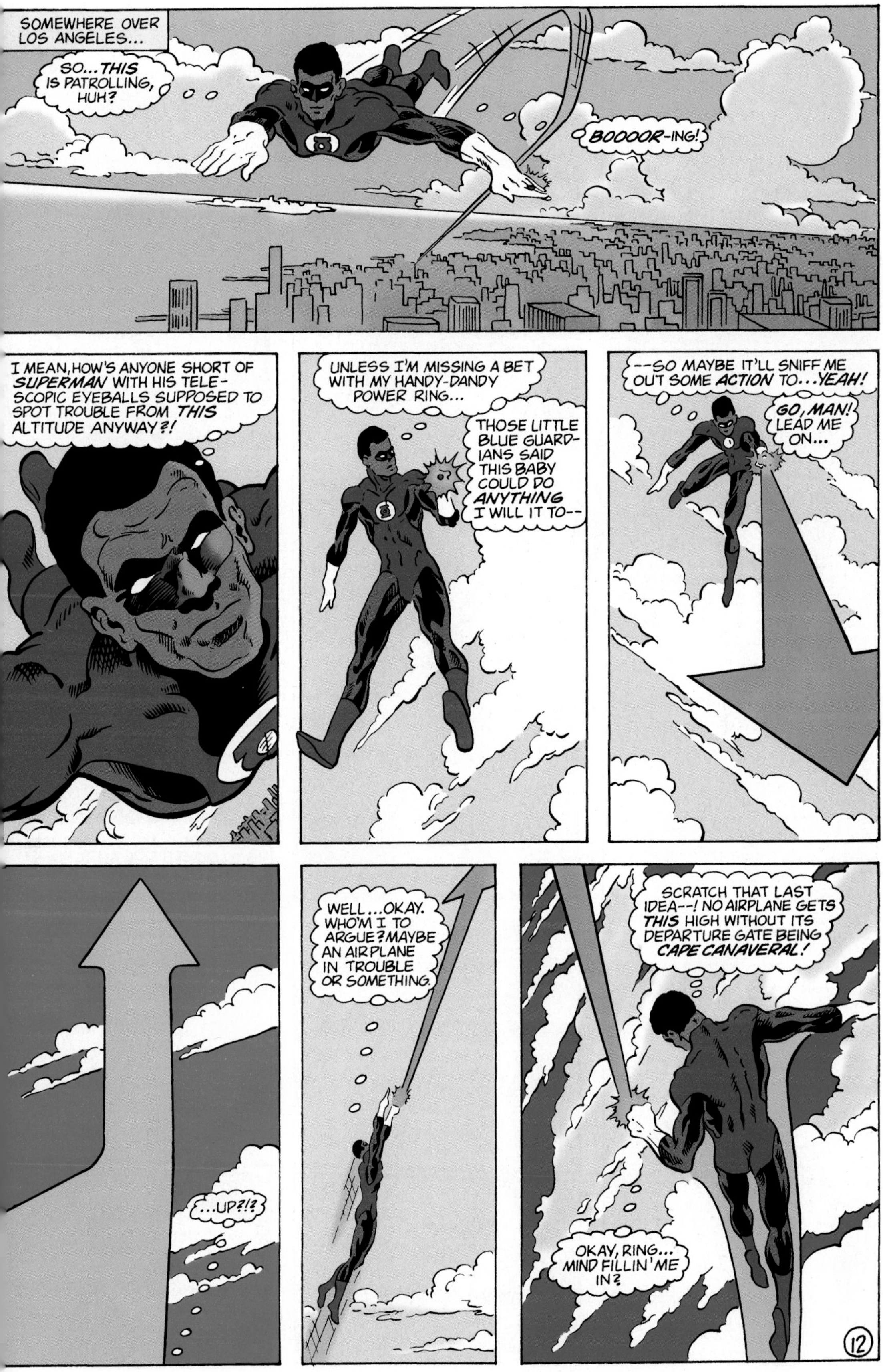
SOMEWHERE OVER LOS ANGELES...
SO...THIS IS PATROLLING, HUH?
BOOOOR-ING!
I MEAN, HOW'S ANYONE SHORT OF SUPERMAN WITH HIS TELE-SCOPIC EYEBALLS SUPPOSED TO SPOT TROUBLE FROM THIS ALTITUDE ANYWAY?!
UNLESS I'M MISSING A BET WITH MY HANDY-DANDY POWER RING...
THOSE LITTLE BLUE GUARD-IANS SAID THIS BABY COULD DO ANYTHING I WILL IT TO--
--SO MAYBE IT'LL SNIFF ME OUT SOME ACTION TO...YEAH!
GO, MAN! LEAD ME ON...
...UP?!?
WELL...OKAY. WHO'M I TO ARGUE? MAYBE AN AIRPLANE IN TROUBLE OR SOMETHING.
SCRATCH THAT LAST IDEA--! NO AIRPLANE GETS THIS HIGH WITHOUT ITS DEPARTURE GATE BEING CAPE CANAVERAL!
OKAY, RING... MIND FILLIN' ME IN?
12

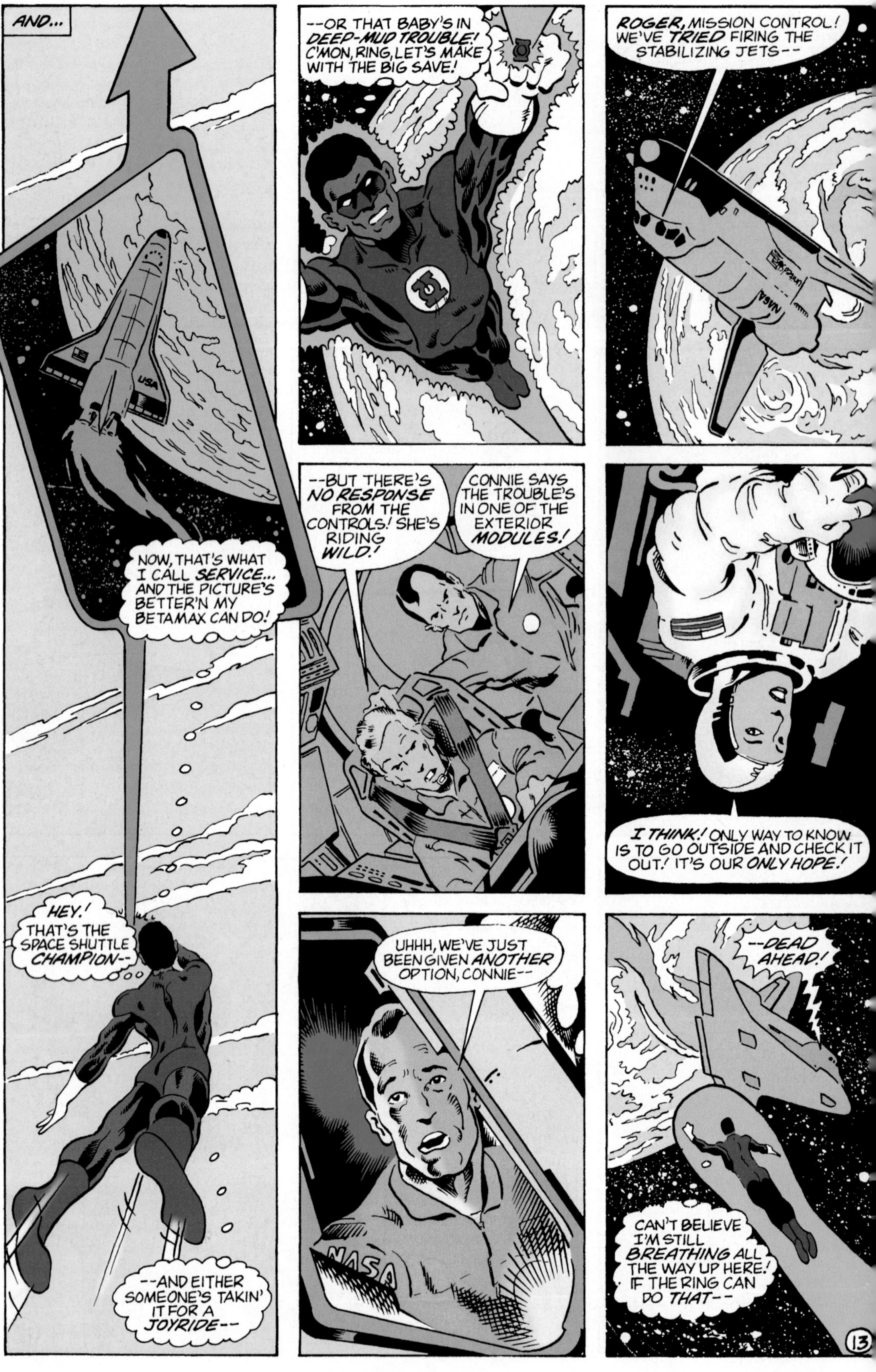
AND...
NOW, THAT'S WHAT I CALL SERVICE... AND THE PICTURE'S BETTER'N MY BETAMAX CAN DO!
HEY! THAT'S THE SPACE SHUTTLE CHAMPION--
--AND EITHER SOMEONE'S TAKIN' IT FOR A JOYRIDE--
--OR THAT BABY'S IN DEEP-MUD TROUBLE! C'MON, RING, LET'S MAKE WITH THE BIG SAVE!
ROGER, MISSION CONTROL! WE'VE TRIED FIRING THE STABILIZING JETS--
--BUT THERE'S NO RESPONSE FROM THE CONTROLS! SHE'S RIDING WILD!
CONNIE SAYS THE TROUBLE'S IN ONE OF THE EXTERIOR MODULES!
I THINK! ONLY WAY TO KNOW IS TO GO OUTSIDE AND CHECK IT OUT! IT'S OUR ONLY HOPE!
UHHH, WE'VE JUST BEEN GIVEN ANOTHER OPTION, CONNIE--
--DEAD AHEAD!
CAN'T BELIEVE I'M STILL BREATHING ALL THE WAY UP HERE! IF THE RING CAN DO THAT--
13

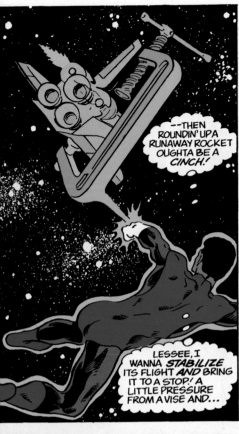

--THEN ROUNDIN' UP A RUNAWAY ROCKET OUGHTA BE A *CINCH!*

LESSEE, I WANNA *STABILIZE* ITS FLIGHT *AND* BRING IT TO A STOP! A LITTLE PRESSURE FROM A VISE AND...

NO! I APPLIED TOO MUCH *PRESSURE!* I'M TRASHIN' THE SHUTTLE!

GREAT! NASA SPENDS *MILLIONS* OF DOLLARS COMIN' UP WITH A WAY TO STICK THOSE SPECIAL TILES ON THE SHUTTLE'S HULL--

--AND I UNDO IT ALL BY STICKIN' MY *TWO CENTS* IN!

ALL RIGHT. NO BIG DEAL. I CAN PATCH UP THE TEARS EASY ENOUGH--

--IT'S JUST THE MORE *COMPLICATED* STUFF THAT THROWS ME!

I DON'T LIKE THE WAY THIS LOOKS, COMMANDER! I'M TAKING THAT *E.V.A.*--

--JUST *IN CASE* THE HERO'S PERFORMANCE DOESN'T GET ANY *BETTER!*

SHOOT! BANK ROBBERS... FALLIN' BRIDGES... KITTENS IN TREES...

...*THAT* I CAN HANDLE, NO SWEAT!

BUT THIS'S THE *BIG TIME,* MAN... AND THERE AIN'T *NOTHIN'* BETWEEN THOSE ASTRONAUTS AND *DEATH*...

...'CEPT *ME!*

14

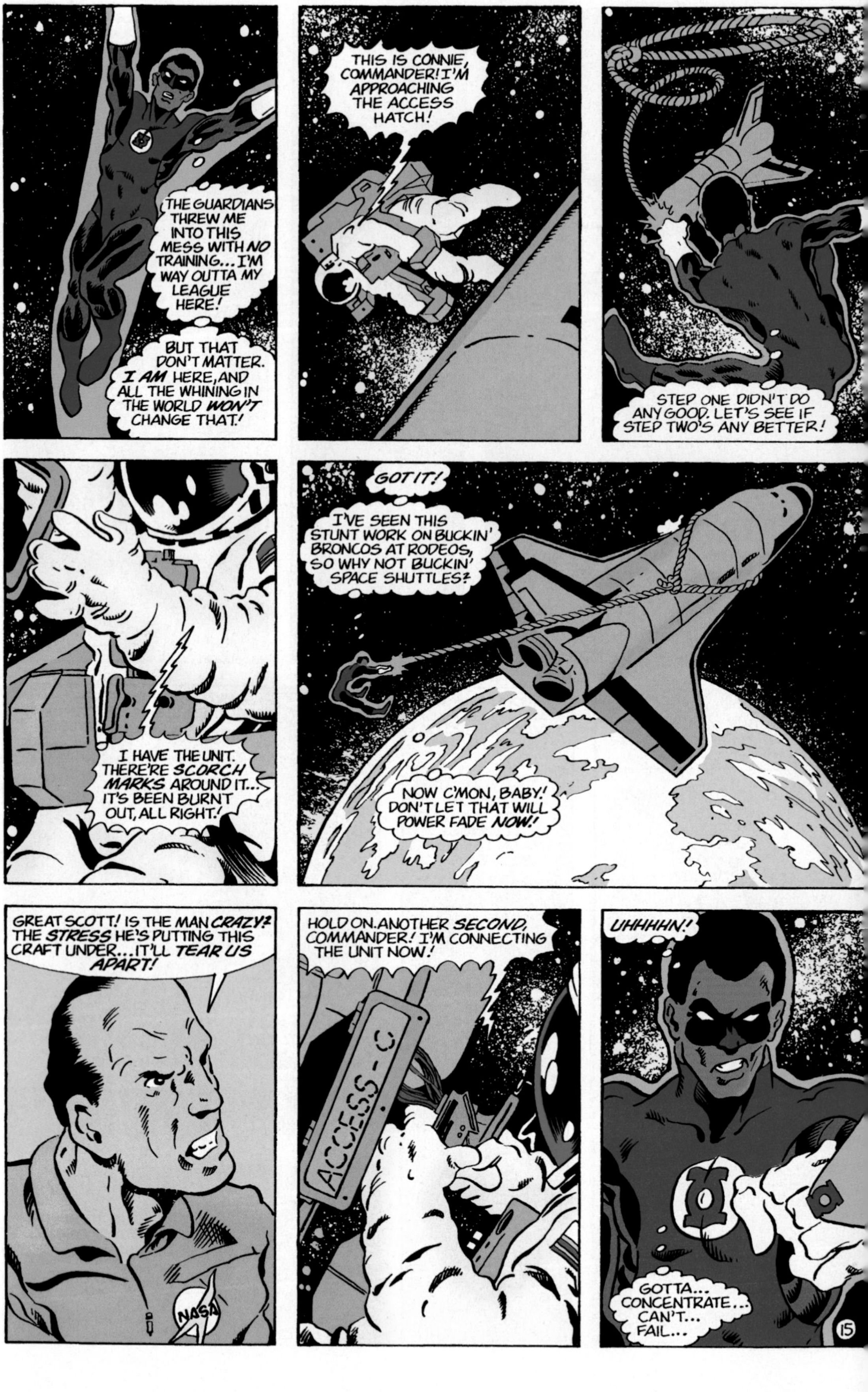
THE GUARDIANS THREW ME INTO THIS MESS WITH NO TRAINING... I'M WAY OUTTA MY LEAGUE HERE!
BUT THAT DON'T MATTER. I AM HERE, AND ALL THE WHINING IN THE WORLD WON'T CHANGE THAT!
THIS IS CONNIE, COMMANDER! I'M APPROACHING THE ACCESS HATCH!
STEP ONE DIDN'T DO ANY GOOD. LET'S SEE IF STEP TWO'S ANY BETTER!
I HAVE THE UNIT. THERE'RE SCORCH MARKS AROUND IT... IT'S BEEN BURNT OUT, ALL RIGHT!
GOT IT!
I'VE SEEN THIS STUNT WORK ON BUCKIN' BRONCOS AT RODEOS, SO WHY NOT BUCKIN' SPACE SHUTTLES?
NOW C'MON, BABY! DON'T LET THAT WILL POWER FADE NOW!
GREAT SCOTT! IS THE MAN CRAZY? THE STRESS HE'S PUTTING THIS CRAFT UNDER... IT'LL TEAR US APART!
NASA
HOLD ON. ANOTHER SECOND, COMMANDER! I'M CONNECTING THE UNIT NOW!
ACCESS-C
UHHHHN!
GOTTA... CONCENTRATE... CAN'T... FAIL...
15

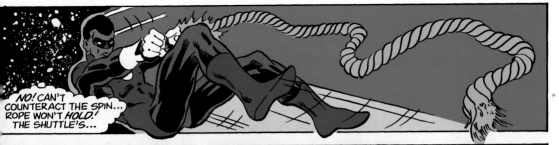

NO! CAN'T COUNTERACT THE SPIN... ROPE WON'T *HOLD!* THE SHUTTLE'S...

...SAVED!

TRY FIRING THE BACK-UP SYSTEMS NOW, COMMANDER!

OOOOFF! FORGOT ALL ABOUT BEIN' IN A *VACUUM!* IF I DON'T BRING MYSELF TO A STOP--

--I'LL KEEP GOIN' UNTIL I HIT *MARS...*

...AND THAT'S A TRIP THE SHUTTLE ASTRONAUTS CAN'T AFFORD ME TO TAKE!

BETTER GET BACK THERE *PRONTO,* BEFORE IT'S *TOO LATE!*

WELL, I'LL BE...! THEY'RE *BACK IN CONTROL*--

--AND THEY DID IT WITHOUT ME!

AWWW, WHOM I *KIDDIN'...*

...THEY DID IT *IN SPITE* OF ME! *DAMN!*

I GOTTA MAKE SURE SOMETHIN' LIKE THIS DOESN'T *EVER* HAPPEN AGAIN, AND THE PLACE TO DO THAT...

16

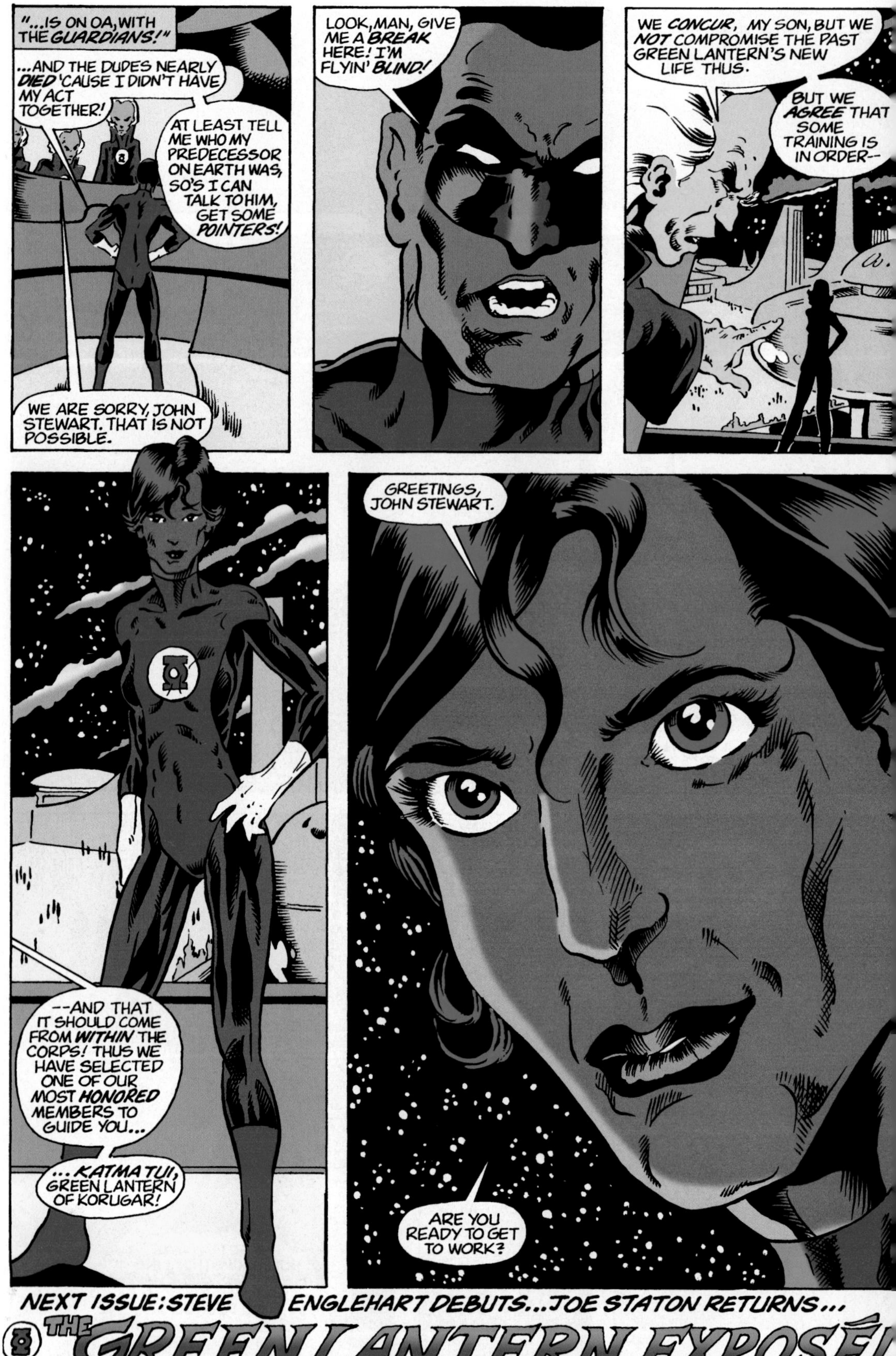

"...IS ON OA, WITH THE GUARDIANS!"
...AND THE DUDES NEARLY DIED 'CAUSE I DIDN'T HAVE MY ACT TOGETHER!
AT LEAST TELL ME WHO MY PREDECESSOR ON EARTH WAS, SO'S I CAN TALK TO HIM, GET SOME POINTERS!
WE ARE SORRY, JOHN STEWART. THAT IS NOT POSSIBLE.
LOOK, MAN, GIVE ME A BREAK HERE! I'M FLYIN' BLIND!
WE CONCUR, MY SON, BUT WE NOT COMPROMISE THE PAST GREEN LANTERN'S NEW LIFE THUS.
BUT WE AGREE THAT SOME TRAINING IS IN ORDER--
--AND THAT IT SHOULD COME FROM WITHIN THE CORPS! THUS WE HAVE SELECTED ONE OF OUR MOST HONORED MEMBERS TO GUIDE YOU...
...KATMA TUI, GREEN LANTERN OF KORUGAR!
GREETINGS, JOHN STEWART.
ARE YOU READY TO GET TO WORK?
NEXT ISSUE: STEVE ENGLEHART DEBUTS...JOE STATON RETURNS...
"THE GREEN LANTERN EXPOSÉ!"

Cover art by Joe Staton & Bruce Patterson

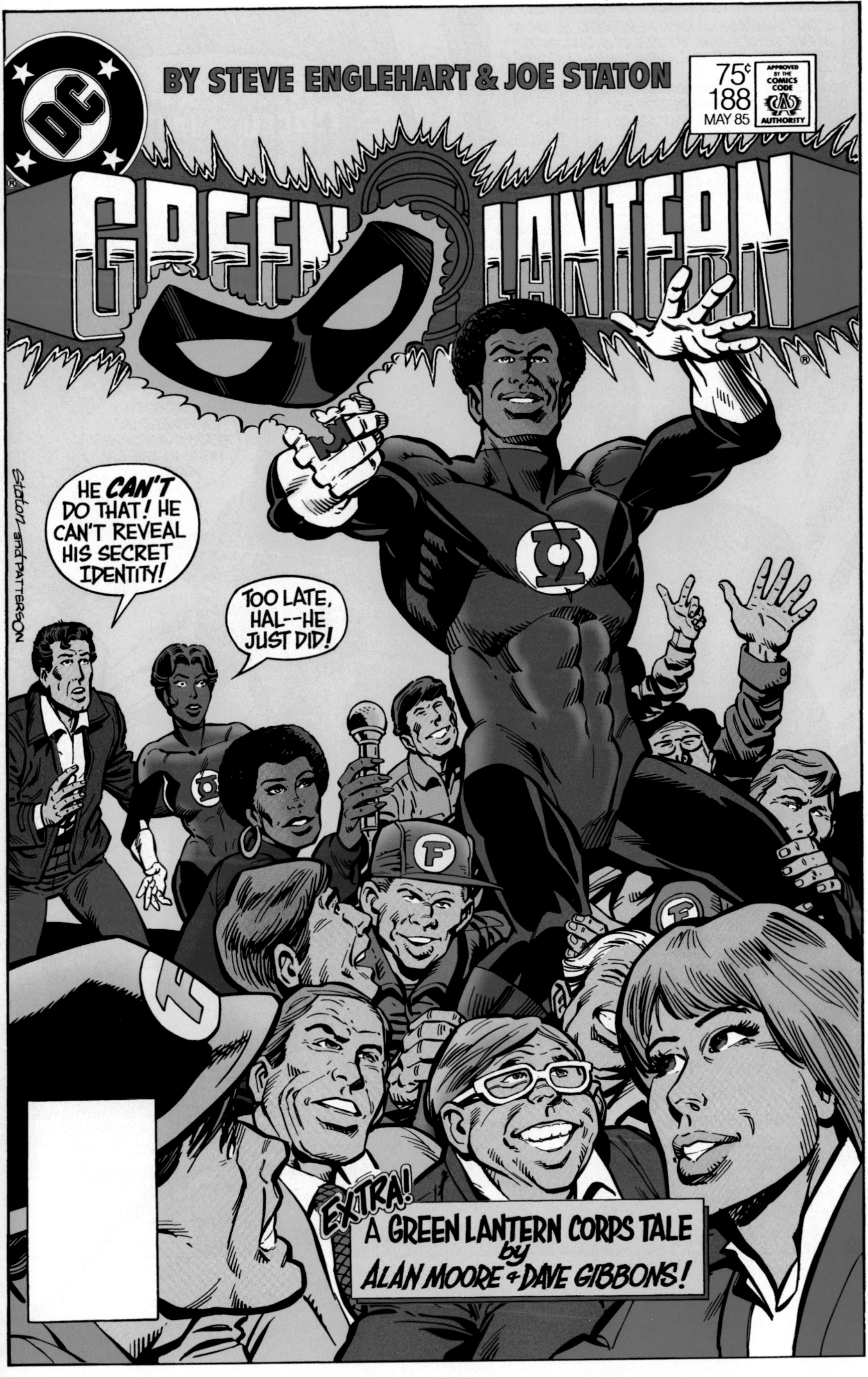
BY STEVE ENGLEHART & JOE STATON
75¢
188
MAY 85
APPROVED BY THE COMICS CODE AUTHORITY
GREEN LANTERN
STATON AND PATTERSON
HE CAN'T DO THAT! HE CAN'T REVEAL HIS SECRET IDENTITY!
TOO LATE, HAL--HE JUST DID!
EXTRA!
A GREEN LANTERN CORPS TALE by ALAN MOORE & DAVE GIBBONS!

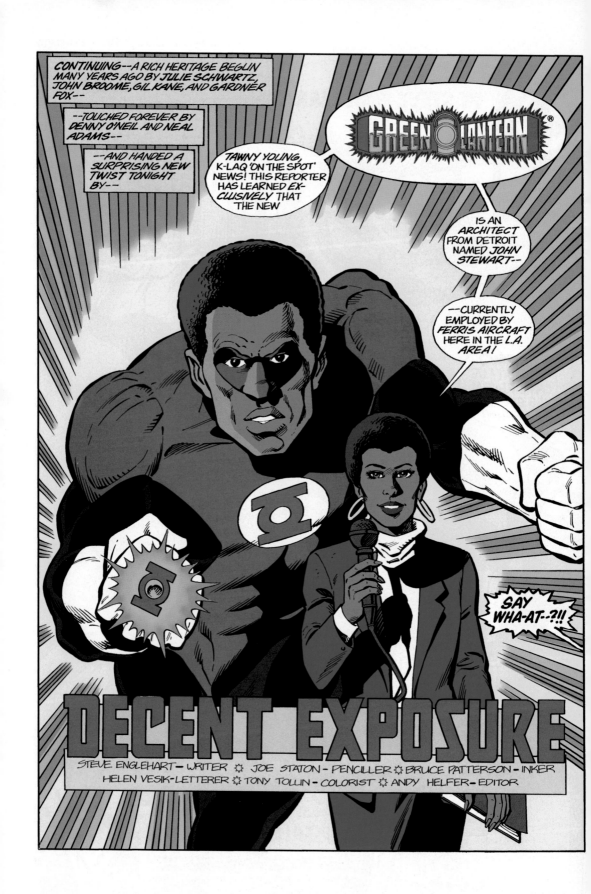

CONTINUING--A RICH HERITAGE BEGUN MANY YEARS AGO BY JULIE SCHWARTZ, JOHN BROOME, GIL KANE, AND GARDNER FOX--

--TOUCHED FOREVER BY DENNY O'NEIL AND NEAL ADAMS--

--AND HANDED A SURPRISING NEW TWIST TONIGHT BY--

TAWNY YOUNG, K-LAQ 'ON THE SPOT' NEWS! THIS REPORTER HAS LEARNED EX-CLUSIVELY THAT THE NEW

GREEN LANTERN

IS AN ARCHITECT FROM DETROIT NAMED JOHN STEWART--

--CURRENTLY EMPLOYED BY FERRIS AIRCRAFT HERE IN THE L.A. AREA!

SAY WHA-AT--?!!

DECENT EXPOSURE

STEVE ENGLEHART--WRITER ✿ JOE STATON - PENCILLER ✿ BRUCE PATTERSON--INKER
HELEN VESIK-LETTERER ✿ TONY TOLLIN - COLORIST ✿ ANDY HELFER--EDITOR

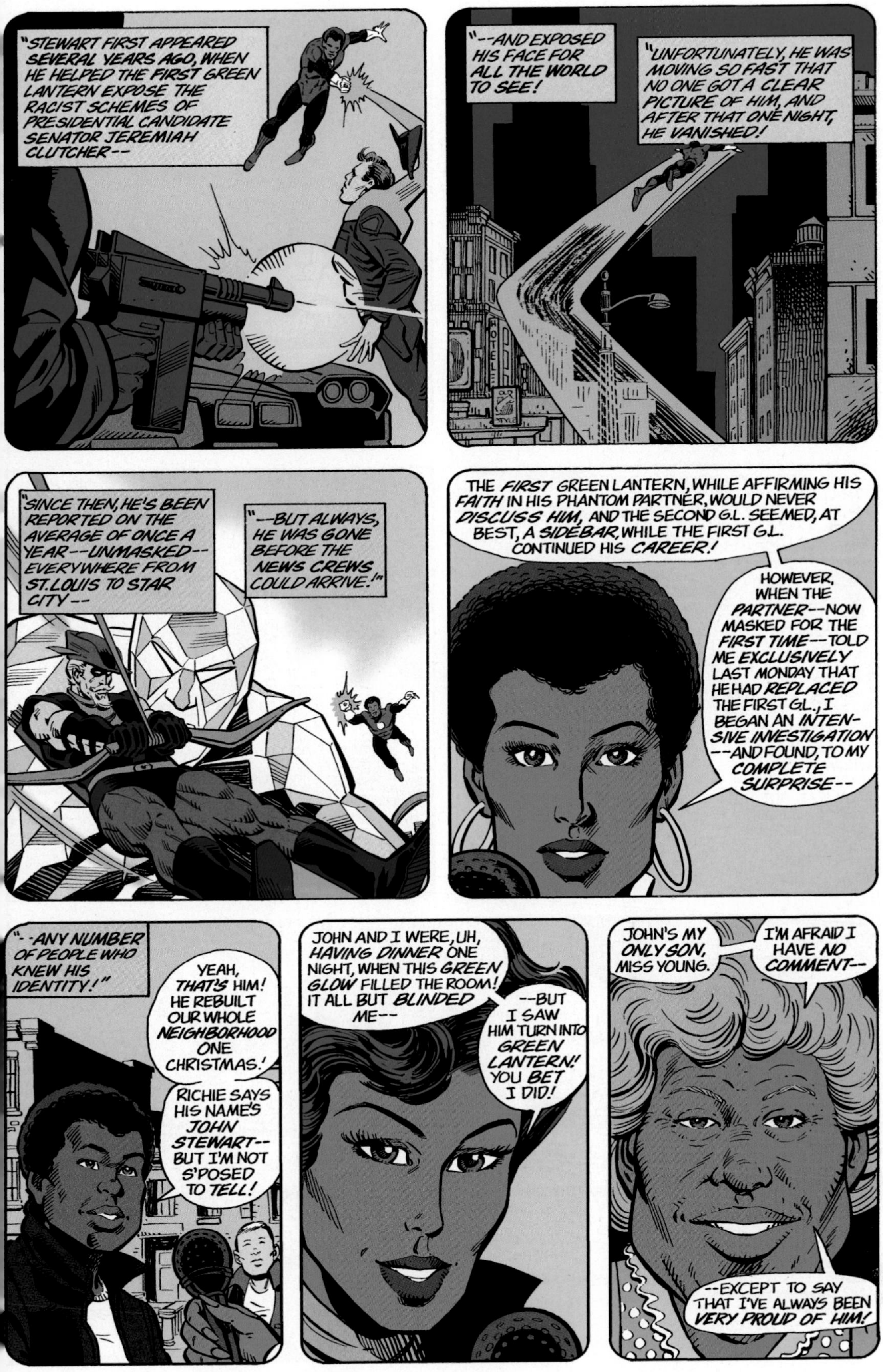
"STEWART FIRST APPEARED SEVERAL YEARS AGO, WHEN HE HELPED THE FIRST GREEN LANTERN EXPOSE THE RACIST SCHEMES OF PRESIDENTIAL CANDIDATE SENATOR JEREMIAH CLUTCHER--
"--AND EXPOSED HIS FACE FOR ALL THE WORLD TO SEE!
"UNFORTUNATELY, HE WAS MOVING SO FAST THAT NO ONE GOT A CLEAR PICTURE OF HIM, AND AFTER THAT ONE NIGHT, HE VANISHED!
HOTEL
"SINCE THEN, HE'S BEEN REPORTED ON THE AVERAGE OF ONCE A YEAR--UNMASKED--EVERYWHERE FROM ST. LOUIS TO STAR CITY--
"--BUT ALWAYS, HE WAS GONE BEFORE THE NEWS CREWS COULD ARRIVE!"
THE FIRST GREEN LANTERN, WHILE AFFIRMING HIS FAITH IN HIS PHANTOM PARTNER, WOULD NEVER DISCUSS HIM, AND THE SECOND G.L. SEEMED, AT BEST, A SIDEBAR, WHILE THE FIRST G.L. CONTINUED HIS CAREER!
HOWEVER, WHEN THE PARTNER--NOW MASKED FOR THE FIRST TIME--TOLD ME EXCLUSIVELY LAST MONDAY THAT HE HAD REPLACED THE FIRST G.L., I BEGAN AN INTENSIVE INVESTIGATION--AND FOUND, TO MY COMPLETE SURPRISE--
"--ANY NUMBER OF PEOPLE WHO KNEW HIS IDENTITY!"
YEAH, THAT'S HIM! HE REBUILT OUR WHOLE NEIGHBORHOOD ONE CHRISTMAS!
RICHIE SAYS HIS NAME'S JOHN STEWART--BUT I'M NOT S'POSED TO TELL!
JOHN AND I WERE, UH, HAVING DINNER ONE NIGHT, WHEN THIS GREEN GLOW FILLED THE ROOM! IT ALL BUT BLINDED ME--
--BUT I SAW HIM TURN INTO GREEN LANTERN! YOU BET I DID!
JOHN'S MY ONLY SON, MISS YOUNG.
I'M AFRAID I HAVE NO COMMENT--
--EXCEPT TO SAY THAT I'VE ALWAYS BEEN VERY PROUD OF HIM!

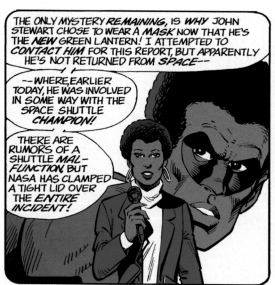

THE ONLY MYSTERY *REMAINING*, IS *WHY* JOHN STEWART CHOSE TO WEAR A *MASK* NOW THAT HE'S THE *NEW* GREEN LANTERN! I ATTEMPTED TO *CONTACT HIM* FOR THIS REPORT, BUT APPARENTLY HE'S NOT RETURNED FROM *SPACE*--

--WHERE, EARLIER TODAY, HE WAS INVOLVED IN SOME WAY WITH THE SPACE SHUTTLE *CHAMPION!*

THERE ARE RUMORS OF A SHUTTLE *MALFUNCTION*, BUT NASA HAS CLAMPED A TIGHT LID OVER THE *ENTIRE* INCIDENT!

"I DID, HOWEVER, SPEAK WITH *SUPERMAN* AND *GREEN ARROW*--"

HE'S A *GOOD MAN*-- A *BRAVE MAN* --!

ABSOLUTELY!

--SO, IN CONCLUSION, WE MAY BE SURE THAT *JOHN STEWART*, THE *NEW* GREEN LANTERN, WILL CONTINUE TO BE A *HOT STORY* FOR MANY MONTHS TO COME!

WE MAY NEVER KNOW WHAT HAPPENED TO THE *OLD* G.L., BUT THE *NEW* ONE LOOKS TO BE *JUST AS GOOD*, IF NOT *BETTER*--

FUNNY THING, TELEVISION! NOTHING ELSE TOUCHES SO MANY PEOPLE SO DIRECTLY, AND ALL AT THE SAME TIME...

CLIK!

IN MALIBU--

WOW!

HAL--?

IT'S ALL RIGHT, CAROL! I WAS JUST WONDERING WHAT I'D HAVE DONE IF THEY'D ANNOUNCED *MY* SECRET IDENTITY ON THE TUBE!

ALL THE TROUBLE I WENT THROUGH TO *KEEP* THAT SECRET--TRUSTING ONLY *YOU* AND *TOM** IN THE NON-SUPER WORLD FOR ALL THOSE YEARS--!

BUT SHE'S *RIGHT!* JOHN'S NEVER *CARED!*

*KALMAKU, HAL'S RIGHT-HAND MAN. --A.

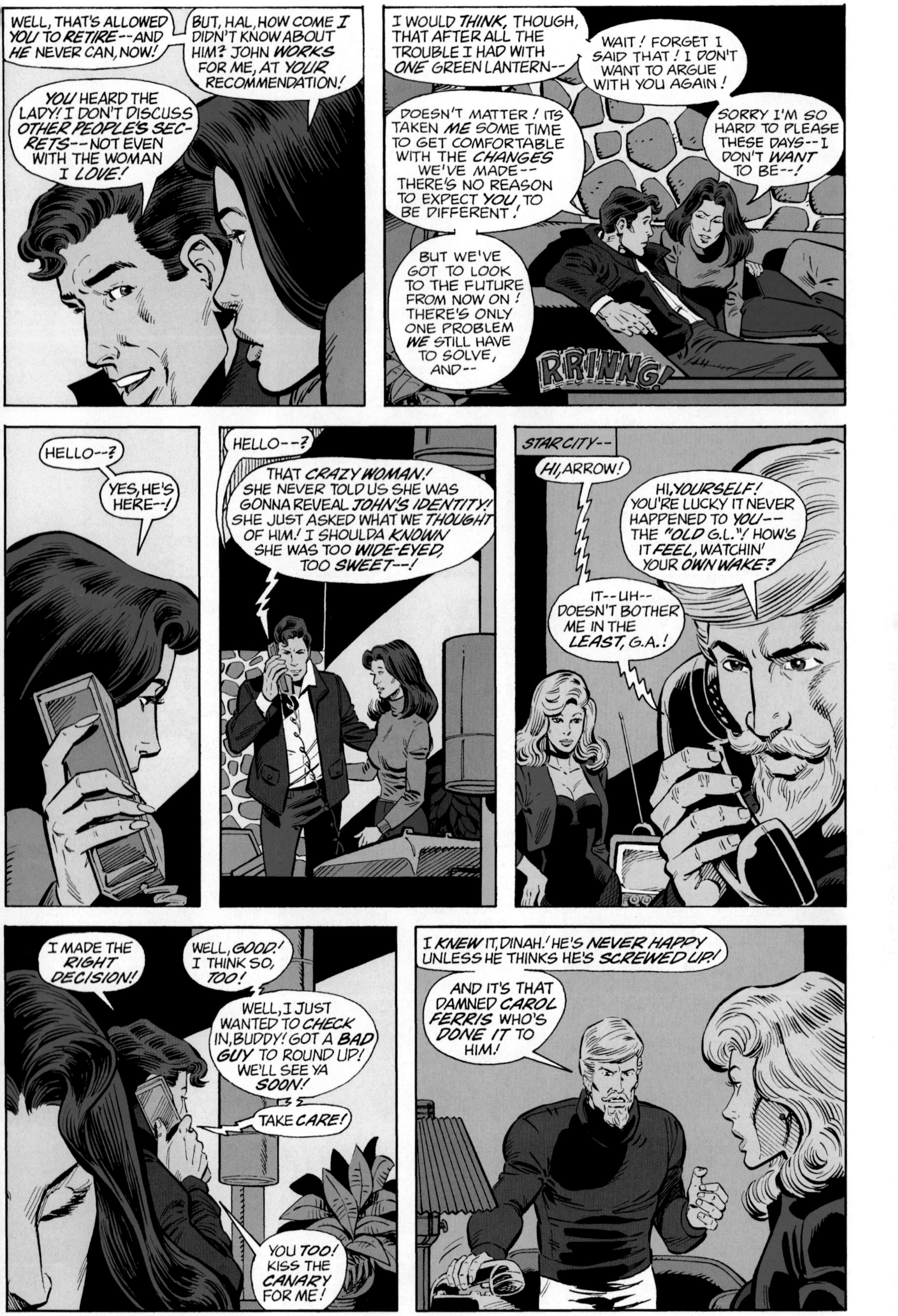

WELL, THAT'S ALLOWED YOU TO RETIRE--AND HE NEVER CAN, NOW!
BUT, HAL, HOW COME I DIDN'T KNOW ABOUT HIM? JOHN WORKS FOR ME, AT YOUR RECOMMENDATION!
YOU HEARD THE LADY! I DON'T DISCUSS OTHER PEOPLE'S SECRETS--NOT EVEN WITH THE WOMAN I LOVE!
I WOULD THINK, THOUGH, THAT AFTER ALL THE TROUBLE I HAD WITH ONE GREEN LANTERN--
WAIT! FORGET I SAID THAT! I DON'T WANT TO ARGUE WITH YOU AGAIN!
DOESN'T MATTER! ITS TAKEN ME SOME TIME TO GET COMFORTABLE WITH THE CHANGES WE'VE MADE--THERE'S NO REASON TO EXPECT YOU, TO BE DIFFERENT!
SORRY I'M SO HARD TO PLEASE THESE DAYS--I DON'T WANT TO BE--!
BUT WE'VE GOT TO LOOK TO THE FUTURE FROM NOW ON! THERE'S ONLY ONE PROBLEM WE STILL HAVE TO SOLVE, AND--
RRINNG!
HELLO--?
YES, HE'S HERE--!
HELLO--?
THAT CRAZY WOMAN! SHE NEVER TOLD US SHE WAS GONNA REVEAL JOHN'S IDENTITY! SHE JUST ASKED WHAT WE THOUGHT OF HIM! I SHOULDA KNOWN SHE WAS TOO WIDE-EYED, TOO SWEET--!
STAR CITY--
HI, ARROW!
HI, YOURSELF! YOU'RE LUCKY IT NEVER HAPPENED TO YOU--THE "OLD G.L."! HOW'S IT FEEL, WATCHIN' YOUR OWN WAKE?
IT--UH--DOESN'T BOTHER ME IN THE LEAST, G.A.!
I MADE THE RIGHT DECISION!
WELL, GOOD! I THINK SO, TOO!
WELL, I JUST WANTED TO CHECK IN, BUDDY! GOT A BAD GUY TO ROUND UP! WE'LL SEE YA SOON!
TAKE CARE!
YOU TOO! KISS THE CANARY FOR ME!
I KNEW IT, DINAH! HE'S NEVER HAPPY UNLESS HE THINKS HE'S SCREWED UP!
AND IT'S THAT DAMNED CAROL FERRIS WHO'S DONE IT TO HIM!

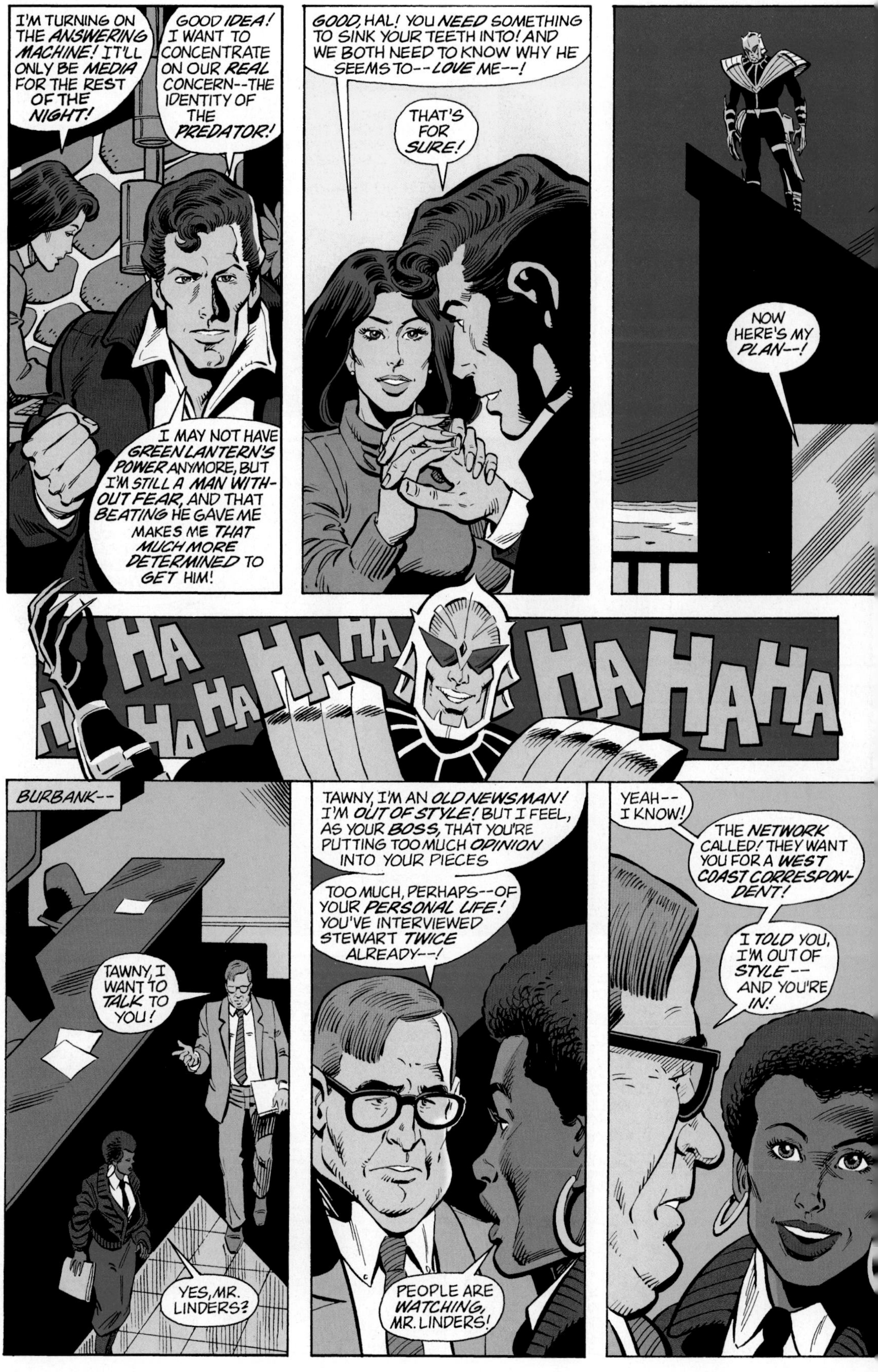
I'M TURNING ON THE ANSWERING MACHINE! IT'LL ONLY BE MEDIA FOR THE REST OF THE NIGHT!
GOOD IDEA! I WANT TO CONCENTRATE ON OUR REAL CONCERN--THE IDENTITY OF THE PREDATOR!
I MAY NOT HAVE GREEN LANTERN'S POWER ANYMORE, BUT I'M STILL A MAN WITHOUT FEAR, AND THAT BEATING HE GAVE ME MAKES ME THAT MUCH MORE DETERMINED TO GET HIM!
GOOD, HAL! YOU NEED SOMETHING TO SINK YOUR TEETH INTO! AND WE BOTH NEED TO KNOW WHY HE SEEMS TO--LOVE ME--!
THAT'S FOR SURE!
NOW HERE'S MY PLAN--!
HA HA HA HA HA HA HA HA HA HA HA
BURBANK--
TAWNY, I WANT TO TALK TO YOU!
YES, MR. LINDERS?
TAWNY, I'M AN OLD NEWSMAN! I'M OUT OF STYLE! BUT I FEEL, AS YOUR BOSS, THAT YOU'RE PUTTING TOO MUCH OPINION INTO YOUR PIECES
TOO MUCH, PERHAPS--OF YOUR PERSONAL LIFE! YOU'VE INTERVIEWED STEWART TWICE ALREADY--!
PEOPLE ARE WATCHING, MR. LINDERS!
YEAH--I KNOW!
THE NETWORK CALLED! THEY WANT YOU FOR A WEST COAST CORRESPONDENT!
I TOLD YOU, I'M OUT OF STYLE--AND YOU'RE IN!

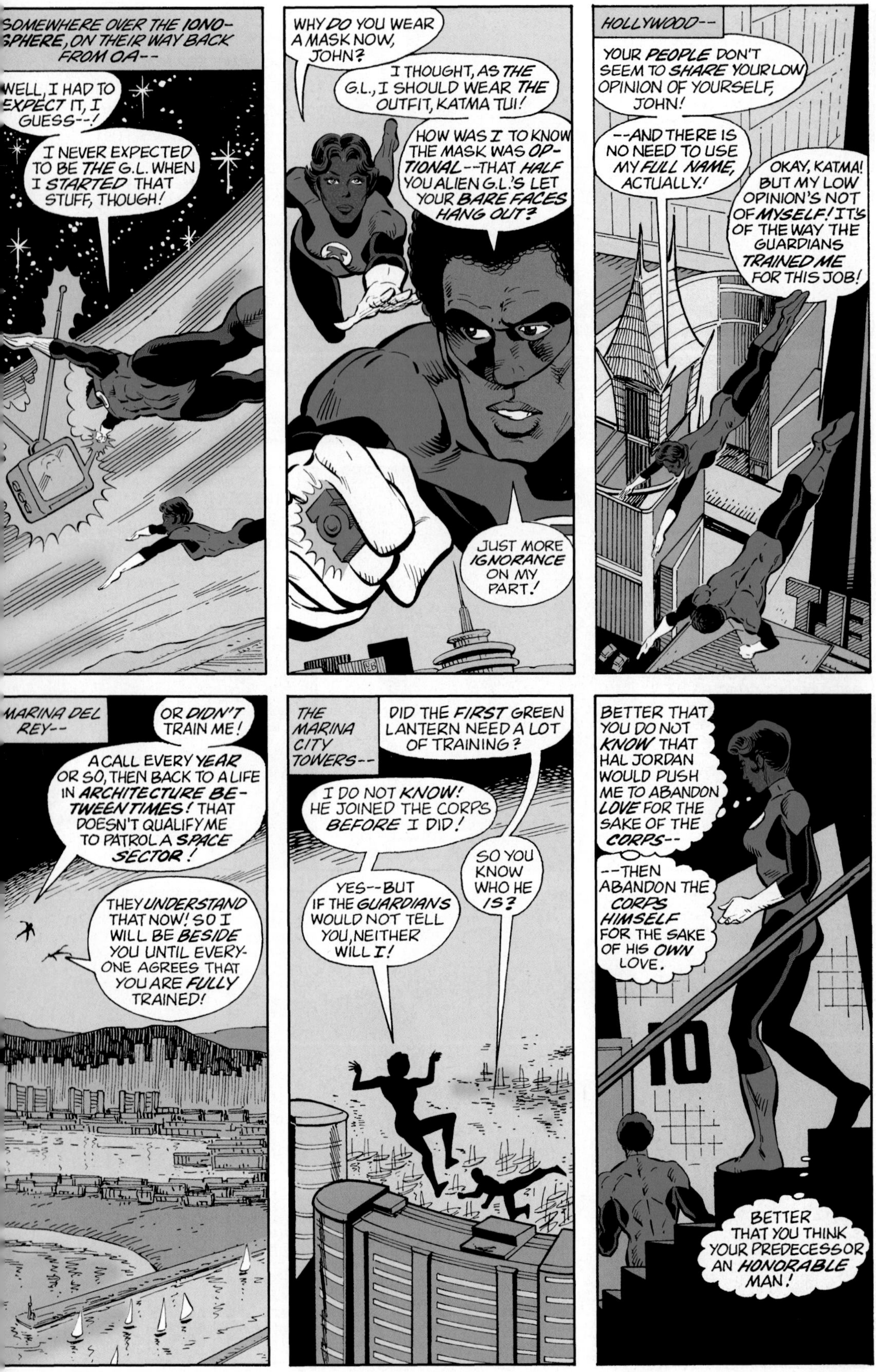
SOMEWHERE OVER THE IONO-SPHERE, ON THEIR WAY BACK FROM OA--
WELL, I HAD TO EXPECT IT, I GUESS--!
I NEVER EXPECTED TO BE THE G.L. WHEN I STARTED THAT STUFF, THOUGH!
WHY DO YOU WEAR A MASK NOW, JOHN?
I THOUGHT, AS THE G.L., I SHOULD WEAR THE OUTFIT, KATMA TUI!
HOW WAS I TO KNOW THE MASK WAS OPTIONAL--THAT HALF YOU ALIEN G.L.'S LET YOUR BARE FACES HANG OUT?
JUST MORE IGNORANCE ON MY PART!
HOLLYWOOD--
YOUR PEOPLE DON'T SEEM TO SHARE YOUR LOW OPINION OF YOURSELF, JOHN!
--AND THERE IS NO NEED TO USE MY FULL NAME, ACTUALLY!
OKAY, KATMA! BUT MY LOW OPINION'S NOT OF MYSELF! IT'S OF THE WAY THE GUARDIANS TRAINED ME FOR THIS JOB!
MARINA DEL REY--
OR DIDN'T TRAIN ME!
A CALL EVERY YEAR OR SO, THEN BACK TO A LIFE IN ARCHITECTURE BETWEEN TIMES! THAT DOESN'T QUALIFY ME TO PATROL A SPACE SECTOR!
THEY UNDERSTAND THAT NOW! SO I WILL BE BESIDE YOU UNTIL EVERYONE AGREES THAT YOU ARE FULLY TRAINED!
THE MARINA CITY TOWERS--
DID THE FIRST GREEN LANTERN NEED A LOT OF TRAINING?
I DO NOT KNOW! HE JOINED THE CORPS BEFORE I DID!
SO YOU KNOW WHO HE IS?
YES--BUT IF THE GUARDIANS WOULD NOT TELL YOU, NEITHER WILL I!
BETTER THAT YOU DO NOT KNOW THAT HAL JORDAN WOULD PUSH ME TO ABANDON LOVE FOR THE SAKE OF THE CORPS--
--THEN ABANDON THE CORPS HIMSELF FOR THE SAKE OF HIS OWN LOVE.
BETTER THAT YOU THINK YOUR PREDECESSOR AN HONORABLE MAN!

WELL, MAKE YOURSELF AT *HOME!* IT'S JUST A *SUBLET,* FOR WHILE I'M *ON THE COAST,* BUT YOU CAN *STAY* HERE IF YOU WANT --THAT IS, IF YOU DON'T MIND MY HAVING *LADIES* OVER NOW AND AGAIN--

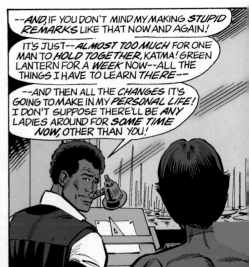

--*AND,* IF YOU DON'T MIND MY MAKING *STUPID REMARKS* LIKE THAT NOW AND AGAIN!

IT'S JUST-- *ALMOST TOO MUCH* FOR ONE MAN TO *HOLD TOGETHER,* KATMA! GREEN LANTERN FOR A *WEEK* NOW--ALL THE THINGS I HAVE TO LEARN *THERE*--

--AND THEN ALL THE *CHANGES* IT'S GOING TO MAKE IN MY *PERSONAL LIFE!* I DON'T SUPPOSE THERE'LL BE *ANY* LADIES AROUND FOR *SOME TIME NOW,* OTHER THAN YOU!

SEE, WHAT YOU HAVE TO *UNDERSTAND* IS, I NEVER *WANTED* THIS JOB!

I SAW MYSELF MORE AS THE *BACKUP QUARTER-BACK* --YOU ONLY PLAY WHEN THE *REAL GUY'S HURT*--AND ONLY UNTIL HE GETS *BETTER!*

THAT'S THE ATTITUDE YOU *HAVE TO* HAVE! IF I'D SAT AROUND *CHAFING AT THE BIT,* WITH *MONTHS BETWEEN CALL UPS,* I'D HAVE GONE *CRAZY!*

AND HEY-- I LOVE *ARCHITECTURE!* THEY CALL ME "SQUARE" JOHN STEWART FOR A *REASON!*

BUT DON'T WORRY--I'M NOT *ABOUT* TO LET THE *TEAM DOWN!* IF I'M GOING TO *PLAY,* I'M GOING TO BE THE *BEST THERE EVER WAS* AT THIS GAME! BETTER EVEN THAN THE *LAST GUY, WHOEVER* HE WAS!

THAT'S WHY MY *LACK OF TRAINING* REALLY BUGS ME!

BUT WITH YOUR HELP, I--

WHA--

WOW!

I THOUGHT I WOULD DRAW *STARES* WITH *CRIMSON SKIN,* SO I USED MY RING TO MATCH *YOUR* COLOR, JOHN!

GUESS *WHAT,* LADY--YOU'RE *STILL* GONNA DRAW *STARES--!*

MOSTLY *MINE--!*

NOW, JOHN--

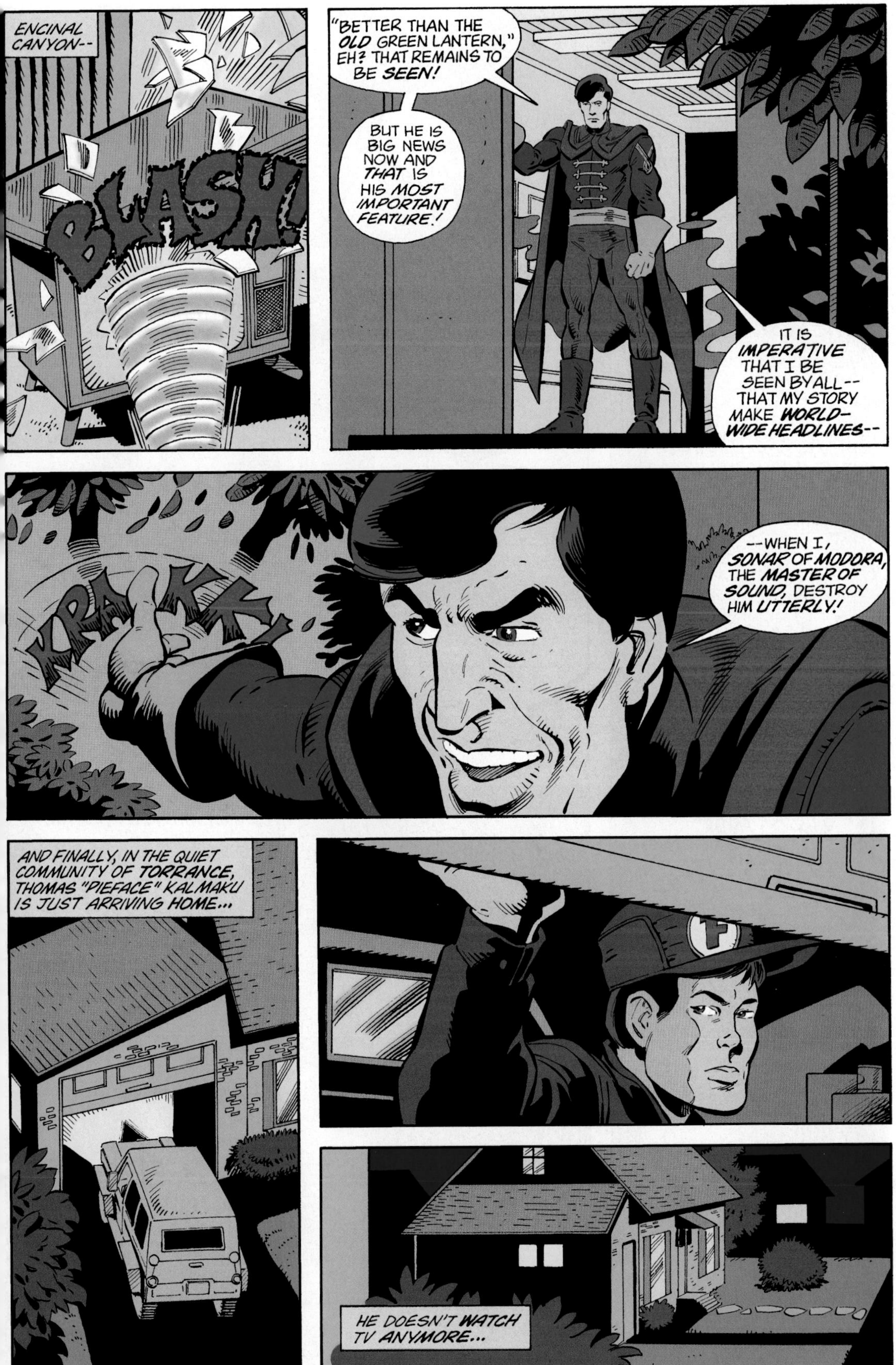
ENCINAL CANYON--
BLASH!
"BETTER THAN THE OLD GREEN LANTERN," EH? THAT REMAINS TO BE SEEN!
BUT HE IS BIG NEWS NOW AND THAT IS HIS MOST IMPORTANT FEATURE!
IT IS IMPERATIVE THAT I BE SEEN BY ALL-- THAT MY STORY MAKE WORLD-WIDE HEADLINES--
KRAKK!
--WHEN I, SONAR OF MODORA, THE MASTER OF SOUND, DESTROY HIM UTTERLY!
AND FINALLY, IN THE QUIET COMMUNITY OF TORRANCE, THOMAS "PIEFACE" KALMAKU IS JUST ARRIVING HOME...
HE DOESN'T WATCH TV ANYMORE...

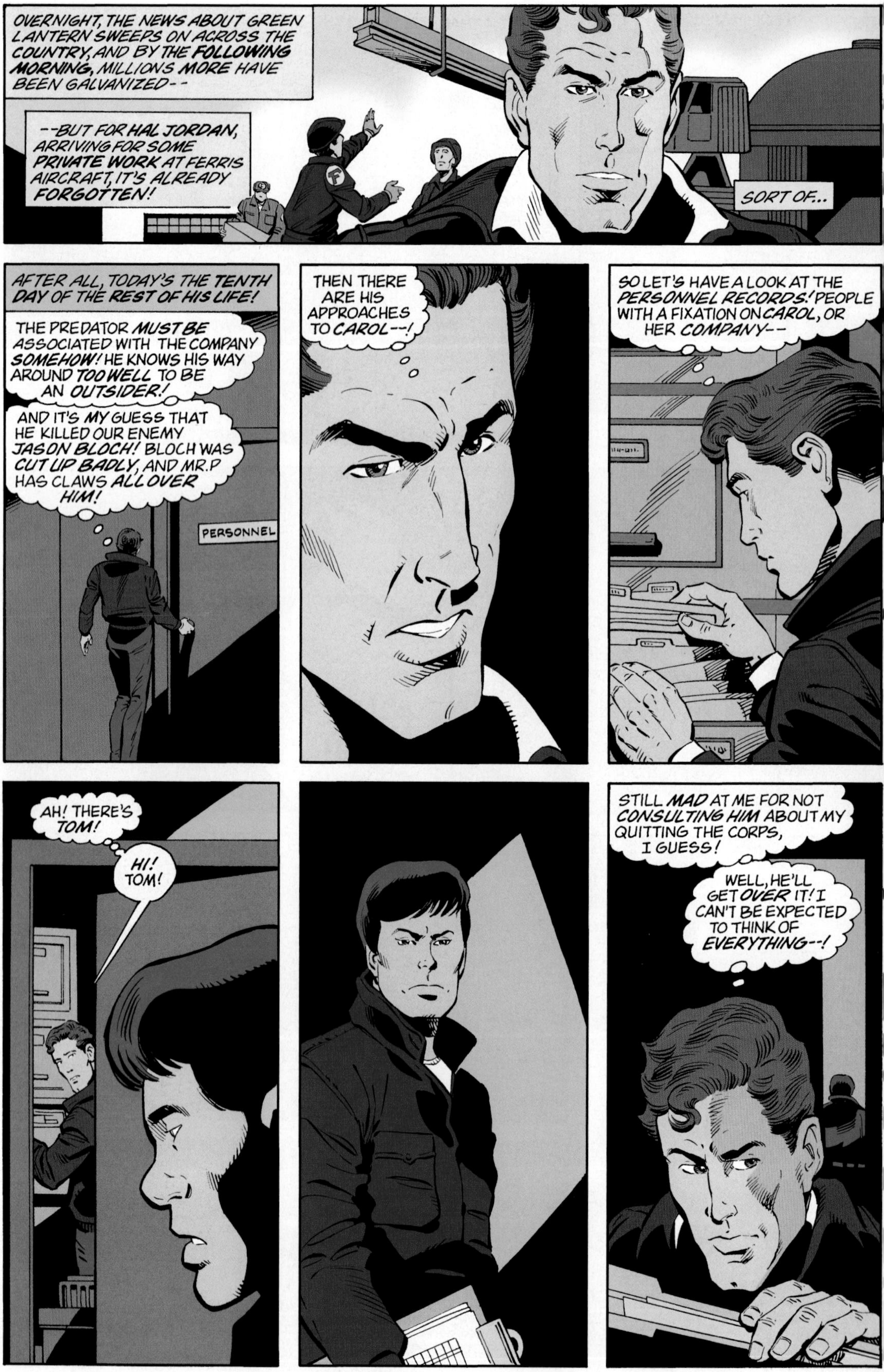

OVERNIGHT, THE NEWS ABOUT GREEN LANTERN SWEEPS ON ACROSS THE COUNTRY, AND BY THE FOLLOWING MORNING, MILLIONS MORE HAVE BEEN GALVANIZED--
--BUT FOR HAL JORDAN, ARRIVING FOR SOME PRIVATE WORK AT FERRIS AIRCRAFT, IT'S ALREADY FORGOTTEN!
SORT OF...
AFTER ALL, TODAY'S THE TENTH DAY OF THE REST OF HIS LIFE!
THE PREDATOR MUST BE ASSOCIATED WITH THE COMPANY SOMEHOW! HE KNOWS HIS WAY AROUND TOO WELL TO BE AN OUTSIDER!
AND IT'S MY GUESS THAT HE KILLED OUR ENEMY JASON BLOCH! BLOCH WAS CUT UP BADLY, AND MR.P HAS CLAWS ALL OVER HIM!
PERSONNEL
THEN THERE ARE HIS APPROACHES TO CAROL--!
SO LET'S HAVE A LOOK AT THE PERSONNEL RECORDS! PEOPLE WITH A FIXATION ON CAROL, OR HER COMPANY--
AH! THERE'S TOM!
HI! TOM!
STILL MAD AT ME FOR NOT CONSULTING HIM ABOUT MY QUITTING THE CORPS, I GUESS!
WELL, HE'LL GET OVER IT! I CAN'T BE EXPECTED TO THINK OF EVERYTHING--!

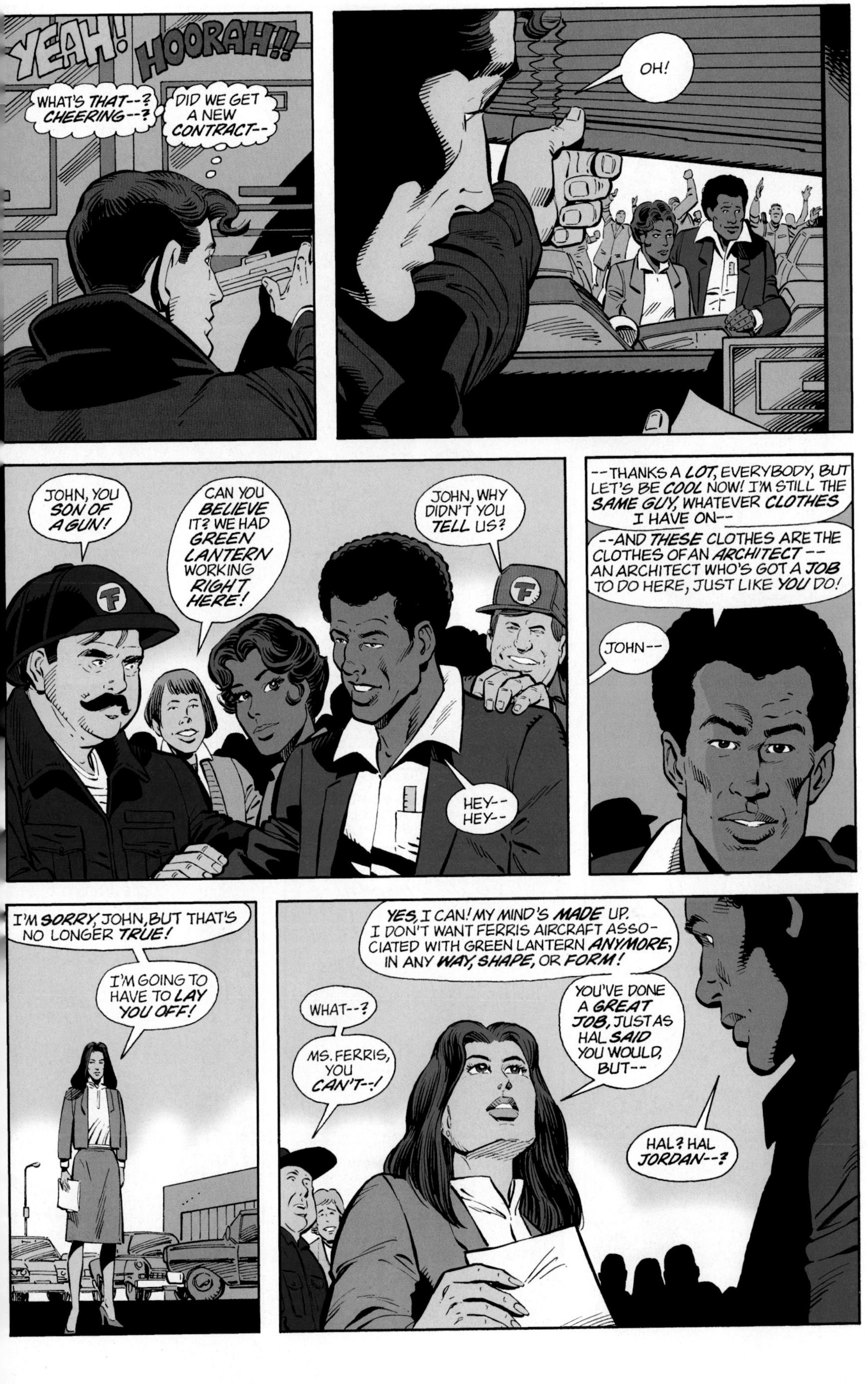
YEAH! HOORAH!!
WHAT'S THAT--? CHEERING--?
DID WE GET A NEW CONTRACT--
OH!
JOHN, YOU SON OF A GUN!
CAN YOU BELIEVE IT? WE HAD GREEN LANTERN WORKING RIGHT HERE!
JOHN, WHY DIDN'T YOU TELL US?
HEY-- HEY--
--THANKS A LOT, EVERYBODY, BUT LET'S BE COOL NOW! I'M STILL THE SAME GUY, WHATEVER CLOTHES I HAVE ON--
--AND THESE CLOTHES ARE THE CLOTHES OF AN ARCHITECT -- AN ARCHITECT WHO'S GOT A JOB TO DO HERE, JUST LIKE YOU DO!
JOHN--
I'M SORRY, JOHN, BUT THAT'S NO LONGER TRUE!
I'M GOING TO HAVE TO LAY YOU OFF!
YES, I CAN! MY MIND'S MADE UP. I DON'T WANT FERRIS AIRCRAFT ASSOCIATED WITH GREEN LANTERN ANYMORE, IN ANY WAY, SHAPE, OR FORM!
WHAT--?
MS. FERRIS, YOU CAN'T--!
YOU'VE DONE A GREAT JOB, JUST AS HAL SAID YOU WOULD, BUT--
HAL? HAL JORDAN--?

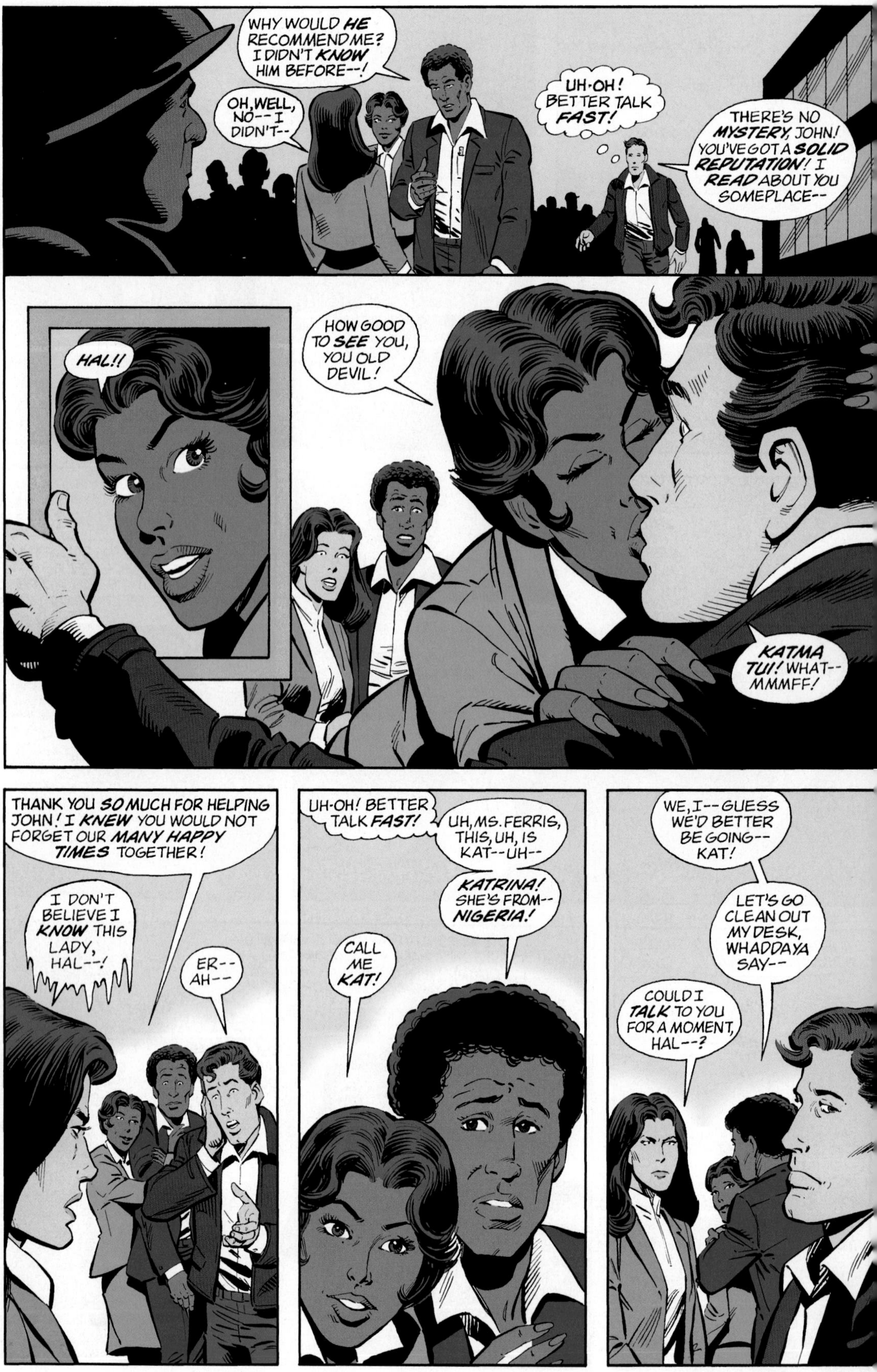

WHY WOULD HE RECOMMEND ME? I DIDN'T KNOW HIM BEFORE--!
OH, WELL, NO-- I DIDN'T--
UH-OH! BETTER TALK FAST!
THERE'S NO MYSTERY, JOHN! YOU'VE GOT A SOLID REPUTATION! I READ ABOUT YOU SOMEPLACE--
HAL!!
HOW GOOD TO SEE YOU, YOU OLD DEVIL!
KATMA TUI! WHAT-- MMMFF!
THANK YOU SO MUCH FOR HELPING JOHN! I KNEW YOU WOULD NOT FORGET OUR MANY HAPPY TIMES TOGETHER!
I DON'T BELIEVE I KNOW THIS LADY, HAL--!
ER-- AH--
UH-OH! BETTER TALK FAST!
UH, MS. FERRIS, THIS, UH, IS KAT--UH--
KATRINA! SHE'S FROM-- NIGERIA!
CALL ME KAT!
WE, I--GUESS WE'D BETTER BE GOING-- KAT!
LET'S GO CLEAN OUT MY DESK, WHADDAYA SAY--
COULD I TALK TO YOU FOR A MOMENT, HAL--?

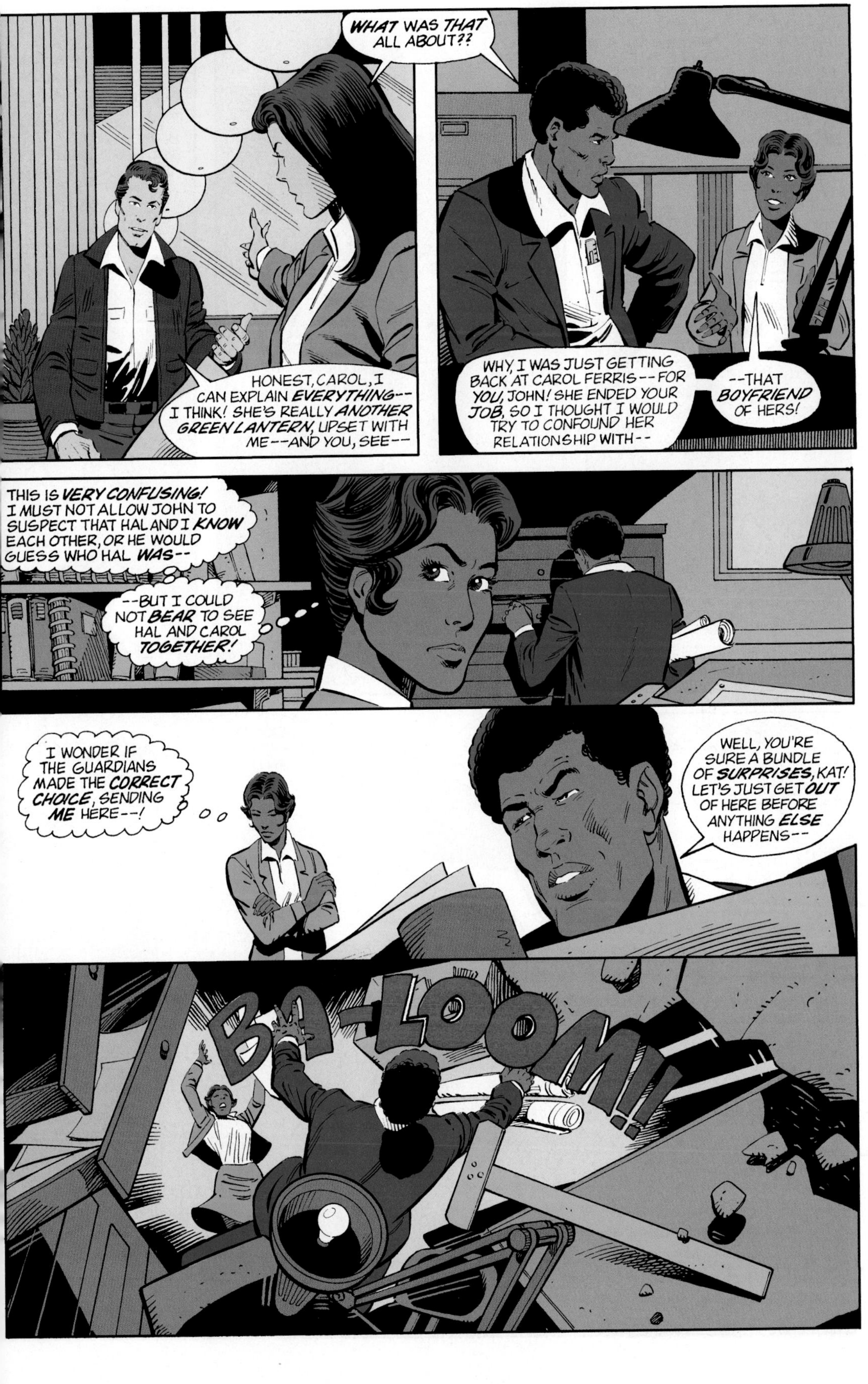
WHAT WAS THAT ALL ABOUT??
HONEST, CAROL, I CAN EXPLAIN EVERYTHING-- I THINK! SHE'S REALLY ANOTHER GREEN LANTERN, UPSET WITH ME--AND YOU, SEE--
WHY, I WAS JUST GETTING BACK AT CAROL FERRIS--FOR YOU, JOHN! SHE ENDED YOUR JOB, SO I THOUGHT I WOULD TRY TO CONFOUND HER RELATIONSHIP WITH--
--THAT BOYFRIEND OF HERS!
THIS IS VERY CONFUSING! I MUST NOT ALLOW JOHN TO SUSPECT THAT HAL AND I KNOW EACH OTHER, OR HE WOULD GUESS WHO HAL WAS--
--BUT I COULD NOT BEAR TO SEE HAL AND CAROL TOGETHER!
I WONDER IF THE GUARDIANS MADE THE CORRECT CHOICE, SENDING ME HERE--!
WELL, YOU'RE SURE A BUNDLE OF SURPRISES, KAT! LET'S JUST GET OUT OF HERE BEFORE ANYTHING ELSE HAPPENS--
BA-LOOM!!

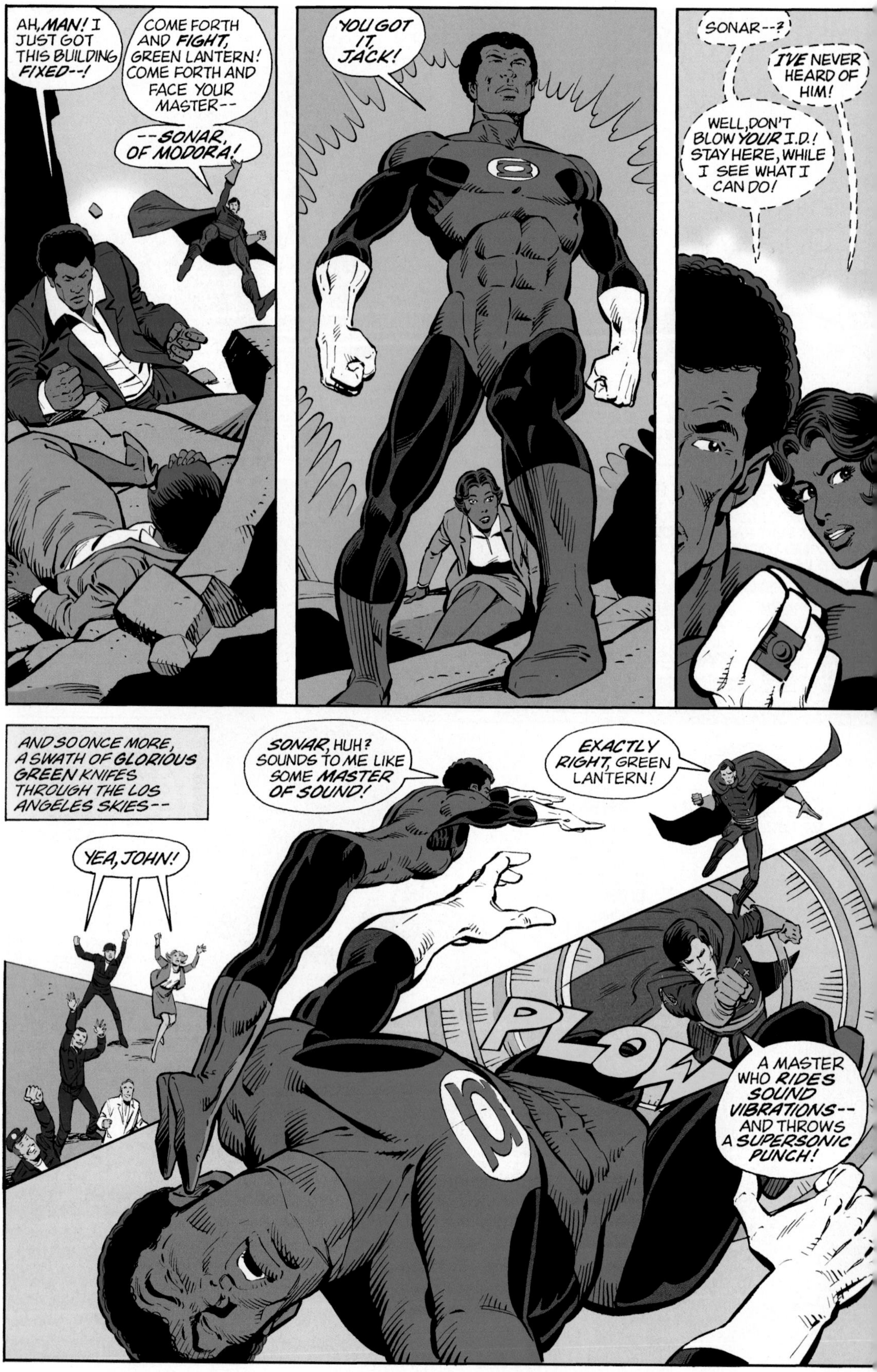

AH, MAN! I JUST GOT THIS BUILDING FIXED--!
COME FORTH AND FIGHT, GREEN LANTERN! COME FORTH AND FACE YOUR MASTER--
--SONAR, OF MODORA!
YOU GOT IT, JACK!
SONAR--?
I'VE NEVER HEARD OF HIM!
WELL, DON'T BLOW YOUR I.D.! STAY HERE, WHILE I SEE WHAT I CAN DO!
AND SO ONCE MORE, A SWATH OF GLORIOUS GREEN KNIFES THROUGH THE LOS ANGELES SKIES--
SONAR, HUH? SOUNDS TO ME LIKE SOME MASTER OF SOUND!
EXACTLY RIGHT, GREEN LANTERN!
YEA, JOHN!
PLOW
A MASTER WHO RIDES SOUND VIBRATIONS-- AND THROWS A SUPERSONIC PUNCH!

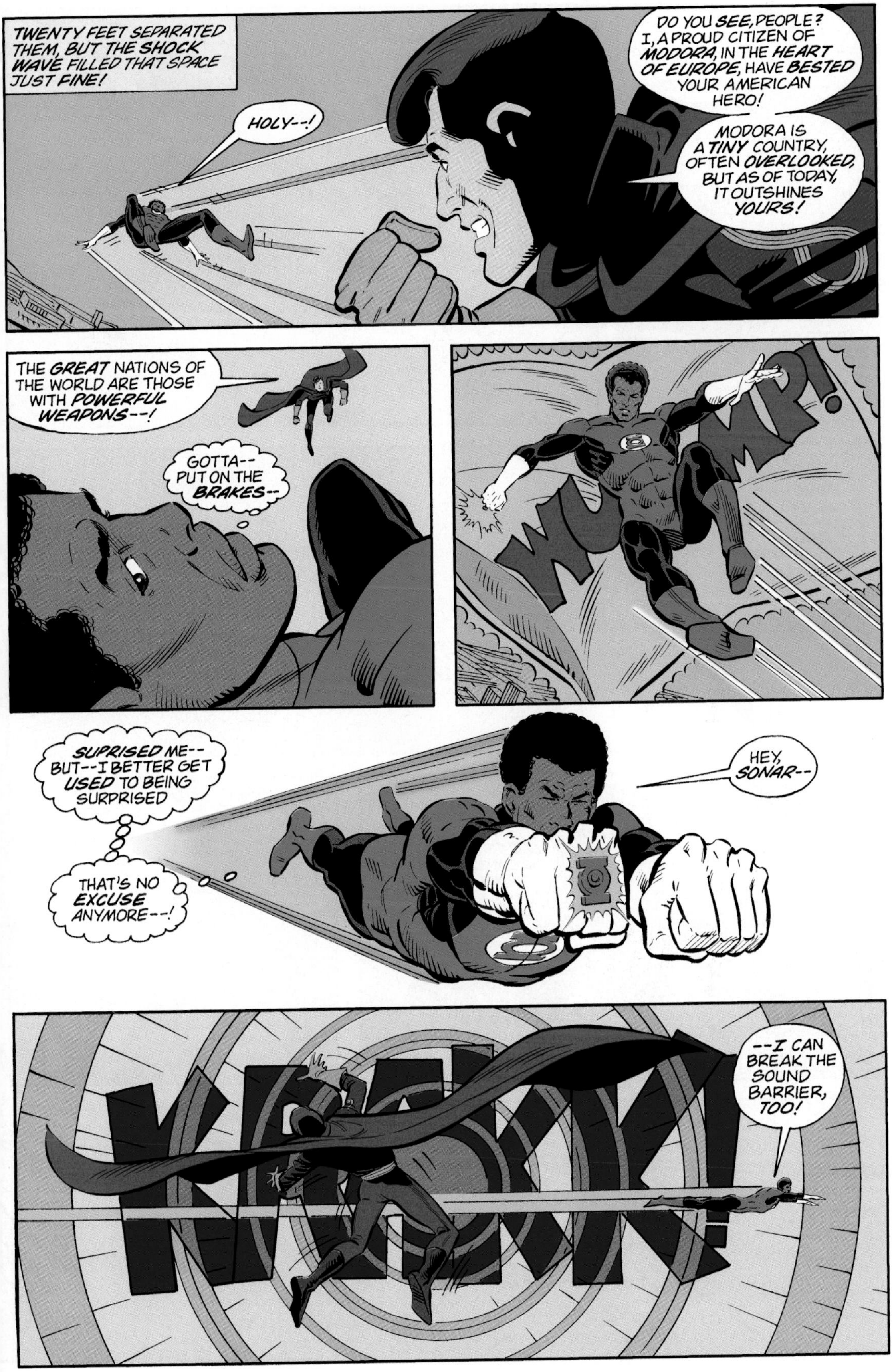
TWENTY FEET SEPARATED THEM, BUT THE SHOCK WAVE FILLED THAT SPACE JUST FINE!
DO YOU SEE, PEOPLE? I, A PROUD CITIZEN OF MODORA, IN THE HEART OF EUROPE, HAVE BESTED YOUR AMERICAN HERO!
HOLY--!
MODORA IS A TINY COUNTRY, OFTEN OVERLOOKED, BUT AS OF TODAY, IT OUTSHINES YOURS!
THE GREAT NATIONS OF THE WORLD ARE THOSE WITH POWERFUL WEAPONS--!
GOTTA-- PUT ON THE BRAKES--
SUPRISED ME-- BUT--I BETTER GET USED TO BEING SURPRISED
HEY, SONAR--
THAT'S NO EXCUSE ANYMORE--!
--I CAN BREAK THE SOUND BARRIER, TOO!

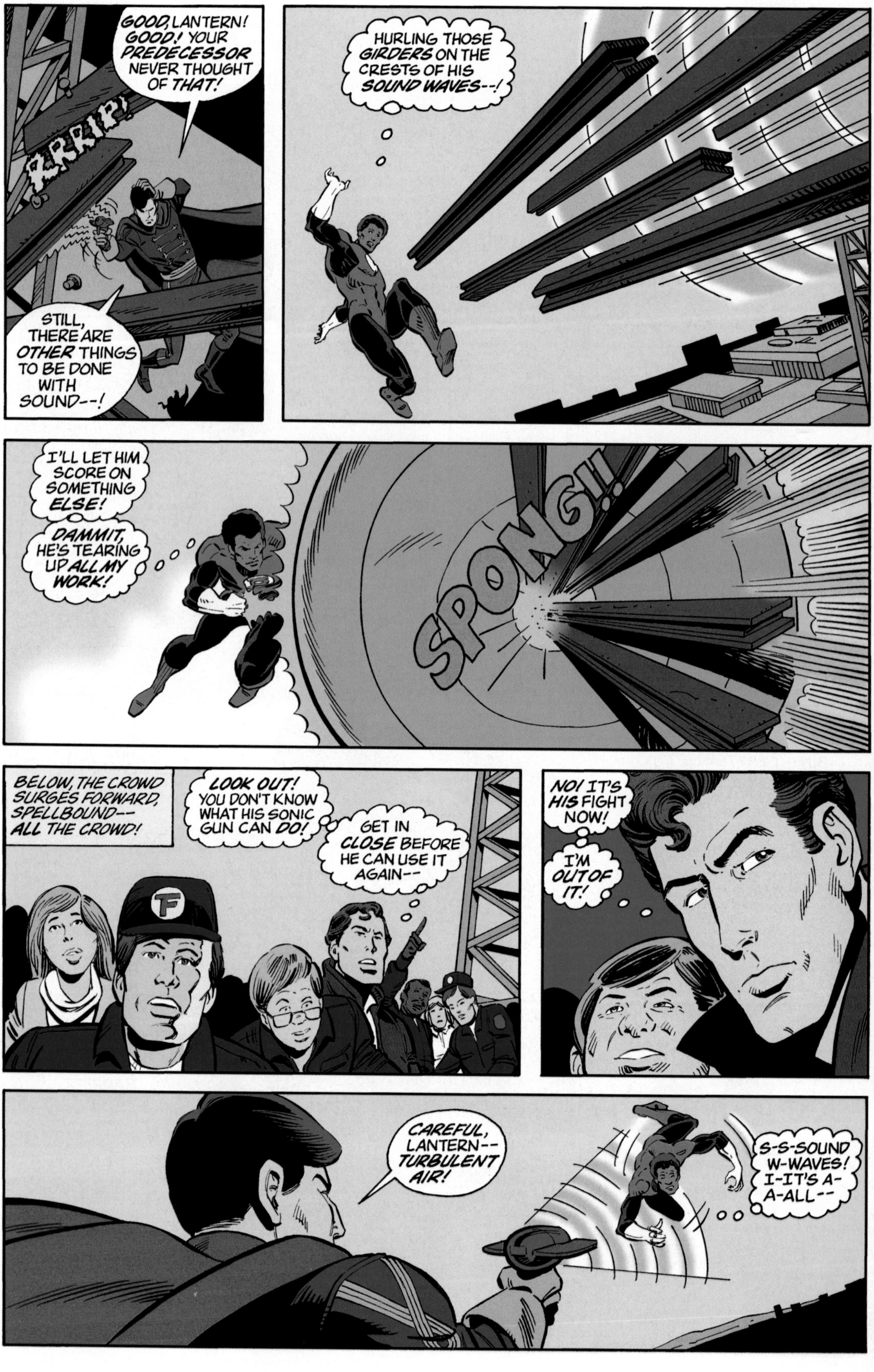
GOOD, LANTERN! GOOD! YOUR PREDECESSOR NEVER THOUGHT OF THAT!
RRRIP!
STILL, THERE ARE OTHER THINGS TO BE DONE WITH SOUND--!
HURLING THOSE GIRDERS ON THE CRESTS OF HIS SOUND WAVES--!
I'LL LET HIM SCORE ON SOMETHING ELSE!
DAMMIT, HE'S TEARING UP ALL MY WORK!
SPONG!!
BELOW, THE CROWD SURGES FORWARD, SPELLBOUND-- ALL THE CROWD!
LOOK OUT! YOU DON'T KNOW WHAT HIS SONIC GUN CAN DO!
GET IN CLOSE BEFORE HE CAN USE IT AGAIN--
NO! IT'S HIS FIGHT NOW!
I'M OUT OF IT!
CAREFUL, LANTERN-- TURBULENT AIR!
S-S-SOUND W-WAVES! I-IT'S A-A-ALL--

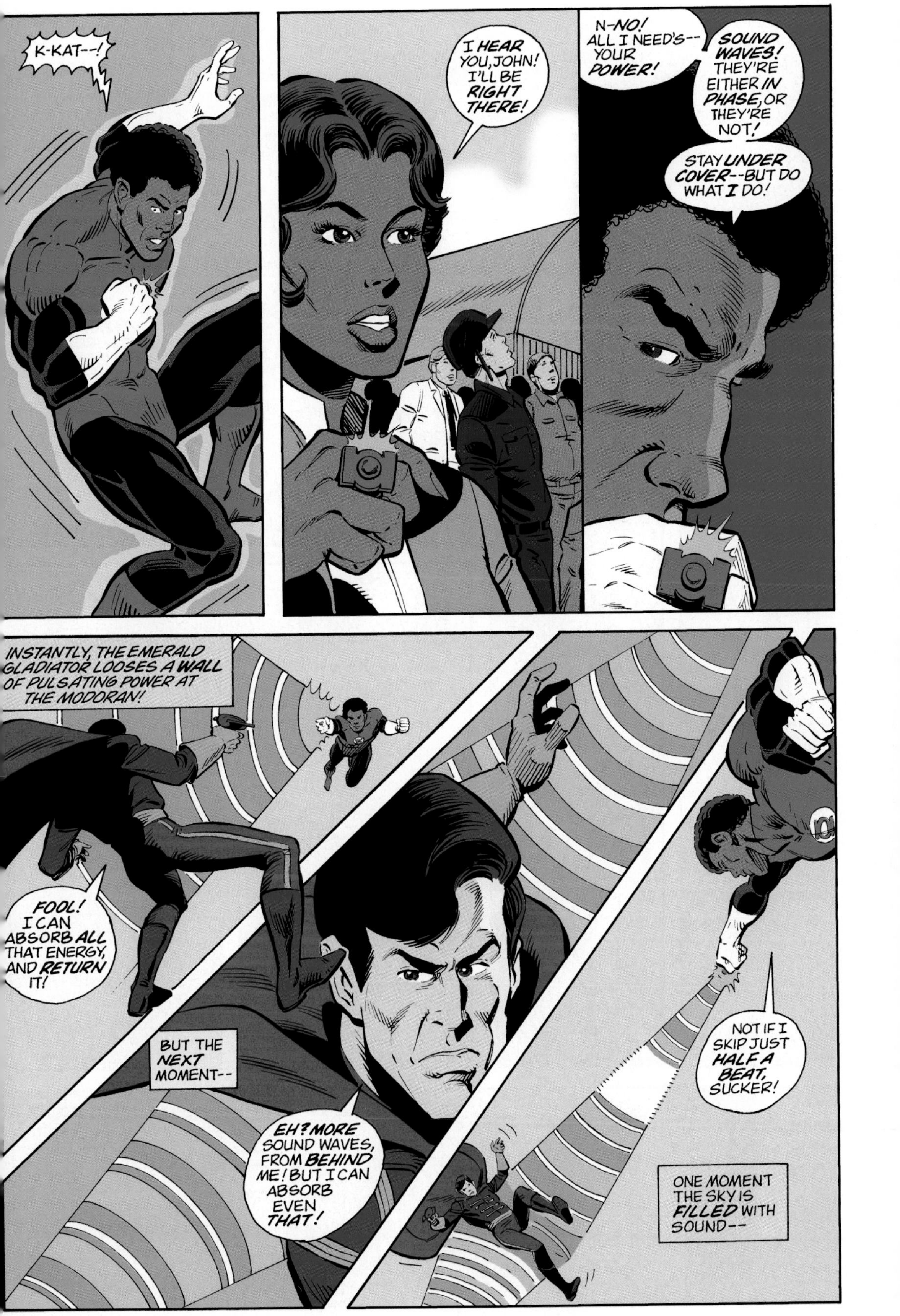

K-KAT--!
I HEAR YOU, JOHN! I'LL BE RIGHT THERE!
N-NO! ALL I NEED'S-- YOUR POWER!
SOUND WAVES! THEY'RE EITHER IN PHASE, OR THEY'RE NOT!
STAY UNDER COVER--BUT DO WHAT I DO!
INSTANTLY, THE EMERALD GLADIATOR LOOSES A WALL OF PULSATING POWER AT THE MODORAN!
FOOL! I CAN ABSORB ALL THAT ENERGY, AND RETURN IT!
BUT THE NEXT MOMENT--
EH? MORE SOUND WAVES, FROM BEHIND ME! BUT I CAN ABSORB EVEN THAT!
NOT IF I SKIP JUST HALF A BEAT, SUCKER!
ONE MOMENT THE SKY IS FILLED WITH SOUND--

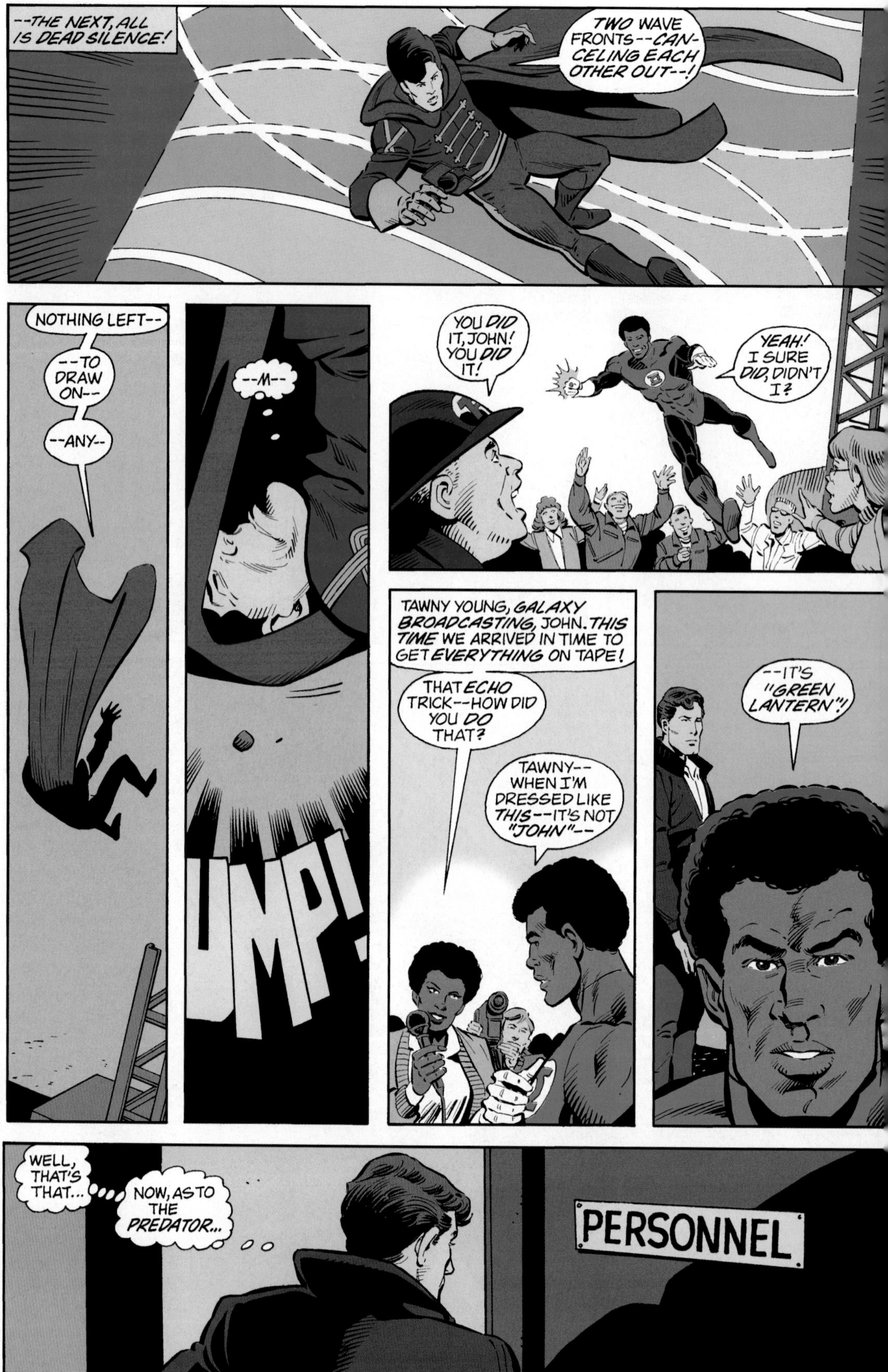
--THE NEXT, ALL IS DEAD SILENCE!
TWO WAVE FRONTS--CANCELING EACH OTHER OUT--!
NOTHING LEFT--
--TO DRAW ON--
--ANY--
--M--
UMP!
YOU DID IT, JOHN! YOU DID IT!
YEAH! I SURE DID, DIDN'T I?
TAWNY YOUNG, GALAXY BROADCASTING, JOHN. THIS TIME WE ARRIVED IN TIME TO GET EVERYTHING ON TAPE!
THAT ECHO TRICK--HOW DID YOU DO THAT?
TAWNY--WHEN I'M DRESSED LIKE THIS--IT'S NOT "JOHN"--
--IT'S "GREEN LANTERN"!
WELL, THAT'S THAT...
NOW, AS TO THE PREDATOR...
PERSONNEL

Cover art by Joe Staton & Bruce Patterson

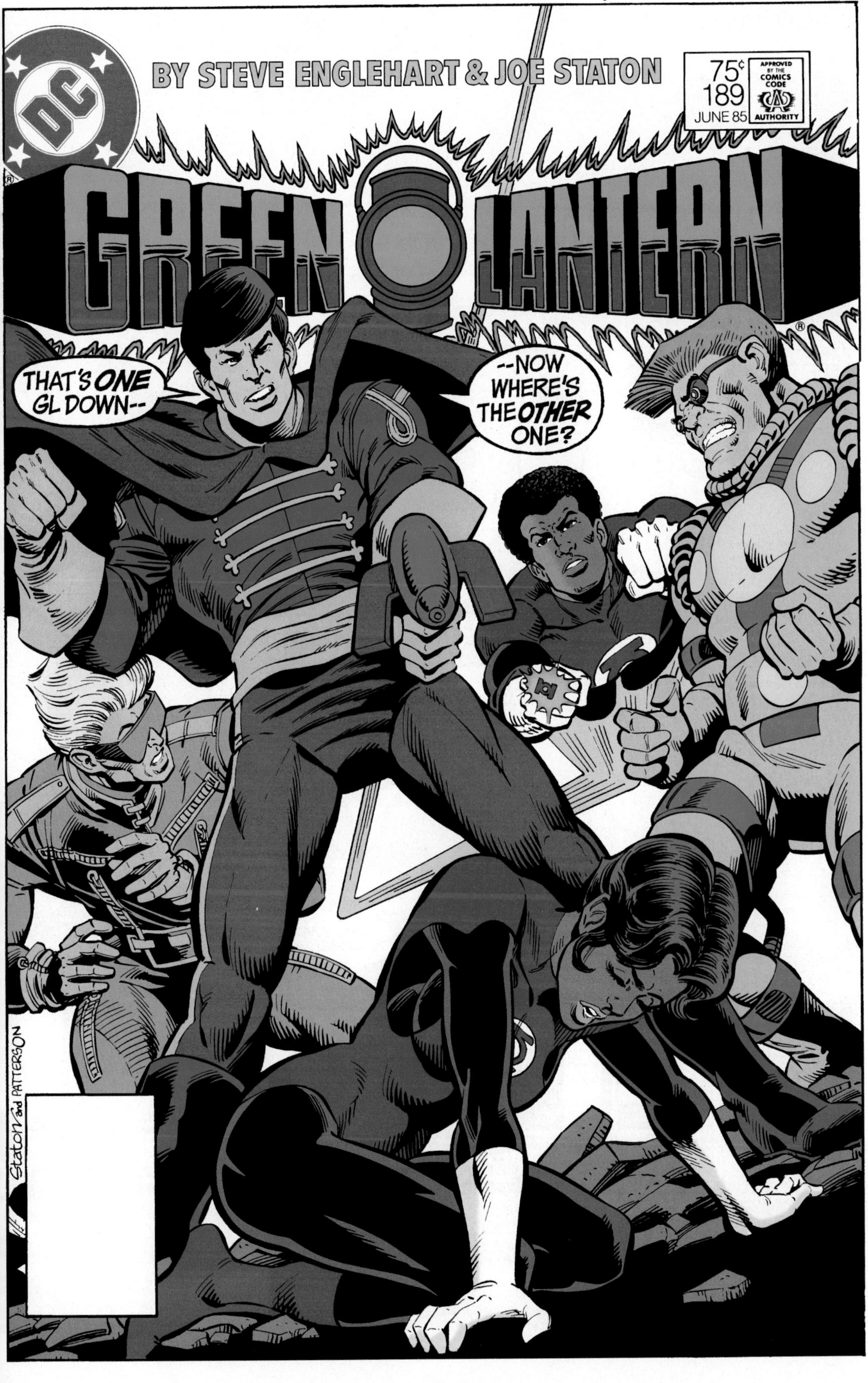
BY STEVE ENGLEHART & JOE STATON
75¢
189
JUNE 85
APPROVED BY THE COMICS CODE AUTHORITY
GREEN LANTERN
THAT'S ONE GL DOWN--
--NOW WHERE'S THE OTHER ONE?
Staton and PATTERSON

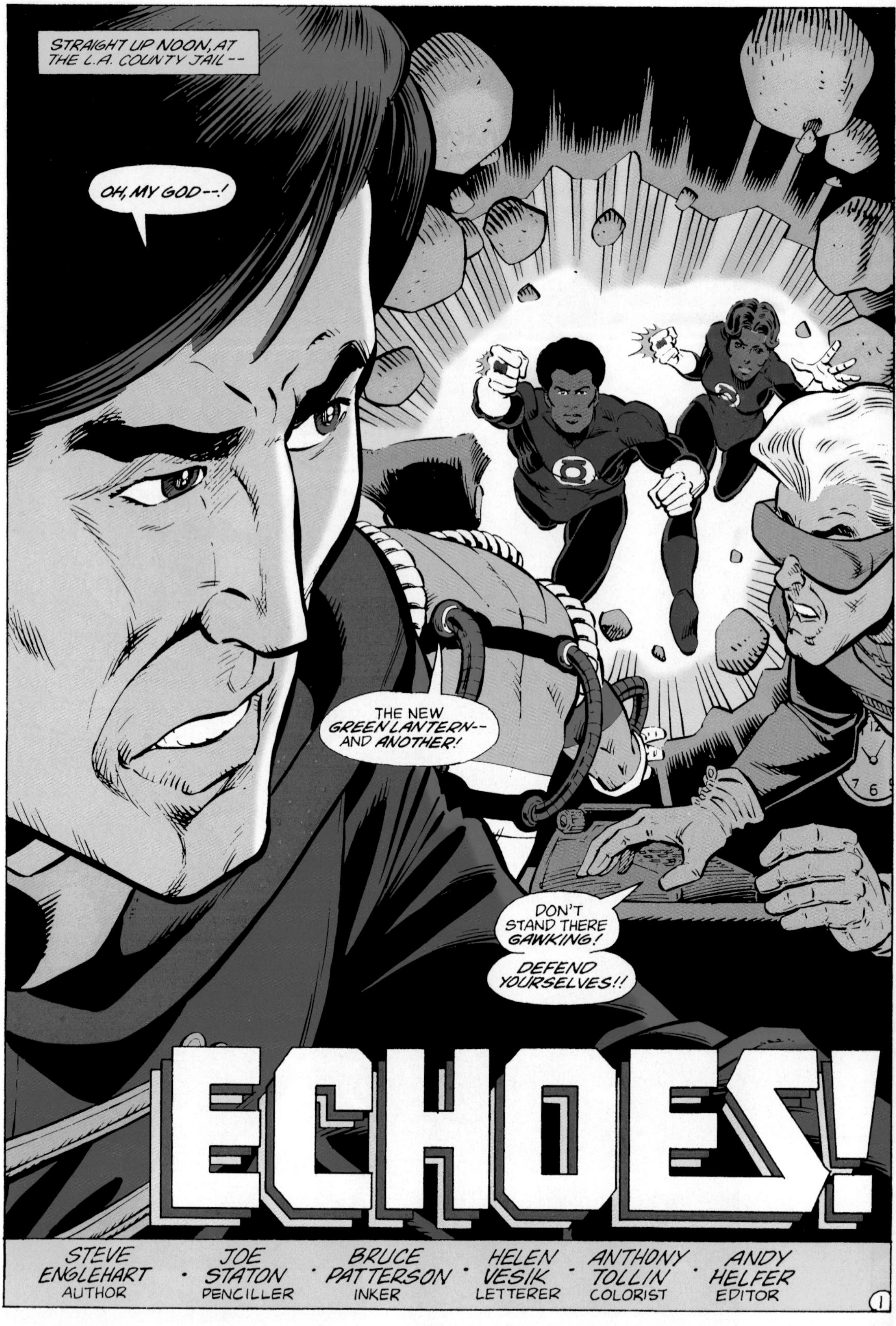
STRAIGHT UP NOON, AT THE L.A. COUNTY JAIL--
OH, MY GOD--!
THE NEW GREEN LANTERN-- AND ANOTHER!
DON'T STAND THERE GAWKING! DEFEND YOURSELVES!!
ECHOES!
STEVE ENGLEHART AUTHOR · JOE STATON PENCILLER · BRUCE PATTERSON INKER · HELEN VESIK LETTERER · ANTHONY TOLLIN COLORIST · ANDY HELFER EDITOR
1

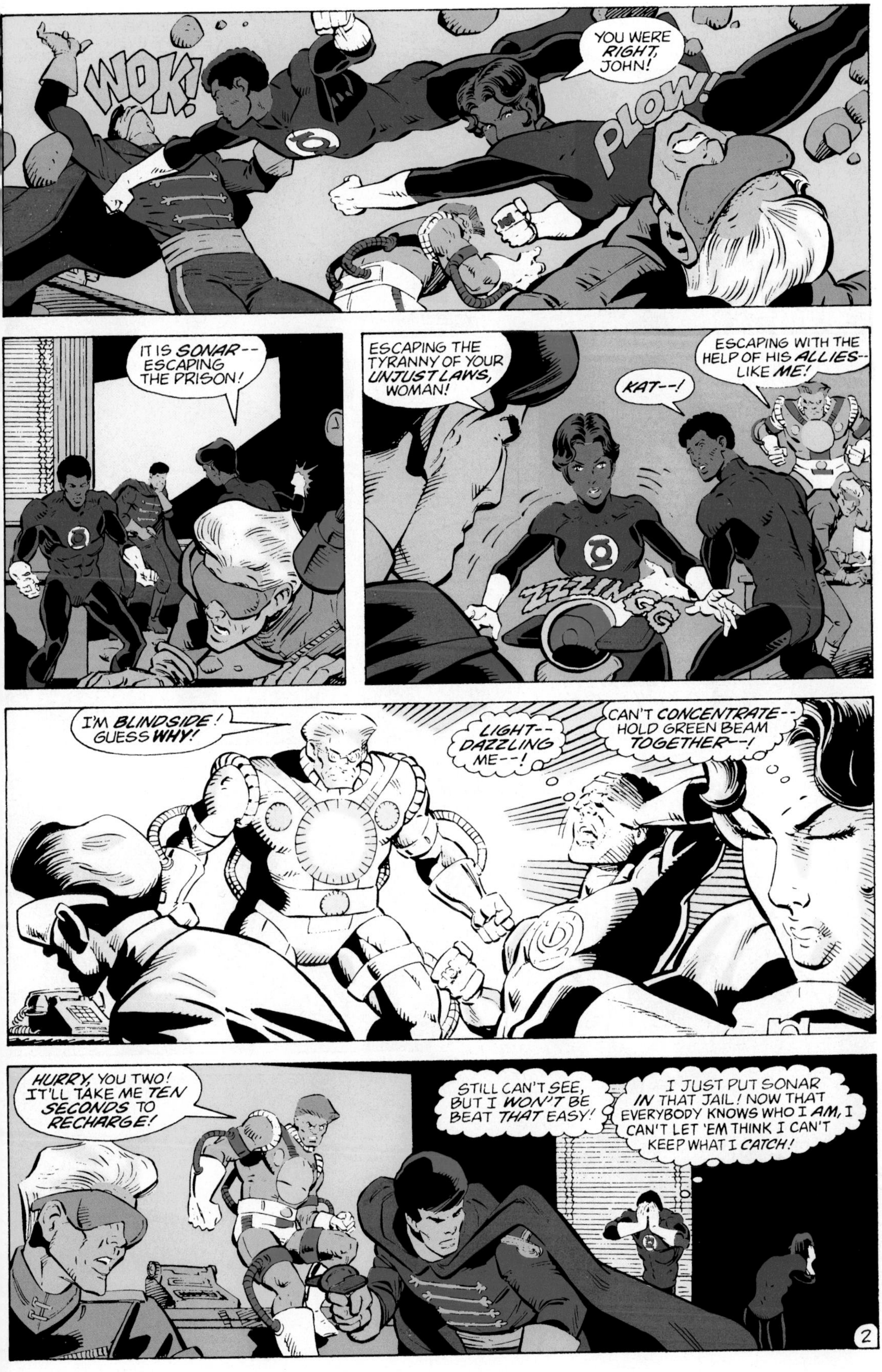
WOK!
YOU WERE RIGHT, JOHN!
PLOW!
IT IS SONAR-- ESCAPING THE PRISON!
ESCAPING THE TYRANNY OF YOUR UNJUST LAWS, WOMAN!
KAT--!
ESCAPING WITH THE HELP OF HIS ALLIES-- LIKE ME!
ZZZINGG
I'M BLINDSIDE! GUESS WHY!
LIGHT-- DAZZLING ME--!
CAN'T CONCENTRATE-- HOLD GREEN BEAM TOGETHER--!
HURRY, YOU TWO! IT'LL TAKE ME TEN SECONDS TO RECHARGE!
STILL CAN'T SEE, BUT I WON'T BE BEAT THAT EASY!
I JUST PUT SONAR IN THAT JAIL! NOW THAT EVERYBODY KNOWS WHO I AM, I CAN'T LET 'EM THINK I CAN'T KEEP WHAT I CATCH!
2

HERE'S *SOMEBODY*-- AND IT DOESN'T SMELL LIKE *KAT!*

IT IS DIFFICULT TO ESCAPE EVEN A *BEDAZ-ZLED* GREEN LANTERN, FELONS!

≡UNNH!≡

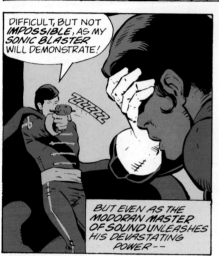

DIFFICULT, BUT NOT *IMPOSSIBLE*, AS MY *SONIC BLASTER* WILL DEMONSTRATE!

BUT EVEN AS THE *MODORAN MASTER OF SOUND* UNLEASHES HIS *DEVASTATING POWER*--

--*KATMA TUI* STRIKES FIRST!

A *SHIELD* TO *REFLECT* HIS NOISE--! *CHILD'S PLAY!*

AND--MY *EYES!* I'M BEGINNING TO *SEE* AGAIN--!

IT'LL DO YOU *NO GOOD*, LANTERNS--

--'CAUSE IT'S *TIME* FOR YOU TO MEET *THROTTLE!*

I CAN SPEED UP ANY MOVING THING, SO EVEN A *CLOCK* CAN BECOME A *DEADLY WEAPON!*

HOLY--! EVERYTHING'S FLYIN' AROUND THE *ROOM!*

GOTTA THROW A *SHIELD* AROUND KAT 'N' ME--!

BUT HOW DO YOU THROW A SHIELD LIKE THAT WITHOUT CATCHING *SOME* MOVING OBJECT *INSIDE?*

RRUMMBL

ANSWER: *YOU DON'T!*

3

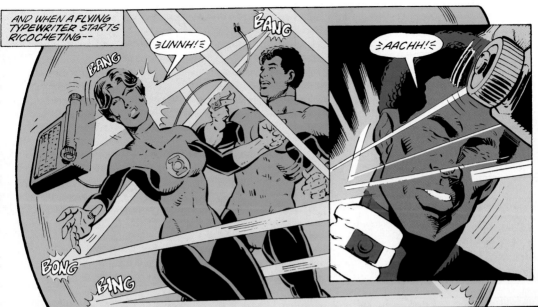

AND WHEN A FLYING TYPEWRITER STARTS RICOCHETING--

BANG

BANG

≡UNNH!≡

≡AACHH!≡

BONG

BING

HE'S OUT! THERE GOES HIS GREEN SHIELD!

NOW I CAN CRUSH THEM AT MY LEISURE!

WOULD THAT IT WERE SO, THROTTLE, BUT ONE CANNOT KILL A GREEN LANTERN SO LONG AS HIS RING RETAINS POWER! IT PROTECTS ITS BEARER AUTOMATICALLY!

OH, WELL, IT'S STILL A PRETTY SIGHT!

WONK!!

AND WE BEAT 'EM--THAT'S WHAT COUNTS!

IT MIGHT HAVE BEEN DIFFERENT AGAINST THE FIRST GREEN LANTERN--!

WHAT DO WE CARE? THESE GREEN LANTERNS ARE THE ONLY ONES WE HAVE TO FACE!

THE OLD G.L. MEANS NOTHIN' ANYMORE!

YEAH? WHADDA YOU WANT?

MR. PETER GRANTLAND? WE'D LIKE TO TALK WITH YOU, IF WE MAY!

THIS IS CAROL FERRIS-- I'M HAL JORDAN...!

YOU'RE NOTHIN' TO ME, BUDDY--

4

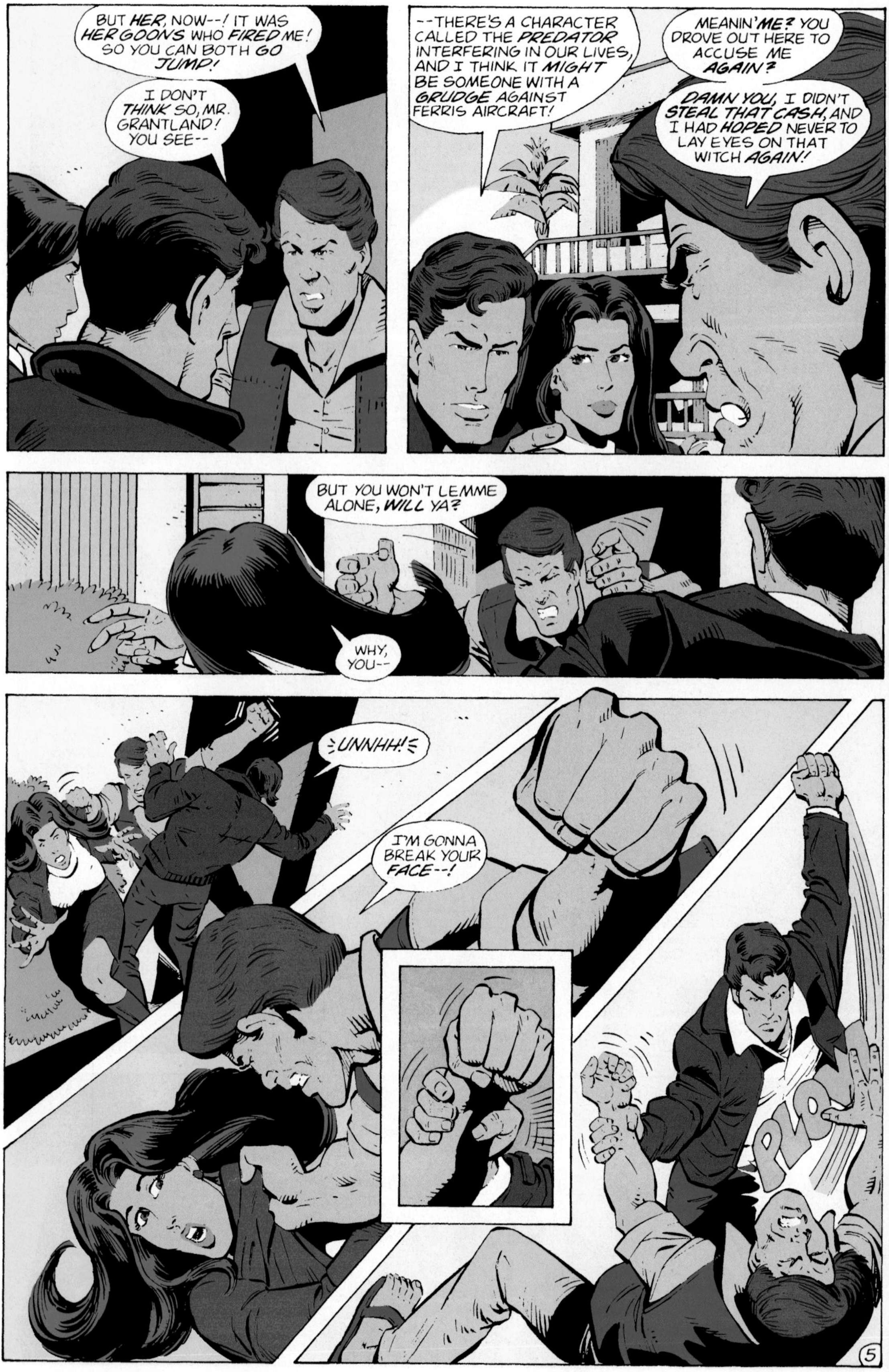
BUT HER, NOW--! IT WAS HER GOONS WHO FIRED ME! SO YOU CAN BOTH GO JUMP!
I DON'T THINK SO, MR. GRANTLAND! YOU SEE--
--THERE'S A CHARACTER CALLED THE PREDATOR INTERFERING IN OUR LIVES, AND I THINK IT MIGHT BE SOMEONE WITH A GRUDGE AGAINST FERRIS AIRCRAFT!
MEANIN' ME? YOU DROVE OUT HERE TO ACCUSE ME AGAIN?
DAMN YOU, I DIDN'T STEAL THAT CASH, AND I HAD HOPED NEVER TO LAY EYES ON THAT WITCH AGAIN!
BUT YOU WON'T LEMME ALONE, WILL YA?
WHY, YOU--
UNNHH!
I'M GONNA BREAK YOUR FACE--!
5

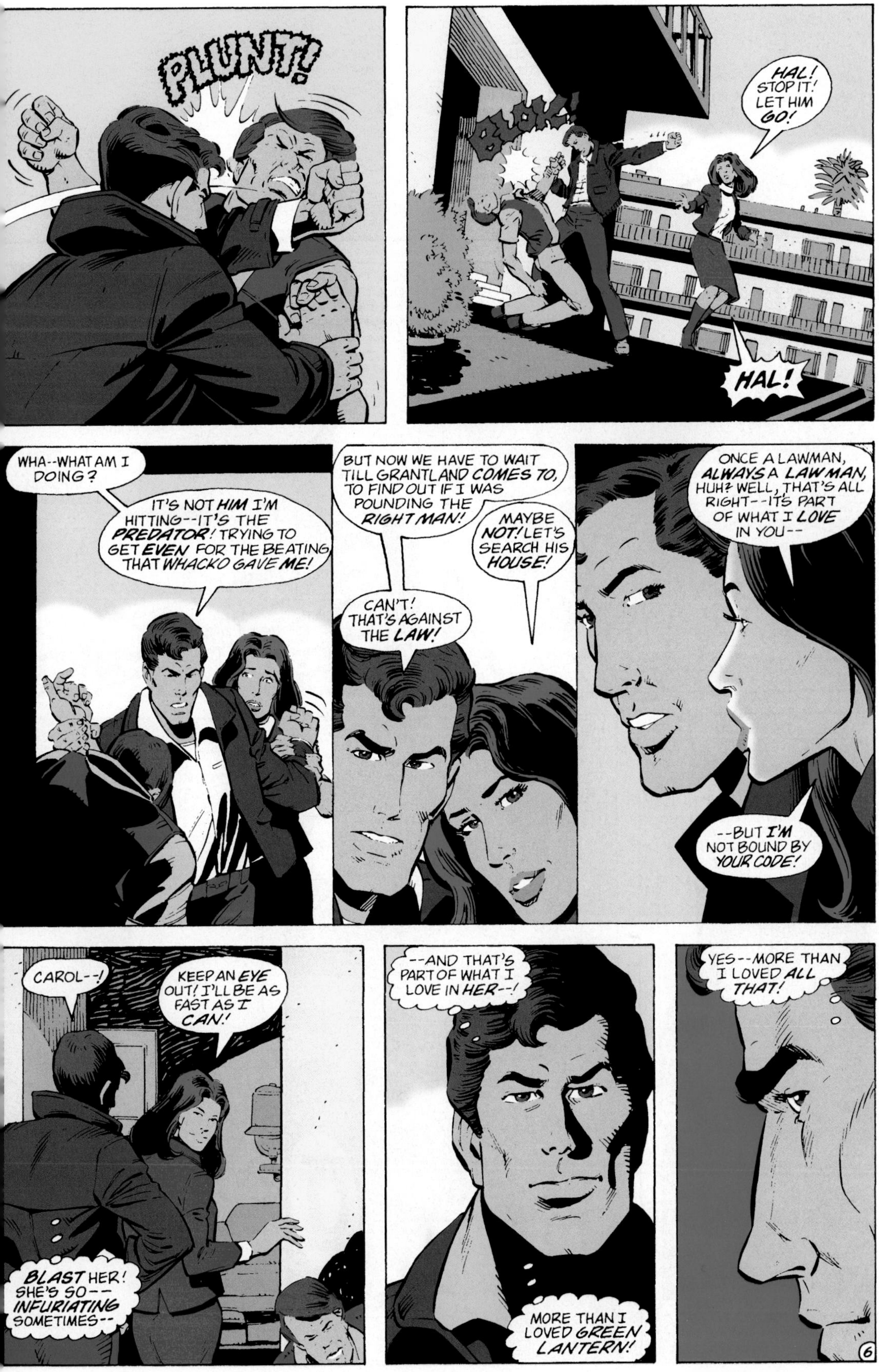
PLUNT!
HAL! STOP IT! LET HIM GO!
BLOK!
HAL!
WHA--WHAT AM I DOING?
IT'S NOT HIM I'M HITTING--IT'S THE PREDATOR! TRYING TO GET EVEN FOR THE BEATING THAT WHACKO GAVE ME!
BUT NOW WE HAVE TO WAIT TILL GRANTLAND COMES TO, TO FIND OUT IF I WAS POUNDING THE RIGHT MAN!
MAYBE NOT! LET'S SEARCH HIS HOUSE!
CAN'T! THAT'S AGAINST THE LAW!
ONCE A LAWMAN, ALWAYS A LAWMAN, HUH? WELL, THAT'S ALL RIGHT--IT'S PART OF WHAT I LOVE IN YOU--
--BUT I'M NOT BOUND BY YOUR CODE!
CAROL--!
KEEP AN EYE OUT! I'LL BE AS FAST AS I CAN!
BLAST HER! SHE'S SO--INFURIATING SOMETIMES--
--AND THAT'S PART OF WHAT I LOVE IN HER--!
MORE THAN I LOVED GREEN LANTERN!
YES--MORE THAN I LOVED ALL THAT!
6

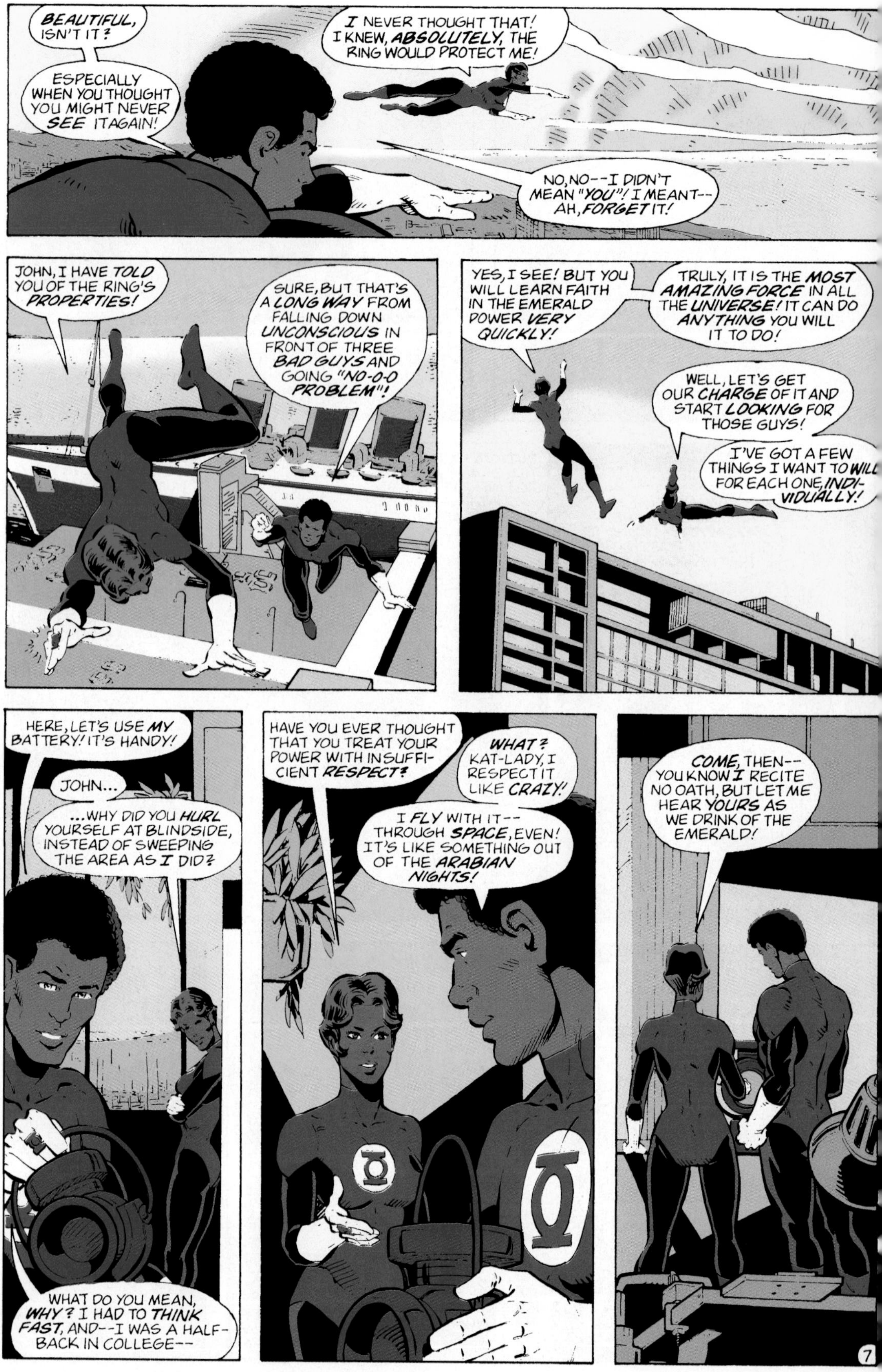
BEAUTIFUL, ISN'T IT?
ESPECIALLY WHEN YOU THOUGHT YOU MIGHT NEVER SEE IT AGAIN!
I NEVER THOUGHT THAT! I KNEW, ABSOLUTELY, THE RING WOULD PROTECT ME!
NO, NO--I DIDN'T MEAN "YOU"! I MEANT--AH, FORGET IT!
JOHN, I HAVE TOLD YOU OF THE RING'S PROPERTIES!
SURE, BUT THAT'S A LONG WAY FROM FALLING DOWN UNCONSCIOUS IN FRONT OF THREE BAD GUYS AND GOING "NO-O-O PROBLEM"!
YES, I SEE! BUT YOU WILL LEARN FAITH IN THE EMERALD POWER VERY QUICKLY!
TRULY, IT IS THE MOST AMAZING FORCE IN ALL THE UNIVERSE! IT CAN DO ANYTHING YOU WILL IT TO DO!
WELL, LET'S GET OUR CHARGE OF IT AND START LOOKING FOR THOSE GUYS!
I'VE GOT A FEW THINGS I WANT TO WILL FOR EACH ONE, INDIVIDUALLY!
HERE, LET'S USE MY BATTERY! IT'S HANDY!
JOHN...
...WHY DID YOU HURL YOURSELF AT BLINDSIDE, INSTEAD OF SWEEPING THE AREA AS I DID?
WHAT DO YOU MEAN, WHY? I HAD TO THINK FAST, AND--I WAS A HALF-BACK IN COLLEGE--
HAVE YOU EVER THOUGHT THAT YOU TREAT YOUR POWER WITH INSUFFICIENT RESPECT?
WHAT? KAT-LADY, I RESPECT IT LIKE CRAZY!
I FLY WITH IT--THROUGH SPACE, EVEN! IT'S LIKE SOMETHING OUT OF THE ARABIAN NIGHTS!
COME, THEN--YOU KNOW I RECITE NO OATH, BUT LET ME HEAR YOURS AS WE DRINK OF THE EMERALD!
7

IN BRIGHTEST DAY, IN BLACKEST NIGHT, NO EVIL SHALL ESCAPE MY SIGHT! LET THOSE WHO WORSHIP EVIL'S MIGHT-- BEWARE MY POWER-- GREEN LANTERN'S LIGHT!

WHAT IS YOUR *OATH* TO YOU, JOHN?

WHAT IS THIS, A *POP QUIZ?*

AN *EXAMINATION,* YOU MEAN? YES! I AM HERE TO *TRAIN* YOU!

WHAT IS YOUR *OATH* TO YOU?

WELL-- A PLEDGE TO USE THIS POWER-- TO MAKE BAD GUYS *BEWARE*--

"BAD GUYS," AND *EVERYTHING ELSE* THAT THREATENS PUBLIC SAFETY!

THERE IS *MUCH* EVIL IN THE UNIVERSE, JOHN--AND ONLY *ONE GROUP* ORGANIZED TO *COMBAT IT!*

WE ARE THAT GROUP!

YOU ARE A *GREEN LANTERN*-- ONE OF *3600* IN *ALL THE UNIVERSE!* YOU ARE RESPONSIBLE FOR A *SECTOR* OF THE UNIVERSE-- RESPONSIBLE FOR PROTECTING ALL THAT IS *GOOD* WITHIN IT!

WHETHER WE *SPEAK* IT OR NOT, THAT IS *EVERY* GREEN LANTERN'S PERSONAL PLEDGE, AND IT IS *NOT* TO BE TAKEN *LIGHTLY*--

--AS YOUR *PREDECESSOR* DID IN THE *END!*

I DO SEE THAT, KAT! IT'S JUST THAT IT'S *TAKING* A WHILE TO *ACCUSTOM* MYSELF--

-- NOT *JUST* TO THE RESPON- SIBILITY--BUT TO TAKING *ANOTHER* MAN'S PLACE!

I GUESS--I'VE BEEN FEELING A LITTLE *GUILTY,* EVEN THOUGH I HAD *NOTHING TO DO* WITH HIS *LEAVING!* I LIKED THE FIRST GUY--I DON'T WANT TO STEP ON HIS *TOES,* WHEREVER HE IS!

BUT LIFE *DOES* GO ON, DOESN'T IT--

--IF IT GETS THE *CHANCE!*

SO, YEAH-- YOU'RE ABSOLUTELY *RIGHT!* I'M THE *LANTERN!*

AND LET THOSE WHO WORSHIP EVIL'S MIGHT--

AND LET THOSE WHO WORSHIP EVIL'S MIGHT--

BEWARE MY POWER!

8

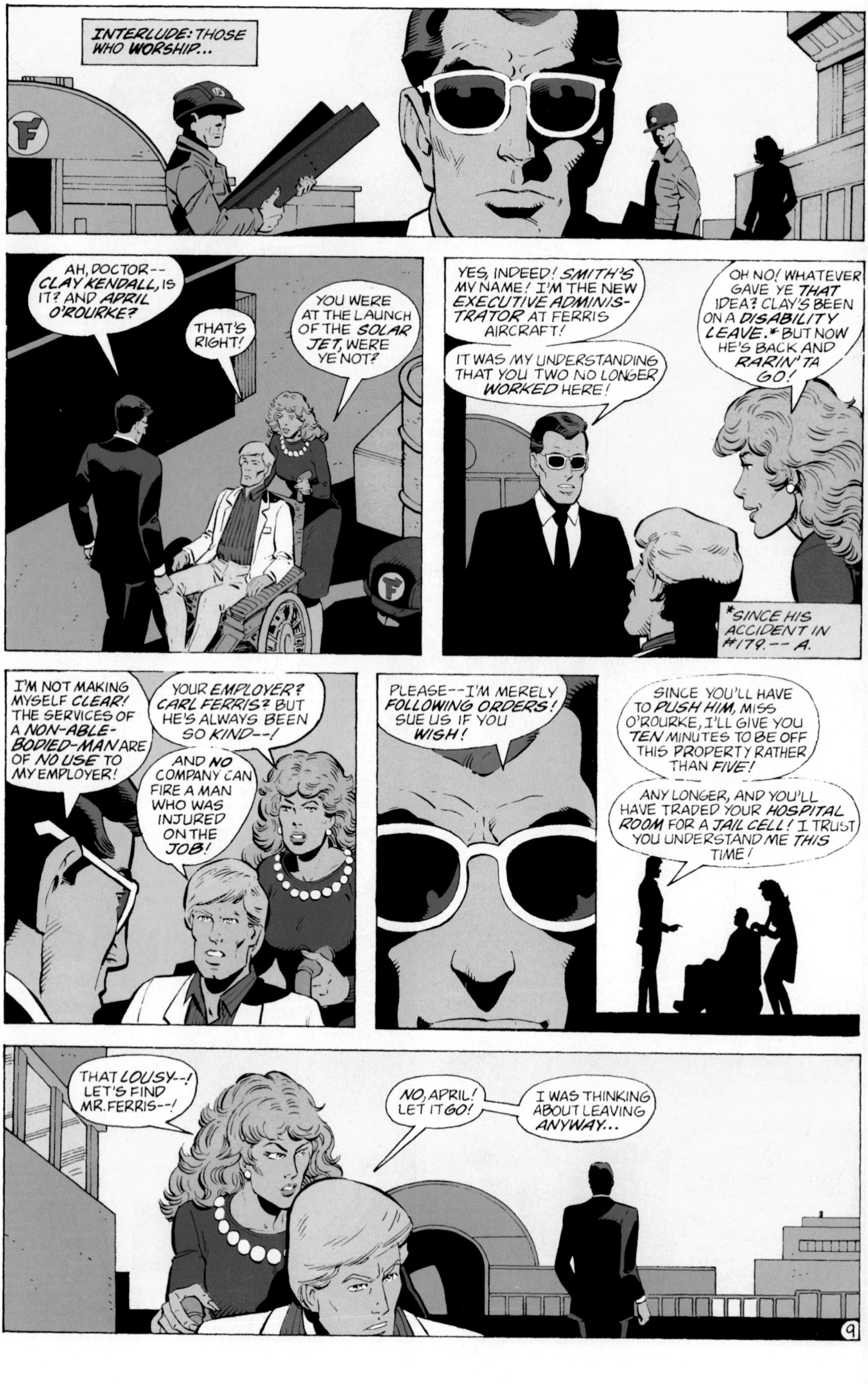
INTERLUDE: THOSE WHO WORSHIP...
AH, DOCTOR-- CLAY KENDALL, IS IT? AND APRIL O'ROURKE?
THAT'S RIGHT!
YOU WERE AT THE LAUNCH OF THE SOLAR JET, WERE YE NOT?
YES, INDEED! SMITH'S MY NAME! I'M THE NEW EXECUTIVE ADMINISTRATOR AT FERRIS AIRCRAFT!
IT WAS MY UNDERSTANDING THAT YOU TWO NO LONGER WORKED HERE!
OH NO! WHATEVER GAVE YE THAT IDEA? CLAY'S BEEN ON A DISABILITY LEAVE.* BUT NOW HE'S BACK AND RARIN' TA GO!
*SINCE HIS ACCIDENT IN #179. -- A.
I'M NOT MAKING MYSELF CLEAR! THE SERVICES OF A NON-ABLE-BODIED-MAN ARE OF NO USE TO MY EMPLOYER!
YOUR EMPLOYER? CARL FERRIS? BUT HE'S ALWAYS BEEN SO KIND--!
AND NO COMPANY CAN FIRE A MAN WHO WAS INJURED ON THE JOB!
PLEASE--I'M MERELY FOLLOWING ORDERS! SUE US IF YOU WISH!
SINCE YOU'LL HAVE TO PUSH HIM, MISS O'ROURKE, I'LL GIVE YOU TEN MINUTES TO BE OFF THIS PROPERTY RATHER THAN FIVE!
ANY LONGER, AND YOU'LL HAVE TRADED YOUR HOSPITAL ROOM FOR A JAIL CELL! I TRUST YOU UNDERSTAND ME THIS TIME!
THAT LOUSY--! LET'S FIND MR. FERRIS--!
NO, APRIL! LET IT GO!
I WAS THINKING ABOUT LEAVING ANYWAY...
9

IT'S WORKING SO VERY *SMOOTHLY!* DAY BY DAY I EXTEND *CON-TROL'S, AH,* CONTROL OVER FERRIS OPERATIONS, EXACTLY AS YOU *PLANNED--*

--*PREDATOR!*

NATURALLY! AND MY COURTSHIP OF *CAROL FERRIS* PROCEEDS *JUST* AS SMOOTHLY, *SMITH!*

SOON, IT WILL *ALL* BE MINE! *FERRIS AIRCRAFT,* AND *CAROL HERSELF--* EVERYTHING I'VE EVER REALLY *WANTED* IN THIS WORLD!

SOON--SO VERY SOON-- I'LL HAVE BEATEN *GREEN LANTERN* AT *LAST!*

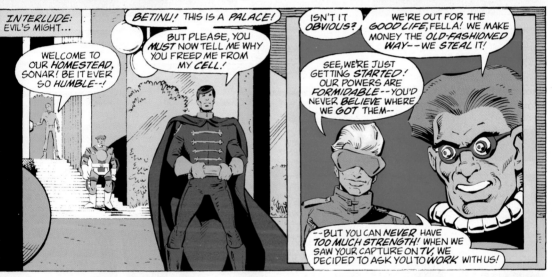

INTERLUDE: EVIL'S MIGHT...

BETINU! THIS IS A *PALACE!*

BUT PLEASE, YOU *MUST* NOW TELL ME WHY YOU *FREED* ME FROM MY *CELL!*

WELCOME TO OUR *HOMESTEAD,* SONAR! BE IT EVER SO *HUMBLE--!*

ISN'T IT *OBVIOUS?*

WE'RE OUT FOR THE *GOOD LIFE,* FELLA! WE MAKE MONEY THE *OLD-FASHIONED WAY--WE STEAL* IT!

SEE, WE'RE JUST GETTING *STARTED!* OUR POWERS ARE *FORMIDABLE--* YOU'D NEVER *BELIEVE* WHERE WE *GOT* THEM--

--BUT YOU CAN *NEVER* HAVE *TOO MUCH STRENGTH!* WHEN WE SAW YOUR CAPTURE ON *TV,* WE DECIDED TO ASK YOU TO *WORK* WITH US!

BUT I AM NO--*ENTREPRENEUR!* I AM ALREADY A *LEADING CITIZEN* IN MY NATIVE *MODORA!* I SEEK ONLY WORLD RECOGNITION OF ITS SPECIAL *GRANDEUR!*

AND YET--

AND YET-- PERHAPS WE *SHOULD* BECOME ALLIES! YOU *DO* HAVE GREAT POWER, AND I HAVE *EXPERIENCE* IN FIGHTING *GREEN LANTERNS!*

IF I WERE TO *LEAD THE ATTACK* WHICH DEFEATED THIS *LATEST* ONE--!

END OF INTERLUDES...

10

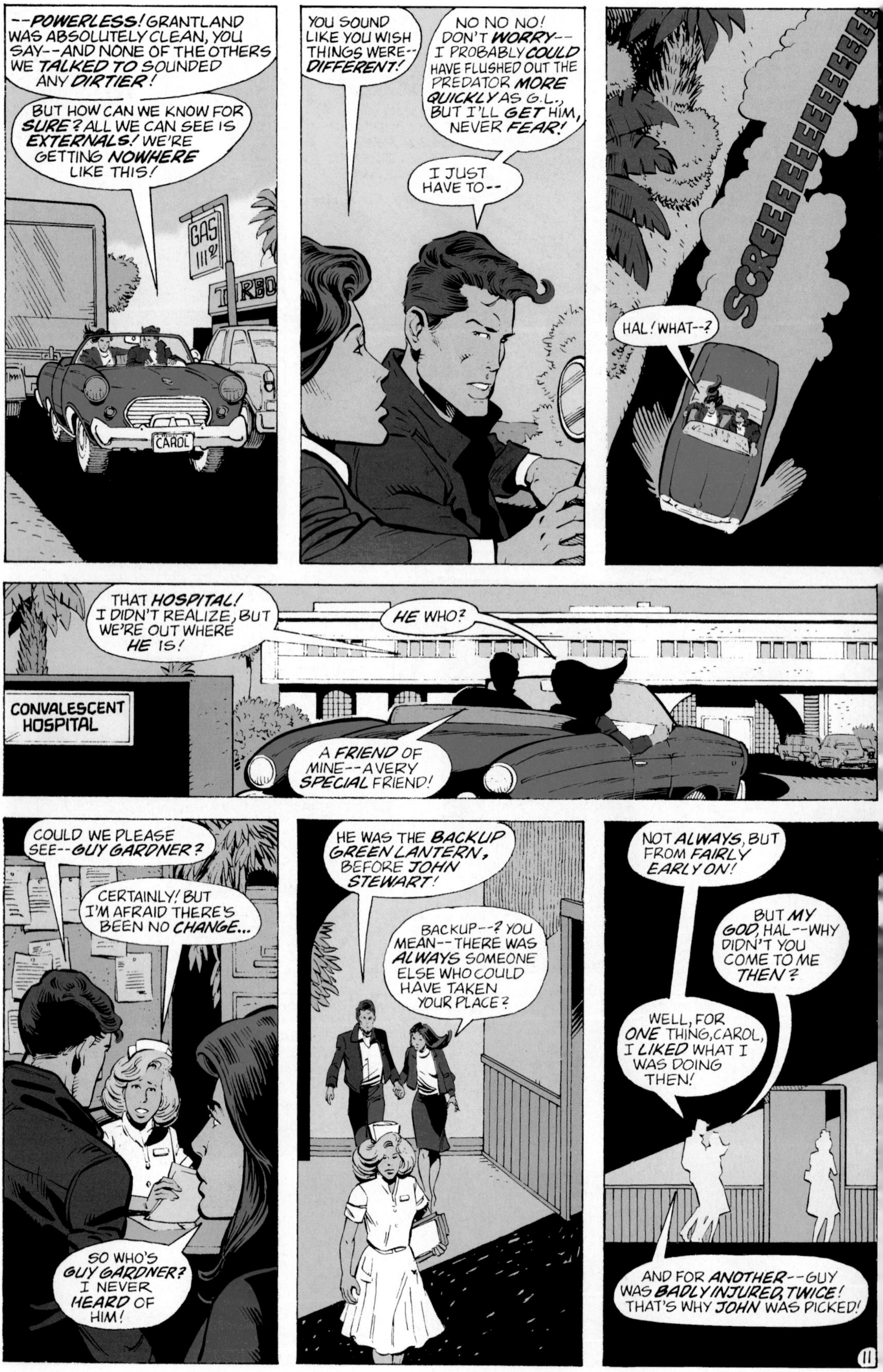
--POWERLESS! GRANTLAND WAS ABSOLUTELY CLEAN, YOU SAY--AND NONE OF THE OTHERS WE TALKED TO SOUNDED ANY DIRTIER!
BUT HOW CAN WE KNOW FOR SURE? ALL WE CAN SEE IS EXTERNALS! WE'RE GETTING NOWHERE LIKE THIS!
GAS 111 9/10
TURBO
CAROL
YOU SOUND LIKE YOU WISH THINGS WERE--DIFFERENT!
NO NO NO! DON'T WORRY--I PROBABLY COULD HAVE FLUSHED OUT THE PREDATOR MORE QUICKLY AS G.L., BUT I'LL GET HIM, NEVER FEAR!
I JUST HAVE TO--
SCREEEEEEEEEEEEE
HAL! WHAT--?
THAT HOSPITAL! I DIDN'T REALIZE, BUT WE'RE OUT WHERE HE IS!
HE WHO?
CONVALESCENT HOSPITAL
A FRIEND OF MINE--A VERY SPECIAL FRIEND!
COULD WE PLEASE SEE--GUY GARDNER?
CERTAINLY! BUT I'M AFRAID THERE'S BEEN NO CHANGE...
SO WHO'S GUY GARDNER? I NEVER HEARD OF HIM!
HE WAS THE BACKUP GREEN LANTERN, BEFORE JOHN STEWART!
BACKUP--? YOU MEAN--THERE WAS ALWAYS SOMEONE ELSE WHO COULD HAVE TAKEN YOUR PLACE?
NOT ALWAYS, BUT FROM FAIRLY EARLY ON!
BUT MY GOD, HAL--WHY DIDN'T YOU COME TO ME THEN?
WELL, FOR ONE THING, CAROL, I LIKED WHAT I WAS DOING THEN!
AND FOR ANOTHER--GUY WAS BADLY INJURED, TWICE! THAT'S WHY JOHN WAS PICKED!
11

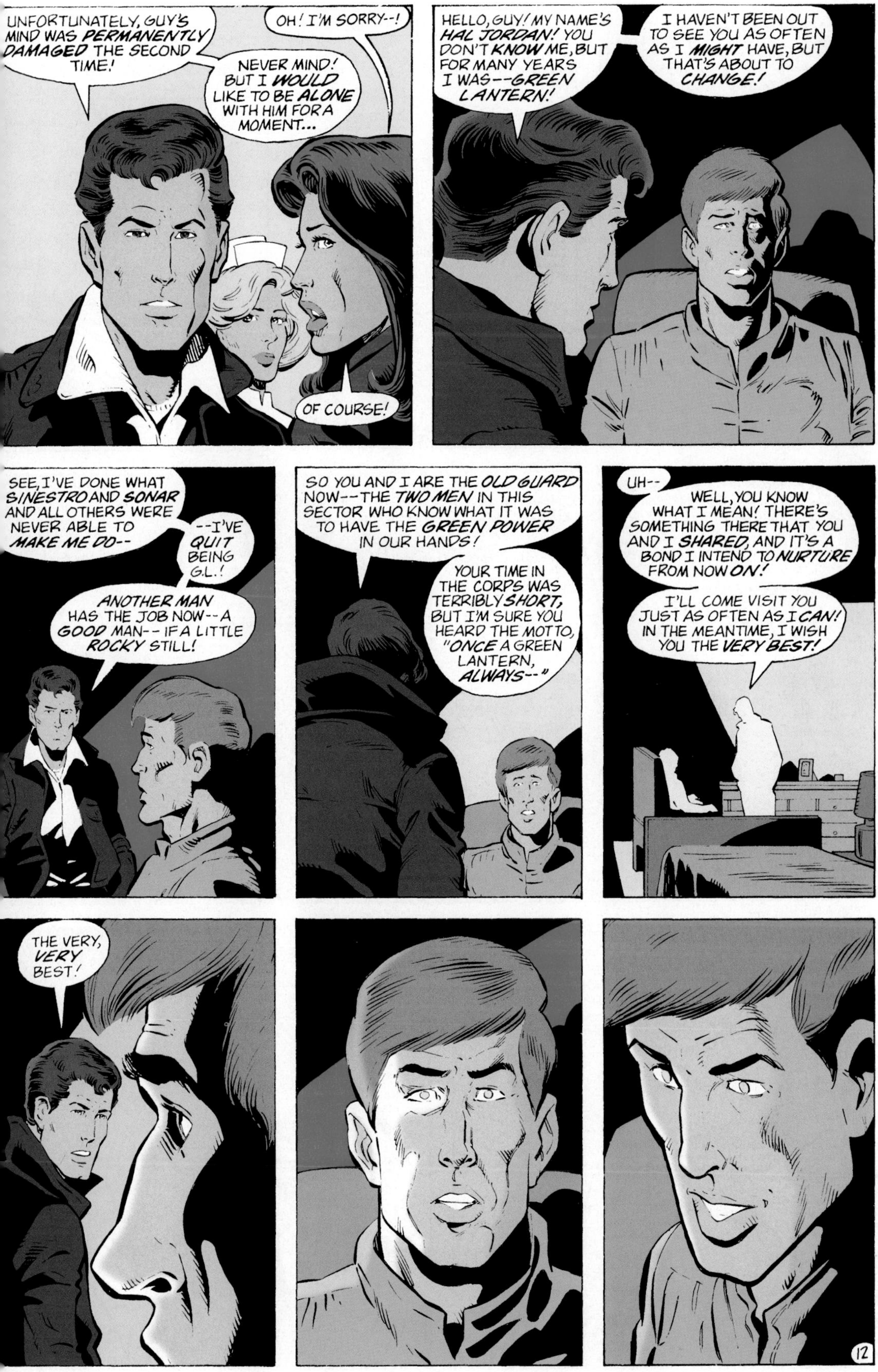
UNFORTUNATELY, GUY'S MIND WAS PERMANENTLY DAMAGED THE SECOND TIME!
OH! I'M SORRY--!
NEVER MIND! BUT I WOULD LIKE TO BE ALONE WITH HIM FOR A MOMENT...
OF COURSE!
HELLO, GUY! MY NAME'S HAL JORDAN! YOU DON'T KNOW ME, BUT FOR MANY YEARS I WAS--GREEN LANTERN!
I HAVEN'T BEEN OUT TO SEE YOU AS OFTEN AS I MIGHT HAVE, BUT THAT'S ABOUT TO CHANGE!
SEE, I'VE DONE WHAT SINESTRO AND SONAR AND ALL OTHERS WERE NEVER ABLE TO MAKE ME DO--
--I'VE QUIT BEING G.L.!
ANOTHER MAN HAS THE JOB NOW--A GOOD MAN-- IF A LITTLE ROCKY STILL!
SO YOU AND I ARE THE OLD GUARD NOW--THE TWO MEN IN THIS SECTOR WHO KNOW WHAT IT WAS TO HAVE THE GREEN POWER IN OUR HANDS!
YOUR TIME IN THE CORPS WAS TERRIBLY SHORT, BUT I'M SURE YOU HEARD THE MOTTO, "ONCE A GREEN LANTERN, ALWAYS--"
UH--
WELL, YOU KNOW WHAT I MEAN! THERE'S SOMETHING THERE THAT YOU AND I SHARED, AND IT'S A BOND I INTEND TO NURTURE FROM NOW ON!
I'LL COME VISIT YOU JUST AS OFTEN AS I CAN! IN THE MEANTIME, I WISH YOU THE VERY BEST!
THE VERY, VERY BEST!
12

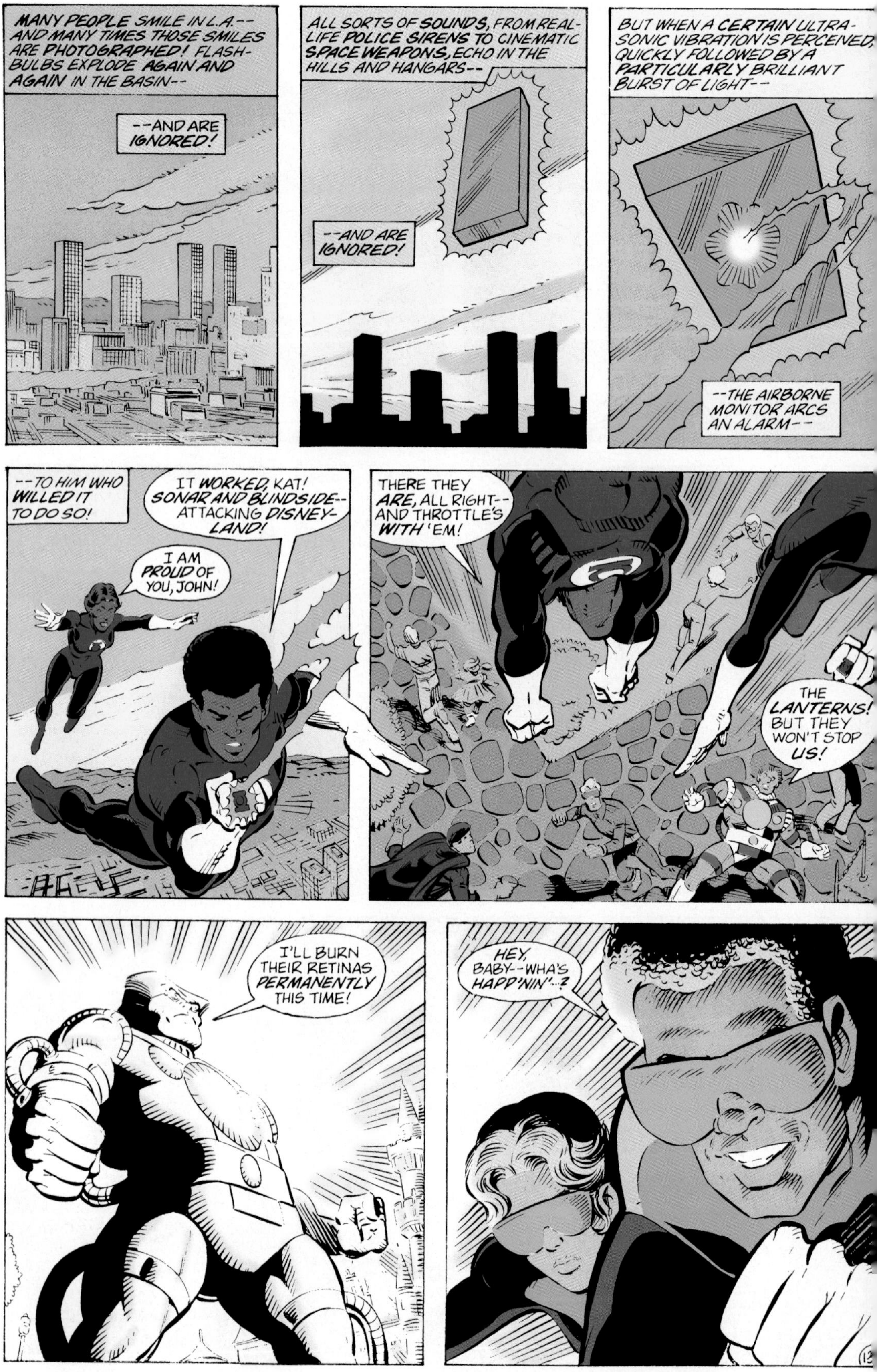
MANY PEOPLE SMILE IN L.A.-- AND MANY TIMES THOSE SMILES ARE PHOTOGRAPHED! FLASH-BULBS EXPLODE AGAIN AND AGAIN IN THE BASIN--
--AND ARE IGNORED!
ALL SORTS OF SOUNDS, FROM REAL-LIFE POLICE SIRENS TO CINEMATIC SPACE WEAPONS, ECHO IN THE HILLS AND HANGARS--
--AND ARE IGNORED!
BUT WHEN A CERTAIN ULTRA-SONIC VIBRATION IS PERCEIVED, QUICKLY FOLLOWED BY A PARTICULARLY BRILLIANT BURST OF LIGHT--
--THE AIRBORNE MONITOR ARCS AN ALARM--
--TO HIM WHO WILLED IT TO DO SO!
IT WORKED, KAT! SONAR AND BLINDSIDE-- ATTACKING DISNEY-LAND!
I AM PROUD OF YOU, JOHN!
THERE THEY ARE, ALL RIGHT-- AND THROTTLE'S WITH 'EM!
THE LANTERNS! BUT THEY WON'T STOP US!
I'LL BURN THEIR RETINAS PERMANENTLY THIS TIME!
HEY, BABY--WHA'S HAPP'NIN'...?
13

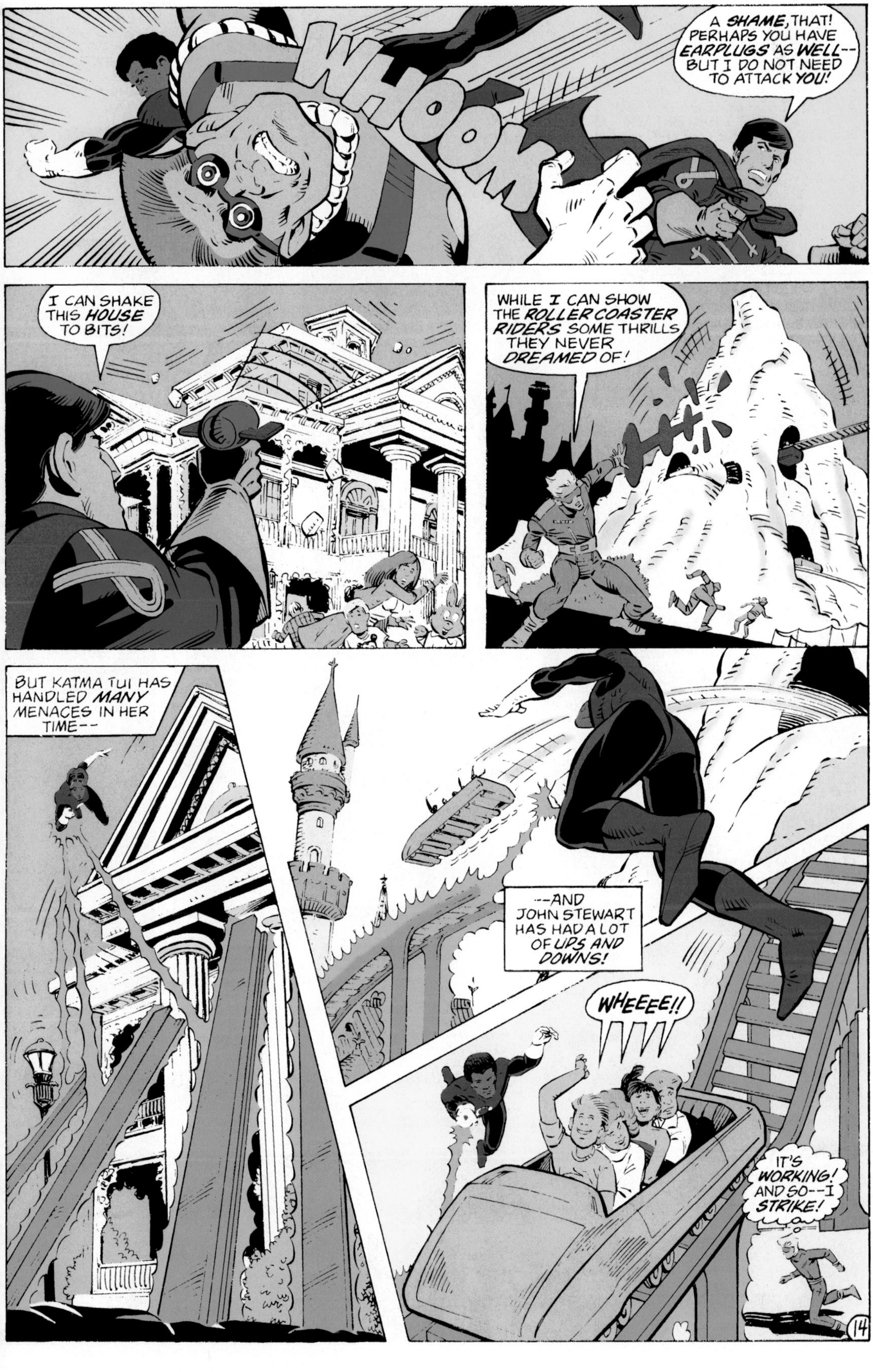

WHOOM
A SHAME, THAT! PERHAPS YOU HAVE EARPLUGS AS WELL-- BUT I DO NOT NEED TO ATTACK YOU!
I CAN SHAKE THIS HOUSE TO BITS!
WHILE I CAN SHOW THE ROLLER COASTER RIDERS SOME THRILLS THEY NEVER DREAMED OF!
BUT KATMA TUI HAS HANDLED MANY MENACES IN HER TIME--
--AND JOHN STEWART HAS HAD A LOT OF UPS AND DOWNS!
WHEEEE!!
IT'S WORKING! AND SO--I STRIKE!
14

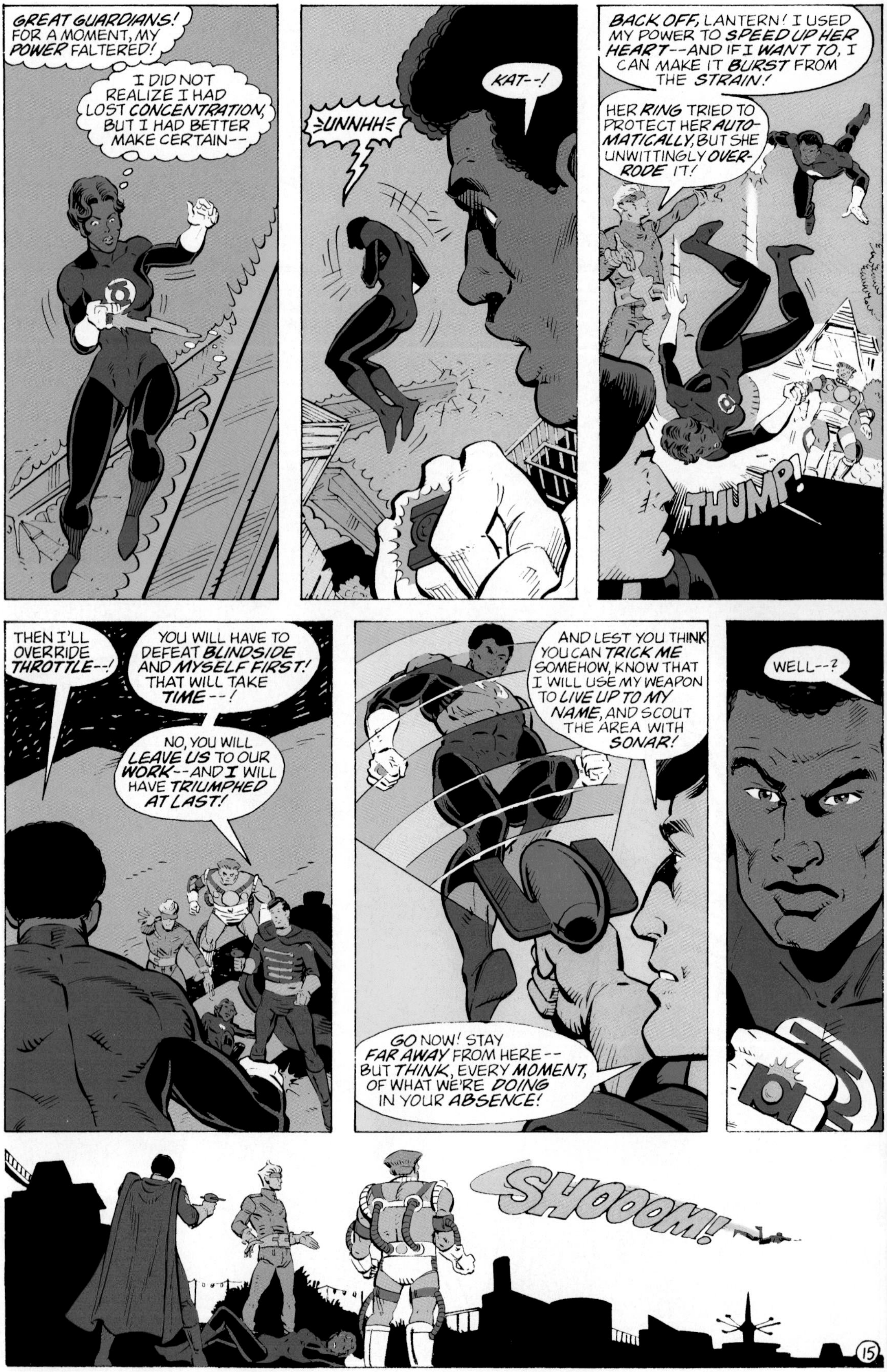
GREAT GUARDIANS! FOR A MOMENT, MY POWER FALTERED!
I DID NOT REALIZE I HAD LOST CONCENTRATION, BUT I HAD BETTER MAKE CERTAIN--
UNNHH
KAT--!
BACK OFF, LANTERN! I USED MY POWER TO SPEED UP HER HEART--AND IF I WANT TO, I CAN MAKE IT BURST FROM THE STRAIN!
HER RING TRIED TO PROTECT HER AUTOMATICALLY, BUT SHE UNWITTINGLY OVERRODE IT!
THUMP!
THEN I'LL OVERRIDE THROTTLE--!
YOU WILL HAVE TO DEFEAT BLINDSIDE AND MYSELF FIRST! THAT WILL TAKE TIME--!
NO, YOU WILL LEAVE US TO OUR WORK--AND I WILL HAVE TRIUMPHED AT LAST!
AND LEST YOU THINK YOU CAN TRICK ME SOMEHOW, KNOW THAT I WILL USE MY WEAPON TO LIVE UP TO MY NAME, AND SCOUT THE AREA WITH SONAR!
GO NOW! STAY FAR AWAY FROM HERE--BUT THINK, EVERY MOMENT, OF WHAT WE'RE DOING IN YOUR ABSENCE!
WELL--?
SHOOOM!
15

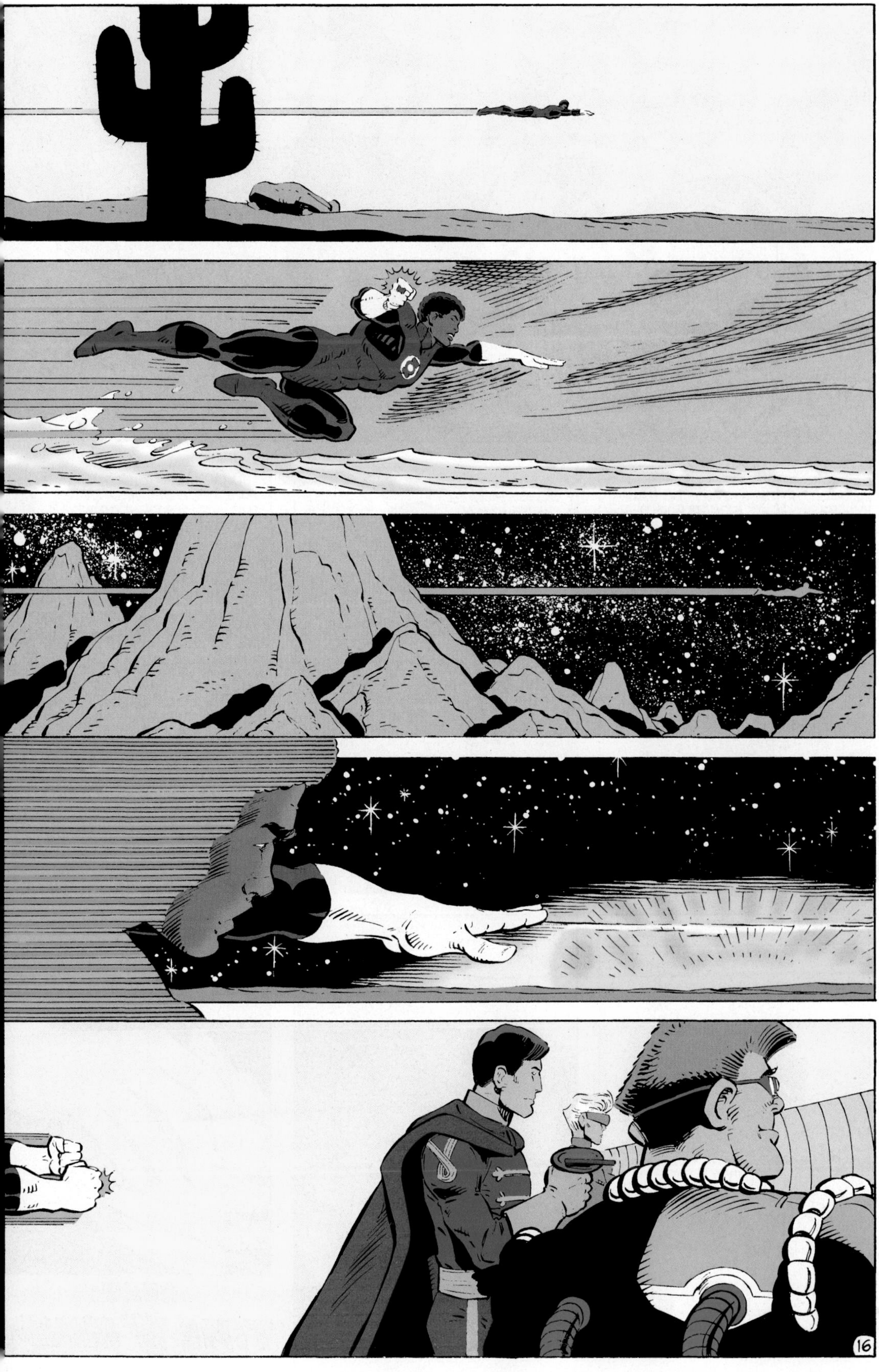
16

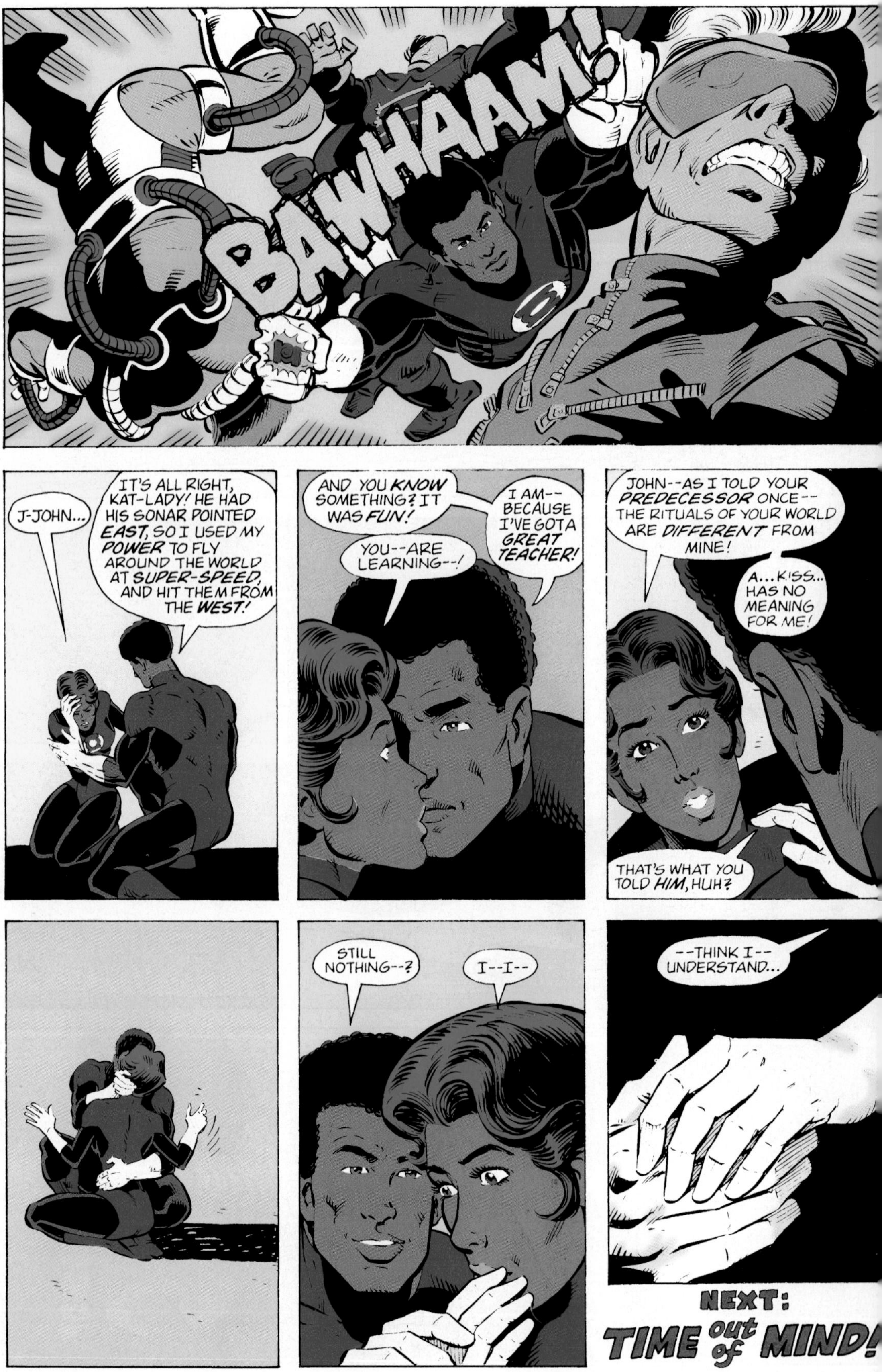
BAWHAAM!
J-JOHN...
IT'S ALL RIGHT, KAT-LADY! HE HAD HIS SONAR POINTED EAST, SO I USED MY POWER TO FLY AROUND THE WORLD AT SUPER-SPEED, AND HIT THEM FROM THE WEST!
AND YOU KNOW SOMETHING? IT WAS FUN!
YOU--ARE LEARNING--!
I AM--BECAUSE I'VE GOT A GREAT TEACHER!
JOHN--AS I TOLD YOUR PREDECESSOR ONCE--THE RITUALS OF YOUR WORLD ARE DIFFERENT FROM MINE!
A...KISS...HAS NO MEANING FOR ME!
THAT'S WHAT YOU TOLD HIM, HUH?
STILL NOTHING--?
I--I--
--THINK I--UNDERSTAND...
NEXT:
TIME out of MIND!

Cover art by Joe Staton & Bruce Patterson

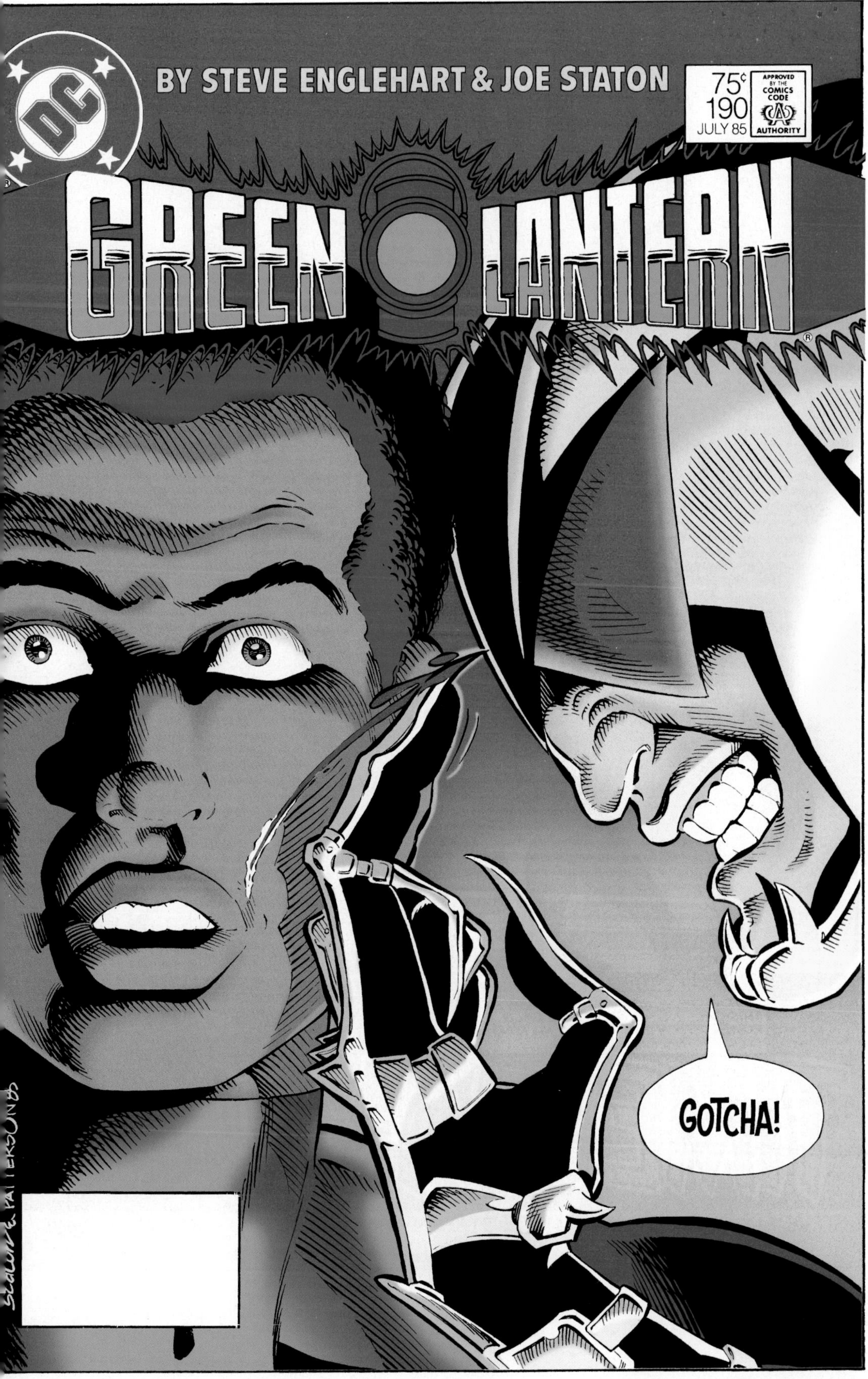
BY STEVE ENGLEHART & JOE STATON
75¢
190
JULY 85
APPROVED BY THE COMICS CODE AUTHORITY
GREEN LANTERN
GOTCHA!

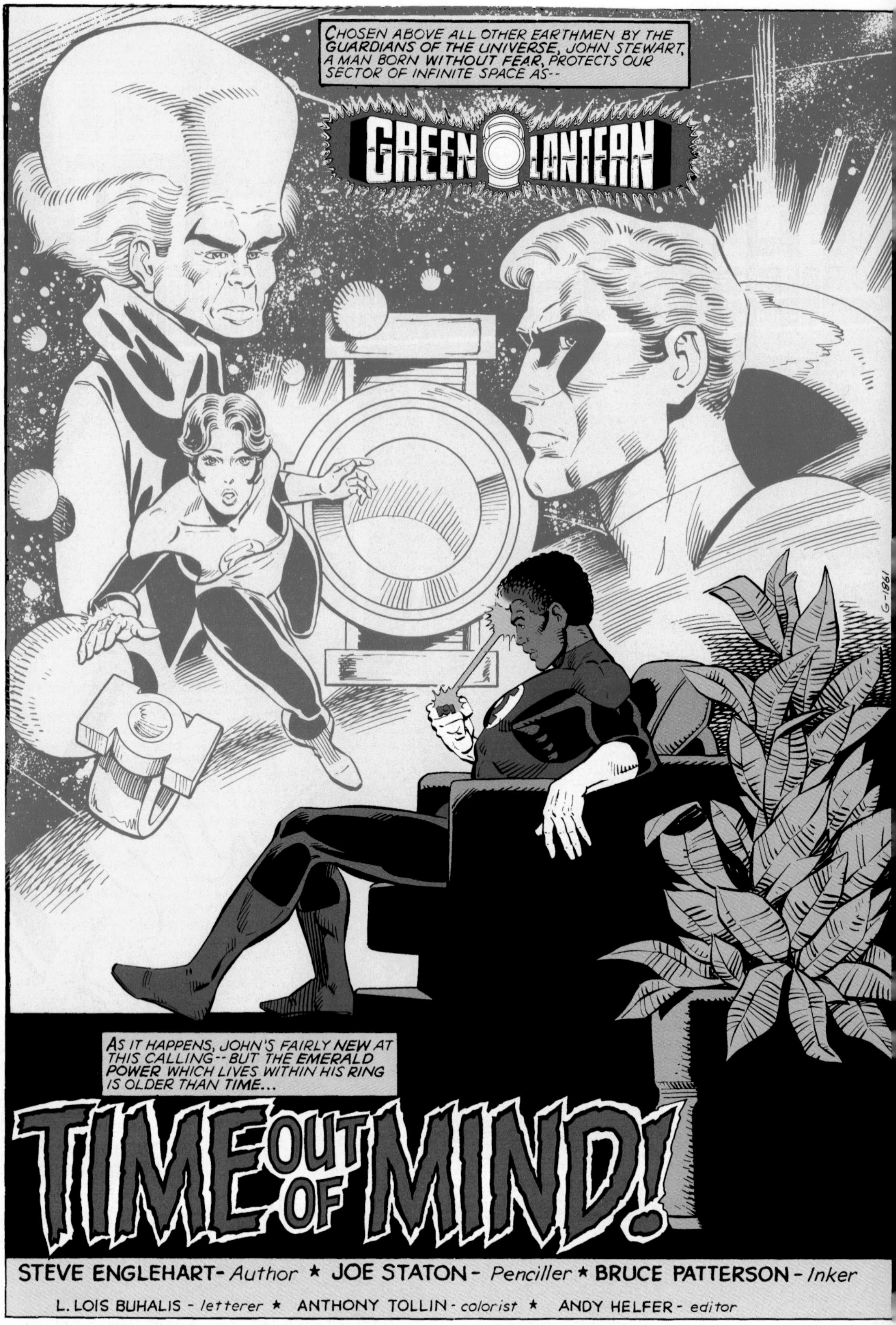

CHOSEN ABOVE ALL OTHER EARTHMEN BY THE GUARDIANS OF THE UNIVERSE, JOHN STEWART, A MAN BORN WITHOUT FEAR, PROTECTS OUR SECTOR OF INFINITE SPACE AS--
GREEN LANTERN
G-1861
AS IT HAPPENS, JOHN'S FAIRLY NEW AT THIS CALLING--BUT THE EMERALD POWER WHICH LIVES WITHIN HIS RING IS OLDER THAN TIME...
TIME OUT OF MIND!
STEVE ENGLEHART-Author ★ JOE STATON-Penciller ★ BRUCE PATTERSON-Inker
L. LOIS BUHALIS-letterer ★ ANTHONY TOLLIN-colorist ★ ANDY HELFER-editor

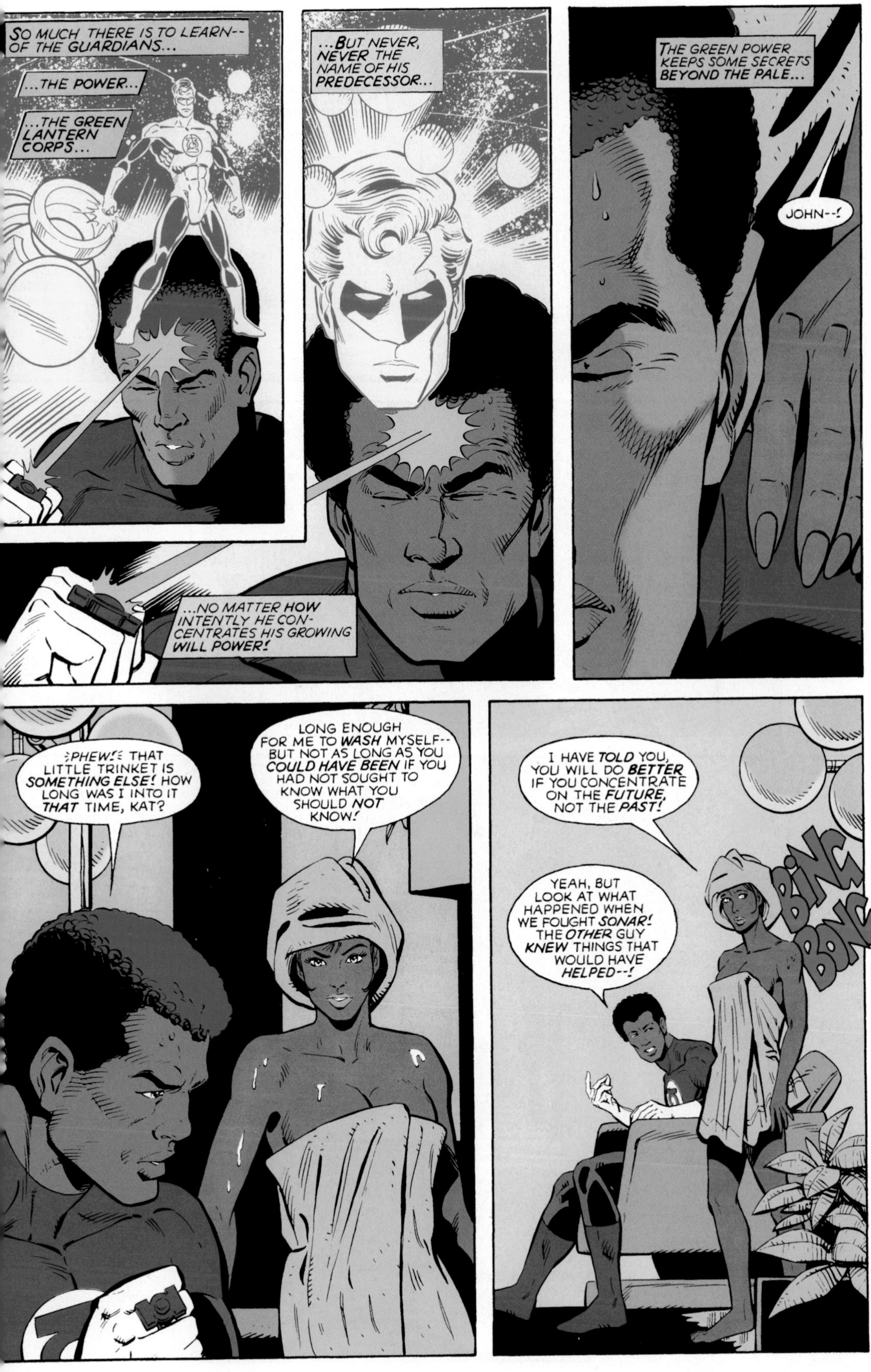
SO MUCH THERE IS TO LEARN-- OF THE GUARDIANS...
...THE POWER...
...THE GREEN LANTERN CORPS...
...BUT NEVER, NEVER THE NAME OF HIS PREDECESSOR...
...NO MATTER HOW INTENTLY HE CONCENTRATES HIS GROWING WILL POWER!
THE GREEN POWER KEEPS SOME SECRETS BEYOND THE PALE...
JOHN--!
PHEW! THAT LITTLE TRINKET IS SOMETHING ELSE! HOW LONG WAS I INTO IT THAT TIME, KAT?
LONG ENOUGH FOR ME TO WASH MYSELF-- BUT NOT AS LONG AS YOU COULD HAVE BEEN IF YOU HAD NOT SOUGHT TO KNOW WHAT YOU SHOULD NOT KNOW!
I HAVE TOLD YOU, YOU WILL DO BETTER IF YOU CONCENTRATE ON THE FUTURE, NOT THE PAST!
YEAH, BUT LOOK AT WHAT HAPPENED WHEN WE FOUGHT SONAR! THE OTHER GUY KNEW THINGS THAT WOULD HAVE HELPED--!
BING BONG

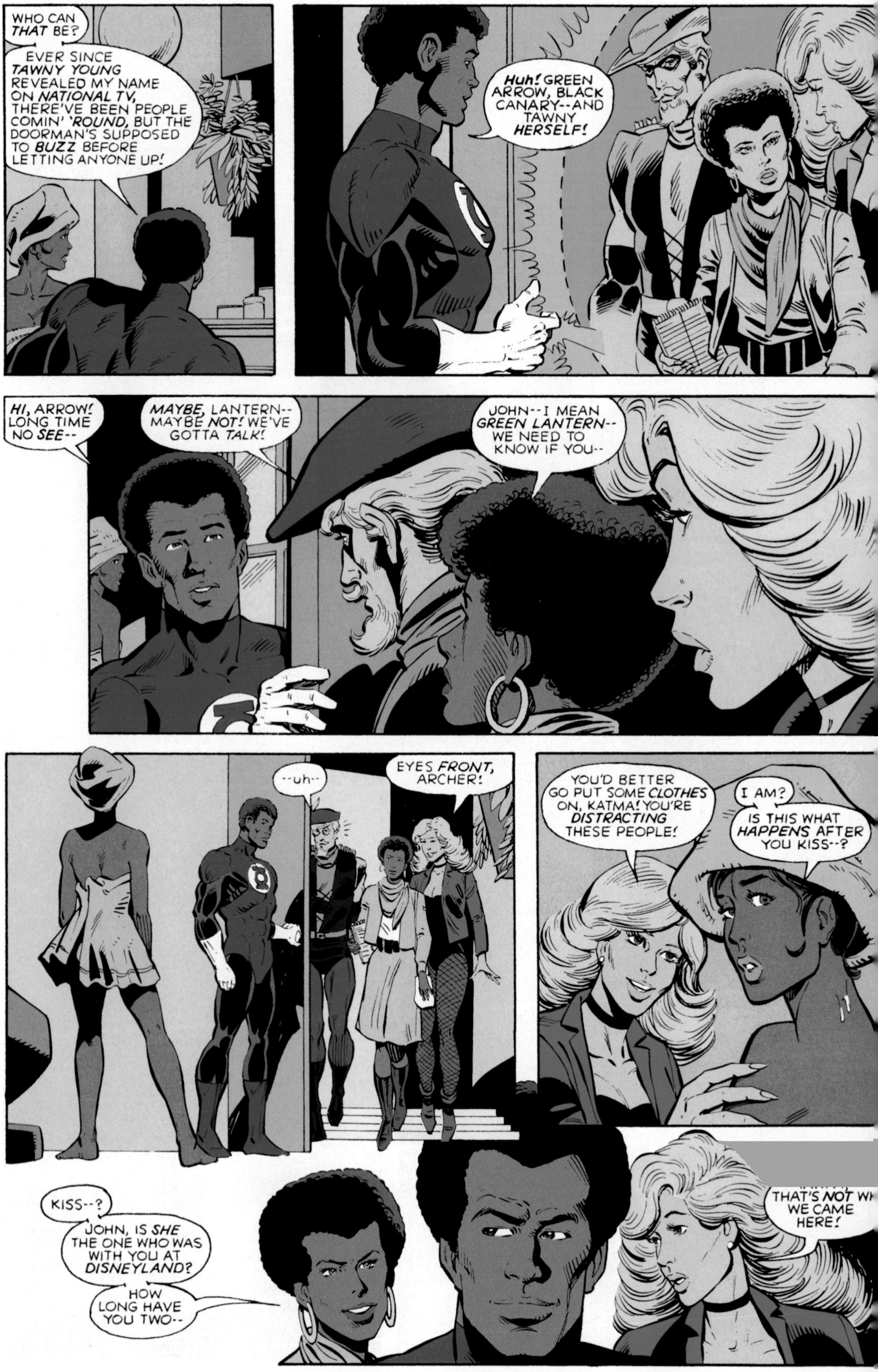
WHO CAN THAT BE?
EVER SINCE TAWNY YOUNG REVEALED MY NAME ON NATIONAL TV, THERE'VE BEEN PEOPLE COMIN' 'ROUND, BUT THE DOORMAN'S SUPPOSED TO BUZZ BEFORE LETTING ANYONE UP!
Huh! GREEN ARROW, BLACK CANARY--AND TAWNY HERSELF!
HI, ARROW! LONG TIME NO SEE--
MAYBE, LANTERN--MAYBE NOT! WE'VE GOTTA TALK!
JOHN--I MEAN GREEN LANTERN--WE NEED TO KNOW IF YOU--
--uh--
EYES FRONT, ARCHER!
YOU'D BETTER GO PUT SOME CLOTHES ON, KATMA! YOU'RE DISTRACTING THESE PEOPLE!
I AM?
IS THIS WHAT HAPPENS AFTER YOU KISS--?
KISS--?
JOHN, IS SHE THE ONE WHO WAS WITH YOU AT DISNEYLAND?
HOW LONG HAVE YOU TWO--
THAT'S NOT W WE CAME HERE!

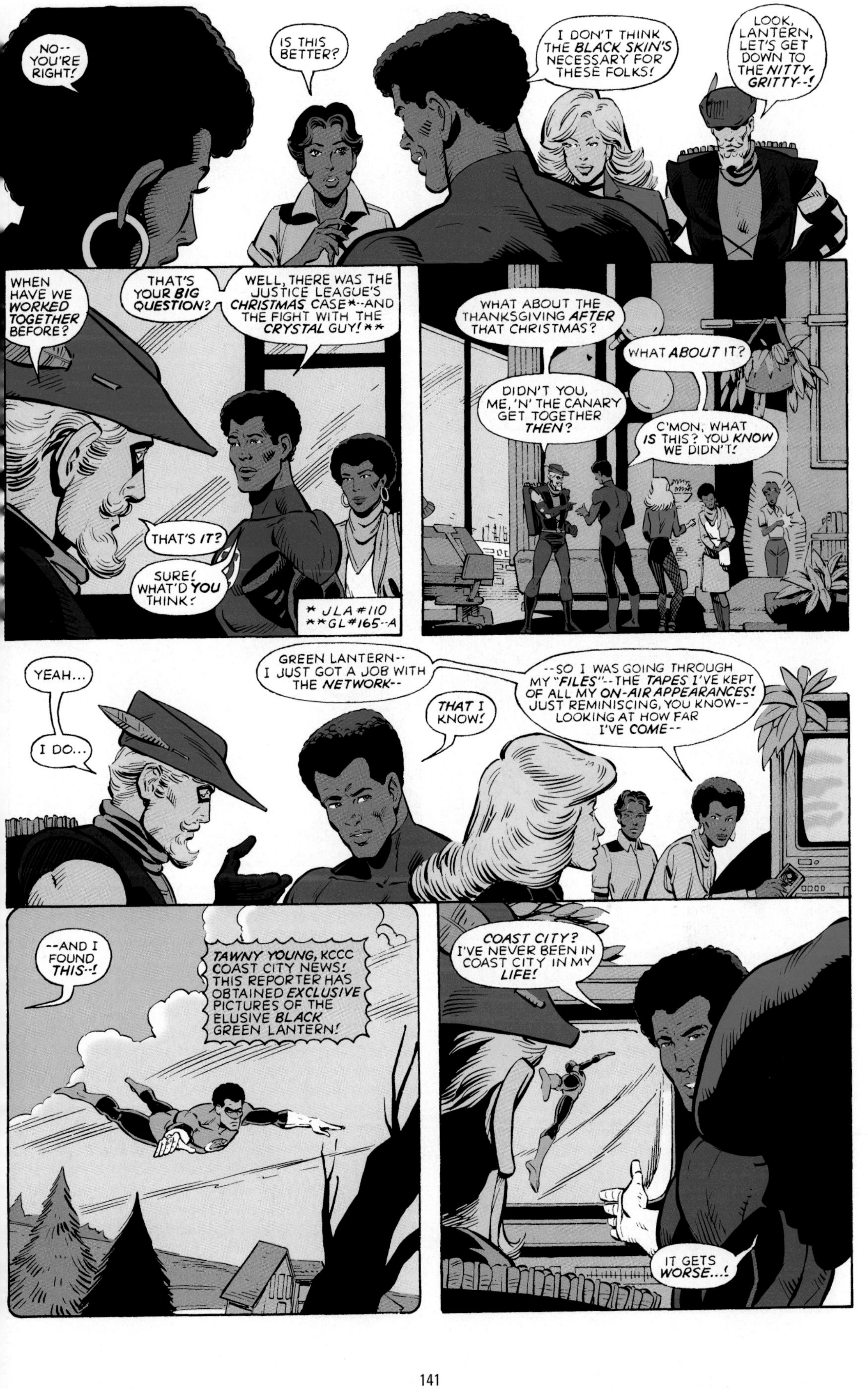
NO-- YOU'RE RIGHT!
IS THIS BETTER?
I DON'T THINK THE BLACK SKIN'S NECESSARY FOR THESE FOLKS!
LOOK, LANTERN, LET'S GET DOWN TO THE NITTY-GRITTY--!
WHEN HAVE WE WORKED TOGETHER BEFORE?
THAT'S YOUR BIG QUESTION?
WELL, THERE WAS THE JUSTICE LEAGUE'S CHRISTMAS CASE*--AND THE FIGHT WITH THE CRYSTAL GUY!**
THAT'S IT?
SURE! WHAT'D YOU THINK?
* JLA #110 **GL #165--A
WHAT ABOUT THE THANKSGIVING AFTER THAT CHRISTMAS?
WHAT ABOUT IT?
DIDN'T YOU, ME, 'N' THE CANARY GET TOGETHER THEN?
C'MON, WHAT IS THIS? YOU KNOW WE DIDN'T!
YEAH...
I DO...
GREEN LANTERN-- I JUST GOT A JOB WITH THE NETWORK--
THAT I KNOW!
--SO I WAS GOING THROUGH MY "FILES"--THE TAPES I'VE KEPT OF ALL MY ON-AIR APPEARANCES! JUST REMINISCING, YOU KNOW-- LOOKING AT HOW FAR I'VE COME--
--AND I FOUND THIS--!
TAWNY YOUNG, KCCC COAST CITY NEWS! THIS REPORTER HAS OBTAINED EXCLUSIVE PICTURES OF THE ELUSIVE BLACK GREEN LANTERN!
COAST CITY? I'VE NEVER BEEN IN COAST CITY IN MY LIFE!
IT GETS WORSE...!

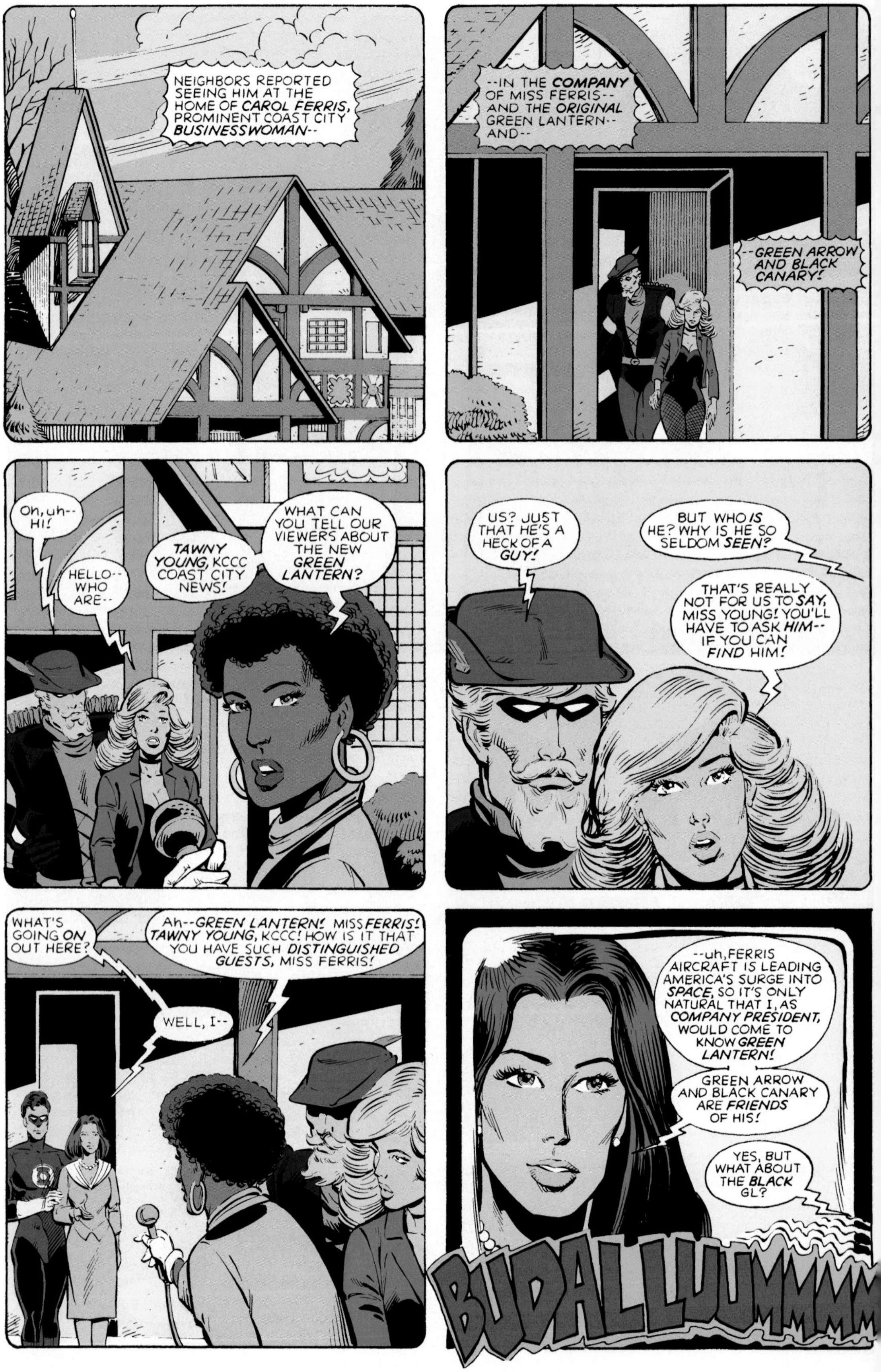
NEIGHBORS REPORTED SEEING HIM AT THE HOME OF CAROL FERRIS, PROMINENT COAST CITY BUSINESSWOMAN--
--IN THE COMPANY OF MISS FERRIS-- AND THE ORIGINAL GREEN LANTERN-- AND--
--GREEN ARROW AND BLACK CANARY!
Oh, uh-- HI!
HELLO-- WHO ARE--
TAWNY YOUNG, KCCC COAST CITY NEWS!
WHAT CAN YOU TELL OUR VIEWERS ABOUT THE NEW GREEN LANTERN?
US? JUST THAT HE'S A HECK OF A GUY!
BUT WHO IS HE? WHY IS HE SO SELDOM SEEN?
THAT'S REALLY NOT FOR US TO SAY, MISS YOUNG! YOU'LL HAVE TO ASK HIM-- IF YOU CAN FIND HIM!
WHAT'S GOING ON OUT HERE?
Ah--GREEN LANTERN! MISS FERRIS! TAWNY YOUNG, KCCC! HOW IS IT THAT YOU HAVE SUCH DISTINGUISHED GUESTS, MISS FERRIS!
WELL, I--
--uh, FERRIS AIRCRAFT IS LEADING AMERICA'S SURGE INTO SPACE, SO IT'S ONLY NATURAL THAT I, AS COMPANY PRESIDENT, WOULD COME TO KNOW GREEN LANTERN!
GREEN ARROW AND BLACK CANARY ARE FRIENDS OF HIS!
YES, BUT WHAT ABOUT THE BLACK GL?
BUDALLUUMMMM

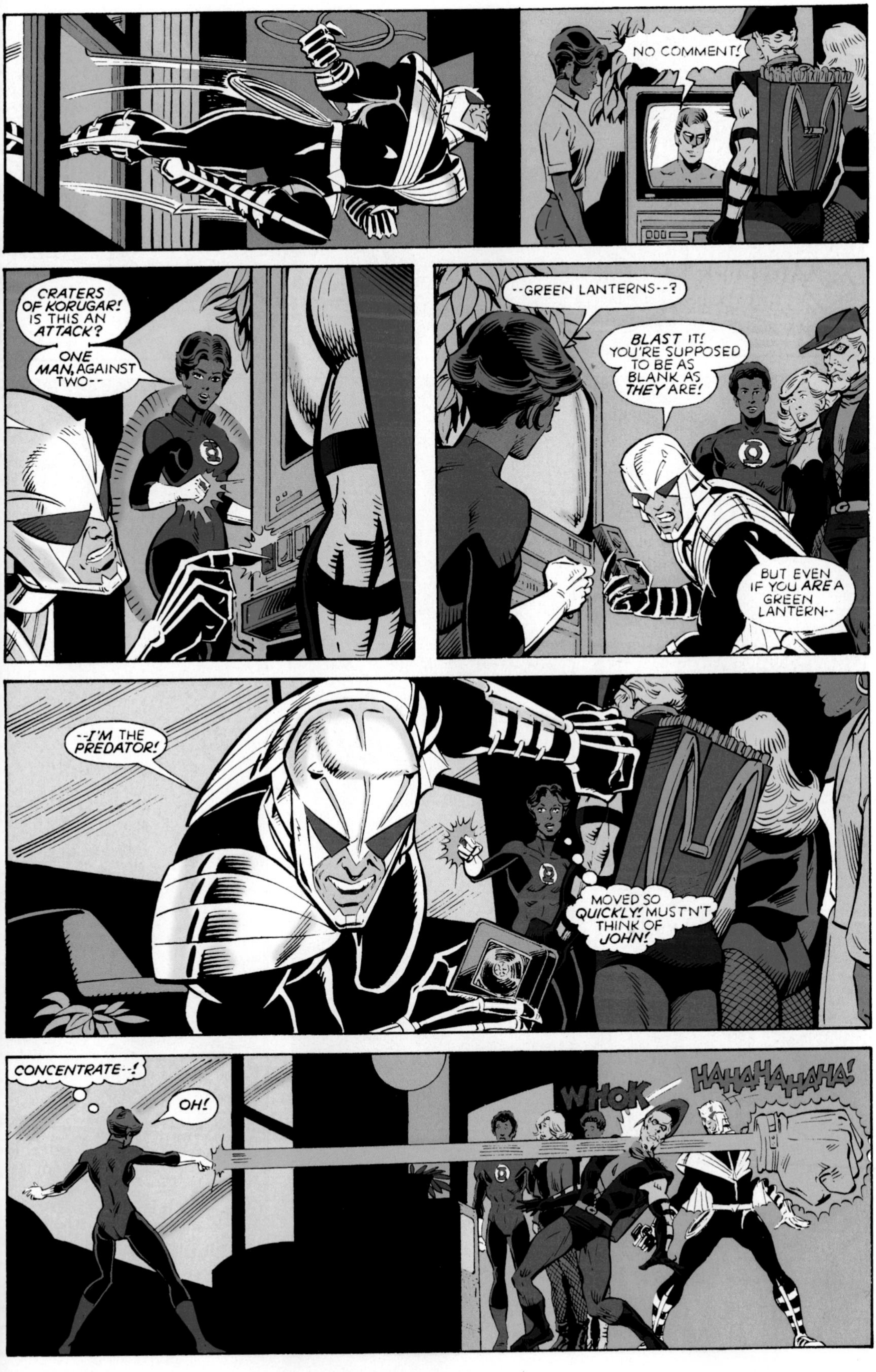
NO COMMENT!
CRATERS OF KORUGAR! IS THIS AN ATTACK?
ONE MAN, AGAINST TWO--
--GREEN LANTERNS--?
BLAST IT! YOU'RE SUPPOSED TO BE AS BLANK AS THEY ARE!
BUT EVEN IF YOU ARE A GREEN LANTERN--
--I'M THE PREDATOR!
MOVED SO QUICKLY! MUSTN'T THINK OF JOHN!
CONCENTRATE--!
OH!
WHOK
HAHAHAHAHAHA!

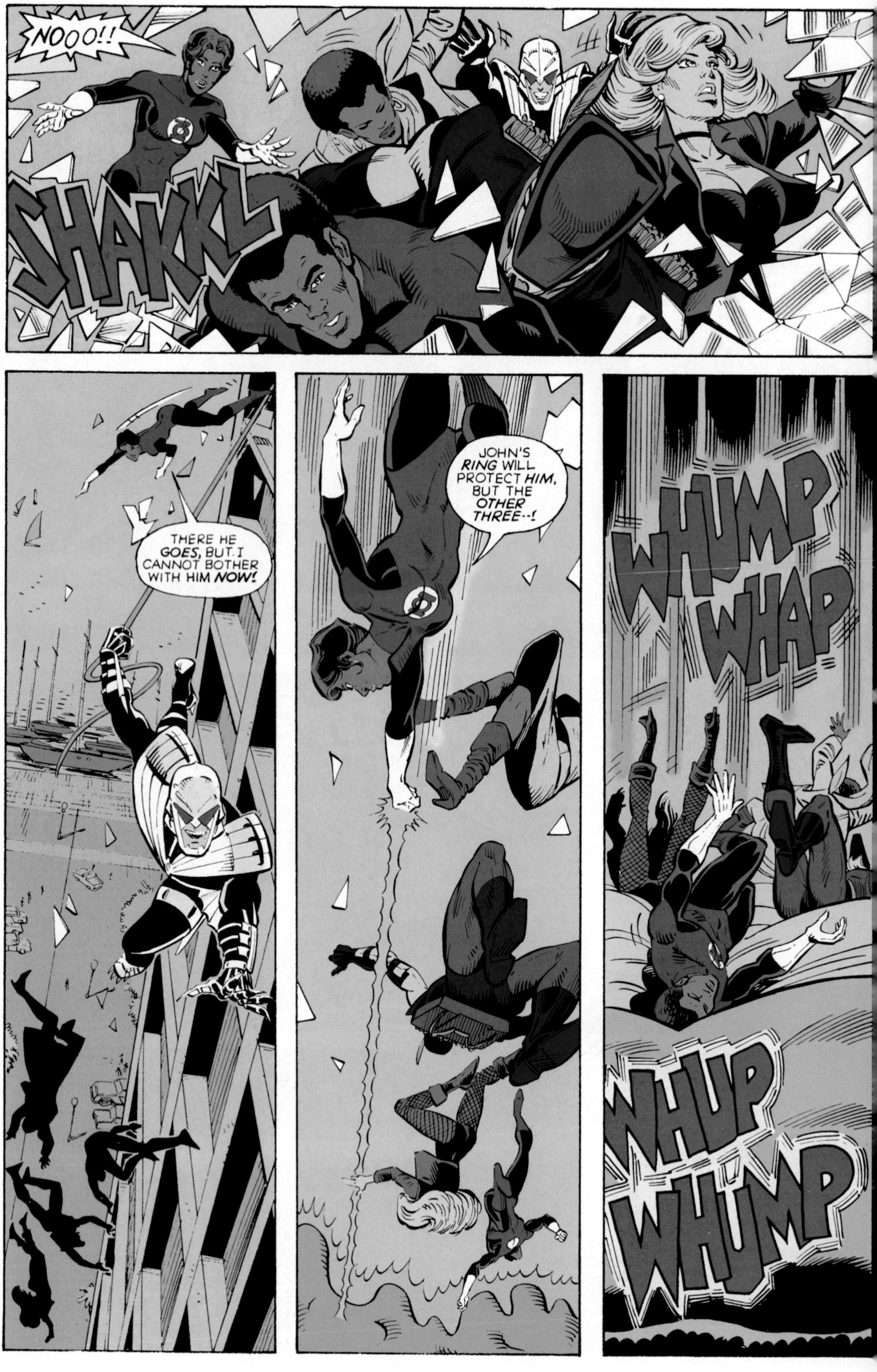
NOOO!!
SHAKKL
THERE HE GOES, BUT I CANNOT BOTHER WITH HIM NOW!
JOHN'S RING WILL PROTECT HIM, BUT THE OTHER THREE--!
WHUMP
WHAP
WHUP
WHUMP
WHUMP

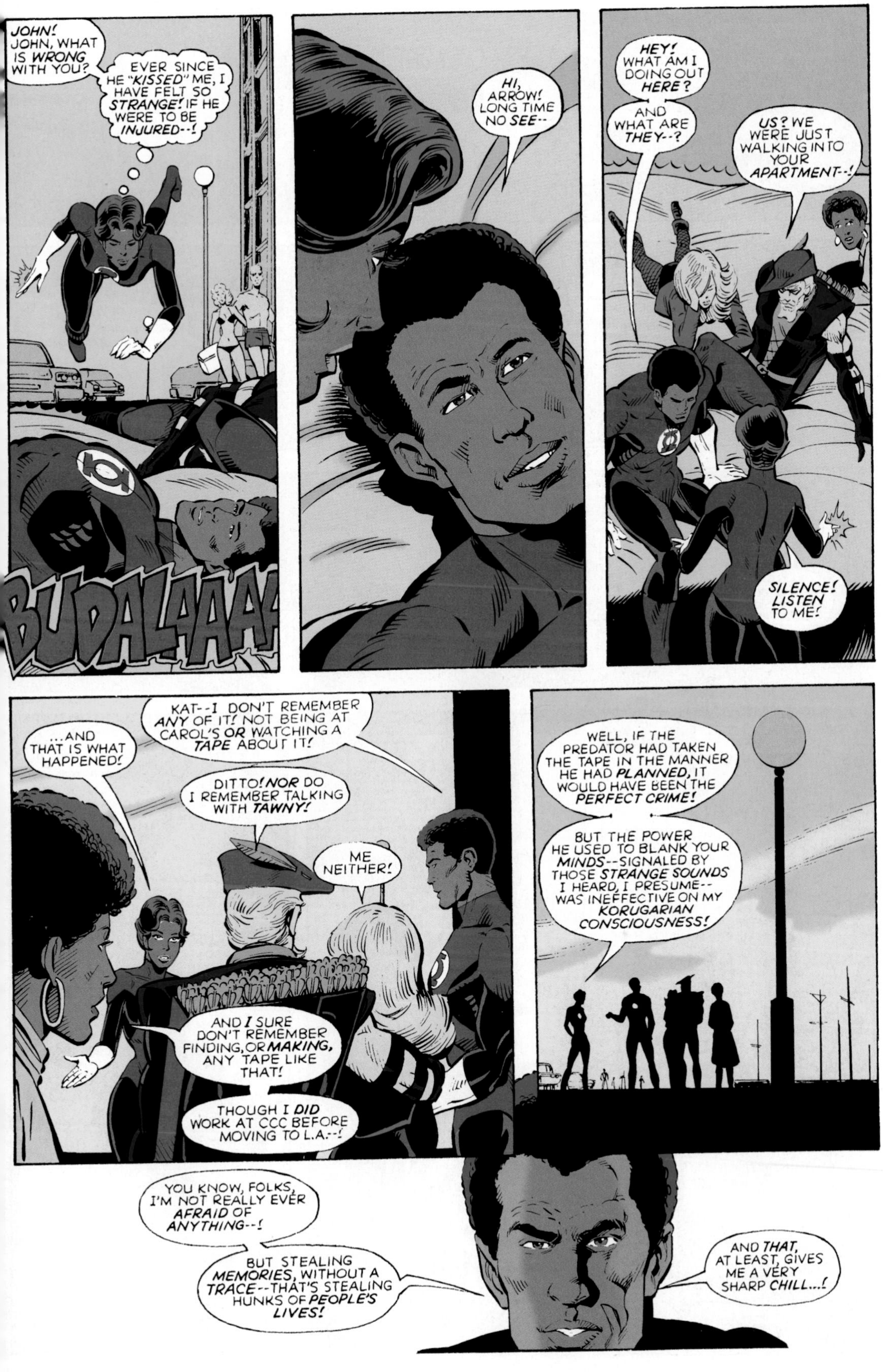

JOHN! JOHN, WHAT IS WRONG WITH YOU?
EVER SINCE HE "KISSED" ME, I HAVE FELT SO STRANGE! IF HE WERE TO BE INJURED--!
BUDALAAAA
HI, ARROW! LONG TIME NO SEE--
HEY! WHAT AM I DOING OUT HERE?
AND WHAT ARE THEY--?
US? WE WERE JUST WALKING INTO YOUR APARTMENT--!
SILENCE! LISTEN TO ME!
...AND THAT IS WHAT HAPPENED!
KAT--I DON'T REMEMBER ANY OF IT! NOT BEING AT CAROL'S OR WATCHING A TAPE ABOUT IT!
DITTO! NOR DO I REMEMBER TALKING WITH TAWNY!
ME NEITHER!
AND I SURE DON'T REMEMBER FINDING, OR MAKING, ANY TAPE LIKE THAT!
THOUGH I DID WORK AT CCC BEFORE MOVING TO L.A.--!
WELL, IF THE PREDATOR HAD TAKEN THE TAPE IN THE MANNER HE HAD PLANNED, IT WOULD HAVE BEEN THE PERFECT CRIME!
BUT THE POWER HE USED TO BLANK YOUR MINDS--SIGNALED BY THOSE STRANGE SOUNDS I HEARD, I PRESUME--WAS INEFFECTIVE ON MY KORUGARIAN CONSCIOUSNESS!
YOU KNOW, FOLKS, I'M NOT REALLY EVER AFRAID OF ANYTHING--!
BUT STEALING MEMORIES, WITHOUT A TRACE--THAT'S STEALING HUNKS OF PEOPLE'S LIVES!
AND THAT, AT LEAST, GIVES ME A VERY SHARP CHILL...!

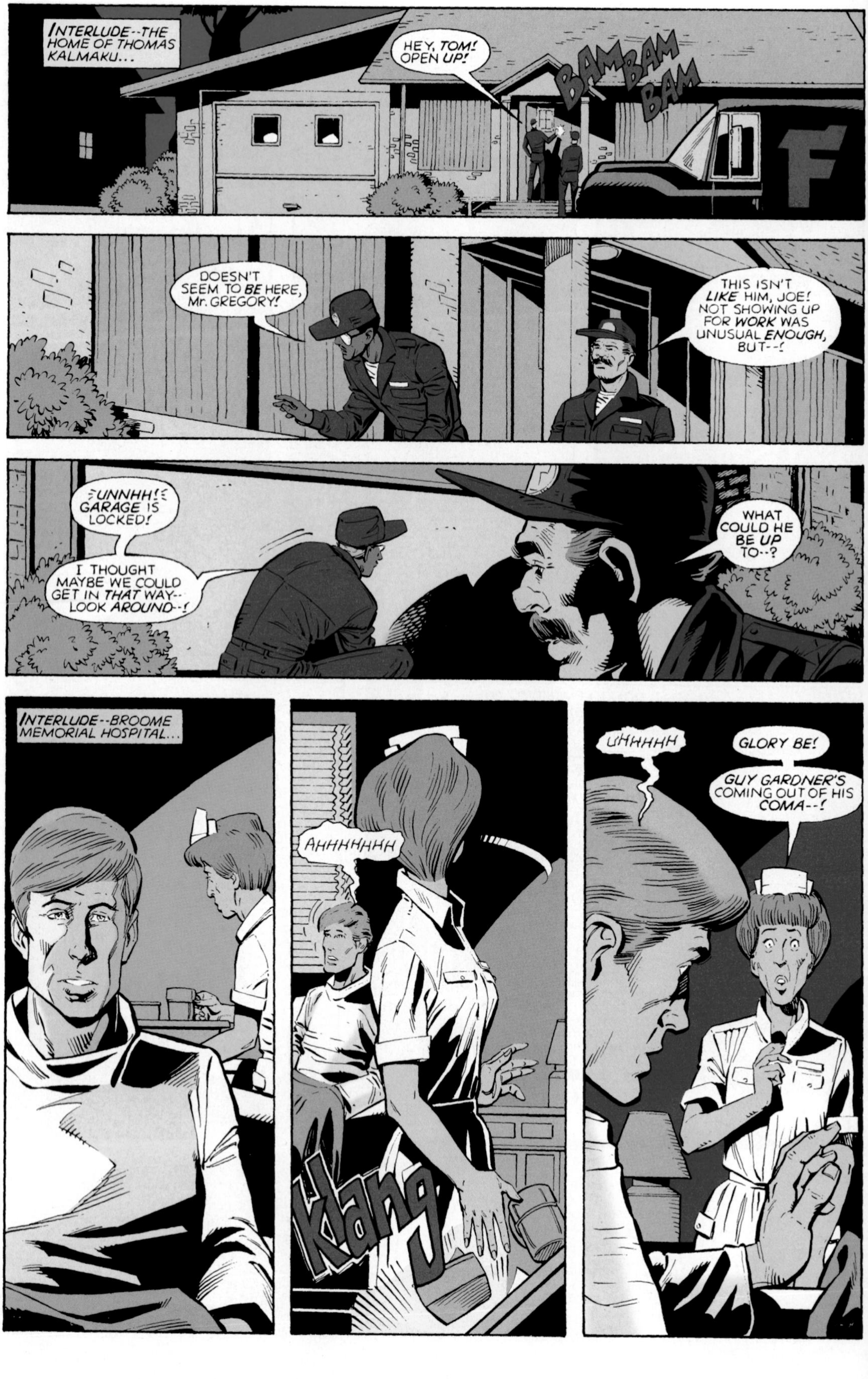
INTERLUDE--THE HOME OF THOMAS KALMAKU...
HEY, TOM! OPEN UP!
BAMBAMBAM
DOESN'T SEEM TO BE HERE, Mr. GREGORY!
THIS ISN'T LIKE HIM, JOE! NOT SHOWING UP FOR WORK WAS UNUSUAL ENOUGH, BUT--!
UNNHH! GARAGE IS LOCKED!
I THOUGHT MAYBE WE COULD GET IN THAT WAY-- LOOK AROUND--!
WHAT COULD HE BE UP TO--?
INTERLUDE--BROOME MEMORIAL HOSPITAL...
AHHHHHHH
KLANG
UHHHHH
GLORY BE!
GUY GARDNER'S COMING OUT OF HIS COMA--!

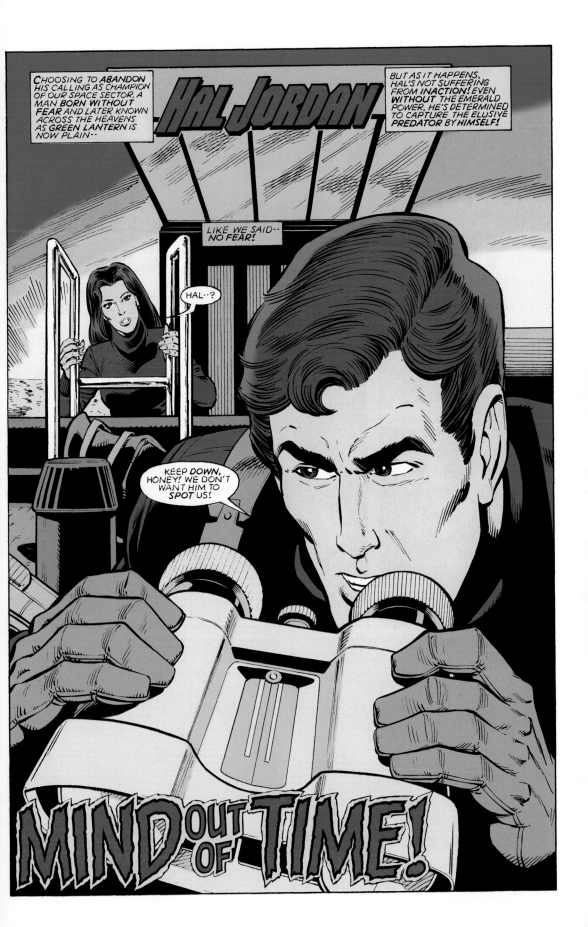

CHOOSING TO ABANDON HIS CALLING AS CHAMPION OF OUR SPACE SECTOR, A MAN BORN WITHOUT FEAR AND LATER KNOWN ACROSS THE HEAVENS AS GREEN LANTERN IS NOW PLAIN--

HAL JORDAN

BUT AS IT HAPPENS, HAL'S NOT SUFFERING FROM INACTION! EVEN WITHOUT THE EMERALD POWER, HE'S DETERMINED TO CAPTURE THE ELUSIVE PREDATOR BY HIMSELF!

LIKE WE SAID-- NO FEAR!

HAL--?

KEEP DOWN, HONEY! WE DON'T WANT HIM TO SPOT US!

MIND OUT OF TIME!

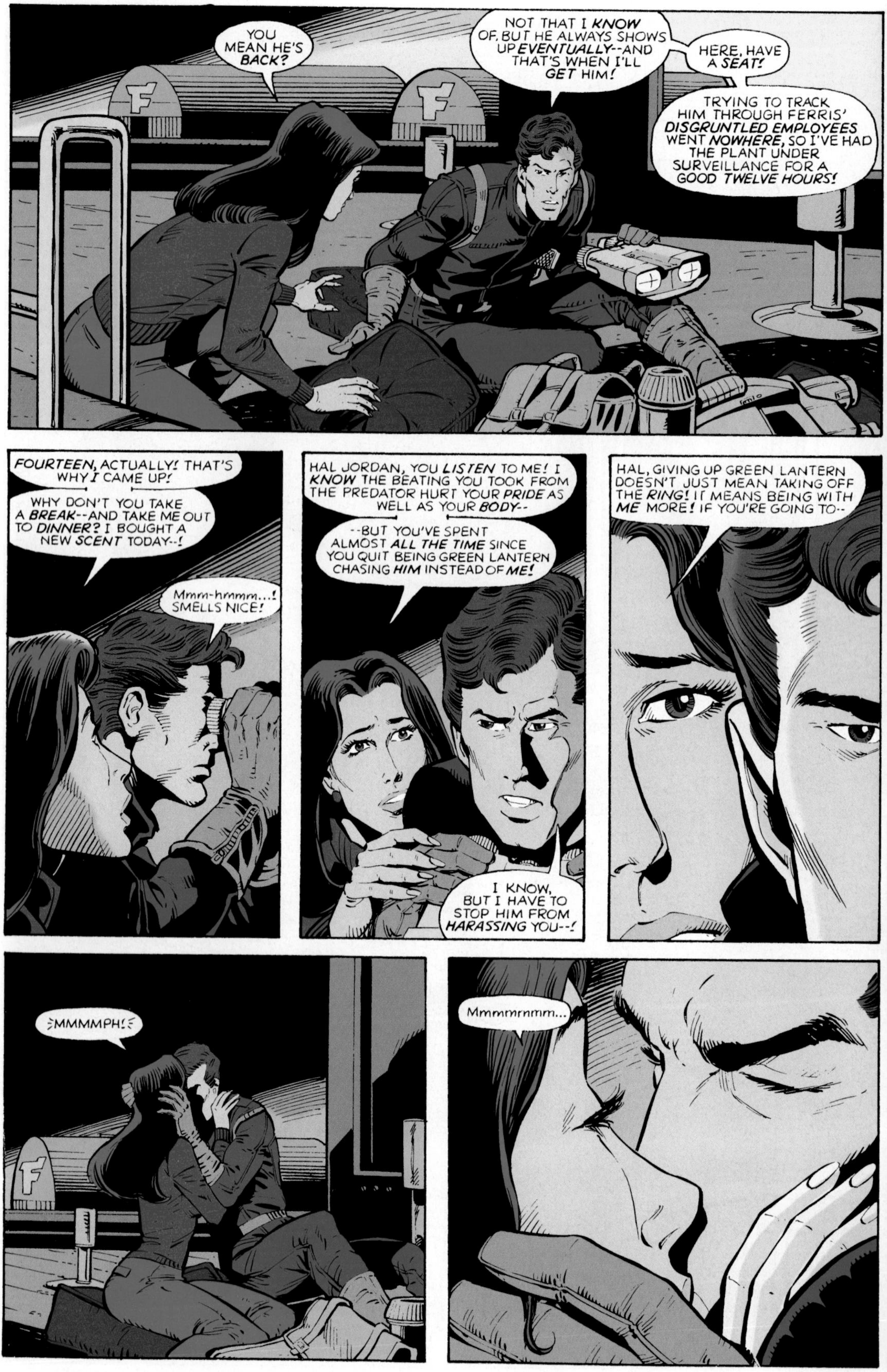
YOU MEAN HE'S BACK?
NOT THAT I KNOW OF, BUT HE ALWAYS SHOWS UP EVENTUALLY--AND THAT'S WHEN I'LL GET HIM!
HERE, HAVE A SEAT!
TRYING TO TRACK HIM THROUGH FERRIS' DISGRUNTLED EMPLOYEES WENT NOWHERE, SO I'VE HAD THE PLANT UNDER SURVEILLANCE FOR A GOOD TWELVE HOURS!
FOURTEEN, ACTUALLY! THAT'S WHY I CAME UP!
WHY DON'T YOU TAKE A BREAK--AND TAKE ME OUT TO DINNER? I BOUGHT A NEW SCENT TODAY--!
Mmm-hmmm...! SMELLS NICE!
HAL JORDAN, YOU LISTEN TO ME! I KNOW THE BEATING YOU TOOK FROM THE PREDATOR HURT YOUR PRIDE AS WELL AS YOUR BODY--
--BUT YOU'VE SPENT ALMOST ALL THE TIME SINCE YOU QUIT BEING GREEN LANTERN CHASING HIM INSTEAD OF ME!
I KNOW, BUT I HAVE TO STOP HIM FROM HARASSING YOU--!
HAL, GIVING UP GREEN LANTERN DOESN'T JUST MEAN TAKING OFF THE RING! IT MEANS BEING WITH ME MORE! IF YOU'RE GOING TO--
MMMMPH!
Mmmmmmm...

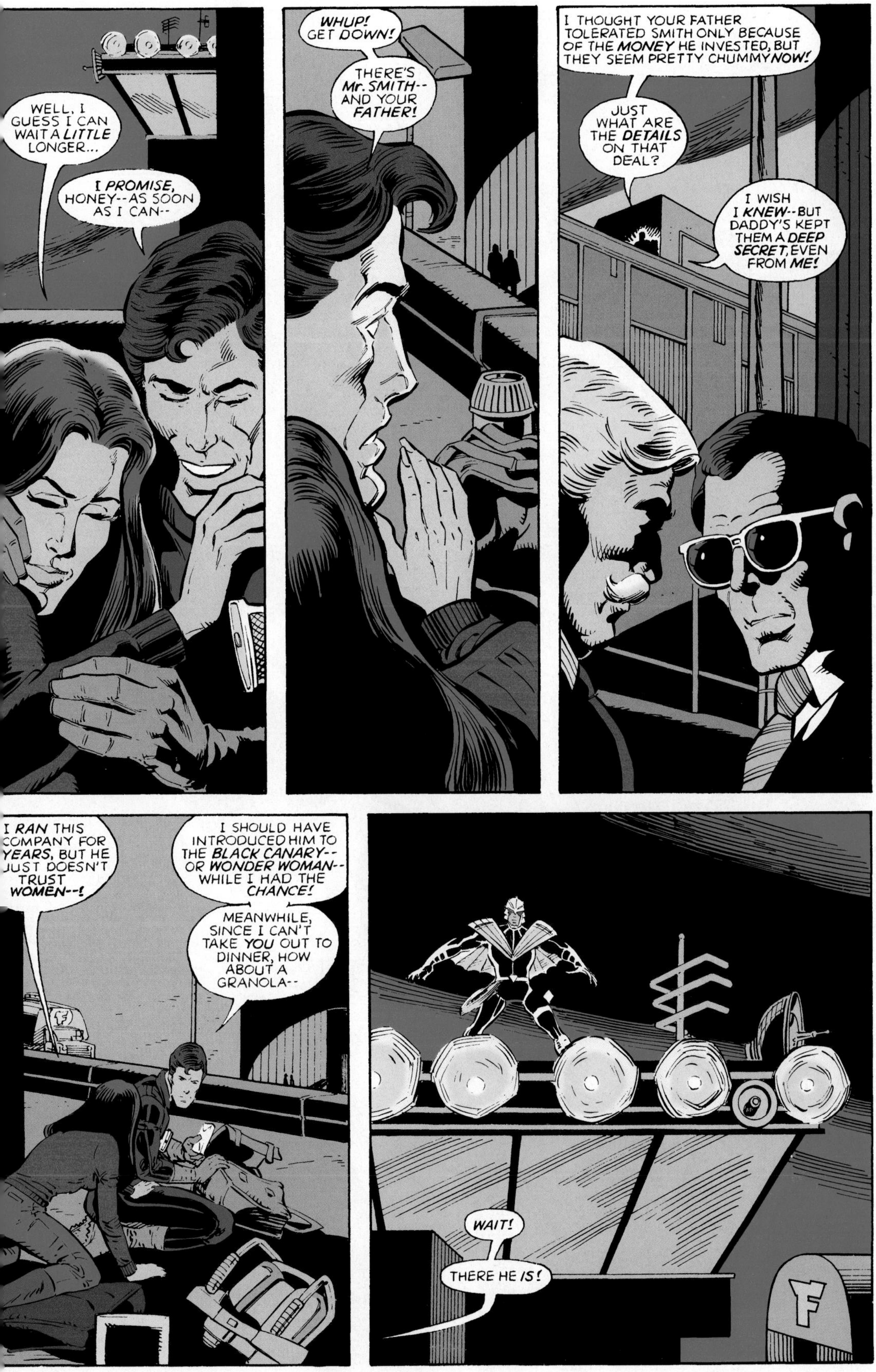

WELL, I GUESS I CAN WAIT A *LITTLE* LONGER...
I PROMISE, HONEY--AS SOON AS I CAN--
WHUP! GET *DOWN!*
THERE'S *Mr. SMITH--* AND YOUR *FATHER!*
I THOUGHT YOUR FATHER TOLERATED SMITH ONLY BECAUSE OF THE *MONEY* HE INVESTED, BUT THEY SEEM PRETTY CHUMMY *NOW!*
JUST WHAT ARE THE *DETAILS* ON THAT DEAL?
I WISH I *KNEW*--BUT DADDY'S KEPT THEM A *DEEP SECRET,* EVEN FROM *ME!*
I *RAN* THIS COMPANY FOR *YEARS,* BUT HE JUST DOESN'T TRUST *WOMEN--!*
I SHOULD HAVE INTRODUCED HIM TO THE *BLACK CANARY--* OR *WONDER WOMAN--* WHILE I HAD THE *CHANCE!*
MEANWHILE, SINCE I CAN'T TAKE *YOU* OUT TO DINNER, HOW ABOUT A GRANOLA--
WAIT!
THERE HE *IS!*

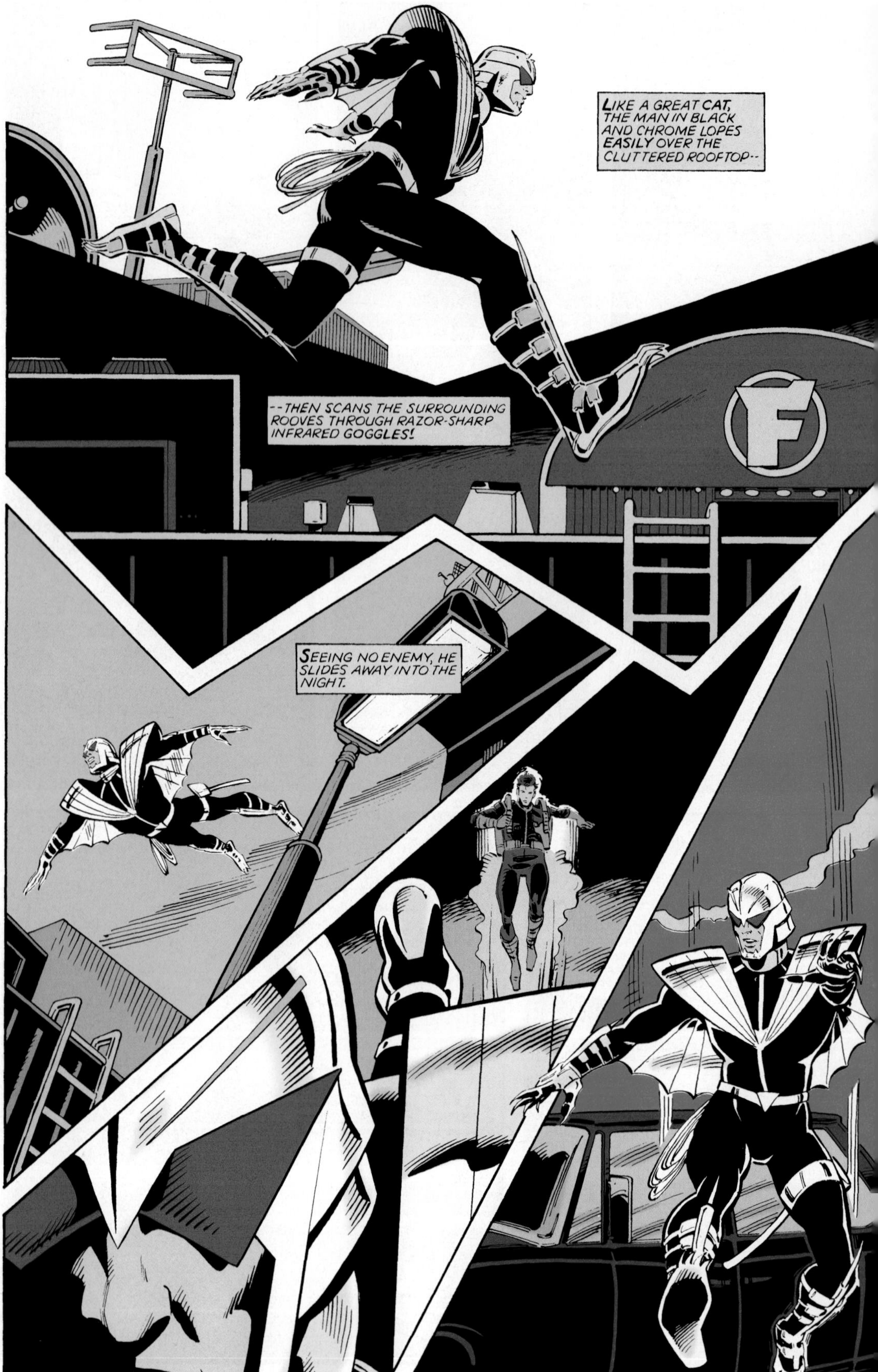
LIKE A GREAT CAT, THE MAN IN BLACK AND CHROME LOPES EASILY OVER THE CLUTTERED ROOFTOP--
--THEN SCANS THE SURROUNDING ROOVES THROUGH RAZOR-SHARP INFRARED GOGGLES!
SEEING NO ENEMY, HE SLIDES AWAY INTO THE NIGHT.

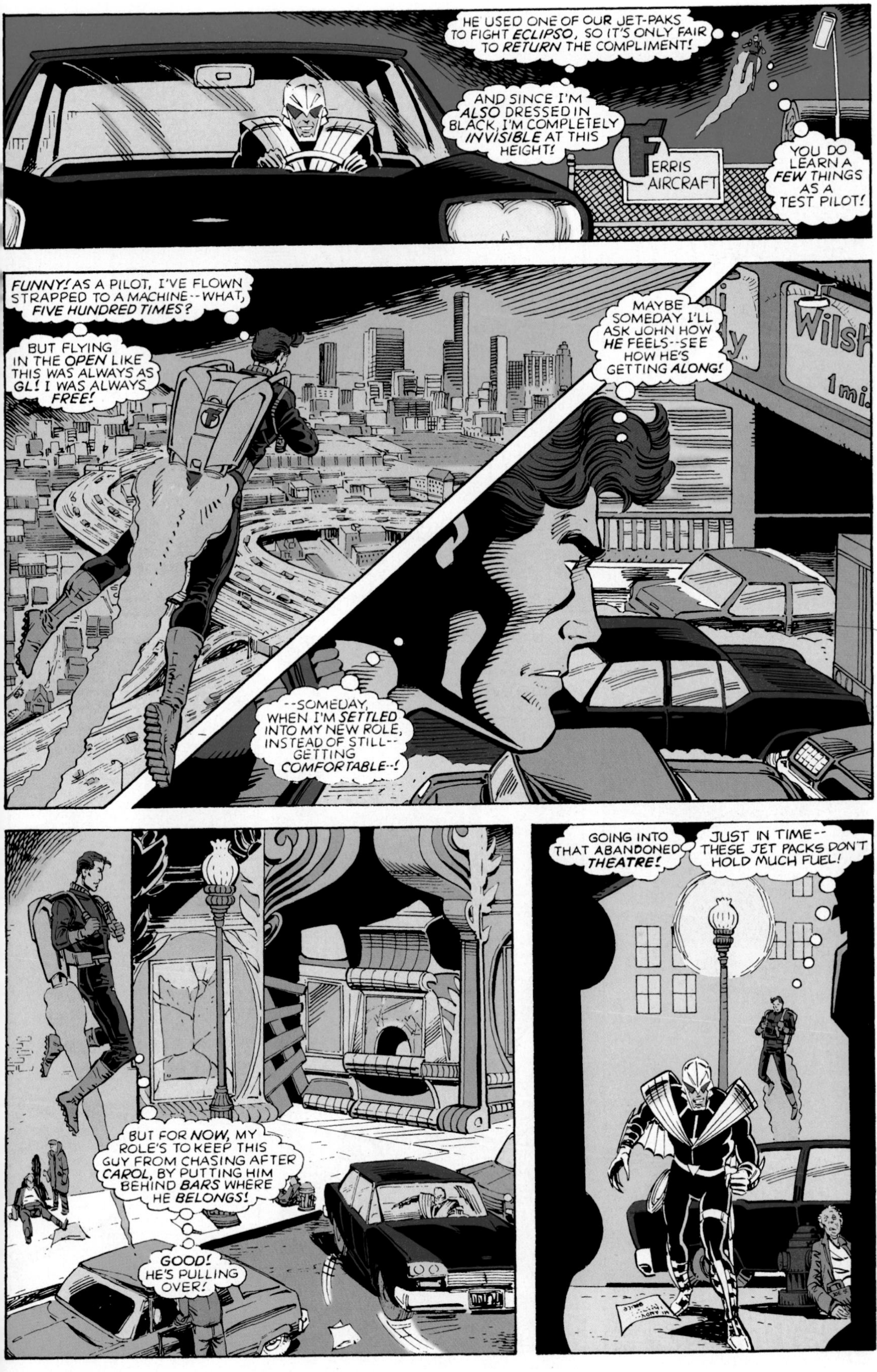
HE USED ONE OF OUR JET-PAKS TO FIGHT ECLIPSO, SO IT'S ONLY FAIR TO RETURN THE COMPLIMENT!
AND SINCE I'M ALSO DRESSED IN BLACK, I'M COMPLETELY INVISIBLE AT THIS HEIGHT!
FERRIS AIRCRAFT
YOU DO LEARN A FEW THINGS AS A TEST PILOT!
FUNNY! AS A PILOT, I'VE FLOWN STRAPPED TO A MACHINE--WHAT, FIVE HUNDRED TIMES?
BUT FLYING IN THE OPEN LIKE THIS WAS ALWAYS AS GL! I WAS ALWAYS FREE!
MAYBE SOMEDAY I'LL ASK JOHN HOW HE FEELS--SEE HOW HE'S GETTING ALONG!
--SOMEDAY, WHEN I'M SETTLED INTO MY NEW ROLE, INSTEAD OF STILL--GETTING COMFORTABLE--!
BUT FOR NOW, MY ROLE'S TO KEEP THIS GUY FROM CHASING AFTER CAROL, BY PUTTING HIM BEHIND BARS WHERE HE BELONGS!
GOOD! HE'S PULLING OVER!
GOING INTO THAT ABANDONED THEATRE!
JUST IN TIME--THESE JET PACKS DON'T HOLD MUCH FUEL!

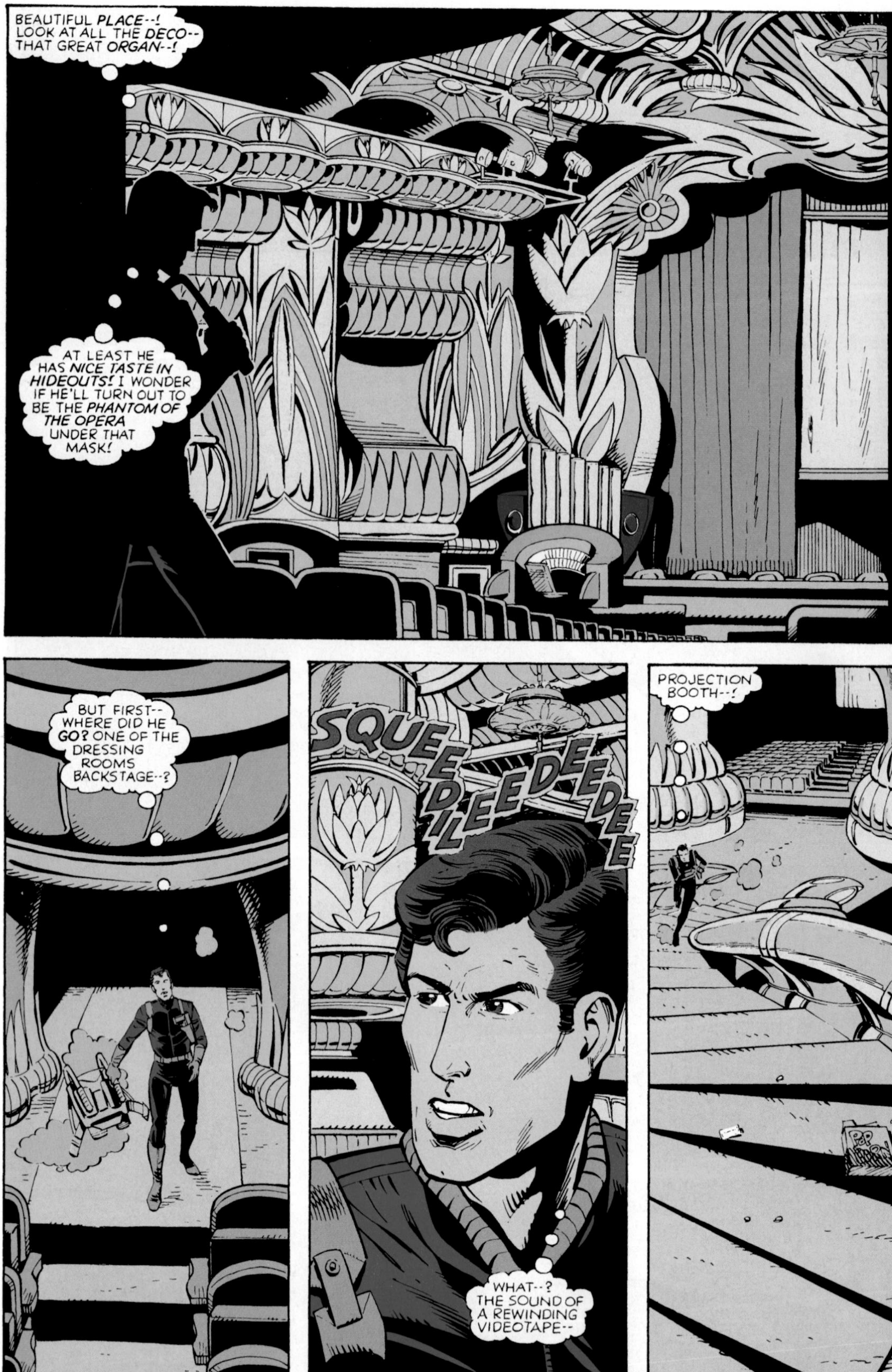
BEAUTIFUL PLACE--! LOOK AT ALL THE DECO-- THAT GREAT ORGAN--!
AT LEAST HE HAS NICE TASTE IN HIDEOUTS! I WONDER IF HE'LL TURN OUT TO BE THE PHANTOM OF THE OPERA UNDER THAT MASK!
BUT FIRST-- WHERE DID HE GO? ONE OF THE DRESSING ROOMS BACKSTAGE--?
SQUEEEDILEEDEEDEE
WHAT--? THE SOUND OF A REWINDING VIDEOTAPE--
PROJECTION BOOTH--!

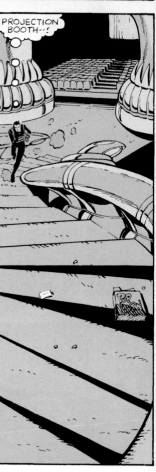

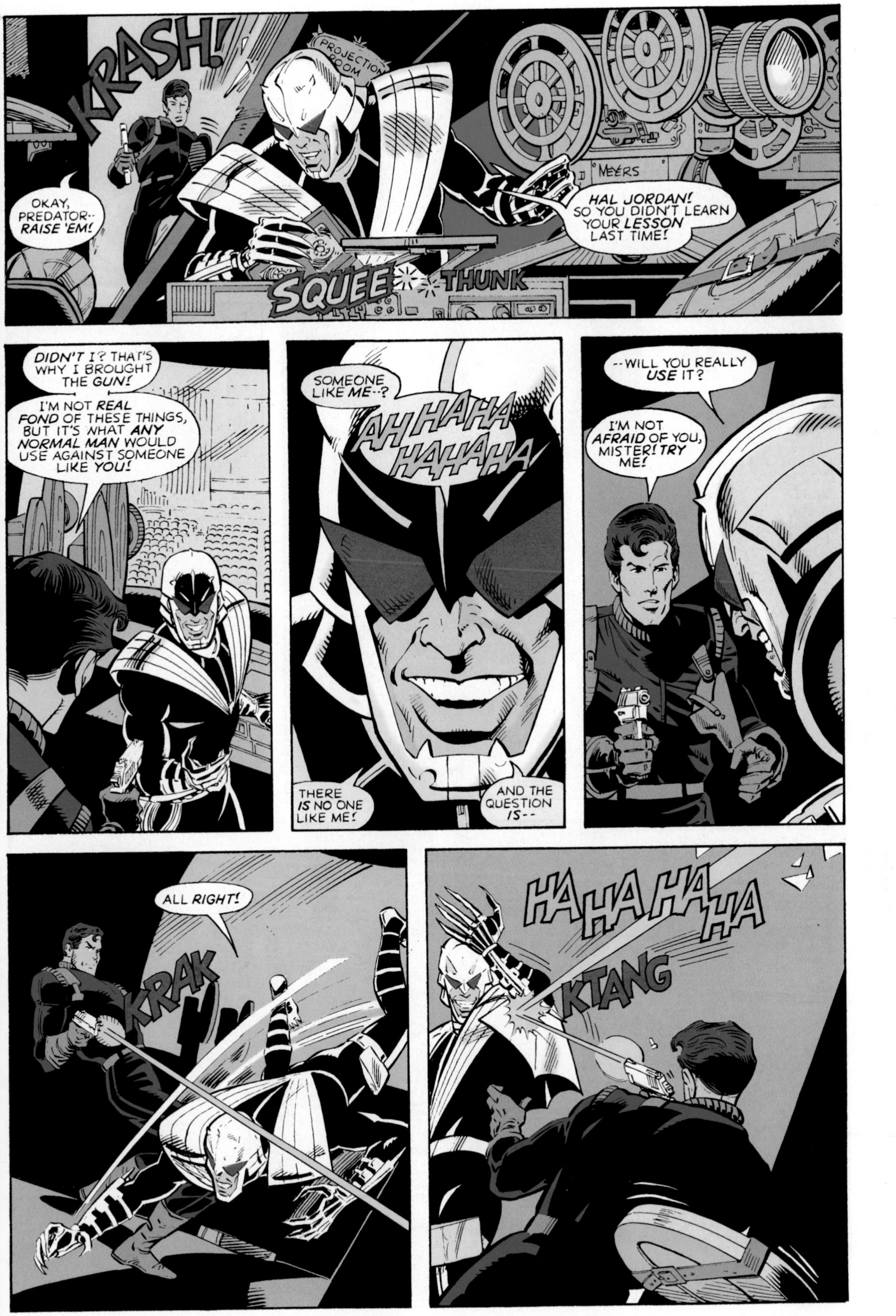
KRASH!
PROJECTION ROOM
OKAY, PREDATOR-- RAISE 'EM!
MEYERS
HAL JORDAN! SO YOU DIDN'T LEARN YOUR LESSON LAST TIME!
SQUEE
THUNK
DIDN'T I? THAT'S WHY I BROUGHT THE GUN!
I'M NOT REAL FOND OF THESE THINGS, BUT IT'S WHAT ANY NORMAL MAN WOULD USE AGAINST SOMEONE LIKE YOU!
SOMEONE LIKE ME--?
AH HAHA HAHAHA
THERE IS NO ONE LIKE ME!
AND THE QUESTION IS--
--WILL YOU REALLY USE IT?
I'M NOT AFRAID OF YOU, MISTER! TRY ME!
ALL RIGHT!
KRAK
HA HA HA HA HA HA
KTANG

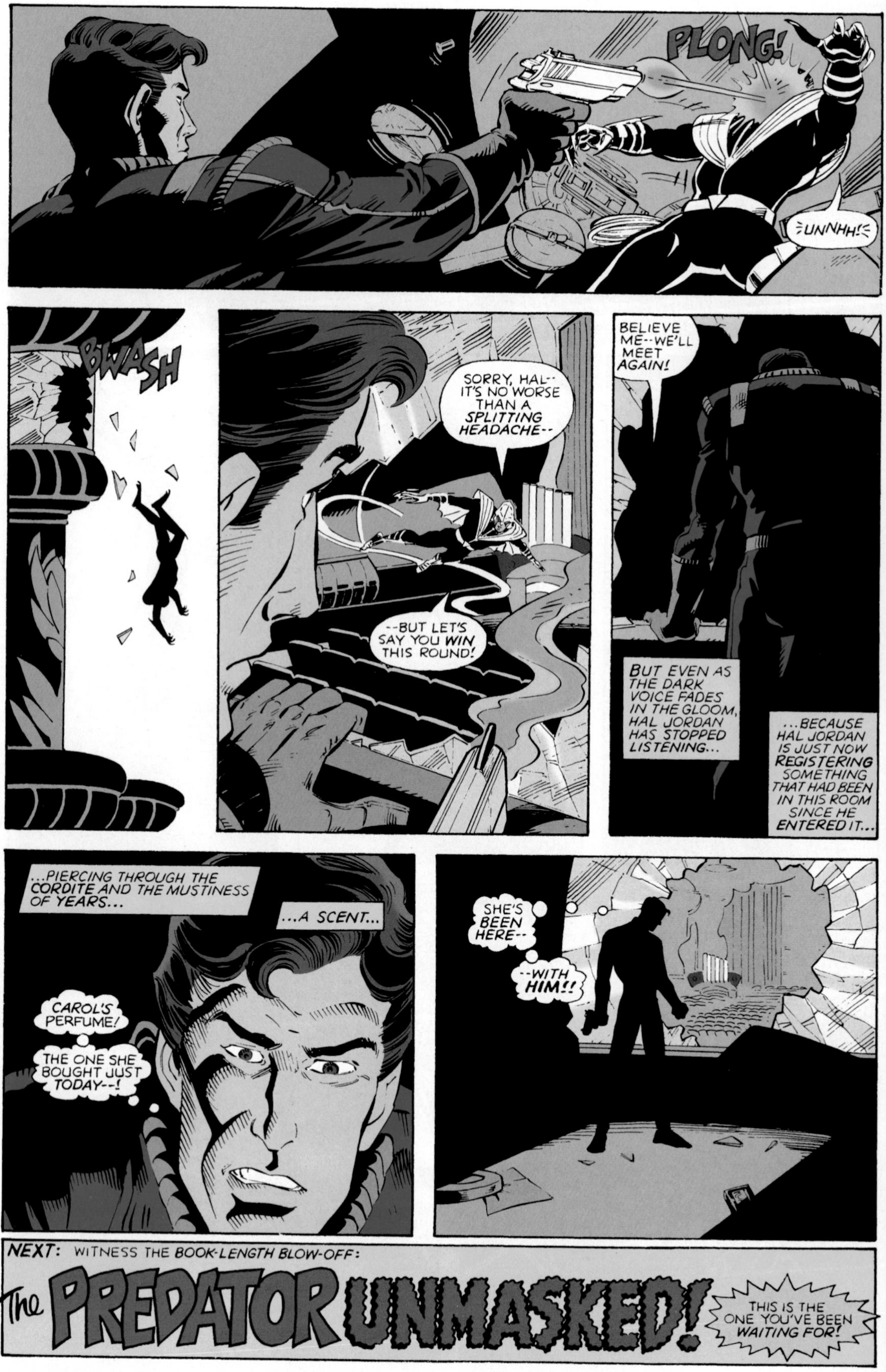
PLONG!
UNNHH!
BWASH
SORRY, HAL-- IT'S NO WORSE THAN A *SPLITTING HEADACHE*--
--BUT LET'S SAY YOU *WIN* THIS ROUND!
BELIEVE ME--WE'LL MEET *AGAIN!*
BUT EVEN AS THE DARK VOICE FADES IN THE GLOOM, HAL JORDAN HAS STOPPED LISTENING...
...BECAUSE HAL JORDAN IS JUST NOW *REGISTERING* SOMETHING THAT HAD BEEN IN THIS ROOM SINCE HE *ENTERED* IT...
...PIERCING THROUGH THE *CORDITE* AND THE *MUSTINESS* OF *YEARS*...
...A SCENT...
CAROL'S PERFUME!
THE ONE SHE BOUGHT JUST *TODAY*--!
SHE'S *BEEN* HERE--
--WITH *HIM!!*
NEXT: WITNESS THE *BOOK-LENGTH BLOW-OFF*:
The PREDATOR UNMASKED!
THIS IS THE ONE YOU'VE BEEN *WAITING FOR!*

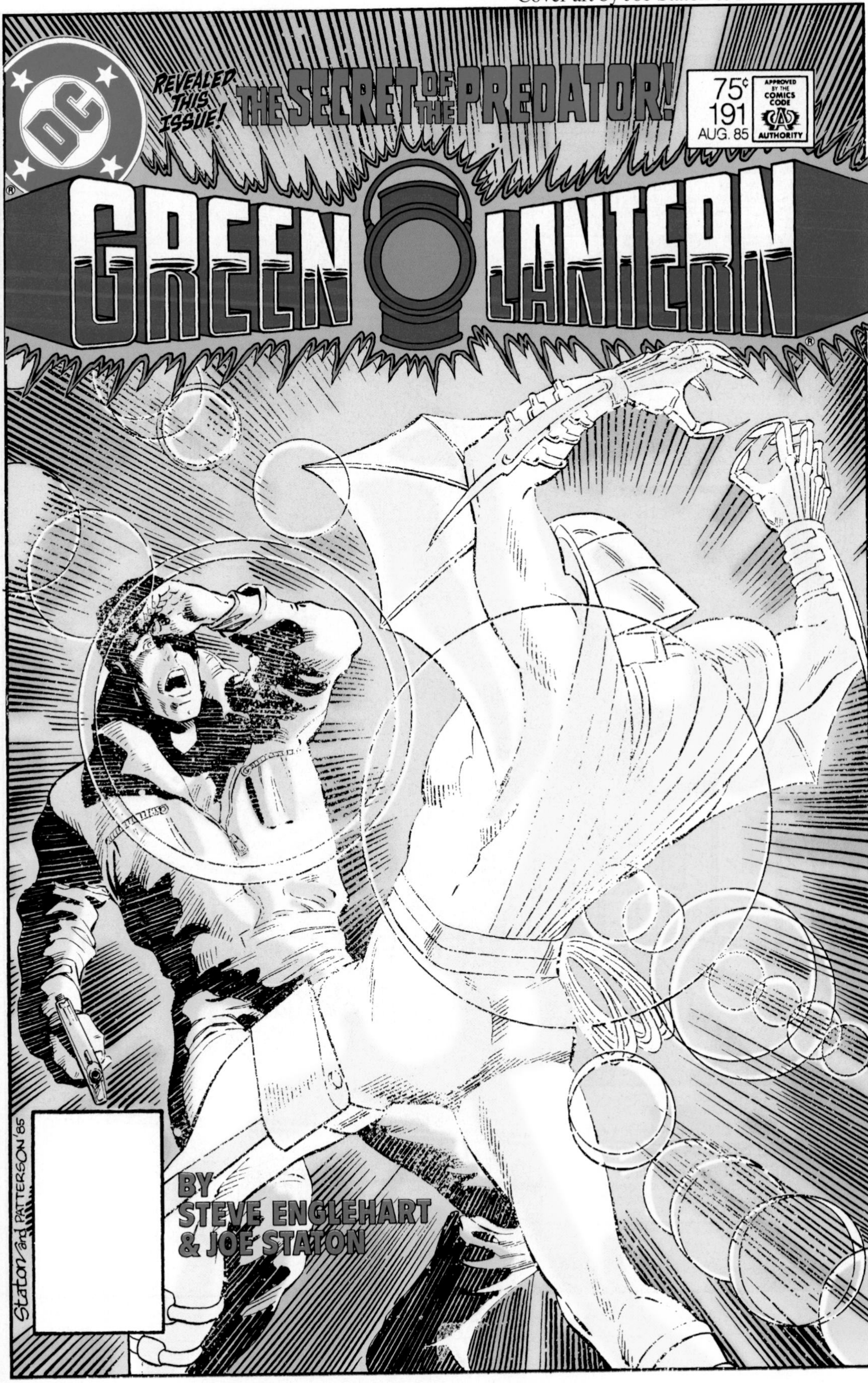
REVEALED THIS ISSUE!
THE SECRET OF THE PREDATOR!
75¢
191
AUG. 85
APPROVED BY THE COMICS CODE AUTHORITY
GREEN LANTERN
Staton and PATTERSON '85
BY STEVE ENGLEHART & JOE STATON

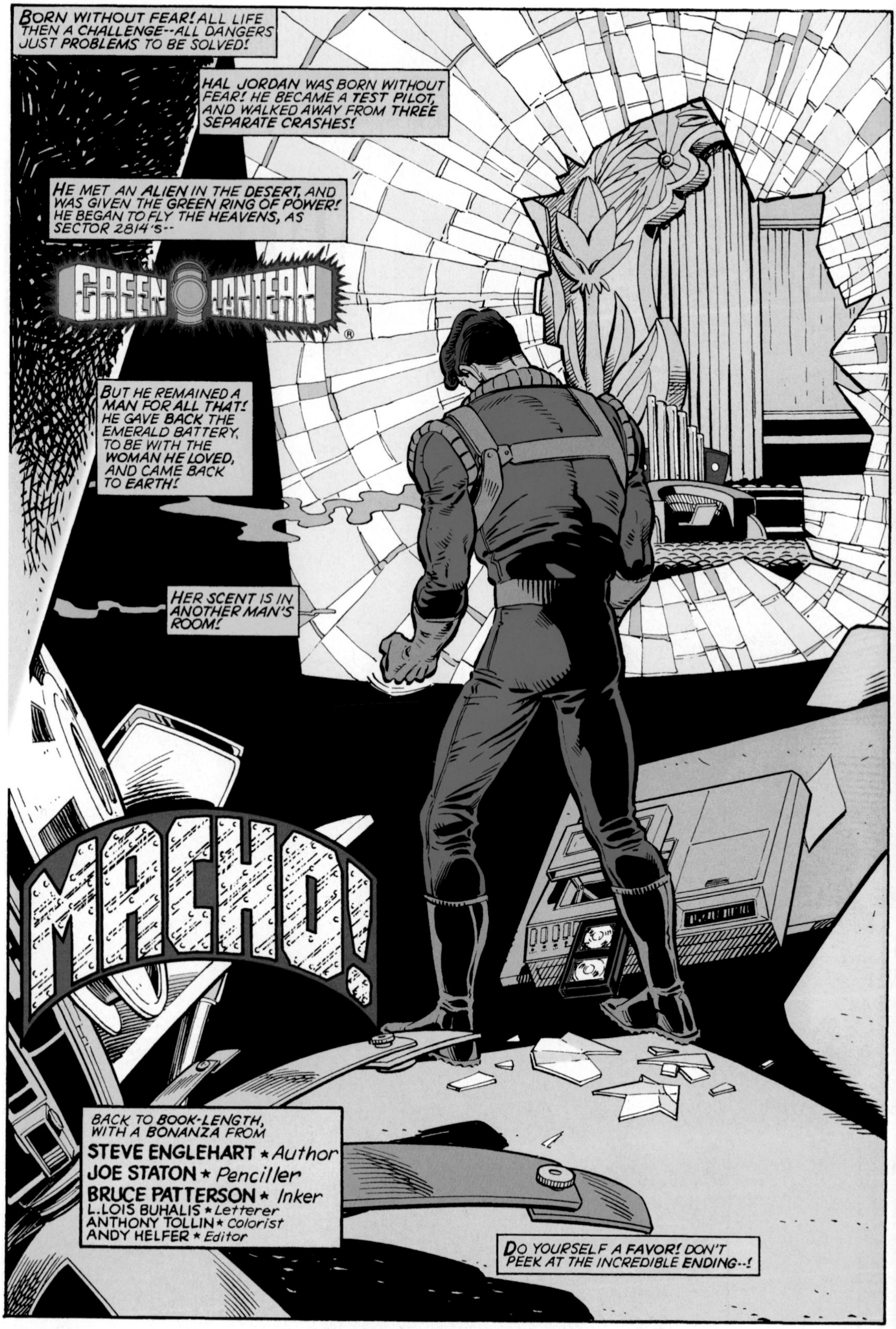
BORN WITHOUT FEAR! ALL LIFE THEN A CHALLENGE--ALL DANGERS JUST PROBLEMS TO BE SOLVED!
HAL JORDAN WAS BORN WITHOUT FEAR! HE BECAME A TEST PILOT, AND WALKED AWAY FROM THREE SEPARATE CRASHES!
HE MET AN ALIEN IN THE DESERT, AND WAS GIVEN THE GREEN RING OF POWER! HE BEGAN TO FLY THE HEAVENS, AS SECTOR 2814'S--
GREEN LANTERN ®
BUT HE REMAINED A MAN FOR ALL THAT! HE GAVE BACK THE EMERALD BATTERY, TO BE WITH THE WOMAN HE LOVED, AND CAME BACK TO EARTH!
HER SCENT IS IN ANOTHER MAN'S ROOM!
MACHO!
BACK TO BOOK-LENGTH, WITH A BONANZA FROM
STEVE ENGLEHART ★ Author
JOE STATON ★ Penciller
BRUCE PATTERSON ★ Inker
L.LOIS BUHALIS ★ Letterer
ANTHONY TOLLIN ★ Colorist
ANDY HELFER ★ Editor
DO YOURSELF A FAVOR! DON'T PEEK AT THE INCREDIBLE ENDING--!

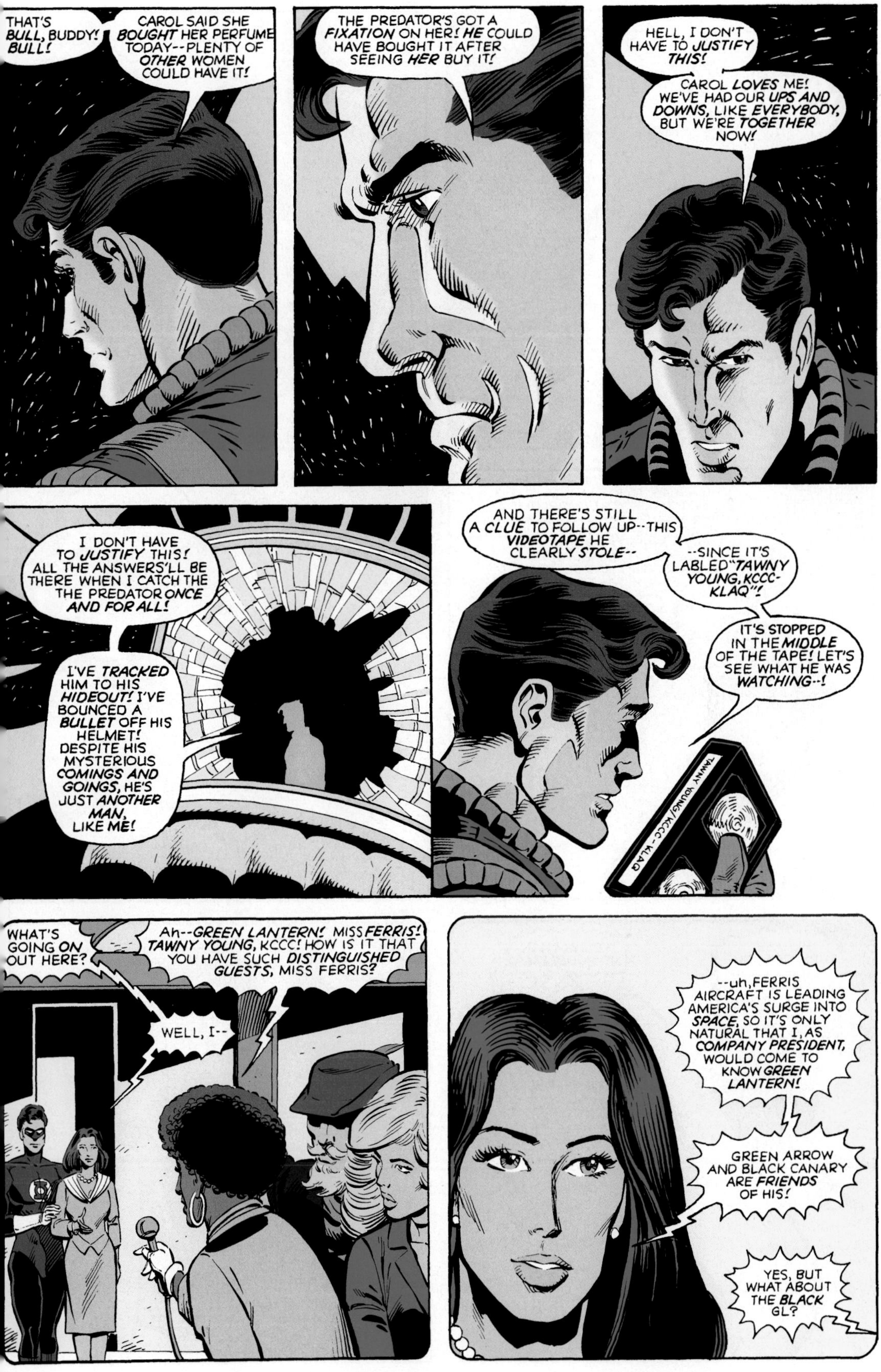
THAT'S BULL, BUDDY! BULL!
CAROL SAID SHE BOUGHT HER PERFUME TODAY--PLENTY OF OTHER WOMEN COULD HAVE IT!
THE PREDATOR'S GOT A FIXATION ON HER! HE COULD HAVE BOUGHT IT AFTER SEEING HER BUY IT!
HELL, I DON'T HAVE TO JUSTIFY THIS!
CAROL LOVES ME! WE'VE HAD OUR UPS AND DOWNS, LIKE EVERYBODY, BUT WE'RE TOGETHER NOW!
I DON'T HAVE TO JUSTIFY THIS! ALL THE ANSWERS'LL BE THERE WHEN I CATCH THE THE PREDATOR ONCE AND FOR ALL!
I'VE TRACKED HIM TO HIS HIDEOUT! I'VE BOUNCED A BULLET OFF HIS HELMET! DESPITE HIS MYSTERIOUS COMINGS AND GOINGS, HE'S JUST ANOTHER MAN, LIKE ME!
AND THERE'S STILL A CLUE TO FOLLOW UP--THIS VIDEOTAPE HE CLEARLY STOLE--
--SINCE IT'S LABLED "TAWNY YOUNG, KCCC-KLAQ"!
IT'S STOPPED IN THE MIDDLE OF THE TAPE! LET'S SEE WHAT HE WAS WATCHING--!
TAWNY YOUNG/KCCC-KLAQ
WHAT'S GOING ON OUT HERE?
Ah--GREEN LANTERN! MISS FERRIS! TAWNY YOUNG, KCCC! HOW IS IT THAT YOU HAVE SUCH DISTINGUISHED GUESTS, MISS FERRIS?
WELL, I--
--uh, FERRIS AIRCRAFT IS LEADING AMERICA'S SURGE INTO SPACE, SO IT'S ONLY NATURAL THAT I, AS COMPANY PRESIDENT, WOULD COME TO KNOW GREEN LANTERN!
GREEN ARROW AND BLACK CANARY ARE FRIENDS OF HIS!
YES, BUT WHAT ABOUT THE BLACK GL?

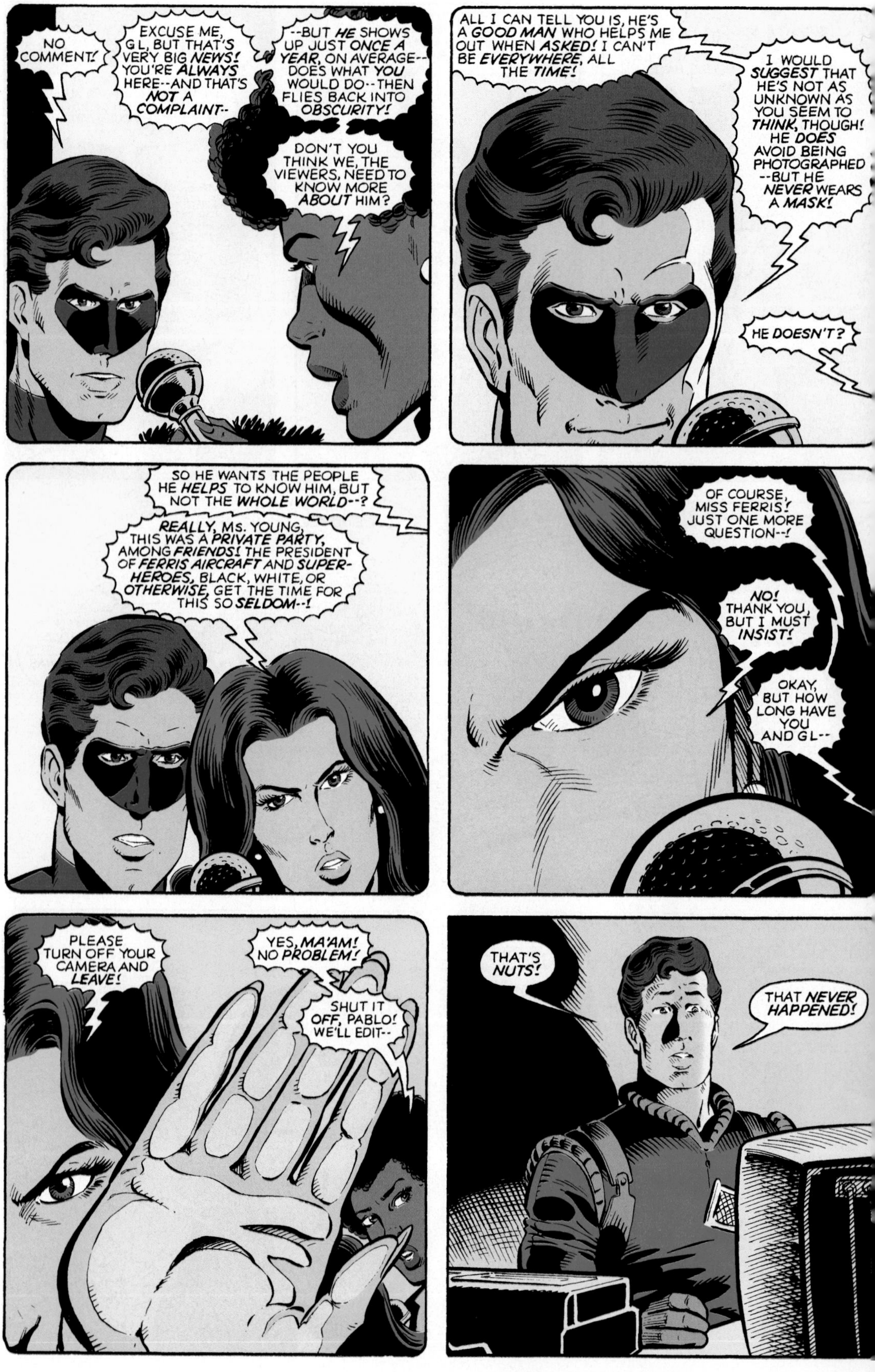
NO COMMENT!
EXCUSE ME, GL, BUT THAT'S VERY BIG NEWS! YOU'RE ALWAYS HERE--AND THAT'S NOT A COMPLAINT--
--BUT HE SHOWS UP JUST ONCE A YEAR, ON AVERAGE-- DOES WHAT YOU WOULD DO--THEN FLIES BACK INTO OBSCURITY!
DON'T YOU THINK WE, THE VIEWERS, NEED TO KNOW MORE ABOUT HIM?
ALL I CAN TELL YOU IS, HE'S A GOOD MAN WHO HELPS ME OUT WHEN ASKED! I CAN'T BE EVERYWHERE, ALL THE TIME!
I WOULD SUGGEST THAT HE'S NOT AS UNKNOWN AS YOU SEEM TO THINK, THOUGH! HE DOES AVOID BEING PHOTOGRAPHED --BUT HE NEVER WEARS A MASK!
HE DOESN'T?
SO HE WANTS THE PEOPLE HE HELPS TO KNOW HIM, BUT NOT THE WHOLE WORLD--?
REALLY, Ms. YOUNG, THIS WAS A PRIVATE PARTY, AMONG FRIENDS! THE PRESIDENT OF FERRIS AIRCRAFT AND SUPER-HEROES, BLACK, WHITE, OR OTHERWISE, GET THE TIME FOR THIS SO SELDOM--!
OF COURSE, MISS FERRIS! JUST ONE MORE QUESTION--!
NO! THANK YOU, BUT I MUST INSIST!
OKAY, BUT HOW LONG HAVE YOU AND GL--
PLEASE TURN OFF YOUR CAMERA AND LEAVE!
YES, MA'AM! NO PROBLEM!
SHUT IT OFF, PABLO! WE'LL EDIT--
THAT'S NUTS!
THAT NEVER HAPPENED!

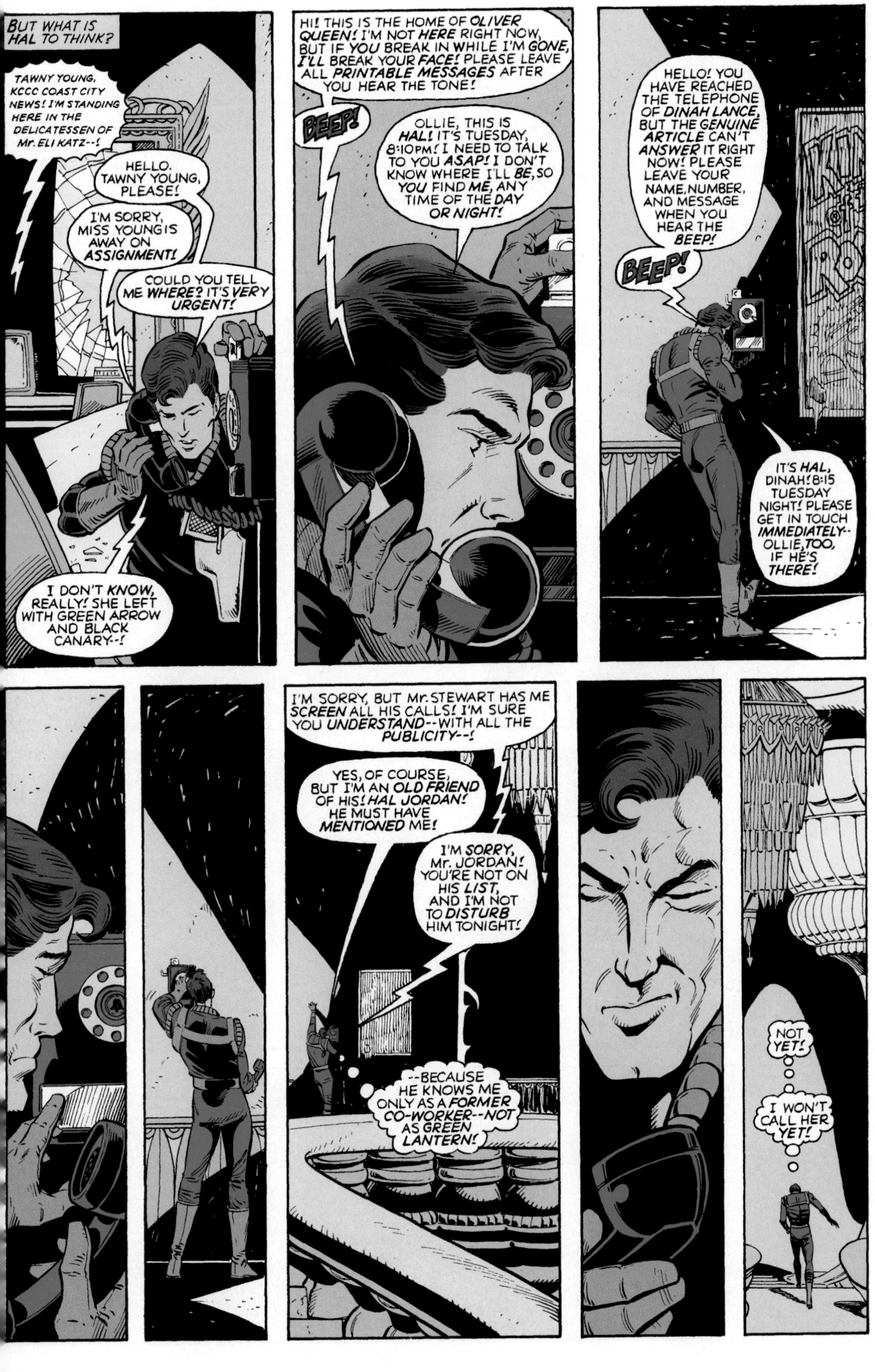
BUT WHAT IS HAL TO THINK?
TAWNY YOUNG, KCCC COAST CITY NEWS! I'M STANDING HERE IN THE DELICATESSEN OF Mr. ELI KATZ--!
HELLO. TAWNY YOUNG, PLEASE!
I'M SORRY, MISS YOUNG IS AWAY ON ASSIGNMENT!
COULD YOU TELL ME WHERE? IT'S VERY URGENT!
I DON'T KNOW, REALLY! SHE LEFT WITH GREEN ARROW AND BLACK CANARY--!
HI! THIS IS THE HOME OF OLIVER QUEEN! I'M NOT HERE RIGHT NOW, BUT IF YOU BREAK IN WHILE I'M GONE, I'LL BREAK YOUR FACE! PLEASE LEAVE ALL PRINTABLE MESSAGES AFTER YOU HEAR THE TONE!
BEEP!
OLLIE, THIS IS HAL! IT'S TUESDAY, 8:10PM! I NEED TO TALK TO YOU ASAP! I DON'T KNOW WHERE I'LL BE, SO YOU FIND ME, ANY TIME OF THE DAY OR NIGHT!
HELLO! YOU HAVE REACHED THE TELEPHONE OF DINAH LANCE, BUT THE GENUINE ARTICLE CAN'T ANSWER IT RIGHT NOW! PLEASE LEAVE YOUR NAME, NUMBER, AND MESSAGE WHEN YOU HEAR THE BEEP!
BEEP!
IT'S HAL, DINAH! 8:15 TUESDAY NIGHT! PLEASE GET IN TOUCH IMMEDIATELY--OLLIE, TOO, IF HE'S THERE!
I'M SORRY, BUT Mr. STEWART HAS ME SCREEN ALL HIS CALLS! I'M SURE YOU UNDERSTAND--WITH ALL THE PUBLICITY--!
YES, OF COURSE, BUT I'M AN OLD FRIEND OF HIS! HAL JORDAN! HE MUST HAVE MENTIONED ME!
I'M SORRY, Mr. JORDAN! YOU'RE NOT ON HIS LIST, AND I'M NOT TO DISTURB HIM TONIGHT!
--BECAUSE HE KNOWS ME ONLY AS A FORMER CO-WORKER--NOT AS GREEN LANTERN!
NOT YET!
I WON'T CALL HER YET!

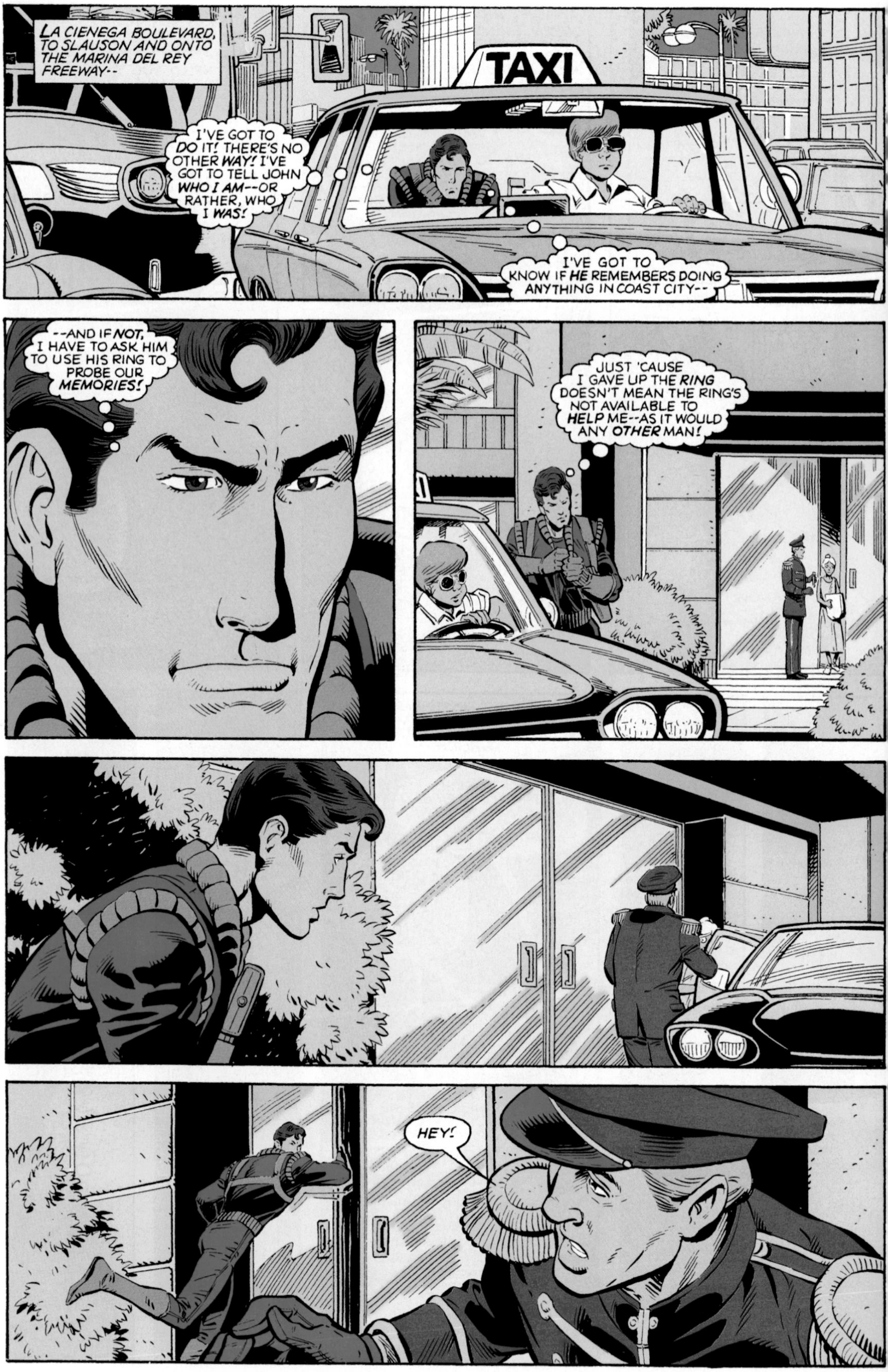
LA CIENEGA BOULEVARD, TO SLAUSON AND ONTO THE MARINA DEL REY FREEWAY--
TAXI
I'VE GOT TO DO IT! THERE'S NO OTHER WAY! I'VE GOT TO TELL JOHN WHO I AM--OR RATHER, WHO I WAS!
I'VE GOT TO KNOW IF HE REMEMBERS DOING ANYTHING IN COAST CITY--
--AND IF NOT, I HAVE TO ASK HIM TO USE HIS RING TO PROBE OUR MEMORIES!
JUST 'CAUSE I GAVE UP THE RING DOESN'T MEAN THE RING'S NOT AVAILABLE TO HELP ME--AS IT WOULD ANY OTHER MAN!
HEY!

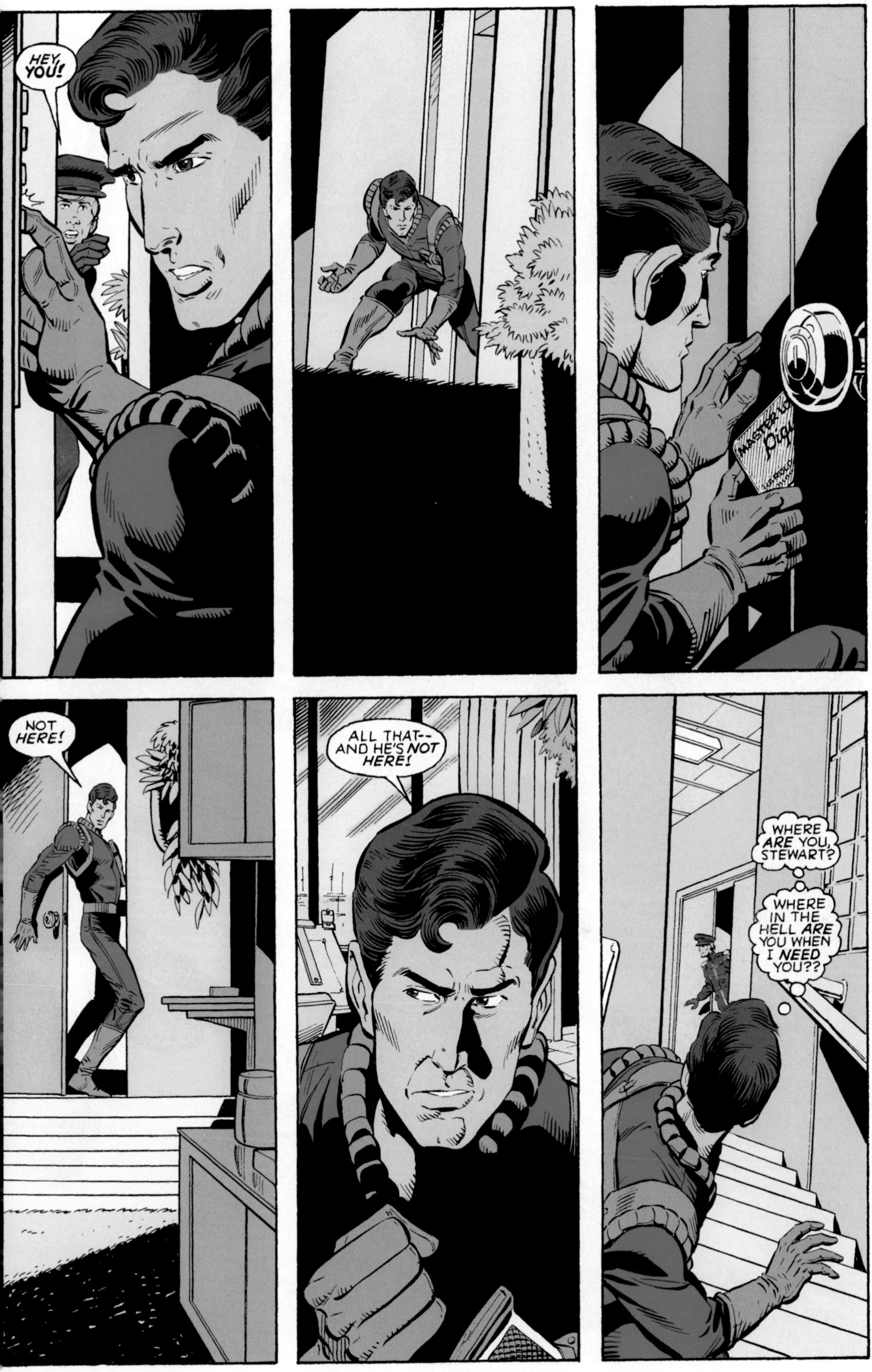
HEY, YOU!
NOT HERE!
ALL THAT-- AND HE'S NOT HERE!
WHERE ARE YOU, STEWART?
WHERE IN THE HELL ARE YOU WHEN I NEED YOU??

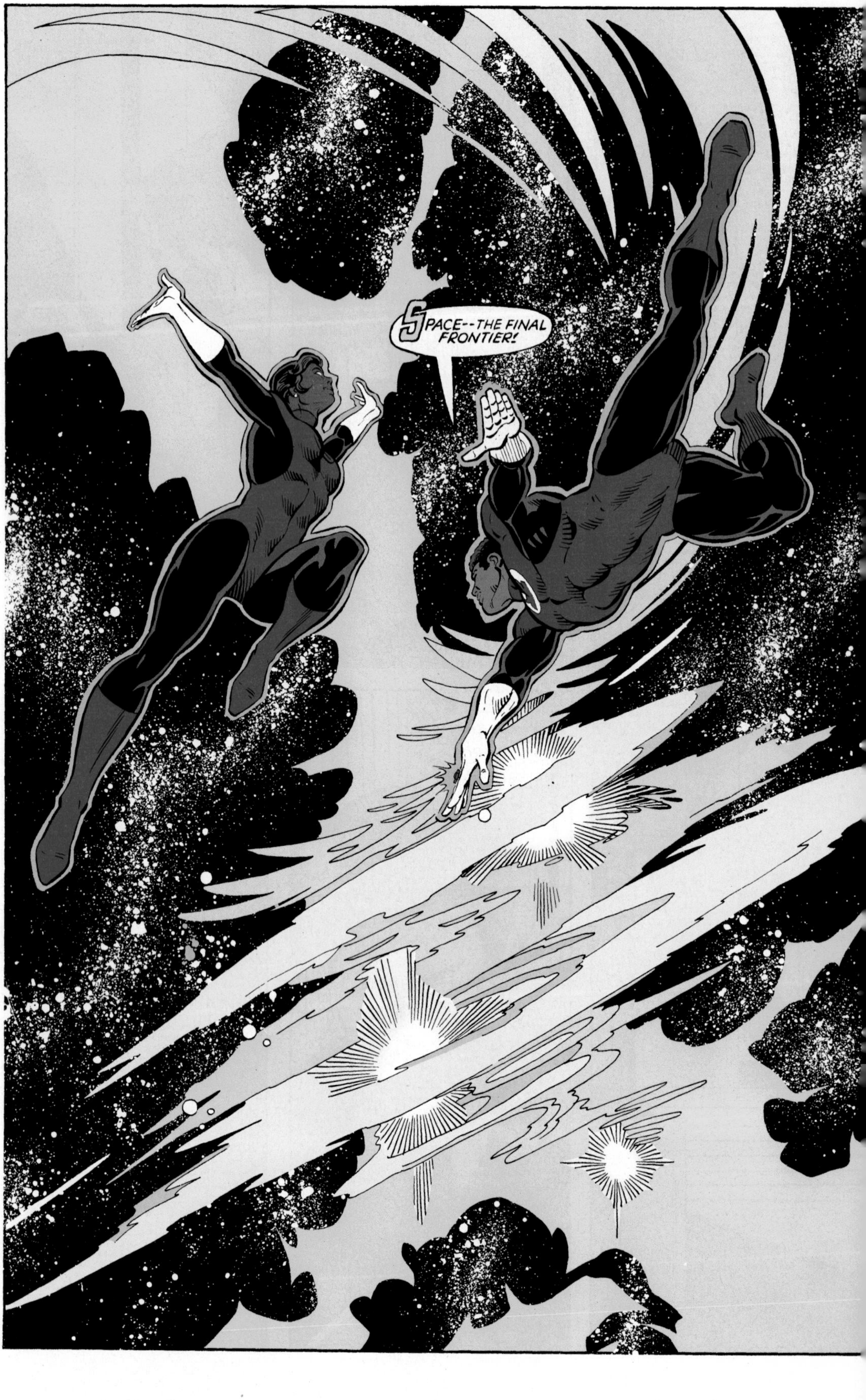
SPACE--THE FINAL FRONTIER!

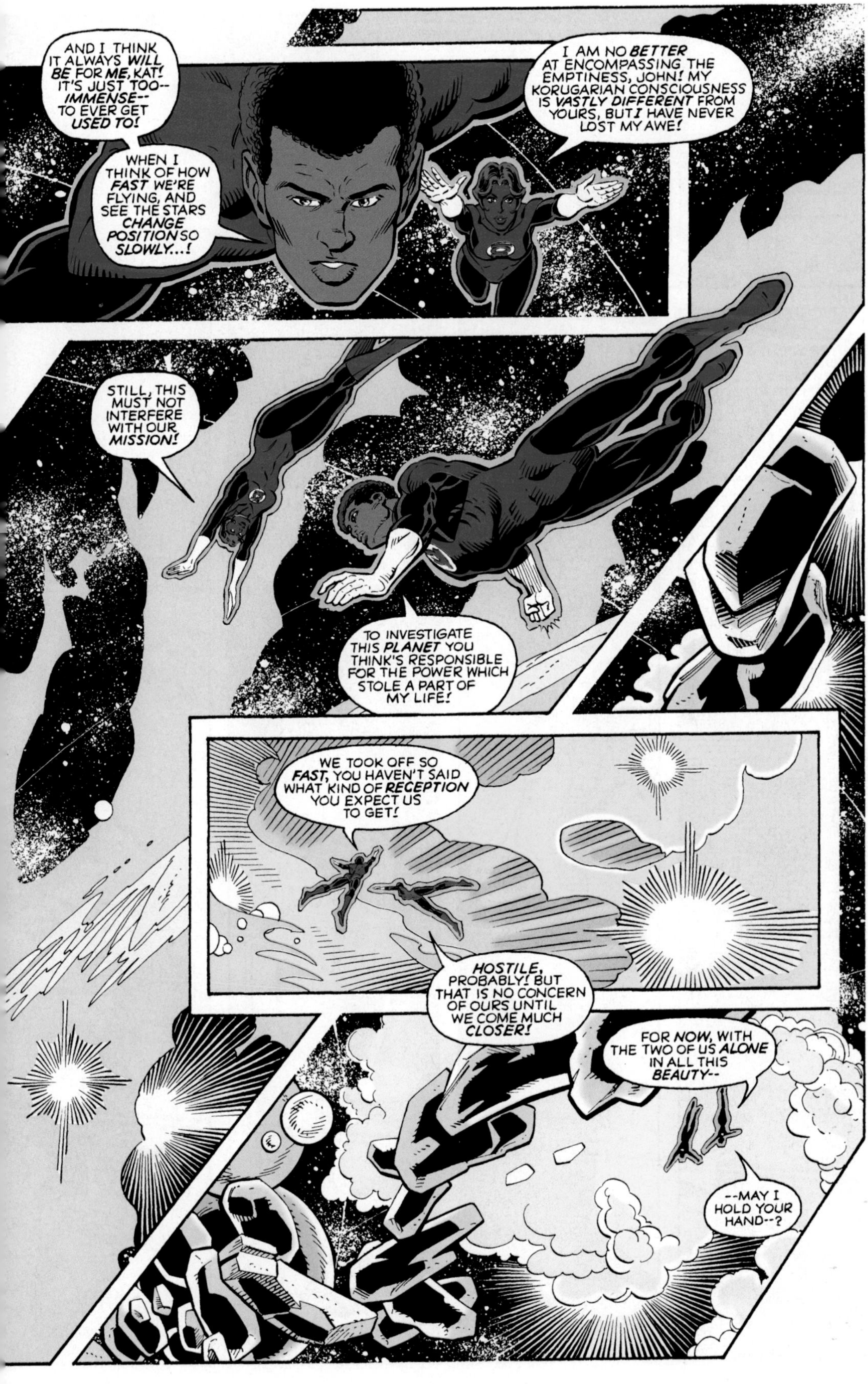
AND I THINK IT ALWAYS WILL BE FOR ME, KAT! IT'S JUST TOO-- IMMENSE-- TO EVER GET USED TO!
WHEN I THINK OF HOW FAST WE'RE FLYING, AND SEE THE STARS CHANGE POSITION SO SLOWLY...!
I AM NO BETTER AT ENCOMPASSING THE EMPTINESS, JOHN! MY KORUGARIAN CONSCIOUSNESS IS VASTLY DIFFERENT FROM YOURS, BUT I HAVE NEVER LOST MY AWE!
STILL, THIS MUST NOT INTERFERE WITH OUR MISSION!
TO INVESTIGATE THIS PLANET YOU THINK'S RESPONSIBLE FOR THE POWER WHICH STOLE A PART OF MY LIFE!
WE TOOK OFF SO FAST, YOU HAVEN'T SAID WHAT KIND OF RECEPTION YOU EXPECT US TO GET!
HOSTILE, PROBABLY! BUT THAT IS NO CONCERN OF OURS UNTIL WE COME MUCH CLOSER!
FOR NOW, WITH THE TWO OF US ALONE IN ALL THIS BEAUTY--
--MAY I HOLD YOUR HAND--?

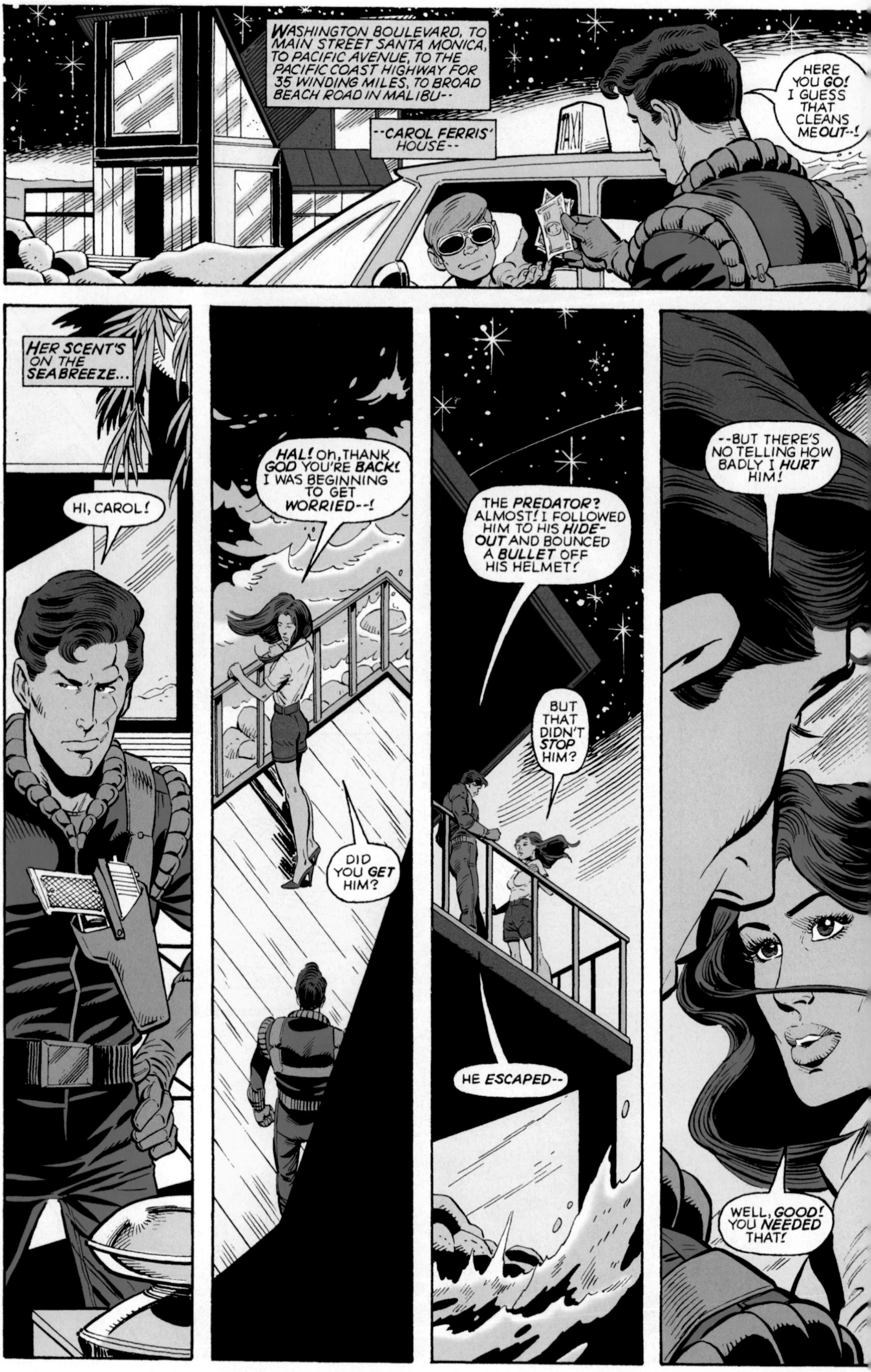
WASHINGTON BOULEVARD, TO MAIN STREET SANTA MONICA, TO PACIFIC AVENUE, TO THE PACIFIC COAST HIGHWAY FOR 35 WINDING MILES, TO BROAD BEACH ROAD IN MALIBU--
--CAROL FERRIS' HOUSE--
TAXI
HERE YOU GO! I GUESS THAT CLEANS ME OUT--!
HER SCENT'S ON THE SEABREEZE...
HI, CAROL!
HAL! Oh, THANK GOD YOU'RE BACK! I WAS BEGINNING TO GET WORRIED--!
DID YOU GET HIM?
THE PREDATOR? ALMOST! I FOLLOWED HIM TO HIS HIDE-OUT AND BOUNCED A BULLET OFF HIS HELMET!
BUT THAT DIDN'T STOP HIM?
HE ESCAPED--
--BUT THERE'S NO TELLING HOW BADLY I HURT HIM!
WELL, GOOD! YOU NEEDED THAT!

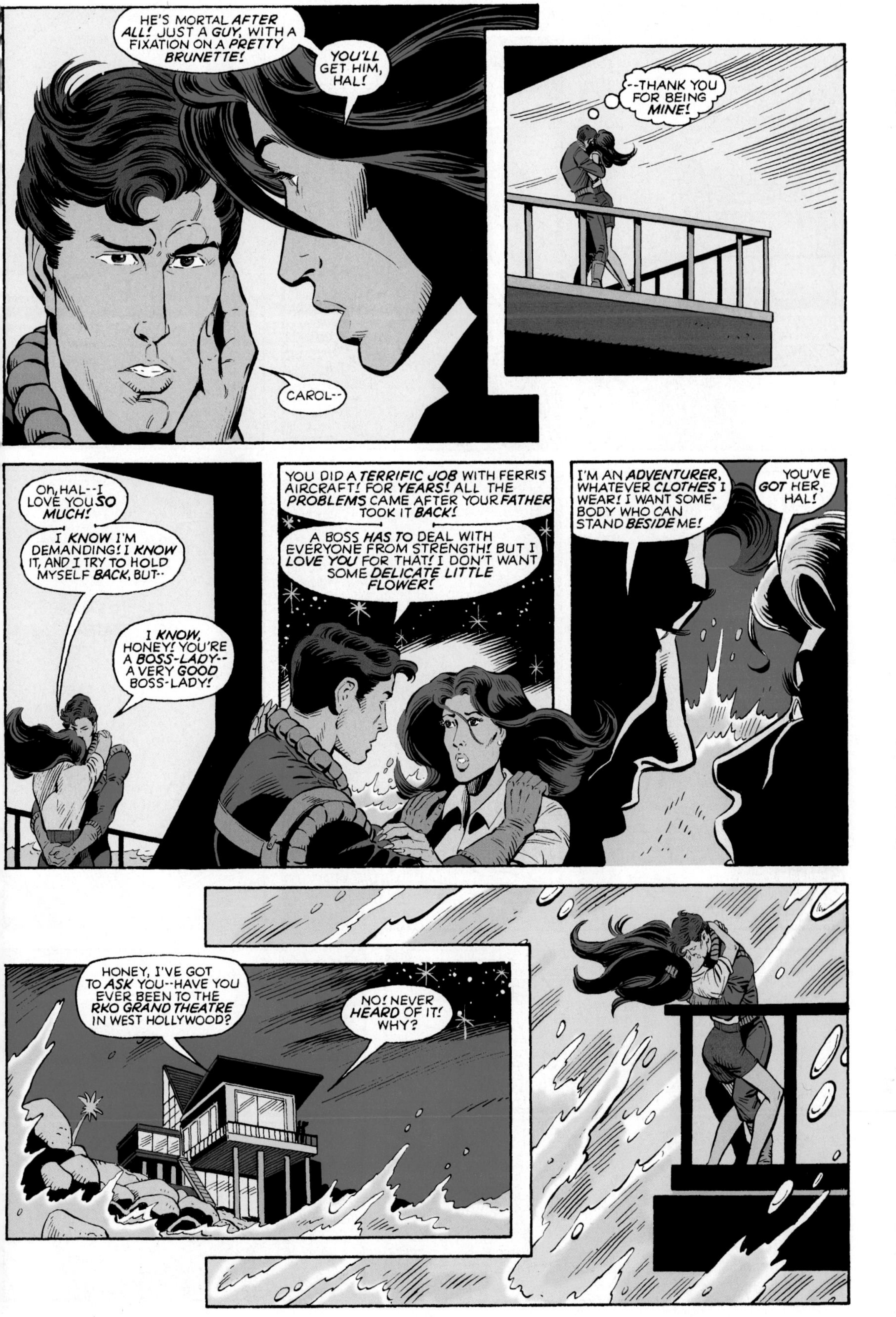

HE'S MORTAL AFTER ALL! JUST A GUY, WITH A FIXATION ON A PRETTY BRUNETTE!
YOU'LL GET HIM, HAL!
CAROL--
--THANK YOU FOR BEING MINE!
Oh, HAL--I LOVE YOU SO MUCH!
I KNOW I'M DEMANDING! I KNOW IT, AND I TRY TO HOLD MYSELF BACK, BUT--
I KNOW, HONEY! YOU'RE A BOSS-LADY-- A VERY GOOD BOSS-LADY!
YOU DID A TERRIFIC JOB WITH FERRIS AIRCRAFT! FOR YEARS! ALL THE PROBLEMS CAME AFTER YOUR FATHER TOOK IT BACK!
A BOSS HAS TO DEAL WITH EVERYONE FROM STRENGTH! BUT I LOVE YOU FOR THAT! I DON'T WANT SOME DELICATE LITTLE FLOWER!
I'M AN ADVENTURER, WHATEVER CLOTHES I WEAR! I WANT SOMEBODY WHO CAN STAND BESIDE ME!
YOU'VE GOT HER, HAL!
HONEY, I'VE GOT TO ASK YOU--HAVE YOU EVER BEEN TO THE RKO GRAND THEATRE IN WEST HOLLYWOOD?
NO! NEVER HEARD OF IT! WHY?

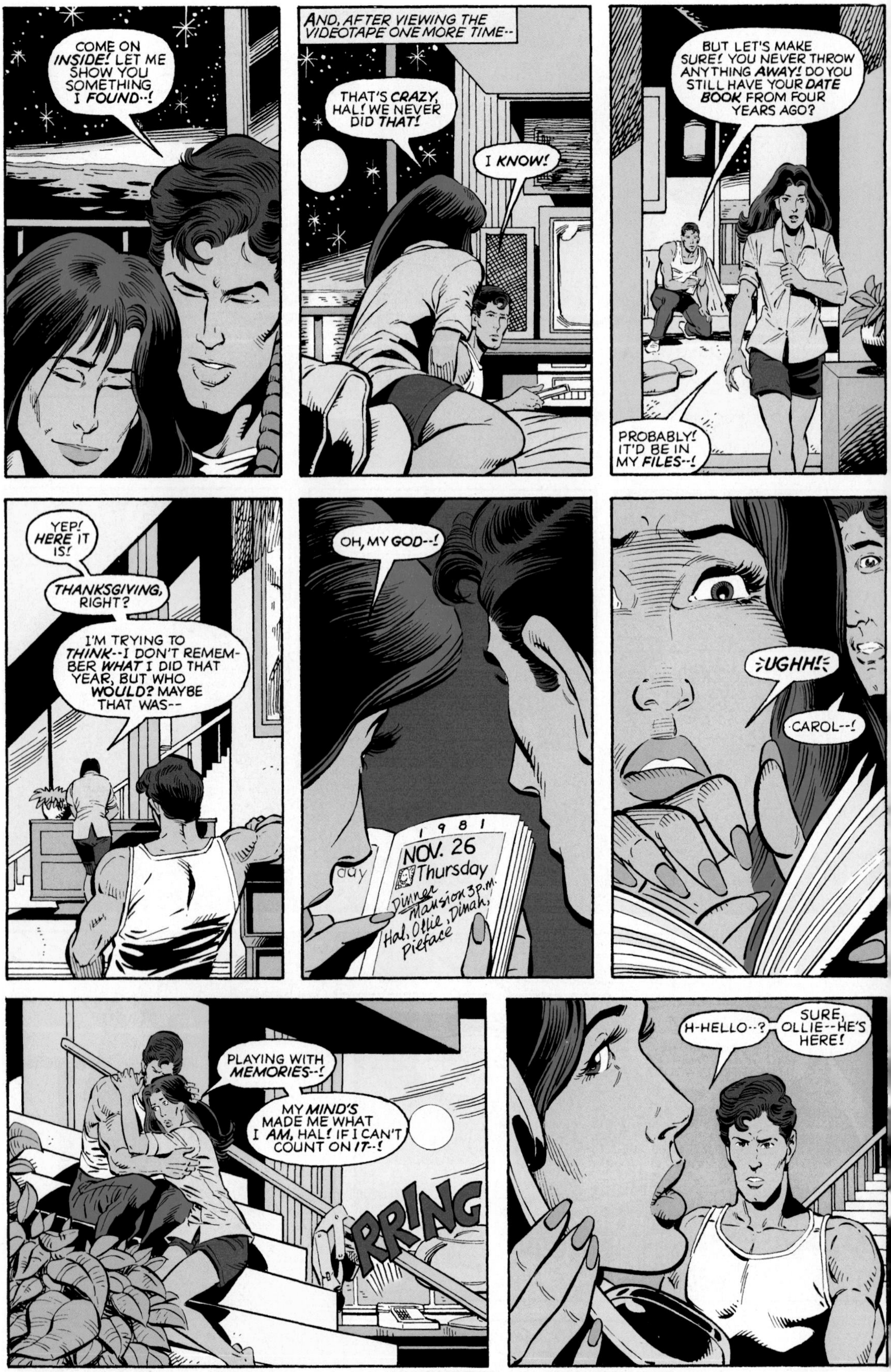
COME ON INSIDE! LET ME SHOW YOU SOMETHING I FOUND--!
AND, AFTER VIEWING THE VIDEOTAPE ONE MORE TIME--
THAT'S CRAZY, HAL! WE NEVER DID THAT!
I KNOW!
BUT LET'S MAKE SURE! YOU NEVER THROW ANYTHING AWAY! DO YOU STILL HAVE YOUR DATE BOOK FROM FOUR YEARS AGO?
PROBABLY! IT'D BE IN MY FILES--!
YEP! HERE IT IS!
THANKSGIVING, RIGHT?
I'M TRYING TO THINK--I DON'T REMEMBER WHAT I DID THAT YEAR, BUT WHO WOULD? MAYBE THAT WAS--
OH, MY GOD--!
1981
NOV. 26
Thursday
Dinner
Mansion 3p.m.
Hal, Ollie, Dinah,
Pieface
UGHH!
CAROL--!
PLAYING WITH MEMORIES--!
MY MIND'S MADE ME WHAT I AM, HAL! IF I CAN'T COUNT ON IT--!
RRING
H-HELLO--?
SURE, OLLIE--HE'S HERE!

11

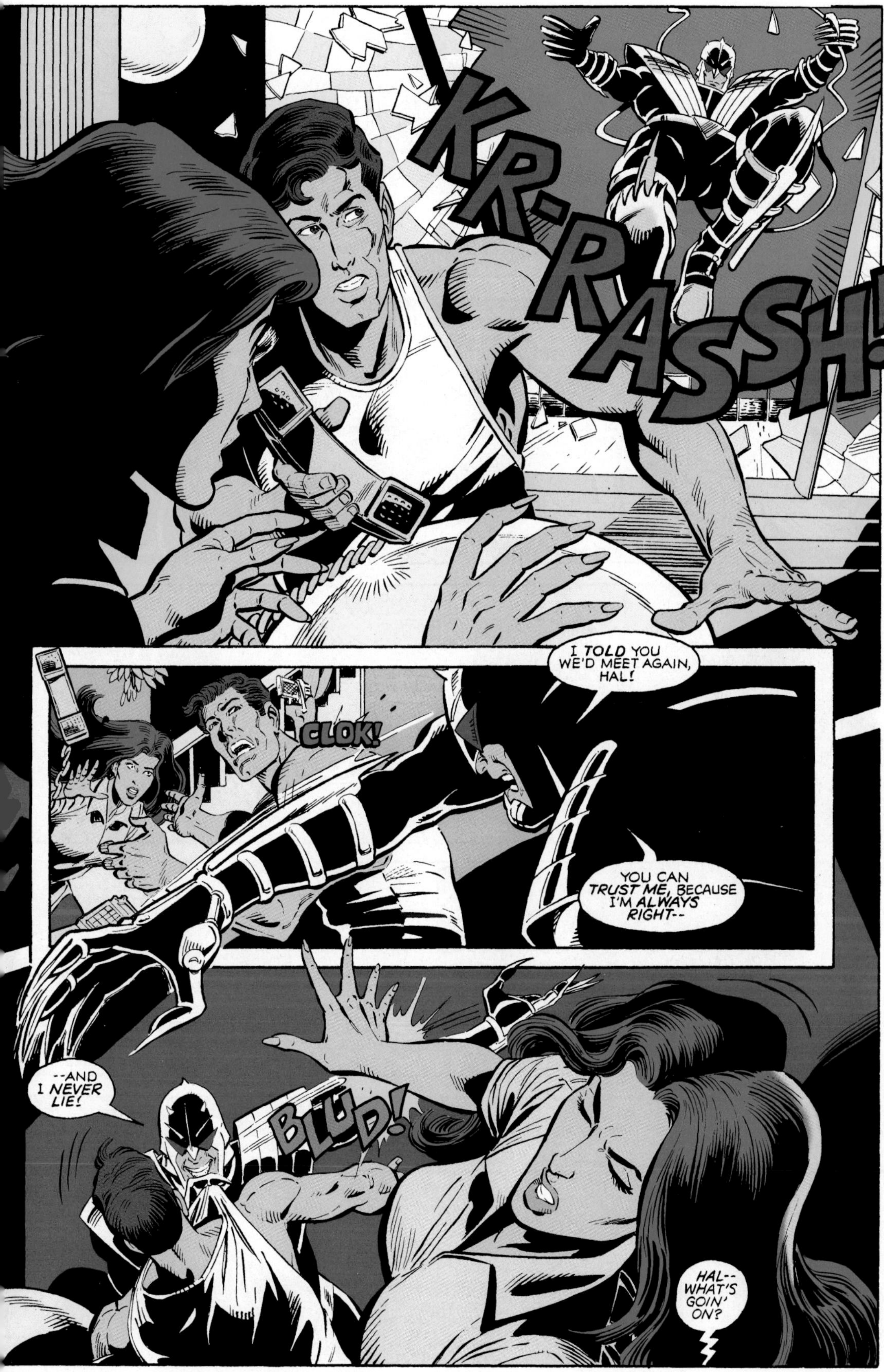
KR-RASSH!
I TOLD YOU WE'D MEET AGAIN, HAL!
CLOK!
YOU CAN TRUST ME, BECAUSE I'M ALWAYS RIGHT--
--AND I NEVER LIE!
BLUD!
HAL--WHAT'S GOIN' ON?

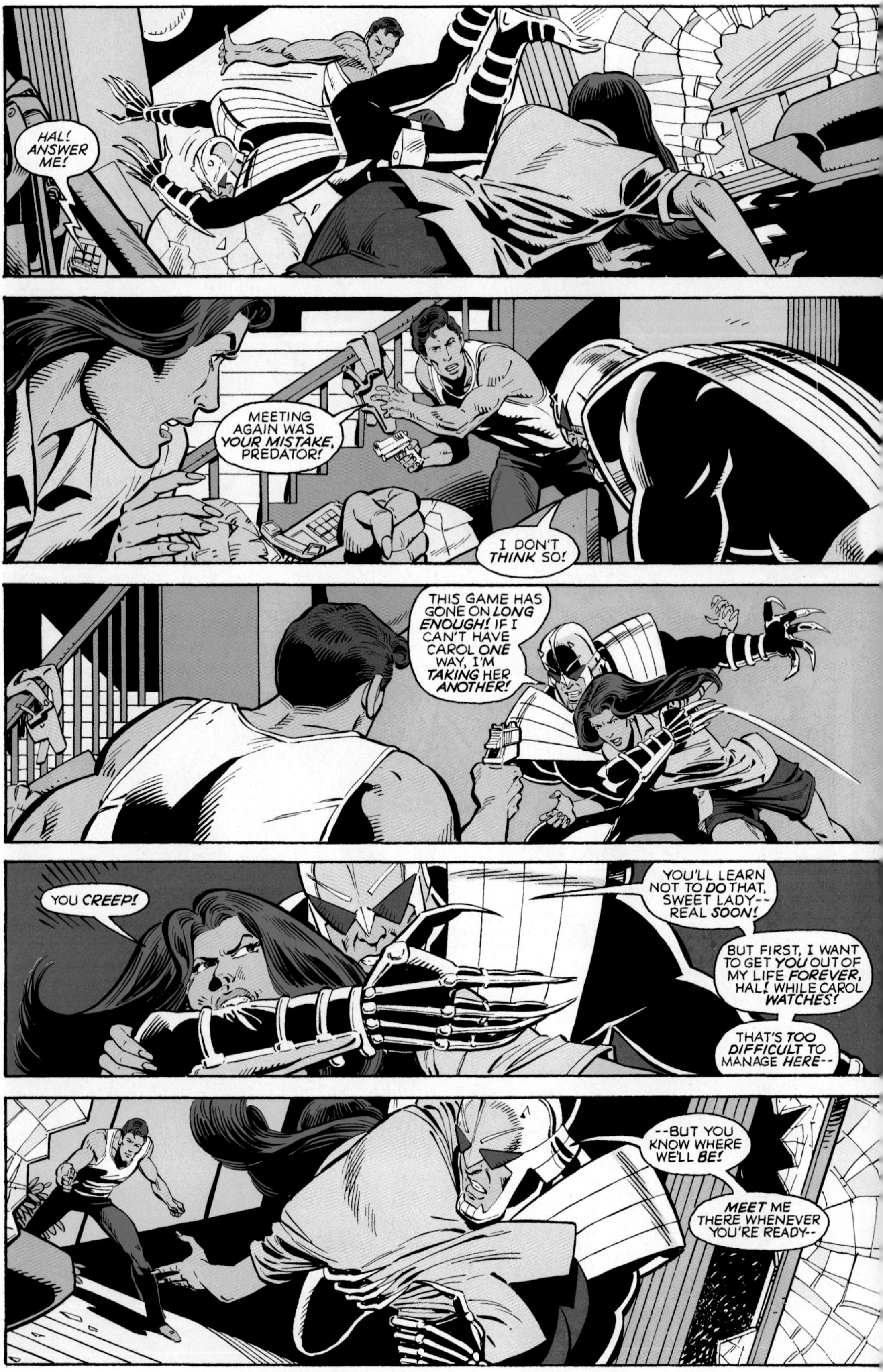
HAL! ANSWER ME!
MEETING AGAIN WAS YOUR MISTAKE, PREDATOR!
I DON'T THINK SO!
THIS GAME HAS GONE ON LONG ENOUGH! IF I CAN'T HAVE CAROL ONE WAY, I'M TAKING HER ANOTHER!
YOU CREEP!
YOU'LL LEARN NOT TO DO THAT, SWEET LADY--REAL SOON!
BUT FIRST, I WANT TO GET YOU OUT OF MY LIFE FOREVER, HAL! WHILE CAROL WATCHES!
THAT'S TOO DIFFICULT TO MANAGE HERE--
--BUT YOU KNOW WHERE WE'LL BE!
MEET ME THERE WHENEVER YOU'RE READY--

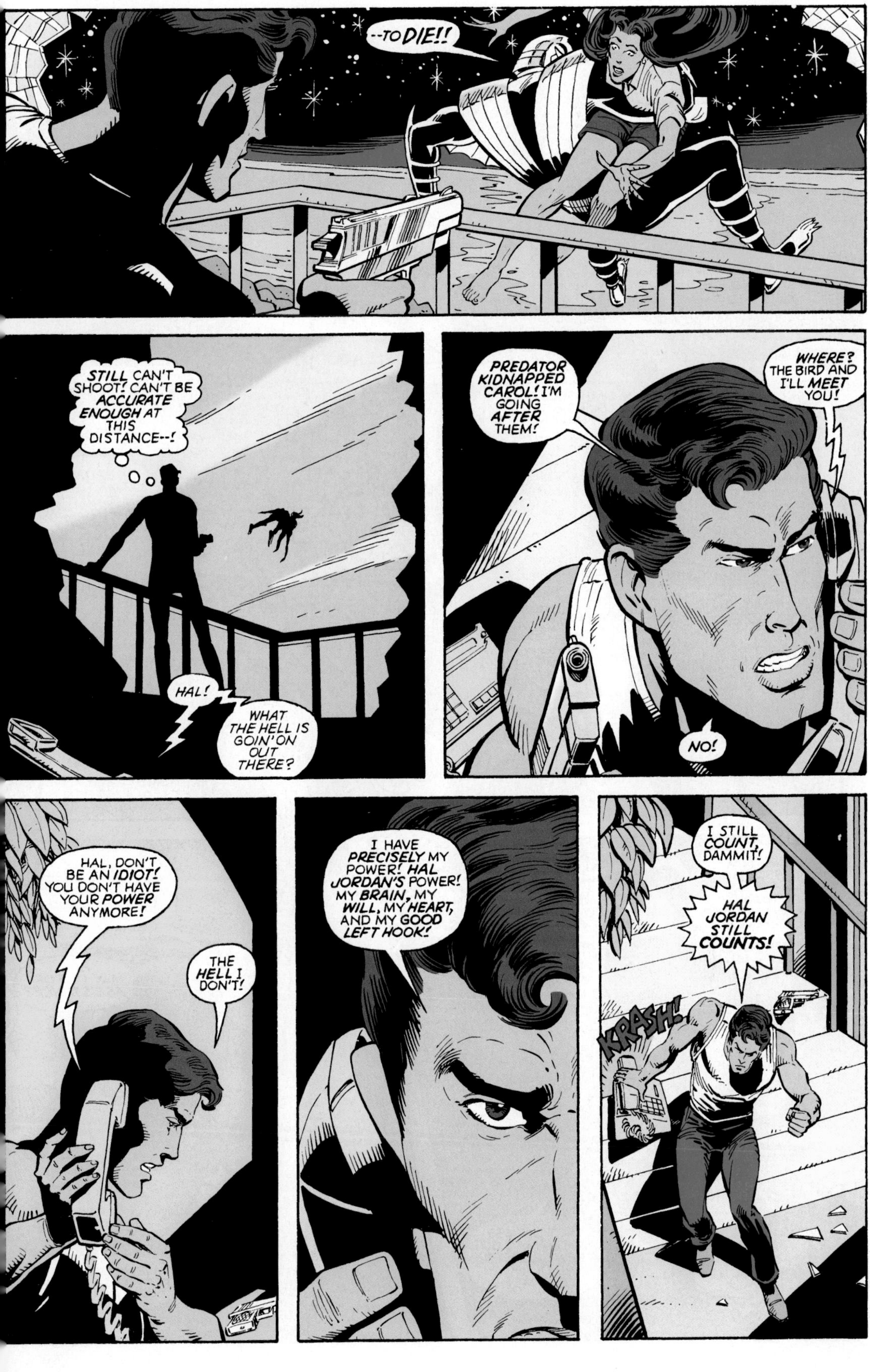
--TO DIE!!
STILL CAN'T SHOOT! CAN'T BE ACCURATE ENOUGH AT THIS DISTANCE--!
HAL!
WHAT THE HELL IS GOIN' ON OUT THERE?
PREDATOR KIDNAPPED CAROL! I'M GOING AFTER THEM!
WHERE? THE BIRD AND I'LL MEET YOU!
NO!
HAL, DON'T BE AN IDIOT! YOU DON'T HAVE YOUR POWER ANYMORE!
THE HELL I DON'T!
I HAVE PRECISELY MY POWER! HAL JORDAN'S POWER! MY BRAIN, MY WILL, MY HEART, AND MY GOOD LEFT HOOK!
I STILL COUNT, DAMMIT!
HAL JORDAN STILL COUNTS!
KRASH!

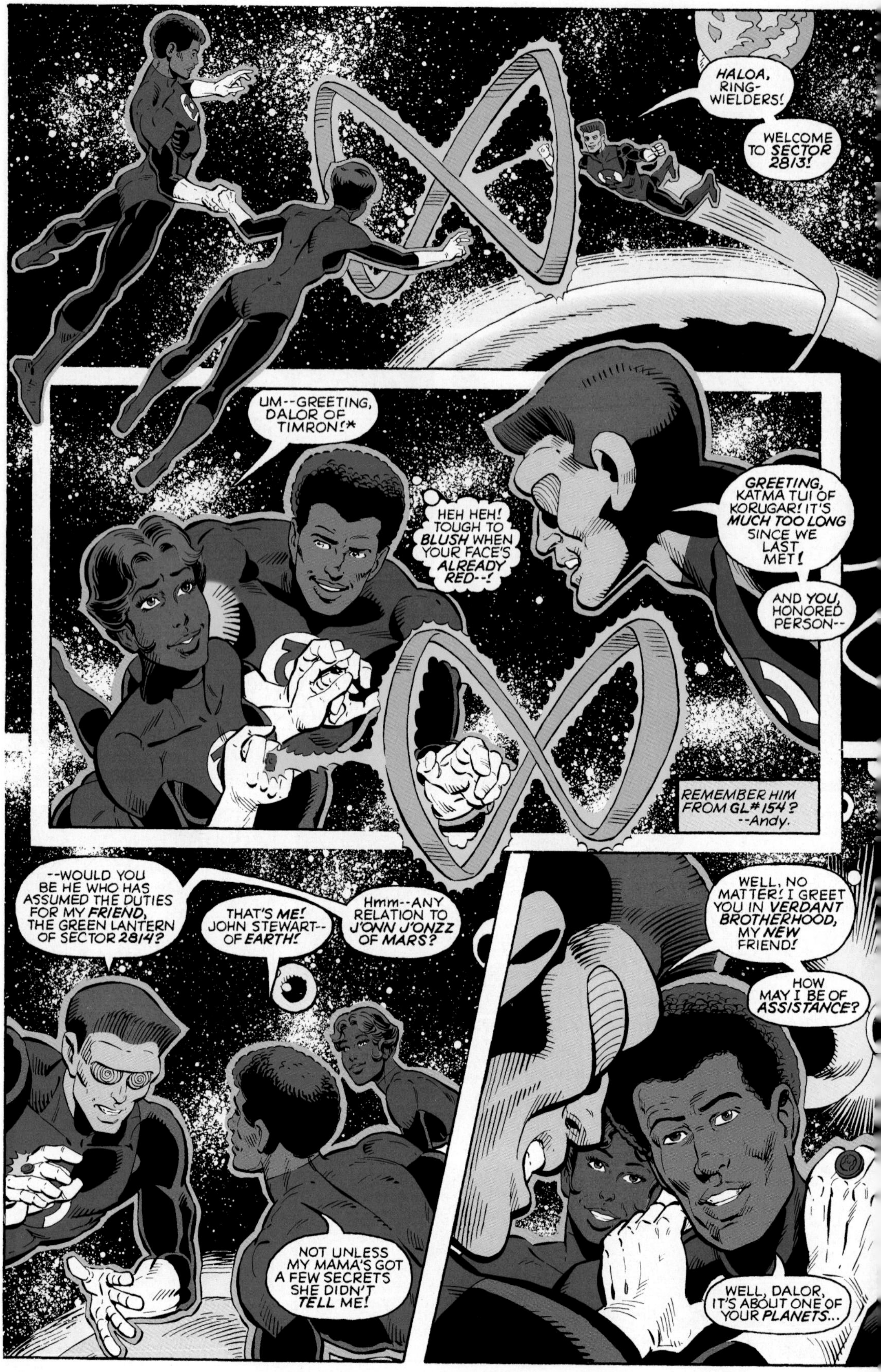
HALOA, RING-WIELDERS!
WELCOME TO SECTOR 2813!
UM--GREETING, DALOR OF TIMRON!*
HEH HEH! TOUGH TO BLUSH WHEN YOUR FACE'S ALREADY RED--!
GREETING, KATMA TUI OF KORUGAR! IT'S MUCH TOO LONG SINCE WE LAST MET!
AND YOU, HONORED PERSON--
REMEMBER HIM FROM GL#154? --Andy.
--WOULD YOU BE HE WHO HAS ASSUMED THE DUTIES FOR MY FRIEND, THE GREEN LANTERN OF SECTOR 2814?
THAT'S ME! JOHN STEWART-- OF EARTH!
Hmm--ANY RELATION TO J'ONN J'ONZZ OF MARS?
NOT UNLESS MY MAMA'S GOT A FEW SECRETS SHE DIDN'T TELL ME!
WELL, NO MATTER! I GREET YOU IN VERDANT BROTHERHOOD, MY NEW FRIEND!
HOW MAY I BE OF ASSISTANCE?
WELL, DALOR, IT'S ABOUT ONE OF YOUR PLANETS...

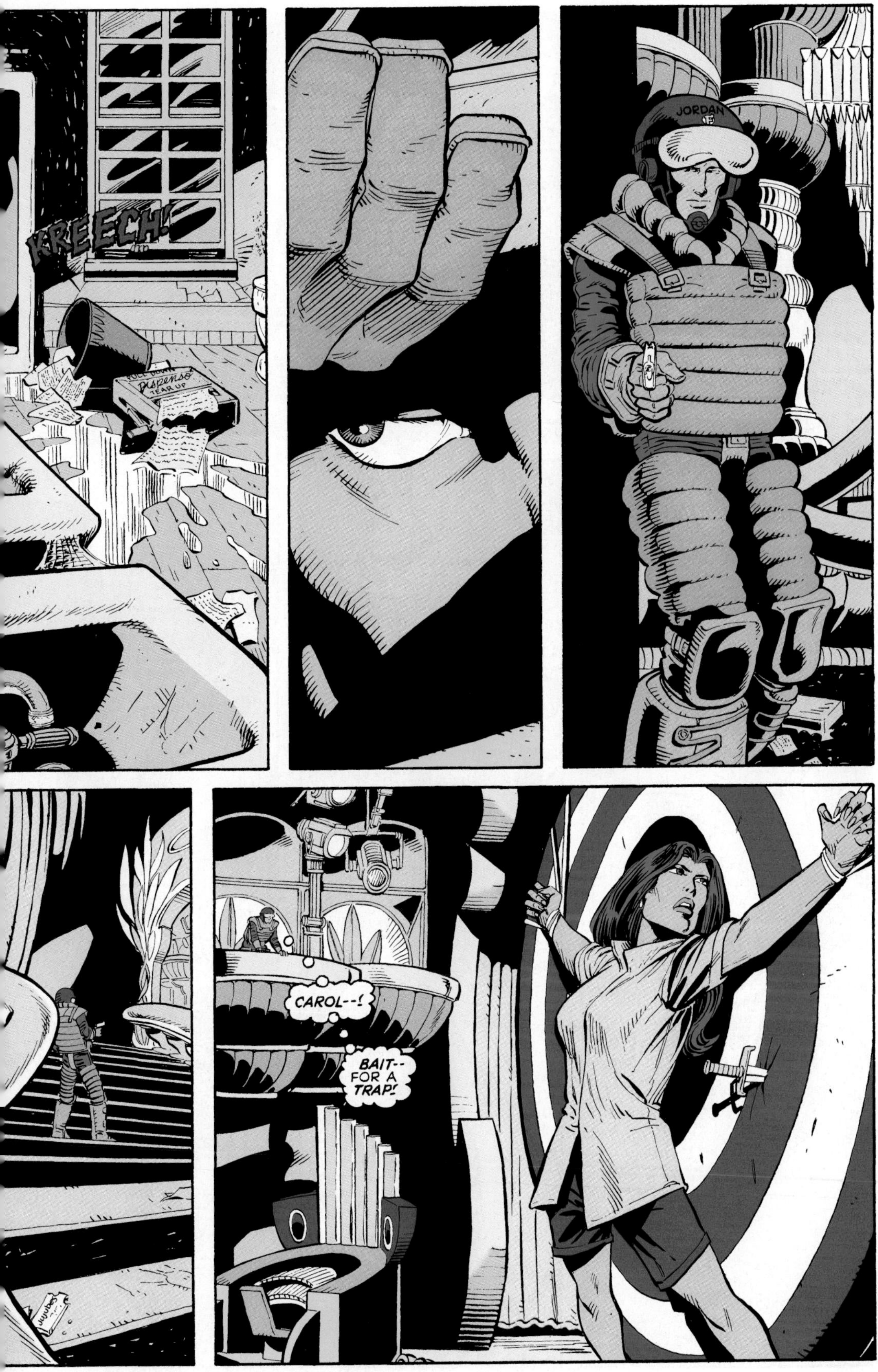
KREECH!
Dispenso
TEAR UP
JORDAN
CAROL--!
BAIT--
FOR A
TRAP!

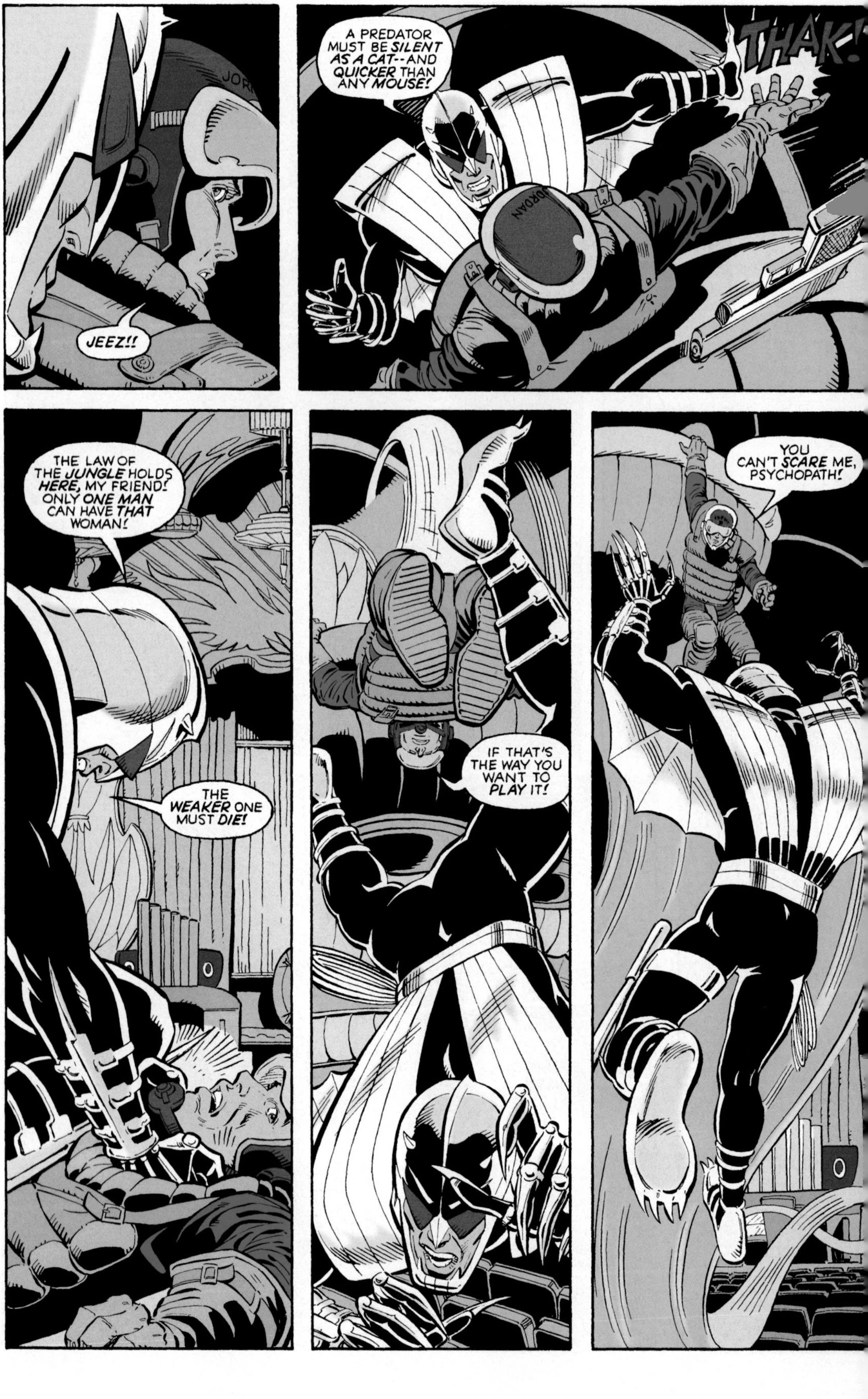
JEEZ!!
A PREDATOR MUST BE SILENT AS A CAT--AND QUICKER THAN ANY MOUSE!
THAK!
THE LAW OF THE JUNGLE HOLDS HERE, MY FRIEND! ONLY ONE MAN CAN HAVE THAT WOMAN!
THE WEAKER ONE MUST DIE!
IF THAT'S THE WAY YOU WANT TO PLAY IT!
YOU CAN'T SCARE ME, PSYCHOPATH!

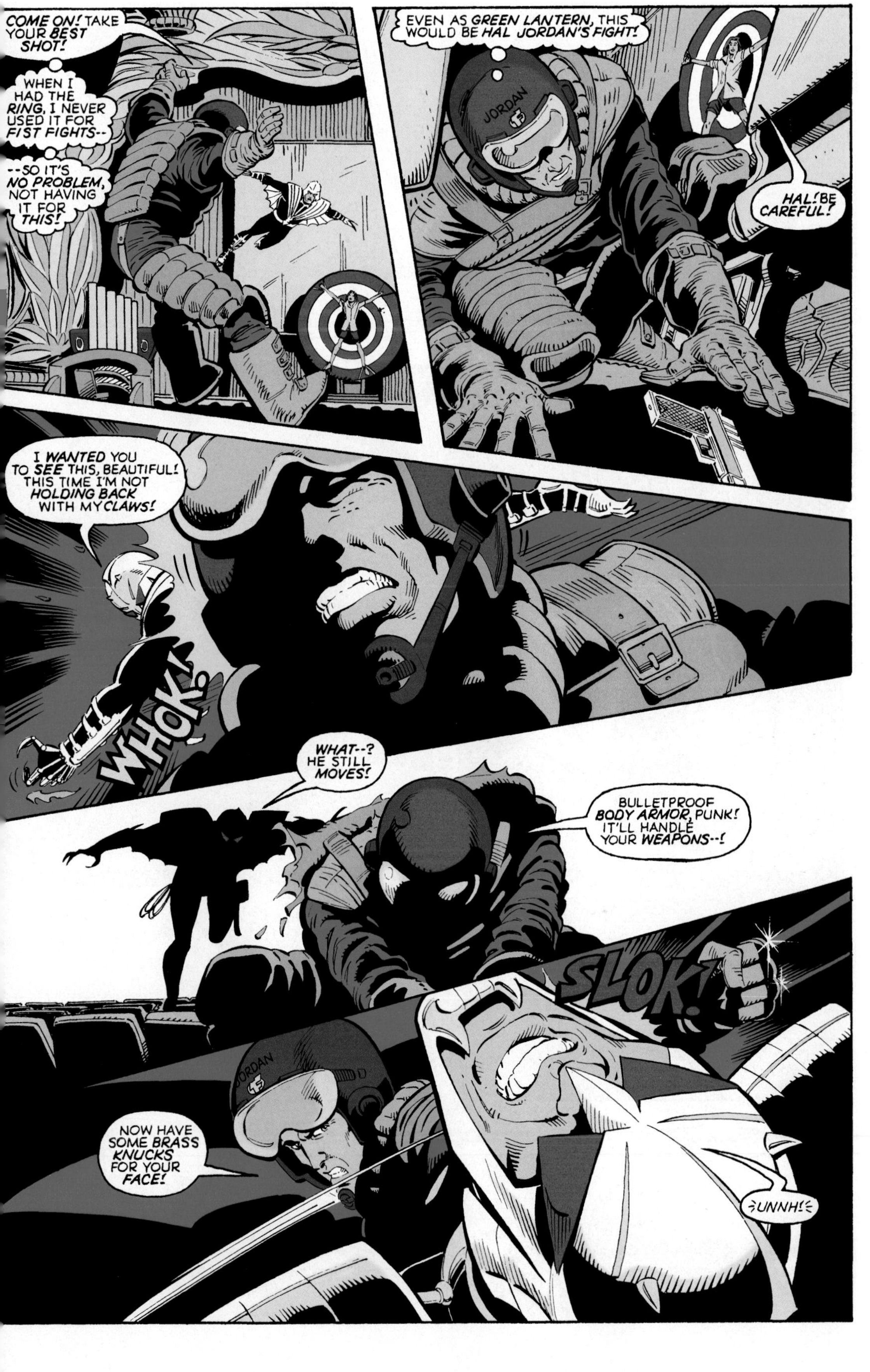
COME ON! TAKE YOUR BEST SHOT!
WHEN I HAD THE RING, I NEVER USED IT FOR FIST FIGHTS--
--SO IT'S NO PROBLEM, NOT HAVING IT FOR THIS!
EVEN AS GREEN LANTERN, THIS WOULD BE HAL JORDAN'S FIGHT!
JORDAN
HAL! BE CAREFUL!
I WANTED YOU TO SEE THIS, BEAUTIFUL! THIS TIME I'M NOT HOLDING BACK WITH MY CLAWS!
WHOK!
WHAT--? HE STILL MOVES!
BULLETPROOF BODY ARMOR, PUNK! IT'LL HANDLE YOUR WEAPONS--!
SLOK!
JORDAN
NOW HAVE SOME BRASS KNUCKS FOR YOUR FACE!
UNNH!

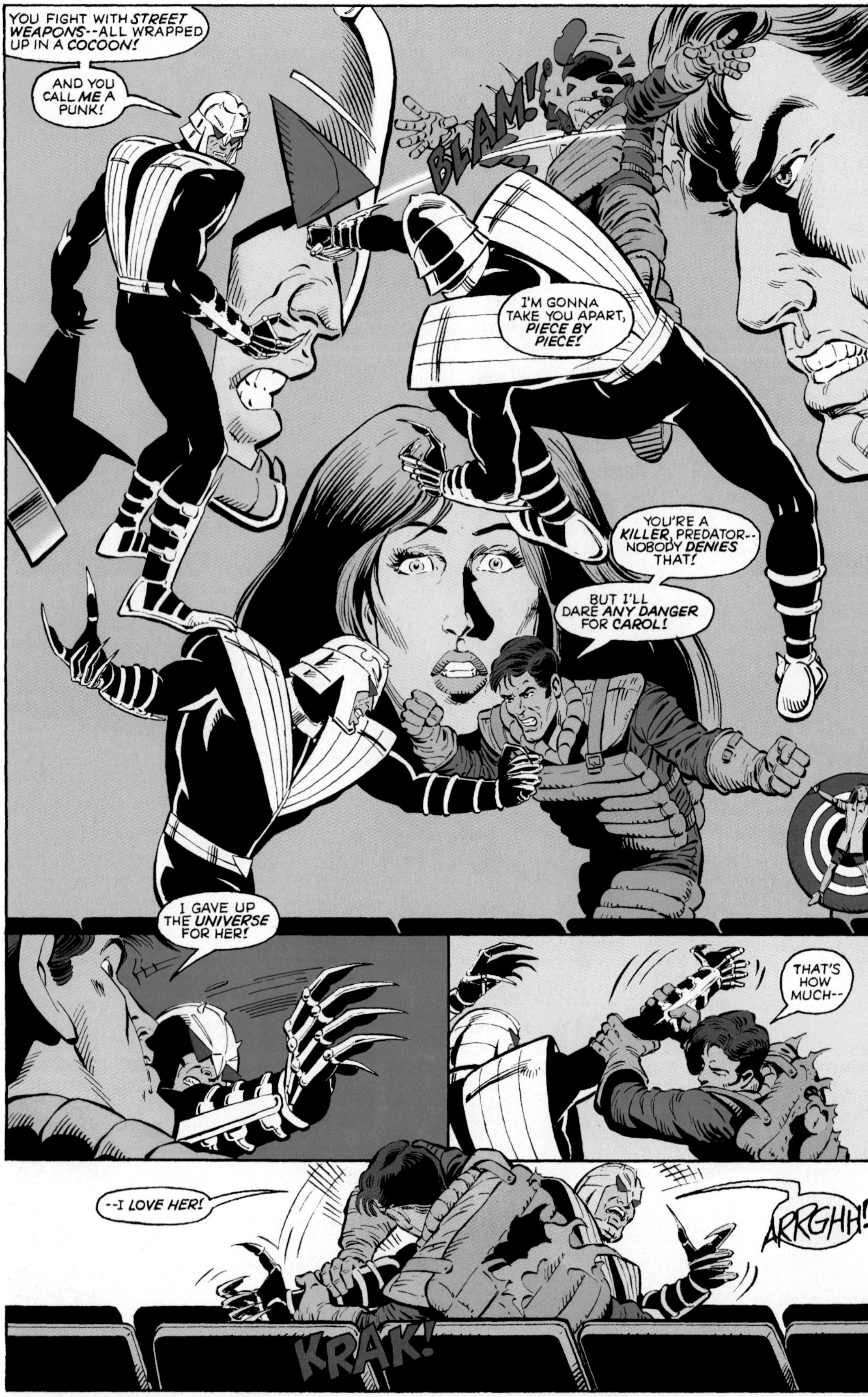

YOU FIGHT WITH STREET WEAPONS--ALL WRAPPED UP IN A COCOON!
AND YOU CALL ME A PUNK!
BLAM!
I'M GONNA TAKE YOU APART, PIECE BY PIECE!
YOU'RE A KILLER, PREDATOR--NOBODY DENIES THAT!
BUT I'LL DARE ANY DANGER FOR CAROL!
I GAVE UP THE UNIVERSE FOR HER!
THAT'S HOW MUCH--
--I LOVE HER!
ARRGHH!
KRAK!

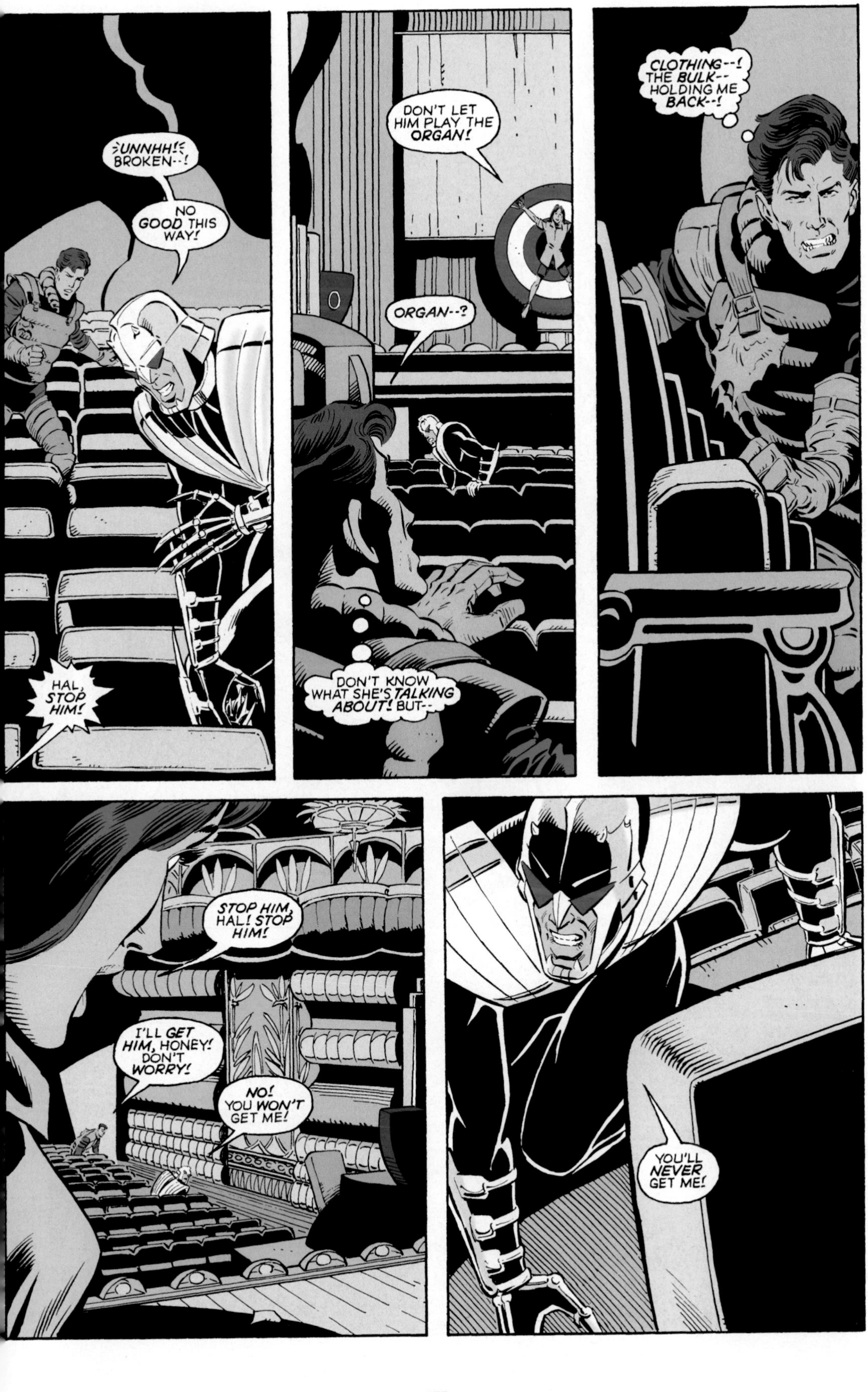

UNNHH! BROKEN--!
NO GOOD THIS WAY!
HAL, STOP HIM!
DON'T LET HIM PLAY THE ORGAN!
ORGAN--?
DON'T KNOW WHAT SHE'S TALKING ABOUT! BUT--
CLOTHING--! THE BULK-- HOLDING ME BACK--!
STOP HIM, HAL! STOP HIM!
I'LL GET HIM, HONEY! DON'T WORRY!
NO! YOU WON'T GET ME!
YOU'LL NEVER GET ME!

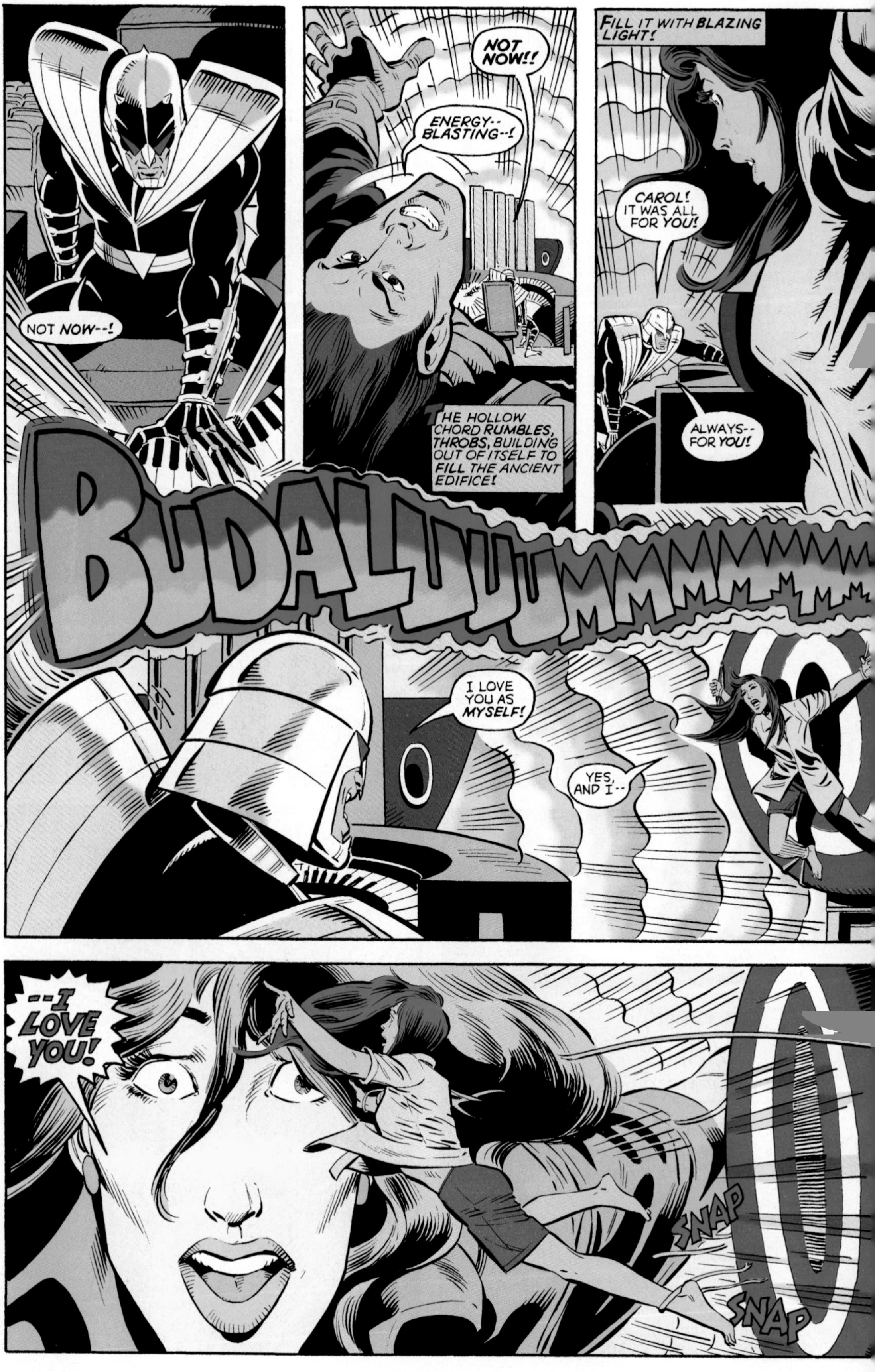
NOT NOW--!
NOT NOW!!
ENERGY-- BLASTING--!
THE HOLLOW CHORD RUMBLES, THROBS, BUILDING OUT OF ITSELF TO FILL THE ANCIENT EDIFICE!
FILL IT WITH BLAZING LIGHT!
CAROL! IT WAS ALL FOR YOU!
ALWAYS-- FOR YOU!
BUDALUUUMMMMMMMM
I LOVE YOU AS MYSELF!
YES, AND I--
--I LOVE YOU!
SNAP
SNAP

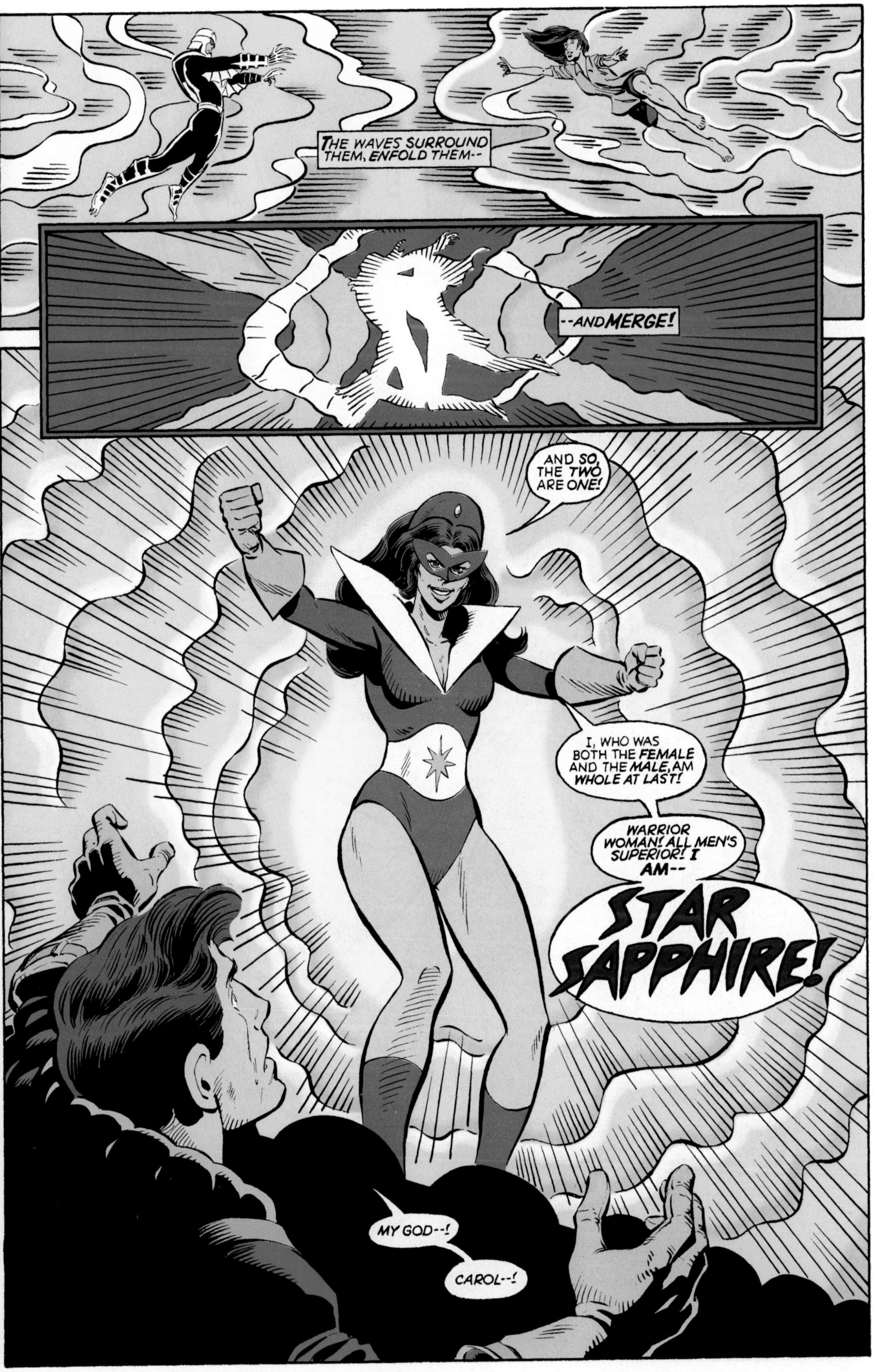
THE WAVES SURROUND THEM, ENFOLD THEM--
--AND MERGE!
AND SO, THE TWO ARE ONE!
I, WHO WAS BOTH THE FEMALE AND THE MALE, AM WHOLE AT LAST!
WARRIOR WOMAN! ALL MEN'S SUPERIOR! I AM--
STAR SAPPHIRE!
MY GOD--!
CAROL--!

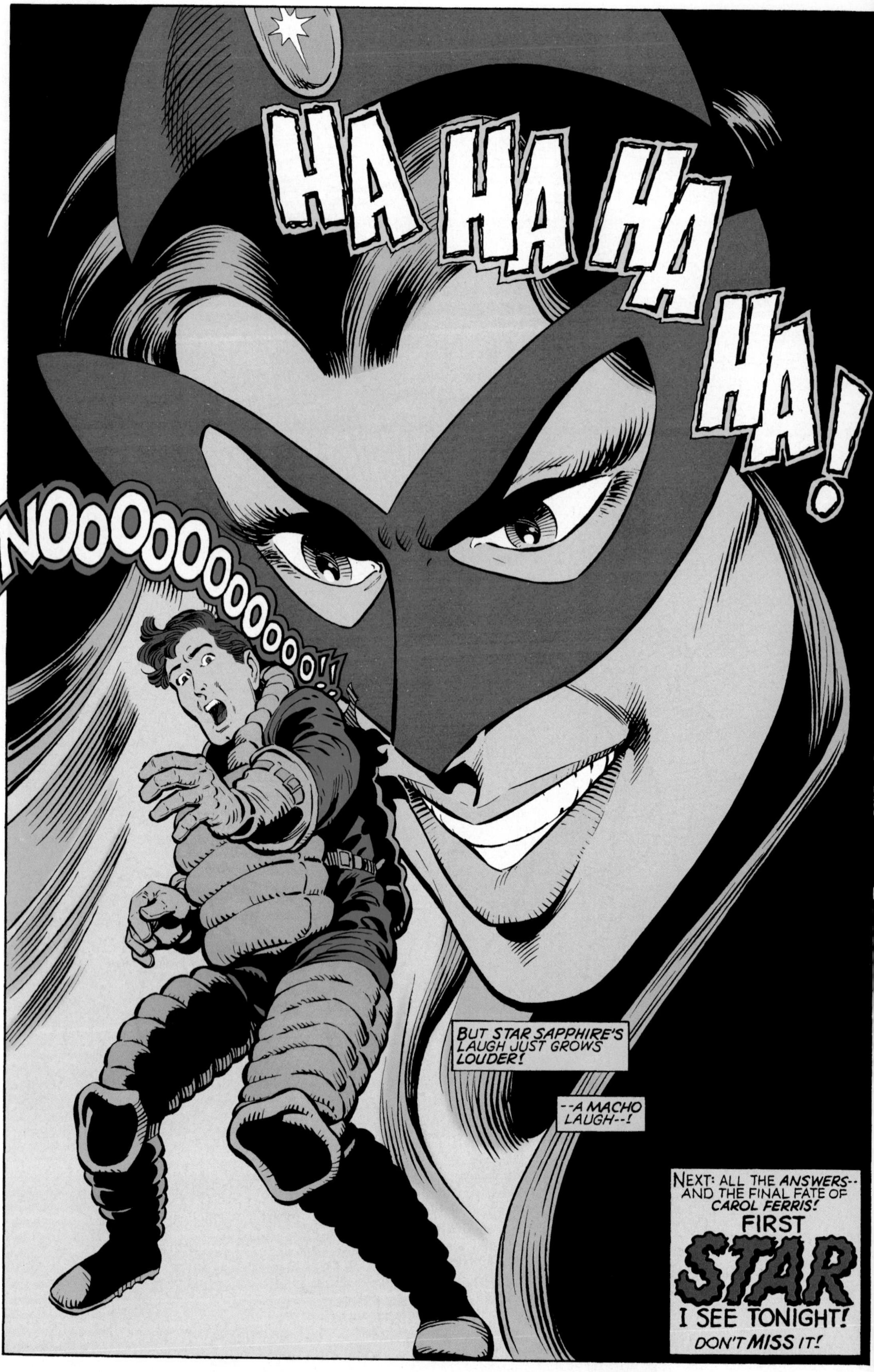
HA HA HA HA HA!
NOOOOOOOOOOOOOO!!
BUT STAR SAPPHIRE'S LAUGH JUST GROWS LOUDER!
--A MACHO LAUGH--!
NEXT: ALL THE ANSWERS-- AND THE FINAL FATE OF CAROL FERRIS!
FIRST STAR I SEE TONIGHT!
DON'T MISS IT!

Cover art by Joe Staton & Bruce Patterson

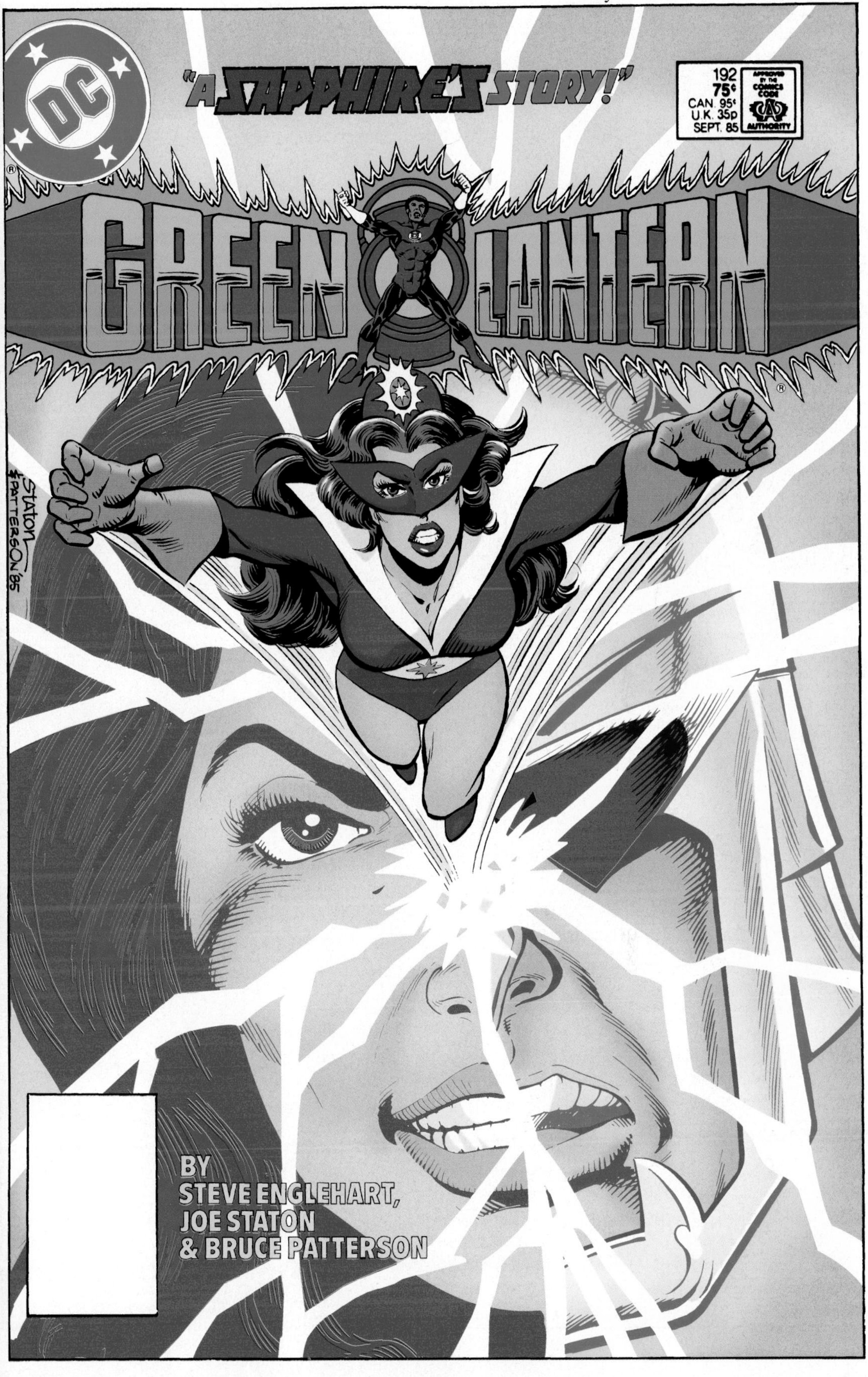
"A SAPPHIRE'S STORY!"
192
75¢
CAN. 95¢
U.K. 35p
SEPT. 85
APPROVED BY THE COMICS CODE AUTHORITY
GREEN LANTERN
STATON & PATTERSON '85
BY
STEVE ENGLEHART,
JOE STATON
& BRUCE PATTERSON

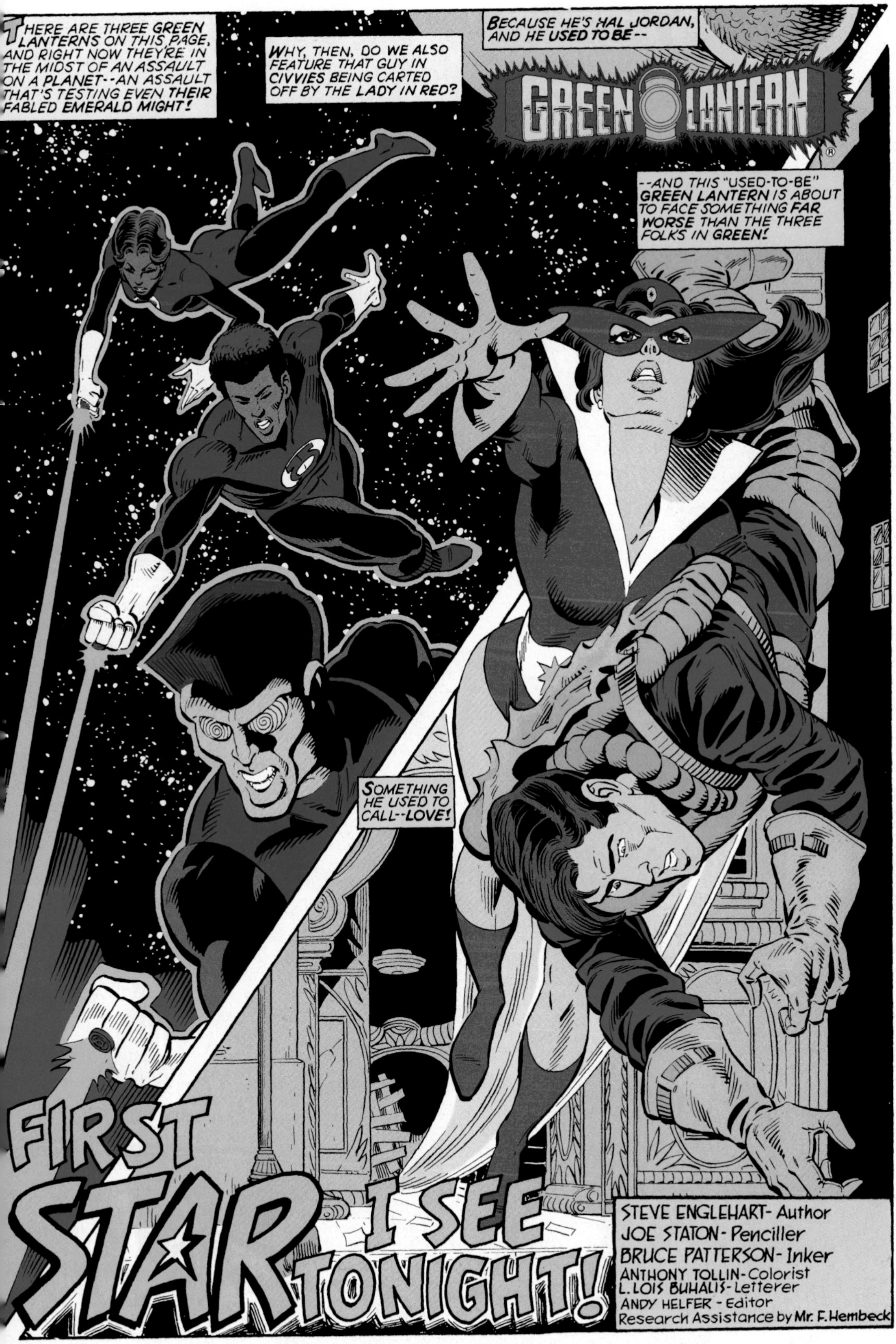
THERE ARE THREE GREEN LANTERNS ON THIS PAGE, AND RIGHT NOW THEY'RE IN THE MIDST OF AN ASSAULT ON A PLANET--AN ASSAULT THAT'S TESTING EVEN THEIR FABLED EMERALD MIGHT!
WHY, THEN, DO WE ALSO FEATURE THAT GUY IN CIVVIES BEING CARTED OFF BY THE LADY IN RED?
BECAUSE HE'S HAL JORDAN, AND HE USED TO BE--
GREEN LANTERN
--AND THIS "USED-TO-BE" GREEN LANTERN IS ABOUT TO FACE SOMETHING FAR WORSE THAN THE THREE FOLKS IN GREEN!
SOMETHING HE USED TO CALL--LOVE!
FIRST STAR I SEE TONIGHT!
STEVE ENGLEHART- Author
JOE STATON- Penciller
BRUCE PATTERSON- Inker
ANTHONY TOLLIN- Colorist
L. LOIS BUHALIS- Letterer
ANDY HELFER - Editor
Research Assistance by Mr. F. Hembeck

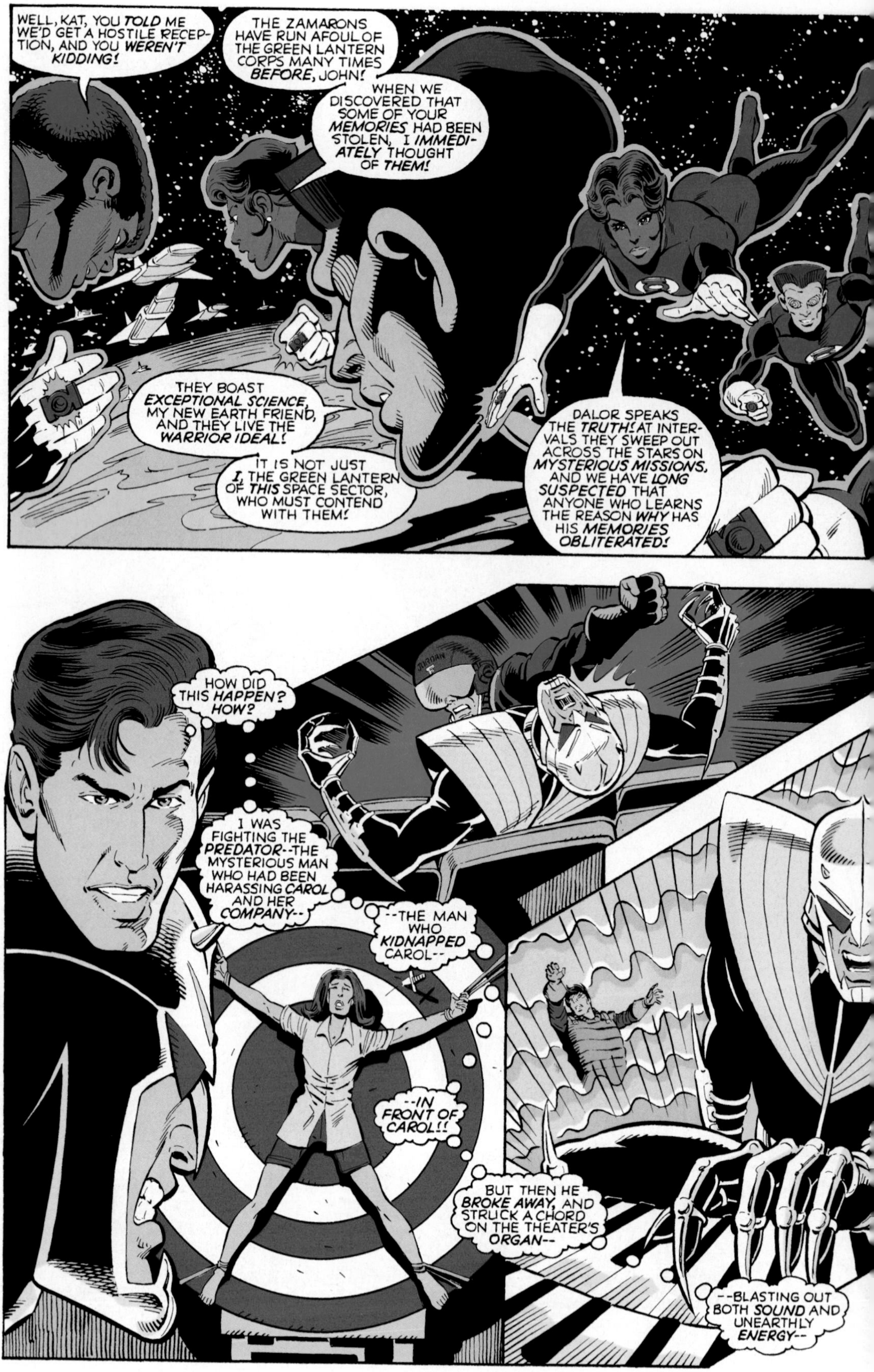
WELL, KAT, YOU TOLD ME WE'D GET A HOSTILE RECEPTION, AND YOU WEREN'T KIDDING!
THE ZAMARONS HAVE RUN AFOUL OF THE GREEN LANTERN CORPS MANY TIMES BEFORE, JOHN!
WHEN WE DISCOVERED THAT SOME OF YOUR MEMORIES HAD BEEN STOLEN, I IMMEDIATELY THOUGHT OF THEM!
THEY BOAST EXCEPTIONAL SCIENCE, MY NEW EARTH FRIEND, AND THEY LIVE THE WARRIOR IDEAL!
IT IS NOT JUST I, THE GREEN LANTERN OF THIS SPACE SECTOR, WHO MUST CONTEND WITH THEM!
DALOR SPEAKS THE TRUTH! AT INTERVALS THEY SWEEP OUT ACROSS THE STARS ON MYSTERIOUS MISSIONS, AND WE HAVE LONG SUSPECTED THAT ANYONE WHO LEARNS THE REASON WHY HAS HIS MEMORIES OBLITERATED!
HOW DID THIS HAPPEN? HOW?
I WAS FIGHTING THE PREDATOR--THE MYSTERIOUS MAN WHO HAD BEEN HARASSING CAROL AND HER COMPANY--
--THE MAN WHO KIDNAPPED CAROL--
--IN FRONT OF CAROL!!
BUT THEN HE BROKE AWAY, AND STRUCK A CHORD ON THE THEATER'S ORGAN--
--BLASTING OUT BOTH SOUND AND UNEARTHLY ENERGY--

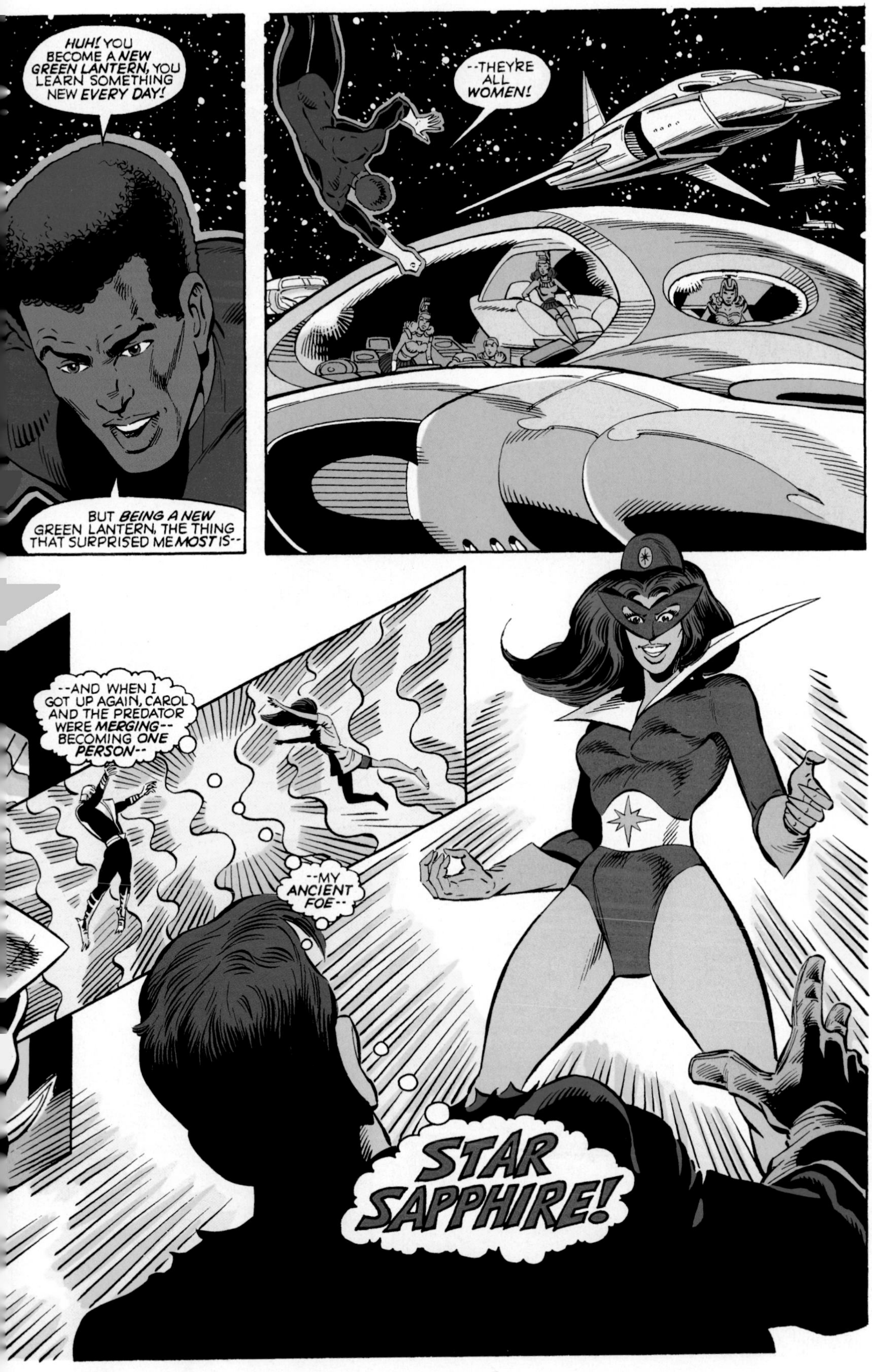
HUH! YOU BECOME A NEW GREEN LANTERN, YOU LEARN SOMETHING NEW EVERY DAY!
BUT BEING A NEW GREEN LANTERN, THE THING THAT SURPRISED ME MOST IS--
--THEY'RE ALL WOMEN!
--AND WHEN I GOT UP AGAIN, CAROL AND THE PREDATOR WERE MERGING-- BECOMING ONE PERSON--
--MY ANCIENT FOE--
STAR SAPPHIRE!

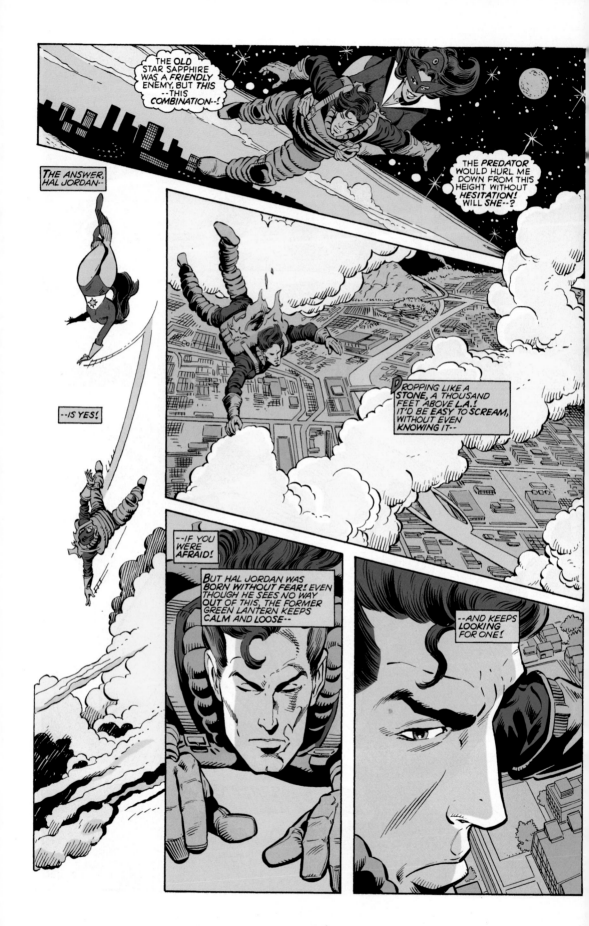

THE OLD STAR SAPPHIRE WAS A *FRIENDLY* ENEMY, BUT *THIS* --THIS *COMBINATION*--!

THE *PREDATOR* WOULD HURL ME DOWN FROM THIS HEIGHT WITHOUT *HESITATION!* WILL *SHE*--?

THE *ANSWER*, HAL JORDAN--

--IS *YES!*

*D*ROPPING LIKE A *STONE*, A *THOUSAND* FEET ABOVE *L.A.!* IT'D BE *EASY* TO *SCREAM*, WITHOUT EVEN *KNOWING* IT--

--IF YOU *WERE* AFRAID!

BUT HAL JORDAN WAS *BORN WITHOUT FEAR!* EVEN THOUGH HE SEES *NO WAY OUT* OF THIS, THE FORMER GREEN LANTERN KEEPS *CALM* AND *LOOSE*--

--AND KEEPS *LOOKING* FOR ONE!

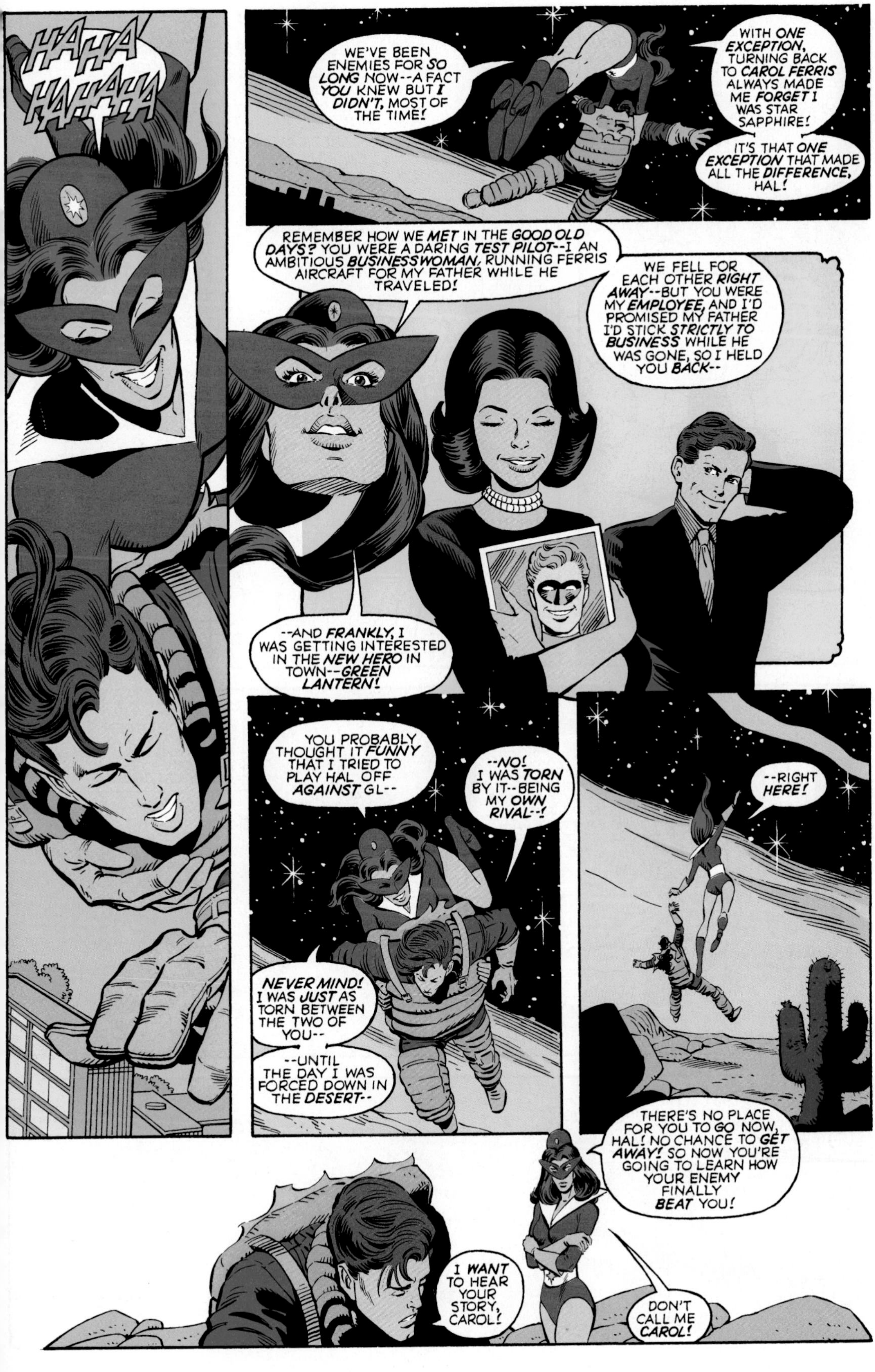
HAHA HAHAHA
WE'VE BEEN ENEMIES FOR SO LONG NOW--A FACT YOU KNEW BUT I DIDN'T, MOST OF THE TIME!
WITH ONE EXCEPTION, TURNING BACK TO CAROL FERRIS ALWAYS MADE ME FORGET I WAS STAR SAPPHIRE!
IT'S THAT ONE EXCEPTION THAT MADE ALL THE DIFFERENCE, HAL!
REMEMBER HOW WE MET IN THE GOOD OLD DAYS? YOU WERE A DARING TEST PILOT--I AN AMBITIOUS BUSINESSWOMAN, RUNNING FERRIS AIRCRAFT FOR MY FATHER WHILE HE TRAVELED!
WE FELL FOR EACH OTHER RIGHT AWAY--BUT YOU WERE MY EMPLOYEE, AND I'D PROMISED MY FATHER I'D STICK STRICTLY TO BUSINESS WHILE HE WAS GONE, SO I HELD YOU BACK--
--AND FRANKLY, I WAS GETTING INTERESTED IN THE NEW HERO IN TOWN--GREEN LANTERN!
YOU PROBABLY THOUGHT IT FUNNY THAT I TRIED TO PLAY HAL OFF AGAINST GL--
--NO! I WAS TORN BY IT--BEING MY OWN RIVAL--!
NEVER MIND! I WAS JUST AS TORN BETWEEN THE TWO OF YOU--
--UNTIL THE DAY I WAS FORCED DOWN IN THE DESERT--
--RIGHT HERE!
THERE'S NO PLACE FOR YOU TO GO NOW, HAL! NO CHANCE TO GET AWAY! SO NOW YOU'RE GOING TO LEARN HOW YOUR ENEMY FINALLY BEAT YOU!
I WANT TO HEAR YOUR STORY, CAROL!
DON'T CALL ME CAROL!

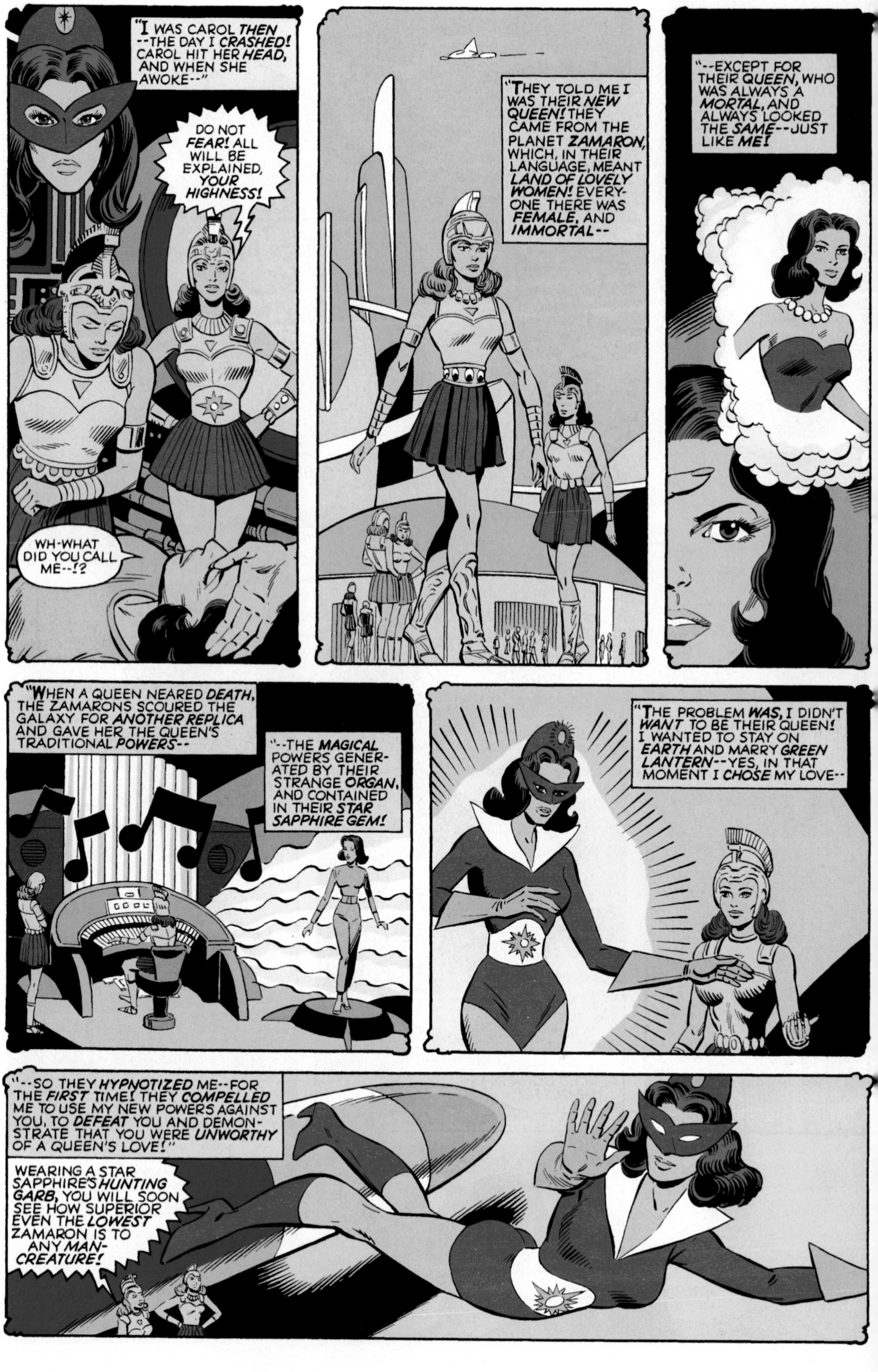
"I WAS CAROL THEN --THE DAY I CRASHED! CAROL HIT HER HEAD, AND WHEN SHE AWOKE--"
DO NOT FEAR! ALL WILL BE EXPLAINED, YOUR HIGHNESS!
WH-WHAT DID YOU CALL ME--!?
"THEY TOLD ME I WAS THEIR NEW QUEEN! THEY CAME FROM THE PLANET ZAMARON, WHICH, IN THEIR LANGUAGE, MEANT LAND OF LOVELY WOMEN! EVERYONE THERE WAS FEMALE, AND IMMORTAL--
"--EXCEPT FOR THEIR QUEEN, WHO WAS ALWAYS A MORTAL, AND ALWAYS LOOKED THE SAME--JUST LIKE ME!
"WHEN A QUEEN NEARED DEATH, THE ZAMARONS SCOURED THE GALAXY FOR ANOTHER REPLICA AND GAVE HER THE QUEEN'S TRADITIONAL POWERS--
"--THE MAGICAL POWERS GENERATED BY THEIR STRANGE ORGAN, AND CONTAINED IN THEIR STAR SAPPHIRE GEM!
"THE PROBLEM WAS, I DIDN'T WANT TO BE THEIR QUEEN! I WANTED TO STAY ON EARTH AND MARRY GREEN LANTERN--YES, IN THAT MOMENT I CHOSE MY LOVE--
"--SO THEY HYPNOTIZED ME--FOR THE FIRST TIME! THEY COMPELLED ME TO USE MY NEW POWERS AGAINST YOU, TO DEFEAT YOU AND DEMONSTRATE THAT YOU WERE UNWORTHY OF A QUEEN'S LOVE!"
WEARING A STAR SAPPHIRE'S HUNTING GARB, YOU WILL SOON SEE HOW SUPERIOR EVEN THE LOWEST ZAMARON IS TO ANY MAN-CREATURE!

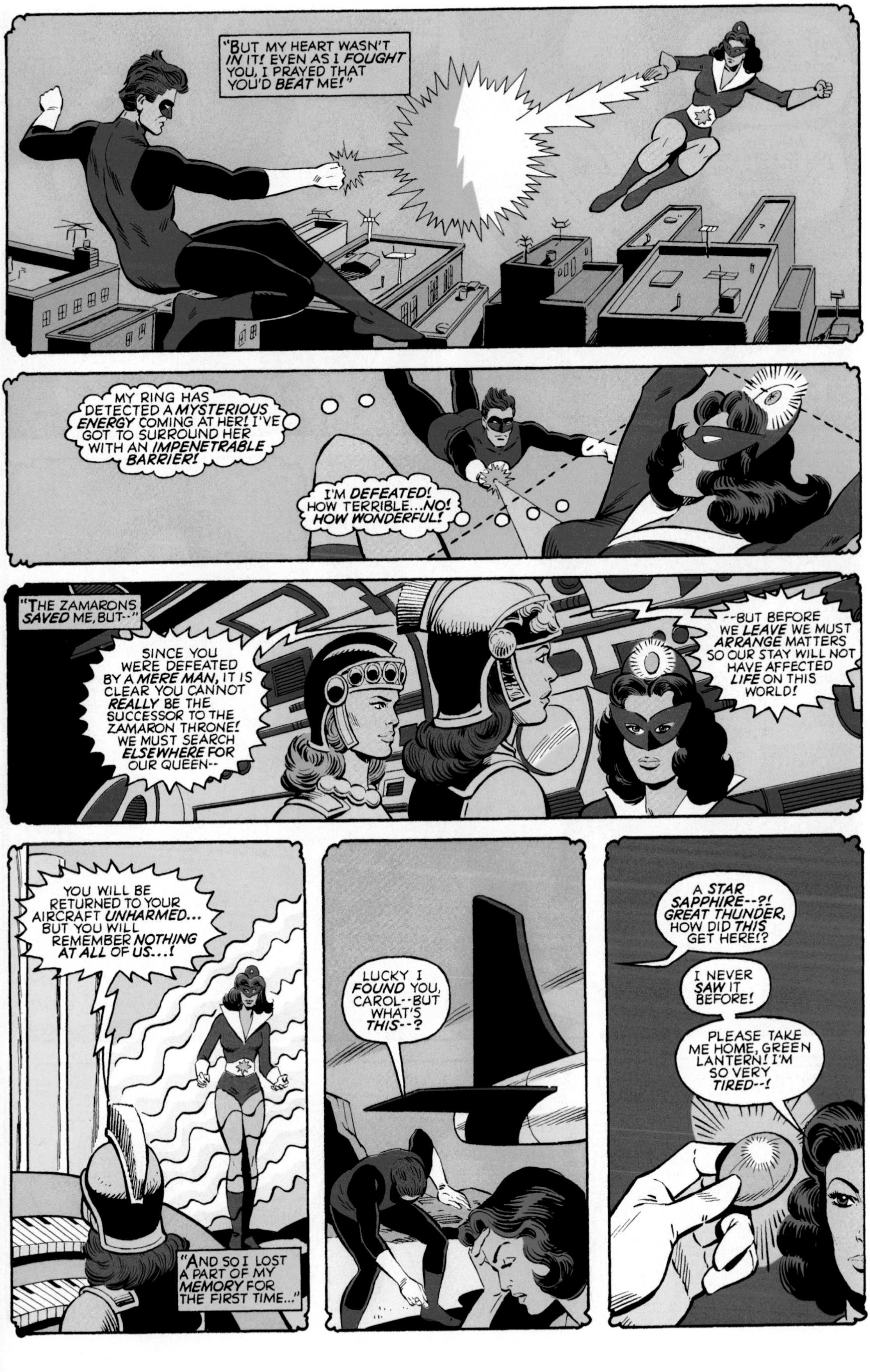
"BUT MY HEART WASN'T IN IT! EVEN AS I FOUGHT YOU, I PRAYED THAT YOU'D BEAT ME!"
MY RING HAS DETECTED A MYSTERIOUS ENERGY COMING AT HER! I'VE GOT TO SURROUND HER WITH AN IMPENETRABLE BARRIER!
I'M DEFEATED! HOW TERRIBLE...NO! HOW WONDERFUL!
"THE ZAMARONS SAVED ME, BUT--"
SINCE YOU WERE DEFEATED BY A MERE MAN, IT IS CLEAR YOU CANNOT REALLY BE THE SUCCESSOR TO THE ZAMARON THRONE! WE MUST SEARCH ELSEWHERE FOR OUR QUEEN--
--BUT BEFORE WE LEAVE WE MUST ARRANGE MATTERS SO OUR STAY WILL NOT HAVE AFFECTED LIFE ON THIS WORLD!
YOU WILL BE RETURNED TO YOUR AIRCRAFT UNHARMED... BUT YOU WILL REMEMBER NOTHING AT ALL OF US...!
"AND SO I LOST A PART OF MY MEMORY FOR THE FIRST TIME..."
LUCKY I FOUND YOU, CAROL--BUT WHAT'S THIS--?
A STAR SAPPHIRE--?! GREAT THUNDER, HOW DID THIS GET HERE!?
I NEVER SAW IT BEFORE!
PLEASE TAKE ME HOME, GREEN LANTERN! I'M SO VERY TIRED--!

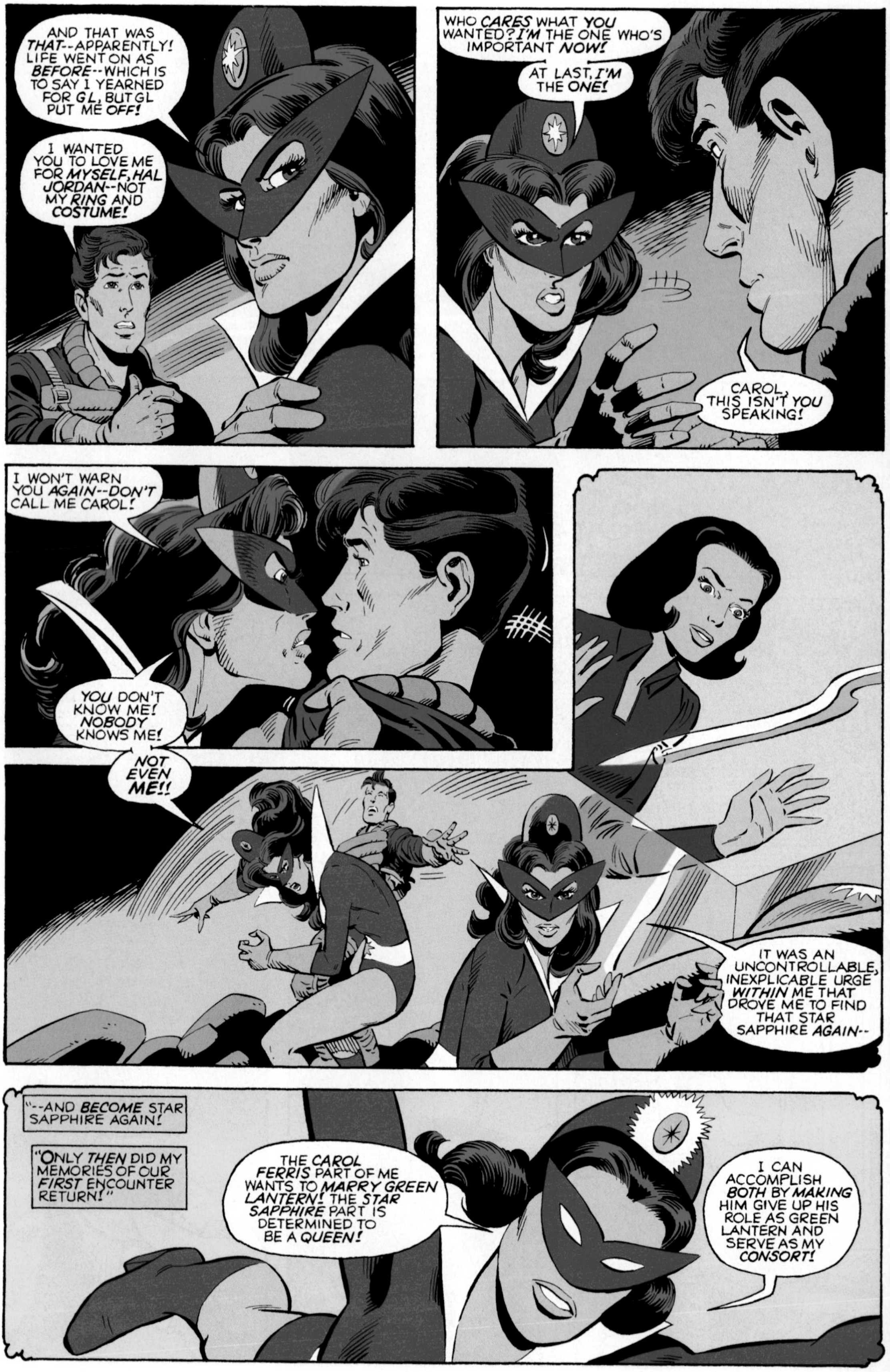
AND THAT WAS THAT--APPARENTLY! LIFE WENT ON AS BEFORE--WHICH IS TO SAY I YEARNED FOR GL, BUT GL PUT ME OFF!
I WANTED YOU TO LOVE ME FOR MYSELF, HAL JORDAN--NOT MY RING AND COSTUME!
WHO CARES WHAT YOU WANTED? I'M THE ONE WHO'S IMPORTANT NOW!
AT LAST, I'M THE ONE!
CAROL, THIS ISN'T YOU SPEAKING!
I WON'T WARN YOU AGAIN--DON'T CALL ME CAROL!
YOU DON'T KNOW ME! NOBODY KNOWS ME!
NOT EVEN ME!!
IT WAS AN UNCONTROLLABLE, INEXPLICABLE URGE WITHIN ME THAT DROVE ME TO FIND THAT STAR SAPPHIRE AGAIN--
"--AND BECOME STAR SAPPHIRE AGAIN!
"ONLY THEN DID MY MEMORIES OF OUR FIRST ENCOUNTER RETURN!"
THE CAROL FERRIS PART OF ME WANTS TO MARRY GREEN LANTERN! THE STAR SAPPHIRE PART IS DETERMINED TO BE A QUEEN!
I CAN ACCOMPLISH BOTH BY MAKING HIM GIVE UP HIS ROLE AS GREEN LANTERN AND SERVE AS MY CONSORT!

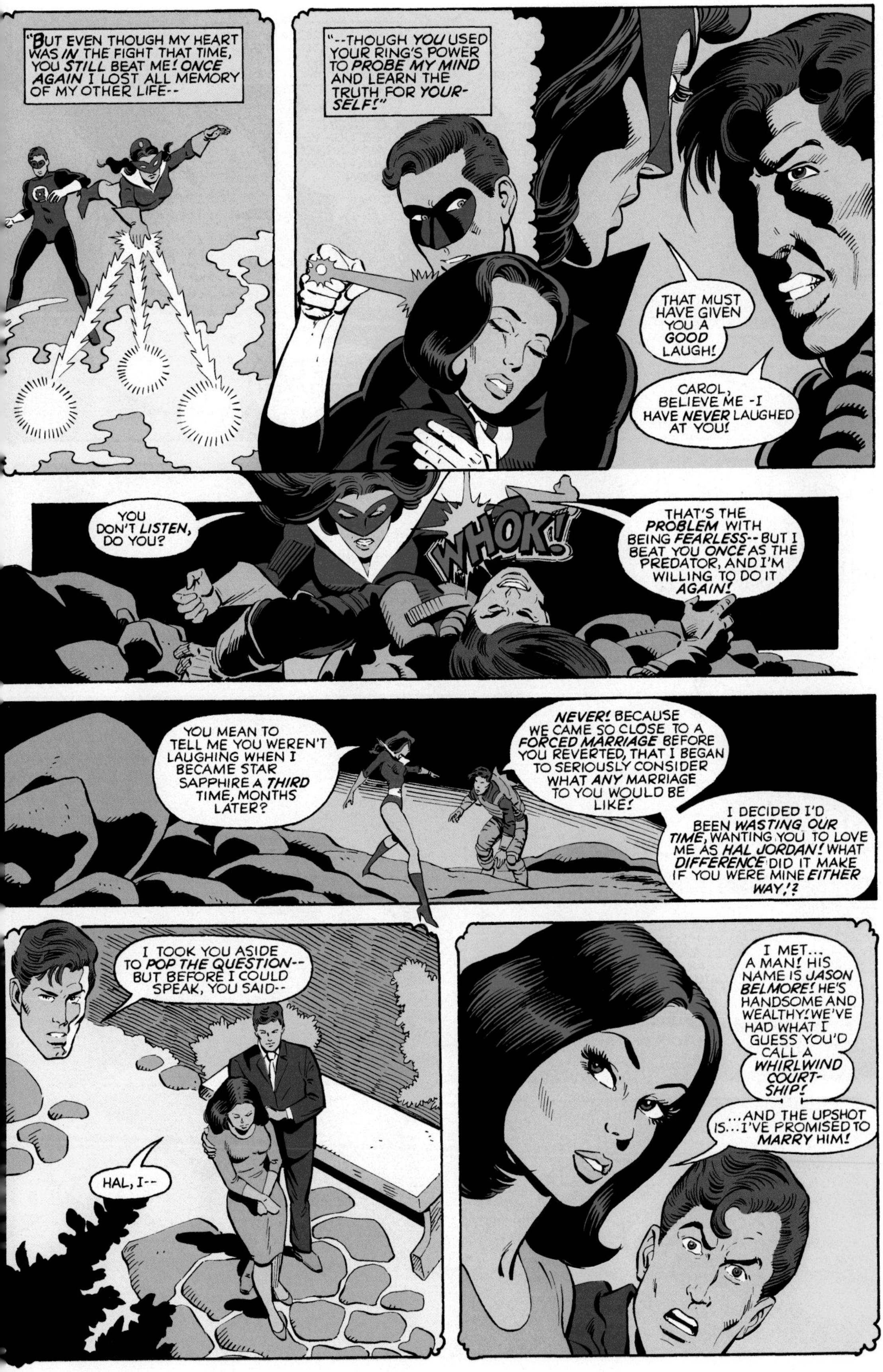
"BUT EVEN THOUGH MY HEART WAS IN THE FIGHT THAT TIME, YOU STILL BEAT ME! ONCE AGAIN I LOST ALL MEMORY OF MY OTHER LIFE--
"--THOUGH YOU USED YOUR RING'S POWER TO PROBE MY MIND AND LEARN THE TRUTH FOR YOURSELF!"
THAT MUST HAVE GIVEN YOU A GOOD LAUGH!
CAROL, BELIEVE ME -I HAVE NEVER LAUGHED AT YOU!
YOU DON'T LISTEN, DO YOU?
WHOK!
THAT'S THE PROBLEM WITH BEING FEARLESS--BUT I BEAT YOU ONCE AS THE PREDATOR, AND I'M WILLING TO DO IT AGAIN!
YOU MEAN TO TELL ME YOU WEREN'T LAUGHING WHEN I BECAME STAR SAPPHIRE A THIRD TIME, MONTHS LATER?
NEVER! BECAUSE WE CAME SO CLOSE TO A FORCED MARRIAGE BEFORE YOU REVERTED, THAT I BEGAN TO SERIOUSLY CONSIDER WHAT ANY MARRIAGE TO YOU WOULD BE LIKE!
I DECIDED I'D BEEN WASTING OUR TIME, WANTING YOU TO LOVE ME AS HAL JORDAN! WHAT DIFFERENCE DID IT MAKE IF YOU WERE MINE EITHER WAY!?
I TOOK YOU ASIDE TO POP THE QUESTION--BUT BEFORE I COULD SPEAK, YOU SAID--
HAL, I--
I MET... A MAN! HIS NAME IS JASON BELMORE! HE'S HANDSOME AND WEALTHY! WE'VE HAD WHAT I GUESS YOU'D CALL A WHIRLWIND COURTSHIP!
...AND THE UPSHOT IS...I'VE PROMISED TO MARRY HIM!

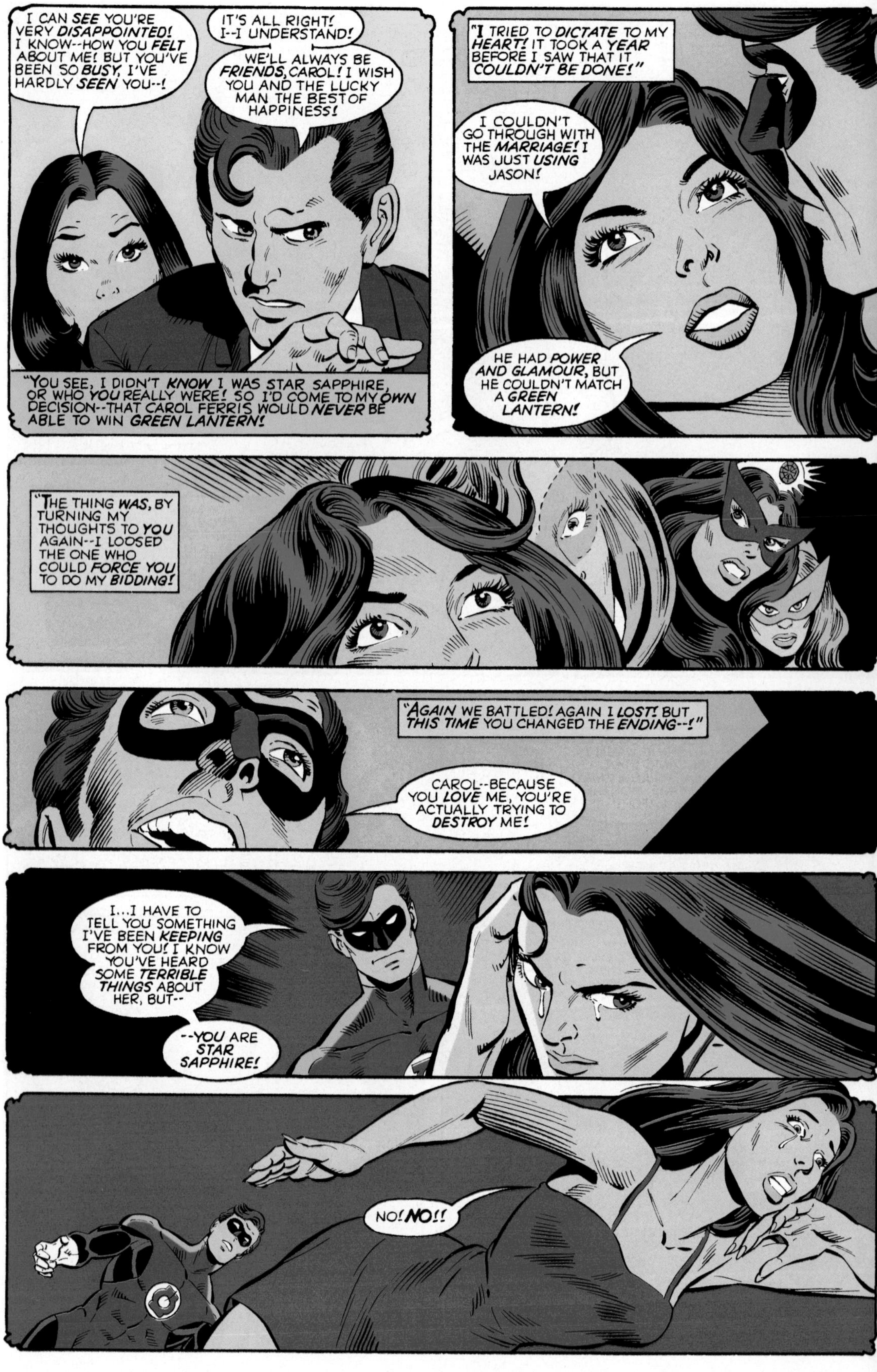
I CAN SEE YOU'RE VERY DISAPPOINTED! I KNOW--HOW YOU FELT ABOUT ME! BUT YOU'VE BEEN SO BUSY, I'VE HARDLY SEEN YOU--!
IT'S ALL RIGHT! I--I UNDERSTAND!
WE'LL ALWAYS BE FRIENDS, CAROL! I WISH YOU AND THE LUCKY MAN THE BEST OF HAPPINESS!
"YOU SEE, I DIDN'T KNOW I WAS STAR SAPPHIRE, OR WHO YOU REALLY WERE! SO I'D COME TO MY OWN DECISION--THAT CAROL FERRIS WOULD NEVER BE ABLE TO WIN GREEN LANTERN!
"I TRIED TO DICTATE TO MY HEART! IT TOOK A YEAR BEFORE I SAW THAT IT COULDN'T BE DONE!"
I COULDN'T GO THROUGH WITH THE MARRIAGE! I WAS JUST USING JASON!
HE HAD POWER AND GLAMOUR, BUT HE COULDN'T MATCH A GREEN LANTERN!
"THE THING WAS, BY TURNING MY THOUGHTS TO YOU AGAIN--I LOOSED THE ONE WHO COULD FORCE YOU TO DO MY BIDDING!
"AGAIN WE BATTLED! AGAIN I LOST! BUT THIS TIME YOU CHANGED THE ENDING--!"
CAROL--BECAUSE YOU LOVE ME, YOU'RE ACTUALLY TRYING TO DESTROY ME!
I...I HAVE TO TELL YOU SOMETHING I'VE BEEN KEEPING FROM YOU! I KNOW YOU'VE HEARD SOME TERRIBLE THINGS ABOUT HER, BUT--
--YOU ARE STAR SAPPHIRE!
NO! NO!!

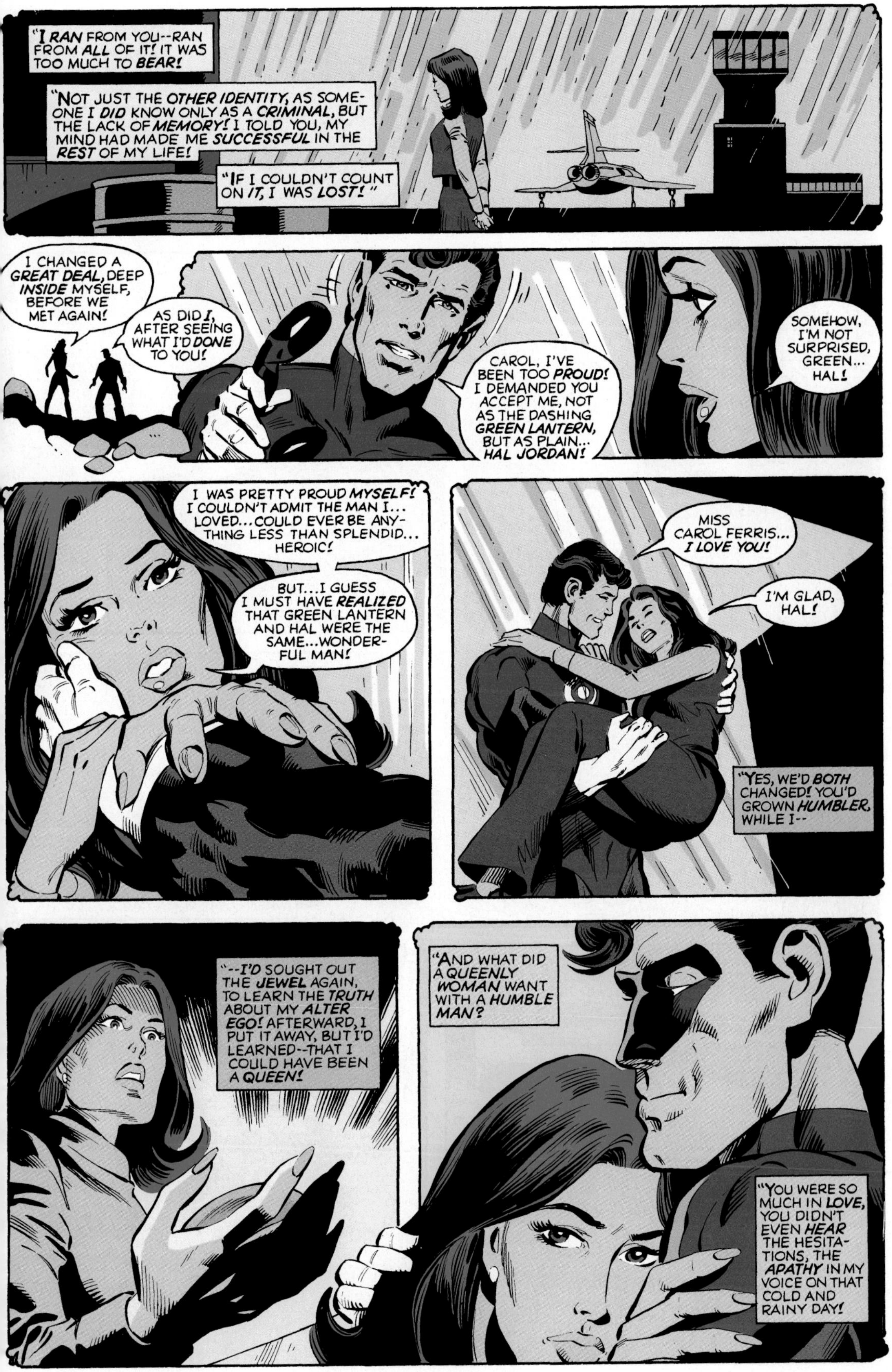
"I RAN FROM YOU--RAN FROM ALL OF IT! IT WAS TOO MUCH TO BEAR!
"NOT JUST THE OTHER IDENTITY, AS SOMEONE I DID KNOW ONLY AS A CRIMINAL, BUT THE LACK OF MEMORY! I TOLD YOU, MY MIND HAD MADE ME SUCCESSFUL IN THE REST OF MY LIFE!
"IF I COULDN'T COUNT ON IT, I WAS LOST!"
I CHANGED A GREAT DEAL, DEEP INSIDE MYSELF, BEFORE WE MET AGAIN!
AS DID I, AFTER SEEING WHAT I'D DONE TO YOU!
CAROL, I'VE BEEN TOO PROUD! I DEMANDED YOU ACCEPT ME, NOT AS THE DASHING GREEN LANTERN, BUT AS PLAIN... HAL JORDAN!
SOMEHOW, I'M NOT SURPRISED, GREEN... HAL!
I WAS PRETTY PROUD MYSELF! I COULDN'T ADMIT THE MAN I... LOVED... COULD EVER BE ANYTHING LESS THAN SPLENDID... HEROIC!
BUT... I GUESS I MUST HAVE REALIZED THAT GREEN LANTERN AND HAL WERE THE SAME... WONDERFUL MAN!
MISS CAROL FERRIS... I LOVE YOU!
I'M GLAD, HAL!
"YES, WE'D BOTH CHANGED! YOU'D GROWN HUMBLER, WHILE I--
"--I'D SOUGHT OUT THE JEWEL AGAIN, TO LEARN THE TRUTH ABOUT MY ALTER EGO! AFTERWARD, I PUT IT AWAY, BUT I'D LEARNED--THAT I COULD HAVE BEEN A QUEEN!
"AND WHAT DID A QUEENLY WOMAN WANT WITH A HUMBLE MAN?
"YOU WERE SO MUCH IN LOVE, YOU DIDN'T EVEN HEAR THE HESITATIONS, THE APATHY IN MY VOICE ON THAT COLD AND RAINY DAY!

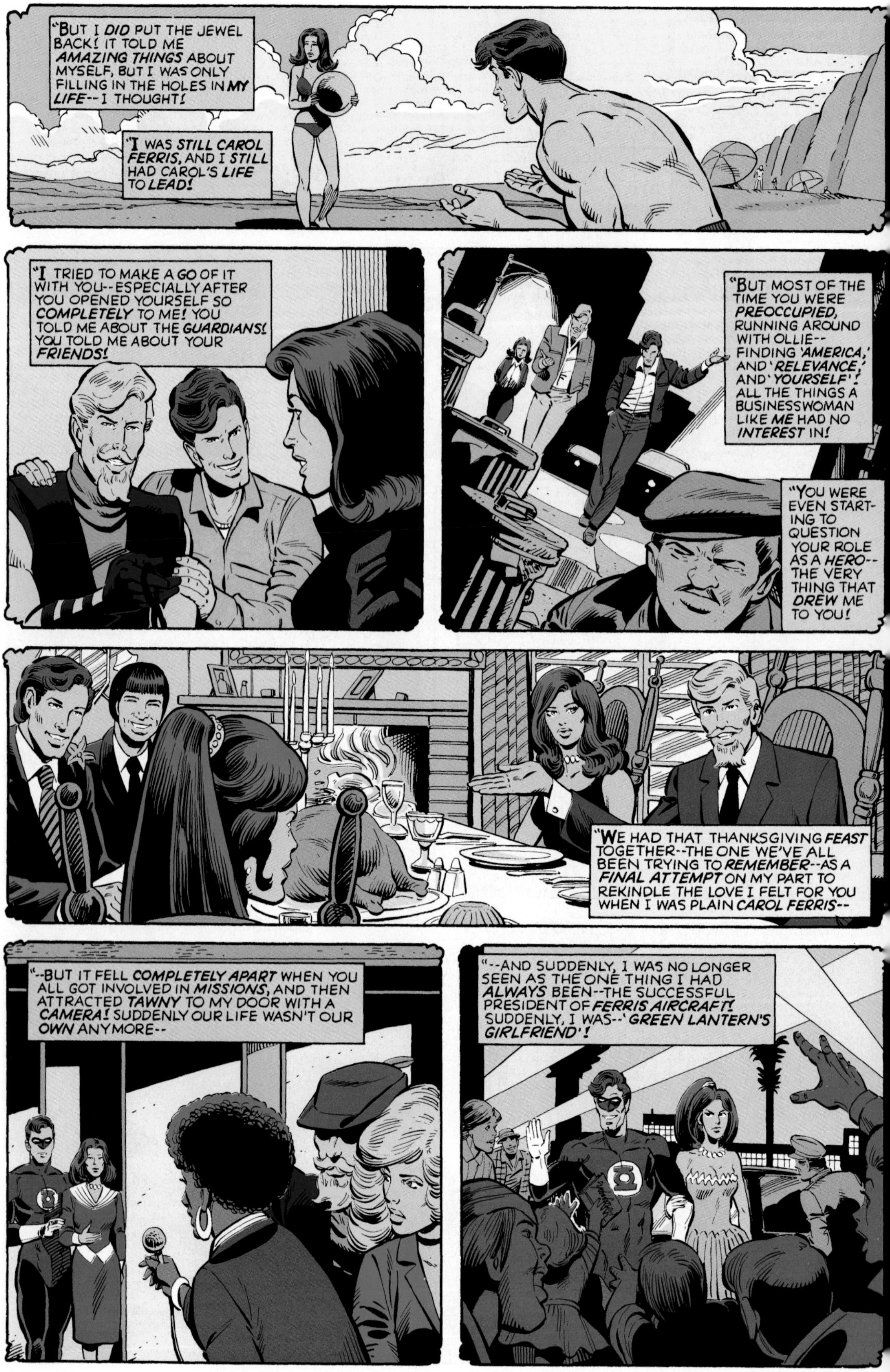
"BUT I DID PUT THE JEWEL BACK! IT TOLD ME AMAZING THINGS ABOUT MYSELF, BUT I WAS ONLY FILLING IN THE HOLES IN MY LIFE--I THOUGHT!
"I WAS STILL CAROL FERRIS, AND I STILL HAD CAROL'S LIFE TO LEAD!
"I TRIED TO MAKE A GO OF IT WITH YOU--ESPECIALLY AFTER YOU OPENED YOURSELF SO COMPLETELY TO ME! YOU TOLD ME ABOUT THE GUARDIANS! YOU TOLD ME ABOUT YOUR FRIENDS!
"BUT MOST OF THE TIME YOU WERE PREOCCUPIED, RUNNING AROUND WITH OLLIE--FINDING 'AMERICA,' AND 'RELEVANCE,' AND 'YOURSELF'! ALL THE THINGS A BUSINESSWOMAN LIKE ME HAD NO INTEREST IN!
"YOU WERE EVEN STARTING TO QUESTION YOUR ROLE AS A HERO--THE VERY THING THAT DREW ME TO YOU!
"WE HAD THAT THANKSGIVING FEAST TOGETHER--THE ONE WE'VE ALL BEEN TRYING TO REMEMBER--AS A FINAL ATTEMPT ON MY PART TO REKINDLE THE LOVE I FELT FOR YOU WHEN I WAS PLAIN CAROL FERRIS--
"--BUT IT FELL COMPLETELY APART WHEN YOU ALL GOT INVOLVED IN MISSIONS, AND THEN ATTRACTED TAWNY TO MY DOOR WITH A CAMERA! SUDDENLY OUR LIFE WASN'T OUR OWN ANYMORE--
"--AND SUDDENLY, I WAS NO LONGER SEEN AS THE ONE THING I HAD ALWAYS BEEN--THE SUCCESSFUL PRESIDENT OF FERRIS AIRCRAFT! SUDDENLY, I WAS--'GREEN LANTERN'S GIRLFRIEND'!

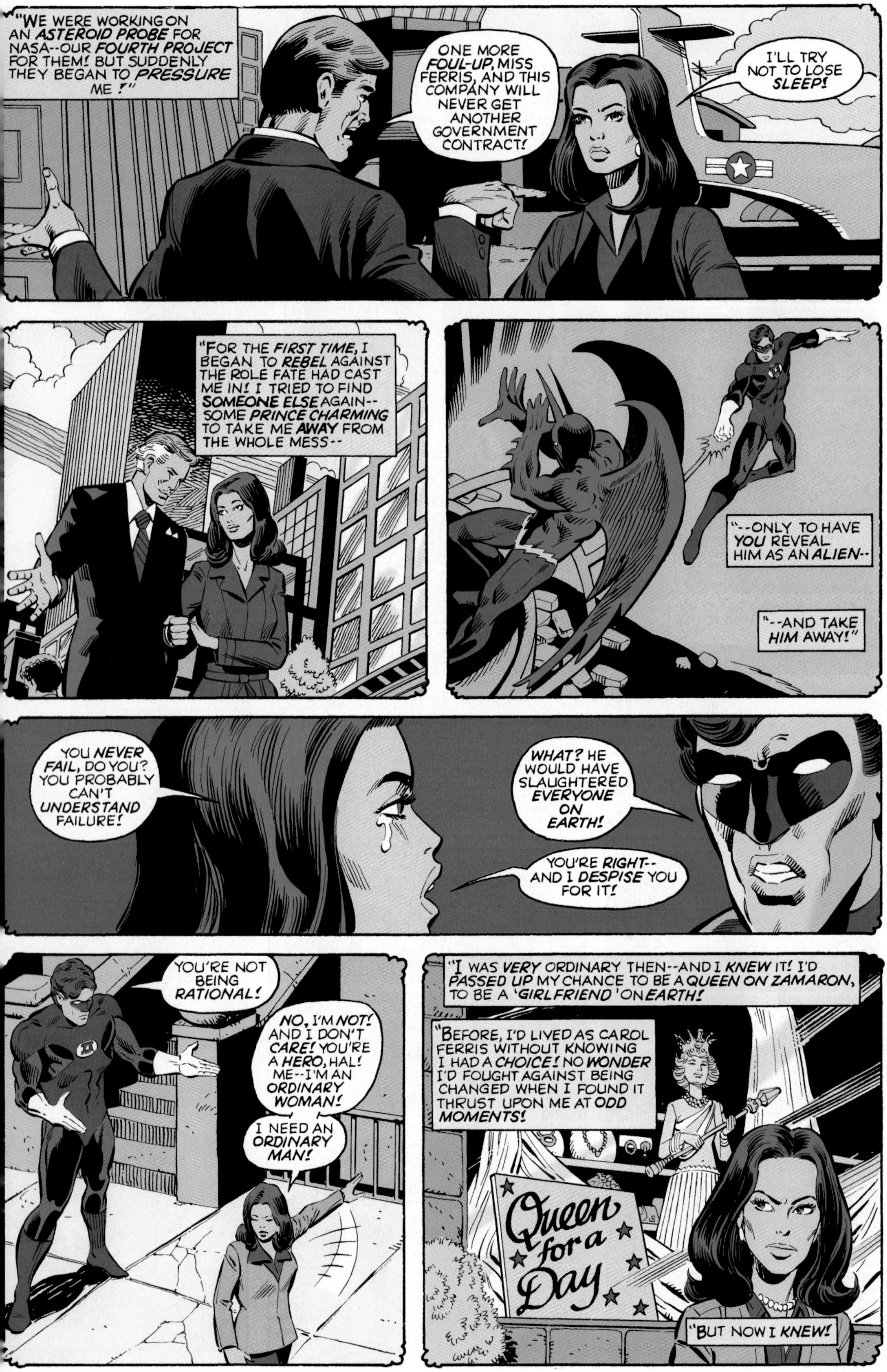

"WE WERE WORKING ON AN ASTEROID PROBE FOR NASA--OUR FOURTH PROJECT FOR THEM! BUT SUDDENLY THEY BEGAN TO PRESSURE ME!"
ONE MORE FOUL-UP, MISS FERRIS, AND THIS COMPANY WILL NEVER GET ANOTHER GOVERNMENT CONTRACT!
I'LL TRY NOT TO LOSE SLEEP!
"FOR THE FIRST TIME, I BEGAN TO REBEL AGAINST THE ROLE FATE HAD CAST ME IN! I TRIED TO FIND SOMEONE ELSE AGAIN-- SOME PRINCE CHARMING TO TAKE ME AWAY FROM THE WHOLE MESS--
"--ONLY TO HAVE YOU REVEAL HIM AS AN ALIEN--
"--AND TAKE HIM AWAY!"
YOU NEVER FAIL, DO YOU? YOU PROBABLY CAN'T UNDERSTAND FAILURE!
WHAT? HE WOULD HAVE SLAUGHTERED EVERYONE ON EARTH!
YOU'RE RIGHT-- AND I DESPISE YOU FOR IT!
YOU'RE NOT BEING RATIONAL!
NO, I'M NOT! AND I DON'T CARE! YOU'RE A HERO, HAL! ME--I'M AN ORDINARY WOMAN!
I NEED AN ORDINARY MAN!
"I WAS VERY ORDINARY THEN--AND I KNEW IT! I'D PASSED UP MY CHANCE TO BE A QUEEN ON ZAMARON, TO BE A 'GIRLFRIEND' ON EARTH!
"BEFORE, I'D LIVED AS CAROL FERRIS WITHOUT KNOWING I HAD A CHOICE! NO WONDER I'D FOUGHT AGAINST BEING CHANGED WHEN I FOUND IT THRUST UPON ME AT ODD MOMENTS!
Queen for a Day
"BUT NOW I KNEW!

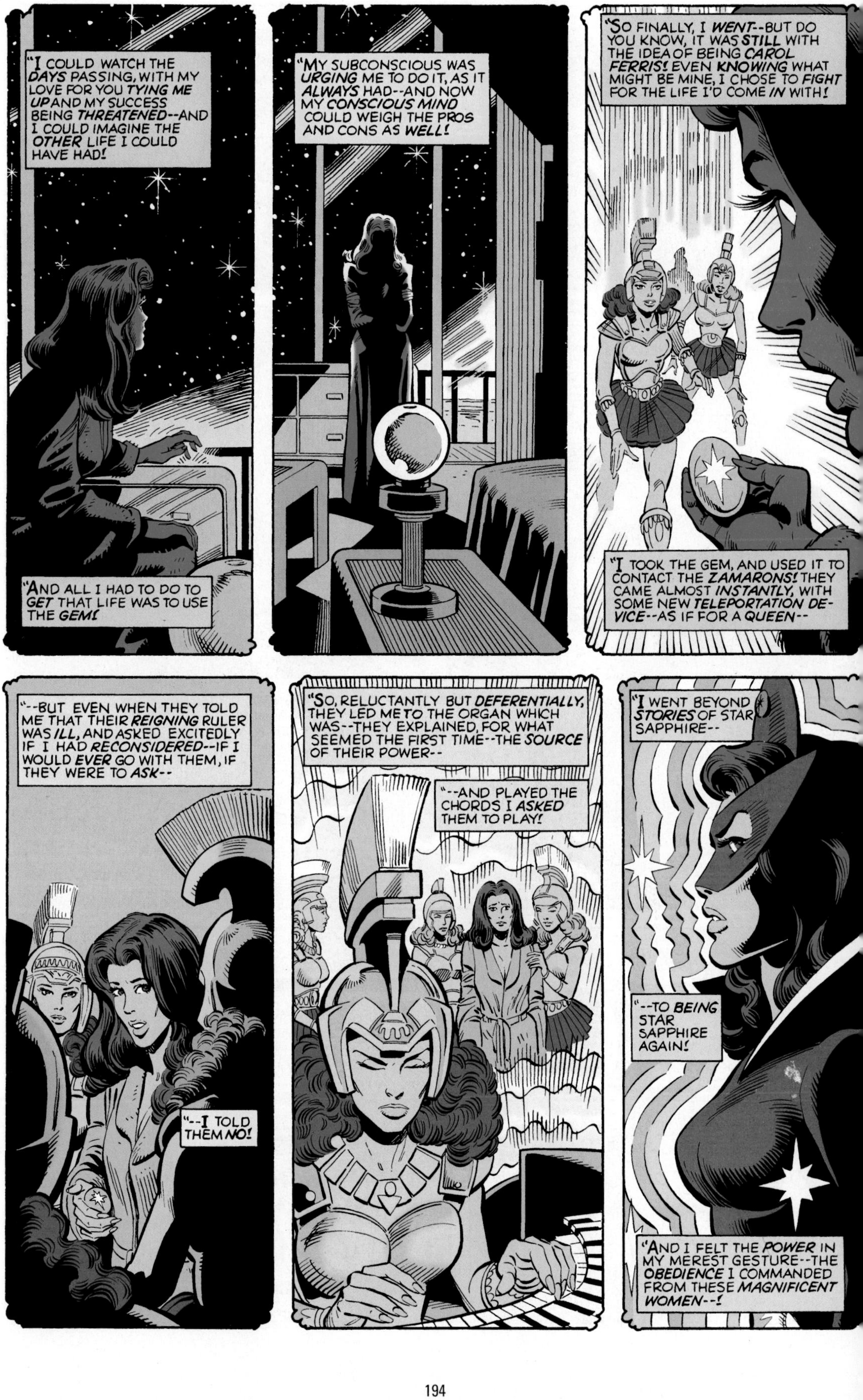
"I COULD WATCH THE DAYS PASSING, WITH MY LOVE FOR YOU TYING ME UP AND MY SUCCESS BEING THREATENED--AND I COULD IMAGINE THE OTHER LIFE I COULD HAVE HAD!
"AND ALL I HAD TO DO TO GET THAT LIFE WAS TO USE THE GEM!
"MY SUBCONSCIOUS WAS URGING ME TO DO IT, AS IT ALWAYS HAD--AND NOW MY CONSCIOUS MIND COULD WEIGH THE PROS AND CONS AS WELL!
"SO FINALLY, I WENT--BUT DO YOU KNOW, IT WAS STILL WITH THE IDEA OF BEING CAROL FERRIS! EVEN KNOWING WHAT MIGHT BE MINE, I CHOSE TO FIGHT FOR THE LIFE I'D COME IN WITH!
"I TOOK THE GEM, AND USED IT TO CONTACT THE ZAMARONS! THEY CAME ALMOST INSTANTLY, WITH SOME NEW TELEPORTATION DEVICE--AS IF FOR A QUEEN--
"--BUT EVEN WHEN THEY TOLD ME THAT THEIR REIGNING RULER WAS ILL, AND ASKED EXCITEDLY IF I HAD RECONSIDERED--IF I WOULD EVER GO WITH THEM, IF THEY WERE TO ASK--
"--I TOLD THEM NO!
"SO, RELUCTANTLY BUT DEFERENTIALLY, THEY LED ME TO THE ORGAN WHICH WAS--THEY EXPLAINED, FOR WHAT SEEMED THE FIRST TIME--THE SOURCE OF THEIR POWER--
"--AND PLAYED THE CHORDS I ASKED THEM TO PLAY!
"I WENT BEYOND STORIES OF STAR SAPPHIRE--
"--TO BEING STAR SAPPHIRE AGAIN!
"AND I FELT THE POWER IN MY MEREST GESTURE--THE OBEDIENCE I COMMANDED FROM THESE MAGNIFICENT WOMEN--!

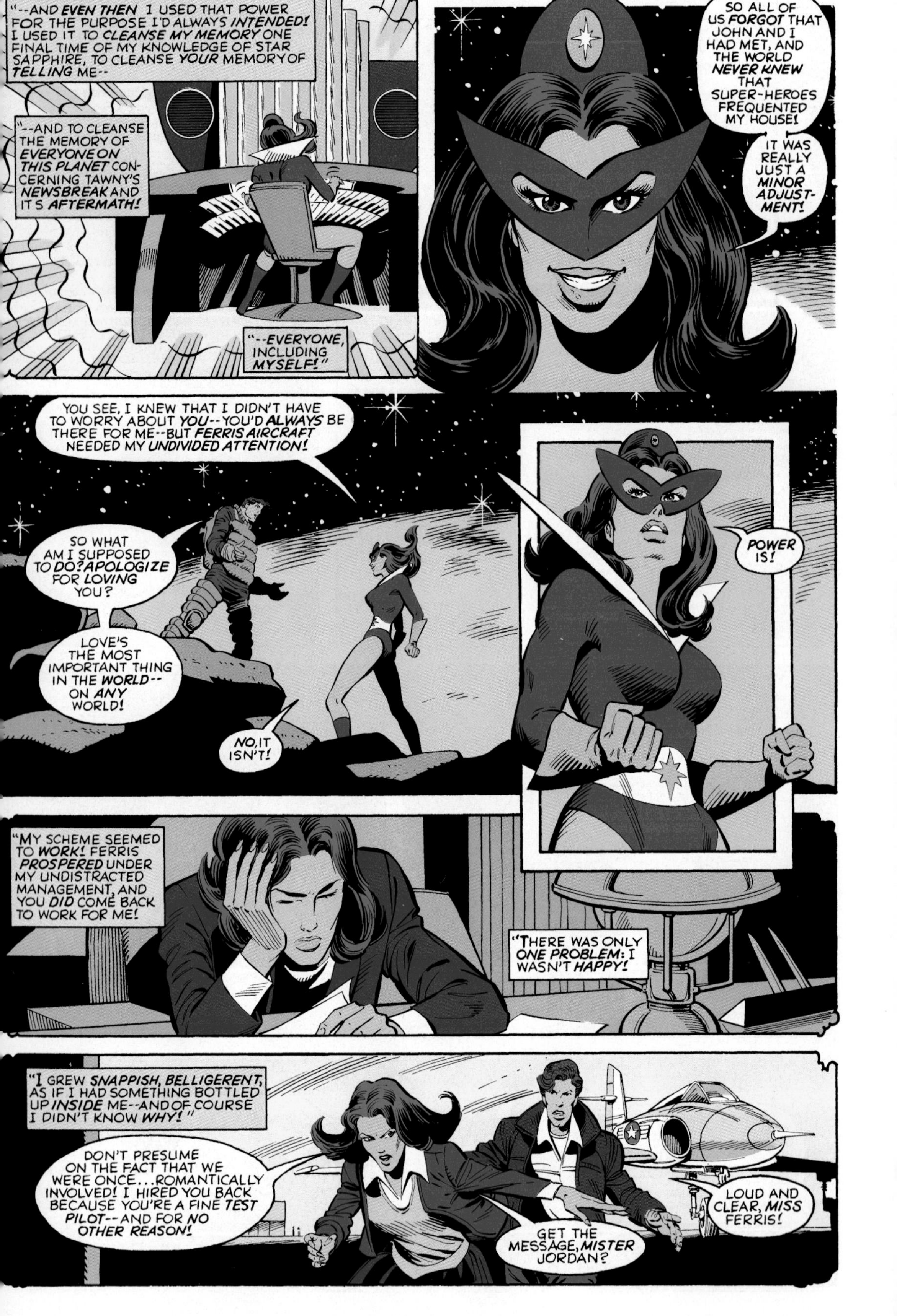
"--AND EVEN THEN I USED THAT POWER FOR THE PURPOSE I'D ALWAYS INTENDED! I USED IT TO CLEANSE MY MEMORY ONE FINAL TIME OF MY KNOWLEDGE OF STAR SAPPHIRE, TO CLEANSE YOUR MEMORY OF TELLING ME--
"--AND TO CLEANSE THE MEMORY OF EVERYONE ON THIS PLANET CONCERNING TAWNY'S NEWSBREAK AND ITS AFTERMATH!
"--EVERYONE, INCLUDING MYSELF!"
SO ALL OF US FORGOT THAT JOHN AND I HAD MET, AND THE WORLD NEVER KNEW THAT SUPER-HEROES FREQUENTED MY HOUSE!
IT WAS REALLY JUST A MINOR ADJUSTMENT!
YOU SEE, I KNEW THAT I DIDN'T HAVE TO WORRY ABOUT YOU--YOU'D ALWAYS BE THERE FOR ME--BUT FERRIS AIRCRAFT NEEDED MY UNDIVIDED ATTENTION!
SO WHAT AM I SUPPOSED TO DO? APOLOGIZE FOR LOVING YOU?
LOVE'S THE MOST IMPORTANT THING IN THE WORLD-- ON ANY WORLD!
NO, IT ISN'T!
POWER IS!
"MY SCHEME SEEMED TO WORK! FERRIS PROSPERED UNDER MY UNDISTRACTED MANAGEMENT, AND YOU DID COME BACK TO WORK FOR ME!
"THERE WAS ONLY ONE PROBLEM: I WASN'T HAPPY!
"I GREW SNAPPISH, BELLIGERENT, AS IF I HAD SOMETHING BOTTLED UP INSIDE ME--AND OF COURSE I DIDN'T KNOW WHY!"
DON'T PRESUME ON THE FACT THAT WE WERE ONCE...ROMANTICALLY INVOLVED! I HIRED YOU BACK BECAUSE YOU'RE A FINE TEST PILOT--AND FOR NO OTHER REASON!
GET THE MESSAGE, MISTER JORDAN?
LOUD AND CLEAR, MISS FERRIS!

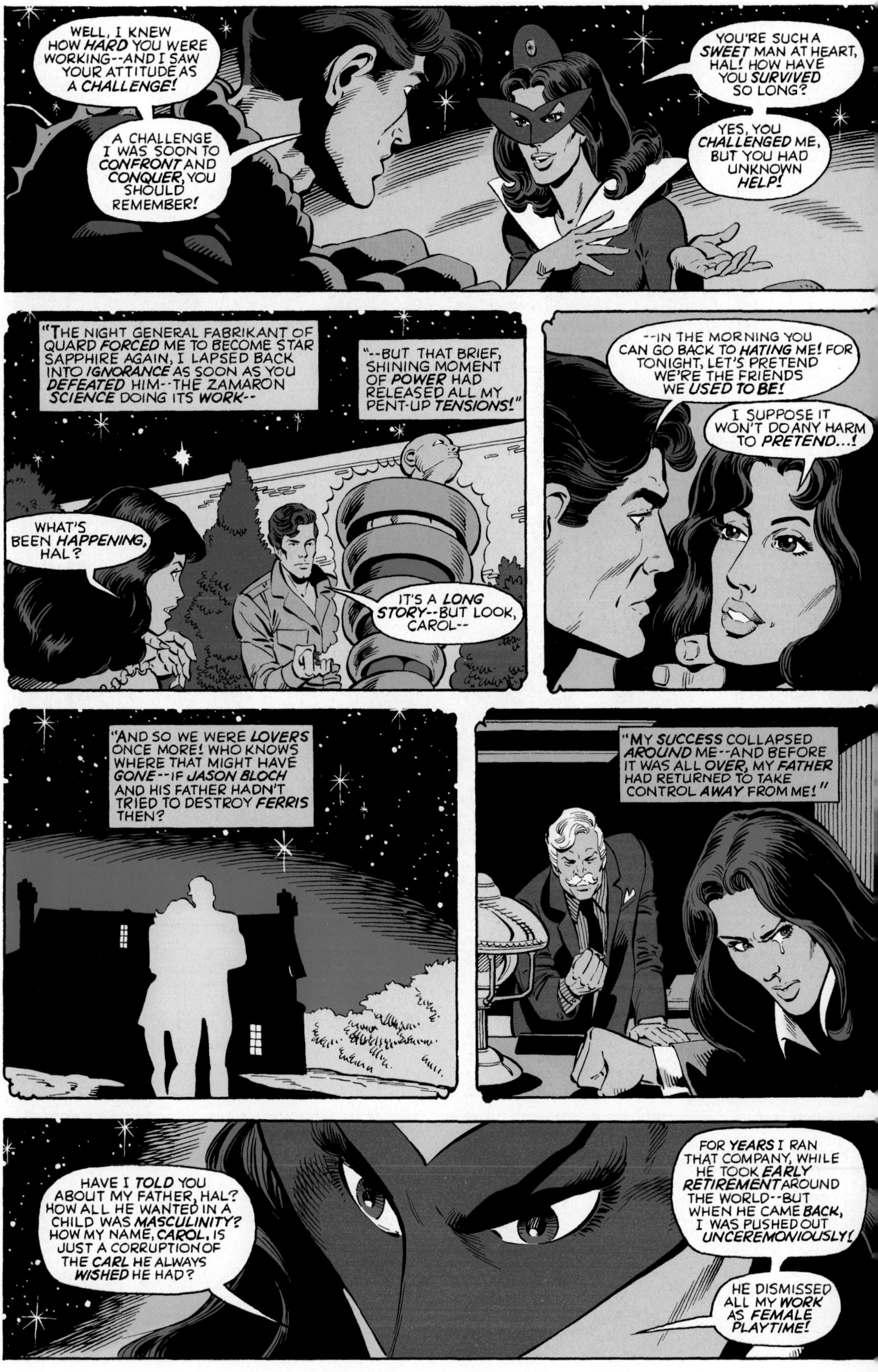
WELL, I KNEW HOW HARD YOU WERE WORKING--AND I SAW YOUR ATTITUDE AS A CHALLENGE!
A CHALLENGE I WAS SOON TO CONFRONT AND CONQUER, YOU SHOULD REMEMBER!
YOU'RE SUCH A SWEET MAN AT HEART, HAL! HOW HAVE YOU SURVIVED SO LONG?
YES, YOU CHALLENGED ME, BUT YOU HAD UNKNOWN HELP!
"THE NIGHT GENERAL FABRIKANT OF QUARD FORCED ME TO BECOME STAR SAPPHIRE AGAIN, I LAPSED BACK INTO IGNORANCE AS SOON AS YOU DEFEATED HIM--THE ZAMARON SCIENCE DOING ITS WORK--
"--BUT THAT BRIEF, SHINING MOMENT OF POWER HAD RELEASED ALL MY PENT-UP TENSIONS!"
WHAT'S BEEN HAPPENING, HAL?
IT'S A LONG STORY--BUT LOOK, CAROL--
--IN THE MORNING YOU CAN GO BACK TO HATING ME! FOR TONIGHT, LET'S PRETEND WE'RE THE FRIENDS WE USED TO BE!
I SUPPOSE IT WON'T DO ANY HARM TO PRETEND...!
"AND SO WE WERE LOVERS ONCE MORE! WHO KNOWS WHERE THAT MIGHT HAVE GONE--IF JASON BLOCH AND HIS FATHER HADN'T TRIED TO DESTROY FERRIS THEN?
"MY SUCCESS COLLAPSED AROUND ME--AND BEFORE IT WAS ALL OVER, MY FATHER HAD RETURNED TO TAKE CONTROL AWAY FROM ME!"
HAVE I TOLD YOU ABOUT MY FATHER, HAL? HOW ALL HE WANTED IN A CHILD WAS MASCULINITY? HOW MY NAME, CAROL, IS JUST A CORRUPTION OF THE CARL HE ALWAYS WISHED HE HAD?
FOR YEARS I RAN THAT COMPANY, WHILE HE TOOK EARLY RETIREMENT AROUND THE WORLD--BUT WHEN HE CAME BACK, I WAS PUSHED OUT UNCEREMONIOUSLY!
HE DISMISSED ALL MY WORK AS FEMALE PLAYTIME!

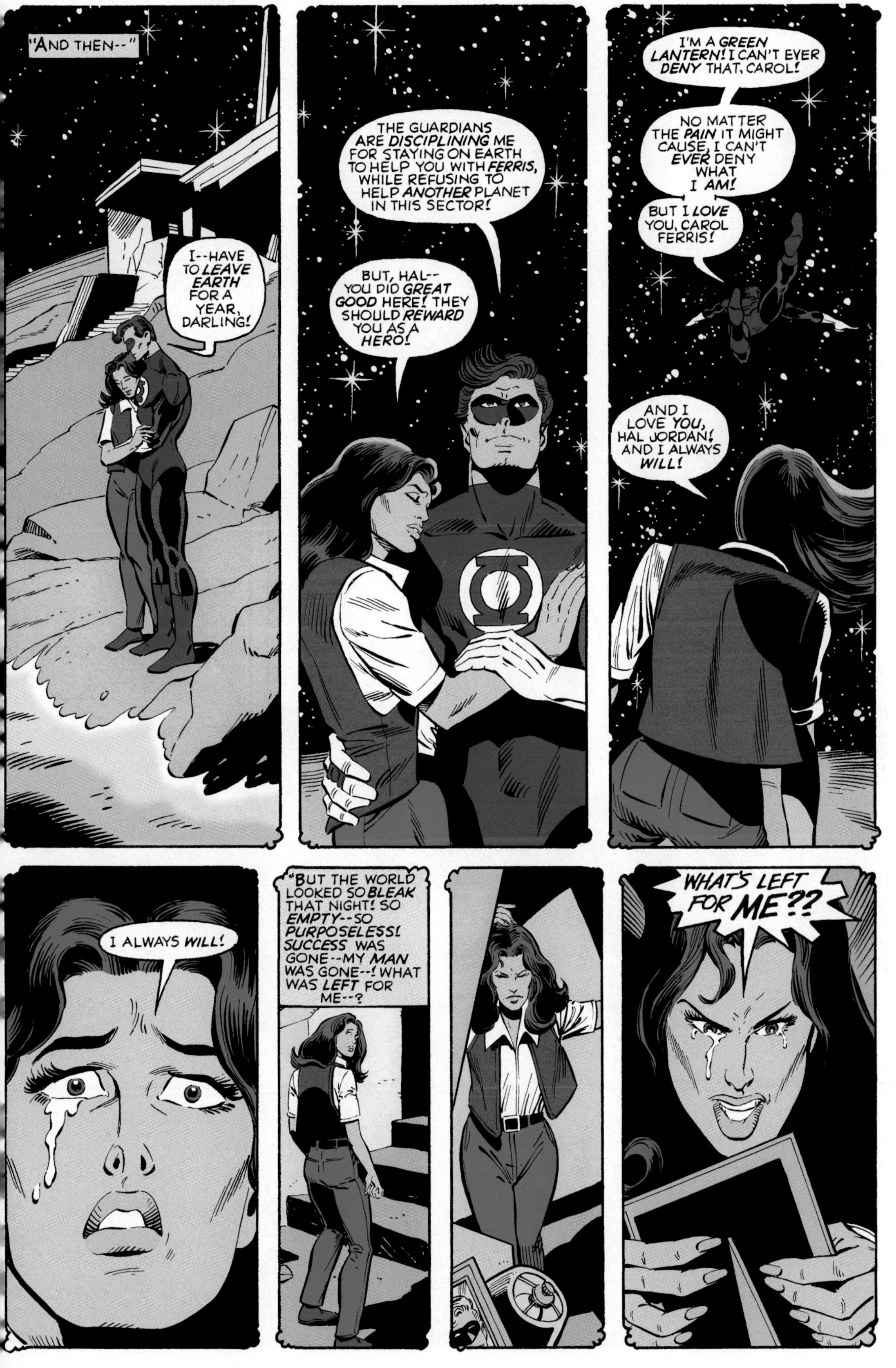
"AND THEN--"
I--HAVE TO LEAVE EARTH FOR A YEAR, DARLING!
THE GUARDIANS ARE DISCIPLINING ME FOR STAYING ON EARTH TO HELP YOU WITH FERRIS, WHILE REFUSING TO HELP ANOTHER PLANET IN THIS SECTOR!
BUT, HAL--YOU DID GREAT GOOD HERE! THEY SHOULD REWARD YOU AS A HERO!
I'M A GREEN LANTERN! I CAN'T EVER DENY THAT, CAROL!
NO MATTER THE PAIN IT MIGHT CAUSE, I CAN'T EVER DENY WHAT I AM!
BUT I LOVE YOU, CAROL FERRIS!
AND I LOVE YOU, HAL JORDAN! AND I ALWAYS WILL!
I ALWAYS WILL!
"BUT THE WORLD LOOKED SO BLEAK THAT NIGHT! SO EMPTY--SO PURPOSELESS! SUCCESS WAS GONE--MY MAN WAS GONE--! WHAT WAS LEFT FOR ME--?
WHAT'S LEFT FOR ME??

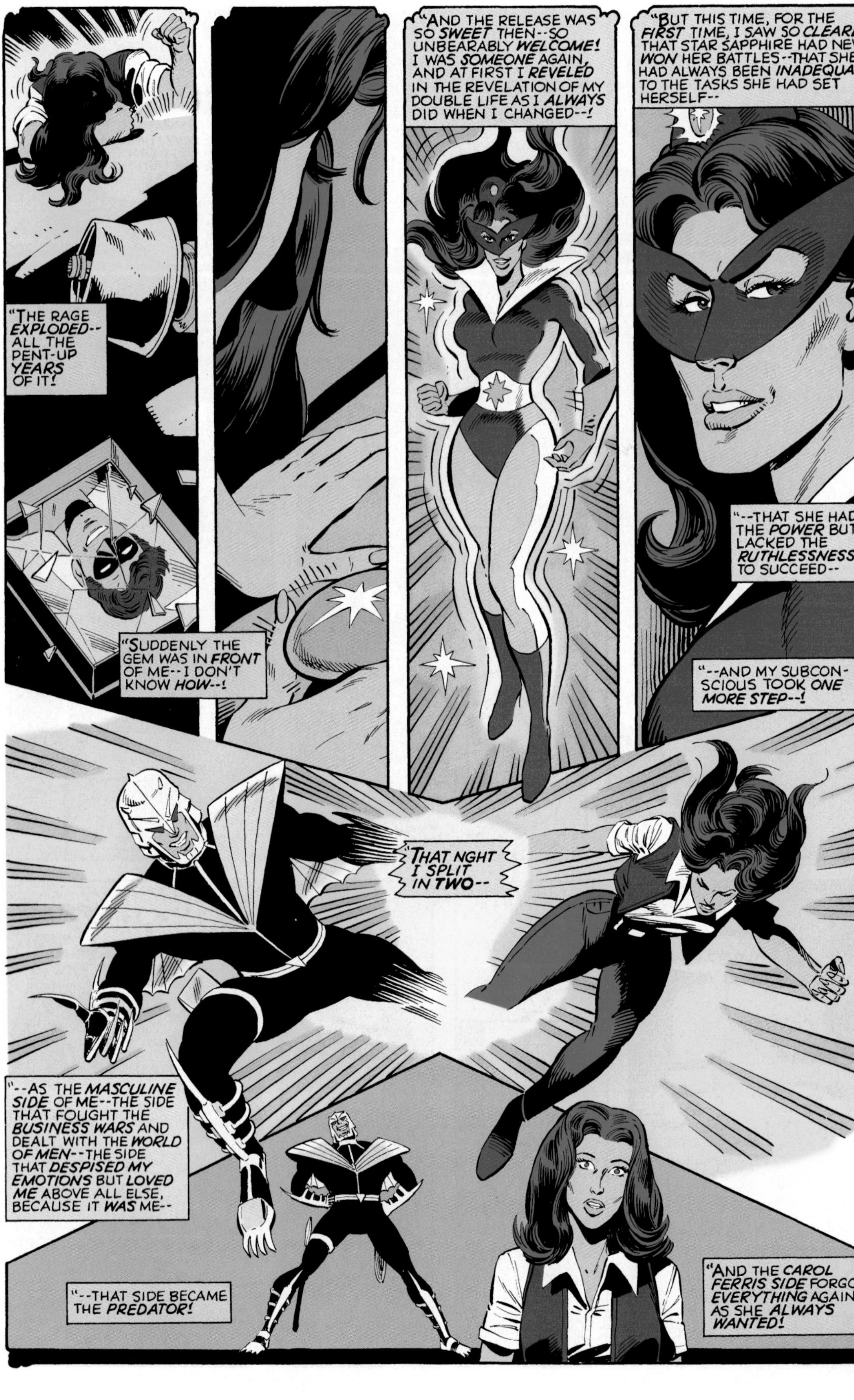
"THE RAGE EXPLODED-- ALL THE PENT-UP YEARS OF IT!
"SUDDENLY THE GEM WAS IN FRONT OF ME--I DON'T KNOW HOW--!
"AND THE RELEASE WAS SO SWEET THEN--SO UNBEARABLY WELCOME! I WAS SOMEONE AGAIN, AND AT FIRST I REVELED IN THE REVELATION OF MY DOUBLE LIFE AS I ALWAYS DID WHEN I CHANGED--!
"BUT THIS TIME, FOR THE FIRST TIME, I SAW SO CLEARLY THAT STAR SAPPHIRE HAD NEVER WON HER BATTLES--THAT SHE HAD ALWAYS BEEN INADEQUATE TO THE TASKS SHE HAD SET HERSELF--
"--THAT SHE HAD THE POWER BUT LACKED THE RUTHLESSNESS TO SUCCEED--
"--AND MY SUBCONSCIOUS TOOK ONE MORE STEP--!
"THAT NGHT I SPLIT IN TWO--
"--AS THE MASCULINE SIDE OF ME--THE SIDE THAT FOUGHT THE BUSINESS WARS AND DEALT WITH THE WORLD OF MEN--THE SIDE THAT DESPISED MY EMOTIONS BUT LOVED ME ABOVE ALL ELSE, BECAUSE IT WAS ME--
"--THAT SIDE BECAME THE PREDATOR!
"AND THE CAROL FERRIS SIDE FORGOT EVERYTHING AGAIN, AS SHE ALWAYS WANTED!

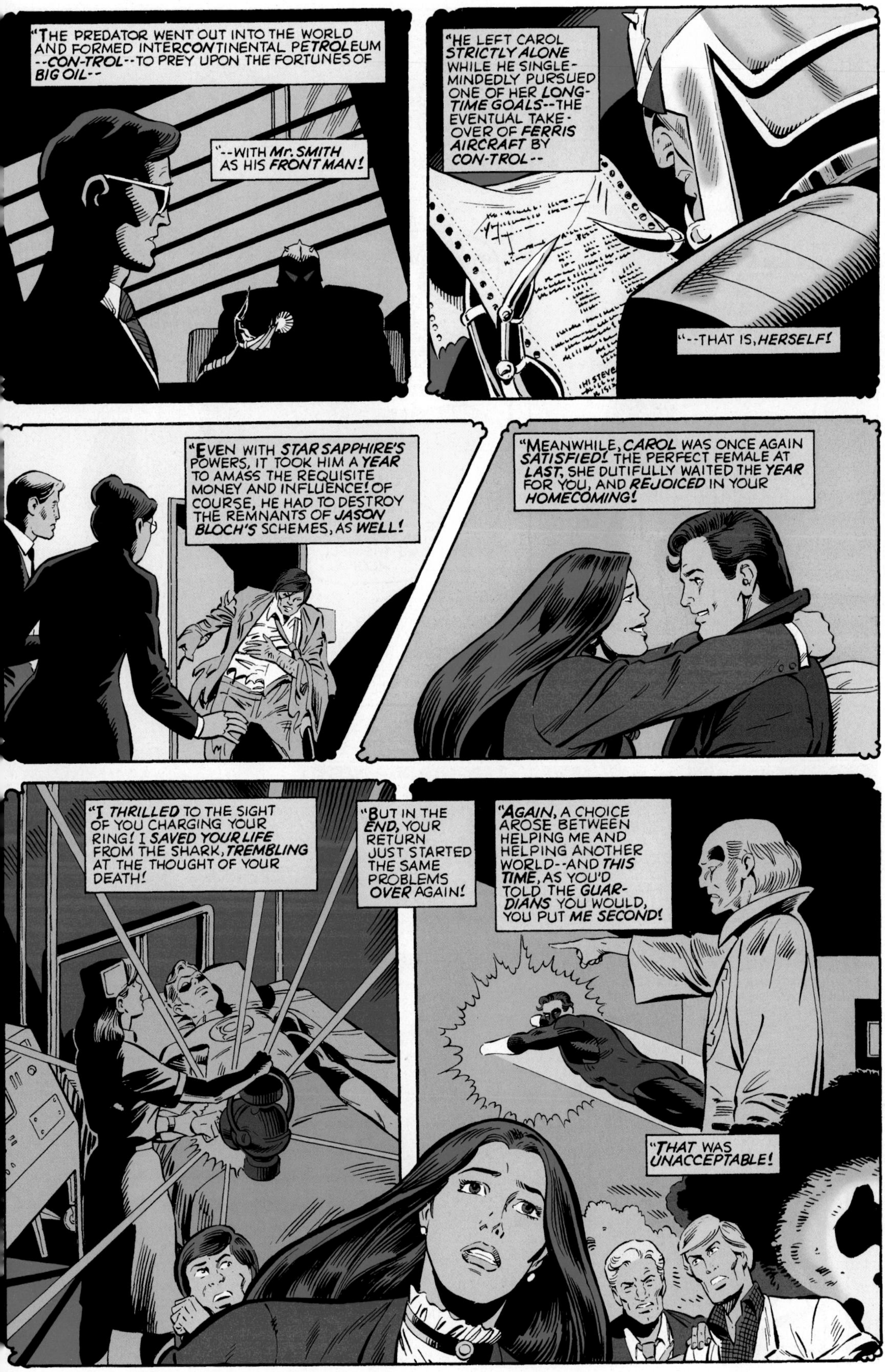
"THE PREDATOR WENT OUT INTO THE WORLD AND FORMED INTERCONTINENTAL PETROLEUM --CON-TROL--TO PREY UPON THE FORTUNES OF BIG OIL--
"--WITH Mr. SMITH AS HIS FRONT MAN!
"HE LEFT CAROL STRICTLY ALONE WHILE HE SINGLE-MINDEDLY PURSUED ONE OF HER LONG-TIME GOALS--THE EVENTUAL TAKE-OVER OF FERRIS AIRCRAFT BY CON-TROL--
"--THAT IS, HERSELF!
"EVEN WITH STAR SAPPHIRE'S POWERS, IT TOOK HIM A YEAR TO AMASS THE REQUISITE MONEY AND INFLUENCE! OF COURSE, HE HAD TO DESTROY THE REMNANTS OF JASON BLOCH'S SCHEMES, AS WELL!
"MEANWHILE, CAROL WAS ONCE AGAIN SATISFIED! THE PERFECT FEMALE AT LAST, SHE DUTIFULLY WAITED THE YEAR FOR YOU, AND REJOICED IN YOUR HOMECOMING!
"I THRILLED TO THE SIGHT OF YOU CHARGING YOUR RING! I SAVED YOUR LIFE FROM THE SHARK, TREMBLING AT THE THOUGHT OF YOUR DEATH!
"BUT IN THE END, YOUR RETURN JUST STARTED THE SAME PROBLEMS OVER AGAIN!
"AGAIN, A CHOICE AROSE BETWEEN HELPING ME AND HELPING ANOTHER WORLD--AND THIS TIME, AS YOU'D TOLD THE GUARDIANS YOU WOULD, YOU PUT ME SECOND!
"THAT WAS UNACCEPTABLE!

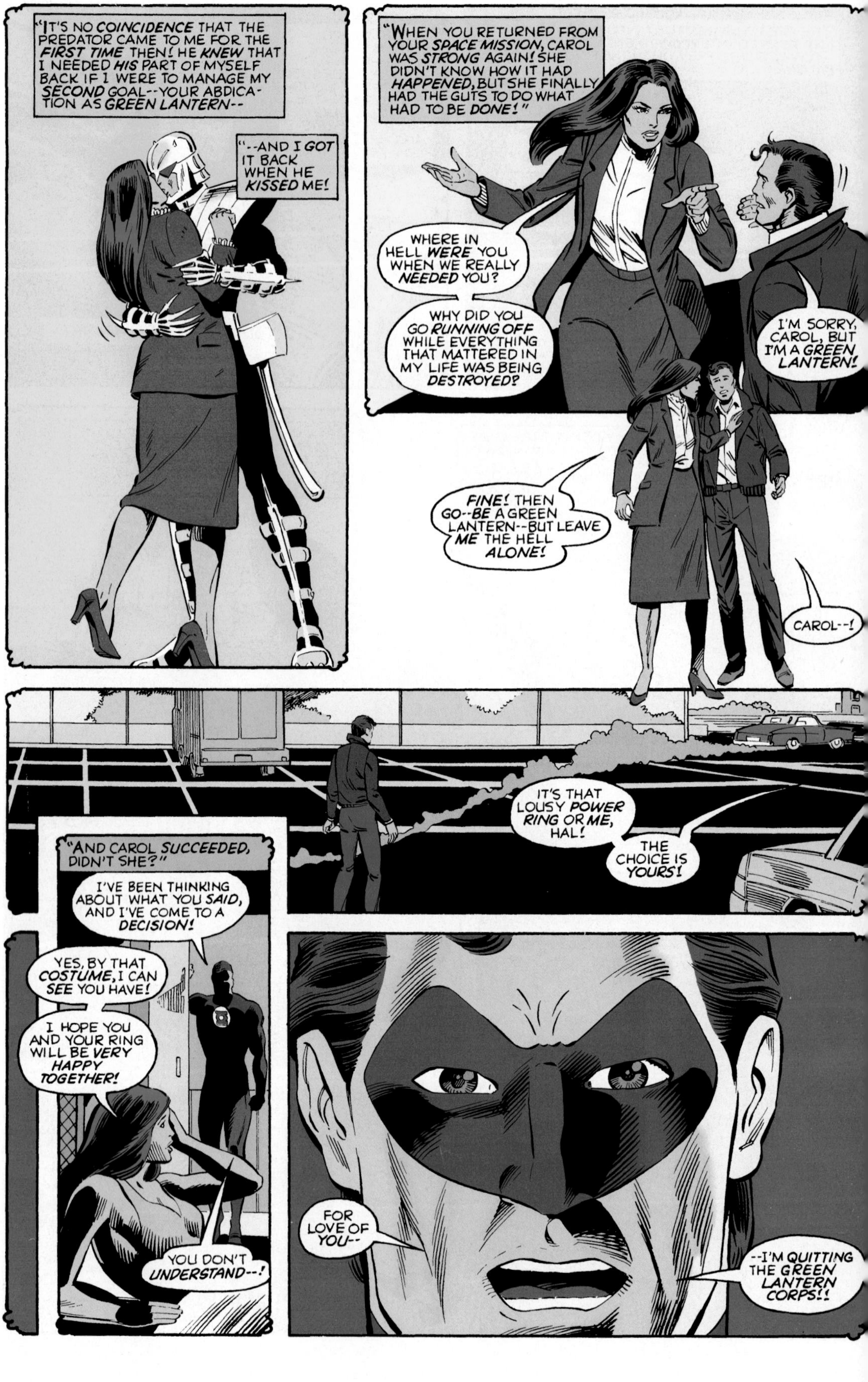
"IT'S NO COINCIDENCE THAT THE PREDATOR CAME TO ME FOR THE FIRST TIME THEN! HE KNEW THAT I NEEDED HIS PART OF MYSELF BACK IF I WERE TO MANAGE MY SECOND GOAL--YOUR ABDICATION AS GREEN LANTERN--
"--AND I GOT IT BACK WHEN HE KISSED ME!
"WHEN YOU RETURNED FROM YOUR SPACE MISSION, CAROL WAS STRONG AGAIN! SHE DIDN'T KNOW HOW IT HAD HAPPENED, BUT SHE FINALLY HAD THE GUTS TO DO WHAT HAD TO BE DONE!"
WHERE IN HELL WERE YOU WHEN WE REALLY NEEDED YOU?
WHY DID YOU GO RUNNING OFF WHILE EVERYTHING THAT MATTERED IN MY LIFE WAS BEING DESTROYED?
I'M SORRY, CAROL, BUT I'M A GREEN LANTERN!
FINE! THEN GO--BE A GREEN LANTERN--BUT LEAVE ME THE HELL ALONE!
CAROL--!
IT'S THAT LOUSY POWER RING OR ME, HAL!
THE CHOICE IS YOURS!
"AND CAROL SUCCEEDED, DIDN'T SHE?"
I'VE BEEN THINKING ABOUT WHAT YOU SAID, AND I'VE COME TO A DECISION!
YES, BY THAT COSTUME, I CAN SEE YOU HAVE!
I HOPE YOU AND YOUR RING WILL BE VERY HAPPY TOGETHER!
YOU DON'T UNDERSTAND--!
FOR LOVE OF YOU--
--I'M QUITTING THE GREEN LANTERN CORPS!!

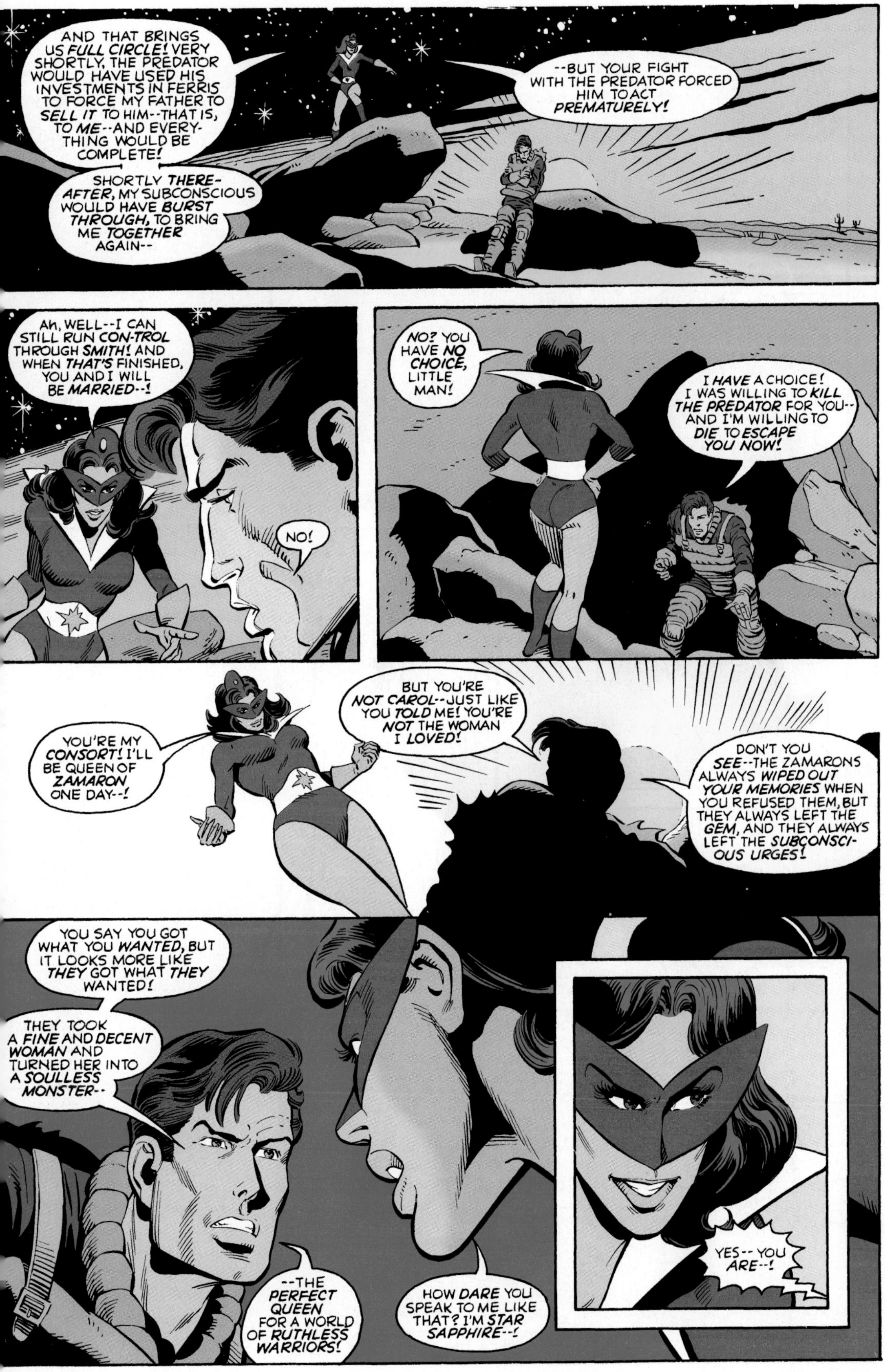

AND THAT BRINGS US FULL CIRCLE! VERY SHORTLY, THE PREDATOR WOULD HAVE USED HIS INVESTMENTS IN FERRIS TO FORCE MY FATHER TO SELL IT TO HIM--THAT IS, TO ME--AND EVERYTHING WOULD BE COMPLETE!
SHORTLY THERE-AFTER, MY SUBCONSCIOUS WOULD HAVE BURST THROUGH, TO BRING ME TOGETHER AGAIN--
--BUT YOUR FIGHT WITH THE PREDATOR FORCED HIM TO ACT PREMATURELY!
Ah, WELL--I CAN STILL RUN CON-TROL THROUGH SMITH! AND WHEN THAT'S FINISHED, YOU AND I WILL BE MARRIED--!
NO!
NO? YOU HAVE NO CHOICE, LITTLE MAN!
I HAVE A CHOICE! I WAS WILLING TO KILL THE PREDATOR FOR YOU--AND I'M WILLING TO DIE TO ESCAPE YOU NOW!
YOU'RE MY CONSORT! I'LL BE QUEEN OF ZAMARON ONE DAY--!
BUT YOU'RE NOT CAROL--JUST LIKE YOU TOLD ME! YOU'RE NOT THE WOMAN I LOVED!
DON'T YOU SEE--THE ZAMARONS ALWAYS WIPED OUT YOUR MEMORIES WHEN YOU REFUSED THEM, BUT THEY ALWAYS LEFT THE GEM, AND THEY ALWAYS LEFT THE SUBCONSCIOUS URGES!
YOU SAY YOU GOT WHAT YOU WANTED, BUT IT LOOKS MORE LIKE THEY GOT WHAT THEY WANTED!
THEY TOOK A FINE AND DECENT WOMAN AND TURNED HER INTO A SOULLESS MONSTER--
--THE PERFECT QUEEN FOR A WORLD OF RUTHLESS WARRIORS!
HOW DARE YOU SPEAK TO ME LIKE THAT? I'M STAR SAPPHIRE--!
YES--YOU ARE--!

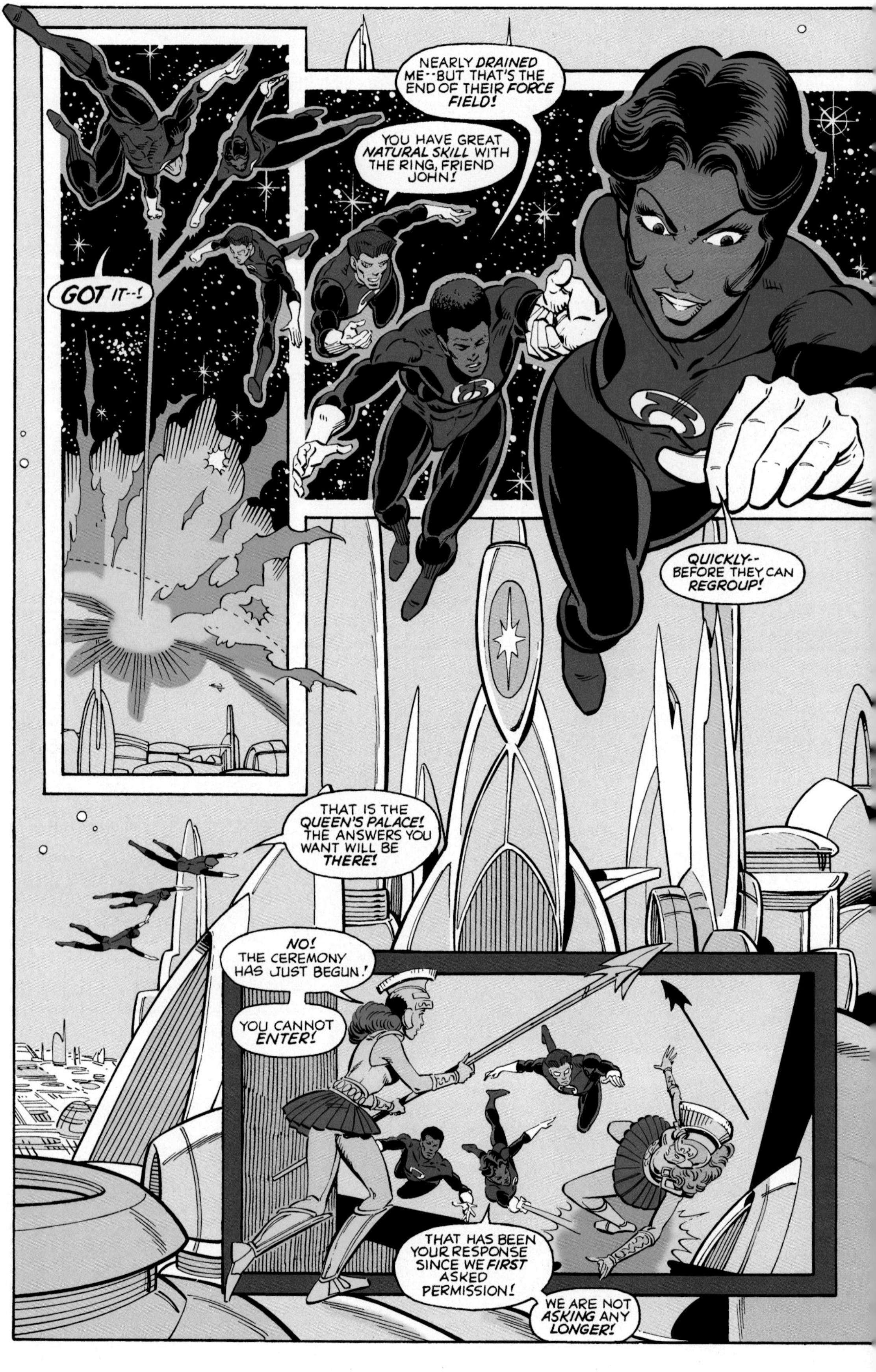
GOT IT--!
NEARLY DRAINED ME--BUT THAT'S THE END OF THEIR FORCE FIELD!
YOU HAVE GREAT NATURAL SKILL WITH THE RING, FRIEND JOHN!
QUICKLY-- BEFORE THEY CAN REGROUP!
THAT IS THE QUEEN'S PALACE! THE ANSWERS YOU WANT WILL BE THERE!
NO! THE CEREMONY HAS JUST BEGUN!
YOU CANNOT ENTER!
THAT HAS BEEN YOUR RESPONSE SINCE WE FIRST ASKED PERMISSION!
WE ARE NOT ASKING ANY LONGER!

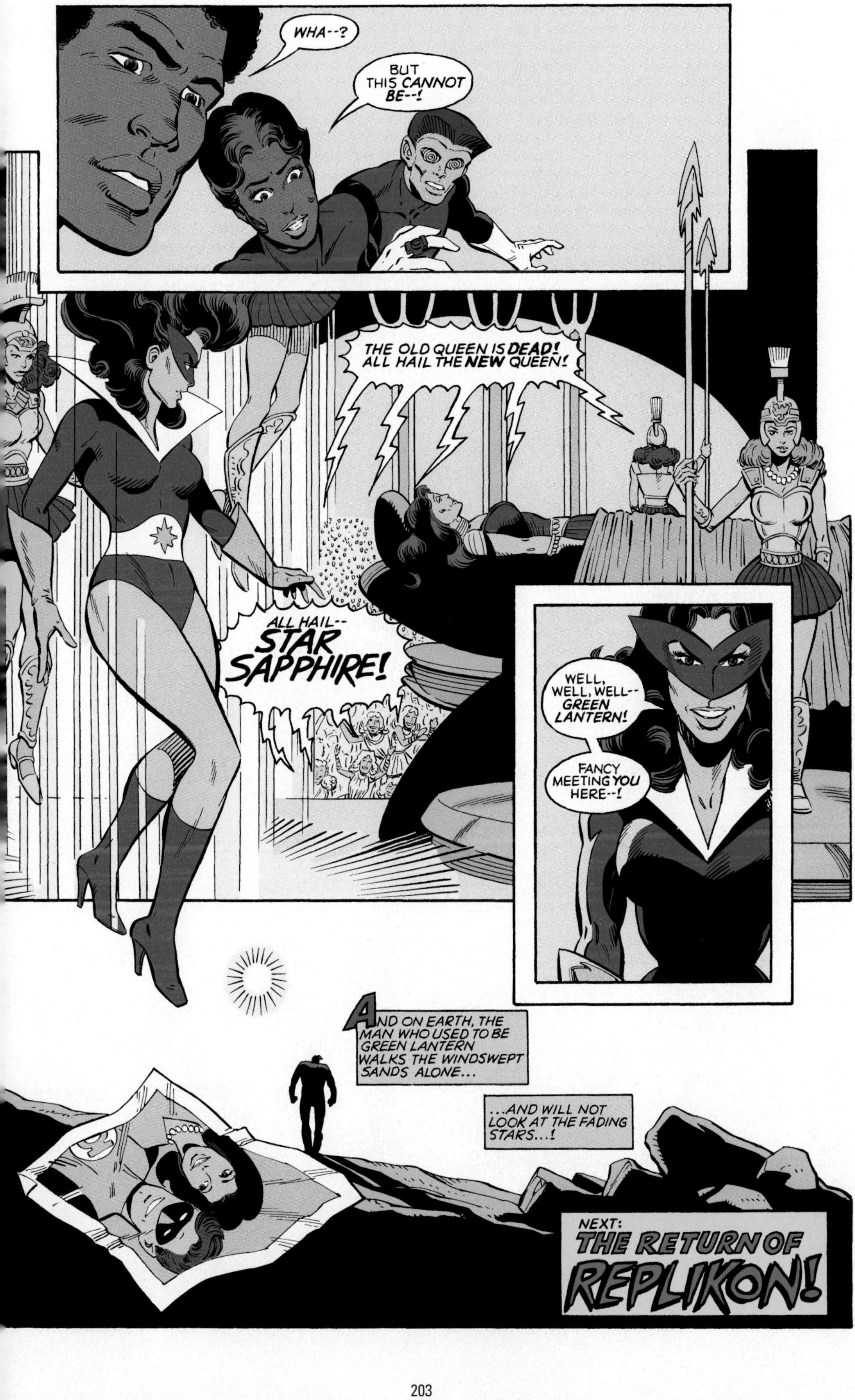
WHA--?
BUT THIS CANNOT BE--!
THE OLD QUEEN IS DEAD! ALL HAIL THE NEW QUEEN!
ALL HAIL-- STAR SAPPHIRE!
WELL, WELL, WELL-- GREEN LANTERN!
FANCY MEETING YOU HERE--!
AND ON EARTH, THE MAN WHO USED TO BE GREEN LANTERN WALKS THE WINDSWEPT SANDS ALONE...
...AND WILL NOT LOOK AT THE FADING STARS...!
NEXT: THE RETURN OF REPLIKON!

Cover art by Joe Staton & Bruce Patterson

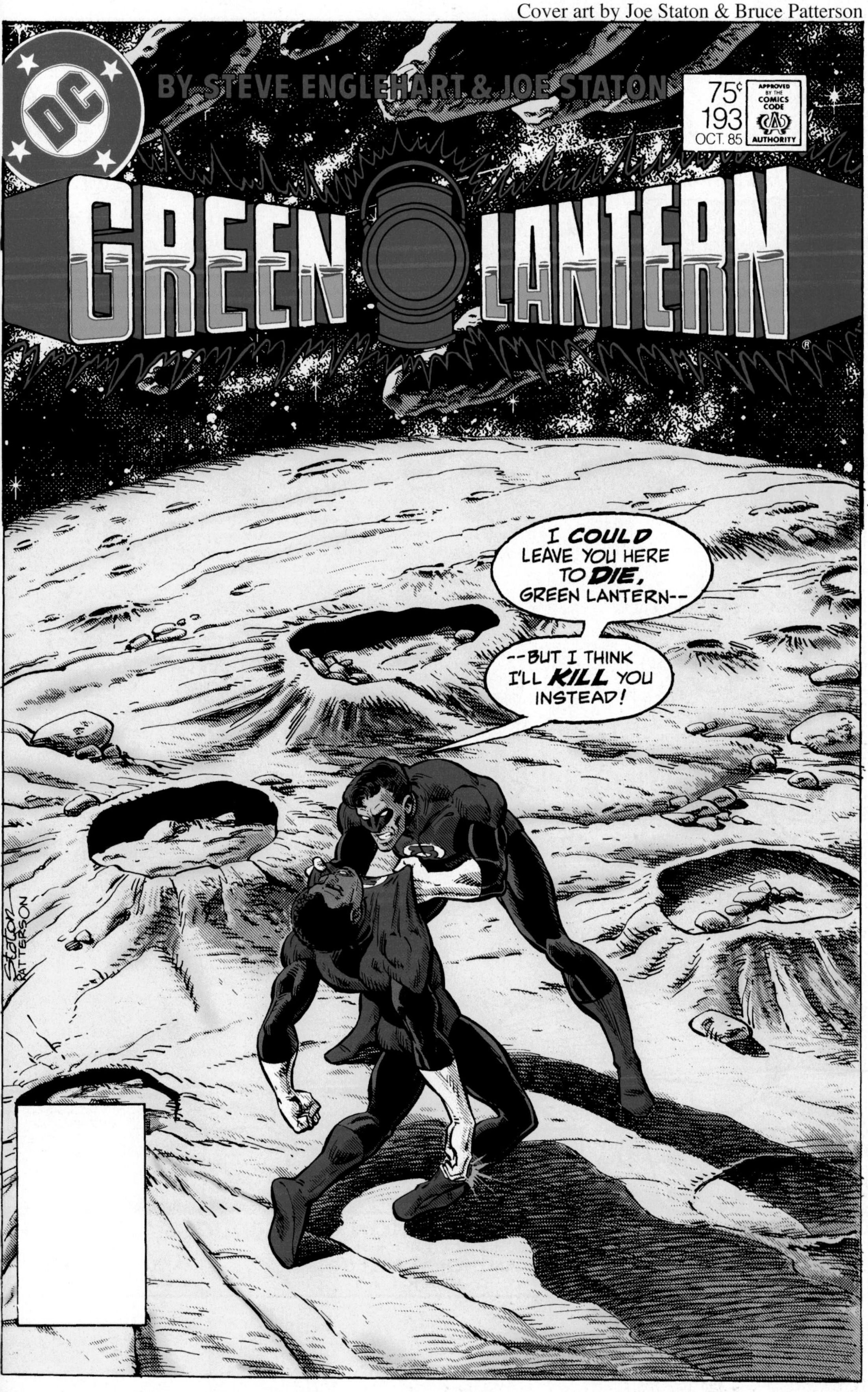
DC
BY STEVE ENGLEHART & JOE STATON
75¢
193
OCT. 85
APPROVED BY THE COMICS CODE AUTHORITY
GREEN LANTERN
I COULD LEAVE YOU HERE TO DIE, GREEN LANTERN--
--BUT I THINK I'LL KILL YOU INSTEAD!
STATON
PATTERSON

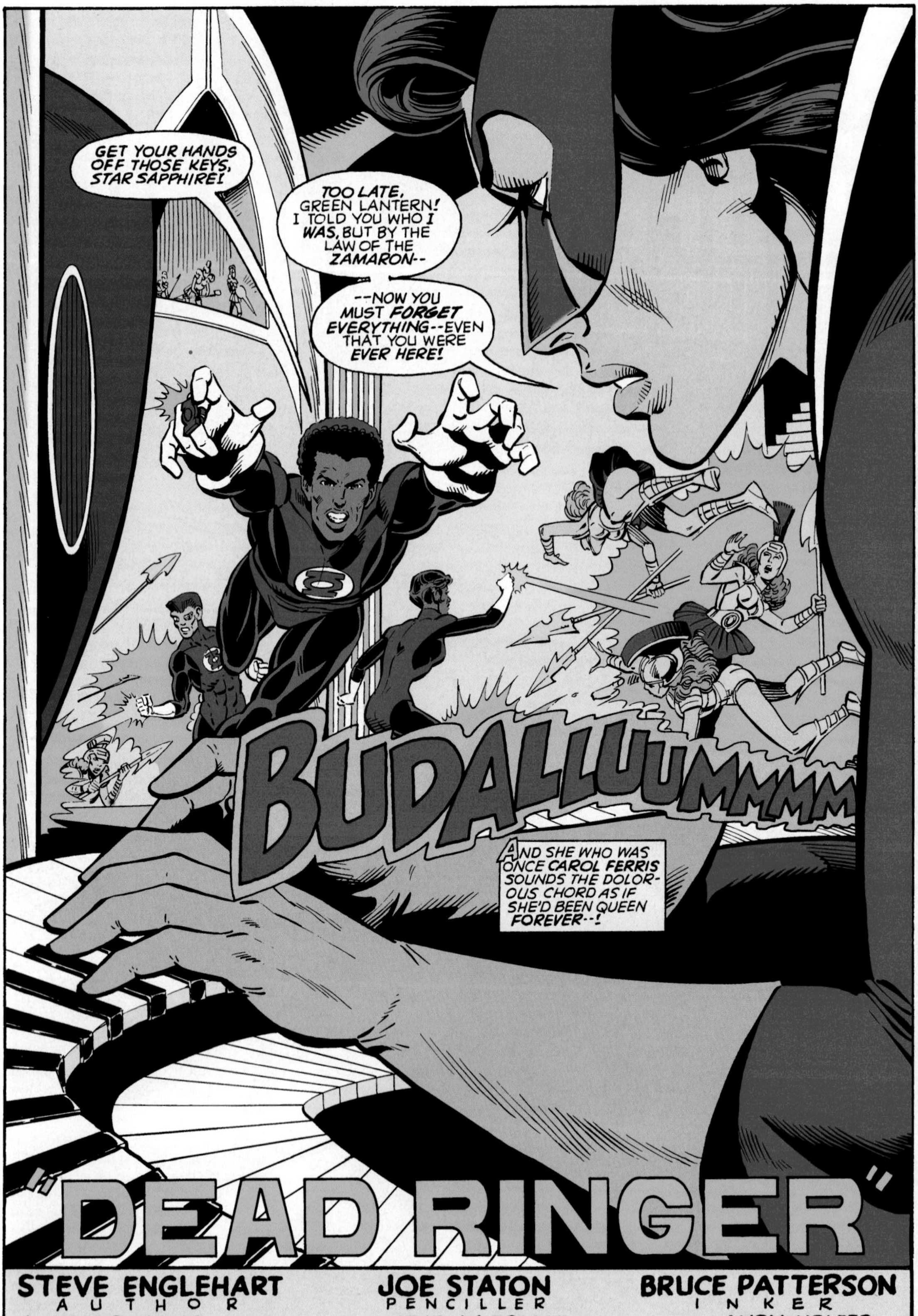
GET YOUR HANDS OFF THOSE KEYS, STAR SAPPHIRE!
TOO LATE, GREEN LANTERN! I TOLD YOU WHO I WAS, BUT BY THE LAW OF THE ZAMARON--
--NOW YOU MUST FORGET EVERYTHING--EVEN THAT YOU WERE EVER HERE!
BUDALLUUMMMMM
AND SHE WHO WAS ONCE CAROL FERRIS SOUNDS THE DOLOROUS CHORD AS IF SHE'D BEEN QUEEN FOREVER--!
"DEAD RINGER"
STEVE ENGLEHART AUTHOR
JOE STATON PENCILLER
BRUCE PATTERSON INKER
L. LOIS BUHALIS LETTERER
ANTHONY TOLLIN COLORIST
ANDY HELFER EDITOR

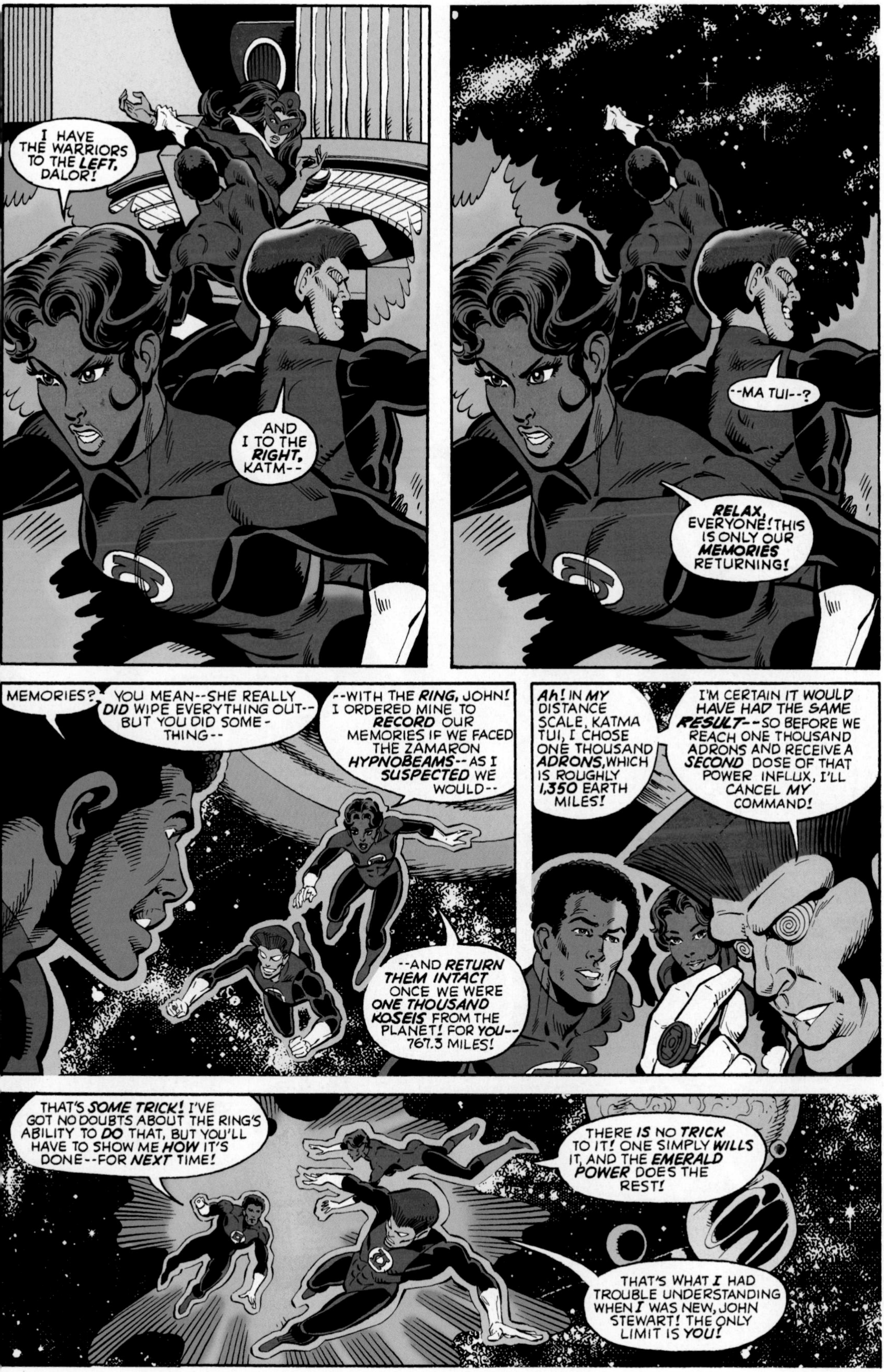
I HAVE THE WARRIORS TO THE LEFT, DALOR!
AND I TO THE RIGHT, KATM--
--MA TUI--?
RELAX, EVERYONE! THIS IS ONLY OUR MEMORIES RETURNING!
MEMORIES?
YOU MEAN--SHE REALLY DID WIPE EVERYTHING OUT-- BUT YOU DID SOME-THING--
--WITH THE RING, JOHN! I ORDERED MINE TO RECORD OUR MEMORIES IF WE FACED THE ZAMARON HYPNOBEAMS--AS I SUSPECTED WE WOULD--
--AND RETURN THEM INTACT ONCE WE WERE ONE THOUSAND KOSEIS FROM THE PLANET! FOR YOU--767.3 MILES!
AH! IN MY DISTANCE SCALE, KATMA TUI, I CHOSE ONE THOUSAND ADRONS, WHICH IS ROUGHLY 1,350 EARTH MILES!
I'M CERTAIN IT WOULD HAVE HAD THE SAME RESULT--SO BEFORE WE REACH ONE THOUSAND ADRONS AND RECEIVE A SECOND DOSE OF THAT POWER INFLUX, I'LL CANCEL MY COMMAND!
THAT'S SOME TRICK! I'VE GOT NO DOUBTS ABOUT THE RING'S ABILITY TO DO THAT, BUT YOU'LL HAVE TO SHOW ME HOW IT'S DONE--FOR NEXT TIME!
THERE IS NO TRICK TO IT! ONE SIMPLY WILLS IT, AND THE EMERALD POWER DOES THE REST!
THAT'S WHAT I HAD TROUBLE UNDERSTANDING WHEN I WAS NEW, JOHN STEWART! THE ONLY LIMIT IS YOU!

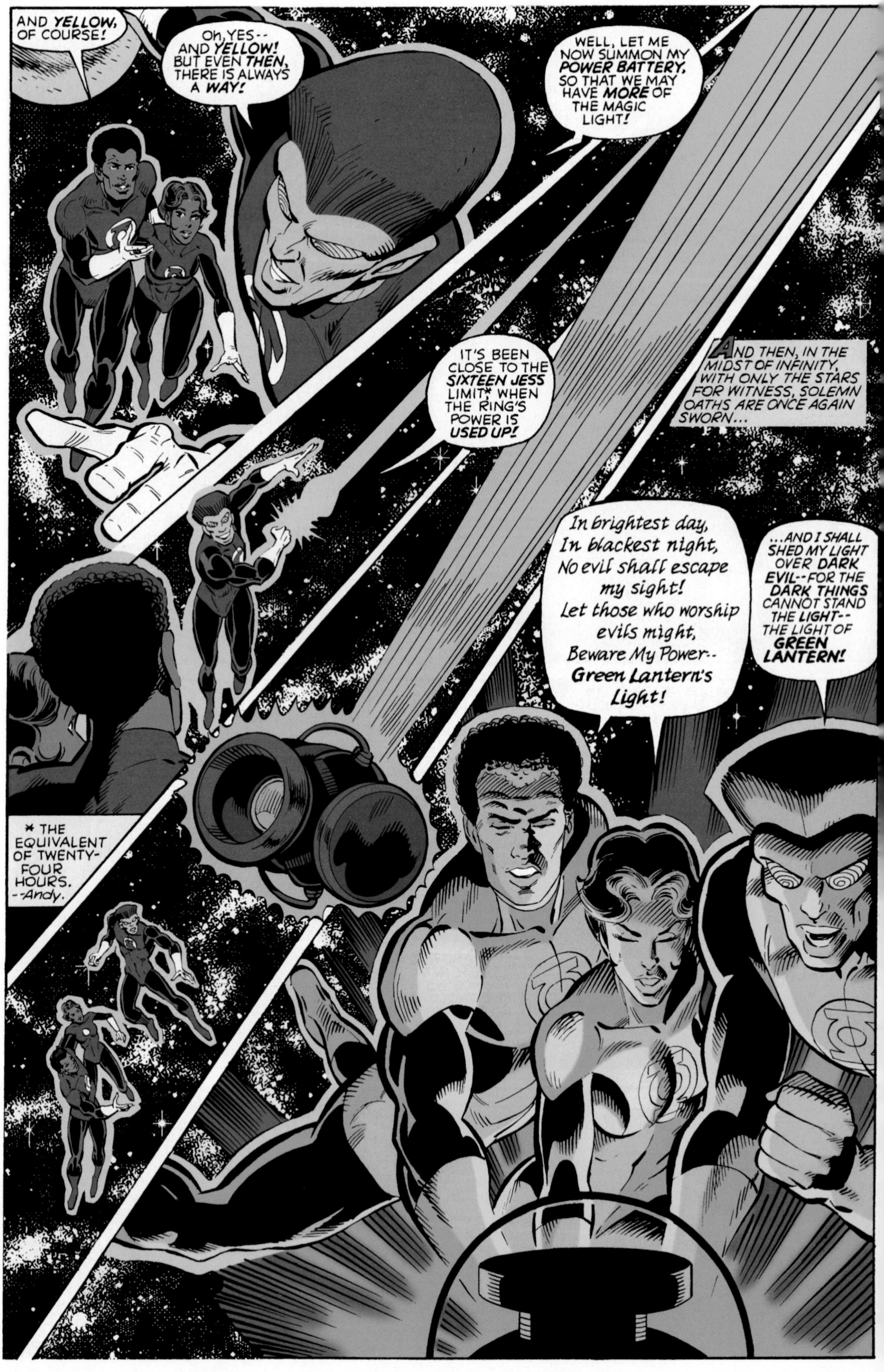
AND YELLOW, OF COURSE!
Oh, YES-- AND YELLOW! BUT EVEN THEN, THERE IS ALWAYS A WAY!
WELL, LET ME NOW SUMMON MY POWER BATTERY, SO THAT WE MAY HAVE MORE OF THE MAGIC LIGHT!
IT'S BEEN CLOSE TO THE SIXTEEN JESS LIMIT* WHEN THE RING'S POWER IS USED UP!
AND THEN, IN THE MIDST OF INFINITY, WITH ONLY THE STARS FOR WITNESS, SOLEMN OATHS ARE ONCE AGAIN SWORN...
In brightest day,
In blackest night,
No evil shall escape my sight!
Let those who worship evils might,
Beware My Power--
Green Lantern's Light!
...AND I SHALL SHED MY LIGHT OVER DARK EVIL--FOR THE DARK THINGS CANNOT STAND THE LIGHT-- THE LIGHT OF GREEN LANTERN!
* THE EQUIVALENT OF TWENTY-FOUR HOURS. --Andy.

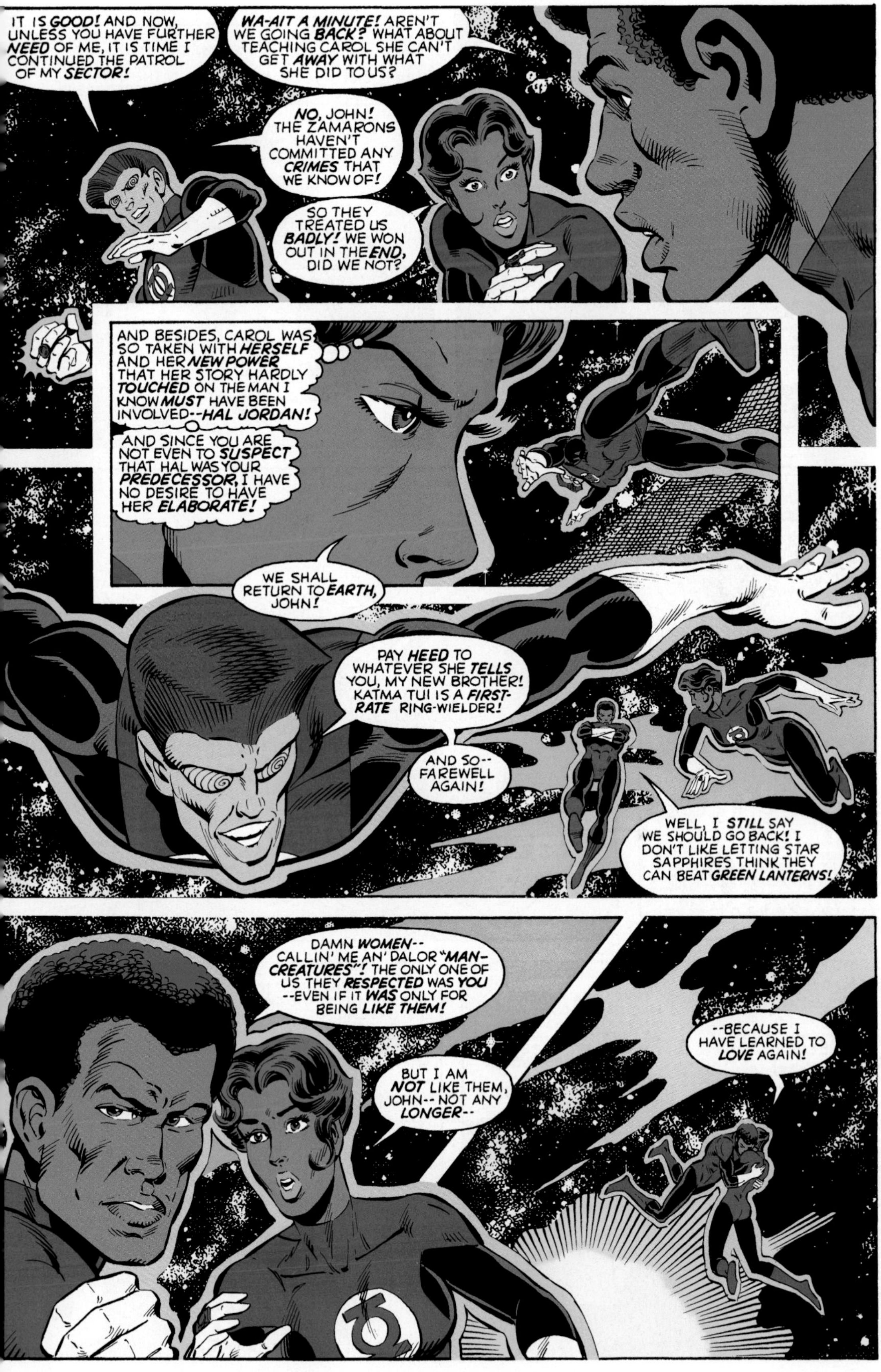
IT IS GOOD! AND NOW, UNLESS YOU HAVE FURTHER NEED OF ME, IT IS TIME I CONTINUED THE PATROL OF MY SECTOR!
WA-AIT A MINUTE! AREN'T WE GOING BACK? WHAT ABOUT TEACHING CAROL SHE CAN'T GET AWAY WITH WHAT SHE DID TO US?
NO, JOHN! THE ZAMARONS HAVEN'T COMMITTED ANY CRIMES THAT WE KNOW OF!
SO THEY TREATED US BADLY! WE WON OUT IN THE END, DID WE NOT?
AND BESIDES, CAROL WAS SO TAKEN WITH HERSELF AND HER NEW POWER THAT HER STORY HARDLY TOUCHED ON THE MAN I KNOW MUST HAVE BEEN INVOLVED--HAL JORDAN!
AND SINCE YOU ARE NOT EVEN TO SUSPECT THAT HAL WAS YOUR PREDECESSOR, I HAVE NO DESIRE TO HAVE HER ELABORATE!
WE SHALL RETURN TO EARTH, JOHN!
PAY HEED TO WHATEVER SHE TELLS YOU, MY NEW BROTHER! KATMA TUI IS A FIRST-RATE RING-WIELDER!
AND SO-- FAREWELL AGAIN!
WELL, I STILL SAY WE SHOULD GO BACK! I DON'T LIKE LETTING STAR SAPPHIRES THINK THEY CAN BEAT GREEN LANTERNS!
DAMN WOMEN-- CALLIN' ME AN' DALOR "MAN-CREATURES"! THE ONLY ONE OF US THEY RESPECTED WAS YOU --EVEN IF IT WAS ONLY FOR BEING LIKE THEM!
BUT I AM NOT LIKE THEM, JOHN-- NOT ANY LONGER--
--BECAUSE I HAVE LEARNED TO LOVE AGAIN!

YOU NEVER TOLD ME HOW YOU LOST YOUR *FIRST* LOVE...

IT IS NOT A *PLEASANT MEMORY* IN THESE TIMES, JOHN--!

"HIS NAME WAS *IMI KANN!* HE WAS ONE OF MY PLANET *KORUGAR'S* MOST BRILLIANT *SCIENTISTS!*

"I WAS JUST COMPLETING A *PROBATION PERIOD* THE GUARDIANS HAD SET FOR ME, AND I TOLD THEM THAT, ALTHOUGH I'D *PASSED* THEIR INSPECTION, I PLANNED *NOT* TO *CONTINUE!*

"IN RESPONSE, THEY SENT H-- YOUR *PREDECESSOR!*

I AM SORRY, BUT I FEEL I MUST DEVOTE MY LIFE TO THE *CHILDREN* IMI AND I PLAN TO HAVE! I *CANNOT* BE GREEN LANTERN!

MAYBE SO,...BUT OUR MASTERS ORDERED ME TO USE *EVERY POSSIBLE MEANS* TO CHANGE YOUR MIND--

--AND AS YOU KNOW, I'M *DUTY-BOUND* TO CARRY OUT MY *MISSION!*

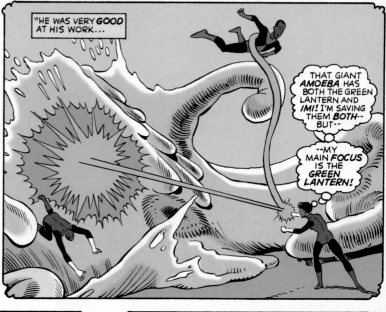

"HE WAS VERY *GOOD* AT HIS WORK...

THAT GIANT *AMOEBA* HAS BOTH THE GREEN LANTERN AND *IMI!* I'M SAVING THEM *BOTH*--BUT--

--MY MAIN *FOCUS* IS THE *GREEN LANTERN!*

YOU SEE, YOUR *LOYALTY* TO THE *CORPS* OUTWEIGHED YOUR *LOVE!*

THERE ARE *OTHERS* WHO CAN BECOME WIVES AND MOTHERS! THERE ARE *VERY FEW*--WOMEN OR MEN--FIT TO BE *GREEN LANTERNS!*

I DON'T WANT TO *HURT* YOU, BUT BEING A GREEN LANTERN IS YOUR *DESTINY!*

YOU ARE ONE OF *US,* KATMA TUI! AND *ONCE* A GREEN LANTERN-- *ALWAYS* A GREEN LANTERN!

"LATER I LEARNED THAT *HE* HAD *CREATED* THE AMOEBA--BUT HE WAS *RIGHT* ABOUT ME, SO I *FORGAVE* HIM!"

210

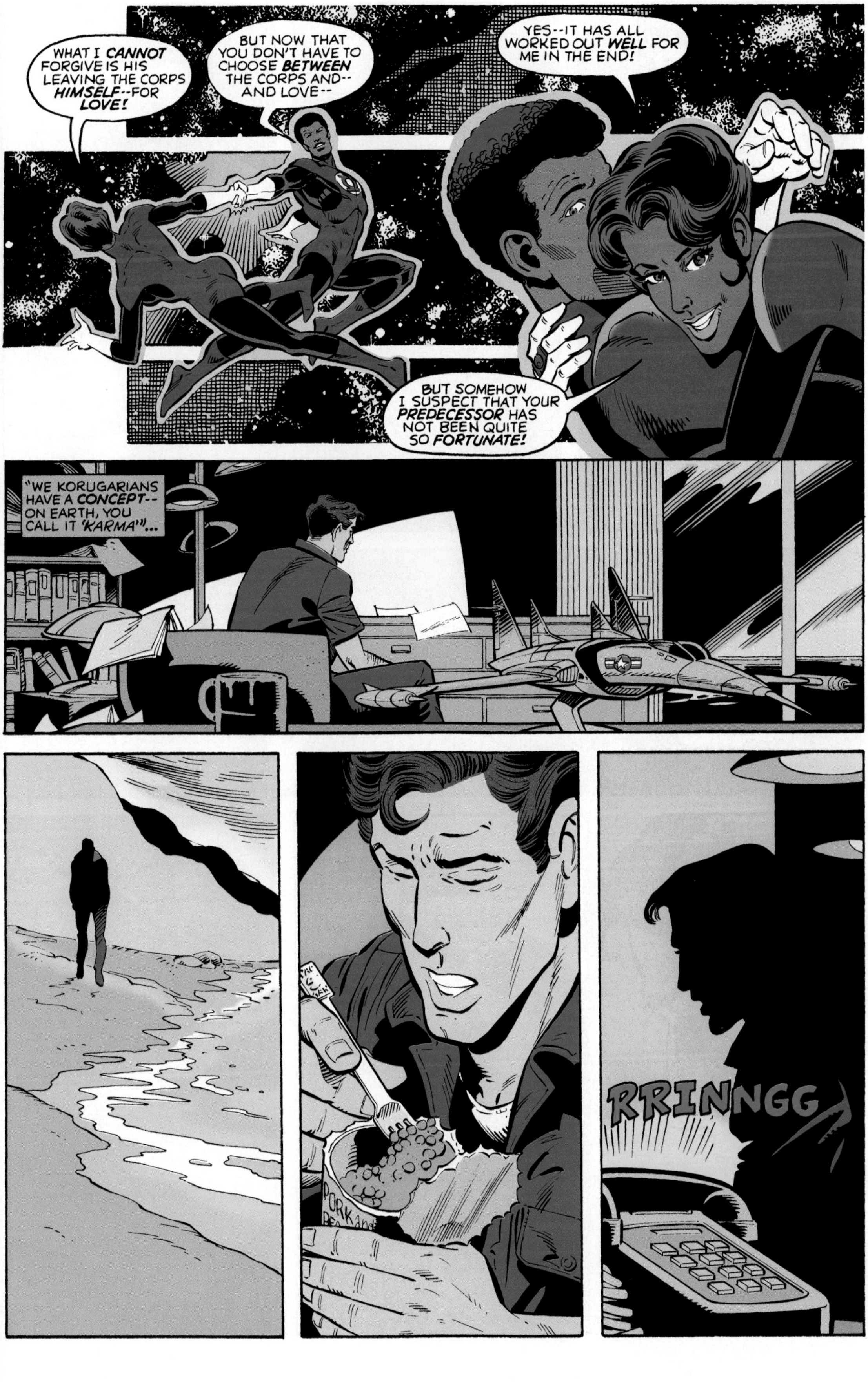
WHAT I CANNOT FORGIVE IS HIS LEAVING THE CORPS HIMSELF--FOR LOVE!
BUT NOW THAT YOU DON'T HAVE TO CHOOSE BETWEEN THE CORPS AND--AND LOVE--
YES--IT HAS ALL WORKED OUT WELL FOR ME IN THE END!
BUT SOMEHOW I SUSPECT THAT YOUR PREDECESSOR HAS NOT BEEN QUITE SO FORTUNATE!
"WE KORUGARIANS HAVE A CONCEPT--ON EARTH, YOU CALL IT 'KARMA'"...
PORK and
RRINNGG

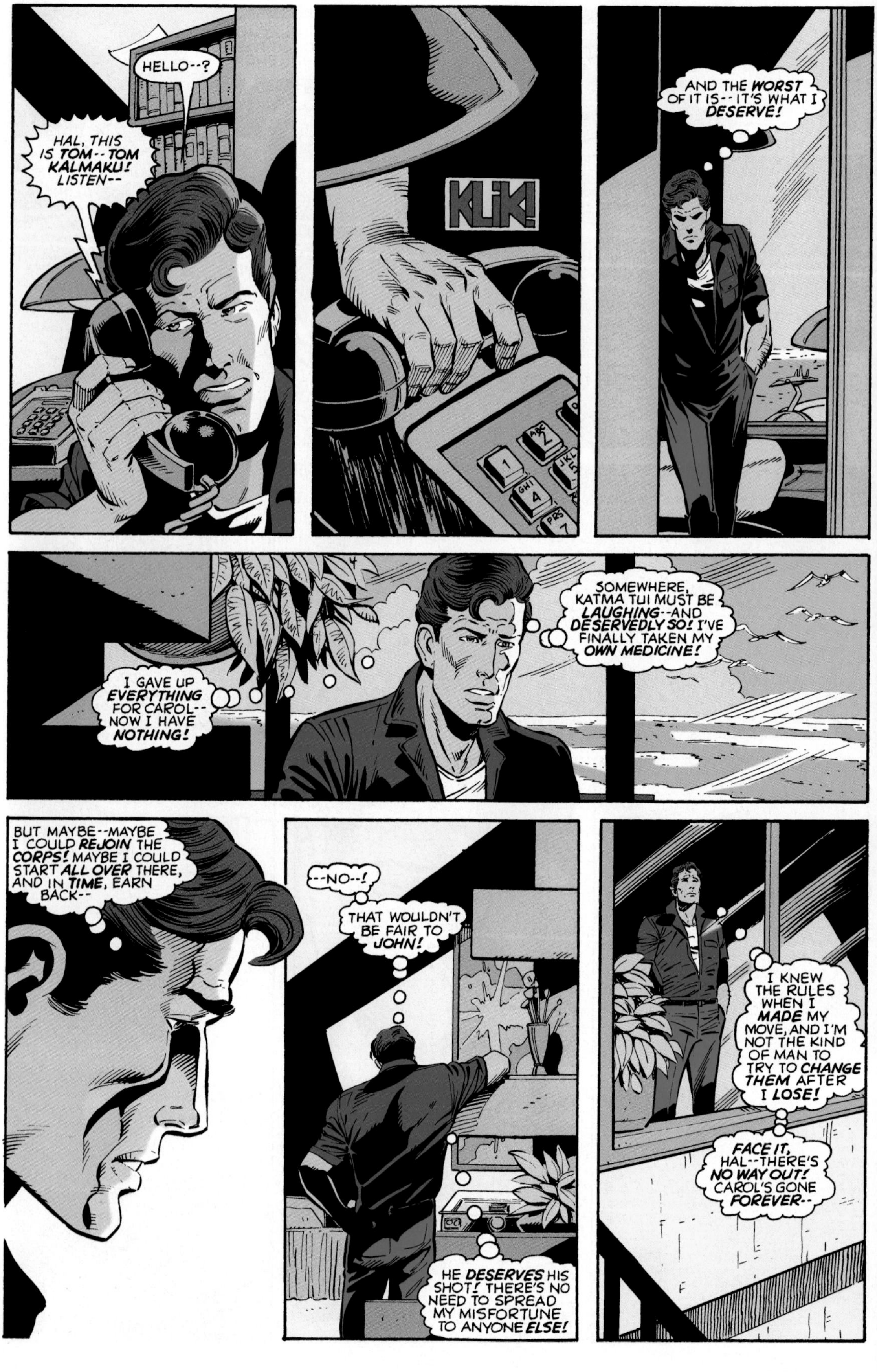
HELLO--?
HAL, THIS IS TOM--TOM KALMAKU! LISTEN--
KLIK!
AND THE WORST OF IT IS--IT'S WHAT I DESERVE!
I GAVE UP EVERYTHING FOR CAROL--NOW I HAVE NOTHING!
SOMEWHERE, KATMA TUI MUST BE LAUGHING--AND DESERVEDLY SO! I'VE FINALLY TAKEN MY OWN MEDICINE!
BUT MAYBE--MAYBE I COULD REJOIN THE CORPS! MAYBE I COULD START ALL OVER THERE, AND IN TIME, EARN BACK--
--NO--!
THAT WOULDN'T BE FAIR TO JOHN!
HE DESERVES HIS SHOT! THERE'S NO NEED TO SPREAD MY MISFORTUNE TO ANYONE ELSE!
I KNEW THE RULES WHEN I MADE MY MOVE, AND I'M NOT THE KIND OF MAN TO TRY TO CHANGE THEM AFTER I LOSE!
FACE IT, HAL--THERE'S NO WAY OUT! CAROL'S GONE FOREVER--

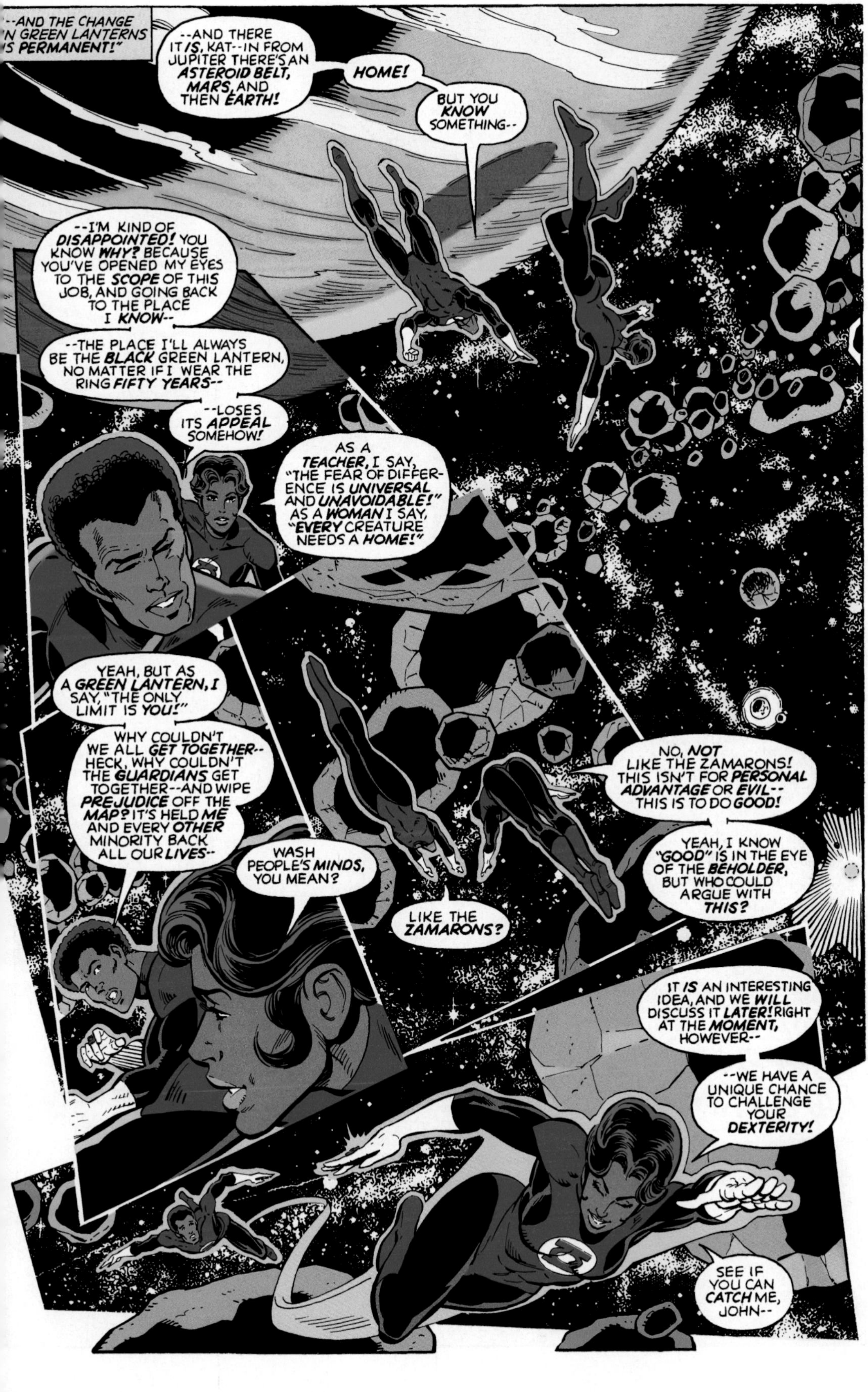
--AND THE CHANGE 'N GREEN LANTERNS 'S PERMANENT!"
--AND THERE IT IS, KAT--IN FROM JUPITER THERE'S AN ASTEROID BELT, MARS, AND THEN EARTH!
HOME!
BUT YOU KNOW SOMETHING--
--I'M KIND OF DISAPPOINTED! YOU KNOW WHY? BECAUSE YOU'VE OPENED MY EYES TO THE SCOPE OF THIS JOB, AND GOING BACK TO THE PLACE I KNOW--
--THE PLACE I'LL ALWAYS BE THE BLACK GREEN LANTERN, NO MATTER IF I WEAR THE RING FIFTY YEARS--
--LOSES ITS APPEAL SOMEHOW!
AS A TEACHER, I SAY, "THE FEAR OF DIFFERENCE IS UNIVERSAL AND UNAVOIDABLE!" AS A WOMAN I SAY, "EVERY CREATURE NEEDS A HOME!"
YEAH, BUT AS A GREEN LANTERN, I SAY, "THE ONLY LIMIT IS YOU!"
WHY COULDN'T WE ALL GET TOGETHER--HECK, WHY COULDN'T THE GUARDIANS GET TOGETHER--AND WIPE PREJUDICE OFF THE MAP? IT'S HELD ME AND EVERY OTHER MINORITY BACK ALL OUR LIVES--
WASH PEOPLE'S MINDS, YOU MEAN?
LIKE THE ZAMARONS?
NO, NOT LIKE THE ZAMARONS! THIS ISN'T FOR PERSONAL ADVANTAGE OR EVIL--THIS IS TO DO GOOD!
YEAH, I KNOW "GOOD" IS IN THE EYE OF THE BEHOLDER, BUT WHO COULD ARGUE WITH THIS?
IT IS AN INTERESTING IDEA, AND WE WILL DISCUSS IT LATER! RIGHT AT THE MOMENT, HOWEVER--
--WE HAVE A UNIQUE CHANCE TO CHALLENGE YOUR DEXTERITY!
SEE IF YOU CAN CATCH ME, JOHN--

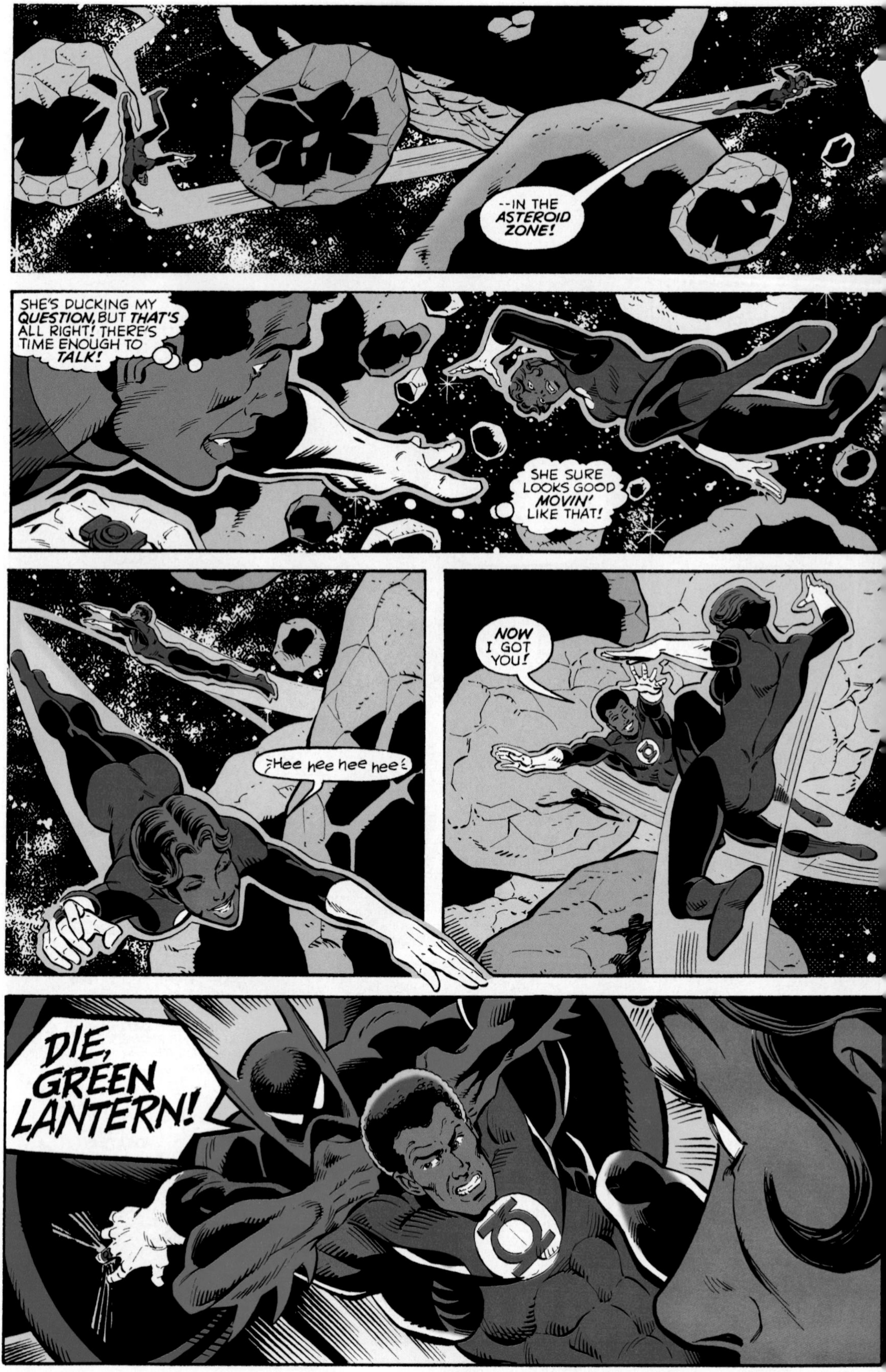
--IN THE ASTEROID ZONE!
SHE'S DUCKING MY QUESTION, BUT THAT'S ALL RIGHT! THERE'S TIME ENOUGH TO TALK!
SHE SURE LOOKS GOOD MOVIN' LIKE THAT!
Hee hee hee hee
NOW I GOT YOU!
DIE, GREEN LANTERN!

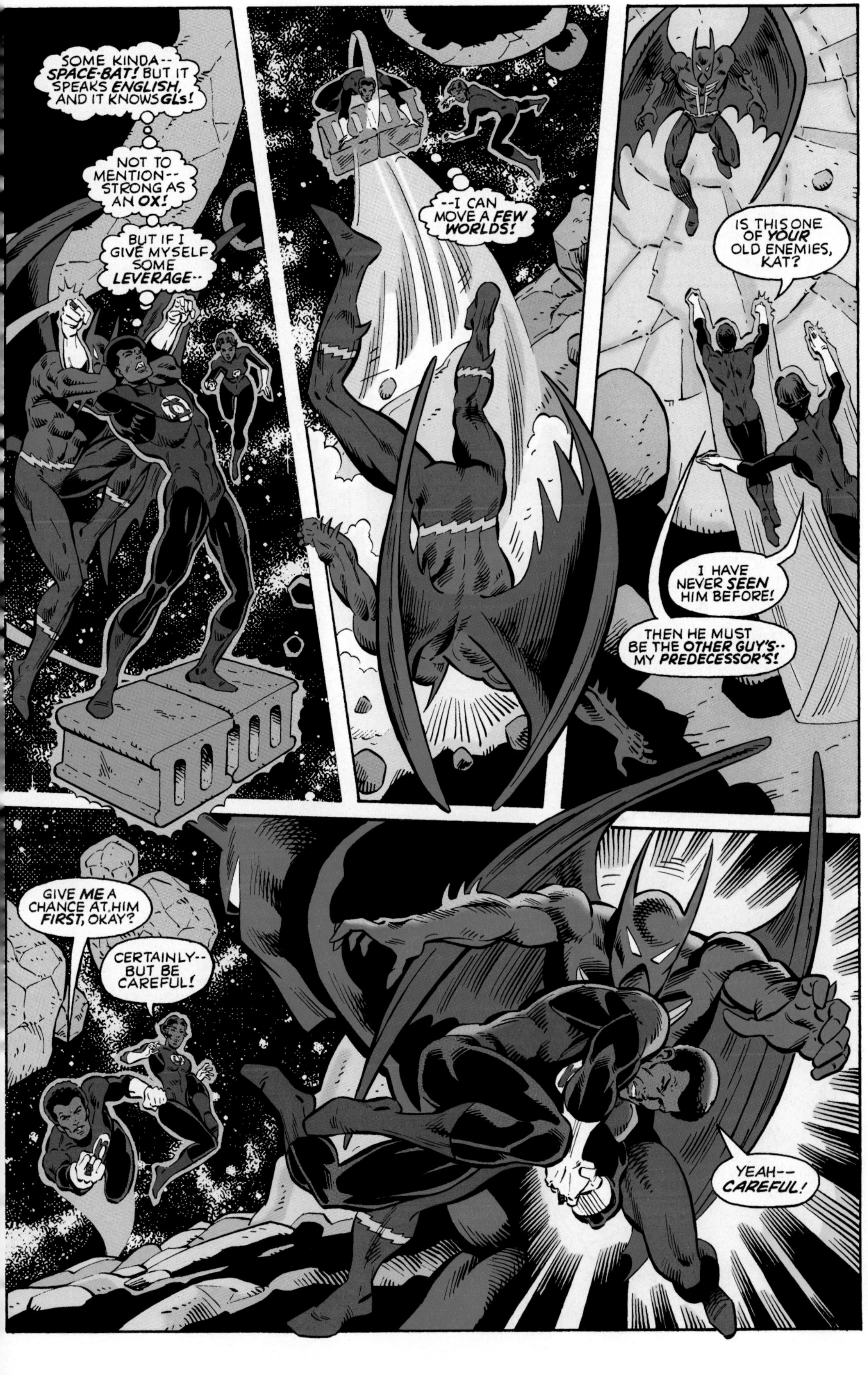
SOME KINDA-- SPACE-BAT! BUT IT SPEAKS ENGLISH, AND IT KNOWS GLs!
NOT TO MENTION-- STRONG AS AN OX!
BUT IF I GIVE MYSELF SOME LEVERAGE--
--I CAN MOVE A FEW WORLDS!
IS THIS ONE OF YOUR OLD ENEMIES, KAT?
I HAVE NEVER SEEN HIM BEFORE!
THEN HE MUST BE THE OTHER GUY'S-- MY PREDECESSOR'S!
GIVE ME A CHANCE AT HIM FIRST, OKAY?
CERTAINLY-- BUT BE CAREFUL!
YEAH-- CAREFUL!

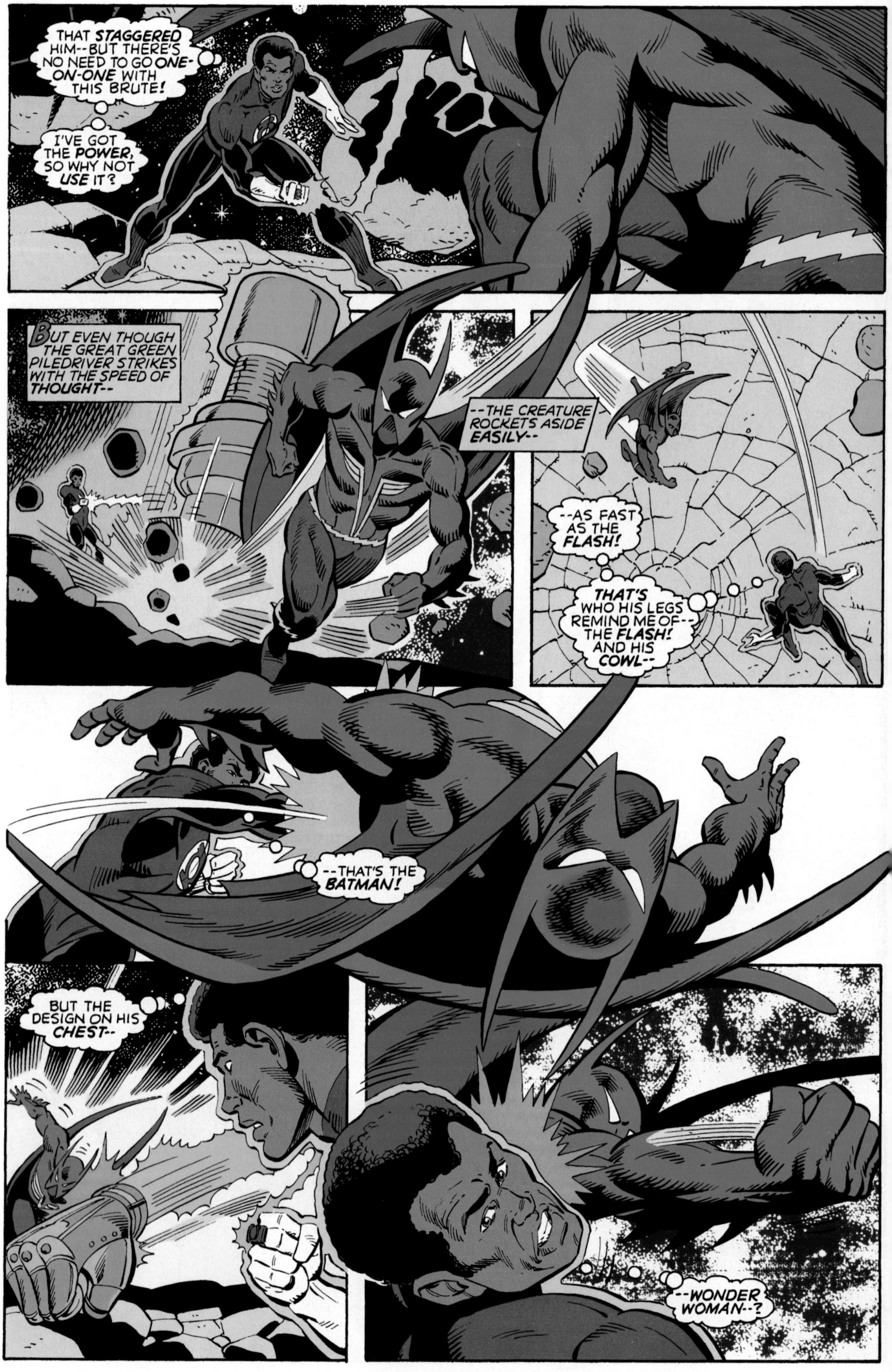
THAT STAGGERED HIM--BUT THERE'S NO NEED TO GO ONE-ON-ONE WITH THIS BRUTE!
I'VE GOT THE POWER, SO WHY NOT USE IT?
BUT EVEN THOUGH THE GREAT GREEN PILEDRIVER STRIKES WITH THE SPEED OF THOUGHT--
--THE CREATURE ROCKETS ASIDE EASILY--
--AS FAST AS THE FLASH!
THAT'S WHO HIS LEGS REMIND ME OF--THE FLASH! AND HIS COWL--
--THAT'S THE BATMAN!
BUT THE DESIGN ON HIS CHEST--
--WONDER WOMAN--?

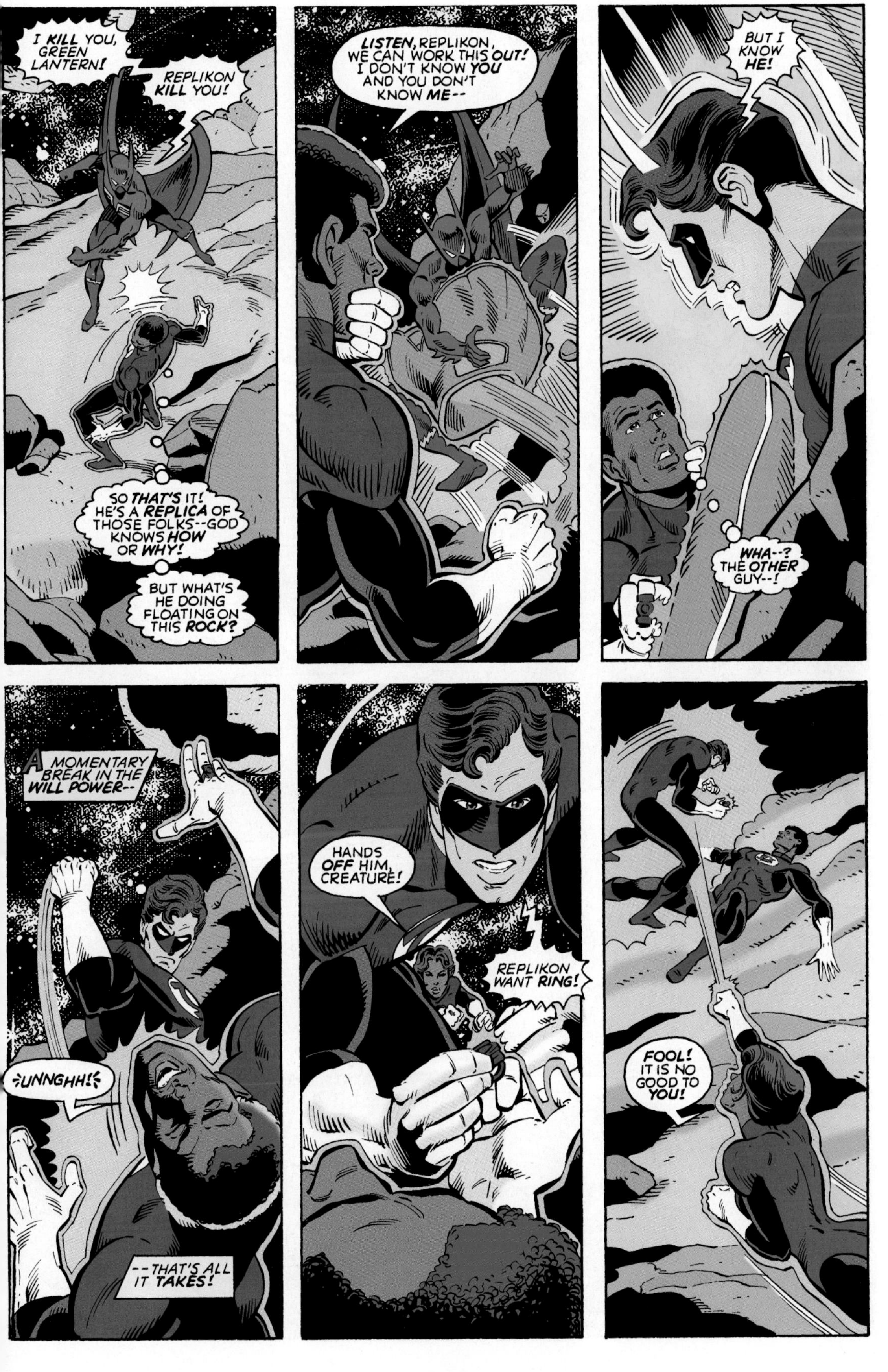
I KILL YOU, GREEN LANTERN!
REPLIKON KILL YOU!
SO THAT'S IT! HE'S A REPLICA OF THOSE FOLKS--GOD KNOWS HOW OR WHY!
BUT WHAT'S HE DOING FLOATING ON THIS ROCK?
LISTEN, REPLIKON, WE CAN WORK THIS OUT! I DON'T KNOW YOU AND YOU DON'T KNOW ME--
BUT I KNOW HE!
WHA--? THE OTHER GUY--!
A MOMENTARY BREAK IN THE WILL POWER--
UNNGHH!
--THAT'S ALL IT TAKES!
HANDS OFF HIM, CREATURE!
REPLIKON WANT RING!
FOOL! IT IS NO GOOD TO YOU!

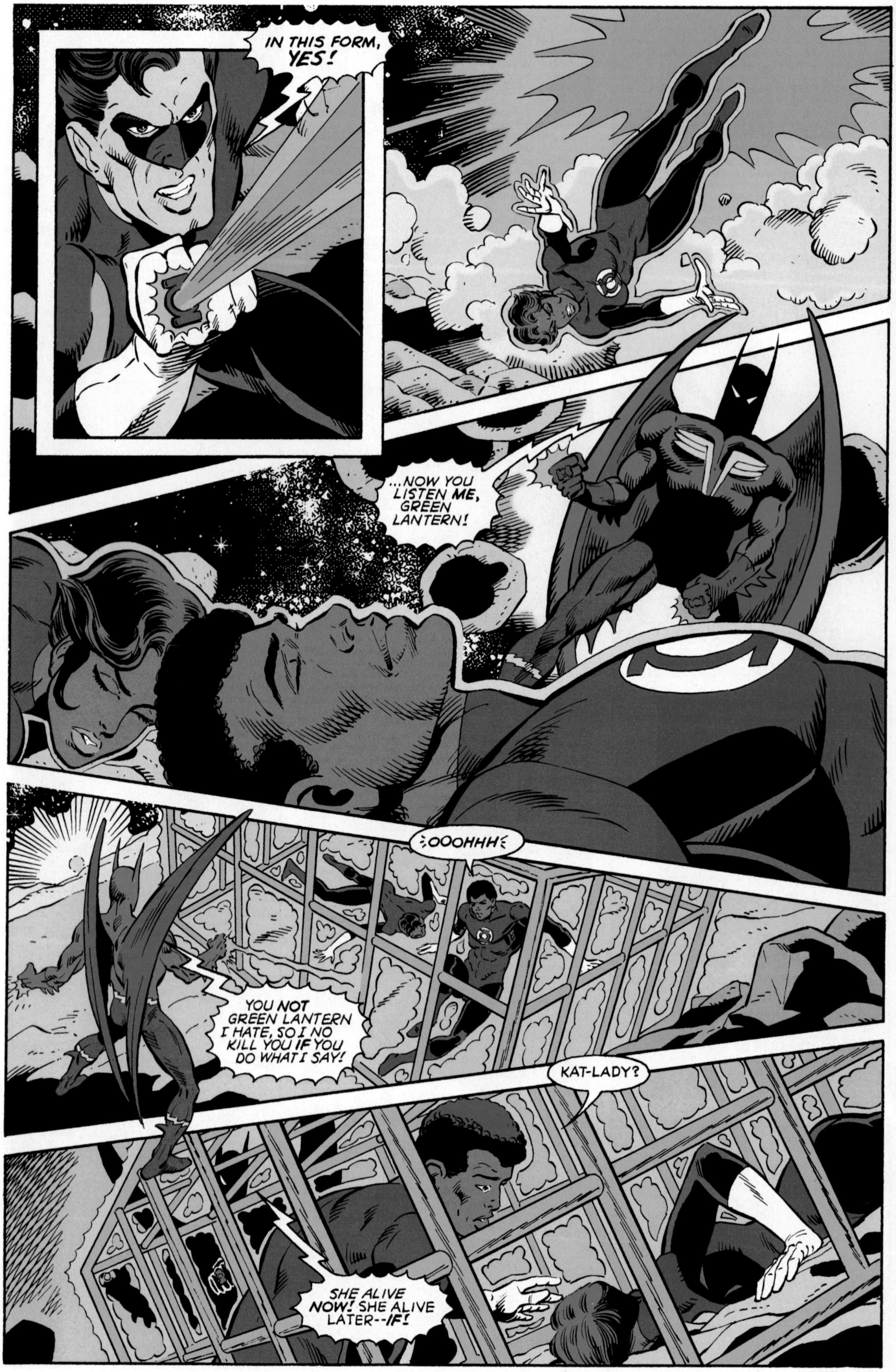
IN THIS FORM, YES!
...NOW YOU LISTEN ME, GREEN LANTERN!
OOOHHH
YOU NOT GREEN LANTERN I HATE, SO I NO KILL YOU IF YOU DO WHAT I SAY!
KAT-LADY?
SHE ALIVE NOW! SHE ALIVE LATER--IF!

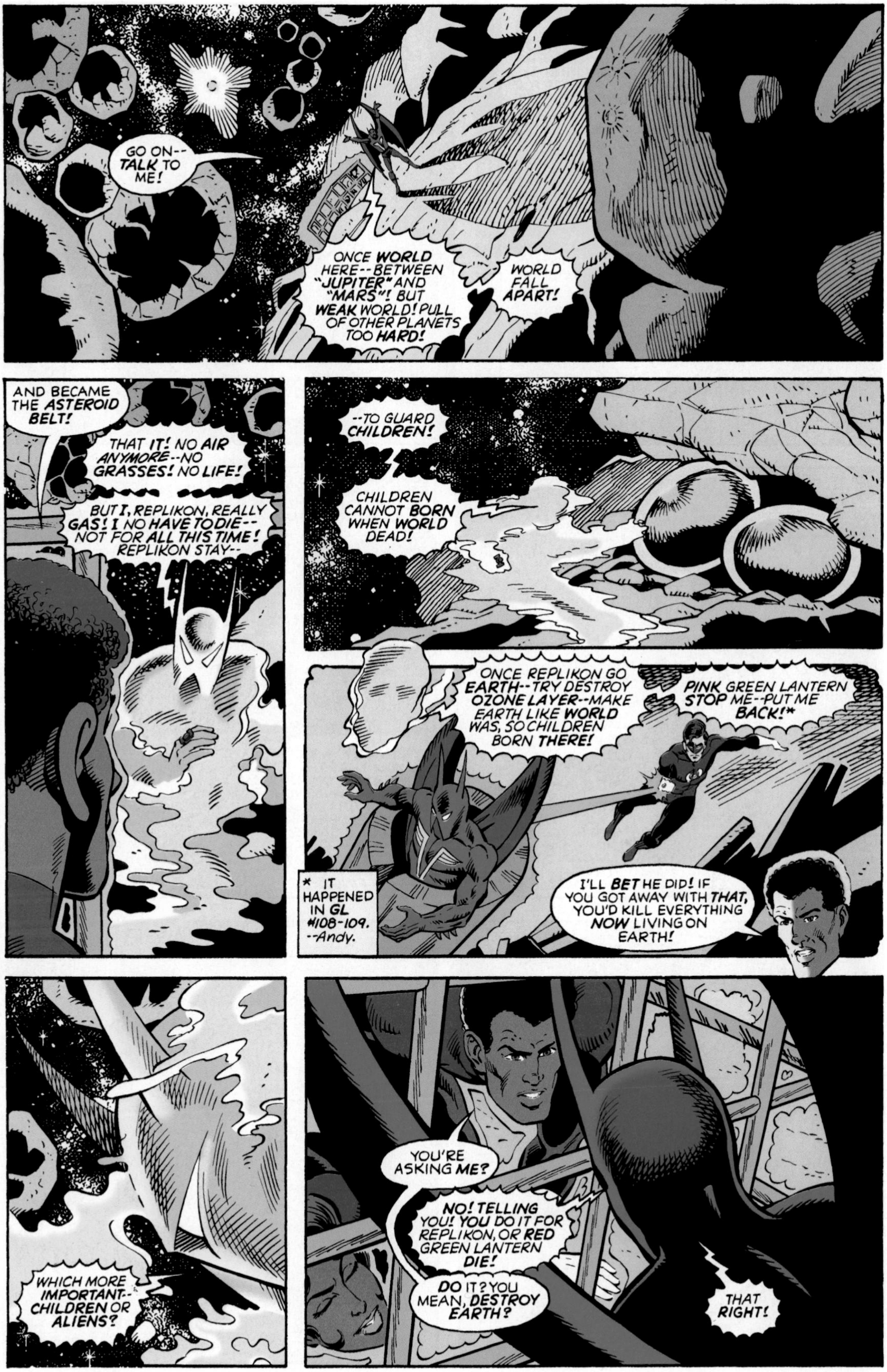

GO ON--
TALK TO ME!
ONCE WORLD HERE--BETWEEN "JUPITER" AND "MARS"! BUT WEAK WORLD! PULL OF OTHER PLANETS TOO HARD!
WORLD FALL APART!
AND BECAME THE ASTEROID BELT!
THAT IT! NO AIR ANYMORE--NO GRASSES! NO LIFE!
BUT I, REPLIKON, REALLY GAS! I NO HAVE TO DIE--NOT FOR ALL THIS TIME! REPLIKON STAY--
--TO GUARD CHILDREN!
CHILDREN CANNOT BORN WHEN WORLD DEAD!
ONCE REPLIKON GO EARTH--TRY DESTROY OZONE LAYER--MAKE EARTH LIKE WORLD WAS, SO CHILDREN BORN THERE!
PINK GREEN LANTERN STOP ME--PUT ME BACK!*
* IT HAPPENED IN GL #108-109. --Andy.
I'LL BET HE DID! IF YOU GOT AWAY WITH THAT, YOU'D KILL EVERYTHING NOW LIVING ON EARTH!
WHICH MORE IMPORTANT--CHILDREN OR ALIENS?
YOU'RE ASKING ME?
NO! TELLING YOU! YOU DO IT FOR REPLIKON, OR RED GREEN LANTERN DIE!
DO IT? YOU MEAN, DESTROY EARTH?
THAT RIGHT!

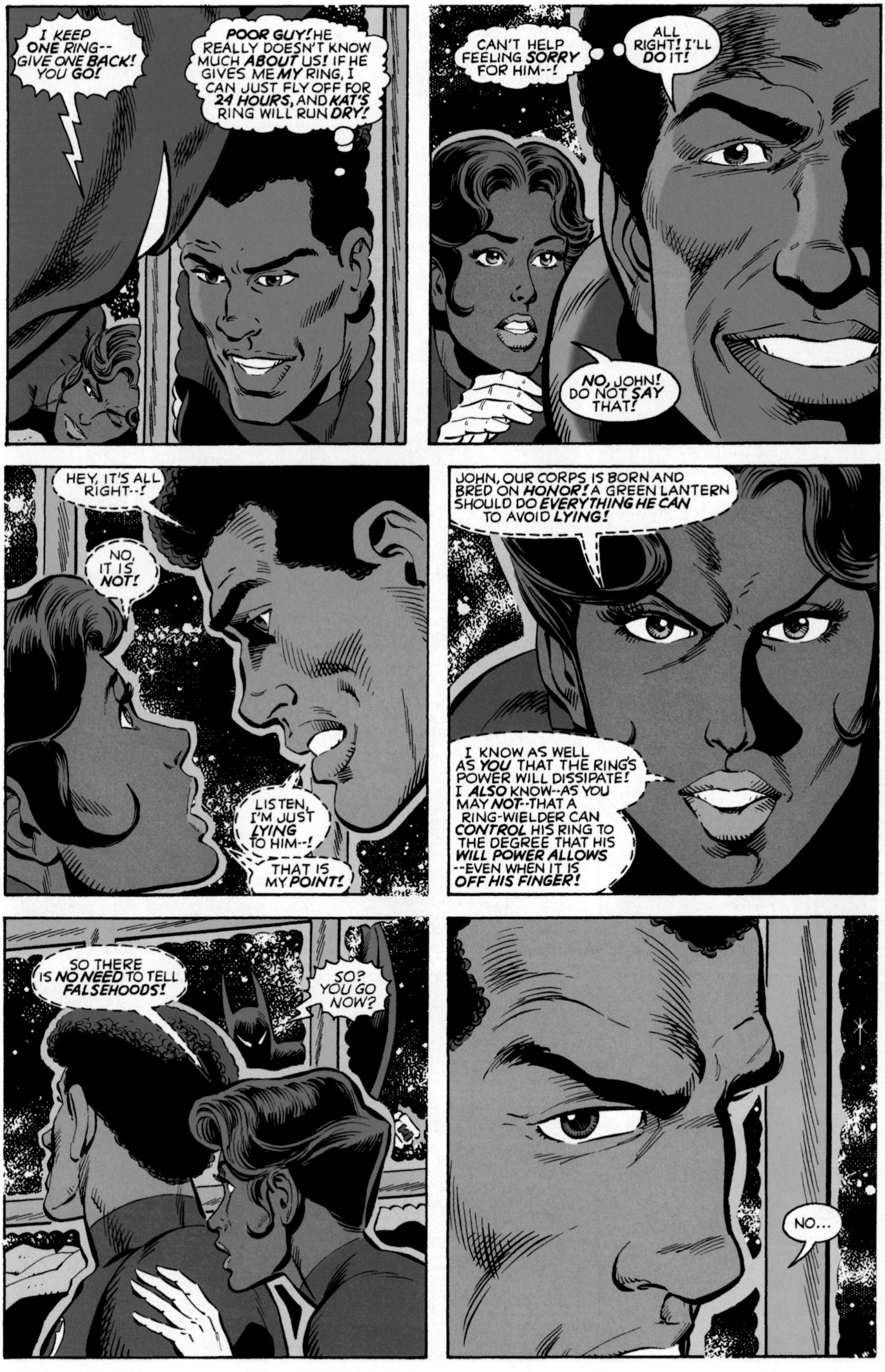
I KEEP ONE RING-- GIVE ONE BACK! YOU GO!
POOR GUY! HE REALLY DOESN'T KNOW MUCH ABOUT US! IF HE GIVES ME MY RING, I CAN JUST FLY OFF FOR 24 HOURS, AND KAT'S RING WILL RUN DRY!
CAN'T HELP FEELING SORRY FOR HIM--!
ALL RIGHT! I'LL DO IT!
NO, JOHN! DO NOT SAY THAT!
HEY, IT'S ALL RIGHT--!
NO, IT IS NOT!
LISTEN, I'M JUST LYING TO HIM--!
THAT IS MY POINT!
JOHN, OUR CORPS IS BORN AND BRED ON HONOR! A GREEN LANTERN SHOULD DO EVERYTHING HE CAN TO AVOID LYING!
I KNOW AS WELL AS YOU THAT THE RING'S POWER WILL DISSIPATE! I ALSO KNOW--AS YOU MAY NOT--THAT A RING-WIELDER CAN CONTROL HIS RING TO THE DEGREE THAT HIS WILL POWER ALLOWS --EVEN WHEN IT IS OFF HIS FINGER!
SO THERE IS NO NEED TO TELL FALSEHOODS!
SO? YOU GO NOW?
NO...

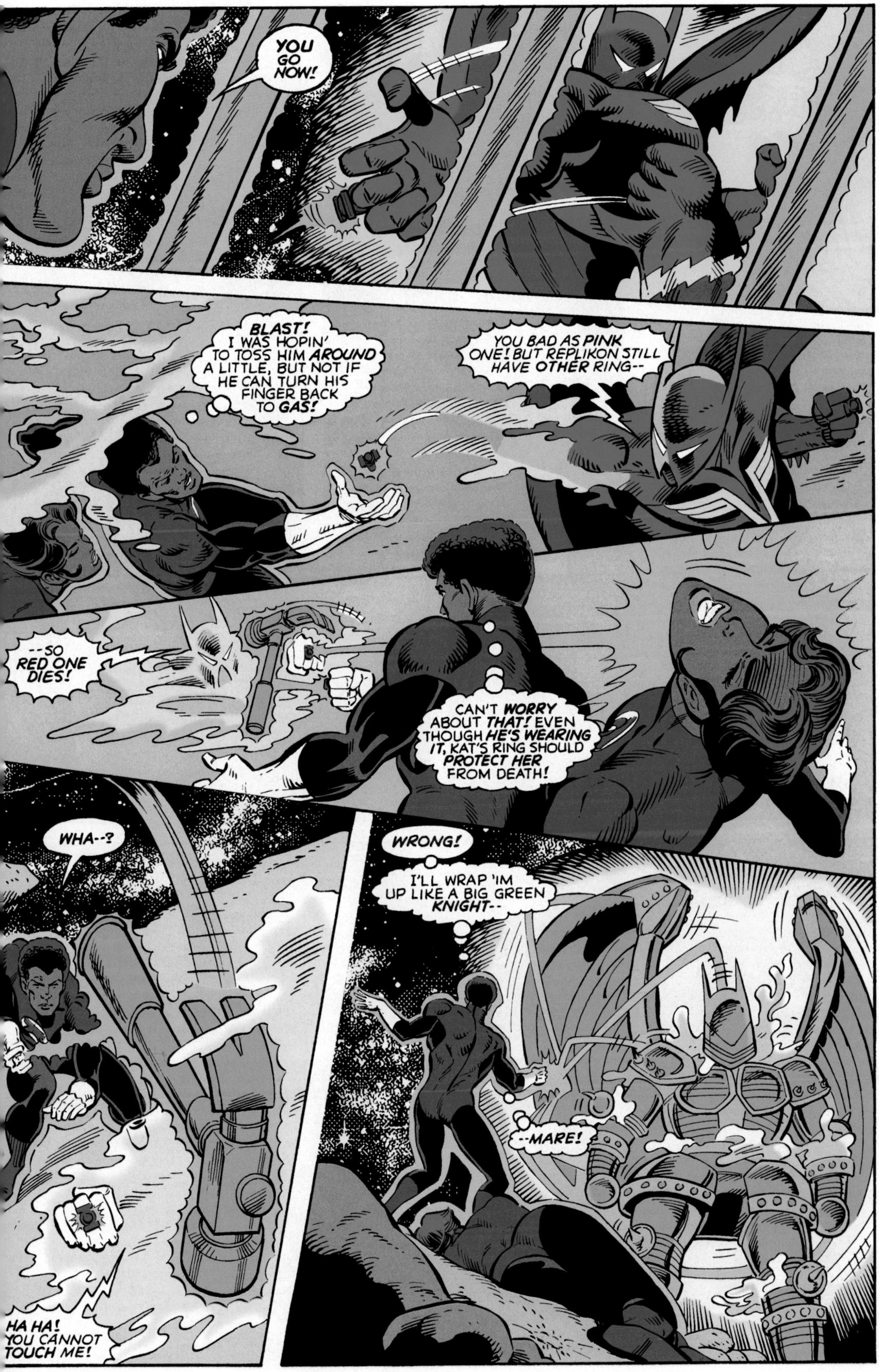
YOU GO NOW!
BLAST! I WAS HOPIN' TO TOSS HIM AROUND A LITTLE, BUT NOT IF HE CAN TURN HIS FINGER BACK TO GAS!
YOU BAD AS PINK ONE! BUT REPLIKON STILL HAVE OTHER RING--
--SO RED ONE DIES!
CAN'T WORRY ABOUT THAT! EVEN THOUGH HE'S WEARING IT, KAT'S RING SHOULD PROTECT HER FROM DEATH!
WHA--?
HA HA! YOU CANNOT TOUCH ME!
WRONG!
I'LL WRAP 'IM UP LIKE A BIG GREEN KNIGHT--
--MARE!

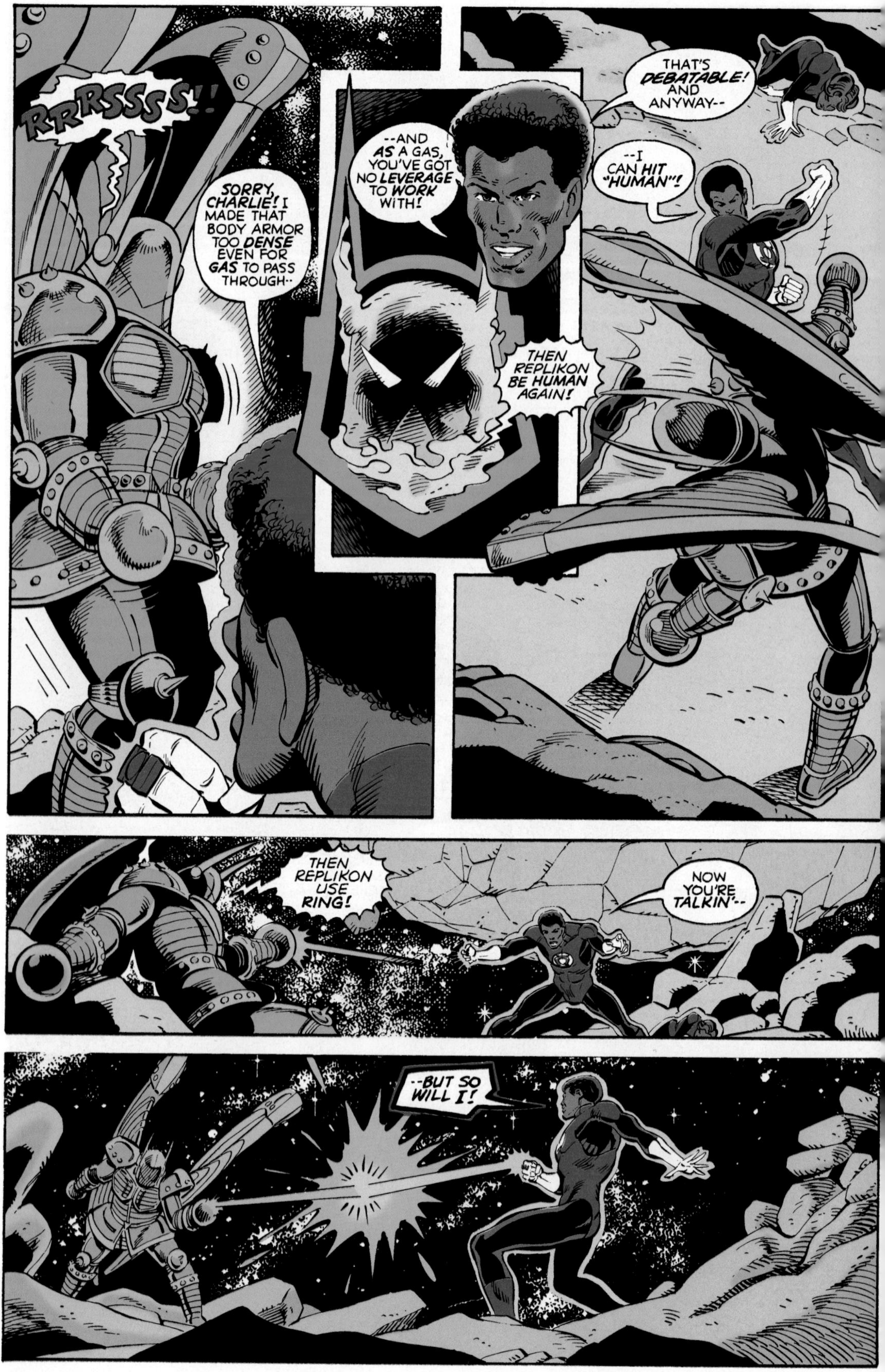
RRRSSSS!!
SORRY, CHARLIE! I MADE THAT BODY ARMOR TOO DENSE EVEN FOR GAS TO PASS THROUGH--
--AND AS A GAS, YOU'VE GOT NO LEVERAGE TO WORK WITH!
THEN REPLIKON BE HUMAN AGAIN!
THAT'S DEBATABLE! AND ANYWAY--
--I CAN HIT "HUMAN"!
THEN REPLIKON USE RING!
NOW YOU'RE TALKIN'--
--BUT SO WILL I!

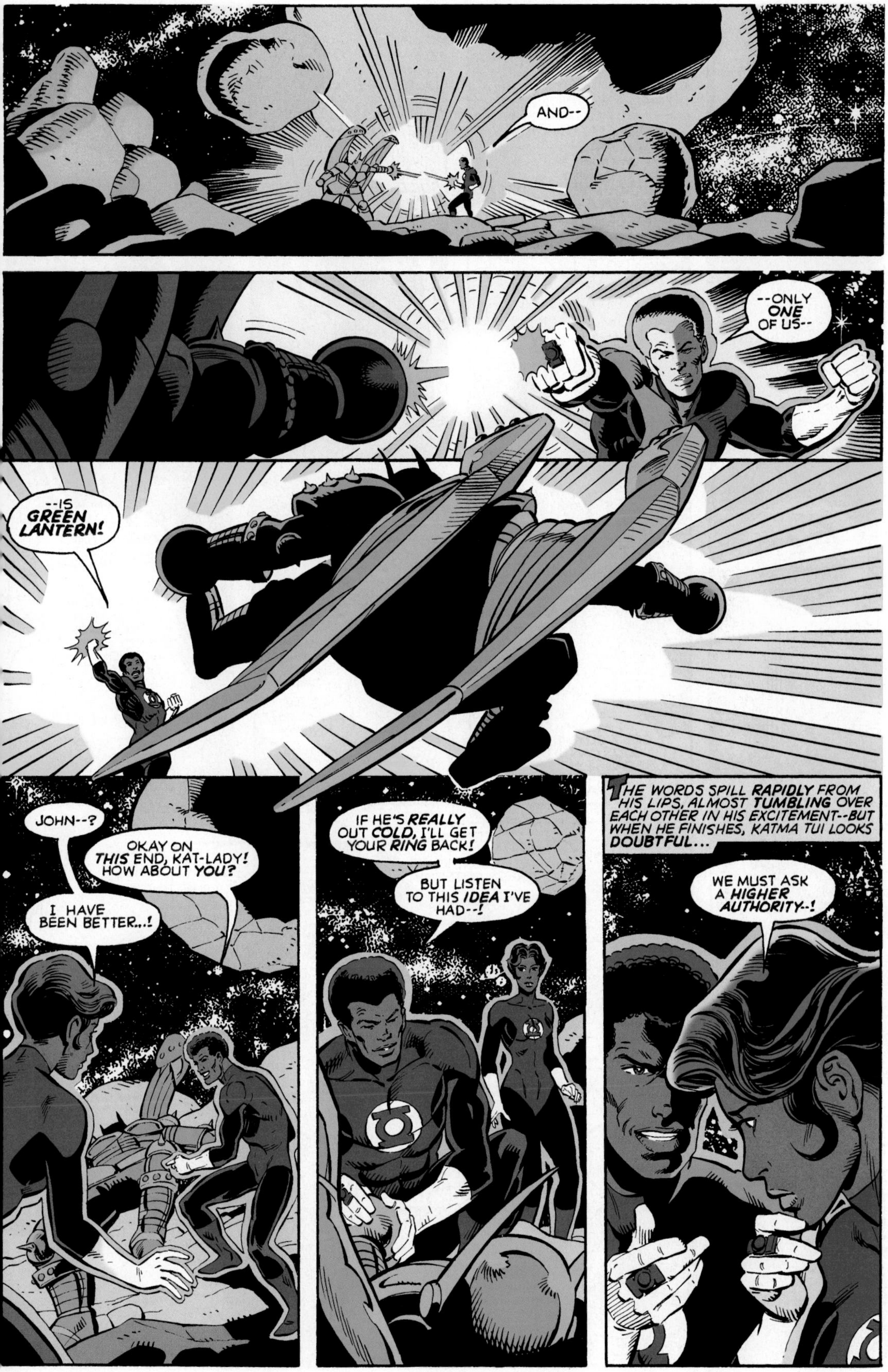
AND--
--ONLY ONE OF US--
--IS GREEN LANTERN!
JOHN--?
OKAY ON THIS END, KAT-LADY! HOW ABOUT YOU?
I HAVE BEEN BETTER...!
IF HE'S REALLY OUT COLD, I'LL GET YOUR RING BACK!
BUT LISTEN TO THIS IDEA I'VE HAD--!
THE WORDS SPILL RAPIDLY FROM HIS LIPS, ALMOST TUMBLING OVER EACH OTHER IN HIS EXCITEMENT--BUT WHEN HE FINISHES, KATMA TUI LOOKS DOUBTFUL...
WE MUST ASK A HIGHER AUTHORITY--!

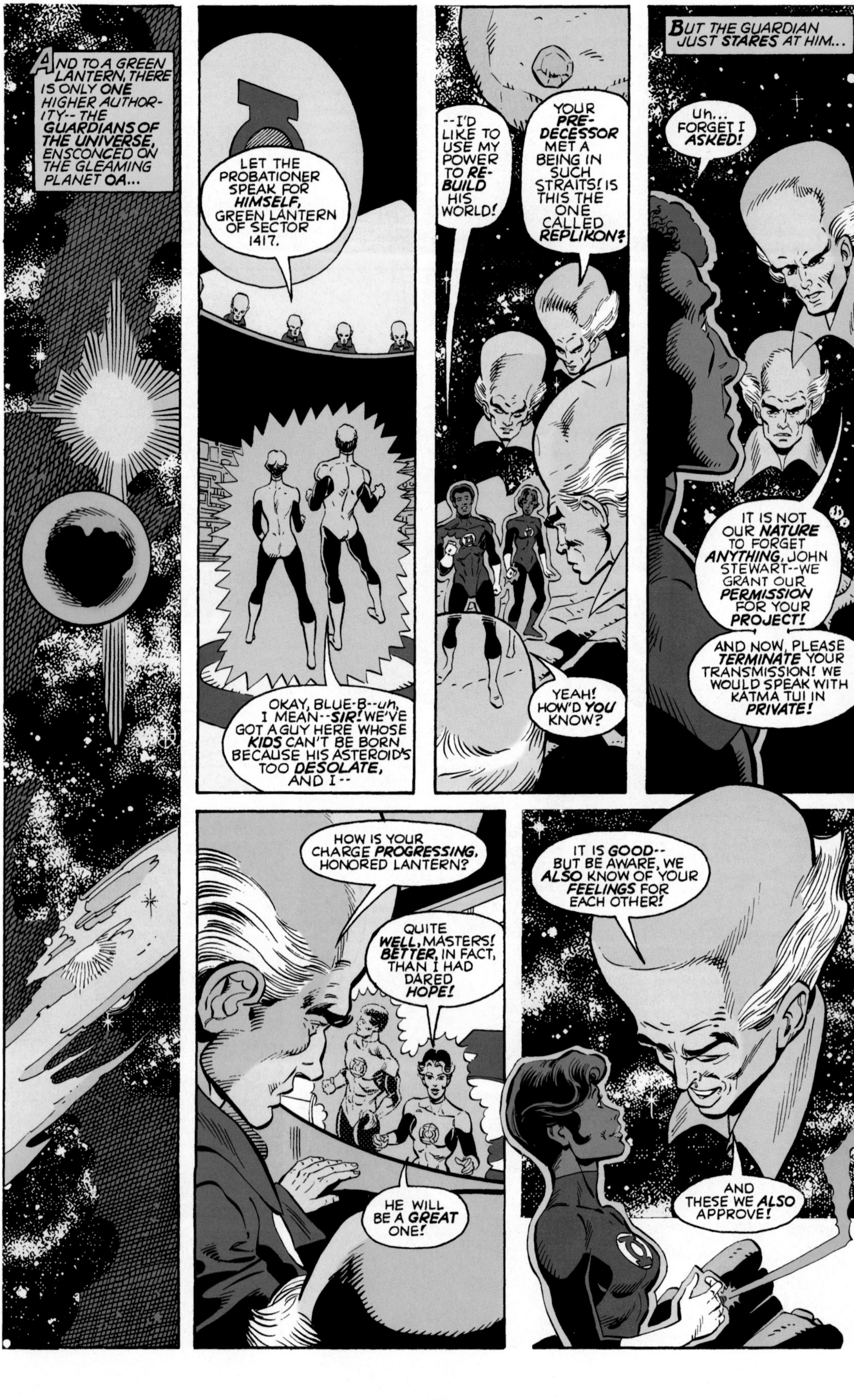
AND TO A GREEN LANTERN, THERE IS ONLY ONE HIGHER AUTHORITY-- THE GUARDIANS OF THE UNIVERSE, ENSCONCED ON THE GLEAMING PLANET OA...
LET THE PROBATIONER SPEAK FOR HIMSELF, GREEN LANTERN OF SECTOR 1417.
OKAY, BLUE-B--uh, I MEAN--SIR! WE'VE GOT A GUY HERE WHOSE KIDS CAN'T BE BORN BECAUSE HIS ASTEROID'S TOO DESOLATE, AND I--
--I'D LIKE TO USE MY POWER TO REBUILD HIS WORLD!
YOUR PREDECESSOR MET A BEING IN SUCH STRAITS! IS THIS THE ONE CALLED REPLIKON?
YEAH! HOW'D YOU KNOW?
BUT THE GUARDIAN JUST STARES AT HIM...
Uh... FORGET I ASKED!
IT IS NOT OUR NATURE TO FORGET ANYTHING, JOHN STEWART--WE GRANT OUR PERMISSION FOR YOUR PROJECT!
AND NOW, PLEASE TERMINATE YOUR TRANSMISSION! WE WOULD SPEAK WITH KATMA TUI IN PRIVATE!
HOW IS YOUR CHARGE PROGRESSING, HONORED LANTERN?
QUITE WELL, MASTERS! BETTER, IN FACT, THAN I HAD DARED HOPE!
HE WILL BE A GREAT ONE!
IT IS GOOD-- BUT BE AWARE, WE ALSO KNOW OF YOUR FEELINGS FOR EACH OTHER!
AND THESE WE ALSO APPROVE!

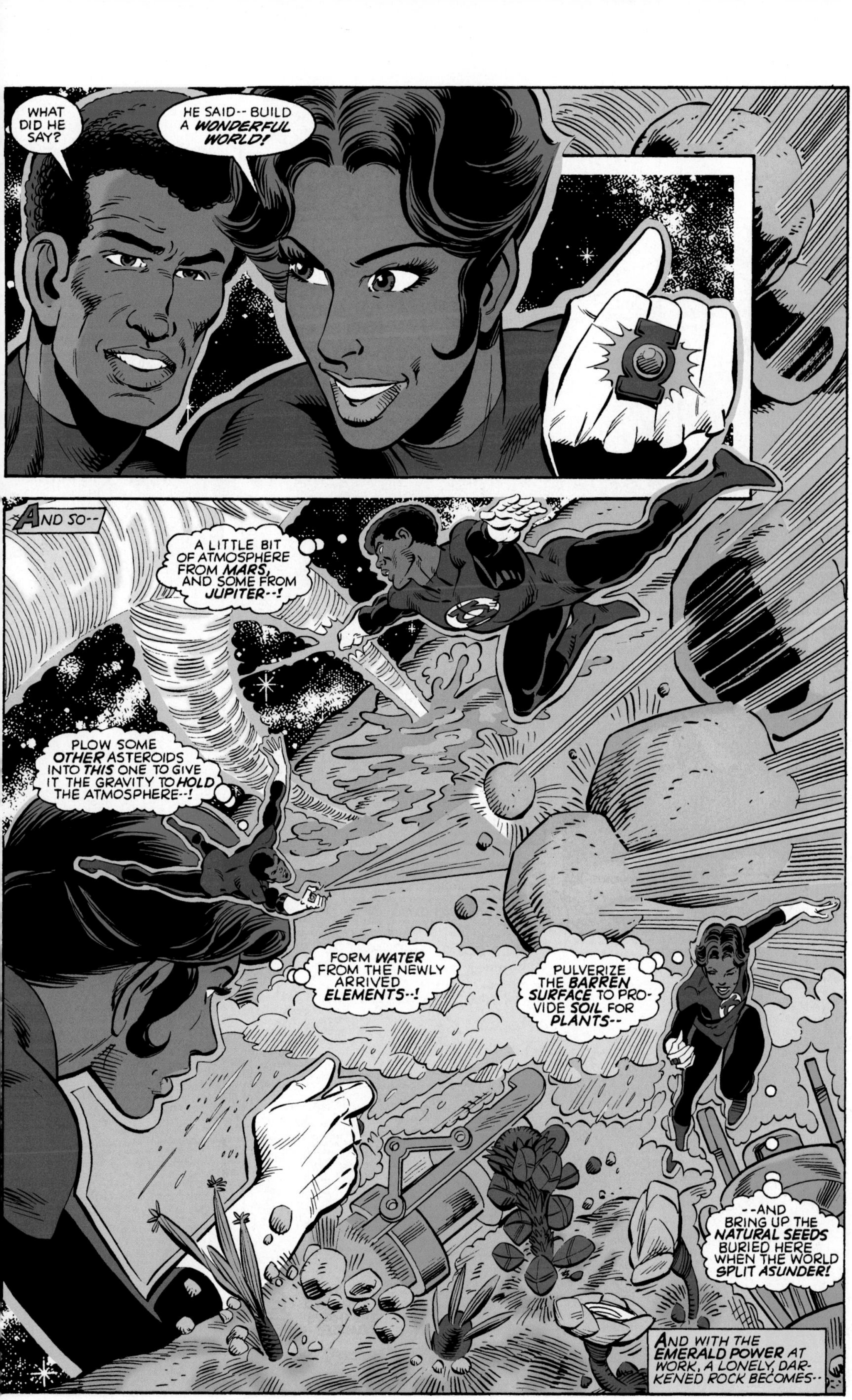
WHAT DID HE SAY?
HE SAID-- BUILD A WONDERFUL WORLD!
AND SO--
A LITTLE BIT OF ATMOSPHERE FROM MARS, AND SOME FROM JUPITER--!
PLOW SOME OTHER ASTEROIDS INTO THIS ONE TO GIVE IT THE GRAVITY TO HOLD THE ATMOSPHERE--!
FORM WATER FROM THE NEWLY ARRIVED ELEMENTS--!
PULVERIZE THE BARREN SURFACE TO PROVIDE SOIL FOR PLANTS--
--AND BRING UP THE NATURAL SEEDS BURIED HERE WHEN THE WORLD SPLIT ASUNDER!
AND WITH THE EMERALD POWER AT WORK, A LONELY, DARKENED ROCK BECOMES--

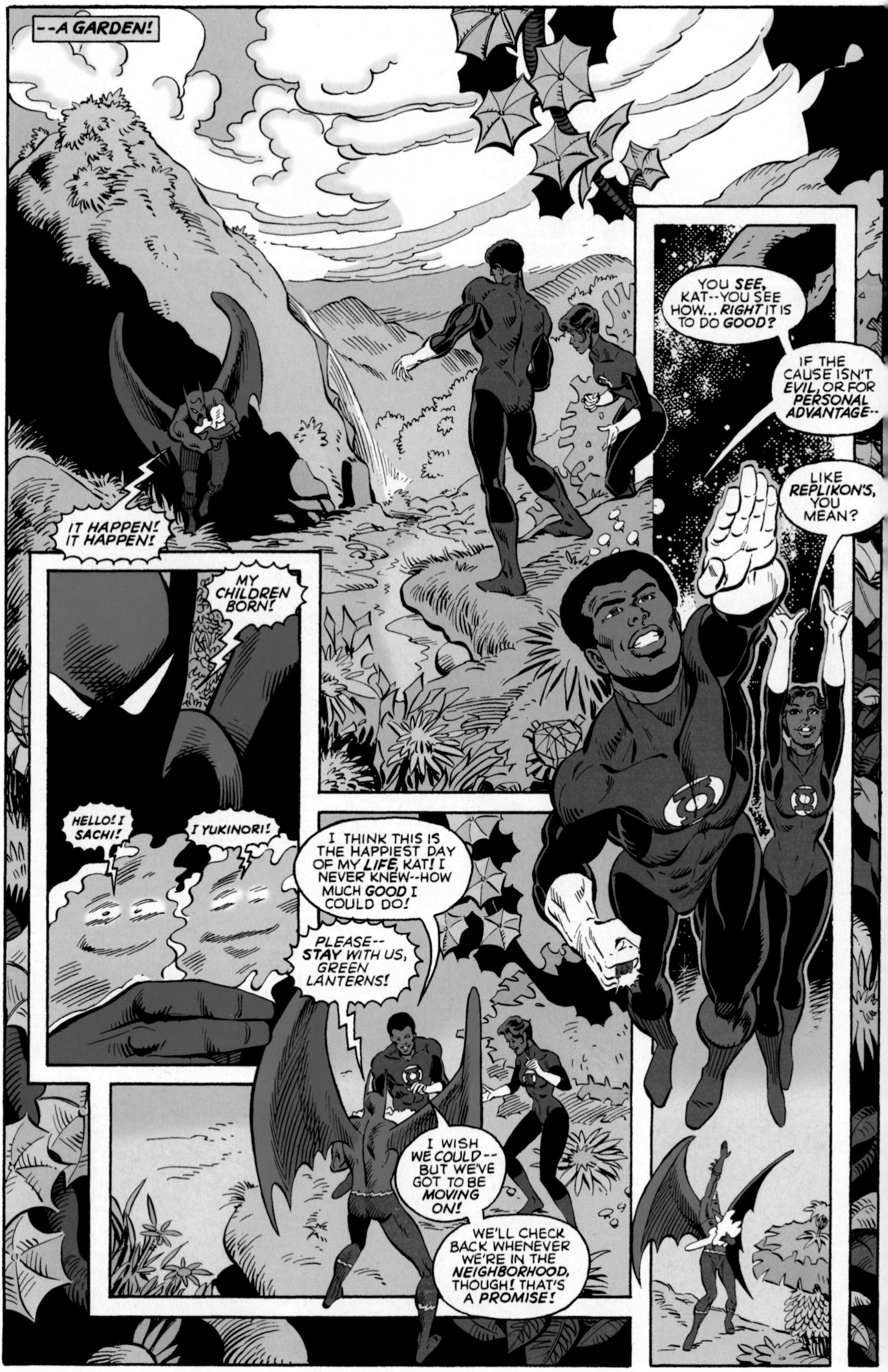
--A GARDEN!
IT HAPPEN! IT HAPPEN!
MY CHILDREN BORN!
HELLO! I SACHI!
I YUKINORI!
I THINK THIS IS THE HAPPIEST DAY OF MY LIFE, KAT! I NEVER KNEW--HOW MUCH GOOD I COULD DO!
PLEASE--STAY WITH US, GREEN LANTERNS!
I WISH WE COULD--BUT WE'VE GOT TO BE MOVING ON!
WE'LL CHECK BACK WHENEVER WE'RE IN THE NEIGHBORHOOD, THOUGH! THAT'S A PROMISE!
YOU SEE, KAT--YOU SEE HOW... RIGHT IT IS TO DO GOOD?
IF THE CAUSE ISN'T EVIL, OR FOR PERSONAL ADVANTAGE--
LIKE REPLIKON'S, YOU MEAN?

HUH?

DO YOU NOT SEE, JOHN-- REPLIKON'S DESIRE TO GIVE HIS CHILDREN LIFE *FITS* YOUR CRITERIA FOR GOOD! HIS INTENTIONS WERE *ADMIRABLE*-- YET IF HE HAD SUCCEEDED IN HIS PLAN OF *DESTROYING EARTH*, GREAT *EVIL* WOULD HAVE RESULTED!

ALL I WISH TO *SAY* IS THAT I CANNOT *POSSIBLY* FORESEE ALL THE CONSEQUENCES OF CHANGING THE PERSONALITY OF *EVERYONE IN THE UNIVERSE*--

--SO I *REFRAIN!*

THE ONLY LIMIT TO THE POWER IS *YOU*--BUT *YOU* MUST LIMIT *YOURSELF!*

Hmmmm...

Y'KNOW, KAT-- WHEN WE FIRST MET REPLIKON, I ASKED YOU IF YOU *KNEW* HIM, AND YOU SAID, "I'VE NEVER *SEEN* HIM BEFORE!"

BUT IF THE *GUARDIANS* KNEW HIM FROM THE OTHER GL'S *REPORTS*--THEY MIGHT HAVE TOLD *YOU* ABOUT HIM!

YOU MIGHT HAVE *SUSPECTED* THAT WE'D *RUN INTO HIM* IN THE ASTEROID BELT!

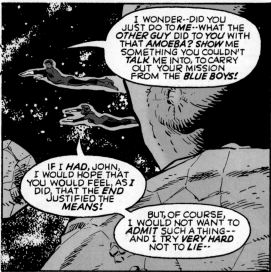

I WONDER--DID YOU JUST DO TO *ME*--WHAT THE *OTHER GUY* DID TO YOU WITH THAT *AMOEBA? SHOW* ME SOMETHING YOU COULDN'T *TALK* ME INTO, TO CARRY OUT YOUR MISSION FROM THE *BLUE BOYS!*

IF I *HAD*, JOHN, I WOULD HOPE THAT YOU WOULD FEEL, AS *I* DID, THAT THE *END* JUSTIFIED THE *MEANS!*

BUT, OF COURSE, I WOULD NOT WANT TO *ADMIT* SUCH A THING-- AND I TRY *VERY HARD* NOT TO *LIE*--

--SO LAST ONE BACK TO EARTH IS A DENEBIAN QUARXL!

227

THAT'S ODD...

WHAT?

ON THE MONITOR OF *UNIVERSAL ANOMALIES*-- A *NEW POWER* HAS BEEN DETECTED! IF IT WERE WHAT IT *APPEARS* TO BE-- IT COULD DESTROY WHOLE *WORLDS*--!

PERHAPS THERE IS AN *ERROR!* TRACK IT CAREFULLY UNTIL YOU ARE *CERTAIN!*

AFTER ALL, JOHN STEWART HAS JUST *ADDED* A WORLD TO THE UNIVERSE! WE WOULD NOT WANT TO *LOSE* ANY!

YES, IT IS FOR EVENTS SUCH AS *THIS* THAT WE CALL OURSELVES-- THE *GUARDIANS* OF THE UNIVERSE--!

*I*T IS JULY 1985! SIX MONTHS AGO, YOU WITNESSED THE INITIATION OF THE *CRISIS ON INFINITE EARTHS*--BUT FOR THESE PEOPLE NOW--IT *BEGINS*...

...AND IN THE MONTHS TO *COME,* THE FUTURE OF *GREEN LANTERN* WILL BE TIGHTLY TIED TO THOSE *CATACLYSMIC* EVENTS!

*B*UT, AS YET, LIFE CONTINUES ON AN *UNCHANGED* COURSE--!

SEE *THERE?* THE SKY'S *DEFINITELY* TURNING *RED*--!

HEY! HOW ABOUT SOME *SERVICE?* I'M CHECKING OUT!

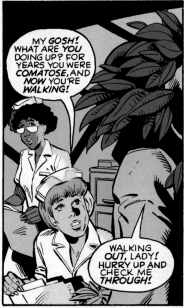

MY *GOSH!* WHAT ARE *YOU* DOING UP? FOR YEARS YOU WERE *COMATOSE,* AND NOW YOU'RE *WALKING!*

WALKING *OUT,* LADY! HURRY UP AND CHECK ME *THROUGH!*

GUY GARDNER HAS A LONG-OVERDUE *APPOINTMENT*--

--WITH A *RING!*

Y'KNOW-- I *FINALLY FEEL* LIKE I'M *REALLY GREEN LANTERN*...

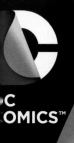

"This is the perfect place for people wary of the Green Lantern to start reading his adventures in order to see just how dynamic his world really is."
—COMPLEX MAGAZINE

START AT THE BEGINNING!

GREEN LANTERN VOLUME 1: SINESTRO

GREEN LANTERN CORPS VOLUME 1: FEARSOME

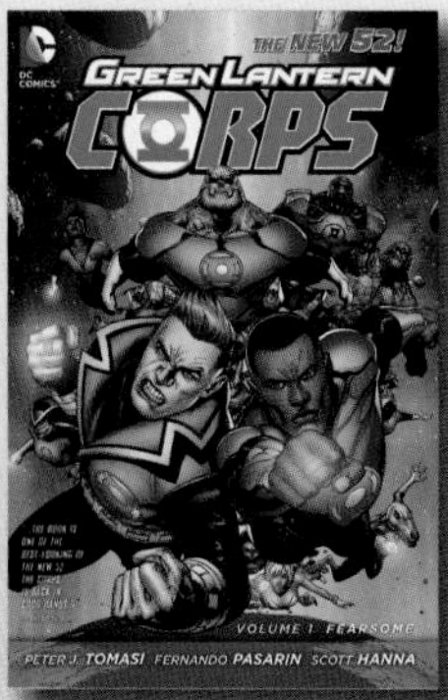
THE NEW 52!
GREEN LANTERN CORPS
VOLUME 1 FEARSOME
PETER J. TOMASI FERNANDO PASARIN SCOTT HANNA

RED LANTERNS VOLUME 1: BLOOD AND RAGE

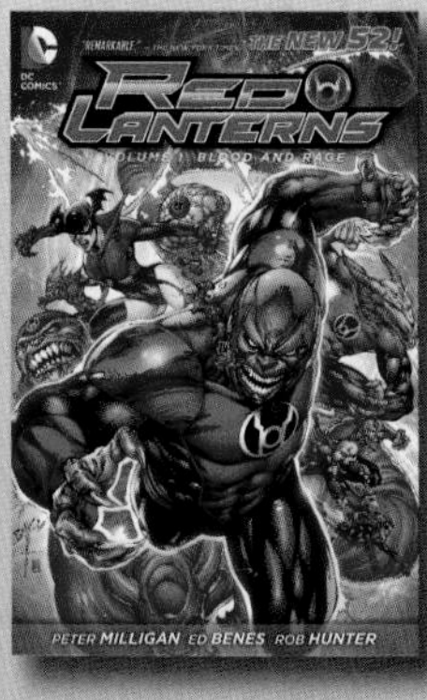
THE NEW 52!
RED LANTERNS
VOLUME 1 BLOOD AND RAGE
PETER MILLIGAN ED BENES ROB HUNTER

GREEN LANTERN: NEW GUARDIANS VOLUME 1: THE RING BEARER

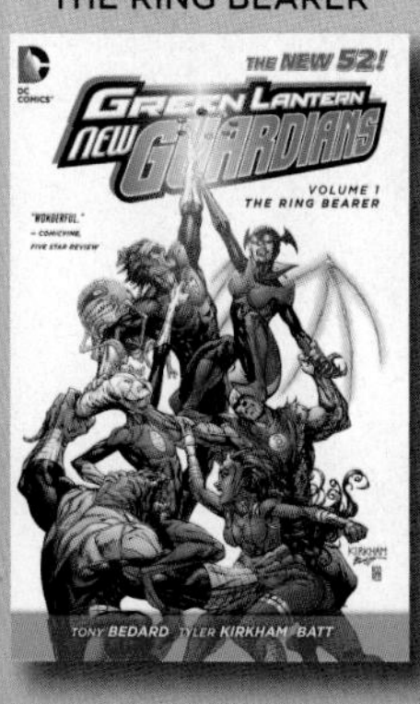
THE NEW 52!
GREEN LANTERN NEW GUARDIANS
VOLUME 1 THE RING BEARER
TONY BEDARD TYLER KIRKHAM BATT

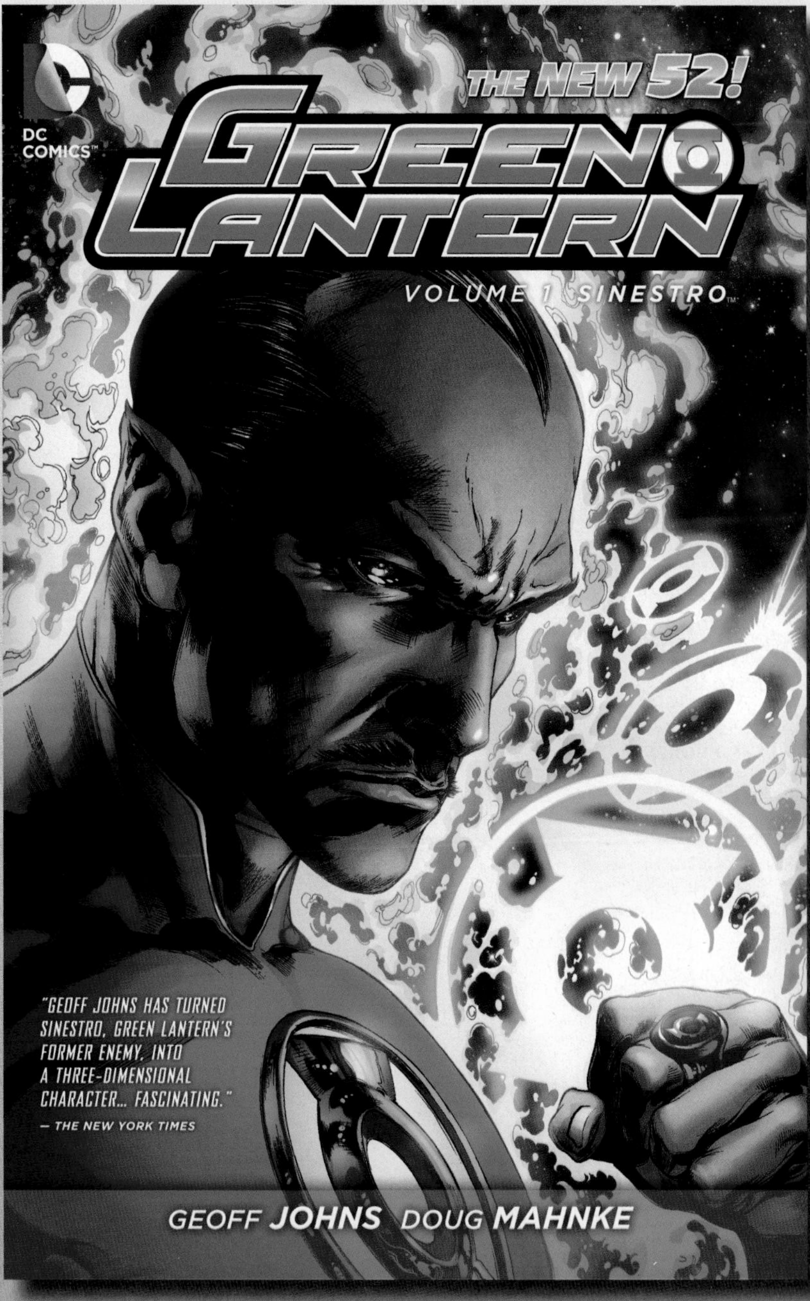
DC COMICS
THE NEW 52!
GREEN LANTERN
VOLUME 1 SINESTRO
"GEOFF JOHNS HAS TURNED SINESTRO, GREEN LANTERN'S FORMER ENEMY, INTO A THREE-DIMENSIONAL CHARACTER... FASCINATING."
– THE NEW YORK TIMES
GEOFF JOHNS DOUG MAHNKE

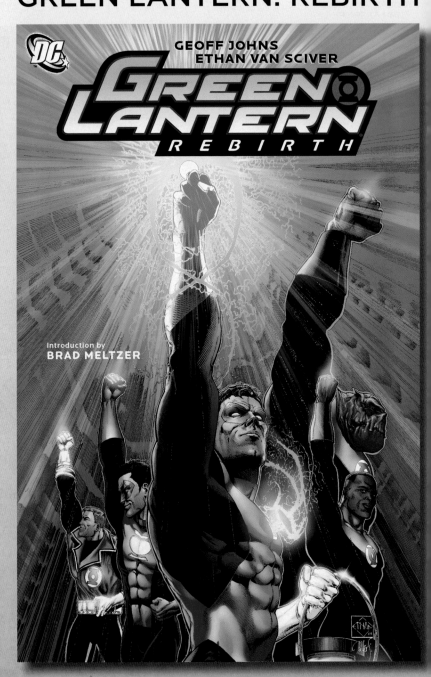

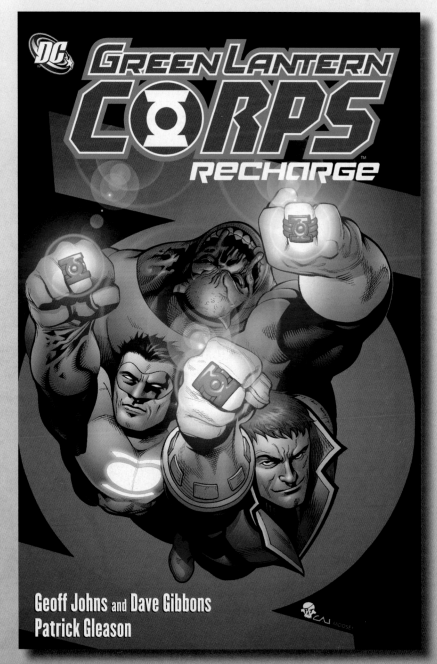

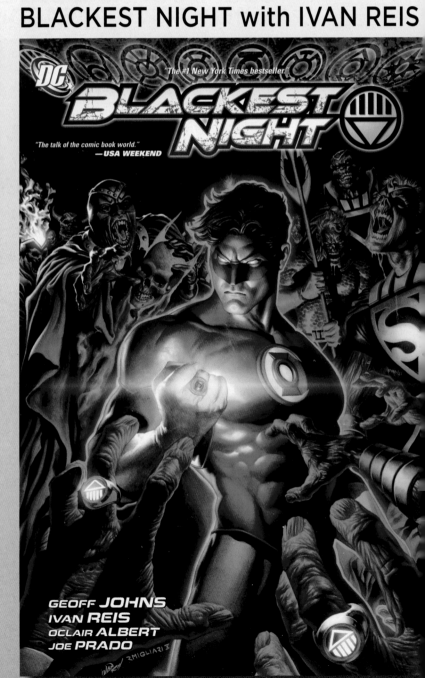